To the Wisconsin Conference
of the United Church of Christ,
with gratitude.

Frederick R. Trost

Advent
2018

NORTH AMERICAN CHURCHES AND THE COLD WAR

North American Churches and the Cold War

Edited by
Paul Mojzes

WILLIAM B. EERDMANS PUBLISHING COMPANY

GRAND RAPIDS, MICHIGAN

Wm. B. Eerdmans Publishing Co.
2140 Oak Industrial Drive NE, Grand Rapids, Michigan 49505
www.eerdmans.com

27 26 25 24 23 22 21 20 19 18   1 2 3 4 5 6 7 8 9 10

ISBN 978-0-8028-7526-6

Library of Congress Cataloging-in-Publication Data

Names: Mojzes, Paul, editor.
Title: North American churches and the Cold War / edited by Paul Mojzes.
Description: Grand Rapids : Eerdmans Publishing Co., 2018. | Includes
     bibliographical references and index.
Identifiers: LCCN 2018006892 | ISBN 9780802875266 (hardcover : alk. paper)
Subjects: LCSH: Christianity and politics—United States—History—20th
     century. | Christianity and politics—Canada—History—20th century. |
     Cold War. | Canada—Foreign relations—20th century. | United
     States—Foreign relations—20th century.
Classification: LCC BR516 .N68 2018 | DDC 261.7097/0904—dc23
     LC record available at https://lccn.loc.gov/2018006892

CONTENTS

US Mainline Protestant Approaches

Roman Catholic Approaches

Eastern Orthodox Approaches

CONTENTS

Evangelical Approaches

Peace Activities

Lessons Learned

PREFACE

The idea for this book was generated in faraway Finland by the Lutheran churchman Risto Lehtonen, who proposed an exploration of the impact the Cold War had on Christian communities worldwide. He visited a number of us in the United States, and we responded positively, but vaguely. This was about a decade ago. In 2011 a conference took place at the Lutheran Theological Faculty at Comenius University in Bratislava, Slovakia, which resulted in a book, *Christian World Community and the Cold War*, containing the conference papers. A consensus developed in favor of publishing multiple volumes on the general topic that would deal with issues in different parts of the world. Due to inadequate coordination and cooperation of supporters of the worldwide project, only several regional groups have advanced toward completion of their task.

The group acting as facilitators for the North American area, consisting of Canada and the USA (Mexico was to be grouped with other Latin American countries in the Third World response to the Cold War), was determined to complete the task. After many meetings, consultations, and teleconferences, largely focused on (mostly unsuccessful) attempts to get support from foundations for authors' workshops, the project limped along. As things turned out, persistence is more important than money, at least where the dedication of churchpeople is concerned. After four or five years of determined effort, the project finally bore fruit with the publication of this book.

Of the many people who were helpful in this process, the most important were a loosely organized ecumenical "group" of dedicated individuals like Norman Hjelm, Bruce Rigdon, Albert Pennybacker, Joan Brown Campbell, Leonid Kishkovsky, Martin Bailey, Joseph Loya, OSA, John Lindner, Rodney Petersen, James Christie, and David Little. My role as editor emerged somehow by default. Serene Jones, president of Union Theological Seminary in New York, and some of her colleagues, especially Gary Dorrien and Frederick Davie, were a great help.

The organizing structure was based on the natural clustering of churches in North America. At first, many US authors agreed to participate, and then with the help of James Christie, we obtained the cooperation of a substantial group of Canadian authors. Accordingly, the five chapters on Canada (by Lois Wilson, Gayle Thrift, Bill Blaikie, Gordon Heath, and Jim Christie) were included after the introduction (by Norman Hjelm). A sixth chapter by a Canadian, Lucian Turcescu, discussing the Romanian Orthodox community in North America, was placed in the section on the Orthodox churches for greater consistency. The Canadian section is introduced and concluded by its editor, James Christie. As the result of the Canadian contribution, a remarkable insight emerged, namely, that from a Canadian Christian perspective, the USA was nearly as big a problem to Canadians during the Cold War as the Communist superpower.

To provide a logical structure, the chapters on the American experience were clustered into four sections: mainline Protestants, Roman Catholics, Eastern Orthodox, and evangelical Christians, who, while Protestants, increasingly displayed an identity distinguishable from their mainline counterparts.

The Cold War was a huge challenge for all American Christians, though the various churches responded very differently, thereby accentuating tensions that already existed among them. The tensions were particularly acute between mainline and evangelical Protestants. The authors who wrote the chapters on the mainline Protestant approaches were Jill K. Gill; Bruce Rigdon, Barbara Green, and John Lindner, who coauthored a chapter; Gary Dorrien; Frederick Trost; Peter Eisenstadt; the late James E. Will; and Charles West.

American Roman Catholics displayed a rather unified anti-Communist approach until the Second Vatican Council (1962–1965). Thereafter, a significant shift in favor of détente took place, although it was opposed by a significant body of conservative opinion. Chapters on the Catholic response were authored by Dianne Kirby, Michael Graziano, Todd Scribner, and Raymond Haberski Jr.

The Orthodox churches, many of which had their canonical homes in Communist bloc nations, were often riven by great rivalries and schisms. The divisions were based on whether the churches functioning in America gave their loyalties to the mother church located behind the Iron Curtain or refused to cooperate, considering the mother church subservient to the Communist governments. Orthodox churches are typically organized according to national identity, and because there are so many such churches in North America, only several were selected for this collection. The authors of the Orthodox section are Leonid Kishkovsky; Nicholas Denysenko; Andrei Psarev and

Nadzieszda Kizenko, who coauthored a chapter; Lucian Turcescu; and Dellas Oliver Herbel.

The chapters describing the evangelical responses were contributed by Axel Schäfer, Dan Hummel, Jeremy Hatfield, Steve Tipton, and Mark Edwards. Edwards provides a helpful reminder that the approaches between liberals and conservatives in regard to the challenges of the Cold War were not always as radically distinct as might be imagined.

The penultimate section of the book deals with Christians who devoted themselves more explicitly to peace building. Walter Sawatsky writes about the historic peace churches; Joseph Loya, about participants in an ecumenical organization; and Paul Mojzes, about participants in a dialogical process between Christians and Marxists, a process that risked misunderstanding in order to build bridges between the two camps.

A guiding principle of the authors was to write primarily as Christians to Christians, as well as being committed to historical and critical accuracy. The authors did not write only so that this most dangerous of ideological confrontations, one that could have easily resulted in nuclear holocaust, is not forgotten. They also wished to provide insights to future generations, based on their examination of the past, as to how to cope more effectively with the great challenges that are yet to take place. Are there lessons Christians can glean in the near and not-so-near future from this collection? James Christie addresses that question in regard to the Canadian chapters, and David Little in regard to the American chapters, as both writers attempt to identify commonalities and lessons where they exist.

In the euphoria over the fall of Communism, many people considered the Cold War over. However, now we see more soberly not only distressing aftereffects, but also new causes of tension and anxiety between Russia and the West that are partly reminiscent of the Cold War, such as a novel cyber-conflict and new proxy wars in Ukraine and Syria.

We are thankful to Wm. B. Eerdmans Publishing Company for accepting this voluminous book and making it available to individuals and churches, scholars and libraries.

PAUL MOJZES, Editor

ABBREVIATIONS

ABM	antiballistic missile
ACCC	American Council of Christian Churches
ACNSAS	National Council for the Study of the Securitate Archives, Bucharest, Romania
ADA	Americans for Democratic Action
AFIE	Armed Forces Information and Education
AFL	American Federation of Labor
AFL-CIO	American Federation of Labor and Congress of Industrial Organizations
AFSC	American Friends Service Committee
AFSCME	Auto Workers, Machinists, Food Workers, and Government Employees
AGDF	Action Committee Service for Peace
AGOA	Archives of the Greek Orthodox Archdiocese
AID	Agency for International Development
AIFLD	American Institute for Free Labor Development
AMBS	Anabaptist Mennonite Biblical Seminary
BESS	Board of Evangelism and Social Service
BGEA	Billy Graham Evangelistic Association
BSC	Brethren Service Committee
CALCAV	Clergy and Laity Concerned about Vietnam
CAREE	Christians Associated for Relationships with Eastern Europe
CBC	Canadian Broadcasting Corporation
CCC	Canadian Council of Churches
CCCB	Canadian Conference of Catholic Bishops
CCIA (UCC)	Committee on the Church and International Affairs
CCIA (WCC)	Commission of the Churches on International Affairs
CCT	Christian Churches Together
CIA	Central Intelligence Agency

CIDA	Canadian International Development Agency
CIO	Congress of Industrial Organizations
CND	Campaign for Nuclear Disarmament
CO	conscientious objector
COPE	Committee on Political Education
CORE	Congress of Racial Equality
CP	Communist Party
CPC	Christian Peace Conference
CPS	Civilian Public Service
CPSU	Communist Party of the Soviet Union
CRALOG	Council of Relief Agencies Licensed to Operate in Germany
CSCE	Commission on Security Cooperation in Europe
CUSO	Canadian University Students Overseas
CWS	Church World Service
DCI	Director of Central Intelligence
DCLW	Division of Christian Life and Work
DDR	Deutsche Demokratische Republik (East Germany)
DOV	Decade to Overcome Violence
DSA	Democratic Socialists of America
EACC	East Asia Christian Conference
EFC	Evangelical Fellowship of Canada
EI	Ecumenical Institute
EKU	Evangelical Church of the Union
END	European Nuclear Disarmament
FBI	Federal Bureau of Investigation
FCC	Federal Council of Churches
FGMF	Fort Garry Mennonite Fellowship
FRG	Federal Republic of Germany
FSLN	Sandinista National Liberation Front
GARF	State Archive of the Russian Federation
GATT	General Agreement on Tariffs and Trade
GCAH	General Commission of Archives and History United Methodist Church
GDR	German Democratic Republic (East Germany)
GOP	Grand Old Party (Republican Party)
HMC	Home Missions Council
HPC	historic peace churches
HUAC	House Un-American Activities Committee
ICC	International Control Commission
ICL	International Christian Leadership

IFOR	International Fellowship of Reconciliation
IPU	Institute for Peace and Understanding
IRD	Institute on Religion and Democracy
IRS	Internal Revenue Service
KGB	Komitet Gosudarstvennoy Bezopasnosti (in English: Committee for State Security)
KJV	King James Version
LAC	Library Archives Canada
MAD	mutual assured destruction
MCC	Mennonite Central Committee
MIRV	multiple independently targeted reentry vehicle
MIT	Massachusetts Institute of Technology
MP	Member of Parliament
MP	Moscow Patriarchate
MRA	Moral Re-Armament
MSU	Michigan State University
MWC	Mennonite World Conference
NAE	National Association of Evangelicals
NAII	National Archives II
NATO	North American Treaty Organization
NCC (also NCCC)	National Council of Churches of Christ in the USA
NCCJ	National Conference on Christians and Jews
NCCNYO	National Council of Churches Communication and Research Department Office Files, New York
NCWC	National Catholic War Council (later, National Catholic Welfare Conference)
NDP	New Democratic Party
NFB	National Film Board
NORAD	North American Air Defense Command
NSBRO	National Service Board for Religious Objectors
OCA	Orthodox Church in America
OPREE	*Occasional Papers on Religion in Eastern Europe*
OSCE	Organization for Security and Cooperation in Europe
OSS	Office of Strategic Services
PCUSA	Presbyterian Church USA
PFSS	Peace, Freedom, and Security Studies
POV	Programme to Overcome Violence
PRC	People's Republic of China
PROK	Presbyterian Church of the Republic of Korea

PUSRG	Provisional US Regional Group
RCA	Russian Church Abroad
RCMP	Royal Canadian Mounted Police
ROC	Russian Orthodox Church
ROCOR	Russian Orthodox Church Outside of Russia
ROEA	Romanian Orthodox Episcopate of America
ROMA	Romanian Orthodox Metropolia in the Americas
RomOC	Romanian Orthodox Church
R2P	responsibility to protect
SALT	Strategic Arms Limitation Talks
SBC	Southern Baptist Convention
SCLC	Southern Christian Leadership Conference
SCM	Student Christian Movement
SDI	Strategic Defense Initiative
SDS	Students for a Democratic Society
SD/USA	Social Democrats, USA
SEATO	Southeast Asia Treaty Organization
SHAPE	Strategic Headquarters Allied Powers Europe
SJ	Society of Jesus
UAOC	Ukrainian Autocephalous Orthodox Church
UCC	United Church of Canada
UCC	United Church of Christ
UCCA	United Church of Canada Archives
UCO	*United Church Observer*
UDA	Union for Democratic Action
UGCC	Ukrainian Greco-Catholic Church
UN	United Nations
UNSSOD	United Nations Special Session on Disarmament
UOC	Ukrainian Orthodox Church (USA)
UOW	*Ukrainian Orthodox Word*
USAID	US Agency for International Development
USCCB	United States Conference of Catholic Bishops
USSR	Union of Soviet Socialist Republics
UW	*Ukrainian Weekly*
WCC	World Council of Churches
WCCD	Winnipeg Coordinating Committee for Disarmament
WRC	World Relief Corporation
WWI	World War I
WWII	World War II
YMCA	Young Men's Christian Association

Introduction

NORMAN A. HJELM

The issue of the "Cold War" remains a vexing one for the global, ecumenical Christian community. We commonly date the end of that "war" in 1989 or 1990, and for the writing of history the interval between that date and the present is not long. The question could well be asked whether or not mature and responsible historical judgments can yet be made concerning a forty-five-year period of human history that ended so recently and still casts so ominous a shadow over the lives of persons, nations, and churches. But then again, perhaps the time has come.

For the past few years, a number of church historians and church leaders—largely, as Paul Mojzes points out in the preface to the present book, under the determined leadership of the Finnish scholar and church leader Risto Lehtonen—have been asking questions about the role of churches and ecumenical organizations during the period from 1945 to 1989 or 1990 commonly referred to as "the Cold War." This book, prepared by authors from both Canada and the United States, is the product of a study begun about a decade ago. It is a North American contribution to an international research project that examines a period of history of crucial significance both to nations and to churches.

Sir Lawrence Freedman of King's College, London, began a review of *The Cambridge History of the Cold War*, "Decoding the Cold War, Twenty Years Later," in the following way: the period is "an undifferentiated chunk of history that stretched across time and space with a vast cast of characters and occasional moments of drama."[1] Most analytical studies of the Cold War, a "chunk of history" of great importance, have looked at it through the lenses of political, diplomatic, economic, social, and surely military conflict. But do

1. Lawrence D. Freedman, "Frostbitten: Decoding the Cold War 20 Years Later," *Foreign Affairs,* March/April 2010.

those angles of vision tell the whole story? It has become increasingly clear to some that the time has surely come for a thoughtful and honest study of the role of the Christian community, in its many and various manifestations, during that tense and crucial period of human history. This is, in point of fact, an unwritten chapter, a missing piece in any comprehensive understanding of our recent common past.

To be sure, there is a growing body of literature that views the Cold War from particular ecclesial angles. One can point to the important collection of essays edited by Klaus Koschorke of Munich, *Falling Walls: The Year 1989/90 as a Turning Point in the History of World Christianity*,[2] or to the four German volumes published between 2002 and 2007 assessing the role of the churches of Eastern Europe and the end of Communist rule, edited by notable scholars such as Jens Holger Schjørring, Peter Maser, Hartmut Lehmann, and Katharina Kunter.[3]

In English, however, such literature is at best meager. General historical studies of the Cold War—by scholars such as John Lewis Gaddis, Melvyn Leffler, or Carole Fink[4]—do not pay much attention to the role of religion in general or churches in particular.[5] Exceptions to this generalization are two collections of essays on the role of religion during the Cold War: *Religion and the Cold War*, edited by Dianne Kirby, and *Religion and the Cold War: A Global Perspective*, edited by Philip Muehlenbeck.[6] What is clearly yet to

---

2. Klaus Koschorke, ed., *Falling Walls: The Year 1989/90 as a Turning Point in the History of World Christianity* (Wiesbaden: Harrassowitz Verlag, 2009).

3. Peter Maser and Jens Holger Schjørring, eds., *Zwischen den Mühlsteinen. Protestantische Kirchen in der Phase der Errichtung der kommunistischen Herrschaft im östlichen Europa* (Erlangen, 2002); Hartmut Lehmann and Jens Holger Schjørring, eds., *Im Räderwerk des 'real existierenden Sozialismus.' Kirchen in Ostmittel- und Osteuropa von Stalin bis Gorbatschow* (Erlangen, 2003); Peter Maser and Jens Holger Schjørring, eds., *Wie die Träumenden? Protestantische Kirchen in der Phase des Zusammenbruchs der kommunistischen Herrschaft im Östlichen Europa* (Erlangen, 2003); and Katharina Kunter and Jens Holger Schjørring, eds., *Die Kirchen und das Erbe des Kommunismus. Die Zeit nach 1989—Zäsur, Vergangenheitsbewältigung und Neubeginn. Fallstudien aus Mittel und Osteuropa und Bestands-aufnahme aus der Ökumene* (Erlangen, 2007).

4. John Lewis Gaddis, *We Now Know: Rethinking Cold War History* (Oxford: Oxford University Press, 1997), and *The Cold War: A New History* (New York: Penguin Books, 2005); Melvyn P. Leffler, *For the Soul of Mankind: The United States, the Soviet Union, and the Cold War* (New York: Hill and Wang, 2007); Carole K. Fink, *Cold War: An International History* (Boulder, CO: Westview Press, 2014).

5. An exception, although more limited in time and focus, is William Inboden, *Religion and American Foreign Policy, 1945–1960: The Soul of Containment* (Cambridge: Cambridge University Press, 2008).

6. Dianne Kirby, ed., *Religion and the Cold War* (Basingstroke, UK: Palgrave Macmillan,

be undertaken is a genuinely comprehensive and ecumenical study of the role of the churches during the Cold War, a study not limited to the Northern Hemisphere or to ideological conflicts originating solely in Moscow and Washington.

The present volume, *North American Churches and the Cold War*, is a step in that direction, a contribution from Canada and the United States to a much-needed international and ecumenical study. The decade-long process leading up to its composition and publication is outlined in Paul Mojzes's preface: initial consultations in Cambridge, Frankfurt, and Bratislava; a first international research conference in 2011 in Bratislava;[7] regional conferences and publications in the Nordic countries;[8] and throughout that decade intense consultation and reflection in North America.

What can this research contribute to our overall understanding of the era that is generally described as the "Cold War"? (The phrase itself has perhaps taken on ideological overtones that are questionable. Although the term originally had a straightforward meaning appropriated on both sides of the Iron Curtain, in the post-1990 climate the phrase "Cold War" came to imply to some that one side was the clear victor in the struggle. While many throughout the world affirm that victory, others, in the aftermath of 1990, seriously question "win/lose" conclusions.)[9] The questions to be faced are indeed many, and they are complex and vexing. We are not seeking in this volume, however, simply to uncover historical details or conclusions that may or may not be important or even interesting. Authors in this book are largely concerned with how the many churches and organizations—of virtually all theological and ecclesial persuasions—can appropriate the meaning of the Cold War in order to clarify their future mission, witness, and service.

It can be suggested that in a comprehensive sense this endeavor is an attempt to illuminate two questions: What was the role of North American

---

2003, 2013), and Philip E. Muehlenbeck, ed., *Religion and the Cold War: A Global Perspective* (Nashville: Vanderbilt University Press, 2012).

7. Julius Filo, ed., *Christian World Community and the Cold War: International Research Conference in Bratislava on 5–8 September 2011* (Bratislava, Slovakia: International Višegrad-fund, 2012).

8. Most recently, Matti Kotiranta, ed., *The Finnish and Estonian Churches during the Cold War* (Joensu, Finland, 2016).

9. At the time of the preparation of this volume, an article, "The Cold War Is Over," by Peter Hitchens, appeared in the journal *First Things* (no. 266 [October 2016]). Under the rubric of distinguishing "the Russian nation from the Soviet empire," the article is an example of wishful thinking quite far removed from immediate geopolitical tensions.

churches and Christian—ecumenical, evangelical, and other—organizations in Cold War events and developments? And what have been the effects of the Cold War on those same churches and organizations? Not only was the Christian community a player—a victim, yet also, perhaps, a perpetrator—in the world divided by this forty-five-year struggle, but that community has also itself been at points bitterly and for some enduringly divided by the ideological and political struggles of the era.

A random sampling of Cold War tensions and developments shows both the breadth and the depth of the unwritten chapter concerning the Christian community that this volume is addressing. Let five of those tensions and developments be identified. The number could be multiplied beyond measure. These five instances are international in scope and had ecumenical implications affecting Protestants, Roman Catholics, and Orthodox. They provide a large portion of the framework within which the issues discussed in the following pages should be seen.

First, the debate in 1948, in Amsterdam when the World Council of Churches was established, between the American Presbyterian who later became secretary of state, John Foster Dulles (1888–1959), and the Czech theologian Josef Hromádka (1889–1969). This encounter did much to set the terms for theological and ideological divisions between Protestant Christians during the Cold War. In the recent words of Peter Morée of Prague, Dulles "outlined the role of the churches for freedom and democracy and underlined the atheist character of the Soviet Union." Hromádka defended his sympathy for Communism and for the Soviet Union by criticizing those who called for disapproval of the Communist ideology as "showing a lack of trust in the way God is moving the history of the world."[10] In a certain sense, the terms of that debate were transferred to relations *both between and within* churches on both sides of the Berlin Wall, deeply wounding many Christians and several churches in ways that have not yet been fully healed.

Second, it was Hromádka again who was instrumental in the establishment of the Christian Peace Conference (CPC) in 1958. With its headquarters in Prague, the CPC once worked in some ninety countries and had especially close contact with church bodies not affiliated with the World Council of Churches. It was initially seen as a forum in which Christians from a divided Europe could talk with one another about the issues involved in their painful separations. After the 1968 invasion/occupation of Prague by the Soviet Union,

---

10. Peter Morée, "Theology in the Struggle for Survival of the Church," in Filo, *Christian World Community and the Cold War*, 300.

however, the CPC found its activities increasingly reduced, and in December 1989, the fateful year of the *Wende* for both East and West, its leadership issued a statement that read in part: "Our movement had an important mission to fulfill, in that it became an ecumenical forum for the churches in Eastern Europe and in other parts of the world where socialist states had been established, and it tried to make visible the presence of the Christian faith in those countries. It is true that during the difficult period of the cold war and in an atmosphere of strong ideological pressure, the CPC accepted some compromises, made mistakes, and in some cases gave way to pressure. We need to do penance for this."[11]

Third, the Second Vatican Council marked a serious shift in Roman Catholic social theory. One of the effects of the council was a move from single-minded anti-Communism through *Ostpolitik* to a diversification of socio-ethical concerns. The fathers of the council were not of one mind regarding proposals to single out Communism as the primary enemy. Subsequent papal encyclicals—*Centesimus Annus* of John Paul II (1991) and *Caritas in Veritate* of Benedict XVI (2009)—represented the considerable movement in Roman Catholic social theory, movement that has, not without controversy, marked post–Cold War Roman Catholicism as it has moved into the twenty-first century.[12]

Fourth, there was serious reflection during the Cold War, particularly perhaps in the evangelical churches of the German Democratic Republic (East Germany), concerning *Kirche im Sozialismus*, the nature and mission of the church when placed in a socialist society. This was an issue of serious dialogue both within churches and the entire ecumenical movement and between churches and socialist governments. But as one scholar, Katharina Kunter, has said: "The end of GDR socialism therefore also marked the end of the alternative idea of a committed church in an atheistic and socialistic environment. The loss of this concept in the 1990s left not only the former GDR, but also ecumenia in an ecclesiological and political vacuum."[13]

Finally among these tensions and developments, it needs to be acknowledged that the boundaries of the Cold War were not confined to terms of

11. Károly Tóth, "Christian Peace Conference," in *The Encyclopedia of Christianity*, ed. Erwin Fahlbusch et al., vol. 1 (Grand Rapids: Eerdmans; Leiden: Brill, 1999), 445–46.

12. Cf. Peter J. Casarella, ed., *Jesus Christ: The New Face of Social Progress* (Grand Rapids: Eerdmans, 2015).

13. Katharina Kunter, "The End of the 'Kirche im Sozialismus': 1989/90 as a Turning Point for Protestant Churches and Christians in the German Democratic Republic (GDR)," in Koschorke, *Falling Walls*, 41.

East-West, Soviet Union–America, or the divided Europe. In question are the implications for the churches of the fact that "one of the central paradoxes of the Cold War is that hot wars took place only in the Third World and Europe had the longest sustained period of peace in modern history during the period. Both superpowers . . . intervened in the Third World in various ways to promote their own strategic and economic interests and to extend their spheres of influence."[14] The same scholar who made those assertions, the late Ninan Koshy from India, also maintained at the 2011 Bratislava conference that the end of the Cold War meant the beginning of the age of the American empire. How has that reality affected the churches of North America?

The essays in this book deal with how those North American churches and Christian communities and organizations approached the global tensions of the Cold War: the churches of Canada, the ecumenical Protestant churches of the United States, the Roman Catholic Church, the churches that compose the Orthodox Church, evangelical churches, and the historic peace churches and movements. This wide variety of Christian bodies acted both during and following the Cold War in sometimes deeply different ways. Labels such as "liberal" and "conservative" were, it will be seen, not always accurate or helpful. Geopolitical and sociological realities were treated in widely disparate ways. Some movements—dialogues between Marxists and Christians, for example—came to an abrupt and perhaps regrettable halt after 1990. The "lessons" drawn from these reflections are themselves by no means uniform. The points, however, are many: political, economic, ethnic, and, for Christians, theological, socio-ethical, and surely ecclesial.

This entire project—Christian community and the Cold War—is, moreover, to be seen as future-oriented. What have we—the world—learned, and in our still-precarious time, can those learnings help guide the future? The late historian Tony Judt, whose reflections on the twentieth century remain among the most penetrating, was among the most frequent commentators on the Cold War, both during that period of contemporary history and immediately after its "end" in 1989–1990. Two elements of that time—the fact that the "alignments and divisions in Europe became intertwined with the politics of national independence movements and of decolonization in Asia, Africa, Latin America, and the Middle East, with seriously misleading consequences" and "the presence of nuclear weapons"—led him to stark conclusions:

14. Ninan Koshy, "Churches and the Cold War: A Third World Perspective with Special Reference to Asia," in Filo, *Christian World Community and the Cold War*, 239.

Because of these two new elements, the cold war seemed to change its nature and become something radically different from anything that had gone before. And when it ended, with the collapse of one adversary, there were therefore some who supposed that we had entered a new era in human history. Since 1990 we can see that this was not altogether the case. The world has utterly changed since 1950: the horses are gone and so has the coal, together with the social dispositions and forms of work that they symbolized.

The great reforming projects are gone, too, at least for the time being. But now that we won the cold war we can see better than we could before that some of the dilemmas it addressed (or screened from view) are still with us. Recent history suggests that the solution will be as elusive as ever.[15]

The essays in this volume are designed—from the viewpoint of the Christian faith and the Christian churches—to help us deal with intractable issues and elusive solutions that still beset the world even a quarter of a century after what we thought was the end of the Cold War.

---

15. Tony Judt, "Why the Cold War Worked," in Tony Judt, *When the Facts Change: Essays, 1995–2010*, ed. Jennifer Homans (New York: Penguin Press, 2015), 81–83.

Canadian Christian Approaches to the Cold War

Notes from the Least Comfortable Chair in the Room

James Christie

Canadians are a curious lot. Though regularly and vigorously defending our unique global contributions as a nation, we do so while constantly striving to be noticed by our American cousins, as if our identity as the second-largest geopolitical entity on the planet depends entirely in the interest of strangers, to paraphrase Tennessee Williams. Hence the quasi dismay of many Canadians that the average weather map generated for network media in the United States shows a blank "canvas" north of the forty-ninth parallel.

Canadians are unsure of their place in the world and in world history. Hence the too-close-to-home accuracy of journalist Peter C. Newman's trenchant observation to the author at an international conference of military chaplains in the capital, Ottawa, in January of 2007: "A Canadian is someone who walks into a room and takes the least comfortable chair." Canada is like an awkward teenager at a high school dance, perched on the sidelines, uncertain of how to get up and shake his booty. Canada is easy to take for granted, our greatest attributes modestly stated by a 1970s tourist brochure circulated widely in US markets that Canada is "foreign, familiar, friendly and near."

This more than applies to Canada's role, and more particularly to the role of Canada's church communities, during the Cold War, broadly defined as stretching from 1945 to 1989. Canadian Christians experienced those years and that undeclared but very real, very deadly conflict as a distant second fiddle to the great Cold Warrior nation in whose shadow Canadians live.

Former prime minister Pierre Elliott Trudeau observed famously that "living next to the United States is like sleeping with an elephant: no matter how benign the beast, one is aware of its every toss and turn in the night." Much of the content and perspective of the following chapters, the "Canadian section" of this book, will reflect that quote.

Four very distinct contributions by four very distinct and distinguished Canadians, two recognized and accomplished scholars, and two scholar-activists, will be followed by a concluding and reflective chapter. Given the time period addressed and the complexity of the subject, the contributions from the north are necessarily far from exhaustive. The reader may find it most helpful to consider each chapter a snapshot from the Cold War album of the Canadian churches. Two of the snapshots are sharply focused—high definition, one might say. Two are more panoramic in nature, like those nearly 360-degree wraparound shots so beloved of visitors to the Canadian Rockies. Each offers a valuable window into the experience of Canadian Christians during the Cold War. Each reflects in some measure the broad impact of the Cold War on Canadian Christians from across the spectrum. After all, all wars have unintended consequences for noncombatants, the Cold War being no exception.

The opening chapter is offered by the Honorable, the Very Reverend Dr. Lois Wilson: "Canadian Churches and the Cold War, 1975–1990." Dr. Wilson is one of the most distinguished church leaders and Canadian citizens of the past half century and more. During the height of the Cold War, she served as the first woman moderator of the United Church of Canada (UCC), Canada's largest Protestant denomination; a codirector of the Ecumenical Forum of Canada; and president of both the Canadian Council of Churches and the World Council of Churches (WCC). A companion of the Order of Canada, Dr. Wilson was named in 1998 to the Senate of Canada by Prime Minister Jean Chretien. She continues as an activist, author, speaker, and mentor. In her contribution, she concentrates on the peace work of the United Church and of the ecumenical partners with which the denomination was and is inextricably linked. Dr. Wilson has been one of the most prominent proponents of the Christian Left in Canada, and her impact, especially through her work with the WCC and the Senate, has had a global impact, especially among women theologians and politicians.

Subsequent to Dr. Wilson's reflections, Dr. Gayle Thrift of St. Mary's University explores in fine detail the impact of the Canadian Protestant Left in her chapter entitled "'Has God a Lobby in Ottawa?' The Protestant Left in the United Church of Canada during the Vietnam War, 1966–1968." Dr. Thrift's work concentrates on the Cold War in Canada: Protestantism; social movements; disarmament, pacifism, and protest. She not only delineates the actions of the UCC during the Vietnam War as an expression of the Cold War overall, but also devotes energy and offers insight into the effect of the Cold War debates on the life of the denomination.

The Honorable, the Reverend Dr. William Alexander Blaikie follows Dr. Thrift with "The Cruise Missile Debate in the Canadian Parliament." Rev.

Bill Blaikie served the riding of Elmwood Transcona from 1979 to 2008 as a member of the federal parliament for the New Democratic Party. He was the longest-serving MP during Canada's Thirty-Eighth and Thirty-Ninth Parliaments, and thus was recognized as dean of the House of Commons. Upon his retirement from the House of Commons, Rev. Blaikie served for two years in the Manitoba provincial legislature as minister of conservation and the Government House Leader. He teaches in the area of faith and politics in the United Centre for Theological Studies at the University of Winnipeg. A minister of the United Church of Canada, his career has been spent as a leader of the New Democratic Party, Canada's social democratic party. The United Church was, although mostly in the past, referred to by wags as "the New Democratic Party at prayer." His chapter provides an insider's view of the intersection between faith and politics during a particularly tense period between Canada and the United States during the Cold War.

Dr. Gordon Heath, of McMaster Divinity College, concludes this collection of four "snapshots" with "Watson Kirkconnell's Covert War against Communism." Dr. Heath is an ordained minister with the Canadian Baptists of Ontario and Quebec, and he has taught the history of Christianity since 1999. He serves as director of the Canadian Baptist Archives. His research focuses on church-state relations and church-war issues. As Dr. Thrift offers an in-depth reflection on the United Church as the key expression of the Protestant Left, of which Dr. Wilson is a key exemplar, so Dr. Heath offers a counterpoint of sorts to Dr. Blaikie's Christian expression of social democracy through an in-depth study of one of Canada's most conservative church leaders of the Cold War, the polymath polemicist Watson Kirkconnell.

The author concludes the Canadian section of this book with a chapter reflecting on the overall Canadian experience; acknowledging some of the gaps that require further research, study, and reflection; providing a congregational case study of yet another aspect of the Cold War; and noting emergent initiatives that owe their genesis to the Canadian Cold War experience.

Canadian Churches and the Cold War, 1975–1990

Lois Wilson

During the Cold War period between 1975 and 1990, Canadian churches were very active on peace issues on many fronts. This chapter aims to describe the myriad activities and policies adopted by the United Church of Canada (a 1925 union of the Methodist Church, Canada; the Congregational Union of Ontario and Quebec; the Association of Local Union Churches; and many congregations of the Presbyterian Church in Canada; it now also includes the Evangelical United Brethren Church); by the Canadian Ecumenical Coalitions for Justice; and by the United Church's reciprocal relationship to both the Canadian Council of Churches and the World Council of Churches.

The Peace Work of the United Church of Canada

The great wave of antiwar sentiment had started as a ripple in the seventies, when underdevelopment and violations of human rights were understood by Canadian churches as being contrary to the gospel. Gradually they began to understand through their own experience as partners with churches in other continents that repression was linked to economic theories, to anti-Communist ideology, and, later, to the nuclear threat.

Their peace work must be placed in the context of the period from the 1970s to the 1990s. For example, the Canadian churches' historic involvement in South America was galvanized with the 1973 Chilean coup by USA-backed Augusto Pinochet that removed Salvador Allende, the socialist head of state. The resulting systematic denial of human rights by the repressive regime, and the economic model that supported the regime, prompted a strong reaction in Canadian churches, which eventually formed the ecumenical coalition the Inter-Church Committee on Human Rights in Latin America. Apartheid was well ingrained in South Africa, but the Soweto massacre and news of the death of black activist Steve Biko, who died of injuries while in police custody, provoked outrage in Canadian churches. After the Korean War of the early 1950s, the historic north-south division of the country in the 1950s and the role played by the Soviet and American power blocs gave Canadian churches renewed energy to support peace efforts on the peninsula. They had shared a hundred years of history with the Korean churches and had firsthand knowledge of the suffering and disorientation that resulted from the division of the country. News from United Church personnel in South Korea about dictatorial policies in the 1970s and 1980s and knowledge of the immense repression of prodemocracy students led to renewed calls for peace and reconciliation on the Korean peninsula. President Reagan's 1983 speeches about the "evil empire" and "Star Wars," which depicted the Cold War as a struggle of good against evil, helped change the ripple to a wave among ordinary church members. His Strategic Defense Initiative (SDI) renewed the peace movement, and a network of peace groups, both secular and religious, sprang up across the country; Operation Dismantle, Canadian Physicians for the Prevention of Nuclear War, and the Canadian Peace Alliance worked closely with church-sponsored groups. Later, a prominent Quaker peace activist, Prof. Ursula Franklin, at the University of Toronto, led an exit of the faculty at the University of Toronto on the occasion of the university conferring an honorary degree on President George H. W. Bush.

At the 1983 meeting of the Sixth Assembly of the WCC in Vancouver, many church members heard of the rapid militarization of many countries, the involvement of Canada in economic and military activity and in arms sales, and the dangers of nuclear war. By the mid-1980s peace education had become a high priority for the United Church of Canada, symbolized by the moderator of the church, Rev. Clarke McDonald, standing on a boat off Vancouver in 1983, protesting the presence of 560-foot-long Trident submarines in Canadian waters. Increasing awareness of the futility of settling conflicts through war and a growing trend to support nuclear abolition gained credence. The ecumenical coalition Project Ploughshares made it known that weapons such as nuclear warheads and air-to-air missiles, under the custody of the USA, were located on Canadian territory.[1] A few people actually built bomb shelters in their backyards, and grassroots folk demanded action from church officials.

In 1983 the International Affairs Committee of the Toronto Conference of the United Church produced a disarmament kit for congregations with the name "Let's Try Peace." Its table of contents is interesting:

---

1. See Ernie Regehr, *Let's Try Peace: A Disarmament Kit* (Toronto: United Church of Canada, Toronto Conference, International Affairs Committee, 1983), 4.

1. Biblical *Reflections on War in a Nuclear Age*, included emphasis on the freedom of people and security lying in covenantal relationship with God, not in arms.
2. *Unquestioned Beliefs About Security*, common myths about security reinterpreted from a Christian perspective.
3. *Factual Information on Militarism and the Arms Race*, including the statement of Canada's Prime Minister Pierre Trudeau at the UN in 1978 advocating "a strategy of suffocation by depriving the arms race of the oxygen it needs."[2]

In this kit, the United Church of Canada pressed the Canadian government to adopt a policy that ensured that Canada became a nuclear-free zone, to be accomplished by refusing storage or passage through Canada of any nuclear, biological, or chemical weapons and of any electronic guidance systems. In addition, the church issued study material on the issue for use in local congregations, presbyteries, and its highest governing body, the General Council, while calling for "a deep spiritual awaking . . . and exploration of our spiritual roots of peacemaking."[3]

A section addressed to the church also recommended that theological faculties strengthen peace and conflict studies; support ecumenical efforts for peace and disarmament concerns through the Canadian Council of Churches and the World Council of Churches; endorse the Peace Tax Fund and a defense fund for people who undertake peace tax resistance; encourage twinning projects with Eastern bloc countries; and initiate Community Conversion Committees in cooperation with other denominations, labor, business, and government to redirect military spending to serve human needs. It also made recommendations to the government and the private sector supporting these initiatives.

In her book *A Million for Peace*, Shirley Farlinger documents the strategies for peacemaking of the United Church of Canada from 1985 to 1990 and following years.[4] In 1984, at the church's General Council, David Wright proposed that the United Church demonstrate its responsibility for peacemaking by establishing a well-funded peace program supported by half a million dollars. The 1986 General Council, recognizing a profound need to explore the

---

2. Regehr, *Let's Try Peace.*
3. Regehr, *Let's Try Peace,* 5–6.
4. Shirley Farlinger, *A Million for Peace* (Toronto: United Church of Canada, 1995). Information about the myriad number of peace initiatives is gleaned from this book.

theological roots of peace, made peace education a priority for the next five years, and two initiatives followed.

The first was the decision to establish a Peacemaking Fund that was to be operative for five years, of which 75 percent went to support peacemaking projects by local grassroots groups during the Cold War. The fund raised a million dollars from church members, which figure was matched by the church, and extended far beyond church groups. Grants were made to groups committed to eliminating nuclear weapons; working for common security as understood by policy statements of the United Church of Canada; discouraging Canada's participation in NATO; strengthening the international economic order; controlling arms production and trade with militarized countries; and linking security concerns with ecology, justice, and human rights. A second track to the Peacemaking Fund was a theological track, to which 25 percent of the fund was dedicated. At the 1990 General Council the church produced a pamphlet for study called *Statement of Faith on Peace in a Nuclear Age*.

We can't begin to write of all the programs that arose, initiated by volunteers and supported by free donated spaces in churches, so, of the 216 projects and the thirty peace and justice organizations spawned, we mention only a few.

One was the 1988 Peace Pilgrims' Walk from Kingston to Parliament Hill in Ottawa—190 kilometers and usually a two-hour drive! Organized by theological student Chris Levan out of Queens Theological Seminary, it took seven days and included a ritual symbolic foot washing of one another's feet. There were the Raging Grannies, a group of senior women who dressed as grandmas and sang outrageous antiwar lyrics in every possible public venue. The Peace Fund backed videotaping of sermons on peace and distributed them widely. In 1986–1987 it helped fund a cross-Canada tour of four Montreal students who took a year off school and addressed one of every twenty high school students in 350 Canadian schools, speaking against cruise missiles and of the possibility of global annihilation by nuclear means. A documentary film, *Mile Zero*, was produced by distinguished film producer Bonnie Klein, the mother of Naomi (author of *This Changes Everything*) and of Seth Klein, one of the four touring students. Cooperative games were introduced to wean children off war games. An annual citywide peace walk in Toronto raised money for the fund and drew attention to peace initiatives. The ecumenical coalition Ten Days for World Development, which was dedicated to education on global issues (which had been more widely known due to the song "We Are the World"), mounted a campaign, "Cancel the Copters," which demonstrated opposition to money spent on the new military helicopters instead of famine relief. There was a growing acceptance by the public of the relationship of disarmament to development.

A plethora of audiovisual resources was promoted and used widely by the church: *No More Hiroshima* and *Speaking for Peace*, highlighting influential Canadians such as Margaret Laurence, the novelist, and Ursula Franklin, the Quaker pacifist. A film, *This Is Only a Test*, documented those who walked from the Canadian Forces base in Cold Lake to Edmonton, Alberta, protesting cruise-missile testing in Canada's north. And there were others: *Be Not Afraid*—a video of why Christians rejected American nuclear policies; *In Our Own Backyard*—a documentary of the Nanoose Bay Conversion Campaign to end underwater testing of nuclear weapons by the USA in the Georgia Straits, British Columbia; and *On Track for Disarmament*, a video by the interchurch peace coalition Project Ploughshares suggesting strategies for disarmament.

Groups of United Church of Canada women made it a practice to meet USSR ships docking in Cornerbrook, Newfoundland, in order to invite the crew to a home-cooked meal in a Canadian home. This practice continued for some years, even though the language barrier complicated communication.

Mixed Reaction to Peace Activities by Christian Congregations and Churches

There was some pushback from local congregations. According to the author's 1981 diary, one local United Church congregation that had invited her to preach told the official board of the congregation, "She can say anything she likes on the Saturday (the day of the Peace rally) but we don't want her preaching about peace here on Sunday."

On Good Friday, April 9, 1982, the author preached at Bloor Street United Church, Toronto, about victims of wars around the world (on the basis of her visits with WCC delegations to Hiroshima, Pearl Harbor, and Bergen-Belsen). The service was picketed by demonstrators on the adjoining street who were also against the subsequent march organized by church peace activists whose purpose was to picket the Toronto office of Litton Systems Canada. Litton is a large defense contractor in the USA that manufactures navigation communications and electronic warfare equipment and guidance systems for cruise missiles. Despite counterpicketing, worshipers *did* proceed to picket Litton.

In 1989 in Labrador City, Newfoundland, the author was involved in a Project Ploughshares consultation with the Innu on an acceptable solution to the low-level flying exercises of the proposed NATO forces' tactical training base at nearby Goose Bay. Peacemakers understood the exercises as a violation of the rights of the Innu. Under the sponsorship of Project Ploughshares, protests were made public. There was plenty of pushback from members of the United Church of Canada who were employed on the NATO base.

Yet the United Nations (Canada) Association has awarded the prestigious United Nations Pearson Peace Medal (in honor of the Honorable Lester B. Pearson, Nobel Peace Prize winner and former prime minister of Canada) to citizens who have publicly worked for peace. The awards ceremony is open to the public and is frequently attended by the governor general. A number of such recipients have been drawn from Canadian religious communities and churches.

The United Church and the Canadian Council of Churches (CCC)

The United Church has participated in peace initiatives of the Canadian Council over the years, particularly through Project Ploughshares. But sometimes the CCC seconded its staff, such as happened with Bonnie Greene, the staff person for the United Church for human rights and international affairs (1975–1990). Her work is not widely known by ordinary church members even today, but it was an important and essential contribution to peaceful relationships between countries antagonistic to one another. She was heavily involved in the Churches' Human Rights Program for the Implementation of the Helsinki Final Act (1975), which represented a commitment to peaceful resolutions of conflicts between states and to détente between governments on both sides of the Cold War. It involved a commitment by participating states to pursue human rights, security, and peace as interrelated goals. Three agreements were reached on military matters and measures to halt the arms race; on matters such as economics, technology, and environment; and on humanitarian concerns. European and North American churches began to push their governments through consensus building, networking and case studies, and monitoring of and contributing to the Helsinki process within each country. Exchanges of people between the churches of a region demolished stereotypes of the "enemy." It also developed a framework for reviewing Canada's compliance with human rights commitments on the home front. The Helsinki Accords linked peace and human rights as interdependent and therefore encouraged peaceful resolution of conflicts. This behind-the-scenes work made these subjects part of the diplomatic discourse between East and West during the Cold War. And the Canadian churches were central to it.[5]

5. Excerpt from a typed report of a June 1984 summary prepared for the Church and

World Council of Churches Peace Initiatives
Impacting Canadian Churches

The WCC Sixth Assembly, held for the first time on Canadian soil in Vancouver, British Columbia, in August 1983, had a profound effect on Canadian churches. During plenary sessions, speakers from all over the world pointed to nuclear war as one of the greatest threats to life itself.

Former Korean Presbyterian moderator Hyung Kyu Park said, "We want to die in freedom, rather than to live under the nuclear umbrella."[6] The Australian antiwar activist Helen Caldicott described the effects of an arms race and a nuclear war: "Seven hundred billion dollars are spent per year on the conventional and nuclear arms races, and the wealthy Western nations—the USA and Europe—and the Soviet Union are peddlers of death and armaments to Third World countries. The bomb destroys the fullness of life Christ has promised us." Darlene Keju-Johnson from the Marshall Islands told delegates that the explosion of nuclear weapons tested at Bikini and Enewetak "continue to affect the people today." She herself recently had a tumor removed, and had three more in her body. All these testimonies lodged in the hearts and minds of delegates, culminating on August 5–6 to commemorate the earth-shattering nuclear explosion that devastated Hiroshima thirty-eight years earlier to the day. The final statement (informed by Canadian churches as well as others) stated that "the churches must unequivocally declare that the production and deployment as well as the use of nuclear weapons are a crime against humanity, and that such activities must be condemned on ethical and theological grounds. . . . We call upon the churches . . . to begin immediately to reduce and then eliminate altogether present nuclear forces."

However, working against the nuclear threat was not enough in the struggle by churches for a peaceful world. At that same assembly, Anglican bishop Henry Okullu of Kenya stated, "More than ever it is imperative that Christians and churches join their struggles for peace and justice. . . . The world economic crisis has contributed to an even greater injustice for the developing countries, denying millions the basic necessities of life. There can be no peace as long as millions in Africa die of hunger while millions in the North die of overeating."

International Affairs Committee, the United Church of Canada, given to the author by Bonnie Greene. Extensive information can be had from Bonnie Greene, *Canadian Churches and Foreign Policy* (Toronto: James Lorimer and Co., 1990).

6. WCC Sixth Assembly, Vancouver, 1983. *One World*, a monthly magazine of the World Council of Churches, no. 89 (Geneva: Communications Department of WCC, 1983). This quote and all subsequent quotes are taken from this source, 5–11, 24.

The statement also linked the arms race to massive injustice and violations of human rights as well as the lack of development particularly in the North-South context, including the Southern Cone and Central America. It vigorously opposed any overt or covert military action in South America by the USA or any other government, noting Guatemala and El Salvador as examples. In the early seventies, Canadian churches had perceived the link between militarism and repression by analyzing their relationships with churches in South Africa and Central America. This was cemented at the Vancouver Assembly when Desmond Tutu, of the South African Council of Churches, arrived at midnight on August 5 to express his public opposition to apartheid. The Canadian churches' experience strengthened the witness of the ecumenical community through the World Council at Vancouver. The dynamic was reciprocal.

Additional WCC-related events focused on the theme of peace and justice. In January 1989, the WCC sponsored an international interfaith meeting of women in Toronto. Included were forty-five women from nine faith traditions: Christian, Hindu, Muslim, Buddhist, Wiccan, Aboriginal, Parsee, Judaic, Sikh; also included were women representing divisions within a particular tradition—for example, Christian delegates were from Orthodox, Catholic, and Protestant traditions. No papers were presented. Instead, the conference laid the groundwork for peacemaking by establishing strong interpersonal relationships, emphasizing our common experience as women, and undermining stereotypes. It encouraged the art of peacemaking and the gift of listening. It encouraged participants to abandon hard-core negative positions fixed in stone in order to be able to listen to "the other." The agenda included land claims and the way in which religion was used in defense of a supposedly unique faith status, or ways in which religion was used to support violence. Women from the West Bank and Israel participated, as did those from Sudan and the Punjab. Up front was the cost of peacemaking where religion is used to sanction repression and mutual disrespect, to abuse and shape the identity of some women and to deface or diminish the identity of others. Participants discovered that at the core of every faith was a vision of the peaceable kingdom, and the symbol of the lion and lamb lying down together is duplicated in every religion, albeit with different imagery. Tensions emerged between openness to others and withdrawal from "the other." The women investigated how in every tradition the interpretation made about war and peace had been prescribed by males. The ripples of this international meeting filtered into many faith communities around the world, and was documented on film and distributed by Canada's National Film Board.[7]

7. From the 1989 diary of Lois Wilson.

Another small WCC-related event was a Canadian Theological Students' Study Tour to the Soviet Union at Orthodox Easter 1985 that arose out of the work of the Ecumenical Forum of Canada. An ecumenical group of fifteen students and others were received by His Holiness and Beatitude Ilya II, Orthodox patriarch of all Georgia, who had previously been a president of the WCC. In addition, the tour visited Smolensk and Moscow through colleagues on the WCC Central Committee who facilitated the visit. Students made a point of meeting with an official, Georgi Arbatov, a member of the Central Committee, who said to the delegation, "In North America, millions sleep out on the streets in the cold. The capitalist system has generated the most threatening arms race in human history. So please—a little humility when you come to talk about human rights to us. The rate of unemployment in the West is a grave violation of human rights."[8] Both covenants—that of economic, social, and cultural rights, and that of civil and political rights—are included in the UN Declaration on Human Rights.

Canada's Ecumenical Coalitions for Justice

The 1960s civil rights movement in the USA was a time of ferment, bringing with it an increased awareness of the sanctity of human rights and of the ties between racism and economic underdevelopment. Hope abounded in Canadian church circles. The Second Vatican Council unleashed fresh ecumenical relationships, and this surge of Catholic renewal and energy invited the Protestant churches to do likewise. Poverty was thought to be a problem that could be solved, and the government of Canada was asking the churches' help in establishing a guaranteed annual income. Human rights emerged in common parlance. The churches collaborated in human rights law and reception of refugees. Awareness of international as well as national problems also increased as Canada, and the Canadian churches, received a stream of American young people fleeing obligation to fight the Vietnam War.[9]

Awareness grew that militarization of the Third World and sharp increases in Canada's military spending went hand in hand. What was becoming known among the churches was Canadian corporate investment in the

---

8. From the 1985 diary of Lois Wilson.

9. For more on Canada's ecumenical coalitions for justice, see Christopher Lind and Joe Mihevc, eds., *Coalitions for Justice: The Story of Canada's Interchurch Coalitions* (Ottawa: Novalis, St. Paul University, 1994). For an excellent article of critique and evaluation, see Lee Cormie, "Seeds of Hope in the New World Disorder," in *Coalitions for Justice*, 370–77.

Vietnam War and in the apartheid system in South Africa. As well, transnational corporations were developing massive projects to exploit the natural resources of the Canadian North without input from aboriginal people. In 1969, a report to the Anglican General Synod, *Beyond Traplines*, penned by Charles Hendry, exposed the need for recognition of treaties for aboriginal rights and land claims.

Theologically, the world exploded with contextual theologies, grounded in the lived experience of oppressed people. James Cone wrote of black oppression in the USA; feminist theologians around the world wrote feminist theology reflecting women's exclusion from decision making; Latin American theologians such as Gustavo Gutiérrez, a Dominican priest dubbed the father of liberation theology, made a "preferential option for the poor" the primary gospel message. Links were recognized by the churches between poverty and the arms race, between violations of human rights and unbridled economic initiatives, and between repression and militarism; also recognized was the necessity of linking peace initiatives with justice concerns.

In this context, a unique way of contributing to the peace and justice agenda of the churches in Canada and worldwide was developed. Interchurch cooperation took a new twist. Staff in these churches and researchers, with the assistance of denominational program officers from several denominations, came together to publish their collective results on issues such as poverty, corporate responsibility, and human rights violations by their church partners in the Third World, which were seen to be inextricably intertwined in the movement to secure a lasting peace. Most of them enlisted local support groups in Protestant and Catholic churches across Canada. The 1970s saw a veritable explosion of these small coalitions. There were at least fourteen of them, and the Canadian government and WCC began to take note of their work. What follows is a brief description of a few of them.

The first one was the PLURA network (Presbyterian, Lutheran, United Church, Roman Catholic, Anglican), which was concerned with *poverty*. It grew out of a 1968 Canadian conference, "Christian Conscience and Poverty," coming mainly out of the Catholic Church, and was committed to involving churches, low-income groups, business, and labor in ending poverty.

Ten Days for World Development urged Canadians to see things from the perspective of the people of Third World countries, who were suffering under burdensome debt loads, and to consider seriously the alternatives and proposals they had developed to address the resulting problems. Countless resource people from the Third World assisted Canadian churches in this goal.

LOIS WILSON

Project Ploughshares became the foremost vehicle of Canadian churches to address the peace agenda. Under the umbrella of the CCC since 1977, it came into being in the mid-1970s. At the time, "militarism, both as an impediment to development and as a means of repression, was the particular preoccupation of Murray Thompson and Ernie Regehr. . . . Thompson at the time was Executive Director of CUSO (Canadian University Students Overseas) and Ernie Regehr had just returned from a three-year Mennonite Central Committee (Canada) study assignment in southern Africa. Both had witnessed firsthand how military spending drained cash and military security obsessions drained energy and confidence from the development enterprise . . . hence 'Project Ploughshares.'"[10] This interchurch coalition eventually involved at least one thousand people from member churches, and in the 1980s a great deal of its activity centered on keeping Canada a nuclear-free zone. Project Ploughshares intervened at both the First and Second Disarmament Sessions in New York (1978 and 1982).

The Inter Church Fund for International Development began around 1973. Its main function was funding overseas development projects on behalf of its member churches, in consultation with the Canadian government. From 1979 to 1989 it entered into full shared partnership with Third World companions in funding projects overseas, and dialogued with the Canadian government's Canadian International Development Agency (CIDA) in policy discussions on structural adjustment and human rights programs.

The Taskforce on the Churches and Corporate Responsibility came into being in 1975. Member churches in Canada were influenced by their American sister churches who, as shareholders, had begun to protest American corporate involvement in the Vietnam War and in the apartheid system in South Africa. Canadian churches began to respond to shareholder resolutions on issues of corporate social responsibility. They helped reduce the flow of military goods from Canadian companies to regional war zones, particularly in South Africa and Central America.

The Inter Church Committee on Human Rights in Latin America came into being in response to the USA-backed bloody coup of September 11, 1973, against the Chilean government, which the American government deemed "Communist"! The coalition itself was not formally established until 1977, when it continued to respond to the deteriorating human rights situations in Chile, Uruguay, and Argentina, through a variety of missions, special reports, and advocacy work with the Canadian government. It gradually extended its

10. Lind and Mihevc, *Coalitions for Justice*, 188–89.

24

work to Central America (Nicaragua, El Salvador, and Guatemala) as well as the Southern Cone and the Andean region.

The Ecumenical Coalition for Economic Justice began in 1973 under its popular name, GATT-FLY. That name comes from a pun on the word "gadfly" and the General Agreement on Tariffs and Trade (GATT). The idea was that GATT-FLY would pester the government on trade and economic justice issues.

Additionally, there were the Aboriginal Rights Coalition (1975), the Inter-Church Coalition in Africa (1984), the Canadian-Asian Working Group (1977), the Canada China Program (1971), and the Inter-Church Committee on Refugees (1979). All these groups were sponsored by Canadian churches and had ties and lines of communication with the WCC as well as with the Canadian government, and with partner churches in developing countries. Their work brought the extra dimension of economic and human justice and rights to the traditional understanding of peacemaking. The reciprocal relationship between Canadian churches and their global partners enhanced all parties. Sometimes the WCC supported the stance of Canadian coalitions; often it was the stance of the coalitions that pushed the WCC or the Canadian government to revise or adopt particular Canadian policies in the face of the pressure of the American government to adopt *its* policies globally. It was a splendid period when the coalitions collectively demonstrated how to "meddle" in the affairs of state on behalf of suffering people and against possible global war.

Contribution of the Society of Friends (Quakers)

We end our general survey with a short comment on the historic and consistent peace policies of the Society of Friends in Canada. The Quakers have always refused to be enemies, and have historically supported those who refused to serve in the military for political or religious reasons. This policy comes from their core conviction that God is found in every human being, and you don't kill God!

The nonviolent resistance of Quakers to war and nuclear annihilation, and their interest in preventing war through peace research, became more widely known in Canada during the 1970s, when they went to court in high-profile cases, attempting to divert taxes for support of the military to a peace fund for international development. Two private members' bill on specific test cases failed to get past a first reading in Parliament, and the members were further blocked from taking their case to the Supreme Court of Canada. But their actions, which were always collective, public, and a sustained effort to establish a peace tax as the norm, gave Christians in mainline denominations some pause, and were supported by the United Church of Canada.

Concluding Observations

The ecumenical coalitions, so unique to Canada, "helped to give birth to new networks of solidarity with oppressed groups across Canada and throughout the world. Through their research and publications they have added immeasurably to our knowledge of major issues confronting the world . . . in many cases they have helped to change government and corporate policies."[11] They strengthened the churches' public witness during the Cold War, confirmed the importance of extensive reliable research in collaboration with those most affected by conflict, and taught the churches the necessity and validity of ecumenical work in the public arena. However, the social justice agenda remained the purview of a minority in most churches. The coalitions failed to find a permanent place within the Christian community, and church budgets began to abandon social justice priorities as membership faltered and survival became the priority. Some felt the social justice agenda had captured the church's agenda at the expense of evangelism. This ongoing tension continues within the Christian community to this day.

While these coalitions and citizen initiatives during the Cold War did stellar work on peace and disarmament, they were never meant to deal with the enormous cultural and transformative changes that have taken place globally since the Cold War, including the emphasis on a highly individualistic culture. Nothing could have prepared them for the global revolution in technology and information dispersal, the seemingly permanent massive movements of refugees, climate change and its serious consequences, nor the increased security concerns that need to be balanced with human rights and civil liberties concerns.

Nevertheless, the work and witness continue, although on a more limited scale. Project Ploughshares and the Taskforce on the Churches and Corporate Responsibility continue their work. Most of the coalitions coalesced under a new umbrella, Kairos, consisting of eleven churches and religious organizations, which advocates with its numerous global partners for ecological justice and human rights both in Canada and overseas. The movement against nuclear

---

11. Lind and Mihevc, *Coalitions for Justice*, 361. See also Greene, *Canadian Churches and Foreign Policy*.

weapons is ongoing. Currently, Quaker Murray Thompson (of Project Plough-shares fame) has mobilized eight hundred recipients of the Order of Canada to advocate for nuclear disarmament and endorsement of the UN's call for a nuclear weapons convention.

The United Church is working for peace in a foundational way to collapse racial stereotypes through ecumenical contacts with recent immigrant con-gregations from Ghana (Methodist) and Colombia (Presbyterian) and with Canada's indigenous population. The church's recent mutual recognition of ministries with the Presbyterian Church of the Republic of Korea (PROK) and the United Church of the Philippines promises a more dynamic relation-ship with immigrants to Canada from those countries. Many United Church congregations are sponsoring Syrian refugee families, and a few are joining with the Muslim community to do so. Emmanuel College in Toronto, a United Church theological college, now offers a master of pastoral studies in Muslim studies, taught by Muslim scholars and open to all.

One of the most helpful contributions of Canadian churches to current peace efforts is the strong emphasis on the importance of interfaith engage-ments. For example, the United Church has issued a series of widely used resource kits for congregations wishing to understand Judaism, Islam, Hin-duism, and aboriginal spirituality.[12] We look to the future with renewed com-mitment and hope, and continue to engage energetically in the enormously complicated issues of peace in the world in our day and generation.

12. All the following works have been published in Toronto by the Theology, Inter-Church and Inter-Faith Committee of the United Church of Canada: *Mending the World: An Ecumenical Vision for Healing and Reconciliation*, 1997; *Bearing Faithful Witness: United Church–Jewish Relations Today*, 2003; *That We May Know Each Other: United Church–Muslim Relations Today*, 2006; *Honoring the Divine in Each Other: United Church–Hindu Relations Today*, 2016. Aboriginal spirituality was affirmed by the United Church adopting additions to the introductory materials to the Basis of Union in the manual, and revising the church's crest to include aboriginal significance and participation.

"Has God a Lobby in Ottawa?"
The Protestant Left in the United Church
of Canada during the Vietnam War, 1966–1968

Gayle Thrift

In an address titled "The American Rape of Vietnam," delivered in Ottawa in June 1966, the Reverend J. R. Hord, a high-profile figure in the United Church of Canada (UCC), attacked the blindness of American foreign policy in opposing what he believed was "a Nationalist Movement towards autonomy and liberation of the people of Vietnam."[1] Describing the war's racial and colonialist overtones, he warned that the United States was losing respect internationally because of its actions and that Canada's reputation had been sullied due to its complicity. Hord compared the Allied bombing of Germany during the Second World War to American bombing in Vietnam. He praised moral authorities such as the National Council of Churches of Christ in the USA (NCC) and the Canadian Council of Churches (CCC) for calling for negotiations to end the fighting because Vietnam, according to Augustinian doctrine, was an unjust war.

The compelling hot-button social issue tailor-made for prophetic social action in Canada at this time was American involvement in the Vietnam War and contravention of just war tenets by its participants. As early as the 1920s, Christian missionaries were vigilant regarding the spread of Communism, their atheistic nemesis, in many of their key mission fields in Asia. However, by the mid to late 1960s, the postcolonial ethos of a new generation prevailed. Clerical antipathy to the excesses of capitalism in Western society generated antiwar speeches and pamphlets that were replete with Marxist-tinged rhetoric and an idealistic identification with the "underdog" Vietnamese in an imperialist American war.

The United Church of Canada, the largest Protestant denomination in the country at this time, leaned to the political left due to its social gospel

---

1. United Church of Canada Archives (hereafter UCCA), 82.250C, Box 18, File 7. Rev. J. R. Hord, "The American Rape of Vietnam," Ottawa, June 29, 1966.

roots, yet it retained a conservative consensus in its highest court, the General Council. The council represented the old guard or "graybeards" of the church, a generation shaped by their experience in fighting the spread of fascism in World War II, who became comfortably ensconced in the existing social order of postwar Canada. Hord, a controversial figure, risked fracturing that consensus. As secretary of the church's Board of Evangelism and Social Service (BESS), Hord was responsible for establishing the church's mandate in social and moral issues. For many years, BESS had aggressively pursued traditional social ills such as drinking, gambling, and public morality. Under Hord's new leadership, the board became increasingly outspoken concerning broader social issues and social change through political involvement, and by the mid-1960s it had focused specifically on the Vietnam conflict. In a "vituperative" sermon delivered to an American Methodist congregation, Hord declared: "Many Canadians do not understand your hysterical fear of communism."[2] A more productive alternative would be "if we in the West would identify with the people . . . spending our money on building up the country, instead of devastating it in war, we could . . . beat communism hands down."[3] Hord attacked "Canada's indirect assistance in the U.S. war effort," and refused to be cowed by the political implications of his remarks when "many large-L Liberals [held] positions of influence in the United Church."[4] Surprisingly, much of the tension surrounding Hord's actions originated from within the church membership and its senior hierarchy.

Where did the dissonance between the conservative consensus of the United Church's General Council and Hord and his supporters originate? What inspired Hord's moral stance over Vietnam? And how did Hord and his controversial views figure in the increasingly tenuous relations between the senior ranks of the United Church and federal officials in Ottawa during the politically charged years of the Vietnam War? This analysis shows that the mobilization of an intransigent and outspoken antiwar Protestant Left, galvanized by Hord, disrupted a long-standing congenial relationship between the United Church and federal politicians, pushing it to the breaking point. Consequently, a conservative backlash occurred within the senior ranks of the church to quell the more radical Left in order to avoid alienating congregants, powerful political friends, and donors. The executive of the General Council not only

2. Loren Lind, "The Backlash Test," *Globe and Mail*, April 27, 1968, A3.
3. Martin O'Malley, "Hail Politics, Power and Protocol: And Pity the Protestant. Amen!" *Globe and Mail*, January 9, 1971, A7.
4. O'Malley, "Hail Politics, Power and Protocol," A7.

publicly censured Hord but also took unprecedented measures to centralize the council's control over who could speak for the church. This remarkable effort to silence debate and dissent by the Protestant Left within its ranks weakened the credibility and moral authority of the church within Canadian society. At a time of doubt and moral crisis, pundits posed the question: "Has God a lobby in Ottawa?"[5]

The United Church, along with other mainline Protestant churches in Canada, enjoyed a surge in membership in the decade after WWII that was subsequently referred to as the Fat Fifties. Dreams of a postwar Protestant revival evaporated when statistics revealed an unexpected decline in membership during and beyond the mid-1960s. Historian S. J. D. Green, in his study of Protestant churches in England, states that to deny that there is ebb and flow in the churches would be to deny that historical change occurs within them.[6] However, scholars have yet to agree on why this reversal occurred and offer different interpretations on what influences contributed to the decline of mainline Protestant churches in Canada. Nancy Christie and Michael Gauvreau, in their social history of religion in Canada, argue against secularization while emphasizing that popular forms of religious expression provide a surer measure of sustained religiosity than membership statistics of religious institutions.[7] Gary Miedema's *For Canada's Sake: Public Religion, Centennial Celebrations, and the Re-making of Canada in the 1960s* (2005) cites the transformative effect of the country's diversifying society, with the arrival of new immigrant groups, for example, mitigating the mainline churches' historical primacy in the public square. A critique commissioned by the Anglican Church of Canada in the sixties, Pierre Berton's *The Comfortable Pew: A Critical Look at Christianity and the Religious Establishment in the New Age* (1965), concluded that Protestant churches were indeed complacent, irrelevant, and too closely aligned with the privilege and status of the establishment. Mark Noll's *What Happened to Christian Canada?* (2007) concurs with Berton's assessment, attributing the marginalization of the mainline denominations to their failure to respond effectively to critical contemporary social issues. Commenting on Noll's essay, Marguerite Van Die agrees, stating that a "congruence between the sacred and the secular" sustained the ideal of a Christian Canada for evan-

5. Carla Courtenay and Patricia Clarke, "Has God a Lobby in Ottawa?," *United Church Observer* (hereafter *UCO*) 28, no. 22 (February 15, 1967): 27.

6. S. J. D. Green, *The Passing of Protestant England: Secularisation and Social Change, c. 1920–1960* (Cambridge: Cambridge University Press, 2011).

7. Nancy Christie and Michael Gauvreau, *Christian Churches and Their Peoples, 1840–1965: A Social History of Religion in Canada* (Toronto: University of Toronto Press, 2010).

gelical Protestants in nineteenth-century Canada but that further research is needed to understand the reasons for "its rapid collapse in the 1960s."[8]

I contend that the interplay between religion and politics warrants more serious consideration when explaining this phenomenon. Paul Boyer's groundbreaking monographs analyze the cultural impact of the atomic bomb upon American society, revealing the powerful confluence of politics, international relations, military technology, and religion during the Cold War. Paul Hollander argues that "the politicization of the churches" contributed to a decline in membership and church attendance in the liberal or mainline Protestant denominations in the United States during the mid-1960s.[9] In addition, Jill Gill's analysis, *Embattled Ecumenism: The National Council of Churches, the Vietnam War, and the Trials of the Protestant Left* (2011), evaluates the effect of the liberal Protestant Left and their antiwar stance upon the NCC during the Vietnam conflict. She concludes that the intersection of faith and politics was damaging for religious institutions.[10]

Traditionally, the concept of the divine in Christianity imbued religion with sacrosanct moral authority in conjunction with the state. The sacred authority and prophetic voice of the church, of speaking truth to power, enhanced the legitimacy of the state, making a case for alignment between the two institutions. During times of crisis, such as war, the Augustinian doctrine of *jus ad bellum* underlay the churches' moral authority. The doctrine required a formal declaration of war to be implemented by a legitimate authority for a tenable cause, with reasonable hope of success. War was justifiable only as a last resort and with a limited response to an aggressor.[11] Critics of the Vietnam War argued that America was fighting an undeclared war in Vietnam without legitimate authority, thereby contravening just war conventions. With the proliferation of nuclear weapons during the Cold War, antiwar proponents also argued that the principle of proportionality was irrelevant. Humanity could

8. Marguerite Van Die, "Mark Noll, What Happened to Christian Canada? A Response from the Perspective of the Canadian Protestant Mainline Denominations," *Church & Faith Trends, a Publication of the Centre for Research on Canadian Evangelicalism* 2, no. 1 (October 2008).

9. Paul Hollander, *Anti-Americanism: Critiques at Home and Abroad, 1965–1990* (New York: Oxford University Press, 1992), 83.

10. Jill K. Gill, *Embattled Ecumenism: The National Council of Churches, the Vietnam War, and the Trials of the Protestant Left* (DeKalb: Northern Illinois University Press, 2011), passim. See also Gill's chapter in this book.

11. Michael Walzer, *Just and Unjust Wars*, 3rd ed. (New York: Perseus Books Group, 1977), 21.

destroy itself many times over with the limitless potential of nuclear technology. Open speculation circulated that tensions between the two superpowers could erupt into an apocalyptic scenario at any moment, as nearly happened during the Cuban missile crisis in October 1962. As the war in Vietnam intensified, public opinion in Canada shifted from deference to protest. Gallup polls reveal that anti-American attitudes among Canadians rose from 27 percent in 1956 to 53 percent a decade later.[12] Private groups led by the Canadian Labour Congress as well as groups of university professors and their students were questioning complicity in Canada's role on the International Control Commission in Vietnam as early as 1966.[13] I argue that the General Council's repudiation of the new evangelism rooted in social activism, combined with efforts by strong conservative forces at work within the church, effectively reduced the controversial prophetic role personified by Hord and his supporters among the Protestant Left. Consequently, the moral authority and credibility of the church as the conscience of the nation were substantially diminished.

The United Church of Canada was founded in 1925 (by an amalgamation of Methodists, Congregationalists, and concurring Presbyterians), and described itself as a "national" and conciliar church. Its courts and boards were comprised of equal representation of clergy and lay members. Leaders expected that the increase in membership after union would result in a stronger political voice, "forc[ing] the government to recognize the status of Protestantism."[14] Church leaders were interested not only in domestic concerns but also in matters of foreign policy and international affairs. With decades of work invested in overseas undertakings in Africa, India, China, Japan, Korea, Trinidad, and elsewhere, the church closely monitored the development of policies that could affect its mission efforts.

Headquartered in Toronto, the church's highest legislative body, the General Council, was comprised of two hundred ministers and two hundred laypeople. Members of the council were elected by the eleven regional conferences and representatives from the Board of Overseas Missions and met biannually. The council established an international affairs committee during the early 1930s. After the revelations of the Gouzenko spy scandal in Ottawa and amid the throes of the Communist advance in China, responsibility for

12. J. L. Granatstein and Robert Bothwell, *Pirouette: Pierre Trudeau and Canadian Foreign Policy* (Toronto: University of Toronto Press, 1990), 41.

13. Thomas Hockin, "External Affairs and Defence," in *Canadian Annual Review of Politics and Public Affairs, 1966*, ed. John Saywell (Toronto: University of Toronto Press, 1967), 189.

14. Neil Semple, *The Lord's Dominion: The History of Canadian Methodism* (Montreal and Kingston: McGill-Queen's University Press, 1996), 424.

the committee was transferred to BESS, where it became a standing committee in 1947. BESS was one of ten boards of the United Church, and a key one, described as "the social conscience of the church."[15]

Although the General Council was designated as the official voice of the church, the Committee on the Church and International Affairs (CCIA) was given considerable autonomy. Terms of reference for the CCIA included gathering and studying relevant materials for the church regarding international developments, providing leadership in formulating and communicating policy recommendations, and most significantly, ensuring that "indifference and complacency" were kept at bay.[16] Major issues such as bipolarity and comparative study of democratic capitalism, socialism, Communism, and totalitarianism were to be researched and discussed, and policies were to be written and submitted to the General Council for approval and subsequent inclusion in the United Church yearbook as official policy statements. The committee was to explore how the church could contribute to better relations between Canada and Asia, in the Pan American Union, and with the USSR. The CCIA's central committee was based in Toronto and met several times a year. Regional committees such as the Toronto and Montreal Round Tables on Atomic Energy met regularly to study and report on specific areas of interest. International affairs experts were invited to give addresses at annual meetings of the General Council, BESS, and the CCIA.

Policies formulated by the CCIA were brought to bear upon the federal government in two ways: directly by communication of church resolutions to the nation's political leaders, and indirectly by influencing public opinion. Access to the public was gained not only through church attendance but also by the print and broadcast media through official press releases. These included the bimonthly periodical, the *United Church Observer*, as well as dissemination of printed CCIA updates or annual CCIA reports that were available in booklet form and were also published as part of the biennial *Record of Proceedings* of the General Council. Members of the CCIA participated in interviews and debates concerning international affairs that were of interest to many Canadians who did not attend church services. The CCIA emerged as part of a large ecumenical network of like-minded organizations that included the Canadian Council of Churches, the British Council of Churches, the National Council of

15. Ken Bagnell, "Ray Hord—the United Church's Great Dissenter," *Star Weekly Magazine* (Toronto), January 27, 1968.

16. UCCA, 88.088C, Box 1, File 1, CCIA, minutes, executive and committee, September 17, 1947.

the Churches of Christ in the USA, and the World Council of Churches. The profusion of conferences and commissions with intermingling representatives produced a community of religious leaders whose combined voice concerning international affairs contributed to the visibility and credibility of the moral authority of the churches in the public square.

The Vietnam conflict was a major flashpoint between East and West during the Cold War. Tensions escalated between the opposing regimes of Communist Hanoi and the American-backed government in Saigon. During the late 1950s and early 1960s, the Canadian government led by Conservative prime minister John Diefenbaker, a staunch anti-Communist, was supportive of US policy in Asia. The American objective was the containment of Communism in Indochina through the support of a non-Communist South Vietnamese government. Despite military assistance programs and the presence of military advisers to prevent a hostile takeover by the North, there were ongoing efforts by the Vietcong, supported by Hanoi, to undermine the stability of the South. The United States, a prominent member of the Southeast Asia Treaty Organization (SEATO), had maintained military personnel in South Vietnam since 1953. The Geneva Accords (1954) ended the First Indochina War and partitioned Vietnam. The accords also established the International Control Commission (ICC) to oversee the uneasy cease-fire and assist with additional matters of disengagement such as troop withdrawal and the return of refugees. At the request of the United States, Canada became an ICC member. Attempts to stabilize the region were not as effective as had been hoped. American president John F. Kennedy, committed to halting the spread of Communism in southeast Asia, provided military aid to South Vietnam in late 1961. American advisers believed that if South Vietnam were defeated, the neighboring states of Cambodia and Laos would, through a domino effect, fall to Communism as well. Both China and the Soviet Union were complicit in providing support to the Communist forces in North Vietnam. Following naval skirmishes between North Vietnamese patrol boats and American warships, Kennedy's successor, Lyndon B. Johnson, signed the Gulf of Tonkin Resolution (August 1964), enabling him to authorize any military action necessary to defend American forces in the region. Without actually declaring war on the North, this measure reduced the risk of China or the Soviet Union becoming openly involved. However, it also committed the United States to ongoing military engagement in Vietnam, straining relations with its geopolitical ally and neighbor, Canada.

A minority Liberal government was elected in April 1963 under the leadership of Lester B. Pearson. During his career, Pearson served in the Department of External Affairs. He was later elected to Parliament, where he was appointed secretary of state for external affairs under Prime Minister Louis St. Laurent. Pearson won the Nobel Peace Prize in recognition of his role in the resolution of the Suez crisis in 1956, which prepared the way for Canada's participation in United Nations (UN) peacekeeping. As a proponent of quiet diplomacy, Pearson wanted to maintain amicable relations with Canada's American ally while ensuring that Canada was not drawn into an unwelcome war. This was not an easy task, since the Liberal election platform included a pledge to honor its NORAD (North American Air Defense Command) commitments for the continental defense of North America by accepting American nuclear tactical weapons and Bomarc warheads. Pearson was concerned that any further increase in American involvement in Indochina might lead to a loss of credibility for the United States, diminishing its influence as a global superpower.[17] His concerns were exacerbated by Operation Rolling Thunder when American forces initiated a series of punitive bombing attacks against North Vietnam. This was in retaliation for an attack by the Communist Vietcong on the American base at Pleiku during the night of February 7, 1965. The bombing was intended to force the North Vietnamese government to the negotiating table. Many Canadians, including the prime minister, were alarmed by the bombing, fearing that China, the most recent nuclear power, would come to the defense of North Vietnam, since the bombing approached its territories. Without intervention, the hostilities could escalate to nuclear conflict.

Pearson expressed his apprehension over the crisis in Vietnam and acknowledged the "growing number of domestic critics of the bombing"—among them, representatives of the UCC.[18] A protest march outside the American embassy in Montreal resulted in several injuries and forty-six arrests.[19] In Vancouver, prominent public figures, including Dr. Brock Chisholm, Dr. Hugh Keenleyside, Dr. N. A. M. MacKenzie, and Bishop G. P. Gower, circulated a statement, "Safeguard World Peace: End the War in Viet Nam."[20] A delegation of Carleton University professors sent the prime minister a petition signed by 306 professors from fourteen universities in various parts of Canada stating:

17. Robert Bothwell, *Canada and the United States: The Politics of Partnership* (Toronto: University of Toronto Press, 1992), 96.

18. Greg Donaghy, *Tolerant Allies: Canada and the United States, 1963–1968* (Montreal and Kingston: McGill-Queen's University Press, 2002), 128. The address to the Canadian Club took place on February 10, 1965, three days after the initiation of Operation Rolling Thunder.

19. Lara Campbell, Dominique Clément, and Gregory S. Kealey, eds., *Debating Dissent: Canada and the Sixties* (Toronto: University of Toronto Press, 2012), 10.

20. F. H. Soward, "External Affairs and Defence," in *Canadian Annual Review of Politics and Public Affairs*, ed. John Saywell (Toronto: University of Toronto Press, 1966), 233.

"It was Canada's duty . . . to seek an end to this war and call for immediate negotiations, to be undertaken without pre-conditions."[21] A group of Toronto clergymen, more than half of them from the United Church, sent a message to Pearson stating their support "for withdrawal of foreign military forces from Vietnam—North and South, neutralization of both areas and a plebiscite to determine the kind of government wanted by the people."[22] Without intervention they believed that continuing American involvement in the civil war in Vietnam "confront[ed] mankind with the grave peril of nuclear war."[23] Anti-American sentiments increased after Pearson's Temple University speech on April 2, where he was to receive the university's World Peace Prize. President Johnson was irate over Pearson's measured remonstrance of his government's bombing policy in Vietnam. Relations between the two allies cooled considerably for the duration of Pearson's tenure, and communication between the two allies was strained.[24]

Increasingly, concerned Canadians joined the antiwar vanguard to voice their protests over American bombing. An unprecedented level of anti-American sentiment would emerge from a young generation of Canadian intellectuals affiliated with the political Left.[25] Many of them believed that Canada's foreign policy was too closely aligned with that of the United States. The Reverend J. Raymond Hord, an intense, outspoken iconoclast, led by example through his unrelenting and withering condemnation of both Pearson and the government's diplomatic stance on Vietnam.

Hord: An Unlikely Prophetic Voice

In 1963, at the age of forty-four, Hord became secretary of the influential Board of Evangelism and Social Service of the United Church. He succeeded James R. Mutchmor, who had distinguished himself as secretary from 1938 to 1963 by

21. Soward, "External Affairs and Defence," 233.

22. "Protest U.S. Policy," *UCO* 27, no. 2 (March 15, 1965): 35.

23. "Protest U.S. Policy," 35. The message was drafted by Dr. Abraham Feinberg, rabbi emeritus of Holy Blossom Temple, and Rev. Glynn Firth of Bathurst Street United Church. The signatories included eight United Church clergymen, two Presbyterian ministers, an Anglican priest, and four rabbis.

24. John English, *The Life of Lester Pearson*, vol. 2, *The Worldly Years, 1949–1972* (Toronto: Knopf, 1992), 368. See John Holmes, "Canada and the Vietnam War," in *Canadian Foreign Policy: Historical Readings*, ed. J. L. Granatstein (Toronto: Copp Clark Pitman, 1986), 204.

25. Donaghy, *Tolerant Allies*, 129.

leading crusades against social problems such as alcohol abuse. According to the *United Church Observer*, the official publication of the UCC, Hord and his colleagues represented the up-and-coming generation, a group concerned about the headline-making issues of the day: the Vietnam War, abortion, divorce, and medicare.[26] There was little to indicate that Hord would become the prophetic voice of the United Church. He was raised in a rural community near London, Ontario, and was ordained at age twenty-three after attending the University of Western Ontario. His first church assignment was in East End, Saskatchewan, where he married and began to raise a family.[27] Hord would later spend a year at Union Theological Seminary in New York, where he was influenced by leading theologians such as Reinhold Niebuhr, Paul Tillich, and John Bennett.[28] Niebuhr was the founder and editor of *Christianity and Crisis*, a periodical that emphasized the importance of integrating Christian realism with international affairs, promoting a doctrine of peace and justice for all through active engagement with social and political issues by the clergy. Niebuhr and other liberals were criticized by conservative European theologian Karl Barth "for reducing the Gospel to a sort of 'Christian Marshall Plan,' a worldly campaign to enact a good society."[29] Niebuhr rejected the view of Barth "that the church's business was not social reconstruction but repentance."[30] Hollander notes that progressive political thought could be traced through the seminaries where many of the clergy received their training. As the churches sought out clergy who were trained at prestigious seminaries with liberal theologies, they were in fact "systematically hiring men who . . . [were] politically more liberal than the constituency of the congregation."[31] He concludes: "In these Protestant churches there has been a growing divergence between the leadership that embraced largely secular and left-of-center causes and the ordinary members of congregations, far less concerned with the favorite issues of the church elite."[32] Hord returned to Saskatchewan a disciple of Niebuhr's philosophy and built Lakeview United Church in Regina into "one

26. Kenneth Bagnell, "The View from the Firing Line," *UCO* 29, no. 12 (September 1, 1967): 5.

27. Bagnell, "The View from the Firing Line," 15. At his death, Hord left his widow and three surviving children.

28. Bagnell, "The View from the Firing Line," 15.

29. Richard Wightman Fox, *Reinhold Niebuhr: A Biography.* (New York: Pantheon Books, 1985), 234.

30. Fox, *Reinhold Niebuhr*, 234.

31. Quoted in Hollander, *Anti-Americanism*, 110.

32. Hollander, *Anti-Americanism*, 84.

of the most vigorous churches in western Canada."[33] His relocation to Toronto in 1959 heralded the realization of his activist praxis.

As American involvement in Vietnam escalated, it emerged as the most contentious issue of all, and the Protestant Left of the United Church found an indefatigable champion in Ray Hord. As early as August 1965, Hord circulated a statement to his fellow United Church clergymen titled "The Christian Conscience and War in Vietnam." He stated, "I am disturbed at American messianism displayed in foreign affairs. The United States is in danger of launching a holy war against Communism."[34] He noted that the World Council of Churches, the British Council of Churches, the Canadian Council of Churches, and several denominations in Canada, including the United Church, had all condemned the escalation of the war in Vietnam. The *United Church Observer* confirmed this in a commentary indicating that "most church leaders have been openly critical" of the legitimacy of the war in Vietnam.[35] For example, the Presbyterian Committee on International Affairs had recommended that Canada not support America's actions in the war by sending military personnel, supplies, or material aid for the purpose of war or even by making statements of support.[36] Hord stressed the importance of bringing China into the UN despite the objections of the United States. He argued, "The most critical challenge which faces the West is to learn to live together with the Chinese who include one-quarter of the world's population. It is outrageous that China has not been included in the United Nations. We Canadians should call on our Government, together with other smaller nations, to challenge the U.S.A. on this issue and vote for Chinese membership."[37] His critique of American policy in Vietnam did not abate. He indicated that the CCIA had stated its opposition to the war on three separate occasions (February, April, and November) in 1965.[38] Almost a quarter of the CCIA's report submitted to the General Council that year focused on the Vietnam conflict, and most

33. Bagnell, "The View from the Firing Line," 15.

34. J. R. Hord, "The Christian Conscience and War in Vietnam," *Christian Outlook*, November 1965, 15. The statement was circulated to United Church ministers, August 9, 1965, and subsequently published in the periodical.

35. "What's New," *UCO* 27, no. 14 (October 15, 1965): 5.

36. The Presbyterian Church in Canada Archives, *The Acts and Proceedings of the Ninety-Second General Assembly of the Presbyterian Church in Canada*, Toronto, Ontario, June 1–9, 1966. Committee on International Affairs, 339.

37. UCCA, Committee on the Church and International Affairs (hereafter CCIA), 82.250C, Box 18, File 7. Hord, "The Christian Conscience and War in Vietnam" (statement), 3.

38. UCCA, CCIA, 82.250C, Box 18, File 7. Hord, "The American Rape of Vietnam."

of its ten-thousand-word text was critical of American policy.[39] The CCIA was increasingly voicing the views of the Canadian Left. Hord argued that "Christians had a good deal to learn from the New Left," since "the old small-l liberals in politics and religion are the new conservatives. Let us admit it. When the crunch is on, us [*sic*] older people . . . are not going to sacrifice our privileged positions. And the crunch is coming."[40] In the spring of 1966, Hord addressed two antiwar protests being held in the prairie cities of Saskatoon and Regina. He had rejected the advice of a Saskatchewan cabinet minister that "he shouldn't join the other protesters because they were 'a bunch of pinks.'"[41] Opposition continued to mount when a group of laymen contacted United Church moderator Ernest Howse to express their concern over Hord's planned attendance. Howse defended Hord's decision, stating, "men in offices of the church are still Canadian citizens and have a perfect right as Canadians to speak where they like."[42] Subsequently, flanked by representatives from the leftist New Democratic Party, the Cooperative Commonwealth Federation, and the Communist Party of Canada, Hord urged the Canadian government to formulate an independent foreign policy depicting the United States as "hell-bent for war with China."[43]

For several years the disagreement over the most effective means to stop Communist expansion had plagued leadership of the church. Despite unprecedented efforts to reach an agreement over defense policy and the question of nuclear weapons, the General Council in 1962 found itself in deadlock. Its compromise was a two-position statement with half its members supporting a theological pacifist position and the rest favoring a policy of credible deterrence.[44] A few weeks later, the convictions of both factions were tested during the thirteen-day Cuban missile crisis. When the Soviet missiles were finally removed from Cuba and the theory of credible deterrence proved effective, many Canadians were firmly convinced that the country deserved more decisive

39. UCCA, *Record of Proceedings of Twenty-second General Council*, Waterloo, September 1966, The United Church of Canada, Toronto, 219.

40. Lind, "The Backlash Test," A3.

41. "Protesting a Protester," *UCO* 28, no. 5 (May 1, 1966): 5. Steve Hewitt, "Sunday Morning Subversion: The Canadian Security State and Organized Religion in the Cold War," in *Love, Hate, and Fear in Canada's Cold War*, ed. Richard Cavell (Toronto: University of Toronto Press, 2004), 57–74.

42. Quoted in "Protesting a Protester," 5. Howse served as moderator for the usual two-year term, September 1964 until September 1966.

43. Quoted in "Protesting a Protester," 5.

44. UCCA, *Record of Proceedings of Twentieth General Council*, London, September 1962, The United Church of Canada, Toronto, 350.

leadership than the Conservative government under Diefenbaker provided and that Canadian defense policies merited serious reconsideration.

One year later, the General Council of the United Church met in Waterloo, Ontario, on September 7, 1966. The 388 delegates in attendance elected Dr. Wilfred C. Lockhart, minister at Kingsway-Lambton United Church in Toronto, as their new moderator. Lockhart was regarded as an experienced consensus builder whose principal task would be to secure the long-awaited union of the Anglican and United Churches, which was in part a response to declining membership.[45] He was fifty-nine, and had been principal of United College in Winnipeg for eleven years and chairman of the Board of Colleges for ten. He was regarded as a leading ecumenical spokesman and a member of the religious establishment.[46]

Lockhart was immediately embroiled in controversy. The more conservative members of the General Council challenged the CCIA's leftist interpretation of American policy in Vietnam. The most problematic section, they argued, was written by Frederick Nossal, considered an expert adviser as the Far East correspondent for the *Toronto Telegram* newspaper. He argued that the Vietnam conflict was not an ideological war between Communists and non-Communists but a war of liberation against colonialism and that the Vietcong guerrilla movement, although predominantly Communist, had attracted adherents of diverse political groups whose common interest was to free Vietnam of foreign domination, American or otherwise. Nossal described growing domestic opposition to American involvement in an undeclared and unnecessary war where seemingly indiscriminate bombing and the use of chemical agents against civilians provoked "voices of protest in Congress, in the churches, the universities, the newspapers and on television and radio."[47] He recommended a cease-fire to facilitate negotiations, reiterating the church's resolutions urging the prime minister to pressure the United States to limit its military action in North and South Vietnam, to begin a phased withdrawal of all foreign troops from South Vietnam, and to install an international force to supervise free elections.[48]

---

45. A. C. Forrest, "The New Moderator: Calm Man for a Tough Time," *UCO* 8, no. 14 (1966): 14. The union was a slow-moving process that had been under discussion for about twenty-two years.

46. "Up Front, Meet the Moderator," *UCO* 28, no. 13 (October 1, 1966): 5.

47. UCCA, *Proceedings*, 1966, 210.

48. UCCA, *Proceedings*, 1966, 220. The resolutions were passed by the International Affairs Committee in February, April, and November and subsequently communicated to the prime minister.

Members of the conservative majority of the General Council believed that although the war in Vietnam was deplorable, it was imperative that it be fought and won in order to contain Communist expansion in Asia. Furthermore, they argued that the CCIA was an inappropriate forum for the dissemination of anti-American propaganda. Subsequently, the council took several steps to distance itself from the recommendations in order to mitigate risk of a public controversy. In efforts to distance itself from the report, the council requested (for the first time) that contributors to the report be listed. In addition, it published a disclaimer stating that the report was not official church policy but merely research presented to stimulate discussion.[49] Most importantly, the CCIA was removed from the jurisdiction of Hord and BESS and placed under the direct supervision of the General Council. The CCIA was reduced in size from fifty to thirty-two members.[50] Donald Evans—an associate professor of philosophy at the University of Toronto, a member of the committee, and a contributor to the report—protested: "The Committee on the Church and International Affairs has been 'cut down to size' both literally and figuratively."[51] The committee investigating Hord's participation in the protest rally in Saskatchewan recommended that "all statements from church boards 'should be channeled through the United Church press officer.' And . . . that 'no board secretary should make a formal policy statement to the press unless his executive or board has approved it.'"[52] Evans described these developments as a move by which members of the executive of the General Council were attempting to centralize authority within the United Church and silence the voice of the Protestant Left.

The General Council reworded the proposed Vietnam resolution, assigning equal culpability to both sides in the conflict rather than placing the onus on the American government to initiate negotiations.[53] The prime minister was to be advised of the resolution and the church's concern over the conflict. The resolution urged the government to refuse to send members of the Canadian forces to fight in Vietnam, to oppose further escalation of the war, and to support the efforts of the United Nations to effect conditions for negotiation, including a cessation of bombing in North Vietnam and a de-escalation of hostilities in the south.[54] Would the resolution evoke a government response?

49. UCCA, *Proceedings*, 1966, 208.

50. UCCA, *Proceedings*, 1966, 379.

51. Donald Evans, "Editor's Commentary: Where Do We Go from Here?," in *Peace, Power and Protest*, ed. Donald Evans (Toronto: Ryerson Press, 1967), 304.

52. O'Malley, "Hail Politics, Power and Protocol," A9.

53. UCCA, *Proceedings*, 1966, 219.

54. UCCA, *Proceedings*, 1966, 274.

The *Observer* investigated the impact of General Council resolutions that were forwarded to the government. Most of these concerned social and economic resolutions submitted to the government by BESS. For example, in 1967 there were more than a dozen resolutions ranging from the recognition of Red China, to the Vietnam conflict, to divorce, birth control, and car insurance. Members of the board countered challenges to its competency in these diverse areas by inviting lay experts to assist in its commissions. There were varying opinions regarding their efficacy. However, David MacDonald, a Conservative MP and United Church minister, commented: "I think some scepticism might exist as to how accurately a general council of roughly 400 adequately represents a church population in the millions."[55] Dr. Ernest Long, the secretary of the General Council, disagreed and argued that the government often provided lengthy responses to resolutions.[56] In the past, former moderator J. R. Mutchmor had cultivated a personal rapport with Ottawa officials and Canadian representatives to the UN through the CCIA.[57] A journalist accounting for Mutchmor's success wrote:

> His influence was so great that he was virtually a minister without portfolio in several federal and provincial governments. He was on good terms with prominent editors and publishers. He either takes credit or has been given credit for the defeat of former Ontario Premier George Drew, for the sacking of a tipsy federal labor minister, for The Toronto Telegram's failure to publish a Sunday newspaper, for the establishment of a separate external affairs department in Ottawa and for unemployment insurance. That he is better known as a former E&SS secretary than as a former United Church moderator says something about the importance of the position.[58]

The *Observer* concluded that "church resolutions are most influential when presented directly to a minister or committee by a prestigious and articulate delegation. And church delegations . . . 'always get past the secretary.'"[59] Mutchmor commented that "during all the years of service of our communion's International Affairs Committee, close contact was maintained with Ottawa and our Canadian representatives at the United Nations."[60] Dr. Paul Fox,

55. Quoted in Courtenay and Clarke, "Has God a Lobby in Ottawa?," 27.
56. Courtenay and Clarke, "Has God a Lobby in Ottawa?," 27.
57. *Mutchmor: The Memoirs of James Ralph Mutchmor* (Toronto: Ryerson Press, 1965), 169.
58. O'Malley, "Hail Politics, Power and Protocol," A6.
59. Courtenay and Clarke, "Has God a Lobby in Ottawa?," 26.
60. *Mutchmor*, 169.

a political science professor, confirmed this: "In the war years, Dr. Mutchmor was on the Ottawa train every week. No one will ever know what went on and what came of it."[61] In his autobiography, Mutchmor remained discreet, saying only that "a senior civil servant told me: 'You had better call to see me at least twice in a year. That is E. P. Taylor's average.'"[62] Mutchmor cultivated a rapport with senior officials in the government: "Sometimes even a brief letter in an hour of crisis was welcomed by our leaders. I recall the Suez trouble and the very hard role Mr. Pearson had in that difficult hour. I sent him a personal note assuring him of our prayers. I treasure his warm handwritten reply. Likewise, and on behalf of the committee, I sent supporting letters when Paul Martin, almost single-handed brought some new nations into the UN. . . . I also wrote to the Right Honourable John G. Diefenbaker to express appreciation of his strong stand against South Africa's policy of apartheid."[63] This, however, was no longer the case, as Peter Newman, a knowledgeable Ottawa correspondent, indicated: "As far as I am aware, God does not now have an effective lobby on Parliament Hill."[64]

Fallout

With Hord's predilection for confrontation, the deference once reserved for governmental authority and reciprocated in kind rapidly dissipated. He criticized Paul Martin, secretary of state for external affairs, for what he perceived to be Martin's refusal to oppose American policy in Vietnam. Hord wanted "a foreign policy that is Canadian, that is clearly stated, courageously and consistently carried through as circumstances permit and which rings with a note of moral concern for the less fortunate and oppressed peoples of the earth."[65] He believed that if the younger generation of Canadians were more knowledgeable about the nation's role in international affairs, there would be a growing level of protest against a Canadian government that was, in his opinion, too closely aligned with an oppressive American foreign policy in Vietnam.[66] Pearson, responding personally to a letter from Hord, stated, "I fully agree with you

61. Courtenay and Clarke, "Has God a Lobby in Ottawa?," 28.

62. *Mutchmor*, 129. Courtenay and Clarke, "Has God a Lobby in Ottawa?," 28.

63. *Mutchmor*, 169–70.

64. Courtenay and Clarke, "Has God a Lobby in Ottawa?," 26.

65. UCCA, CCIA, 82.250C, Box 14, File 4. J. R. Hord, "Canadian Foreign Policy" report, n.d.

66. UCCA, CCIA, 82.250C, Box 14, File 4. Hord, "Canadian Foreign Policy" report.

that the situation in Vietnam is indeed very distressing and I wish to assure you that my Colleagues and I are desirous of seeing the conflict come to an end and that we will do our utmost to assist the parties involved in reaching a settlement which will bring peace to the area."[67] However, Hord continued to openly challenge government policy, causing more headaches for the United Church and the Liberal government.

On May 13, 1967, Walter Gordon, president of the Privy Council, gave a speech calling on Canadians, including Prime Minister Pearson and Secretary of State for External Affairs Paul Martin, to persuade the United States to stop the bombing of Vietnam. Gordon's betrayal of cabinet solidarity provoked a controversy over the right of parliamentary members to speak freely.[68] Hord publicly supported Gordon's remarks and described the prime minister as a "puppy dog on LBJ's leash."[69] The *Globe and Mail* quoted Hord as saying, "God is on the side of the hurt, the maimed and the defenceless and . . . consequently, God must be on the side of the Vietnamese."[70] United Church officials were dismayed at the timing of Hord's defamatory remarks about the prime minister and his government. An official delegation from the United Church was scheduled to visit Martin the following week, and Hord's comments would certainly prejudice their reception.

When Long and Lockhart learned of Hord's remarks, they agreed that an apology was in order to maintain good relations with Ottawa.[71] The apology was drafted without consulting Hord, although he was only two floors away, and released to the press. A reporter at the *Toronto Star* took the apology over the phone and then called Hord to get his reaction. Shortly after the call, Hord received a copy of the apology with a covering letter signed by Long notifying him of their actions. Long expressed his regret over the damage control deemed necessary by senior church officials.[72] The telegram to Lester Pearson began, "In the name of the United Church of Canada I extend sincere apologies to you for the unworthy and unjustified phrase concerning the Prime

67. UCCA, CCIA, 82.250C, Box 14, File 2. Correspondence from Pearson to Hord, January 20, 1967.

68. John Saywell, ed., *Canadian Annual Review of Politics and Public Affairs, 1967* (Toronto: University of Toronto Press, 1968), 212.

69. "PM a Puppy Led by U.S., Hord Says," *Globe and Mail*, May 19, 1967, 27. Bagnell, "The View from the Firing Line," 16.

70. "PM a Puppy Led by U.S., Hord Says," 27.

71. Library Archives Canada (hereafter LAC), RG 146, CSIS, Vol. 1, File AH-2000-00117, Pt. 1.

72. UCCA, CCIA, 82.250C, Box 14, File 2. Correspondence from Long to Hord, May 19, 1967.

Minister of Canada quoted in the C.B.C. and reported in the May 19th issue of the *Globe and Mail* by the Rev. J. R. Hord. . . . The position that the United Church of Canada has taken on the Viet Nam issue is well known. We have expressed our strong opposition to escalation of the war and the bombing of North Viet Nam. We want the war brought to an end. We are in favour of assistance to all who are injured or in distress because of the war, whether such casualties are in the South or in the North." The message concluded: "I wish to make it plain that, while reasserting these opinions, the United Church of Canada dissociates itself from the personal statements made yesterday by the Rev. J. R. Hord and particularly from the manner in which these statements were made."[73] The *Star* reported that Hord remained unrepentant, since he repeated the puppy dog remark a few days later.[74]

Shortly after Hord's faux pas, a committee was established to deal with the "issuing of public statements by headquarters' officers."[75] Hord himself was feeling the pressure. He spoke more guardedly to journalists, explaining, "I have to get on with the rest of the men in the building."[76] Lockhart believed Hord was behaving strategically, ensuring that public opinion was with him before going to the General Council for ratification of controversial recommendations. But the council would not tolerate being reduced to a rubber stamp. Lockhart preferred to have church policy formulated in private, frank discussions, then presented to, and ratified by, the General Council. He questioned Hord's competency to speak on the wide range of issues that he undertook.[77] However, journalist Kenneth Bagnell, writing in the *Observer*, cautioned that although Hord would in future "be more circumspect in taking hard-line positions in the press," he had, through his actions, successfully "attracted and solidified the church's left wing and part of its centre as his base."[78] His critics therefore needed to be cautious if they wanted to avoid further dissension within the church.

73. UCCA, CCIA, 82.250C, Box 14, File 2. Attachment to letter from Long to Hord, May 19, 1967.

74. LAC, RG 146, CSIS. "United Church Cold War: Hord vs. the Brass," *Toronto Daily Star*, October 21, 1967, clipping.

75. Bagnell, "The View from the Firing Line," 13.

76. Bagnell, "The View from the Firing Line," 13.

77. Phyllis D. Airhart, *A Church with the Soul of a Nation: Making and Remaking the United Church of Canada* (Montreal and Kingston: McGill-Queen's University Press, 2014), 226–27. Hord's interests ranged from critiques of big business, to concerns over indigenous rights, to international affairs.

78. Bagnell, "The View from the Firing Line," 16.

Controversy erupted again, however, when Hord sponsored a one-thousand-dollar grant to support Canadian volunteer groups who would provide assistance to American draft dodgers. It was estimated that there were as many as fifteen thousand draft dodgers in Canada, many of them in Toronto, Montreal, and Vancouver. Polls indicated that twenty-somethings were most sympathetic to their plight while the majority of Canadians were ambivalent or disapproving.[79] Hord did not consult or seek approval of the executive of the General Council.[80] His actions sparked debate and furor over the dispersal of church monies for such a contentious political issue. Church leaders feared a reduction in church revenue if major financial contributors chose to boycott the board's decision by withholding their support. The executive of the General Council therefore issued a statement declaring the board's decision: "The United Church does not consider it the province of Canadian citizens to proffer incitement or encouragement for young Americans to break the laws of their own country."[81] It refused to authorize any funds in support of draft dodgers. After its announcement, General Council ordered an investigation of Hord's BESS. The *Globe and Mail* reported that a group of ministers expressed their confidence in Hord and the BESS. The article said, "Forty ministers of the United Church in Toronto have signed a petition criticizing Rt. Rev. Wilfrid Lockhart, moderator of Canada's largest *Protestant faith*, for interfering with one of the church's boards. . . . The ministers also have criticized the General Council which Dr. Lockhart heads for reprimanding Dr. J. Raymond Hord and his Board of Evangelism and Social Service for offering $1,000 to groups aiding U.S. draft-dodgers in Canada." The petition included the signatures of seventy-five lay members of the church in Toronto, and more support was forthcoming from fifteen letters of agreement from across the country. The Reverend Robert Lindsey of Regent Park United Church (Toronto) claimed that the General Council was "a nervous, reactionary group that doesn't want to offend anybody." He noted that "this is the first time in history that the Council has interfered with a church board," and that there was little choice but to "fight for . . . the threatened autonomy of Dr. Hord's board." Hord's supporters believed that "the present controversy is rooted in conflicting views of the role of the church. Members of Dr. Hord's board (and the committee of five and its petitioners) feel the

79. John Saywell, ed., *Canadian Annual Review of Politics and Public Affairs, 1968* (Toronto: University of Toronto Press, 1969), 269–70.
80. Editorial, "D-Dodgers," *UCO* 29, no. 15 (November 1, 1967): 11.
81. Editorial, "D-Dodgers," 11.

church should be on the front lines in the battle for social change. They feel Dr. Lockhart and many of the General Council executives overvalue the financial and membership strength of the church." Lindsey concluded: "What the General Council should be . . . is a collection of men willing 'to take risks,' and allowing its boards freedom to do what they feel is right."[82] Members of the General Council disagreed.

The *Toronto Star* reported that the meeting of the General Council executive had been "very stormy" when Hord was reprimanded for his actions.[83] In an *Observer* editorial, A. C. Forrest described the "left-wing, right-wing struggle" personified by Lockhart and Hord, and he outlined the church's predicament: it desperately needed prophetic leaders who were "alert to the great issues in the modern world," and "one of the great moral issues of 1967" was the unjust and, in Hord's opinion, "evil" Vietnam War. Reflecting upon the controversy, Forrest, with a note of resignation and sadness, concluded: "It is our opinion that prophets in the United Church are few—and that Hord is one of these few."[84] Hord was silenced, and the furor subsided.

Hord's sudden death on March 1, 1968, at the age of forty-nine, left his supporters numb with shock and grief. The *Globe and Mail* reported news of his demise on its front page. The *Regina Leader-Post* described him as "one of the most controversial churchmen in Canada."[85] Newspaper editorials praised Hord's uncompromising moral stance, which could either aggravate or inspire his colleagues.[86] Pierre Berton, who knew him well, described him as a "Christian activist."[87] Forrest, editor of the *Observer*, remarked, "The longer Hord was around the more I suspected he was a prophet. He didn't have any easy time in the job, but he had lots of guts."[88] Family and friends knew that the divisions within the church and the aftermath of the "bitter meeting" took an emotional toll on Hord.[89] In retrospect, Moderator Lockhart stated that

82. "Moderator and General Council Criticized by 40 Toronto Ministers," *Globe and Mail*, October 7, 1967, 1.

83. LAC, RG 146, CSIS. "United Church Cold War: Hord vs. the Brass."

84. Editorial, "D-Dodgers," 11.

85. "Ray Hord Dies Suddenly," *Regina Leader-Post*, March 2, 1968, 4. Reports indicated that he collapsed and died of a pulmonary thrombosis while waiting for a bus, a few blocks from his home.

86. Editorial, "Rev. J. Raymond Hord," *Globe and Mail*, March 2, 1968, 6.

87. Quoted in UCCA, Aubrey Wice, "I Knew Him as a Man of Action," in "A Stranger in Church," *Toronto Telegram*, clipping, n.d.

88. Quoted in UCCA, Ron Lowman, "Death Shocks Canada's Churchmen," *Toronto Star*, March 2, 1968, clipping.

89. O'Malley, "Hail Politics, Power and Protocol," A7.

"while the views expressed by Rev. James Ray Hord . . . were not always acceptable to the entire church, he helped the church to better fulfill its role as 'the conscience of the nation.'"[90]

Although Hord had challenged the authority of the church and the government, particularly over the Vietnam issue, the degree to which he represented a majority or minority of clergy and congregants was uncertain. Subsequently, the *Observer* joined in an opinion poll being conducted by a group of American church magazines to determine whether statements made by churches about Vietnam were representative of the opinions of their congregations. A total of 2,440 readers responded to the one-page mail-in poll.[91] Respondents were asked to check a box indicating their approval, disapproval, or lack of opinion regarding eleven questions and statements. Overall, results indicated that more clergy disapproved of the war than not, while the laity were divided over the issue.[92] Many of the respondents expressed their lack of confidence in partisan reporting about the war, *even when they were hearing it from church leaders.* The editorial concluded, "The recurring wish for information that could be trusted made it obvious that there is a real need which the church could fill if, first, unbiased information is available, and second—perhaps even harder—it could be presented in a way that would be accepted as unbiased."[93] Issues of credibility, as well as differences of opinion evident between the laity and the clergy, therefore raised questions about the competency of church leaders to speak on behalf of their congregants. How can this be accounted for?

In an analysis of the Protestant Left, Gill describes the activist milieu of Union Theological Seminary during the 1950s and 1960s, when Hord was at Union encountering leading theologians such as Niebuhr, Tillich, and Bennett. She states: "Like most of the American public, mainline churches had largely ignored the Vietnam conflict until 1965. The NCC and its denominational members supported America's resistance to communism, but factions within the ecumenical community's leadership had already begun questioning the government's presuppositions underlying Cold War foreign policy. When the Vietnam conflict became America's latest military bulwark against communism, these factions pushed the NCC to take the prophetic lead by organizing

90. "Passion for Social Justice," *Regina Leader-Post*, March 2, 1968.
91. "The Christian and Viet Nam: A Reader-Opinion Poll," *UCO* 29, no. 23 (February 1, 1968): 4.
92. "How You Vote on Viet Nam," *UCO* 30, no. 2 (March 15, 1968): 16.
93. "How You Vote on Viet Nam," 46.

church responses to the war."[94] Gill's findings on the role of ecumenism and the role of church institutions in the antiwar movement of the 1960s are significant and illuminating for the Canadian context.

Additional evidence indicates that leaders of the United Church were aware that clergy were experiencing a latent sense of competition for moral leadership with secular intellectuals. In the latter part of the decade, Mutchmor warned that "the Universities seem to be taking over moral leadership in International Affairs from the Churches."[95] Hollander, too, observes that some clergy attempted to reclaim and expand their moral authority and influence via the secular political realm by "associating themselves with issues attracting the greatest public attention and appearing to have the strongest moral appeal."[96] For Hord and others like him who shared a belief in prophetic social action, this would entail "sponsoring unpopular causes and initiating change on behalf of minorities as well as majorities."[97] Founding documents from church union in 1925 identify the principal responsibility of the church as being to "assist the state to rise above purely temporal matters"; to support it in providing "a coherent and legitimate social and moral role"; and to "guide the country's conscience."[98] To speak prophetically for peace, the church could not merely "echo" the state but needed to "defend and enhance . . . Christian social principles and their practical outworkings in the life of the world."[99] This was prophetic social action.

94. Gill, *Embattled Ecumenism*, 5.

95. UCCA, 88.088C, Box 1, File 4. Minutes, March 30, 1967. Hollander, *Anti-Americanism*, 89.

96. Hollander, *Anti-Americanism*, 85, 82. Hollander's work involved a study of American churches, and he states that "although a cause-and-effect relationship is unclear, the politicization of the churches . . . more or less coincided with the beginning (in the mid-1960s) of a decline of membership and church attendance in the liberal (or mainline) Protestant denominations." Kenneth Minogue, *Encounter*, March 1990, 3–15. Minogue reports similar trends in churches in Britain. Gerald Walton Paul, "The Board of Evangelism and Social Service of the United Church of Canada: An Historical Analysis of the Enterprises of the Board from 1925 to 1968" (MTheol thesis, Vancouver School of Theology, 1974), 117. This is evident in a 1964 decision by the United Church General Council that authorized the National Project of Evangelism and Social Action, which endorsed both social service and social action as being in the purview of the board.

97. Paul, "The Board of Evangelism and Social Service," 119.

98. Semple, *The Lord's Dominion*, 427.

99. UCCA, *Record of Proceedings of Thirteenth General Council, Vancouver*, September 1948, The United Church of Canada, "Part IV Reports of Sessional Committees as Adopted by the General Council: On the Church and International Affairs—the Church's Task," 130–31.

Conclusion

As Cold War tensions developed, the leaders of the United Church of Canada affirmed its responsibility to promote international reconciliation, order, and peace. Determined to be vigilant over the threat of warfare or "signs of danger and weakness" within the Western bloc, they warned that "building peace requires more than the preaching of a few sermons on vague generalities. . . . [It] will involve work in the muck and slime of world affairs as the peace makers dig down to find the sure rock for the permanent structure."[100] However, when Hord, a proponent for the antiwar Protestant Left, challenged the political leaders of the country to speak to the moral question of US actions in Vietnam, he was declared "pink" or too sympathetic to Communism. While some senior officials defended his right to dissent publicly, the most senior ranks of the church chose to censure him, to silence clerical opposition to American involvement in a war that did not meet the precepts of the Augustinian doctrine of *jus ad bellum*.

Was the moral authority of the United Church challenged by Hord's prophetic social action? Yes, and justly so. As Donald Evans, an associate of Hord's, remarked: "General Councils have no hot-line to heaven, no infallibility. No influx of moral wisdom which raises them above all other gatherings or individuals."[101] The CCIA was tasked with formulating the church's stance on foreign policy, and the General Council, as the highest court and official voice of the church, usually approved it. It wasn't until its recommendations proved unpopular with the conservative majority of the General Council, contradicting government policy and risking financial patrons, that problems arose. The church would not risk the loss of good will and friends in powerful places by approving controversial recommendations even when they were meritorious. The executive of the General Council stated shortly before Hord's death that "board officers may speak out as individuals, but 'should exercise discretion in making any public statements.' This announcement, Dr. Long said, was meant to throttle no one. But being discreet was one of Ray Hord's lesser concerns."[102] As Hord stated prior to his death, "How can the church exercise its prophetic ministry when financial contributions are used as the measure of success while intimidation and threats are used against leaders who dare to

100. UCCA, *Record of Proceedings of Sixteenth General Council*, Sackville, N.B., September 1954, The United Church of Canada, Toronto, 126.

101. Evans, "Editor's Commentary," 304.

102. Lind, "The Backlash Test," A3.

speak a word of judgment upon modern society?"[103] Could the Hord incident have been handled with more tact and less damage to the church's reputation? Former moderator Ernest Howse, interviewed in 1966, defended Hord's right to speak as a Canadian citizen. Evans, writing in *Peace, Power, and Protest*, concluded: "The question 'Who speaks for the Church?' becomes manageable if we no longer equate it with 'Who speaks for God?' Nobody does, in that sense."[104] The censure of Hord by the General Council violated the founding principles of the United Church and its commitment to social gospel activism to fulfill its role as conscience of the nation. Edgar File, a defender of Hord, remarked, "They weren't able to steamroller Hord so they set out to emasculate his board."[105] During Mutchmor's tenure as secretary of BESS from 1937 to 1962, he was able to develop it as a national platform for social reform. This was attributed to his ability to be "a United Church politician, and you must always consider politics when you consider the United Church."[106] Hord was more prophet than politician.

In his outgoing address to the Twenty-Third General Council, Moderator Lockhart warned "against social activists who would undermine the very existence of an organized church." He stated: "What we see emerging is a new kind of Protestantism, a movement in which the protest is mainly against authority, since all authority and all power now become suspect." Calling activists "oversimplifiers," he cautioned, "we are challenged on every side to abandon the old forms of Christian life and witness and to become involved in the world, so involved in fact that we must be prepared to surrender the very corporate life of the church so that any taint of identification *with our past* shall be forever obliterated."[107]

Martin O'Malley, a journalist writing three years after the Hord imbroglio, provided an evaluation of the United Church, stating, "described as a longtime moral presence in Canadian life, [BESS] may become much more diminutive than in the days of J. R. Mutchmor and, later, the late Ray Hord."[108] According to a survey of over eight hundred United Church laymen, the most urgent issue facing the church was "a decreasing concern for moral values."[109] In the

---

103. O'Malley, "Hail Politics, Power and Protocol," A9.

104. Evans, "Editor's Commentary," 305.

105. Quoted in O'Malley, "Hail Politics, Power and Protocol," A9.

106. O'Malley, "Hail Politics, Power and Protocol," A7.

107. William Johnson, "Once Robichaud Aid, Runs for Hord Post," *Globe and Mail*, August 28, 1968, 8.

108. O'Malley, "Hail Politics, Power and Protocol," A6.

109. O'Malley, "Hail Politics, Power and Protocol," A6.

same survey, they were asked what the role of the church should be, and the "distant third [choice] was 'to be the conscience of society on social and moral issues.'"[110] As a result of the confrontation between the Protestant Left and the powerful forces of conservatism in the General Council of the United Church during the Vietnam War, the role of the church as moral arbiter in the political realm of Canadian public life was transformed. There was, indeed, no lobby for God in Ottawa.

110. O'Malley, "Hail Politics, Power and Protocol," A9.

The Cruise Missile Debate in the Canadian Parliament

Bill Blaikie

In April 1982 the Standing Committee on External Affairs and National Defense of the Canadian House of Commons submitted a report to Parliament in advance of the second United Nations Special Session on Disarmament (UNSSOD 2) that was to begin in June of that year. What turned out to be significant about the report was not the report itself, but the decision of six members of the committee to file a minority report. The Minority Report on Security and Disarmament, as it came to be known, became the focus of a larger debate in Canada about the proper Canadian response to the nuclear arms race, and the Cold War, as these things presented themselves in the early 1980s.

It is unlikely that the Canadian debate attracted much attention in America. But the debate that the Minority Report helped to catalyze, particularly with respect to cruise missile testing, was not just about the nuclear arms race but was also about how Canadians saw themselves, their security, and their sovereignty in relation to their neighbor to the south and their historic ties to the North Atlantic alliance.

The authorship of the Minority Report is interesting in itself with respect to the relationship between the church and the Cold War, in that three of the six dissenters were MPs with strong faith connections. Walter McLean was a Progressive Conservative MP from Ontario, and a minister in the Presbyterian Church of Canada. Father Bob Ogle, a New Democratic MP from Saskatchewan, was a diocesan Roman Catholic priest who would be forbidden to run for reelection in 1984 by the Vatican. Douglas Roche, a Progressive Conservative from Alberta, was a nationally known Catholic activist and author. The other three signatories were New Democrats Pauline Jewett and Terry Sargeant, and Liberal Paul MacRae, the only MP from the governing party on the committee to sign the report.

The dissenters associated themselves in their report with some 188 members of the United States Congress who had signed a House-Senate joint resolution sponsored by Senator Mark Hatfield, Republican, and Senator Edward Kennedy, Democrat. The quote they highlighted from the resolution in their report was the call on the United States and the USSR to achieve "a mutual and verifiable freeze on the testing, production, and further deployment of nuclear warheads, missiles, and other delivery systems."

Questioning the conventional view of what constitutes security, the Minority Report noted that one of the paradoxes of the modern world was that although defense is necessary, "the arms race itself is a threat to security." Canadian foreign policy, therefore, should be directed toward the building of conditions for peace, and at the UN special session, Canada should press "for the adoption of a Strategy of Suffocation to stop the arms race, including these four elements, a comprehensive test ban to impede the further development of nuclear explosive devices, an agreement to stop the flight testing of all new strategic delivery vehicles, an agreement to prohibit all production of fissionable material for weapons purposes, and an agreement to limit and then progressively reduce military spending on new strategic nuclear weapons systems."[1] To "give weight to this strategy," the report further recommended that

1. Canada should put its full strength into the campaign that was gathering strength in many parts of the world for a global freeze on the testing, production, and deployment of nuclear weapons and their delivery vehicles.
2. The Canadian government should deny the United States permission to test the new cruise missile system in Canada.
3. Canada should press all nations to pledge never to be the first to use nuclear weapons.
4. Canada should pledge that it will devote one-tenth of 1 percent of its defense budget to disarmament efforts.

As it turned out, recommendation number 2 would attract the most attention in the year following the release of the Minority Report, partly because it was already addressed as a question before the Canadian public, and to an even greater extent, because it was doable, or so it seemed. No other nations had to be persuaded for the recommendation to be fully acted upon, and no fiscal challenges were involved. All that had to happen was for the Canadian government to "Refuse the Cruise," in the words of what became the disarmament battle cry at protests and demonstrations.

1. "Security and Disarmament: A Minority Report," April 1982, 7.

The Canadian public was aware that the Canadian and American governments were considering, and perhaps actively negotiating, the terms of a new agreement for the testing of US military equipment on Canadian soil. The testing of cruise missiles was one test being considered. Debate about a possible request to test the cruise missile prompted the recommendation in the Minority Report, and the debate was intensified by the Minority Report, which became a focal point for those arguing against the testing.

It was widely believed that, in addition to the public debate, a lively debate was going on within the government itself. After all, Prime Minister Pierre Trudeau had supported a strategy of suffocation of nuclear weapons in 1978 in the context of the first United Nations Special Session on Disarmament (UNSSOD 1). Was this same prime minister going to approve the testing of a new delivery vehicle that was arguably going to usher in a whole new era of the nuclear arms race? The government seemed to hold off, but on February 10, 1983, Canadian foreign affairs minister Allan MacEachen surprised many by signing the Canada/US Test and Evaluation Program while on a visit to Washington. The five-year agreement, which was renewed in 1988, made provision for the United States to request the testing of unarmed air-launched cruise missiles and various other military-related tests.

Given the political controversy, the minister bought some time by emphasizing that the agreement did not require the testing of the cruise per se but permitted the United States to make a specific request for each test that might fall under the agreement, and that the Canadian government was free to say yes or no to each individual request. There was no requirement on either side of the border for parliamentary or congressional approval. The tests would take place inside a 2,200-kilometer test corridor located in parts of the Northwest Territories, British Columbia, Alberta, and Saskatchewan.

It was only a matter of time before a request did come to test the cruise, and with an actual request, the debate intensified. In the Cold War, thinking about the cruise missile almost always took place in the larger context of debates about the nuclear arms race, nuclear deterrence, nuclear balance, etc. Defenders of the cruise argued that because it was difficult to detect, and therefore increased uncertainty on the Soviet side, it was a positive contribution to the nuclear deterrent capability of the West. Pejoratively speaking, it was the latest installment of the doctrine of mutual assured destruction, otherwise known as MAD.

Opponents of the cruise agreed that difficult detection and the relative unverifiability of the cruise increased Soviet uncertainty and anxiety, and therefore its testing and ultimate deployment would be dangerous in practice and destructive of disarmament negotiations. It was seen as a "first strike" weapon that would contribute to the escalation of the nuclear arms race. For this reason, it is not surprising that the Minority Report recommended against testing the cruise, and for a "no first use" pledge.

The Canadian debate about testing the cruise, and the importance of heeding the Minority Report on Security and Disarmament, took place amid growing anxiety about the nuclear arms race, and American foreign policy in general. For example, in 1982 Jonathan Schell's book about the danger of the nuclear arms race, *The Fate of the Earth*, raised public awareness of the issue.

In Canada, in 1983, a film entitled *If You Love This Planet* was being widely viewed and discussed. A half-hour documentary produced by the National Film Board of Canada, the film presents a lecture by Dr. Helen Caldicott, the Australian-born and -trained president of the American chapter of Physicians for Social Responsibility, in which she argues persuasively and passionately for disarmament as the only way to save humanity from nuclear disaster. The lecture was given at the State University of New York in Plattsburgh. The film won an Academy Award in the Documentary Short Subject category, and was given extra profile by reportedly being labeled as "foreign political propaganda" by the US Department of Justice.

Concerns in Canada about American foreign policy in general tended to focus on the perceived bellicose rhetoric and attitude of President Ronald Reagan, and more specifically on American policy in Central America, and the actions of those that America supported. The 1980 assassination of Archbishop Oscar Romero in El Salvador was still a fresh memory, as was the raping and killing of four religious sisters several months later. The American invasion of Grenada later in 1983, on trumped-up charges whereby a long-planned airport expansion for commercial purposes was cast as a plot to enable Soviet military aircraft to land on the island, would serve to further confirm such concerns.

Distrust of American foreign policy perspectives in one arena tended to bleed into all areas of foreign policy, and an American request to test the cruise missile was no exception. It was also true that high-level Canadians at SHAPE (Strategic Headquarters Allied Powers Europe) in Belgium expressed informally on occasion more concern about trigger-happy American nuclear warriors than about the Russians. To the extent that cruise testing would be billed as integral to Canadian collective security, many Canadians wondered just what kind of collective they were in, and what constituted security.

Also in 1983, something called Operation Dismantle was very active on the Canadian scene. Founded in 1977 by a Canadian named James Stark, Operation Dismantle dreamed of stopping the nuclear arms race through the power of public opinion, ideally through a UN-sponsored global referendum. They advocated municipal referenda all across Canada in support of a nuclear freeze. Operation Dismantle had the support of the Federation of Canadian Municipalities, the Quebec National Assembly, and 140 members of Parliament. In the end there were 195 such referenda, and the issue of cruise testing was front and center in the public debate that accompanied them.

Nationally, 76.2 percent of Canadians voted in favor of Operation Dismantle's proposal for a nuclear freeze. Many of the referenda took place in the fall of 1983 alongside municipal elections, and therefore after the decision to test the cruise was made, in July 1983. Nevertheless, the lead-up to the various referenda, and the debate in communities whether even to hold them, was all part of the context in which Canadians, their Parliament, and their churches were seized by the issue.

Another leader in the fight against testing the cruise in Canada was an ecumenical coalition called Project Ploughshares. This group was founded in 1976 by Ernie Regehr, a Mennonite, and Murray Thomson, a Quaker and son of Christian missionaries. By 1977 it had become a project of the Canadian Council of Churches. It was located, and continues to be located, at Conrad Grebel College in Waterloo, Ontario, and is affiliated with the Institute of Peace and Conflict Studies at Conrad Grebel University College.

Project Ploughshares is a good example of the many ecumenical coalitions active in Canada at that time on issues of peace and justice. At one time there were at least twelve such coalitions. Some of the larger ones, like Project North, were concerned with the rights of aboriginal peoples in Canada, and others, like GATT-FLY, Ten Days for World Development, and the Inter-Church Committee on Human Rights in Latin America, focused on global and regional issues of social and economic justice. The ecumenical energy and spirit that informed these coalitions that involved both Roman Catholic and mainline Protestant denominations did not survive intact the so-called culture wars that began in earnest in the 1980s over issues like abortion, which led to a new ecumenical convergence between Catholic and evangelical churches.

Project Ploughshares saw its membership and financial support soar in the early 1980s, and at one point had fifty branches across Canada. A major focus of the group was always to point out the conflict between Canada's commitment to international law and the commitments involved in Canada's membership in, and allegiance to, NATO. The debate whether to test the cruise is an example of this conflict between traditional "collective security," as expressed in NATO, and what was coming to be called "common security." Common security was not yet part of the general lexicon of the debate about the nuclear arms race, but it eventually would be, as a result of the Palme Report, which was released in 1982. The report was entitled "Common Security: A Programme for Disarmament," and was produced by the Independent Commission on Disarmament and Security Issues, chaired by former Social Democratic prime minister of Sweden, Olof Palme. It was very clear about the fact that a nuclear war can never be won, and must never be fought, and that any idea of a limited nuclear war must be vigorously rejected, along with nuclear first-use policies.

Such was the context in which the Canadian churches were operating in 1982 and 1983 when the debate about the testing of the cruise missile was a political issue in Canada. In early February 1983, just before the announcement of the umbrella testing agreement that would ultimately see a specific request for testing the cruise missile, a letter to the faithful was released. It was signed by the Canadian Conference of Catholic Bishops, the Canadian Council of Churches, the United Church of Canada, the Anglican Church of Canada, the Presbyterian Church in Canada, and the Lutheran Church in America–Canada Section. In the letter Canadians were urged to write their MPs in opposition to the testing of the cruise missile in Canada. The letter argued that Canada had "responsibilities as a sovereign nation" not to assist the United States in the testing because "the moral and ethical costs associated with complicity in the nuclear arms race are too high"; it cited "growing concern about the threat to human survival" posed by the current nuclear arms race between the superpowers; and it claimed that testing the cruise missile would "stand as an important symbol" of Canada's position in the debate about disarmament.[2]

In a February 8, 1983, *Toronto Sun* article about the church leaders' statement, a spokesperson for the Canadian external affairs minister said the church leaders' views were welcome but would not change government policy on cruise missile testing, betraying a conviction that the testing would go ahead when requested. The spokesperson said, "It's easy to say the Cruise missile is evil. But war is evil. And the Cruise missile is meant to prevent war."

These words dovetail nicely with a lesser-known ecclesiastical missive put out on February 9, 1983, one day before the announcement of the umbrella testing agreement. In a telegram to External Affairs Minister Allan MacEachen, the Heritage Forum released "'A Prince of Peace' Position Statement—Urging Peace through Prayer and Proper Preparedness." The Heritage Forum described itself as "an interdenominational council of Canadian

---

2. Quotations from various reports throughout this chapter are from the author's personal files.

Churchpersons articulating the Centrist views of historic Christianity to contemporary Canadian concerns."

The position statement was signed by twelve Canadian evangelical pastors and was clearly meant to disagree with the mainline church leaders' statement of several days before. Three of the twelve were listed as past presidents of the Evangelical Fellowship of Canada. Arguing that "even death is better than submission to the bondage and servitude often superimposed by a totalitarian regime," the pastors called on the government of Canada to "maintain that level of force necessary and commensurate with the safe guarding of our freedom and rights." The theological difficulty posed by the possible death of the whole human race was not addressed.

The debate about the testing of the cruise missile in Canada in 1983 also occurred during the lead-up to the Sixth Assembly of the World Council of Churches scheduled from July 24 to August 10 in Vancouver. At the assembly there would be a night-long vigil for peace on August 5, on the eve of the thirty-eighth anniversary of the atomic bomb being dropped on Hiroshima. It is difficult to imagine that the mainline Canadian church leaders who denounced the testing of the cruise missile were not also influenced, and even encouraged in their stance on the testing, by what they anticipated would be the dominant perspective on the nuclear arms race at the meeting in Vancouver.

According to Hugh McCullum, in *Radical Compassion*, his biography of Archbishop Ted Scott, who served as tenth primate of the Anglican Church of Canada from 1971 to 1986 and moderator of the Central Committee of the WCC from 1975 to 1983, "The 1983 Vancouver assembly informed the two superpowers and their satellites that nuclear warmongering could result in a state of *'status confessionis.'* The churches could make the rejection of nuclear weapons an article of their confessions of faith, similar to what they had done with apartheid in South Africa."[3]

The spring that followed the letter from church leaders and the signing of the umbrella agreement was a spring that saw record-breaking protest marches across Canada against the nuclear arms race in general, and against the testing of the cruise missile in particular. Canadian churches and their members were active participants in these protests. In one march, in Winnipeg, Manitoba, on June 12, 1983, twenty-five thousand paraded to the grounds of the provincial legislature to hear speeches and voice their opposition to cruise testing, and their support for the 1982 Minority Parliamentary Report of the External

---

3. Hugh McCullum, *Radical Compassion: The Life and Times of Archbishop Ted Scott* (Toronto: ABC Publishing, 2004), 407.

Affairs Committee. At the May 1983 monthly meeting of the Winnipeg Presbytery, of the United Church of Canada, a motion was passed to "endorse the
June 12th Peace Parade and Disarmament Rally sponsored by the Winnipeg
Coordinating Committee for Disarmament (WCCD), and fully publicize the
event, calling for United Church members and congregations to participate
in the parade and rally." Member groups of the WCCD were noted in the
motion. Among others, the membership list included the Winnipeg Presby-
tery itself, the local chapter of the Student Christian Movement, Quakers, the
Canadian Catholic Organization for Development and Peace, the Mennonite
Central Committee, World Federalists of Canada, and the United Nations
Association. A motion was also passed that "Presbytery support the view of
the six members of House of Commons Committee on External Affairs and
National Defence, as contained in the document: Security and Disarmament:
A Minority Report, April 1982, and that this support be communicated to
the Prime Minister and to every member of the House of Commons by way
of letter." In the letter, the six MPs were named, and it was noted that among
them were "members of all three political parties." The joy taken in the fact that
the report was signed by MPs from all parties was a temptation to a certain
depoliticization of the issue that will be discussed later.

The United Church was not the only church in Winnipeg to take a stand.
For example, also in May 1983, a more theologically pointed letter was sent to
the prime minister from the Fort Garry Mennonite Fellowship (FGMF) in Winnipeg protesting cruise testing, and "Canada's participation in this un-Christian
approach to solving international conflict and problems." The FGMF letter was
critical of President Reagan's speech before the National Association of Evangelicals in the USA, in which Reagan described the Soviet Union as the focus
of evil in the modern world. The FGMF "firmly reject[ed] this self-righteous
and hypocritical east-west division of the world," where the USA and its allies
represent "the uncritical expression of all that is good." The letter went on to
say that "we are prepared to live without the 'protection' of nuclear weapons."

The prime minister, in answer to questions in the House of Commons
that spring, had been clinging to the hope that NATO's "two-track" approach
would soon bear fruit. The two-track approach combined nuclear modernization with ongoing negotiations for suffocation of the nuclear arms race,
and had been adopted by NATO in the fall of 1979 during the nine months
Trudeau was out of office. Trudeau officially supported the two-track decision,
but also hinted that had he been in Brussels in 1979, he might have sought a
different outcome, presumably one with more emphasis on disarmament than
on rearmament.

But on June 13, 1983, the day after the Winnipeg march, the prime minister announced in the House of Commons that the Americans had requested to test air-launched unarmed cruise missiles in Canada. The prime minister was between a rock and a hard place. The next day, June 14, there was a daylong debate on the issue in the House of Commons provoked by a motion from Ed Broadbent, the leader of the New Democratic Party (NDP) of Canada, whose MPs had made up three of the six MPs who submitted the Minority Report of Security and Disarmament the year before. The motion read as follows: "That this House express its opposition to the escalation of the nuclear arms race by any nation and, in particular, its opposition to Canada's participation by testing in Canada any nuclear weapon, or nuclear weapons delivery vehicle such as, and including, the Cruise missile." In speaking to the motion, Broadbent quoted the words of Pope John Paul II, who had said when he visited Hiroshima in 1981, "In the past it was possible to destroy a village, a town, a region, even a country. Now it is the whole planet that has come under threat. This fact should finally compel everyone to face a basic moral consideration. From now on, it is only through a conscious choice and through a deliberate policy that humanity can survive." The Canadian Parliament was urged to make a conscious choice against the escalation of the nuclear arms race represented by the testing of the cruise missile.

Interestingly, in pointing out the similarity between current Soviet arguments for the SS-20s and NATO arguments for the cruise and the Pershing missiles, Broadbent referred to a conversation he had recently had with a visiting senior member of the Politburo, Mikhail Gorbachev. Broadbent went on to question whether the request to test the air-launched cruise missile was actually related to NATO's strategy, since it was a purely American one and not a NATO request, as NATO's two-track policy referred only to ground-launched cruise missiles.

The minister of national defense replied to Broadbent with a papal quotation about the importance of negotiations, and suggested that the NDP motion was similar to one that had been defeated at a recent meeting of the Anglican General Synod in England, which he characterized as a call for unilateral disarmament. NDP MP and Anglican priest Dan Heap, from Toronto, later took issue with the comparison, as the NDP motion only talked about cruise testing and was far from a call for unilateral disarmament.

There were no other interventions that referred to religion, or churches, and the motion was soundly defeated, 213 to 34. Four Conservatives voted for the NDP motion, including the two who had signed the Minority Report, and one other, who was closely associated with the weekly parliamentary prayer breakfasts. There were six Liberal abstentions, including the Liberal who signed the Minority Report, and one Liberal voted for the NDP motion. A month later, in July 1983, the Liberal government agreed to the testing of the cruise.

The vote in the House of Commons revealed a weakness in the satisfaction that had been taken by churches, and many other Canadians, that the Minority Report had been signed by MPs from all parties. To the extent that the cross-partisan support for the report enabled people to imagine that any and all MPs could be similarly persuaded, the reality of party politics and party discipline, always a very salient reality in Canadian politics, had been obscured. Only the NDP MPs who signed the Minority Report had signed on behalf of, or with the support of, their leader, caucus, and party.

Thus it was that despite all the vocal public opposition to cruise testing in 1983, in 1984 the Conservative Party, the party that had been the least ambiguous in its support for cruise testing, won a huge parliamentary majority. Also, in addition to not adequately addressing the reality of political parties, the church leaders and activists who devoted themselves to opposing the testing of the cruise may have simply underestimated the degree to which the Christians in their own pews quietly thought otherwise.

In his remaining time as prime minister, Pierre Trudeau arguably tried to compensate for this turn of events. Giving in to American pressure was not how a prime minister who had recognized Communist China before America did, and who cultivated a relationship with Fidel Castro, wanted to be remembered. And the American pressure had been heavy. Private comments by highly placed Liberals confirmed that the pressure was intense, and it was American, despite the public defense that the decision was grounded in alliance solidarity and NATO considerations. Trudeau arguably tried to make up for agreeing to the American request to test the air-launched cruise missile by embarking on a peace initiative in late 1983 and early 1984 that bore no visible fruit.

As for the churches, it is likely that their public opposition to cruise testing in Canada helped swell the ranks of the protest marches, but in the end, neither the marches nor the churches themselves had much effect on government policy. Trudeau had told the Canadian Conference of Catholic Bishops to mind their own business when they released a statement on the economy on New Year's Day in 1983. He apparently took a similar view of their advice on the nuclear arms race.

The language of the churches may well have been found more persuasive, and prophetic, at least within the religious community, if it had had the edge found in the concluding words of George F. Kennan's book *The Nuclear Delusion*: "The readiness to use nuclear weapons against other human beings—against people whom we do not know, whom we have never seen, and whose guilt or innocence it is not for us to establish—and in so doing, to place in jeopardy the natural structure upon which all civilization rests, as though the safety and security and the perceived interests of our own generation were more important than everything that has ever taken place or could take place in civilization: this is nothing less than a presumption, a blasphemy, an indignity—an indignity of monstrous dimensions—offered to God."[4]

4. George F. Kennan, *The Nuclear Delusion: Soviet-American Relations in the Atomic Age* (New York: Pantheon Books, 1976), 206–7.

Watson Kirkconnell's Covert War against Communism

GORDON L. HEATH

Soviet Communism was quickly deemed by a number of Canadian church leaders a mortal danger, and efforts were carried out to ensure that the Christian identity of the nation was not undermined by subversive forces.[1] Organizations were formed, statements released, sermons preached, and governments lobbied to ensure that "godless" Communism was discredited and denied opportunities for growth in Canada. One figure associated with those anti-Communist activities was Dr. Watson Kirkconnell (1895–1977).

Watson Kirkconnell

Kirkconnell was a polymath, with wide-ranging interests, responsibilities, accomplishments, and accolades.[2] He held academic posts in three different regions of Canada: professor of English at Wesley College in western

---

1. Gayle Thrift, "The Bible, Anti-Communism, and the A-Bomb: Canadian Protestant Churches in the Cold War Era, 1945–1968" (PhD diss., University of Calgary, 2005); George Egerton, "Between War and Peace: Politics, Religion, and Human Rights in Early Cold War Canada, 1945–1950," in *Religion and the Cold War*, ed. Dianne Kirby (Houndsmill, UK: Palgrave Macmillan, 2003), 163–87. Previous conflicts had seen a similar church-state partnership. For instance, see Gordon L. Heath, *A War with a Silver Lining: Canadian Protestant Churches and the South African War, 1899–1902* (Montreal: McGill-Queen's University Press, 2009); Gordon L. Heath, ed., *Canadian Churches and the First World War* (Eugene, OR: Pickwick, 2014); Charles Thomas Sinclair Faulkner, "'For Christian Civilization': Churches and Canada's War Effort, 1939–1942" (PhD diss., University of Chicago, 1975).

2. For biographical details on Kirkconnell, see Watson Kirkconnell, *A Slice of Canada: Memoirs* (Toronto: University of Toronto Press, 1967); J. R. C. Perkin and James B. Snelson, *Morning in His Heart: The Life and Writings of Watson Kirkconnell* (Wolfville, NS: Lancelot, 1986); J. R. C. Perkin, *The Undoing of Babel: Watson Kirkconnell, the Man and His Work* (Toronto: McClelland and Stewart, 1975).

Canada (1922–1940), head of the English Department at McMaster University in central Canada (1940–1948), and president of Acadia University in eastern Canada (1948–1964). During those years, he became a fellow of the Royal Society of Canada (1936) and played a pivotal role in the establishment of the Humanities Research Council of Canada (1943). He was active in denominational work, serving as moderator of the Red River Association of Baptist Churches (1937) and president of the Baptist Union of Western Canada (1938–1940), and was the founding father of the Canadian Baptist Federation (1944).[3] Kirkconnell mastered approximately fifty languages, and his groundbreaking translations of literature from Canada's ethnic minorities gave a voice to "new Canadians" who were often marginalized by the two founding European peoples, the British and the French.[4] He played a key role in shaping Baptist (and Canadian) views of non–Anglo-Saxon immigrants, contributing to a vision of a multiethnic Canada.[5] His translation efforts also gave him access to (and sympathy for) peoples under Soviet rule in Eastern Europe. His output of scholarship was prodigious.[6] Kirkconnell received numerous accolades, including twelve honorary doctorates, two knighthoods, and the Order of Canada (1968).[7]

Kirkconnell's passionate opposition to Marxism was obvious to his contemporaries, for he rarely passed on an opportunity to declare publicly his contempt for Soviet Communism. However, what would have been surprising to most were his private actions calculated to stop the spread of Communism. One claim made by a number of scholars is the role of Kirkconnell as a spy or informant for the Royal Canadian Mounted Police (RCMP) during the fearful Cold War years. Nicholas Fillmore claims that during "his tenure at Acadia," Kirkconnell spent significant time "sniffing out" Communists, documenting their activities, and corresponding with the RCMP.[8] Judith Woodsworth asserts that he collected material on Communists and "provided the RCMP

---

3. Now known as Canadian Baptist Ministries.

4. Judith Woodsworth, "Watson Kirkconnell and the 'Undoing of Babel': A Little-Known Case in Canadian Translation History," *Meta: journal des traducteurs / Meta: Translator's Journal* 45, no. 1 (2000): 13–28.

5. Robert R. Smale, "For Whose Kingdom? Canadian Baptists, Watson Kirkconnell and the Evangelization of Immigrants, 1880–1939," in *Baptists and Public Life in Canada*, ed. Gordon L. Heath and Paul Wilson (Eugene, OR: Pickwick, 2012), 343–92.

6. For a detailed summary of his works, see Perkin and Snelson, *Morning in His Heart*.

7. For a complete listing of his honors, see Kirkconnell, *A Slice of Canada*, 369–71.

8. Nicholas Fillmore, *Maritime Radical: The Life and Times of Roscoe Fillmore* (Toronto: Between the Lines, 1992), 215.

with information and advice on certain matters."[9] Nigel R. Moses argues that Kirkconnell was not alone, for "the RCMP relied on university presidents such as Watson Kirkconnell at Acadia or Sydney Smith at the University of Toronto to control and monitor campus-based student activism."[10] Similar statements appear elsewhere.[11] However, as of yet no one has detailed Kirkconnell's private correspondence and collaboration with the RCMP or other government officials, so one is left wondering about the nature and extent of such collaboration. Based solely on the contents of Kirkconnell's own personal files at the archives at Acadia University, this chapter will detail Kirkconnell's private anti-Communist communications. It will conclude with some observations on the significance of Kirkconnell's activities.

Public Voice

Kirkconnell's political activism was shaped by a "deep humanitarianism"[12] but driven by a conviction that Communism was a mortal threat to life and liberty. In his own words, Communism was "based on the simple ground that it is a carefully organized drive for power, committed to the systematic extermination of whole strata of the population in every country that it takes over."[13] Elsewhere he referred to the Soviet Union as the "the foulest slave-state in history."[14] His prewar travels in eastern Europe had made him sensitive to the threat of Nazi tyranny, and in 1939 he wrote *Canada, Europe, and Hitler* to sound an alarm. His concerns for the plight of Europeans under totalitarian rule continued into the postwar years when Soviet designs for eastern Europe became apparent. His ability to read eastern European languages gave him unprecedented access to the plight of those under Soviet rule, and meant he could also read Communist publications inaccessible to most Canadians.

9. Woodsworth, "Watson Kirkconnell," 13–28.

10. Nigel Roy Moses, "Canadian Student Movements on the Cold War Battlefield, 1944–1954," *Social History / Histoire sociale* 39 (2006): 363–403.

11. Steve Hewitt, *Spying 101: The RCMP's Secret Activities at Canadian Universities, 1917–1997* (Toronto: University of Toronto Press, 2002), 87–88; Michiel Horn, *Academic Freedom in Canada: A History* (Toronto: University of Toronto Press, 1999), 149; Franca Iacovetta et al., *Enemies Within: Italian and Other Internees in Canada and Abroad* (Toronto: University of Toronto Press, 2000), 142–43.

12. Perkin and Snelson, *Morning in His Heart*, 22.

13. Kirkconnell, *A Slice of Canada*, 330.

14. Watson Kirkconnell Box 55 Folder 12 in Baptist archives at Acadia University: letter dated September 6, 1950.

Kirkconnell's dealing with Communism had both a public and a private element. There was nothing secretive about his anti-Communist sentiments, for his public lectures and publications made it clear that he was an ardent opponent and critic. He had established his anti-Communist credentials through his condemnation of Communism during the Second World War, often even criticizing Canada's wartime ally the Soviet Union. Those attacks provided fuel for his opponents, and they claimed that he was a pro-German Fascist: as one Canadian Communist critic wrote, "His books and babble are without truth because they form an adulterous alliance with the vomits of the brown python of Germany, the spews of the black snake of Italy, and slime of the sun-shark of Japan."[15] After the publication of *Seven Pillars of Freedom* (1944), a book warning of the growth and threat of Communism in Canada, Kirkconnell faced public censure by two Communist members of the Canadian House of Commons, the Russian press, and Canadian Communist publications, one of which called him a "fascist, mad dog, and a traitor."[16] Undeterred by threats (he said he eventually avoided back alleys after dark), he continued his scathing verbal and literary attacks on Soviet Communism into the Cold War years. By the time of his appointment to Acadia in 1948, he had established himself as an outspoken critic of Communism. J. R. C. Perkin states that his appointment as president at Acadia reduced (not eliminated) his public speaking and publishing on the subject.[17] Kirkconnell himself said that by that time he had "gradually dropped" his extensive research on Communism due to other responsibilities.[18] However, as the following details indicate, that was not really the case, for his war against Communism continued in the shadows, out of the glare of public scrutiny.

Private Correspondence

Sources

The Baptist archives at Acadia University contain extensive holdings on Kirkconnell.[19] Included in the collection is his communication with the RCMP, pol-

15. Kirkconnell, *A Slice of Canada*, 316.
16. Perkin and Snelson, *Morning in His Heart*, 26. For Kirkconnell's summary of Communist reactions to his activities, see Kirkconnell, *A Slice of Canada*, chap. 24.
17. Perkin and Snelson, *Morning in His Heart*, 26.
18. Kirkconnell, *A Slice of Canada*, 329.
19. Reference to the material in the archives is by WK Box number and Folder num-

iticians, notable figures, and private citizens on the topic of Communism. The range of messages was from the early 1940s to the 1960s. The earliest piece of correspondence was with M. J. Coldwell, a member of the House of Commons, dated September 19, 1942, inquiring about a speech and the identity of a person in government.[20] The first letter to a member of the police was to Detective Dan Mann of the Toronto police force on August 24, 1943; it included a list of inquiries for Mann to address.[21] The largest volume of correspondence was from the mid-1940s to the mid-1950s, with the last RCMP letter dated December 1957.[22] In a number of items addressed to Kirkconnell, the sender's signature is unclear, or redacted by Kirkconnell.[23] In some cases, the intended recipients of his letters are unclear for similar reasons. However, in most cases the author and recipient are apparent. While the collection is a rich resource of his correspondence, there are gaps and omissions. Letters were sent with no record of response, or letters were responses with no record of what was originally received. Material included in the original correspondence is often missing; in a number of cases, the sender requested material be returned after Kirkconnell had made use of it.

General Pattern

The letters followed a common pattern. They mostly involved inquiries by or to Kirkconnell about the Communist identity or activities of people, publishers, publications, or organizations. Other lines of inquiry pertained to advice on how to proceed when faced with legal challenges or uncertain loyalties. While much of the material directed to Kirkconnell was solicited, Kirkconnell's public anti-Communist reputation led some to write him directly. For instance, one lady found a letter left by a suspicious foreign house guest and immediately sent it to Kirkconnell for translation to ascertain if the person was a spy.[24]

---

ber. For instance, WK B55 F12 is Watson Kirkconnell Box 55 Folder 12. Thanks to archivist Pat Townsend for her assistance in this research on Kirkconnell.

20. WK B58 F1.

21. WK B55 F22.

22. WK B56 F29.

23. Kirkconnell was diligent in disguising identities in the early years, but, by the mid to late 1940s, he paid less attention to concealing identities.

24. WK B55 F20: letters dated July 22, 1953; December 20, 1954. Another example of a request in the mail is one related to the evangelistic group Youth for Christ. Kirkconnell responded with basic information but claimed to not be able to provide much documentation to support or discredit rumors. See WK B55 F20: letters dated November 13, 1947; November 23, 1947.

As for the secretive nature of his correspondence, for those with whom he regularly corresponded he openly spoke of his "informants" and his RCMP contacts. RCMP officers and other sources often reminded Kirkconnell of the sensitive and secretive nature of the information being passed on to him. On that note, a number of documents are files on individuals marked "Secret and Confidential" or "Strictly Confidential," items clearly passed on to him by the RCMP or other government agencies.[25] However, for the uninitiated he made it sound as if he operated solo: "All that I have done to fight Communism has been done as a sort of lone wolf, without help and without connections."[26] When needed, he also downplayed his interest in Communism.[27] Finally, some letters contained personal greetings and good wishes that reveal long-term relationships and even friendships with RCMP officers such as Mervyn Black and the famous counterespionage officer John Leopold.

Kirkconnell's correspondence related to Communism indicates that he communicated with a broad spectrum of people. In his autobiography he acknowledged communicating with a few members of Parliament: Louis S. St. Laurent (then minister of justice), General Léo Richer Laflèche, and Ralph Maybank.[28] However, his letters reveal a much wider network of politicians in Queen's Park (the Ontario provincial legislature) and Ottawa (the nation's capital), as well as university presidents, academics, clergy, prominent citizens, businesspeople, and Americans. The most striking series of contacts were those within the RCMP, with over one hundred extant letters, many on official RCMP letterhead. The following is a brief summary of all these letters, focusing on how Kirkconnell collected or disseminated material, when he gave or received direction, and various themes or issues important to him.

Collection and Dissemination of Information

What often made Kirkconnell's Communist opponents so livid was his access to critical information that bolstered his case. He admitted in his autobiography that former members of the Communist Party passed on to him archival

25. For instance, see WK B58 F1; WK B58 F1; WK B56 F27.

26. WK B55 F20: letter dated October 21, 1947.

27. When someone unknown to Kirkconnell wanted to meet with him in Wolfville, Kirkconnell responded: "I fear that I may not prove very knowledgeable for your purposes. Since I came here 22 years ago, I have had very little contact with Communist developments in Canada." WH B57 F31: letter dated August 7, 1970.

28. Kirkconnell, *A Slice of Canada*, 318, 320.

material as well as mimeographed minutes, booklets, pamphlets, magazines, and other key items of interest.[29] He also made it clear in his autobiography that he spent prodigious amounts of time searching public records at the New York Public Library and the Library of Congress, as well as browsing his subscription to *Pravda*.[30] He was a tenacious researcher, relentlessly sniffing out names and connections, and freely disseminating that information to those he thought could be trusted. However, his network, or anonymous "informants," as he often called them, went beyond what he admitted to the public.

Politicians were one set of important contacts for the gathering and disseminating of information. For instance, Kirkconnell received information from Ottawa on the Communist activities surrounding the sixtieth anniversary of Ukrainians in Canada,[31] or responded to inquiries from MPs such as John Blackmore who sought an opinion on the trustworthiness of the United Nations.[32] Years later, on a different subject, Blackmore reassured Kirkconnell that "we will not quote you." Even later, Blackmore sought information on whether or not the University of New Brunswick was a hotbed for Communism.[33] George Drew, premier of Ontario, requested information that would be used in "strictest confidence."[34] Drew also later requested information as the leader of the opposition.[35] Future prime minister John D. Diefenbaker requested that Kirkconnell look at a file and give his confidential opinion.[36] Kirkconnell shared a number of letters with MP Ernest G. Hansell concerning Communists in the Canadian Broadcasting Corporation (CBC) and National Film Board (NFB). One letter gives a glimpse of some subterfuge in regards to Hansell getting information about CBC personnel: "In order to avoid suspicion I asked our Mr. Low if he would place the appropriate questions on the Order Paper respecting the employees of C.B.C."[37] Kirkconnell also corresponded directly with MP Solon E. Low,[38] and provided a brief to Senator Murdock in the Canadian Senate.[39]

29. Kirkconnell, *A Slice of Canada*, 315.

30. Kirkconnell, *A Slice of Canada*, 326.

31. WK B57 F15: letter dated March 27, 1951.

32. WK B58 F16: letter dated May 10, 1954.

33. WK B57 F33: letters dated June 21, 1956; November 25, 1957.

34. WK B56 F27: letter dated February 26, 1946. See also WK B57 F33, letters dated March 22, 1946; April 17, 1948.

35. WK B57 F33: letter dated April 14, 1950.

36. WK B57 F33: letters dated June 2, 1948; June 5, 1948.

37. WK B56 F4: letter dated October 11, 1945. See also letter dated September 24, 1945.

38. WK B55 F17: letter dated February 18, 1955.

39. WK B57 F33: letter dated July 6, 1946. There is also a handwritten letter from someone at the Senate, but the author's name is illegible. See WK B55 F22: letter dated December 31, 1944.

One example of cross-border sharing of information was his contact with the Committee on Un-American Activities. Kirkconnell received a letter from the committee providing information on Communists that included a request that he reciprocate by sending them any helpful material. Kirkconnell offered to help: "If there is any further way in which I can be of help to you, please do not hesitate to call on me. In one sense, I can give you no inside information since I have never been a member of the Communist Party. I have, however, gathered through the years a great amount of first-hand material from former members of the Party and have been rather closely in touch with the foreign language press in Canada."[40]

Besides former party members, and government officials on both sides of the border, Kirkconnell's sources comprised a wide variety of disparate people.[41] One interesting exchange was with Igor Gouzenko, the famous Russian spy-turned-defector whose actions were "paramount" in the development of the Canadian "national security state."[42] Initially, correspondence was through a third party due to Gouzenko and his family being in hiding, and it dealt primarily with Gouzenko's book *The Fall of a Titan* (1954). However, in 1968 Gouzenko penned a letter to Kirkconnell that provided information on socialism in the Federal Liberal Party and especially in the views of the soon-to-be prime minister Pierre Trudeau. His comments indicated a sense of despair over what could be done to sway public opinion against the Liberals: "Press, radio and television in general failed in this respect. The reason is obvious: there are far too many hidden leftists in the communication media. Trudeau is their darling. They ascribe to him unashamedly the non-existent qualities, while the known facts, like for example his own writings, they ignore with equal disregard of public interest." Nevertheless, Gouzenko urged Kirkconnell to use the enclosed material to sway public opinion against the Liberals. Kirkconnell, however, faced medical issues at the time and apologized for not being able to help. Contact with others indicates a similar pattern of exchanges of information. Kirkconnell urged a church pastor to provide him with an

---

40. WK B57 F31: letters dated October 31, 1949; November 4, 1949.

41. The list of his informants goes beyond what can be identified in his letters, for a number of people mentioned as informants in North America and Europe were never identified by Kirkconnell.

42. Mark Kristmanson, *Plateaus of Freedom: Nationality, Culture, and State Security in Canada, 1940–1960* (Oxford: Oxford University Press, 2003), 141. See also Amy Knight, *How the Cold War Began: The Gouzenko Affair and the Hunt for Soviet Spies* (Toronto: McClelland and Stewart, 2005). For Kirkconnell's Gouzenko correspondence, including his recommendation of Gouzenko's *The Fall of a Titan* for a Nobel Prize, see WK B57 F38.

off-the-record list of suspects.[43] Elsewhere he urged a citizen concerned with Communism in summer school at the University of British Columbia to dig up as much printed material as possible in order to document his claim: "Documentation is essential, but given enough of it I believe that I could blast the outfit. The sooner the evidence is gathered, the better, for the trail soon grows cold. Names of students present would also be of interest, in case some Commies had been planted among them."[44] Kirkconnell was not above admitting mistakes, for he clarified with the president of the University of British Columbia some accusations made about the faculty in Slavonic studies.[45] The need to get the facts right was partly rooted in his belief that exposure of the truth was the best way to fight Communism, but also to avoid libel suits. Consequently, he was meticulous in getting details right, and conferred with his many contacts to do just that.[46]

Perhaps the most striking examples of sharing or obtaining information relate to his contacts in the RCMP. The largest collection of correspondence with the RCMP is filed in one box, which contains just over one hundred letters.[47] Members of the RCMP corresponded with include the following: George McClellan, K. W. N. Hall, John Leopold, Mervyn Black, L. H. Nicholson, and C. W. Harvison.[48] Over the years Kirkconnell had face-to-face meetings with Black and Leopold and perhaps others. Their relationship was often quite cordial, as the following comments from Black to Kirkconnell indicate:

> My wife joins me in sending you and Mrs. Kirkconnell our hearty congratulations and best wishes on your new appointment [to Acadia]. My only regret is that I shall be perforce deprived of the pleasure of our periodic get-togethers. However, distance is no barrier to co-operation and you may be assured that in whatever way I can assist I shall be ready, willing and anxious. When you are next in our City I hope you will call and see me. Insp.

43. WK B55 F20: letter dated December 1950. He was also contacted by Rev. Ivan Morgan for information on a possible Communist. Morgan would later become professor and principal at McMaster Divinity College. See WK B55 F17: letters dated February 25, 1950; February 28, 1950.

44. WK B57 F23: letters dated August 29, 1946; September 1, 1946; September 24, 1946.

45. WK B55 F17: letters dated May 6, 1948; May 13, 1948.

46. For an example of his painstaking attempts to get the facts right, see WK B55 F17: letters dated February 1, 1955; February 3, 1955; February 5, 1955; February 9, 1955; February 10, 1955; February 12, 1955; February 16, 1955; February 18, 1955 (two letters); and March 1, 1955.

47. WK B55 F22.

48. There was also an officer with the last name of Lemieux.

Mathewson would also like to have a talk with you. There is an off chance that he may be able to do something that will further the publishing of your book. . . . The photostats are being prepared and should be in your hands by the beginning of next week.[49]

In the late 1940s Kirkconnell also interacted with recruits and officers when he lectured at Rockcliffe Barracks, Ottawa.[50] His relationship with the RCMP was mutually beneficial, with the RCMP providing information to Kirkconnell, and vice versa. The written correspondence related to a wide range of subjects. Kirkconnell constantly had his eye on suspicious organizations such as various labor movements, the YMCA, or ethnic groups formed by immigrant communities such as Ukrainians, and sought information from the RCMP in regards to their origins, aims, and leaders.[51] For instance, one letter from McClellan to Kirkconnell reads in part: "The organization you refer to namely, the 'Canadian Council of Professional Engineers and Scientists,' 18 Rideau Street, Ottawa, is a perfectly reputable organization according to our information. This is not the group exposed as the Communist front during the espionage case and it is possible that you may have in mind the Association of Scientific Workers. Wartime Information Board which you refer to in your last paragraph is now defunct."[52]

Publications were items of considerable interest, with Kirkconnell relentless in tracking down the intentions of those publishing suspect periodicals and pamphlets.[53] Kirkconnell often sought information in order to build files on people, with the RCMP occasionally asking him for material from his

49. WK B55 F22: letter dated November 18, 1947. See also WK B58 F2: letter dated May 18, 1948.

50. WK B55 F22: letters dated May 1, 1947; May 6, 1947; October 3, 1949; October 5, 1949; October 11, 1949; WK B57 F31: letters dated September 22, 1949; September 27, 1949. One lecture delivered was entitled "The Growth of Communism in Canada with Particular Reference to the Mass Language Groups."

51. WK B56 F29: letter dated December 1957; WK B55 F22: letters dated December 11, 1948; May 8, 1947; April 22, 1946; March 18, 1946; April 16, 1946; April 10, 1945; letters dated December 1944 and January 1945; September 11, 1943; WF B57 F15: 1948. For a detailed chart of the "red network" in Ontario, see WK B58 F1. Kirkconnell wrote the Department of the Attorney General (Ontario) regarding the legality of the Communist Party in Ontario. See WK B58 F1: letter dated November 23, 1944.

52. WK B55 F22: letter dated December 11, 1948.

53. WK B55 F22: letters dated July 11, 1956; July 20, 1956; January 27, 1953; November 22, 1952; September 1, 1950; February 18, 1949; letters dated January and February 1949; WK B58 F16: letters dated December 1952.

files.[54] Kirkconnell managed to assemble quite extensive files on those accused of Communist activities, such as Raymond Arthur Davies,[55] Stewart Smith,[56] or Adrian Arcand.[57]

Queries were made about public figures and private citizens. For example, Kirkconnell inquired of Black for background details on the firing of six Toronto Symphony Orchestra employees. Black provided the confidential details, but made it clear that they were for Kirkconnell's "personal information only."[58] Other examples were when Kirkconnell sought McClellan's input as to the Communist identity of a Wolfville citizen,[59] when Black asked Kirkconnell about a professor he once knew at McMaster,[60] and when in response to information on a Polish person from the president of Alliance College, Cambridge Springs, Pennsylvania, Kirkconnell contacted Harvison and set in motion an exchange where information was proposed to be passed on to the Department of External Affairs.[61] One final example is an exchange between Kirkconnell and McClellan about a woman who worked at the CBC.[62] Kirkconnell was always suspicious of the CBC, and this is quite evident in his letter. "A cousin of the lady concerned mentioned to me last evening that Miss Dorothy Cox, formerly of the University of New Brunswick and now of the headquarters staff of the CBC in Toronto, was a very active Communist in her college days and used to help print the little Party bulletins. It may be that you already have a dossier for her. If not, this may serve as a nest-egg for a subsequent accumulation. She would not be the first Red in the CBC." McClellan responded, "the lady you mention is very well known to us. Our records over the last year or two indicate that she has ceased activity."

54. WK B55 F22: letters dated April 13, 1953; March 24, 1953; November 29, 1949; December 21, 1949; December 5, 1949; May 6, 1949; December 22, 1948; December 16, 1948; December 9, 1949; October 15, 1946; October 23, 1946; August 21, 1945; January 9, 1945; April 20, 1944; December 27, 1944; December 22, 1944. One letter with the date (probably from the 1940s) and names redacted out related to the Communist identity of some Roman Catholic priests.

55. WK B56 F27.

56. WK B55 F17.

57. WK B58 F14.

58. WK B55 F22: letters dated September 18, 1952; September 3, 1952.

59. WK B55 F22: letters dated December 21, 1949; December 5, 1949.

60. WK B55 F22: letter dated October 10, 1950.

61. WK B55 F22: letters dated December 8, 1953; December 3, 1953; November 23, 1953; November 14, 1953.

62. WK B55 F22: letters dated June 5, 1953; June 12, 1953.

Giving or Receiving Direction

The relationship between Kirkconnell and government officials or agencies went beyond just an exchange of information. Both sides often took action based on the information shared. The following are just a few examples to illustrate further the nature of Kirkconnell's activities.

In 1949, Kirkconnell was invited by letter to submit an article to a new magazine entitled *Canadian Life*. Kirkconnell thought he could "catch a faint aroma" of Communism from its editor, so he wrote Inspector Mathewson (they also spoke on the phone) to see if he knew of the editor. Mathewson wrote back saying that he had no evidence of him being a Communist, but suggested to Kirkconnell that he propose submitting an anti-Communist article to test the magazine. Kirkconnell followed instructions.[63]

At least twice Kirkconnell was sought out by the RCMP to supply names for possible recruits. In 1950, Leopold sought a list of names from Kirkconnell, and Kirkconnell obliged.[64] A few years later, RCMP commissioner L. H. Nicholson wrote to Kirkconnell requesting help to find recruits for the Special Branch Headquarter of the RCMP. Once again, Kirkconnell responded positively.[65]

Sometimes unsolicited advice was offered by the RCMP. During labor unrest in Hamilton in 1946, when Kirkconnell was at McMaster, an RCMP officer advised Kirkconnell: "If you have any influence with the Hamilton police or the Crown attorney there inform them that the only way to beat the pickets who are breaking the law is to charge them with 'Obstructing the Police' it worked in Toronto and there is no reason why it would not work there."[66] There is no evidence that Kirkconnell acted on that advice.

Occasionally Kirkconnell ran into legal difficulties due to comments made in publications, and in response to the threat of lawsuits he sought advice and assistance from government officials and the RCMP.[67] In 1946, Kirkconnell faced a libel suit for comments he made about Adrian Arcand in the pamphlet entitled *Canadians All*.[68] Since the pamphlet was published by the Bureau of

63. WK B55 F22: letters dated February 18, 1949; January 27, 1949; January 7, 1949; January 6, 1949.

64. WK B55 F22: letters dated April 4, 1950; March 30, 1950.

65. WK B55 F22: letters dated October 26, 1954; October 25, 1954; October 6, 1954.

66. WK B55 F22: letter dated August 23, 1946. Officer's name redacted.

67. WK B58 F14: letters dated March 1, 1946; March 26, 1946; March 28, 1946; April 5, 1946; April 5, 1946; April 9, 1946; April 12, 1946; April 18, 1946; April 28, 1946.

68. Kirkconnell referred to Arcand as a "right wing extremist." See Kirkconnell, *A Slice of Canada*, 322.

Public Information, then under the Department of National War Services, Kirkconnell immediately wrote to C. H. Payne, deputy minister of the Department of War Services, for instruction. Payne suggested contact be made with the Department of Justice. Kirkconnell then wrote F. P. Varcoe, deputy minister of the Department of Justice. A portion of the letter reads as follows:

> Inasmuch as a college professor like myself is scarcely in a position to handle lawyer's fees and court expense in such a case, and inasmuch as the real publisher was the Dominion Government and not the hack writer who prepared the script, I have wondered if there were any possibility of your Department taking a hand in the defense, either officially or unofficially? I understand from the R.C.M.P. that there is an imposing amount of evidence to implicate Arcand and refute his action, but I am in no position personally to assume the legal costs. As I expect to be in Ottawa on the 12th of April, to consult with Inspector Leopold of the R.C.M.P. as to evidence, I should be most grateful for a clarification of this problem of legal defense.

The end result was no doubt a relief for Kirkconnell, for Varcoe informed him that the Canadian government would pay "reasonable legal expenses incurred" for his defense, and the attorney general would like some input into his selection of counsel. Even better for Kirkconnell was that the lawsuit was never initiated, so no further action was needed.[69]

Another example of legal problems relates to the threat of a lawsuit from Ryerson Press over comments made in Kirkconnell's review of Vera Lysenko's *Men in Sheepskin Coats: A Study in Assimilation* (1957).[70] Lorne Pierce, editor of the press, threatened Kirkconnell with a lawsuit if he went ahead with his claims that the work glorified or whitewashed the work of the Ukrainian Communist Party. Pierce would no doubt have been quite surprised at what he had initiated behind the scenes. Kirkconnell's surreptitious response to the threat reveals his relentless and painstaking approach to gathering evidence. He promptly contacted a number of sources for advice and information. The RCMP provided information on Lysenko as well as Ukrainian Communist organizations.[71] Lawyers and the RCMP offered input to ensure that he was

---

69. Kirkconnell stated that his standard response to such legal threats was to mail the threatening lawyers a partial list of evidence, and that usually ended the matter. See Kirkconnell, *A Slice of Canada*, 321–22.

70. WK B57 F15: see numerous letters from 1948.

71. One letter read: "The information contained in the latter has been largely taken from our official files and great care should be taken when using it for the purpose you have in

safe from legal action. He collaborated with other reviewers of the book, and he reciprocated by providing them with "ammunition" against Lysenko from his sources. Members of Parliament offered their services, with MPs Hlynka and Diefenbaker consulted on the matter.[72] He encouraged others to write to Ryerson Press and protest their publishing of what he deemed Communist propaganda. Kirkconnell incorporated the many suggestions in his final version, and eventually published the review in the July 1948 edition of *Opinion*.

One final issue needs to be addressed: Kirkconnell's anti-Communist activities related to universities. Kirkconnell's association with identifying Communists on Canadian universities has been previously made. However, specific details have been lacking. The extant letters indicate that Kirkconnell did correspond with persons in regards to Communist activity on Canadian campuses, with a focus on the extent of Communist infiltration into campus publications, organizations, and events. For instance, there was correspondence in 1946 with G. B. Gunn (a former intelligence officer in the army during the war) from Ontario related to the "training of Communist professionals" at a summer camp at the University of British Columbia. Kirkconnell wrote back to Gunn with instructions on how to gather details on what he referred to as a "nest of snakes."[73] In 1947, Kirkconnell corresponded with A. C. Lewis, dean at the Ontario College of Education, University of Toronto, regarding a campus paper entitled *Campus*. Lewis mentioned how he was in correspondence with the RCMP (Black and Mathewson) over the issue, and Kirkconnell offered advice on how to determine whether or not the paper was Communist.[74] In 1949 there was correspondence between Kirkconnell at Acadia and the president of the McMaster University Students Council indicating that the president of the student council had used material provided by Kirkconnell to hinder the spread of Communism in student councils.[75] That same year, J. G. Hanley, chaplain of the Newman Club at Queen's University, inquired of Kirkconnell for a sought-after document.[76] Much later, in 1955, George

---

mind. In view of the possibility that the memorandum might prove embarrassing to you (should it be found in your possession), it might be as well to have it returned to me after taking whatever notes you may desire concerning the individuals. You will also note that our file numbers appear in the margin of the memorandum." WK B57 F15: letter dated February 24, 1948.

72. Hlynka supported Kirkconnell's criticism of the book, and asked Kirkconnell for advice on how he could best deal with the subject in Parliament.

73. WK B57 F23: letters dated August 29, 1946; September 1, 1946; September 24, 1946.

74. WK B55 F16: letters dated April 19, 1947; April 17, 1947; April 15, 1947.

75. WK B55 F16: letters dated January 19, 1949; January 10, 1949.

76. WK B55 F16: letters dated January 26, 1949; January 28, 1949.

Barber at Mount Alison University inquired about the Communist identity of the Student Christian Movement (SCM) on campus; after some inquiries, Kirkconnell assured him that there was no Communist threat.[77] There is other documentation that indicates that Kirkconnell had access to confidential information necessary to fulfill his mission to keep a close eye on the activities of the Communists on campuses, such as a list of names of students who attended the World Youth Festival in Budapest in 1949.[78] One difficulty of commenting on Communism on campuses was that it could get him in trouble with his fellow university presidents. In 1949, it was reported in the press that Kirkconnell claimed that McGill University and the University of Toronto were "hotbeds of communism." Constituents of both universities were unimpressed, and Kirkconnell spent a great deal of energy publicly and privately backtracking and clarifying that he had not said such a thing and that what he had said was misconstrued. Presidents of both institutions graciously accepted his explanation and apology.[79]

Conclusion

A number of church leaders were concerned with the spread of Soviet Communism in Canada during the Cold War. Kirkconnell was especially alarmed, for his Eastern European contacts and his ability to read dozens of European languages gave him unprecedented access to the experience of those behind the Iron Curtain. He was convinced that Soviet Communism was intent on global domination, and, based on insider reports coming to him from behind the Iron Curtain, that such a rule would be ruthless and destructive. As a result, he committed a great deal of public and private energy to stopping a similar disaster from happening in Canada. It would be easy to lump Kirkconnell in with the Religious Right, for certainly some of his fears and harsh rhetoric were shared with American fundamentalists.[80] However, he was not a fundamentalist and "not at ease" with their spirituality and politics.[81] Also, despite what his critics thought, he did not consider himself a Canadian version of US Senator

77. WK B55 F16: letters dated November 6, 1955; November 24, 1955; November 28, 1955.
78. See various items in WK B55 F16.
79. WK B55 F16: letters dated February 1, 1949; February 2, 1949; February 3, 1949(a); February 3, 1949(b); February 5, 1949(a); February 5, 1949(b); February 9, 1949; February 14, 1949.
80. Matthew Avery Sutton, *American Apocalypse: A History of Modern Evangelicalism* (Cambridge, MA: Harvard University Press, 2014).
81. Perkin and Snelson, *Morning in His Heart*, 63.

McCarthy. He distanced himself from McCarthy's roughshod tactics: "I have an uneasy feeling that Senator McCarthy messed up an important job by handling it in an offensive and blundering fashion. It is tragic that the very exposure of the Communist infiltration in the United States fell into his hands."[82] Neither was Kirkconnell in favor of banning or outlawing Communist organizations or publications.[83] He was certainly tenacious in his methods (some would say badgering), and was definitely happy to see Communists exposed for what they were. However, he did not advocate for a policy of suppression. His methods were rooted in lofty notions of democracy and freedom of speech, as well as in the pragmatic consideration that exposure was much more effective than suppression. He believed that the publicizing of Soviet actions and intentions was a key component in the war against Communism, and that his covert work was tactically necessary to achieve a larger strategic goal.

However, there are troubling and ironic aspects to his covert war on Communism. Discoveries of collaboration between European clergy and Communist secret police have been startling and disturbing.[84] While Kirkconnell's covert collaboration with the RCMP and other government agencies may not have been as nefarious (no one was sent to a "Canadian gulag" in the Arctic), his relationship with the RCMP raises moral and legal questions regarding the frequent exchange of information between citizens and the police. The coy response of Kirkconnell about the sources of his information certainly makes him appear to be a shifty character with a dual identity: public professor/principal by day, and private informer/spy at night. The ironic element to his role as anti-Communist crusader was his contribution to the growth of a surveillance and security state. The postwar reaction to fears of Communism in Canada led to rapid expansion of state-sanctioned surveillance and the loss of certain privacy rights, and Kirkconnell's covert activities were a move in that very direction. Finally, Kirkconnell's covert activities raise questions as to the extent to which some Canadian church leaders and academics were willing to go in their crusade against Communism. Further exploration into the papers of other Cold Warriors is necessary to reveal whether Kirkconnell's activities were an exception or a rule.

82. WK B57 F1: letter dated January 28, 1955.

83. WK B55 F16: letters dated February 3, 1949; February 5, 1949(a); February 5, 1949(b); WK B55 F22: letter dated February 13, 1951; WK B57 F23: September 1, 1946; WK B57 F23: letters dated April 5, 1956; April 4, 1956.

84. David P. Conradt and Eric Langenbacher, *The German Polity* (Lanham, MD: Rowman and Littlefield, 2013), 178.

Snapshots from the Northern Front:
Canadian Church Experiences during the Cold War

James Christie

In his 1941 essay "Meditation on the Third Commandment," C. S. Lewis, literary critic, Oxford (and Cambridge) don, Anglican lay theologian, novelist and essayist, and evangelical Christian, noted:

> We learn of the growing desire for a Christian "party," a Christian "front," or a Christian "platform" in politics. . . . It remains to ask how the resulting situation will differ from that in which Christians find themselves today. . . . Whatever it calls itself, it will represent, not Christendom, but a part of Christendom. The principle which divides it from its brethren and unites it to its political allies will not be theological. It will have no authority to speak for Christianity; it will have no more power than the political skill of its members gives it to control the behaviour of its unbelieving allies. But there will be a real, and most disastrous, novelty. It will not simply be a *part* of Christendom, but *a part claiming to be the whole*. By the mere act of calling itself the Christian Party it implicitly accuses all Christians who do not join it of apostasy and betrayal. It will be exposed, in an aggravated degree, to that temptation which the Devil spares none of us at any time— the temptation of claiming for our favourite opinions the kind and degree of certainty and authority which really belongs only to our faith.[1]

Setting aside for the moment the question of whether the term "Christendom" holds any real meaning, at least in twenty-first-century Europe and North America, and admitting that in many circles, certainly in the academy, C. S. Lewis has devolved to the dinosaur he claimed to be in his latter years at Cambridge, it must yet be recognized that Lewis remains among the most

---

1. C. S. Lewis, "Meditation on the Third Commandment," in *God in the Dock: Essays on Theology and Ethics* (1941; reprint, London: Fount Books, 1979), 196–98.

popular—in the truest meaning of the term—Christian writers in the English language. This is so primarily because his theological obsession with what he termed "mere Christianity" speaks directly to the intelligent, theologically acute, though not necessarily theologically trained, Christian of all traditions.

Therein lies the theological rub for any discussion of the Cold War and the Christian churches. Theological arguments informed the various positions held by denominations, ecumenical communities, congregations, clergy, and laity from the end of World War II to the fall of the Berlin Wall in 1989, but the dominant discussion was always political and expressed almost exactly as Lewis warned at the height of WWII. As ever, Christian political opinions during the Cold War, as in every age, were radically divided. This begs the question whether it is even possible to undertake a serious theological reflection on the churches and the complexity of the Cold War. It is certainly possible, as the four preceding chapters have superbly demonstrated, to describe the experiences of Christian churches and individual Christians in the Cold War. But the result, of necessity, is ever but a few pieces of the extraordinary jigsaw puzzle that was this most tendentious of periods.

The reader may note, throughout the Canadian contributions to this book, markedly less concern regarding Communism of either the Marxist-Leninist variety or its even more egregious Maoist derivative. More, there emerges a sense that Canadian churches during the Cold War, by and large, consistently demonstrated far more nervousness about the activities of our cousins to the south in the United States than about the potential incursions of the Soviets. This is particularly evident in the offering of Dr. Blaikie, who writes as both a church and a political leader. It is an accurate perspective. Dr. Heath's chapter on the anti-Communism of Watson Kirkconnell is the exception that proves the rule. Possibly the last Communist scare in Canada of any note was during the Winnipeg General Strike of 1919; even that led, not to anti-Communist crackdowns, but to progressive innovations in the collective bargaining process throughout the country. From Dr. Norman Bethune's legendary surgical and teaching contributions during Mao's Long March, to H. Gordon Green's selection as Canada's "Man of the Year" in the late 1950s for his contribution toward Canada's wheat deals with the USSR, to Prime Minister Pierre Elliott Trudeau's friendship with Fidel Castro and his incursion into China before President Nixon's, Canadians in general, and Canadian churches in particular, have aspired to global community rather than to divisive politics based on ideologies of either the left or the right.

As noted in the preface, these Canadian chapters constitute "snapshots" of the churches' experience of the Cold War. They provide much over which to gaze and ponder; but much more is left unexamined, grist for another mill, another day. This chapter will attempt to identify some areas that require further consideration, study, and research in order to render a more complete composite portrait of the period; it will reflect to some extent on certain tensions that the Canadian chapters identify; and it will note further complexities that have emerged during and since the "end" of the Cold War. The text will be, perforce, journalistic in style. Three reasons apply. First, while extensive archives exist for some individual Canadian denominations, archives for the Canadian Council of Churches and the council's peace agency, Project Ploughshares, consist of hundreds and hundreds of file boxes, unsorted and uncatalogued, and are thus of little value in this current exercise. Second, the author has been intimately involved in much of the content already chronicled, and even more since the end of the Cold War as a leader of the United Church of Canada, a longtime governor of the Canadian Council of Churches, including past president and current chair of the Governing Council of Project Ploughshares. The author's memory thus becomes the primary resource in the chronicling. Third, the style lends itself to a story that continues to unfold since the bipolar world of the Cold War has morphed into the multipolar global complexity of the current century.

The Missing Links

Each of the four Canadian chapters is illustrative of the challenges faced by the church communities in Canada, generally and during specific periods. They demonstrate with clarity the actions of individuals, denominational courts, and, to some degree, ecumenical alliances, both domestic and international. Lois Wilson offers the testimony of Canada's preeminent church leaders of the period. Bill Blaikie demonstrates the complete dedication of a Christian of principle to the formal political process as it pertained to the country's role in the Cold War. Gayle Thrift unpacks the vigorous, often acrimonious, exchanges between and among church leaders during the depths of the Vietnam conflict, and the increasingly evident, in hindsight, realization that a rift, eventually a chasm, was growing between denominational leaders and the broad base of church members. With the political activity of the United Church of Canada's leadership, an anecdotal truism has emerged that "Toronto," that is, the denominational leadership of the UCC, has steadily lost touch with the base of its faithful. In his exceptionally detailed exposé of the career of Watson Kirkconnell, Gordon Heath demonstrates the fullness of Lewis's 1941 observation above. Representationally, the chapters are remarkably comprehensive of the Canadian church experience during the Cold War.

And yet, the content of each chapter is entirely Protestant, and embodies a ratio of three to one in favor of the experiences of the United Church of Canada. More, a substantial portion of the content is concerned with the Protestant Left, of which the UCC is the "poster" denomination. This is hardly surprising, given the issues of Cold War and tepid peace with which this study is concerned. When the UCC was established, in 1925, it was intended by its founders to be a "national" church; to be, in fact, *the* national expression of church in Canada: hence, the United Church *of* Canada rather than the United Church *in* Canada, like its antipodean offspring, the Uniting Church *in* Australia. At its peak in the postwar years, the denomination numbered in the millions of members, and without dispute was Canada's largest Protestant denomination. Even in its ongoing decline, with a membership in the neighborhood of half a million, the UCC was the choice of census-completing Canadians. Roughly 10 percent of Canadians indicated membership in the UCC, even if they had never darkened a church door of any tradition since baptism—if baptized they had ever been. During the Cold War, the United Church was the Christian communities' lightning rod of that stormy period.

But the United Church is far from the complete story of the Canadian churches during the Cold War. Riffing on the theologically bankrupt concept of the "God of the gaps," which observed, in the rapid advance of the natural sciences, that God might yet occupy those places that human genius has yet to explore, it must be acknowledged that God was rather busy in those expressions of Christianity in Canada that have perforce been left unexplored in this book.

A very few modest examples follow.

Roman Catholicism in Canada during the Cold War

Herein lies a book in its own right. Numerically, Roman Catholicism remains the most numerous as well as the most ubiquitous expression of Christianity in Canada. Rome led the way during the European incursion into what Canadian indigenous peoples call Turtle Island: North America. Catholicism was the religion of the French explorers, trappers, and settlers; although there are apocryphal suggestions mooted about that the greatest of all these, Samuel de Champlain, may have been secretly Huguenot, a French Protestant. No matter.

From at least 1608 until the English general James Wolfe defeated his French counterpart, Montcalm, in the Battle of the Plains of Abraham in 1759, Lower

Canada, Quebec, was more Catholic than the pope. Like Ireland, Quebec was "ultramontaine," and Canada's new English Protestant masters of the late eighteenth century and onward saw no reason to meddle with a good thing. Religious control of the masses was conservative control of the masses. Among the most egregious examples of this control was the premier of Quebec in the early postwar, Cold War years, Maurice Duplessis. Duplessis cultivated what might be described as an unholy alliance with Roman Catholic authorities that sustained a nearly feudal culture in Quebec. Then two events conspired to change that centuries-old social order: one was world shaking, the other was nation shaping.

In 1958, Eugenio Pacelli, Pope Pius XII, was succeeded by a genuinely humble, genuinely spiritual, genuinely humane Italian peasant, Angelo Giuseppe Roncalli. Roncalli assumed the papal tiara as John XXIII, and promptly convened the Second Vatican Council. He opened the windows of the Roman Church and allowed the wind of the Spirit to "blow where it listeth." The Roman Catholic Church has never been the same since—especially in Quebec.

In 1960, Quebec provincial Liberal leader Jean Lesage took the strangling reins of government from the entirely unlamented Duplessis, and ushered in *La Revolution Tranquille*, the "Quiet Revolution." Among those upon whom he leaned were the three "Magi" from Quebec, who would emerge from relative obscurity to change Canada: Pierre Elliott Trudeau, Gérard Pelletier, and Jean Marchand. Quebec society would never be the same. Catholic social thought and policy would change and evolve in unimaginable ways, most certainly with respect to the Cold War.

With Duplessis gone—dead and gone, in fact—and Vatican II under way in tandem with Quebec's own Quiet Revolution, the leadership of the Roman Catholic community in Quebec and across Canada assumed a new and "progressive stance." Conferences of bishops worldwide were invited to congregate and take greater local leadership. In Quebec, the Canadian Conference of Catholic Bishops (CCCB) was increasingly influenced by the highly educated and social radical Societe de Jesus, the Jesuits. Under the leadership of Jesuit priests of the ilk of Pere Irénée Beaubien, still alive and nearing a hundred at the time of writing, and the great ecumenist Pere Stephane Valiquette, the Jesuits proactively engaged, and often inaugurated, ecumenical dialogue with Protestants and interfaith dialogue with the Jewish community, stimulated by the still very raw and vivid memories of the Shoah. In the 1960s, 1970s, and at least the early 1980s, in some cases echoing, in some anticipating, the theology of liberation articulated by Gustavo Gutiérrez in Latin America, Roman Catholic priests in Quebec, and bishops such as Remi De Roo in British Columbia, adopted a "preferential option for the poor." Cardinal Leger left the princely trappings of the College of Cardinals to minister to lepers in central Africa, and Jean Vanier founded L'Arche for the less fortunate of our brothers and sisters. It is hardly surprising that these leaders should have also raised their voices for economic justice, the plight of the poor, and international collaboration; halcyon days for Canadian ecumenism, these were. Out of this collaboration grew the "PLURA" network: Presbyterian, Lutheran, United Church, Roman Catholic, and Anglican.

But life and churches move in rhythms. As a great old Protestant hymn puts it, "time makes ancient good uncouth." In 1978, following the brief succession of John Paul I, following the long and ecumenically engaged reign of Paul VI, Karol Wojtyla ascended the throne of Saint Peter. On the heels of the 1980 assassination of Archbishop Oscar Romero in El Salvador by reactionary forces, and the stinging rebuke of the CCCB's statement on the economy by Prime Minister Trudeau, himself a Jesuit-trained and devout lifelong Roman Catholic, to "mind your own business," John Paul II directed all priests to desist from overt political activity. As Bill Blaikie has inferred, this impoverished the House of Commons, and led to a much-nuanced Roman Catholic support on issues of peace and global justice, except for, thankfully, specific agencies such as Development and Peace and participation in ecumenical coalitions.

The Orthodox Church (or Rather, Churches) during the Cold War

To many Canadian Christians, the various Orthodox traditions seem somewhat mysterious, even exotic. There are understandable reasons for this. The churches of the East, though among the most ancient in the Christian world, are unknown to much of the West. The eleventh-century split with Rome ensured that western Europeans would have little contact with the Eastern and Oriental rites. The majority of the Orthodox communities enjoy ethnic and linguistic foundations unfamiliar to the mainstream of Canadian society. To many they seem to be the stuff of quaint legends, even today, despite the popularity of the Greek, "green" patriarch, Bartholomew. The Russian Orthodox Church conjures images of strange if beautiful icons; tall hats, long beards, and prurient songs about Rasputin and the fall of the House of Romanov.

Of course, the Orthodox churches are far more than that; found mostly within ethnic minority communities, true, they are vibrant and serious players in Canadian society. Still, even to those involved in the demanding but rewarding ministry of ecumenical relations, the Orthodox are often puzzling. Witnessing to the unity of the church, Orthodoxy yet is made up of distinct, often contesting expression: Armenian, Russian (Orthodox Church in America), Greek, Ethiopian, Coptic, Syrian, Ukrainian. Then there is that curious hybrid, the Ukrainian Greek Catholic Church, practicing the Eastern rites but owing allegiance to Rome.

There is little available to the outsider that chronicles the engagement of the Orthodox churches during the Cold War. Orthodox Christians fix their eyes firmly on the reign of God, and the beauty of their iconography and liturgy as a foretaste of the kingdom to come in its fullness. This is not to say that they are politically inert entities, but that their political concerns have, until recently, been oriented to their own histories. The Armenians have struggled for years for recognition that their massive destruction at the hands of the Ottoman Turks in 1915 might be recognized as genocide. This was finally accomplished through acknowledgment by the government of Canada—with support from the Canadian Council of Churches—in 2004. The Ukrainian Orthodox have, with equal vigor, sought to obtain recognition that Stalin's 1930s' slaughter by famine in Ukraine, the *Holodomor*, was genocide. This was finally recognized by the Canadian Council of Churches during its 2006–2009 triennium, but not without acrimonious debate from the Orthodox Church in America with its global patriarchate in Moscow.

Nevertheless, the Orthodox churches, particularly the Orthodox Church in America and the Ukrainians, have become in recent years far more politically engaged, as a consequence not so much of the Cold War, but of its putative conclusion. In the wake of the implosion of the former Soviet Union, and the rise of the Russian mafia and gang oligarchy, human trafficking has become a significant economic enterprise in all the former USSR satraps. The most dramatically visible of human trafficking victims are the "Natashas," young women from Russia, the Baltic, the Balkans, and especially Ukraine, kidnapped or lured with promises of a better life in the West, especially Canada, who arrive in Vancouver only to find themselves as sex slaves. This has spurred the Orthodox Church in America and Ukrainian Orthodox churches to social engagement hitherto unwitnessed in the Canadian context.

The Evangelical Fellowship of Canada

By the early twenty-first century, the Canadian Council of Churches (CCC; of which more will be said shortly) described itself as representative of 85 percent of the self-declared Christian population of Canada. The balance of the country's Christians was to be found in the membership of the Evangelical Fellowship of Canada (EFC). The CCC is denominationally structured, the membership of the governing board being delegated by the constituent communions.

The EFC has a much different structure, with membership being drawn from denominations, individual congregations, and individual Christians. Membership of any kind in the EFC is contingent upon the acceptance and adherence to a statement of faith, rendering the EFC essentially creedal. Denominational membership in the CCC is based on a national presence as expressed in multiple congregations, and an acceptance of the doctrine of the Trinity.

The CCC was founded in 1944, as Allied victory in WWII seemed ever more likely, and a desire for unity and concord was growing throughout the Western world. Ultimately, the CCC became one of eight regional councils of churches, including the European, AllAfrican, Asia-Pacific, Latin American, Middle East, Caribbean, and National Council of Churches of Christ in the USA (NCC). The distinction between Canada and the United States is significant; more will follow on this curious distinction within a geographical region. The World Council of Churches (WCC) would be established in 1948. It must be noted that regional bodies are not constituent of the WCC.

Watson Kirkconnell, it might be suggested, represented in many ways the founding inspiration for the EFC. In 1961, with the Berlin Wall a shocking new addition to the Cold War European landscape, evangelical Christians in Canada, or at least many of their leaders, became unshakably convinced that the soidisant historical churches within the CCC had become too politically oriented, abandoning the appropriate pietism of Christendom, forgetting, if not outright rejecting, the ideal Pauline relationship between the Christian and the magistrate. As an aside, the author notes that such a hermeneutic is a limited if not woefully inadequate understanding of the rich complexity of Paul's theology.

The EFC was also a product of the late nineteenth-, early twentieth-century conflict between the individualist model of Christian discipleship inherent to the evangelical worldview and the emergent Social Gospel championed by Walter Rauschenbusch of Hell's Kitchen, New York, and Colgate Rochester Seminary in the United States, and J. S. Woodsworth of Winnipeg, founder of the Cooperative Commonwealth Federation, the predecessor to Bill Blaikie's social democratic New Democratic Party of Canada. One of the more dramatic examples of this dichotomy lies in an as yet largely unexplored thesis concerning the founding of the United Church of Canada. In 1925, virtually all the Methodists and Congregationalist in Canada agreed to unite, forming the UCC. Fully one-third of Canadian Presbyterians stayed aloof from the decision, becoming the Continuing Presbyterian Church in Canada. Many contend that this decision was based principally on the discord between the personal piety of evangelical Presbyterians and the Social Gospel orientation of those who voted yes to church union.

The EFC was convoked to be a counterpoint to the CCC, which seemed to many evangelicals to have strayed so far to the left politically as to have become apostate. However, change happens. An increasingly dangerous world and undiminished interreligious strife globally played upon the hearts and minds of both CCC and EFC members through the balance of the Cold War. For reasons to be discussed in the next section, by the turn of this century a spirit of tentative cooperation developed between the two ecumenical communities. An increasing recognition that the Lordship of Jesus trumps politics suggested new possibilities for collaboration on issues, social and theological, of mutual concern. The rigid distinctions that exist between the National Council of Churches of Christ and the National Association of Evangelicals in the United States, in Canada had, by 2002, dwindled to insignificance. And caricatures are unseemly in Christian community. Far from being literalists and fundamentalists, Canadian evangelicals have long prized scholarship and a clearly articulated faith. Canadian evangelicals also have an acute sense of social responsibility, and not only in the arena of personal morality. In the autumn of 2006, Bruce Clemenger, president of the EFC, engaged in table talk with the author while both were guests at the annual convocation of the Canadian Conference of Catholic Bishops at the "Nav" Centre in Cornwall, Ontario.

In January of that year, Stephen Harper, a political conservative and, in the view of many Canadians, an extreme conservative evangelical, had narrowly won a federal election to form a minority government, becoming prime minister. At the time, Canadians of all walks of life and in multiple contexts were still engaged in the now largely settled debate on same-sex marriage. Dr. Clemenger noted that the January 2006 election was the first since the founding of the EFC almost fifty years earlier in which, and by a slim majority, more evangelicals had voted for a conservative party than for a liberal or social democratic option, and solely based on the ongoing contention on the place of same-sex relations in Canadian society.

The Canadian Council of Churches

Considerable comment has been made both above and in Dr. Wilson's chapter in this collection about the CCC, but some further nuance is in order. At the time of writing, the CCC boasts the broadest and deepest denominational membership of any council of churches in the world. The twenty-five member denominations comprise representation from all the major Christian "families" of churches globally extant in the twenty-first century: Roman Catholic, Orthodox, episcopal, historic (Geneva-based) Protestant communions, free church, and evangelical, and with Pentecostal observers. This was not always the case.

The CCC was born out of the same postwar impulse for unity and peace as the World Council of Churches, the United Nations, and even the fragile European Union. But it came to some maturity during the Cold War, and the realities of the Cold War shaped its evolution until the end of the twentieth century.

As an aside, it must be stated that much, if not most, church engagement in Canada since the Second World War has been ecumenical in nature and in practice. This is certainly true for the various church responses to the Cold War. Though perhaps not always perfectly, or even reliably, Canadian churches have sought to adhere to the World Council of Churches' "Lund Principle": to undertake separately only those particularities that cannot be undertaken together.

From its founding in 1944 until the summer of 1997, the CCC operated as a kind of parliament of leading Protestant denominations. True, six Orthodox communions were members, but in the majority of instances, and after the establishment of the WCC, these denominations were required by their "home" offices in Athens, Moscow, Alexandria, and so on to obtain membership in regional councils of churches to remain in good standing in their global communions. The number of representatives of each denomination at the governing board table of the CCC depends on the member status of each denomination. In practical terms, and throughout the first five decades of the council's history, this meant that the council's dominant member denomination was the United Church of Canada, Canada's "national" church. Previous Canadian chapters have more than adequately demonstrated the dominance of the Protestant Left in the UCC, and hence, the CCC was primarily perceived as an amalgamated lobby group for Christian leftist positions—as, in short, a megaphone for the positions of United Church leaders such as Ray Hord, whose career has been so well documented by Gayle Thrift.

By the late 1980s and early 1990s, a sea change was brewing in the council. Perhaps the earthshaking developments in the former USSR had awakened the Orthodox members of the CCC to a new potential for diverse Christian witness globally; perhaps a new ecumenical spring was beginning to bloom; perhaps a new century just over the horizon stirred creative juices in ecumenists; perhaps the numerical and financial diminishing of the "historical" Protestant churches was coming home to roost; for whatever reason, the CCC's status quo was no longer acceptable.

In 1997, at the council's triennial assembly in Ottawa, after much theological discourse and prayerful debate, a new constitution was adopted, ushering in a new operating model: the forum. It was unseemly in a Christian council, reformers argued, that the majority should rule. It was unseemly among brothers and sisters in Christ to adopt the worldly stance that the one who paid the piper called the tune. Under the rubric of "forum," the number of representatives would still be established according to denominational population statistics, ensuring richness of debate, but policy and position decisions would be reached not by majority rule, but by consensus. This was not received graciously by all. The UCC argued passionately against the change, arguing that the voice of progressive Christianity in Canada would be lost, drowned in the overwhelmingly difficult quest for compromise. Endless examples would detract from the major task of this chapter; suffice it to say, that voice was not lost. What did occur was a substantial expansion of the membership of the council, including application by the Canadian Conference of Catholic Bishops, several new evangelical denominations, and the Mennonite Church, Canada. The council does tend to say less as a body; what it says is heard by a variety of audiences, including politicians of all stripes. The forum model has since been studied and adopted by both the WCC and the South African Council of Churches, albeit with modification. The Spirit moveth in sundry places . . .

The fact that the CCC is the only global council that has retained a national as opposed to a regional designation did not happen by accident. From the beginning in 1944, there was a determination to resist any suggestion that the Canadian church community was somehow to be subsumed by that of the USA. Though sometimes vague in particulars, the conviction was clearly held that Canadian views and policies were often, perhaps generally, divergent to those of the NCC, and most certainly of the USA itself. The former has often proved inaccurate; the latter almost invariably on point.

Let there be no mistake: for Canadians, and perhaps especially for Canadian church leaders of all persuasions, the Cold War was as much about resistance to the American empire as it was about the great contest between East and West, Communism and capitalism.

Project Ploughshares

In most respects, Project Ploughshares, founded in 1976 by Ernie Regehr and Murray Thompson, the former a Mennonite, the latter a Quaker, has been adequately addressed by Lois Wilson in an earlier chapter. Since shortly after its inception, Ploughshares has been the peace research arm of the CCC. Its work has been of inestimable value not only to church communities in Canada and beyond, but also to civil society activists and legislators both in Canada and abroad. Ploughshares has earned an international reputation for the excellence of its reports on nuclear nonproliferation treaties; its annual armed conflict inventory; its research on the Arms Trade Treaty; and most recently, its Space Security Index. Throughout the peak years of the Cold War, Ploughshares's motto of Follow the Hardware has kept Canadians, Canadian churches, and by extension the English-speaking world informed on the perils and madness of MAD (mutually assured destruction) and other global follies.

There was little critique of Ploughshares during the Cold War itself; its added value to the church community and others was self-evident. It is thus ironic that it is in the arguably even more dangerous world of the post–Cold War—in this world of multipolar powers, and a nuclearized North Korea, India, Pakistan, and Israel—that Ploughshares has come under attack. Canada's smugness over its peacekeeping history, including the very genesis of twentieth-century UN peacekeeping sprung from the fertile Presbyterian mind of the Nobel Prize–winning prime minister Lester Pearson, is in no small measure delusional. In the aftermath of the Cold War, it has been increasingly evident that in many instances Canada has become the world's small arms and combat vehicle arsenal. In "following the hardware," Ploughshares has never been reticent in naming Canadian complicity in the merchandizing of death. Successive Canadian governments have been embarrassed by the revelations of Ploughshares.

After forty years of distinguished struggle to provide the "intel" to end the Cold War, Ploughshares, which broke the complex and controversial narrative of Canada's 2015 proposed $15 billion sale of light armored vehicles to Saudi Arabia, one of the world's most egregious human rights violators, has been targeted for a "political" audit by the Canada Revenue Agency (the Canadian equivalent of the IRS). The action was instituted by the Conservative Harper regime and continues unrescinded by the supposedly liberal government of Justin Trudeau, son of Pierre Elliott Trudeau, the great friend of Fidel Castro and legendary foe of Richard Milhouse Nixon. The world turns.

And it keeps on turning. In October of 2017, the International Coalition for the Abolition of Nuclear Weapons (ICAN) was awarded the Nobel Peace Prize. Project Ploughshares is a lead Canadian member of ICAN.

Sanctuary and the Defiant Churches

To reiterate, the Canadian church response to and engagement in the Cold War had as much or more to do with Canadian-American relations as with the tensions of a bipolar world. This was perhaps never so sharply delineated as in Canadian perceptions of American engagement, considered by many to be a twentieth-century form of imperialism resting on the very shaky moral foundations of the Monroe Doctrine.

Canadians in general, and the churches in particular, were shocked over decades of American intervention in the affairs of Latin American and Caribbean nations. The United Fruit Company's depredations in Guatemala; the Trujillo assassination in the Dominican Republic; the continuing international embarrassment of America's obsession with Fidel Castro and the subsequent and decades-long embargo of Cuba; the Allende coup by CIA-supported Anaconda Copper; the invasions of Panama and Grenada; the "Contra Gate" of the Reagan presidency—in all these the United States has been seen, regardless of the friendship with Canada, as little better than a rogue state in the context of Latin America.

In late 1983, the personal became political in the city of Beloeil, just southeast of Montreal. Four Christian congregations, one Anglican, one Roman Catholic, and two UCC, banded together to declare sanctuary for the first time in Canadian history. The subject was a young Guatemalan man, codenamed "Raphael," who, fearing for his life should he be deported by the Liberal Trudeau government to his native Guatemala, still torn by civil war, a war many attributed to American interference in the 1930s through United Fruit, sought refugee status in the province of Quebec.

If there is any positive side to the Cold War, it is that the human community has become increasingly aware of human rights abuses on both sides of the Berlin Wall. Gayle Thrift has asked pointedly whether the political activities of leaders of the UCC have been a factor in the decline and loss of influence of that publicly perceived progressive, Protestant Left denomination. It is a fair question, and worthy of extensive research and reflection far beyond the scope of this book. But, in this case at least, confronted by a life-and-death issue and with a face put to the human rights challenges of Cold War tensions, the people of these four congregations, St. Martin's Anglican, Our Lady of Fatima Roman Catholic Parish, Saint Andrew's United Church, and Union United, discovered the meaning of solidarity with the poor, and the "radical hospitality of the Kingdom," in the words of one commentator.

The story is not terribly complicated, but it illustrates ecumenical cooperation in one aspect of the Cold War world. In late 1983, John Paul II and Ronald Reagan were both determined to destroy the "evil empire" of the USSR. The argument is that they succeeded: Mr. Reagan by military spending in an accelerated arms race that bankrupted the Soviet Union; John Paul II through the force of moral suasion. Be that as it may, the global collateral damage of the 1980s and subsequently the 1990s was extensive. In Canada, as Bill Blaikie has so clearly described, Prime Minister Pierre Trudeau walked a fine line between independent policy and offending Canada's closet neighbor and largest trading partner. Hence, Canadian diplomatic witness and American assurance that the thirty-year Guatemalan civil war was in a dormant phase led the Trudeau government to deny refugee status to nearly three hundred Guatemalans resident in Quebec, mostly in Montreal, some of whom were children born in Canada. A coalition of one hundred human rights–oriented lawyers, activists, and church leaders protested, arguing that, as in the Allende coup, any Guatemalans returned to their country faced certain disappearance and death.

By early December the first deportation order had been issued. The coalition was desperate. An eleventh-hour plea was issued for a congregation of any tradition to step forward and declare sanctuary for Raphael. The congregational polity of the UCC provided for the most rapid decision making. In mid-December, the governing body of Saint Andrew's United Church in Beloeil, Quebec, unanimously decided to declare sanctuary for the first time in Canadian church history. To its credit, the Trudeau government, urged by the solicitor general, the Honorable Warren Allmand, agreed to play by the medieval rules of a nearly vanished Christendom; as long as Raphael remained within the confines of the church building, the integrity of the sanctuary action was to be respected.

Meanwhile, the research and activism continued. Raphael lived in a minister's study converted to living quarters from December 1983 to May 1984, when a convinced Prime Minister Trudeau issued an Order in Council (a Cabinet decree) that deportations were to be suspended, and a "special case" was announced permitting all the Guatemalans at risk to remain in Canada. The rest is well-documented history; it became a cause celebre in the national media of the day, and has been documented in a number of articles since.

It proved to be something of a prophetic moment for churches in the Cold War era. Not only did other congregations follow suit in declaring sanctuary, but the episode built upon the outpouring of generosity to the Vietnamese boat people in 1979, and provided a precedent for the welcome of refugees in recent civil strife in Africa and the Middle East.

The episode also foreshadowed the advent of a new concept in global affairs springing from the abuses of the Cold War, and built upon the Social Gospel principles of the Canadian West, so entrenched in both the UCC and the NDP. This new concept is human security, and it issued in the Doctrine of the Responsibility to Protect, now official and normative within the UN system, even though its implementation is fraught and its future uncertain.

It is the product, in large measure, of the fertile genius of the Honorable Lloyd Axworthy, a junior minister in the Trudeau cabinet during the sanctuary experiment.

Lloyd Axworthy and the Responsibility to Protect

The secretary of state in President Bill Clinton's administration, Madeleine Albright, referred to him—mostly affectionately—as "Pink Lloyd" and "St. Lloyd of the North." Lloyd Axworthy was elected to Canada's Parliament in 1979 and served until 1999, holding cabinet posts under both Pierre Elliott Trudeau and Jean Chretien, for both of whom he acted as western lieutenant. His legacy work politically was as minister of foreign affairs and international trade. During four short years, from 1996 to 1999, Axworthy was midwife to the 1997 Land Mines Treaty; actively contributed to the 1998 Rome Treaty process to establish an International Criminal Court; and led in the establishment of the International Commission on Intervention and State. This last launched the concept of the responsibility to protect (R2P).

The essence of R2P is brilliantly, almost painfully, simple. Axworthy's vision is that human security, the security of people everywhere not only from military action but also from any other form of disaster, must come not only to trump but also to replace nation-state security. It grows out of nearly a lifetime's experience of the deadly rhetoric of the Cold War. It follows as the night the day that the first responsibility of every nation-state is to ensure the security of and afford protection to all its citizens—and beyond. If a nation-state is unwilling or unable to exercise its responsibilities to its own citizens, then it is the responsibility of the global community to intervene to ensure the primacy of human security.

R2P is the very antithesis of the Cold War doctrine of mutually assured destruction. And it was generated in a north end Winnipeg United Church Sunday school. Lloyd Axworthy is one of the most celebrated Canadians ever to grace the world stage, but at every turn, in public and in private, he credits his international insights and innovations to his parents, Norman and Gwen, who insisted that he and his siblings attend Sunday school each week. There, he came under the influence of the scholarly "Churchman," Dr. Roy Wilson, and his remarkable partner, Lois (Freeman) Wilson, with whom the reader will be by now intimately familiar.

Quo Vadis?

In the wake of the Cold War, one must wonder whether a Lloyd Axworthy would be possible today. Granted, Sunday schools of the United Church and of all denominations are not quite extinct, but they are endangered. The reader will no doubt recall a number of the points elucidated by Dr. Thrift in her chapter. This is not to say that leaders with a burning passion for justice and a world set on a diametrically opposite course to the world of the Cold War will not emerge from families, religious communities of all world traditions, and the better schools. But the unique contribution of the Christian Left in Canada is, at the very least, in decline. The Sunday morning lessons that nurtured and inspired Lloyd Axworthy in his northern childhood are few and far between.

The reasons for this are many, and a comprehensive analysis must no doubt await the scholarship and reflection of some future generation. Canada and the world are, and perhaps ever will be, in transition. In the early twenty-first century, the forces of secularism hold sway. The abuses of Christendom are still being uncovered; witness the 2016 Best Picture Award for the docudrama on sexual abuse by Roman Catholic priests in the Archdiocese of Boston in the 1990s; or the depredations of the *DAESH* (ISIS). European Christianity has yet to recover from, never mind somehow integrate its complicity in, the Shoah, the industrialized and documented genocide of six million European Jews under the Nazi Third Reich between 1933 and 1945. Perhaps it is natural, given that most troubled of centuries, the twentieth, that all authority would come to be questioned, not only the religious.

The list of travails goes on. And yet, at least for now, though the jury is still out on the ultimate fate of the earth, humanity, too, goes on. The religious impulse does not die. Nine of every ten people on the planet still count themselves adherents to one or another of the great religious traditions. Even in agnostic western Europe and North America, the "spiritual but not religious," as Diana Butler Bass counts them, are emerging as a force to be reckoned with.

An old proverb has it that "what does not kill us makes us stronger." The Cold War did not kill us; who knows if surviving the Cold War will make the global community stronger—other than God? And God, as ever, isn't telling.

The Canadian church community is not what it was in the early days of the Cold War. Perhaps Dr. Thrift is right, and church leaders have lost touch with their constituent bodies. Perhaps this is not entirely a bad thing. Bill Blaikie once reported to the author that the great Canadian theologian Gregory Baum once observed that "the great divide in the church today is not between liberal and conservative, but between those who recognize the end of Christendom and mourn it; and those who recognize the end of Christendom and celebrate it." So, let us "rejoice in the Lord always," and hold fast to the wisdom of Karl Barth, who, and I paraphrase, held to the principle that we "must do theology with the Bible in one hand and the newspaper in the other."

US Mainline Protestant Approaches

The National Council of Churches and the Cold War

JILL K. GILL

World War II infused the ecumenical movement with an urgent goal: foster real global peace rooted in sociopolitical and economic justice. To do so, it had to evangelize about its human rights–based worldview and convert both fellow Christians and governing bodies to embrace the spiritual and secular wisdom of its principles. These, it felt, would not only enhance ecumenism within Christendom, but also provide the right soil for growing the roots of a thriving "responsible society," which was the ecumenical movement's term for what Martin Luther King Jr. later envisioned as a "beloved community." As the American ecumenical movement's flagship body, the National Council of the Churches of Christ in the USA (NCC) championed this effort Stateside. However, the Cold War threatened this ecumenical mission to its core. The assumptions underlying it, and the actions they spawned, were antithetical to ecumenism's goal of a responsible, justice-based society. Therefore, America's Cold War culture forced the council institutionally to make a Faustian choice: push its ecumenical agenda in a prophetic manner and pay the steep financial and political price, or bless America's Cold War narrative with godly authority to retain popularity and easy access to power.

NCC leaders didn't fully realize the price their movement would pay for critiquing Cold War presuppositions and policies. A triumphalism buoyed their prophetic efforts from the late 1940s through the mid-1960s. However, the Vietnam War put their organization into larger crosshairs for rival conservative forces to target, while internal strains within the diverse community of American churches broke open into chasms.

As a result, the Cold War that drove US foreign policy for over four decades, and that lingers in it still, undercut the ecumenical movement's mission and institutions more than perhaps any other single thing. It created a hostile environment for ecumenism by serving as incubator and rationale for a host of ideas, beliefs, and policies that ran diametrically opposite to it.

This included a powerful, hubris-infused Christian nationalism and bipolar worldview that imagined America as God's right arm in a militarized spiritual battle against Communism; that uncritically blessed capitalism, individualism, and the American way of life as godly; and that saw patriotism and Protestantism as fused.[1] Within the Cold War context, dissent against these premises drew charges of disloyalty to God and nation. Because of this, denominational members expected the NCC to be their snowplow on controversial matters, speaking out first to draw and blunt critics' icy flak (including from laity) while forging an ecumenical path in which churches could follow once clergy and laity better understood the issues. However, contentious Cold War concerns and their ramifications also turned fissures within the ecumenical community into full-scale chasms; this occurred especially between clergy and laity, missions and social justice personnel, and activist "new breed" Christians and more traditional process-driven ecumenists. Additionally, antiecumenical evangelicals leveraged Cold War controversies and partisan politics to repeatedly attack the ecumenical movement generally, and the NCC specifically, while seeking cultural and political status for their own organizations. Thus, the international Cold War added new fuel to an ongoing religious cold war within the United States that grew out of the modernist-fundamentalist controversy of the late nineteenth century. In fact, using the Cold War context to their advantage, antiecumenical evangelicals supplanted mainline Protestants as the go-to consultants of government officials, while forging a close partnership with the Republican Party.

Ecumenists with the National Council of Churches saw the Cold War as a time of testing and crisis. They felt the world needed the ecumenical message, and that God called them to share it and fight for it. In practical terms, because the Cold War exacerbated divisions within the body of Christ, ecumenists tried to use Cold War issues as catalysts to ecumenize the churches. They also, simultaneously, tried to mobilize ecumenical witnesses in action, especially within the halls of government. And they worked to meet the spiritual and physical needs of people who became casualties of the Cold War, whether refugees, soldiers, or people persecuted for their beliefs. As the Religious Right and secular Left both rose in the wake of the Vietnam War, the NCC lost the allegiance of many conservative laity as well as liberal young activists disillusioned by bureaucracies, neither of whom understood or bought into the full ecumenical mission in terms of both vision and process. In part, because

---

1. Paul Gordon Lauren, *The Evolution of International Human Rights* (Philadelphia: University of Pennsylvania Press, 2003), 166–264.

ecumenists did not privilege the survival of their institutions over the vision and process that animated their movement, and because evangelicals bested them in media delivery of their messages—ones generally in tune with the political power structure—ecumenical institutions suffered a steady stream of financial and staffing losses throughout the last half of the Cold War and into the current war on terror. As a result, the NCC's administrative structures have weakened considerably. However, its ideas and approach still provide an inspirational, theological, historical, and position-based spine for progressive spiritual communities today.

Born during a snowstorm in late November 1950, under a banner reading "This Nation under God," the NCC felt the sharp chill of Cold War concerns heighten its spiritual focus and sense of mission. Secretary of State Dean Acheson reminded those gathered at its founding assembly of "great danger to the peace in the world" from Red China, which had recently fallen to Mao Zedong's Communist faction.[2] President Harry Truman, in his message to the NCC, thanked its member churches for contributions to "the maintenance of freedom throughout the world," and expected more of the same. Participants visiting from the World Council reminded the NCC to honor its ecumenical mission. With respect to Red China's aggression, O. Frederick Nolde, head of the WCC's Commission of the Churches on International Affairs (CCIA), stressed, "So long as there remains even a marginal possibility of averting total global war we must utilize every means which will not betray conviction nor offend conscience."[3] Realizing that the McCarthyite atmosphere taking hold in America might weaken the NCC's ecumenical backbone, WCC general secretary Willem Visser 't Hooft urged its leaders to make it into a "fighting organization," one that "strove for spiritual values that speak to the crises of the time."[4] Throughout the early 1950s, Visser 't Hooft consciously nurtured global ecumenical bonds with the NCC, hoping these would mitigate the overwhelming pressures upon American church leaders to mute their prophetic ecumenical voices and provide automatic God-cover to US foreign and domestic policy.[5]

2. Nathan H. VanderWerf, *The Times Were Very Full: A Perspective on the First Twenty-Five Years of the National Council of the Churches of Christ in the United States of America, 1950–1975* (New York: NCC, 1975), 19.

3. VanderWerf, *The Times Were Very Full*, 19.

4. VanderWerf, *The Times Were Very Full*, 18–19.

5. Robert S. Bilheimer, telephone interview with author, December 14, 1991; interviews with author, August 5–9, 1993, Collegeville, MN. Jill K. Gill, *Embattled Ecumenism: The National Council of Churches, the Vietnam War, and the Trials of the Protestant Left* (DeKalb: Northern Illinois University Press, 2011), 50.

The red, white, and blue chairs that filled the convention center, combined with the banners of Protestant denominations and flags from every nation, suggested that the NCC was trying to fuse images of American patriotism and global ecumenism for a Cold War–minded public. Evangelicals and fundamentalists had already made sport of red-baiting the NCC's predecessor, the Federal Council, for its social gospel roots and for supporting business regulations, labor rights, and racial equality. In 1947, the fundamentalist American Council of Christian Churches (ACCC), founded by Carl McIntire in 1941, had framed these positions as "Marxian ideas," which it spun instead as "a planned and controlled economy, class strife, and color conflict."[6] Therefore, in the NCC's first message to member churches, it argued that ecumenical ideas dovetailed compatibly with American values of democracy, freedom, and justice for all. It also compared itself to the United Nations, suggesting that the NCC "could do for religion what it was hoped the UN would do for the world."[7] And it tried to distinguish between the sensible anti-Communism held by most NCC leaders and the hysterical freedom-crushing version popularized by Senator Joseph McCarthy.

Though in 1950 the NCC held to a salvation-oriented mind-set and concern for a world-in-crisis similar to that of its conservative brethren, its ecumenical views and worldly justice agenda prevented it from receiving any honeymoon from their attacks. The ACCC struck first with a pamphlet titled *How Red Is the Federal/National Council of Churches?* It charged the NCC with having the same pink people and perspectives as the former Federal Council. The NCC rebutted with its own pamphlet, *Plain Facts about the National Council of the Churches of Christ in the U.S.A.* It cited FBI director J. Edgar Hoover as having never charged the council with harboring Communists, criticized the ACCC for being "unable to distinguish between Communism and support of constructive measures of social advance prompted by Christian conscience," and chided them for "scatter[ing] the adjective 'Red' as indiscriminately as a shotgun blast against all who do not share their own pet ideas."[8] The NCC

6. "Church Council Calls Russia a Tyrant Bent on Enslaving World," *Washington Evening Star*, October 17, 1947, in Federal Bureau of Investigation, Freedom of Information and Privacy Acts, "Subject: National Council of Churches HQ File: 100–50869 Sub A, 1&2, 2/28/36 Through 3/3/76," https://archive.org/details/foia_National_Council_of_Churches-HQ-4 (December 17, 2017), hereafter "NCC FBI file."

7. Robert Wuthnow, *The Restructuring of American Religion: Society and Faith since World War II* (Princeton: Princeton University Press, 1988), 82.

8. *How Red Is the Federal/National Council of Churches?* (New York: American Council of Christian Churches, n.d.). *Plain Facts about the National Council of Churches of Christ in*

encouraged a type of patriotism that preferred loyalty to the whole of Scripture rather than to a two-dimensional political ideology.

The National Association of Evangelicals (NAE, founded in 1942), along with the ACCC, attacked what they viewed as the NCC's so-called secular politicking, even though both conservative groups maintained their own political lobbying arms in Washington. The NAE equated the council's concerns about unregulated capitalism with the Red Menace, and viewed its affection for the UN as proof that it expected humans, rather than God, to save the world.[9]

The NCC's leaders also quickly drew the ire of the House Un-American Activities Committee (HUAC). In 1953, a high-level HUAC investigator claimed that seven thousand Protestant ministers conspired with Communists as "fellow travelers," then levied specific accusations against liberal Methodist bishop G. Bromley Oxnam, who had served in the leadership of all three councils, and once graced the cover of *Time* magazine. McCarthy echoed HUAC's charges in the Senate, basing them on the words of fundamentalist radio host Billy James Hargis.[10] The NCC countered by crafting a resolution and blue-ribbon "Committee on the Maintenance of American Freedom" to monitor the spurious methods of HUAC's investigators. It charged them with "threaten[ing] the freedom and institutions of the United States" and wrongly "pin[ning] a Communist label on social liberals and advocates of reform" without verifiable evidence.[11] Modeling the sort of fighting spirit Visser 't Hooft had sought, Oxnam insisted on the chance to "face his accusers." There, he

the U.S.A. (New York: NCC, n.d.). The first was published about 1951, and the second about 1953. See also the NCC FBI file

9. Allan J. Lichtman, *White Protestant Nation: The Rise of the American Conservative Movement* (New York: Grove Press, 2008), 123–25, 453. See also the history section of the National Association of Evangelicals website. Darren Dochuk, "Evangelicalism Becomes Southern, Politics Becomes Evangelical: From FDR to Ronald Reagan," in *Religion and American Politics from the Colonial Period to the Present*, ed. Mark A. Noll and Luke E. Harlow (New York: Oxford University Press, 2007), 297–325, and Darren Dochuk, *From Bible Belt to Sunbelt: Plain-Folk Religion, Grassroots Politics, and the Rise of Evangelical Conservatism* (New York: Norton, 2011), 118–19, 161–62, 248.

10. Bishop Oxnam served as president of the Federal Council (1944–1946), president of the World Council (1947–1953), and vice president of the National Council's social justice–minded Division of Life and Work (1957–1960). VanderWerf, *The Times Were Very Full*, 114. Edwin Gaustad, *A Religious History of America* (1966; New York: Harper and Row, 1990), 294–96. "Evangelist Hargis 'Ghosted' Attack on Oxnam," *Christian Advocate*, April 6, 1967, 23.

11. "Church Council Raps Methods of Red Hunters," *New York World Telegram and Sun*, March 12, 1953; "Church Freedom Vigil over Congress Set Up," *Philadelphia Inquirer*, May 21, 1953; Marquis Childs, "Critics of Clergy Now in Politics," *Washington Post*, July 7, 1953; all in NCC FBI file.

decimated their claims, excoriated HUAC for disrespecting democratic processes, and asserted that the churches were far more effective at weakening Communism than congressional investigators. In 1957, General Secretary Roy Ross bragged to that year's General Assembly how the young NCC stood strong against witch-hunting anti-Communists. "Let me remind you that the new council did take on Senator McCarthy and McCarthyism at a time when most of Capitol Hill was either afraid, confused, or both."[12] Instead of intimidating the NCC, Cold War issues and anti-Communist attacks drove it toward greater boldness in issuing its peace and justice message, while still defending civil liberties and the separation of church and state.

A group of conservative donors, led by the Presbyterian oilman J. Howard Pew, grew dismayed. Pew had hoped the council would become an uncritical champion of free enterprise and other so-called American values. When this seemed unlikely, he sought power for an influential lay board to veto NCC statements.[13] The council refused. So Pew withdrew his financial support, condemned the NCC as "the most subversive force in the United States," and chastised churches he felt privileged sociopolitical and economic issues over evangelism. He then forged a partnership with evangelist Billy Graham, who helped convince Pew to bankroll the first year of a new evangelical journal, *Christianity Today*, which promised to trumpet a conservative anti-Communist message.[14] It was an early indication that the NCC prioritized its prophetic ecumenical vision ahead of safely buttressing its own institutional resources, while evangelical Christianity proved willing to provide an aura of divine blessing to economic and political forces that propagated an uncritical exceptionalist view of American capitalism, while benefiting handsomely from the partnership.

The massive retaliation philosophy that drove a competitive nuclear arms buildup between the United States and the USSR led NCC leaders to see the Cold War as a crisis that compelled church unity and prophetic boldness.

12. Roy Ross, quoted in VanderWerf, *The Times Were Very Full*, 37.

13. VanderWerf, *The Times Were Very Full*, 36.

14. Donald Meyer, *The Protestant Search for Political Realism, 1919–1941*, 2nd ed. (Middletown, CT: Wesleyan University Press, 1988), 404–5. Henry J. Pratt, *The Liberalization of American Protestantism: A Case Study in Complex Organizations* (Detroit: Wayne State University Press, 1972), 86–104; E. V. Toy Jr., "The National Lay Committee and the National Council of Churches: A Case Study of Protestants in Conflict," *American Quarterly* 21, no. 2 (Summer 1969): 190–209. William Inboden, *Religion and American Foreign Policy, 1945–1960: The Soul of Containment* (New York: Cambridge University Press, 2008), 55, 99. Lichtman, *White Protestant Nation*, 194, 215–17.

Ecumenical unity could both strengthen their churches' influence and model how diverse peoples could bridge differences through justice and respect. NCC president Edwin T. Dahlberg (1957–1960) described massive retaliation as "a feverish philosophy of bomb for bomb, rocket for rocket, Sputnik for Sputnik," something foreign to the Christian gospel. "The task of the Christian Church," he countered, "must be one of massive reconciliation." And this was no Pollyanna cry to him, but rather a matter of human survival. "We are faced now with chemical and mechanical destruction of such colossal scale that nothing more of the world may be left than a radio active ash heap," he stressed, while emphasizing that Communism could be defeated more effectively by delivering justice to the oppressed in foreign lands. "It is not half so important that we send Sputniks circling around the globe as we should send more loaves of bread around the world. It is the hunger and misery of the vast population of the earth . . . that makes for war." And he summoned the NCC's members to exhibit "the evangelistic passion of a Billy Graham" in their own work, while infusing it "with the social insights of a Walter Rauschenbusch."[15]

Although NCC leaders were firm anti-Communists and initially bought into several assumptions of the 1950s-era Cold War consensus, their ecumenical worldviews led them to question US foreign policy methods that seemed counterproductive to loosening Communism's appeal in developing nations. Communism proved attractive to peoples who suffered from colonial exploitation and deprivation. Therefore, they reasoned, the lasting solution lay in bringing human rights and economic justice through the collaborative work of many nations, not via unilateral military action, bipolar arms races, or remaking other nations coercively in America's image. Too many Cold War architects also viewed bolstering American power as an end in itself.[16] The NCC's positions on several Cold War crises of the 1950s revealed these predilections in mild ways. For example, the council urged restraint and a negotiated solution to tensions in the Formosa Strait in 1955, and pressed US policy makers to rely upon the UN during crises in Hungary and the Middle East in 1956. The council even supported the creation of the Southeast Asia Treaty Organization (SEATO) in 1955 to forestall Communism in that region, because it naively assumed SEATO to be a respectable cooperative international body, like NATO. And it championed foreign aid when conservatives urged reduction.[17]

15. VanderWerf, *The Times Were Very Full*, 38.
16. John Bennett, editorial response, *Christianity and Crisis*, May 1, 1972, 106–7.
17. Statement, General Board, November 14, 1954, RG 6, box 13, folder 19; Walter W. Van

However, US China policy drew the NCC into a sharper conflict with the State Department and, more personally, with its former ecumenical colleague, John Foster Dulles. They split over America's decision to withhold recognition from the Communist People's Republic of China (PRC) and deny it representation in the United Nations. As with its vociferous opposition to McCarthyite erosions of civil liberties, the NCC proved again its willingness to speak its truth to power on Cold War issues, despite intense scrutiny and charges of disloyalty.

The clash with Secretary of State Dulles occurred at the council's Fifth World Order Study Conference in 1958, and played out in the media. For years before he joined President Eisenhower's cabinet in 1952, Dulles chaired the Federal Council of Churches' Commission on International Justice and Goodwill, which authored a landmark study called "A Just and Durable Peace" during World War II and helped lay the groundwork for the United Nations. But with his move into the State Department, and as a result of the Cold War, his ecumenical friends noticed a shift in his thinking. According to historian Mark Toulouse, Dulles's ecumenical worldview gave way to one that equated "the American way of life" with the highest good. Like many American Christians of that era, Dulles conflated the nation's purpose with the church's, making the United States "God's redemptive agent in the world."[18] Even the ardent anti-Communist Reinhold Niebuhr sensed danger when he saw government officials like Dulles confuse America's "responsibility for world order" with "a responsibility to impose an American order on the world."[19] The former could be done through international bodies like the UN and be rooted in human rights. The latter could veer into a new form of US imperialism, supplanting one type of injustice with another.

The NCC invited Dulles to present the rationale behind the government's Asia policies at its Fifth World Order Study Conference. Through his radio-

---

Kirk, "Report of Executive Director," Division of Christian Life and Work (DCLW), April 21, 1955, RG 6, box 14, folder 21; both in NCC Records, Presbyterian Historical Society, Philadelphia (hereafter NCC). Report, Department of International Affairs, April 27, 1955; Kenneth Maxwell, "What the Churches Are Doing in International Affairs in the Current Crisis" (report to the General Board, December 4, 1956); Report, "Re Conference with President Eisenhower and Secretary of State Dulles by NCC Officers, April 3, 1957, on Christian Concerns for Foreign Aid Programs and Other Developments to Date"; all three in RG 6, box 14, folder 21, NCC.

18. Mark G. Toulouse, *The Transformation of John Foster Dulles: From Prophet of Realism to Priest of Nationalism* (Macon, GA: Mercer University Press, 1985), 252–53.

19. Robert Stone, "An Interview with Reinhold Niebuhr," *Christianity and Crisis*, March 17, 1969, 48–52.

broadcasted address, Dulles argued that stopping a godless menace like China from extending its regional influence required uncompromising containment.[20] Lacing his words with religious references, he aimed specifically to counter Oxnam's challenging address from earlier that day.

As vice president of the NCC's Division of Christian Life and Work, which handled international affairs, Oxnam presented the ecumenical alternative with bite and wit. He reiterated the foolishness of materialistic arms races and military posturing, which ignored the basic human needs Communists leveraged in their propaganda. Promises of American "freedoms" carried little weight beyond how US policy impacted people's daily lives. "True, we have held certain lines," he noted, "but we have lost vast areas. We have failed to get through to the minds and hearts of the people." Many such observations foreshadowed similar differences between the NCC and the State Department on Vietnam a decade later, and on Iraq in 2003. Oxnam also excoriated how cries for national security led to evermore government secrecy, while civil liberties and the concept of an open society eroded. On China, Oxnam asserted that strict containment would prevent the possibility of reconciliation, as the latter required contact and communication. For many in the audience who still ached over Mao Zedong's termination of their Christian missions, political recognition of China seemed prerequisite to rebooting Christian work there. Simply put, Oxnam asked Christians to lead their nation in a "move from fear to faith" when dealing with foreign policy, marching "into the light, by way of the altar, library and laboratory" in an effort to defeat "segregation, exploitation, and discrimination" globally. Listeners left the Oxnam-Dulles debate with a clear choice: navigate Cold War challenges using ecumenical worldviews and approaches, or keep relying on militaristic ones justified by a providential Christian nationalism championed by conservative evangelicals.[21]

The Fifth World Order Study Conference repudiated US China policy by respectfully urging government officials to reconsider US policy, and to offer the PRC both official recognition and inclusion in the United Nations.

20. State Department policy statement, August 1958, in Robert Smylie, "The China Issue: A Review of the Position of the National Council of Churches," *Christian Century*, October 10, 1973, 1004. John Foster Dulles, Fifth World Order Study Conference, November 18, 1958, RG 6, box 27, folder 24, NCC.

21. Bromley Oxnam, "Christian Responsibility on a Changing Planet" (paper presented at Fifth World Order Study Conference, Cleveland, November 18, 1958, RG 6, box 27, folder 24, NCC). Wallace C. Merwin, "Resume of Approaches to the Chinese Church" (report to the annual meeting of the China Committee, Division of Foreign Missions, March 5, 1958, RG 4, box 21, folder 15, NCC).

Neither suggestion implied "moral approval," said its official message. Rather, they were seen as practical moves benefiting both nations.[22] Nevertheless, after media publicized the conference's report, negative backlash engulfed the council and provided conservatives with additional fodder to discredit ecumenists as disloyal, naive, and overly humanistic.[23] Even more disturbing to the NCC was the clamor of protest against churches speaking out on sociopolitical issues, period.

The council replied with the Hartford Appeal in 1959. It asserted the right and *duty* of religious bodies to apply their faith to every dimension of life—including political, social, economic, and foreign policy matters—and then to make a public witness of these positions. Freedom of conscience and speech, the NCC insisted, "is especially vital to the Church, which owes a duty to lead and to inform, so that its members may be aided in reaching morally valid judgments in light of their common faith."[24] These were essential to the ecumenical discernment process, too; therefore the council urged its members to engage in candid self-reflective discussions of contentious issues despite the flak incurred.

In 1960, the NCC received a fresh dose of accusations from an unanticipated place. The air force published a training manual that repeated specious charges of rampant Communist infiltration in US churches, and mentioned the National Council by name. Using discredited, error-filled sources from the council's most right-wing detractors, the manual warned airmen to distrust Christians who raised critical questions about American policies, actions, or systems. Not only did the NCC's stands on China make it suspect; so, too, did its recently published Revised Standard Version of the Bible. The council hit back hard, obliging the air force to retract the manual and apologize. The fiasco created a brief platform for the NCC to stress again the dangers lurking in any government-coerced "regimentation of expression" that manufactured

22. "It [isolation] helps to preserve a false image of the United States and of other nations in the minds of the Chinese people. It keeps our people in ignorance of what is taking place in China. It hampers negotiations for disarmament. It limits the functioning of international organizations. We have a strong hope that the resumption of relationships between the peoples of China and of the United States may make possible also a restoration of relationships between their churches and ours." Message to the Churches, Fifth World Order Study Conference, in Smylie, "The China Issue," 1004.

23. Smylie, "The China Issue." See also Inboden, *Religion and American Foreign Policy, 1945–1960*, for more on Christian divisions regarding US China policy.

24. The Hartford Appeal, policy statement, NCC General Board, February 25, 1959, National Council of Churches Communication and Research Department Office Files, New York (hereafter NCCNYO).

false litmus tests of loyalty or right belief.[25] Even America's Catholic president John F. Kennedy saw the good in encouraging religious free speech. "The most unfortunate aspect of the Air Force Manual fiasco," he explained, "is that it plays into the hands of those who want to silence the views of the National Council—because they do not share those views. They are not communistic views." Additionally, because controversial issues "involved ethical considerations," Kennedy stressed, "I would expect many church leaders and organizations to feel they have an obligation to speak out on them."[26] Yet this validating moment faded quickly.

Throughout the 1950s, the NCC proved that its commitment to a global ecumenical worldview trumped cultural, political, and religious pressures to provide unquestioning support to US Cold War policies. The council readily backed the federal government when the two aligned in vision, but it also opposed the White House when they clashed. In the early 1960s, the swelling civil rights movement eventually united the White House and the NCC behind advancing racial justice at home. And it boosted the council's sense that churches could facilitate cultural, political, and conceptual transformations in society. However, the council's growing awareness of racial discrimination, as well as the church's ability to drive social movements with prophetic action, also fueled its criticism of US policies that perpetuated a racist paternalistic colonialism under the veil of containing Communism.[27] It also inspired NCC leadership to pursue the insights of Asian ecumenists on America's growing military commitment in Vietnam, and to rely less on government position papers for contextual information.

---

25. The NCC produced the Revised Standard Version of the Bible in 1952; evangelicals largely rejected it, and created their own New International Version. *Air Reserve Training Manual*, student text, NR 45–0050, Incr. V., vol. 7, reserve noncommissioned officer course, US Air Force, New York, January 4, 1960, p. 20. Statement to congressmen for the National Council of Churches, March 23, 1960, RG 17, fox 6, folder 19, NCC.

26. John F. Kennedy, from the *Washington Post*, April 19, 1960, in "Interpretation Manual," Office of Information, April 25, 1961, RG 4, box 36, folder 30, NCC.

27. As Robert Spike, head of the NCC's Commission on Religion and Race, said, "I am more and more persuaded this is a crisis [Vietnam] that ought to trouble the conscience of the leadership of Protestantism in the same way the racial issue has." And he wanted the church globally to engage with it. Robert Spike, memo to R. H. Edwin Espy, July 26, 1965, RG 4, box 33, folder 14, NCC. See also David Hunter, memo to SACVN, February 11, 1966, RB 4, box 33, folder 26, NCC. Some, like J. Irvin Miller, predicted that responding to Vietnam would be more difficult and confusing than racial matters. J. Irwin Miller, in "Background Paper for General Board, IV," in "IV. Background Material," February 21, 1966, RG 4, box 33, folder 26, NCC.

Specifically, throughout 1965, the East Asia Christian Conference (EACC) and the Japan Christian Council for Peace in Vietnam stressed to NCC leaders that racist cultural biases, a nationalistic Christianity, "their too-self-justifying understanding of liberty and democracy," and all-encompassing fear of Communism blinded Americans to the facts of the Vietnam conflict as well as to Asians' perspectives of them.[28] Complicating matters further, America's imperialist reputation in Asia compromised the image of US churches every time they collaborated with the US government to dispense relief in ways that supported US economic and military aims.[29] Within the NCC specifically, its missions and relief arm, Church World Service (CWS), had forged a strong partnership with the federal government wherein the government provided surplus food, transportation, and logistics support, while the churches dispensed supplies through their vast networks. This collaboration threatened the American ecumenical movement's reputation as an independent agent tied first to the global body of Christ, and became a problem that tested the NCC's credibility throughout the Vietnam War.[30]

Pressures within certain US ecumenical circles to take a critical look at the government's Vietnam policy also mounted throughout 1965. Young ecumenists in the National Student Christian Federation, the editorial boards of the *Christian Century* and *Christianity and Crisis*, and some denominational leaders with the United Presbyterian Church, Methodist Church, United Church of Christ, and pacifist denominations each leveraged their influence to pressure the NCC's General Board to challenge US actions in Vietnam.[31]

28. "Japanese Peace Mission Ends American Tour," press release, August 1965; Isamu Omura et al., statement, Japanese Christian Peace Mission to the US, August 15, 1965; Ryozo Hara, letter to "Friend," June 4, 1964; all in RG 6, box 27, folder 1, NCC. U Kyaw Than, "The Crucified in Vietnam" (confidential notes on the EACC and Vietnam, January 6, 1965, RG 6, box 21, folder 1, NCC). Gerhard Elston, interviews by author, December 11, 1991; October 13–22, 1992, Philadelphia. "Report on Visit of NCC Delegation to Southeast Asia" (December 17, 1965, RG 4, box 32, folder 29, NCC).

29. Elston interview, October 16, 1992.

30. See Jill K. Gill, "The Politics of Ecumenical Disunity: The Troubled Marriage of Church World Service and the National Council of Churches," *Religion and American Culture* 14, no. 2 (Summer 2004): 175–300.

31. Elston interviews, October 13 and 22, 1992. Leonard Clough, "The National Student Christian Federation: A Bridge between Independent Organizations and a Unified Movement," *Journal of Ecumenical Studies* 32, no. 3 (Summer 1995): 331. Sixth World Order Study Conference, survey results, RG 6, box 28, folder 19, NCC. Editorial Board, "U.S. Policy in Vietnam: A Statement," *Christianity and Crisis*, June 14, 1965, 125–26. Kyle Haselden, *Christian Century*, June 16, 1965, 766–67. Arthur J. Moore, "The Question of Credibility," *Christianity and Crisis*, June 28, 1965, 133–34. Editors of the *Christian Century* and *Christianity and Crisis*, "On Foreign

These factors led the council to become one of the first major mainstream organizations in America to criticize its government on Vietnam. The content of its December 1965 policy statement cautiously questioned America's unilateral military methods there, not America's goals, presuppositions, or motives; criticism of the latter came with additional time and study. Nevertheless, it gave the council clearance to enter the antiwar movement, and piqued the White House's attention.[32]

Between 1965 and 1973, no other international issue dominated the NCC's attention like the Vietnam War. Only racial justice surpassed it in inspiring organizational urgency and mobilization. And the conceptual ties between the two issues made them seem evermore like two halves of a larger international ecumenical effort to build a reconciling peace on the bedrock of economic, political, and sociocultural justice. Therefore, although the NCC participated in multiple actions to try to halt that war, and to minister to its various victims, the council's motives and goals far surpassed that single issue. To Robert Bilheimer, the NCC's newly hired (1966) head of the Department of International Affairs and its Priority Program for Peace, US Vietnam policy manifested the exceptionalist worldview that drove all of America's most ill-conceived and counterproductive foreign interventions. Therefore, the war became symptomatic of larger ills to which the body of Christ must speak. Bilheimer hoped the church's witness on Vietnam could transform that military tragedy into a mirror through which Americans could analyze their values and actions as Americans—and as Christians. "A basic task of the church," he stressed, "is to help people discover who they are."[33]

Policy: A Joint Appeal to the National Council of Churches," *Christian Century*, July 7, 1965, 863. Alan Geyer, interview by author, June 13, 2003, in Washington, DC. Herman Will, memo to Dudley Ward, July 26, 1965, CS, box 33, 1444-2-1:08, General Commission of Archives and History United Methodist Church, Special Collections and Archives, Madison, NJ (hereafter GCAH). Kenneth G. Neigh, "Don't Tear Down the Wall," *Monday Morning*, November 1966 (special issue), 4–15. The Church of the Brethren's Resolution on the Vietnam War and China, March 25, 1966, RG 6, box 30, folder 32. See David Settje, *Faith and War: How Christians Debated the Cold and Vietnam Wars* (New York: New York University, 2011), for positions and influence of the United Church of Christ.

32. "Policy Statement on Viet-Nam," General Board, December 3, 1965, RG 4, box 36, folder 15, NCC. "A Message to the Churches on Viet-Nam," General Board, December 3, 1965, RG 4, box 36, folder 15, NCC. "Memorandum from President's Special Assistant for National Security Affairs to President Johnson," December 4, 1965, in *Foreign Relations of the United States, 1964–1968*, vol. 3, *Vietnam*, June–December 1965, Department of State Publications 10289, ed. Glenn La Fantasie (Washington, DC: US Government Printing Office, 1996), 600.

33. Quoted in Minutes, Social Education and Action Section, DCLM, NCC Washington

Bilheimer also came to the NCC determined to utilize international issues like Vietnam as a means to further ecumenize America's territorial, action-focused vis-à-vis theology-focused, competitive denominations. His traditional ecumenical approach came from years working at the World Council as Visser 't Hooft's devoted second-in-command. And he shared his mentor's concern that the NCC's member communions often mistook turf-protecting interdenominational collaboration on hot single-shot issues for real ecumenism. After a week's stay in the United States, Visser 't Hooft quipped sarcastically, "every time a couple of Methodists and Baptists get together for a tea party, it's the ecumenical movement."[34] Bilheimer was committed to muscling the NCC's denominations into real ecumenical dialogue, grounded in theological understanding, and then transforming those principles into an action-based, confessing-church witness that spoke truth to power and addressed the presuppositions underlying US Vietnam policy. He expected the council's communions to reconfigure their separate antiwar programs in ways that best served the larger ecumenical effort.[35] This ran counter to the expectations of some denominations' international affairs secretaries, who preferred instead that the NCC serve the needs of the denominations in mounting a church-based wing of the peace movement aimed at simply stopping the war, while filling programmatic gaps that were too impractical or expensive for them to do individually.[36] Although Bilheimer would unite the NCC's members in ecumenical witness on Vietnam by 1968, these internal tensions grew as disgruntled conservative laity withdrew funds and approval from their churches.

In 1966 and 1967, most of the NCC's denominational leaders felt caught between their own growing antiwar views, which generally aligned with the NCC's official position, and the more traditional anti-Communist sentiments of their laity, who tended to support US involvement in Vietnam as righteous and patriotic. Robert Bulkley, of the United Presbyterian Church, warned the activist Methodist leader Dudley Ward to avoid pushing too aggressively ahead

Office, September 5–6, 1968, CS, box 7, 1439-3-1:36, GCAH. Robert S. Bilheimer, "Transition in the American Identity," *Christian Century*, January 1, 1969, 11–14; Robert S. Bilheimer, "Christian Opposition to the Indochina War," General Board, June 10, 1972, RG 6, box 26, folder 1, NCC. Robert S. Bilheimer, "What Kind of People Are We?," *Christianity and Crisis*, June 23, 1969, 176–78.

34. "Warns against Danger of 'Empty' Ecumenicity," *Christian Advocate*, July 1, 1965, 23.

35. Bilheimer interviews. Robert S. Bilheimer, "Sunday Morning Sermon," April 24, 1966, RG 4, box 33, folder 19, NCC.

36. Bilheimer interviews. Clark G. Karsh, "National Council Mirrors Shifting Church Patterns," *Presbyterian Life*, January 15, 1967, 31.

of denominational policies and local members despite holding morally sound views. A church witness driven by bureaucrats alone would be both ineffective and alienating, especially on such a charged issue.[37] Therefore, these denomination heads needed the council, whose General Board was largely comprised of clerics like themselves and therefore not directly bound to lay opinion, to step ahead and lead. NCC general secretary R. H. Edwin Espy noticed that denominational officials spoke and voted far more liberally in NCC meetings on Vietnam than they did when in denominational settings. He likened the council's role in this situation to a snowplow that cleared a path through deep drifts so that the denominations could later follow, while breasting and buffering the icy storms that blew back on these churches from conservative and governmental sources.[38] Although the NCC's staff largely embraced this duty, Espy sometimes resented the fact that, when lay criticism peaked, denomination heads could shield themselves by pointing blame back at the council. Speaking of this, he said, "I have the feeling that sometimes the NCC is being taken for a ride by some who take advantage of the platform the National Council provides." This dynamic fueled the erroneous impression among parishioners that the NCC was behaving in a dismissive and unrepresentative fashion with respect to the denominations.[39] Conservative evangelical critics of the council, often also Cold War hawks, tactically leaned into that growing rift between laity and ecumenical organizations, to help bust it wide open.

Nevertheless, Bilheimer led the NCC's action against the war. It moved on three main fronts: mobilizing the grass roots and denominations, collaborating globally with ecumenists and the interfaith community, and urging government to change its presuppositions and policies. To meet the expressed need of the denominations, the council spearheaded a "debate and action" program designed to engage laity in thought-provoking discussions and activism relative to the war. In this it relied upon the willingness of denominations to utilize the NCC's positions, programs, and materials; it also collaborated broadly with

37. Bulkley to Ward, September 2, 1966. Kurtis Naylor to Oren Baker, October 27, 1966, RG 6, box 26, folder 15, NCC.

38. Leonard Kramer, associate director of the council's International Affairs Commission, clarified the following for a pastor upset by the NCC's controversial positions on Vietnam: "We are not trying to make up anybody's mind for them, but we are interested in having people use their minds. We are not trying to have people agree with us but we are trying to have people focus on the questions." Kramer to Rev. Howard H. Groover, July 14, 1966, RG 6, box 26, folder 16, NCC.

39. Espy to Ed Grant, March 22, 1967, RG 4, box 35, folder 15, NCC. Also R. H. Edwin Espy, interview by author, August 26, 1991, in Doylestown, PA.

religious and secular organizations whose antiwar projects were compatible with the council's evolving position.[40] Perhaps most significantly, it helped birth the popular grassroots organization Clergy and Laity Concerned about Vietnam (CALCAV) in 1966, and provided it invaluable financial and administrative support for years.[41] Although these efforts often polarized laity along liberal and conservative lines, they created enough consensus to allow a sizable number of member denominations to craft official antiwar positions by 1968.[42]

Meanwhile, Bilheimer attempted to interweave the NCC's expanding work on Vietnam with that of other ecumenical organizations globally. In addition to the World Council and the EACC, he tried forging intersecting ties with similar ecumenical bodies in Britain, Japan, and Korea, among others. In 1969, the NCC joined with the Canadian Council of Churches and Swedish congregations to provide safe haven and religious support to American draft resisters.[43] As anticolonial anger rose in non-Western nations, it did also in

40. "Reporting the Ad Hoc Meeting on Vietnam Action, Notes in Lieu of Minutes," January 7, 1967; Robert S. Bilheimer, letter to "The approximately 200 people the telegrams went to," December 22, 1966; both in RG 6, box 26, folder 14, NCC. "A Multi-Media Album to Encourage Debate and Action on Vietnam" (New York: Council Press, NCC, 1967). "Now Available: A Multi-Media Album to Help in Discussing the National Council of Churches 'Appeal for Debate and Action' on Vietnam," February 1967, RG 6, box 26, folder 14, NCC. Elston, memo to James MacCracken, April 10, 1967, RG 6, box 26, folder 13, NCC. Elston, memo to participants in ad hoc meeting on Vietnam, etc., May 12, 1967, RG 6, box 30, folder 23. David Hunter, memo to Elston, May 15, 1967, RG 6, box 26, folder 13, NCC. Elston to Deborah Brewster, January 17, 1967, RG 6, box 30, folder 13, NCC. Kurtis Naylor, Staff Council–International Affairs, January 13, 1967, RG 6, box 15, folder 3, NCC.

41. Mark Hulsether, *Building a Protestant Left: Christianity and Crisis Magazine, 1941–1993* (Knoxville: University of Tennessee Press, 1999), 130. Elston interview, December 11, 1991; Richard Fernandez, interviews by author, October 31 and December 12, 1991, in Philadelphia. Mitchell K. Hall, *Because of Their Faith: CALCAV and Religious Opposition to the Vietnam War* (New York: Columbia University Press, 1990), 15–23. William Sloane Coffin, draft letter to fellow clergy, January 17, 1966; press release, CCAV, January 18, 1966; both in RG 5, box 13, folder 31, NCC. "Clergy Concerned about Vietnam," *Christian Century*, January 26, 1966, 99–100. David Hunter, memo to R. H. Edwin Espy, January 28, 1966, RG 4, box 33, folder 26, NCC. H. LeRoy Brininger, memo to S. Feke and H. Newton Hudson, January 19, 1966; David Hunter, memo to the Executive Committee, CALCAV, May 29, 1967; both in RG 4, box 34, folder 8, NCC.

42. A majority of the NCC's member churches had taken official positions on Vietnam that were largely reflective of the NCC's by 1968. See Gill, *Embattled Ecumenism*, 223–25. See also John Bennett's observations about the gap between church leaders and parishioners on the war: John Bennett, "The War and the Local Church," *Christianity and Crisis*, October 2, 1972, 215–16.

43. Hall, *Because of Their Faith*, 79–89. Herman Will, interview by author, March 17, 1996, in Seattle.

their respective ecumenical bodies; this included the WCC, whose membership was swelling with nonwhite representatives. These sentiments crystallized in criticism against US Vietnam policy and pressure for American churches to make a bold prophetic witness. The perspectives of nonwhite international ecumenists pressed the NCC further into self-reflection and examination of US policies, resulting in a lessening of the NCC's alignment with white mainstream constituencies as it shifted to stand more clearly with the outcast and oppressed.[44] Since Church World Service relied upon grassroots donations and good will for much of its hefty budget, this further strained CWS's relationship with the council's international affairs department.[45]

Bilheimer also built upon ties with Jewish and Catholic organizations that crafted their own peace positions on Vietnam. Although such alliances formed fastest with Jewish groups, Jewish support of the Six-Day War in 1967 led some Jews to moderate their critique of US Vietnam policy as a result. (It proved hard politically to criticize the White House on one war while applauding its support of another.) Collaboration with Catholics grew more slowly, due in part to powerful strains within Catholicism of anti-Communism as well as an affinity for South Vietnam's Catholic president Ngo Dinh Diem, but cooperative efforts accelerated with time.[46]

Finally, Bilheimer invested extensive personal effort in organizing the NCC's witness to government on the Vietnam War, as well as on the larger systemic issues it magnified. The council's status, membership, and reach provided it with sufficient clout to secure meetings upon request with top government leaders. Its global network ensured it access to firsthand data about the war from a broad base of sources well beyond what the State Department

44. One excellent example of this dynamic is the tensions that arose between nonwhite delegates and the joint white American–Western European power bloc in 1968 at the World Council's Fourth Assembly in Uppsala, Sweden. For a description, see Gill, *Embattled Ecumenism*, 218–19.

45. Gill, "The Politics of Ecumenical Disunity."

46. See "Call to Vigil on Vietnam," *Christian Century*, May 12, 1965, 605. "Statement by the Union of American Hebrew Congregations," November 1965; "Excerpts from the Ecumenical Council's Constitution on 'The Church in the Modern World'"; "Pope Paul VI before the United Nations General Assembly," October 4, 1965; all in *Concern*, January 1–5, 1966, 3–6, RG 6, box 27, folder 1, NCC. "Policy Statement on Vietnam, Synagogue Council of America," January 1966, RG 6, box 30, folder 33, NCC. "Summary Notes of a Strategy Meeting Held in the Interchurch Center," January 6, 1967, RG 6, box 26, folder 19, NCC; Elston to Rabbi Henry Siegman, January 26, 1967, RG 6, box 30, folder 33, NCC. On the impact of the Six-Day War, see as examples: Arthur Flemming, telegram to LBJ, June 6, 1967, RG 4, box 33, folder 40, NCC; Kurtis Naylor, memo to Bruce Hanson, January 16, 1969, RG 4, box 35, folder 18, NCC.

chose to share. These helped it transcend the myopic view of the war created by government-supplied misinformation (known as the credibility gap) and formulate nuanced positions that, when delivered by respected clerics, added a certain gravitas to the antiwar message. Few peace groups possessed this range of advantages.

Under Bilheimer's leadership, the NCC not only visited regularly with White House officials and members of Congress; it also spoke with the Selective Service about improving treatment of conscientious objectors, filed numerous *amicus curiae* briefs in court cases related to the war, testified before Congress, and lobbied candidates for public office about their platforms related to peace. It also operated in a nonpartisan way, for, in addition to adhering to the restrictions that accompanied its 501(c)(3) status, the hawkishness it questioned peppered the positions of both major political parties, and the council's own leadership comprised both Democrats and Republicans.[47] In fact, Arthur Flemming, the NCC's president from 1966 to 1969, was a lifelong Republican who had served in the Eisenhower cabinet as secretary of the Department of Health, Education, and Welfare.

Ensuring that ecumenical rationales reached the ears of the nation's decision makers was a core part of the ecumenical "confessing church" mission to speak truth to power. Bilheimer always clarified that this witness must be made regardless of whether government chose to listen, or whether it opened its doors to ecumenical representatives. He certainly hoped the witness would be persuasive, and he adjusted methods in hopes that doing so might enhance receptivity. However, from his perspective, the church's actual success or failure was not measured by the government's response to the message. Rather, it hinged on whether or not the church did due diligence in formulating genuine ecumenical positions and then whether it proclaimed them publicly in a clear, widespread, persistent fashion. This is what he meant by the church being the church.

Between 1966 and 1970, the NCC's Department of International Affairs relied upon the sort of data-driven, liberal, education-and-discussion-based methods of persuasion with government that had worked so well in developing a consensus within ecumenical circles on issues of concern. Many American ecumenists of Bilheimer's generation were also deeply influenced by the works of H. Richard and Reinhold Niebuhr, which emphasized taking a practical, realistic approach when dealing with power structures rather than simply speaking in ethereal moral arguments. So NCC leaders invested considerable

47. Gill, *Embattled Ecumenism*, 391–95.

effort consulting with and assembling teams of experts, collecting the best data available, formulating what they saw as actionable recommendations, grounding these within their ecumenical worldview, and then presenting their findings to the nation's decision makers. In crafting resolutions and policy statements, they often erred on the side of caution to guard against being discounted by political leaders who often tagged antiwar activists "kooks."

However, these methods generally failed to move elected officials, especially those in the White House. Other tactics would have, too, since those in power largely rejected antiwar arguments no matter how they were delivered, or by whom. Rather, their interest in meeting with the council rested not in considering its evolving antiwar positions but in trying to turn the NCC's message and outreach efforts on Vietnam more toward the government's favor. In other words, the NCC's value to government rested on the degree to which the council could be made politically useful to the White House. Bilheimer learned this hard lesson over years of frustrated attempts to make a prophetic witness heard at 1600 Pennsylvania Avenue in Washington, DC.

The fruitless wooing sessions that Bilheimer and Secretary of State Dean Rusk engaged in over Vietnam provide a clear example of this dynamic. The council knew Rusk to be a devout Presbyterian who respected the church's duty to address public issues and who took the NCC's work seriously. Whenever ecumenists asked Rusk for a meeting to discuss foreign policy, Rusk stood with their statements in hand, red-marked, and ready for debate.[48] They also knew Rusk to be a traditional, southern, Cold War liberal—one who filtered global tensions through the lens of the domino theory (if one nation falls to Communism, its neighbors will likely be next), a bipolar view of the world split between Russia's Communist puppets and our democratic alliances, and World War II's Munich analogy (never appease an aggressor).[49]

In 1967, the NCC wanted to sponsor a Mission of Concern to both North and South Vietnam, and Bilheimer asked Rusk for his blessing. A small delegation of ecumenical leaders hoped to visit both areas to express Christian concern, to witness firsthand the nature of the conflict, to interview people from various sides, and to hear people's stories. Since travel to North Vietnam was restricted, the State Department would need to give the council special clearance. Rusk did this, and more. He helped with travel logistics and securing desired meetings with top officials in South Vietnam and the military.

48. Elston interview, October 15, 1992.
49. Elston interview, October 20, 1992. Geyer interview. Advisory Committee on Peace minutes, August 24, 1966, RG 6, box 27, folder 3, NCC.

Bilheimer insisted that no quid pro quos be attached and no manipulative interference be applied to where the ecumenists went or who they interviewed. It thrilled Bilheimer to see the secretary of state respect the independence of the church enough to provide these things.[50]

Bilheimer hoped the Mission of Concern would not only generate actionable independent data on the war, as well as human connections with those struggling on both sides of the conflict; he also wanted their final report to be persuasive to government and laity. So, he composed the delegation and itinerary with an eye toward ensuring that the entire venture would exude rationalism, judiciousness, and expertise that could win respect from laity and policy makers.[51]

Rusk did view the NCC leaders as logical, thoughtful, and patriotic—and that's why he helped them with logistics and visas to visit North Vietnam. He challenged them to use the trip to conduct a new study on the makings of a just and durable peace, just as Dulles had done years earlier. Rusk assumed that, once the ecumenists saw the war firsthand, they'd interpret it as he did, and adopt a more Dullesesque view of world order. Then, perhaps, they'd channel their clout in support of White House policies. As Rusk noted when approving the mission's waiver to visit both sections of Vietnam, the NCC's request fit the State Department's requirement that such trips "serve the national interest." Specifically, it saw the NCC as "a large, influential body" with leaders who "can be expected to conduct themselves in North Vietnam responsibly and in such a manner as to convey to the North Vietnamese people . . . that our quarrel is not with them. The public effect," it stressed, "would reinforce our [i.e., the Johnson administration's] posture of reasonableness and moderation." Rusk trusted that the council's delegation would be measured and respectable, not radical; he hoped the North Vietnamese would meet American church leaders whom "they cannot be sure will share their view of the war and who may correct their misconceptions about the extent and practical effect of dissent in this country."[52]

---

50. Bilheimer interview, December 14, 1991. Barbara Watson of the State Department's Bureau of Security and Consular Affairs recommended to Rusk that he authorize the NCC's request for the reasons outlined here. Rusk approved the passport request in May 1967. Watson, memo to the Dean Rusk, Department of State, May 18, 1967, on the subject of "Validation of Passports for Travel to North Viet-Nam by Study Group from the National Council of Churches," located in Pol. US 27 Viet S, RG 59, box 2784, Department of State, US Government, National Archives II, College Park, MD (hereafter NAII).

51. Bilheimer interviews. Bilheimer to Eugene Carson Blake, June 7, 1967, RG 6, box 16, folder 15, NCC. Elston interviews. Bilheimer to Andre Philip, July 14, 1967, RG 6, box 26, folder 13, NCC.

52. Watson, memo to the secretary, May 18, 1967.

Conversely, Bilheimer hoped the mission's report would shake the Cold War presuppositions of policy makers like Rusk and of laity in the pews. So he took up Rusk's challenge to use this trip to explore, again, the components of a just and durable peace. To his chagrin, North Vietnam refused to issue visas to the Mission of Concern. But the group still went to South Vietnam, Thailand, and Cambodia, where it interviewed top government and military officials and aid workers.[53] The resulting report was as cautious and careful as the delegation that Bilheimer led—so much so that its conclusions disappointed some ecumenists who didn't feel it went far enough in crafting a prophetic critique of the war.[54] But it did question the White House's narrative about the war specifically, and America's approach to the Cold War generally. It insisted that America's vision of freedom could not be imposed militarily upon Vietnam, and in fact, America's military efforts might backfire. The problematic pacification program provided one illustration where military actions were creating more Vietcong than they eliminated. It raised doubts about the simplistic popular view that Communist China puppeteered Hanoi's efforts, and asserted that nationalism was at least as strong a motivational force for "the enemy" as Communism. Finally, to Bilheimer's delight, the report questioned Communism's supposed monolithic nature, America's duty to contain it single-handedly if need be, and the notion that military forces could effectively do this work.[55]

As one might guess, Rusk dismissed its findings, just as he had when other antiwar activists articulated them. He became more dismissive of the council's leadership, too, when its usefulness to government waned. As secretary of state, he measured its value using a political stick: To what degree could it persuade and represent voters? He concluded that the NCC's leaders had become "generals without armies," a coterie of elite bureaucrats with weakening connections to average churchgoers.[56] Prophetic leadership carried a

53. See Bilheimer's handwritten appointment schedule, June 1967; Russell Johnson to Prince Sihanouk, June 6, 1967; William P. Thompson, "Notes on Trip to South East Asia," June 15–July 5, 1967; Bishop George Barrett, journal, June–July 1967; all in RG 6, box 16, folder 15, NCC.

54. Dudley Ward to Bilheimer, July 14, 1967, RG 6, box 16, folder 15, NCC.

55. "NCC Delegation to South East Asia Report," July 5, 1967, RG 6, box 26, folder 13, NCC; "NCC Delegation Returns from Vietnam," International Issues, Department of International Affairs, NCC, July 21, 1967, RG 4, box 33, folder 44, NCC. A copy of the report is also in the State Department files, soc 12–1, RG 59, box 3110, NAII.

56. Dean Rusk, telephone interview with author, January 15, 1992. Barrett journal, epilogue, July 20, 1967. See also Rhodri Jeffreys-Jones, *Peace Now: American Society and the Ending of the Vietnam War* (New Haven: Yale University Press, 1999).

political price that cost the council popularity with laity and, by extension, with elected officials.

Bilheimer forged ahead anyway, crafting a new policy statement that more directly met Rusk's challenge to revisit the makings of just and durable peace. The council adopted "Imperatives of Peace and Responsibilities of Power" in early 1968. This signaled its strategic shift from critiquing specific governmental actions to focusing on the presuppositions that led to wars like Vietnam. Bilheimer considered it the most significant statement produced by the council during his tenure.[57]

"Imperatives" reiterated the long-held ecumenical notion that genuine peace and world order rested on creating justice by expanding human rights; these could not be furthered through colonialism, occupying armies, economic exploitation, or multiplying nuclear warheads. Whenever simple ideologies like capitalism or Communism failed to make justice and human rights priorities, they fueled tensions rather than solutions. And the faulty presuppositions underlying US policies led to what Senator Fulbright described as America's arrogance of power. These suppositions included a bipolar view of power split between the Communist bloc and the allies that opposed it, seeing developing nations as playable pawns "hovering in a neutral vacuum," and assuming America must serve as God's global policeman. The NCC's statement specifically challenged how the United States then used power to magnify its own influence worldwide rather than to help redistribute power and economic resources more equitably. US military actions like those in Vietnam could not solve political problems or build justice, it insisted, nor could occupying soldiers win the hearts and minds of people. Instead, the United States should support resistance to colonialism by those exploited peoples and help create indigenously crafted institutions rather than install US-friendly puppets that would do America's bidding. Favoring a global order that privileged the political, economic, or military needs of the powerful would always breed resentment and war. The NCC spoke these things out of its belief that the church must prophesy for justice and help Americans understand that international policies could become another means of loving one's neighbor as oneself. In this spirit, America should nurture "a new internationalism" that would build respect for diversity, equity, and trust between peoples.[58]

57. Bilheimer interviews. "Imperatives of Peace and Responsibilities of Power," policy statement, NCC General Board, February 21, 1968, NCCNYO.

58. Bilheimer interviews. "Imperatives of Peace and Responsibilities of Power." The General Board in February also passed a new "Resolution on Vietnam," with specific recommendations to which the "imperatives" document directed readers' attention. See also "A Position

The NCC circulated this policy statement to all government and denominational leaders, hoping to inspire consideration and discussion. However, elected officials dismissed it, some denominational leaders viewed it as too academic, and, as Bilheimer's Vietnam expert Gerhard Elston concluded, the council struggled to "sell it to the pews."[59] By 1968 the NCC had largely succeeded in uniting the bulk of its denominational members behind ecumenical positions on the Vietnam War and the Cold War; nevertheless, its relationships with laity and government continued to erode. Savvy politicians like President Richard Nixon used this fact to nurture a growing alliance between his party and conservative evangelicals, which would empower both.

As domestic unrest peaked between 1968 and 1970, and the nation's white majority recoiled, Cold War dynamics further fractured ecumenical relationships. The deliberative council moved more sharply in a contrary direction from Nixon and his silent majority of supporters.

Despite the NCC's intent to transcend cultural pressures produced by interest groups and power centers, the council found itself caught squarely within the cultural battles of the sixties era, including those aspects that divided generations. Young radicals, who challenged the ideological premises undergirding America's "arrogance of power" much as the council did, grew suspicious of how establishments run by white men replicated hegemonies of privilege. While largely in agreement with the NCC's position on Vietnam, race, anti-Communist fears, and the Cold War, young radicals reared within ecumenical communions often saw their own churches as too wedded to the established order to transform it. In December 1969, a series of youth-and-minority-based demonstrations largely hijacked the NCC's triennial General Assembly. A group of Christian renewalists called Jonathan's Wake thought the NCC needed to be killed and reborn as an activist service agency so it could better aid the oppressed. Such a change would gut the council of its full ecumenical identity and mission, including its theological aspects and focus on unity; so Bilheimer opposed this. As he explained, with these renewalists "you have everyone looking at the world through the lenses of their own issues, and not through the vision of all as members of the body of Christ. Everyone has a soapbox and all people can agree on is to let each person have their soapbox

Paper concerning Southern Africa," Department of International Affairs, NCC, March 1968, NCC. Senator William J. Fulbright, "The Arrogance of Power" (lecture, Johns Hopkins University, May 5, 1966).

59. Elston interview, October 20, 1968. Bilheimer interview, August 9, 1993. "Outline of a Proposed Three-Year International Affairs Program of Encounter, Study and Education in USA/Asia Relations," RG 6, box 30, folder 21, NCC.

and write their own reports." That's not ecumenism. Nevertheless, Jonathan's Wake interrupted triennial sessions by parading through with a coffin representing a "dead" NCC; performed a decontamination ceremony to purge the hall of demonic powers such as "exploitation, suppression, and war"; held a mock draft lottery to send triennial delegates to fight on Vietnam's front lines; and when the assembly narrowly voted down a measure to hold a young man's draft card in trust, they threw red paint on the moderator's table, yelling, "The blood of the Vietnamese and Americans is dripping from the minutes [of this assembly] and from our hands."[60] Yippies, Native Americans, women, and black church leaders supportive of James Foreman's Black Manifesto (which demanded economic reparations from white churches) all criticized the NCC's collaboration with oppressive structures and challenged it to do more, use radical means, and push harder for faster results.[61] To them, churches betrayed their own calls for justice by clinging to ineffective, outdated institutionalized methods.[62] CALCAV's New Breed leadership likewise operated from an "act your way into thinking" philosophy that favored skipping discernment-based discussions to take transformative action immediately.[63] Many radical youth left their church folds during these years to do activism through secular means.

Meanwhile, their parents' and grandparents' generations largely adhered to patriotic calls to support their country's efforts against Communism, and remained suspicious of radicals who challenged the status quo. The council's antiwar efforts and critiques of US Cold War policies, as well as its willingness to listen to the complaints of youth and minorities, allowed the media, White

60. Report from Association of Council Secretaries, General Assembly, Detroit, November 30–December 4, 1969, RG 2, box 5, folder 14, NCC. General Assembly minutes, Second Plenary Session, December 1, 1969, Detroit, November 30–December 4, 1969, RG 2, box 4, folder 18, NCC. (See also Seventh–Ninth Plenary Sessions.) Bilheimer interview, August 6, 1993. "Top Church Post Urged for Negro," *New York Times*, December 2, 1969, RG 4, box 35, folder 13, NCC. Free Church of Berkeley, "Part II: The Exorcism, Jonathan's Wake," General Assembly, November 30–December 4, 1969, RG 2, box 5, folder 3, NCC. Edward Fiske, "Church Council's Parley: Several Steps Further to the Left," *New York Times*, December 8, 1969, RG 4, box 35, folder 13, NCC. General Assembly, November 30–December 4, 1969, RG 2, box 5, folder 3, NCC. Alan Geyer, "Joy Box with No Joy: The NCC at Detroit," *Christian Century*, December 17, 1969, 1601–5. Jonathan's Wake, quoted in Nancy Manser, "NCC Elects First Woman President," *Detroit News*, December 5, 1969, RG 4, box 35, folder 13, NCC.

61. For a full description, see Gill, *Embattled Ecumenism*, 266–74.

62. Gill, *Embattled Ecumenism*, 236–37; Mark Hulsether, *Religion, Culture, and Politics in the Twentieth-Century United States* (New York: Columbia University Press, 2007), 158–59.

63. Richard Fernandez, interviews with author, October 31 and December 12, 1991, Philadelphia.

House, and conservative Christians to bundle the NCC with others seen as domestic threats. Disgruntled laity expressed their displeasure by reducing donations to the NCC and its member denominations. In 1969, the council's income dropped by $500,000, signaling a trend that continued for decades. The consensus explanation, as one reporter described, was rooted in "'a backlash among conservative local congregations' against these bodies' liberal policies 'in such areas as race and opposition to the war in Vietnam.'" Media specialist Bob Gildea described the NCC as trapped "in a squeeze play between militant liberals . . . and aggravated conservatives," the former who now channeled their money into secular activist agencies while the latter routed their giving into more traditional evangelical work.[64] Bilheimer realized that laity actually took little interest in foreign policy; therefore, they were unreliable as a financial base for his department's programs. He told denomination heads who understood their value to foot the bills instead.[65] Meanwhile, conservative groups within the NCC's denominations, such as the Presbyterian Lay Committee and the Methodist Good News movement, organized against what they saw as the socialist and secularist drift of their churches.[66] Conservative evangelical reactions such as these both encouraged and fed off of the Nixon administration's chilly treatment of the NCC.

When Nixon first assumed the White House, NCC president Arthur Flemming wrote to share the council's concerns about US policy in Vietnam. Nixon replied invitingly, telling his former colleague from the Eisenhower

64. Roy Branson, "Time to Meet the Evangelicals?," *Christian Century*, December 24, 1969, 1640–43. Bob Gildea, untitled and undated article, RG 4, box 35, folder 1, NCC.

65. Robert S. Bilheimer, "The Peace Priority Program, 1966–1969," draft, April 17, 1969, RG 4, box 35, folder 27, NCC.

66. Aubrey Haines, "Polarization within the Churches," *Christian Century*, September 2, 1970, 1039–41. "A Call to Presbyterian Laymen," *Presbyterian Life*, December 1, 1965, 18–19. "Portland Presbyterians Register an Objection to the Vietnam Declaration," *Presbyterian Layman*, March 1968, 3. Both the Presbyterian Lay Committee and the Good News Methodists continue today as leaders of a conservative movement within mainline Protestantism to turn those denominations back toward what they call "orthodox" or "classic" doctrines, beliefs, and practices. Harold Bosely noted correctly that "The churches' concern for social issues is alienating many of the older generation of churchmen without winning the support of an appreciable number of those—younger and older alike—who, while deeply concerned about social issues, refuse to get involved in the churches." Harold Bosley, "The Quiet Storm in the Churches," *Christian Century*, December 2, 1970, 1449–52. For information on how the John Birch Society collaborated with conservative Christians to exacerbate divisions within mainline churches, see the following articles in *Monday Morning*: "Far Right Attacks the Church," and John Coventry Smith, "It Still Happens," both dated April 20, 1970, 26; and Reverent Richard Ittner, "Moving Forward in the Age of Malaise," January 1, 1973, 3–4.

administration that his team was making fresh evaluations and welcomed input. It "will be an open administration sensitive to a wide variety of efforts and ideas," he assured, and encouraged Flemming to speak directly to Secretary of State Bill Rogers, another mutual friend from Eisenhower's staff.[67] So Bilheimer's team sprung to action, assembling a consultation of about thirty respected cultural, political, religious, and military leaders dubbed the "Wisemen's Conference" to discuss US Vietnam policy and offer Nixon suggestions.[68] Former ambassador Edwin O. Reischauer and four-star general Matthew Ridgway were among them; the latter had commanded allied forces in Korea and warned Eisenhower against rescuing French soldiers caught in the 1954 siege at Dien Bien Phu.[69] The group's report was moderate and practical. It advised Nixon to end the conflict rather than de-Americanize it, by diminishing military efforts in favor of a political solution; the "wisemen" suggested creating a genuinely representative "interim body" in South Vietnam that could form a viable government, send foreign military units home, and negotiate the South's future relationship with the North.[70] The report also urged Nixon to give the Thieu regime an ultimatum: end South Vietnam's denial of basic political freedoms or the United States would sever support.

Following Nixon's suggestion, Flemming set an appointment with Rogers to discuss it. But when six consultation members arrived, it was clear that Rogers hadn't read his advance copy—which surprised and disappointed them. Rather, Rogers verbally cut the group off, showed scant interest in the report's contents, and lectured these "potential public opinion makers" about their patriotic duties during a time of war. After complaining about Fulbright's and George McGovern's supposed "collusion with the enemy," he urged these ecumenists to aid Nixon's agenda.[71] Council leaders were stunned by the administration's dismissive lack of interest in everything except how the NCC might be utilized politically. When the council rejected that possibility, Nixon gave them the cold shoulder and added them to his enemies list. As a result, NCC staffers experienced wiretaps on their phones, harassment through IRS audits (that turned up nothing), and verbal slander from Vice President Spiro

67. Nixon to Flemming, February 22, 1969, RG 4, box 35, folder 12, NCC.

68. "Memo of Understanding: Special Vietnam Program, April 16–June 1, 1969," April 21, 1969, RG 6, box 26, folder 11, NCC.

69. Matthew Ridgway, "Vietnam Options," June 20, 1969, RG 6, box 26, folder 10, NCC.

70. Howard Schomer to members of the Vietnam Policy Consultation, June 13, 1969, RG 4, box 36, folder 15, NCC. Flemming et al. to Nixon, June 30, 1969, RG 3, box 4, folder 12, NCC.

71. Schomer to Bilheimer, July 14, 1969, RG 6, box 26, folder 10, NCC. Elston interview, October 15, 1992.

Agnew designed to please the council's evangelical critics.[72] In a mocking tirade against liberal Protestantism, Agnew slammed the NCC for "cast[ing] morality and theology aside as not relevant and set[ting] as its goal on earth the recognition of Red China and the preservation of the Florida alligators."[73]

Nixon found evangelical leaders eager to slide into seats of political power and willing to provide his administration the sort of God-cover he desired, not to mention traction with a voter base he sought to secure. So he ordered his aide Charles Colson to woo evangelicals at special White House events, a demographic Colson found "to be about the most pliable of any of the special interest groups that we worked with."[74] Nixon also launched a series of Sunday morning worship services, using invitations to reward allies and build bonds with potential political supporters. Evangelicals like Billy Graham largely adopted a patriotic nationalistic stance toward the Vietnam War. This meant they stood behind their country and its elected leaders, whether right or wrong, trusting God to make lemonade out of lemons. It wasn't for the churches to analyze such things too deeply. God was in control, and America was God's chosen nation.[75] Many ecumenists criticized Nixon's politicized Sunday services, as Reinhold Niebuhr did in the sarcastically titled "The King's Chapel and the King's Court."[76] But the public liked them, and they provided Nixon with the moral authority he sought.

Throughout Nixon's first term, the NCC sought a personal meeting, to no avail. Meanwhile, it escalated its antiwar activities. For example, the council participated in the Moratorium demonstrations in the fall of 1969, grew its

72. Elston interviews; a friend of Elston's swept for bugs and confirmed their existence. Hall, *Because of Their Faith*, 92.

73. Agnew, quoted in George Cornell, from AP news features, *Religion in the News*, June 17, 1970, RG 6, box 30, folder 16, NCC.

74. Charles Colson, in William Martin, *With God on Our Side: The Rise of the Religious Right in America* (New York: Morrow, 1991), 99. Charles Colson, *God and Government: An Insider's View on the Boundaries between Faith and Politics* (Grand Rapids: Zondervan, 2007), 348. See also Darren Dochuk, "Evangelicalism Becomes Southern, Politics Becomes Evangelical," 297–325.

75. Martin asserts, "none ever made such a conscious, calculating use of religion as a political instrument as did Richard Nixon," in *With God on Our Side*, 97; see 97–99 for a description of Nixon's Sunday morning worship services. For a description of the similarities and differences between evangelicals and fundamentalists on the Vietnam War, and their reactions to Nixon, see Jill K. Gill, "Religious Communities and the Vietnam War," in *Vietnam War Era: People and Perspectives*, ed. Mitchell Hall (Santa Barbara, CA: ABC-CLIO, 2009), 97–116.

76. Reinhold Niebuhr, "The King's Chapel and the King's Court," *Christianity and Crisis*, August 4, 1969, 211–12.

ministry to war resisters and veterans, took a supportive position of conscientious objectors of particular wars, sent ecumenists to meet with the four delegations negotiating peace in Paris, and joined CALCAV in lobbying Congress to cut the war's funding.[77] Of course, these actions hardened Nixon further against ecumenists. After escalating his bombing campaign in spring 1972, and threatening human catastrophe by extending this to the dikes along North Vietnam's Red River, leaders tied to the National Council of Churches and World Council of Churches released two strong joint condemnations.[78] However, they received little press attention.[79] The charismatic WCC president and former NCC leader Eugene Carson Blake sent several letters to Nixon about the bombing, and appealed again for a meeting. He expected White House doors to open when top mainline Protestant leaders came calling, and could not quite fathom how Nixon repeatedly brushed him off—especially since Nixon willingly conferred with evangelical and Catholic clerics.[80] Bilheimer asked Blake to stop trying, as Nixon's obvious rebuffs made it "degrading" for ecumenists to continue the pursuit.[81] The price of earning face time with Nixon was co-optation, and Bilheimer refused to compromise the ecumenical mission for that. Besides, the mainline Protestant establishment's voice carried less cultural weight than in decades past. As Bilheimer sadly noted, "'Who cares?' was the attitude." Nixon knew this, so felt little political pressure to placate liberal church leaders.

In 1972, due to Nixon's unresponsiveness, Bilheimer shifted the NCC's strategies again—largely abandoning attempts to persuade the White House with data and arguments. Instead, the NCC coordinated a strong *moral* condemnation from the ecumenical community against America's Vietnam poli-

77. The Moratorium to End the War in Vietnam occurred October 15, 1969, and again November 15, 1969.

78. Yves Lacoste, "American Aviation Can Cause Flooding in the North without Directly Hitting the Dikes," *LeMonde*, June 7, 1972, RG 6, box 26, folder 2, NCC. Niilus memo to N. Canh and Epps, July 10, 1972; Epps, memo to Eugene Carson Blake, July 13, 1972; Blake to the president, July 17, 1972; Cynthia Clark Wedel and R. H. Edwin Espy, statement, April 17, 1972; Blake to Espy, April 17, 1972; Untitled, signed statement, April 20, 1972; statement by church leaders, St. John's Church, Washington, DC, May 11, 1972; all in RG 6, box 26, folder 1, NCC. "This Old and New War," *Christian Century*, April 19, 1972, 439.

79. Bilheimer to Cynthia Wedel, May 15, 1972, RG 6, box 26, folder 1, NCC.

80. Stephen Rose, "Eugene Carson Blake: A Welcome-Home Interview," *Christian Century*, October 18, 1972, 1036–39. Blake to Nixon, April 26, 1972; Blake to the president, May 16, 1972; Blake to Dr. John McLaughlin, June 6, 1972; James A. Wechsler, "A Studied Evasion," *New York Post*, July 25, 1972; all in RG 6, box 26, folder 1, NCC.

81. Bilheimer to Blake, July 13, 1972, RG 6, box 26, folder 1, NCC.

cies that was designed to challenge the sense of divine blessing Nixon received from his evangelical inner circle. The council's huge international "Ecumenical Witness" conference in Kansas City, Missouri, raised up a loud, expansive ecumenical voice against the sins being committed by the United States in Southeast Asia, and purposefully separated the ecumenical voice from what Bilheimer called the predominant "national religion" of Nixon's evangelical allies.[82] As Bilheimer said, "I wanted the conference to be a real point where the churches exercised self-criticism of themselves, their country, and its policies. I hoped they'd do that in such terms that people in the churches and government would listen."[83] The *New York Times* dubbed it "the most comprehensive religious gathering ever assembled in the United States over the peace issue."[84] But once again, younger, more radical participants chafed at Bilheimer's traditional bureaucratic style and the slowness of institutional church action, while conservative Christians continued to question what they interpreted as the council's political extremism, radical biases, and unthinking willingness to kowtow to disruptive youth.[85] In early 1973, Nixon ended America's military engagement in Vietnam with a treaty that accomplished little beyond disengaging US troops. Burned out, Bilheimer left the NCC shortly thereafter.

Back in 1970, the Reverend Richard John Neuhaus made a prescient prediction about which Christian faction would win the popularity contest with the public after America's impending failure in Vietnam. This prominent liberal who helped found CALCAV, and who shifted into the neoconservative camp in the 1980s, foresaw that evangelicals who remained supportive of their nation's cause regardless of the war's outcome "would feel confirmed . . . and be in a position to congratulate themselves." Conversely, the liberal ecumenists, who condemned the war and exposed its root causes, would be rebuffed by a populace eager to preserve their self-conceptions and nation's identity.[86] He

82. "A Call to an Ecumenical Witness, Kansas City," NCC, January 13–16, 1972, RG 6, box 26, folder 2, NCC.

83. Bilheimer interview, August 6, 1993.

84. Edward Fiske, "Religious Assembly Terms Vietnam Policy Immoral," *New York Times*, January 17, 1972, 35.

85. Bilheimer interview, August 6, 1993. Poikail George, "Ecumenical Witness in Kansas City," January 13–16, 1972, RG 6, box 26, folder 2, NCC. Stephen Brown to Bishop James Armstrong, January 22, 1972, RG 6, box 26, folder 4, NCC. Eugene Pulliam, "Social Action and the Pulpit," *Arizona Republic*, January 30, 1972, RG 6, box 26, folder 2, NCC. Lester Kinsolving, "Disruptions," newspaper article (newspaper unknown), February 5, 1972, RG 6, box 26, folder 6, NCC.

86. Richard John Neuhaus, "War, Churches, and Civil Religion," *Annals of the American Academy of Political and Social Science* 387 (January 1970): 128–40, quoted in Andrew

was correct. Bilheimer had tried to use the Vietnam conflict as a catalyst for transforming the nationalistic Christian exceptionalism that justified US Cold War policies. While the NCC's efforts largely succeeded within the ecumenical establishment, its message failed to resonate widely among laity and therefore also failed to move policy makers.[87] Meanwhile, an ascendant Religious Right escalated its attacks on liberal Christian organizations. As a result, the council experienced decades of financial and staff shrinkage, as well as a loss of political clout, especially with Republican presidential administrations.

During the 1970s and 1980s, the NCC continued to push human rights as the foundation of a just and durable peace. It opened a global Human Rights Office in 1977, from which it organized actions against violations worldwide. The council's efforts to aid the Sanctuary Movement, where congregations hid Latin American refugees fleeing dictators and death squads backed by US Cold War policies, put the NCC squarely in conflict with President Ronald Reagan's international agenda. So, too, did the council's opposition to South Africa's apartheid system, its backing of Palestinian self-determination, its work to negotiate an end to Guatemala's civil war, and its protests of Reagan's renewed nuclear arms buildup.[88] Surrounded by evangelical supporters, Reagan sought to win the Cold War, and willingly made anti-Communist dictators his partners. He also popularized a narrative of the Vietnam War that blamed America's loss on those disloyal liberal spoilers who supposedly helped erode public support, undercut morale, and weakened the military's hand.[89] These spoilers included the NCC. Like Nixon, Reagan ostracized council leaders from the West Wing and felt little political compulsion to do otherwise.

LeRoy Pratt, "Religious Faith and Civil Religion: Evangelical Responses to the Vietnam War, 1964–1973" (PhD diss., Southern Baptist Theological Seminary, 1988), 349–50. Also discussed in Gill, "Religious Communities and the Vietnam War," 113–14.

87. As one example, Rick Nutt describes how the war helped change the foreign policy perspectives of leaders within the Presbyterian Church US (southern Presbyterians). See Rick Nutt, *Toward Peacemaking: Presbyterians in the South and National Security, 1945–1983* (Tuscaloosa: University of Alabama Press, 1994), 69–124.

88. Lester Kurtz and Kelly Goran Fulton, "Love Your Enemies? Protestants and United States Foreign Policy," in *The Quiet Hand of God: Faith-Based Activism and the Public Role of Mainline Protestantism*, ed. Robert Wuthnow and John H. Evans (Berkeley and Los Angeles: University of California Press, 2002), 364–80.

89. Pratt, "Religious Faith," 275–350. See also Billy Hargis's book *Our Vietnam Defeat! What Happened: A Study in International Defeat, Shabby Betrayal, Shameful Retreat* (Neosho, MO: Operation God and Country; Tulsa: Christian Crusade, 1975). Mitchell Hall outlines the "stabbed-in-the-back" thesis popularized by conservatives in *The Vietnam War*, 84–85.

Although the NCC received welcome access to the White House again under President Bill Clinton's leadership, George W. Bush won the office in 2000 and 2004 with powerful evangelical support and, like Nixon and Reagan, saw little need to cater to his ecumenical critics. Bilheimer viewed the Vietnam War as a symptom of skewed worldviews and presuppositions—which, if not altered, would lead to future quagmires. The terrorist attacks on New York's Twin Towers and the Pentagon on September 11, 2001, provided Bush the opportunity to wage a war on terror in the Middle East that relied upon assumptions similar to those undergirding the Cold War. These included a godly American exceptionalism that justified a unilateral attack on Iraq and Afghanistan in March 2003, despite no verifiable evidence that Iraq had anything to do with the 9/11 attacks or possessed weapons of mass destruction. In late 2002 the Reverend Robert Edgar, general secretary of the NCC, who had once protested the Vietnam War, organized a large interreligious effort to visit Iraq, humanize its population in the media, and try to deter invasion.[90] This occurred at a time when few groups dared to raise questions; even the media was largely silent. Bush denied requests from council leaders to hear their concerns. Instead, he relied on conservative evangelicals for interpretations of Scripture that supported invasion.[91] The subsequent incursion into Iraq spiraled into civil war and became another intractable mess for the US military. During this time, Edgar published a book that condemned once again America's use of Christianity to support a "Pax Americana" theology of

90. Letter from US church leaders to George W. Bush, September 12, 2002, at www.nccc usa.org/news/02news83.html. Prior to this letter, thirty-eight churchpeople from the United States, Canada, and Britain wrote one during a meeting at the World Council in which they stated, "the United Nations Charter does not permit states to engage in pre-emptive war." See "Leaders from American, Canadian, British Churches Appeal to U.S. Government: 'Stop the Rush to War,'" August 29, 2002, www.ncccusa.org/news/02news82.html (September 1, 2006). Robert Edgar, *Middle Church: Reclaiming the Moral Values of the Faithful Majority from the Religious Right* (New York: Simon and Schuster, 2006), 65–75. For a description of the NCC's humanitarian mission to Iraq between December 29, 2001, and January 3, 2002, see "NCC-Led Religious Leaders Mission to Iraq Concludes," January 3, 2002, www.ncccusa.org /news/02news104.html. And for the NCC's efforts to persuade Europeans to oppose preemptive war, see "NCC Delegation to Paris Surprises Many with Opposition to War," February 12, 2003, www.ncccusa.org/news/03news10.html. For information on similar sentiments by other religious bodies, see Gill, *Embattled Ecumenism*, 379.

91. Lichtman, *White Protestant Nation*, 429–43. Richard Land et al. to George W. Bush, October 3, 2002, http://www.drrichardland.com/press/entry/the-so-called-land-letter (December 10, 2017). Richard Land, "There Is Just Cause to Remove Saddam Hussein from Power in Iraq," September 9, 2002, http://mail.erlc.com/article/there-is-just-cause-to-remove-saddam -hussein-from-power-in-iraq (December 10, 2017).

empire.[92] In 2011 US combat troops left an Iraq that remained politically divided, undemocratic, and unstable. The invasion of Afghanistan, though more justified, became America's longest war, and one that also failed to establish a stable, self-governing, democratic state. These policy choices and methods illustrated to ecumenists that America still clung to the presuppositions and self-conceptions that fueled earlier Cold War policies.

Decades of opposing these, while parrying right-wing attacks, left the ever-shrinking council marginalized from laity, financially strapped, and relatively insignificant to policy makers.[93] In 2000 Church World Service left the NCC to operate independently. Its missions and relief work were too reliant upon lay contributions and government partnerships to survive being tied to the NCC's more politically polarizing positions—especially when Republicans held power.[94] By 2013, the NCC's institutional operation could sustain a small handful of permanent staff; budget constrictions also forced its departure from its longtime home in New York City's Interchurch Center into a few shared offices in the Methodist Building near Capitol Hill. From there, it continues to lead the shared ecumenical efforts of its thirty-seven denominational members comprising over 45 million people within more than 100,000 congregations.[95]

The noted intellectual historian David Hollinger argues that ecumenical Protestants succeeded greatly in helping move American culture toward acceptance of gender and racial equality as well as enlightenment-based values. Their institutional decline, he suggests, is due in part to the obsolescence created by this success.[96] I argue, however, that they were far less fruitful in challenging assumptions related to foreign policy. American exceptionalism continues to be fueled by both major political parties, and it remains central to the nation's identity. As Reinhold Niebuhr argued in *Moral Man, Immoral*

---

92. Edgar, *Middle Church*, 63–100. For similar sentiments to Edgar's, see Arthur Schlesinger Jr., "Forgetting Reinhold Niebuhr," *New York Times*, September 18, 2005; Jim Wallis, *God's Politics: Why the Right Gets It Wrong and the Left Doesn't Get It* (San Francisco: HarperSanFrancisco, 2006), 108–71; Michael Lerner, *The Left Hand of God: Taking Back Our Country from the Religious Right* (New York: HarperCollins, 2006), 112–13. For a description of Bush's "Pax Americana" perspectives, see Lichtman, *White Protestant Nation*, 439–43.

93. Amy Frykolm, "Culture Changers: David Hollinger on What the Mainline Achieved," *Christian Century*, July 2, 2012.

94. Gill, "The Politics of Ecumenical Disunity," 175–212.

95. National Council of Churches, http://nationalcouncilofchurches.us/about/member-communions.php.

96. David A. Hollinger, "After Cloven Tongues of Fire: Ecumenical Protestantism and the Modern American Encounter with Diversity," *Journal of American History* 98, no. 1 (June 2011): 21–48, http://history.berkeley.edu/sites/default/files/cloventongues.pdf.

Society, institutions protect their own self-interested power first and foremost; justice for those beyond America's borders stimulates few champions Stateside. Whereas cries for racial and gender equity boiled up from within the diverse, interconnected American electorate—and became linked to America's founding ethos—people who live beyond its borders remain fixed as lessers and outsiders. To care for their causes can seem un-American if doing so threatens American power.

The NCC led America's ecumenical churches into battle against Cold War premises and policies. It largely lost that fight in terms of fundamentally transforming US foreign policy and the minds of most Americans. Because the council prioritized its ecumenical mission over institutional survival, it did not moderate its critiques to win back conservative laity and their donations, nor to appease presidents' political agendas. Much like Mark 8:36, which warns, "For what shall it profit a man, if he shall gain the whole world, and lose his own soul?" (KJV), Bilheimer insisted that the church fulfilled its purpose when it proclaimed its transcendent message prophetically and persistently; it failed when it became a tool of politics or culture. As historian Forrest Church concluded in his study of the disestablishment of religion, "When church and state tucked into bed together, it was the church that ended up asking, 'Will you respect me in the morning,' and the answer was almost always 'No.'"[97] While evangelical leaders became the GOP's Cold War bed partners in an effort to grow their political and cultural clout, those in the NCC opted instead to "be the church" as ecumenically defined in the first half of the twentieth century. This contributed to their marginalization as Christian public intellectuals, an ongoing phenomenon that inspires renewed lamentation from people whose ears crane for voices that navigate thoughtfully the culture-war gulf between the Religious Right and the secular Left in the twenty-first century.[98]

Over the last sixty-five years, the council stressed repeatedly that human rights and justice—key expressions of loving one's neighbor as oneself—must become foundational to international policies if peace is to be achieved. Through reams of published studies, messages, policy statements, resolutions, and *amicus curiae* briefs, it produced a body of Christian thought that con-

97. Forrest Church, *So Help Me God: The Founding Fathers and the First Great Battle over Church and State* (New York: Harcourt, 2007), 13.

98. See E. J. Dionne Jr., "In Today's Troubling Times, Where Are Our Faith Leaders?," *Washington Post*, August 24, 2016, https://www.washingtonpost.com/opinions/in-search-of -humble-prophets/2016/08/24/7fa00d86-6a0e-11e6-ba32-5a4bf5aad4fa_story.html?utm_term =.6ff2f734f186, and Alan Jacobs, "The Watchmen: What Became of the Christian Intellectuals?," *Harpers Magazine*, September 2016, http://harpers.org/archive/2016/09/the-watchmen/.

tinues to challenge providential, nationalistic, American exceptionalism and policies that emanate from that. Over the years, its work helped to morally ground and legitimate the broader peace movement. And through its actions and partnerships, the NCC became a hub for building a counterhegemonic network of progressive religious organizations that continues to articulate an ecumenical worldview. Though it paid a political and financial price for prophetic leadership during the Cold War, the council remains an unapologetic advocate of a human rights–based, justice-focused path to peace.

US-USSR Church Relations, 1956–1991

Bruce Rigdon, Barbara Green, and John Lindner

The roots of the Cold War, as it came to be known, are to be found in the ashes of the Second World War itself. The event that more than any other symbolized the recognition of its beginnings can be found in one of Winston Churchill's most famous addresses, "Sinews of Peace," given in the presence of President Harry S. Truman at Westminster College in Fulton, Missouri, on March 5, 1946. In his address Churchill spoke of an "iron curtain" that had descended across the continent of Europe, with the result that "behind that line all the famous cities and the populations around them lie in what I must call the Soviet sphere, and all are subject in one form or another, not only to Soviet influence but to a very high and, in some cases, increasing measure of control from Moscow."[1]

The Cold War came to envelop the entire world in its grip for more than four decades of the twentieth century. This struggle for power and dominance between the Soviet Union and its satellites and the United States and its allies influenced and shaped every aspect of modern life, from science and technology to economics and politics, from arts and culture to social policies and education. Nor was this influence limited to so-called secular areas of life, for it also had profound effects upon religious institutions in both the East and the West.

The subject of the impact and effects of the Cold War upon American religious institutions and their ways of responding to its challenges is too vast to be undertaken in this brief chapter. Instead we will focus on the National Council of Churches, founded in 1950, and the responses that it made during the next forty years to the challenges and possibilities of relations with the churches of the USSR.

1. Winston Churchill, "The Sinews of Peace," quoted in Mark A. Kishlansky, ed., *Sources of World History* (New York: HarperCollins, 1995), 298.

To set the scene, it is well to remember that Americans emerged from WWII with the conviction that they had won a great victory and were clearly the winners in the global conflict. What followed was a period of enormous industrial growth, unprecedented new wealth, and great, new opportunities. Americans felt quite confident about their place in the world and undergirded this sense of being a special people with themes of messianism, which were already present in the nation's history. America was the shining city set on a hill, the new promised land, the place where God was doing a new thing. America's victories and prosperity, its new pride of place in the world of nations, seemed to be confirming signs of the nation's special destiny. That destiny, of course, involved spreading the blessings of democracy and freedom to every corner of the globe.

Russians also had a history of messianic consciousness, beginning with the notion of Moscow as the Third Rome, which dated from the reign of Ivan III following the fall of Constantinople to the Turks in the fifteenth century. Wed to Marxism's convictions about the inevitability of the outcome of human history, Soviets also believed that they were a nation with a messianic mission: to spread socialism and its promised benefits around the world in preparation for the final victory of Communism.

The Cold War was therefore not only a struggle for political and economic dominance, it was also the confrontation of two messianic ideologies that competed for the minds, hearts, and commitments of people everywhere. If anything, this made the conflict the more determined, bitter, and ruthless, and made compromise exceedingly difficult to negotiate. And it posed unique questions and enormous problems of very different sorts for religious communities and institutions on both sides of the conflict.

The 1950s witnessed the first armed conflict in the Cold War, the Korean War, which concluded with a stalemate and the division of the Korean peninsula. It was now clear to Americans that Communism was the nation's primary enemy, and specifically, that meant the Soviet Union and the People's Republic of China. The decade also witnessed the sweeping phenomenon of McCarthyism, a national virus of fear, suspicion, and mistrust that asserted that Communist infiltration and influence in all American institutions constituted such a dangerous threat that the loyalty of all Americans had to undergo careful scrutiny. This sinister mood affected everything in American life from its governmental institutions to its universities and its religious communities. Being a loyal American seemed to imply consent to a worldview in which everything was clearly and simply black or white, good or evil, loyal or disloyal. To have one's loyalty challenged was to have questions raised and suspicions aroused about whether or not one should be considered fit and allowed to govern or to lead. Reputations were destroyed overnight, and institutions began to feel overwhelming pressures to conform to new norms, which resisted the recognition of complexity, the need for free speech, the necessity for intellectual rigor and reflection, and the integrity of honest disagreement and debate. Even after McCarthy had been discredited, popular American political debate, especially about the issues of the Cold War, continued to be rather pragmatic, simplistic, and flat, lacking in subtlety, nuance, and insight. The issue of the threat of nuclear war, of "mutually assured destruction," as in the Cuban missile crisis, did bring a sense of reality and a need for pragmatism to the nation and its leaders, but overall the period of the Cold War missed the opportunity for the conflicting parties to learn a great deal about one another or about themselves and the new world that was emerging.

It was in this context that the first official delegation of the National Council of Churches of Christ in the USA (NCC) made a historic visit to the churches of the USSR, the first of its kind. The date was March 9, 1956, and the ecumenical delegation departing from Idlewild Airport in New York consisted of nine men, headed by Eugene Carson Blake, president of the NCC. The rest of the delegation consisted of NCC staff members, heads of US denominations, a seminary president, and a layperson who served in a major New York law firm. Discussion about including a female in the delegation had taken place, but it was decided not to do so because of the possible negative response from Russian Orthodox officials.

This bold venture was a response to the impetus of the Second Assembly of the World Council of Churches (WCC), meeting in Evanston, Illinois, two years earlier, in 1954, which appealed to representatives of churches in countries "between which tension exists to visit one another, so that they may gain a better understanding of one another, and of the countries in which they live, and thus strengthen the bonds of fellowship, and promote the reconciliation of the nations."[2]

On June 8, 1955, Eugene Carson Blake cabled Alexei I, patriarch of the Russian Orthodox Church, requesting that the Russian Orthodox Church officially invite a group of American church representatives to visit the USSR at an early date. "We desire to participate in this process of conference between Christian leaders as a means of increasing mutual understanding and making manifest the spiritual fellowship which is ours in Christ."[3]

---

2. Douglas R. Brankenridge, "A Beginning Has Been Made: Eugene Carson Blake and the Soviet Union, 1956," *American Presbyterians* 68, no. 2 (1990): 91.

3. Brankenridge, "A Beginning Has Been Made," 89.

Arriving in Moscow on March 11, 1956, after an intermediate stop in Prague, the American delegation was met and warmly welcomed by Metropolitan Nikolai, the chairperson of the Department of External Church Relations of the Moscow Patriarchate. For the next ten days the delegation engaged in rigorous discussions, official receptions, sightseeing, and opportunities to view life in the Soviet Union on a firsthand basis.

From the outset of the official talks between Soviet church representatives and the NCC delegation, Blake stressed the church-to-church character of the deputation's presence. "Our mission to you is a church mission," he said, "it is not a subsidiary supplement to national diplomacy. We come without any instructions from our government. . . . We are here as churchmen [*sic*] with a dedicated loyalty to the Risen Christ. It is in the context of the Christian Gospel, and the bearing of that Gospel upon the conduct of men [*sic*] and of nations that we embark upon these conversations."[4]

The conversations were wide-ranging, and included talk about theological education, human rights, religious freedom, and the importance of sharing scientific and technical skills. Without question, however, all the participants viewed the question of world peace as the most important, urgent, and pressing agenda item. The ensuing conversations were frank, open, and at times conflicting and even confrontational. But the process allowed for the beginning of better understanding of one another's presuppositions, fears, and hopes. The fear of atomic disaster, for example, was shared by both sides, as was the desire to achieve some means of controlling the production and use of atomic weapons. At the conclusion, Dr. Blake and Metropolitan Nikolai issued statements regarding the nature of the East-West dialogue that had just occurred. Both emphasized the importance of world peace and linked the concepts of peace and justice as essential ingredients for any lasting solution to international conflict.

Not surprisingly, the visit of the delegation was severely criticized and condemned by many in both the religious and secular communities in the United States. This, however, gave the participants significant opportunities to talk about their experiences in the Soviet Union, their impressions of the churches with which they had come in contact, and the importance of dialogue as a process of coming to understand those whose lives are very different from our own. This "official" dialogue continued with two visits from the churches in the USSR to the churches in the USA in 1956 and 1961.

These visits produced occasions to talk about and to begin to test the

4. Brankenridge, "A Beginning Has Been Made," 93.

possibility for the churches in the USSR to become members of the World Council of Churches. That very important development took place at the Third Assembly of the WCC in New Delhi in 1961. Its enormous impact was to transform the entire future of the ecumenical movement.

The visit of Blake's delegation took place just six years after the founding of the NCC. The NCC was already heavily engaged in many ways in Cold War issues of all sorts. A council of more than thirty member churches representing the majority of Protestant and Orthodox churches in the USA, the NCC at its height was one of the largest ecumenical organizations in the world, with an annual budget in excess of $30 million. A large percentage of this budget was allocated to a division of the NCC called Church World Service, which provided emergency and development aid to needy people across the world. This in itself involved the council in Cold War issues, since aid was sometimes sent to so-called Communist countries as well as to areas that were at the center of Cold War conflicts.

From the beginning the NCC had an effective office and well-qualified staff devoted to international affairs. It regularly took positions on global issues, held conferences and consultations, published policy papers, developed educational materials, cooperated with international organizations, and advocated on behalf of the churches to various branches of the US government. In doing so, its perceived liberal orientation on such matters regularly brought it under attack from conservative secular and religious groups and organizations. When it spoke in favor of such issues as the recognition of the People's Republic of China and advocated its admission to the UN, when it urged changing US policy toward and treatment of Cuba, when it expressed strong opposition to the Vietnam War, and when it took strong stands for nuclear disarmament and arms control, it brought upon itself stronger and more determined opposition. In the context of this history, the NCC and its member churches found it significant and necessary to establish a new chapter in the dialogue between themselves and the churches of the USSR.

In some respects this dialogue would reflect continuity with the earliest visits and conversations with the members of the churches in the USSR. Most important, of course, was the understanding that all these activities and contacts were of a profound churchly character and purpose. It was because of their common convictions about the gospel and the church that they committed themselves to the disciplines of dialogue, prayer, worship, and witness. If this led them to speak together and work together around issues of peace and justice, it was because of their Christian faith and because it belonged to the mission of their churches.

In other respects, the dialogue took on new forms and new dimensions. The most obvious was that what came into being would involve women, as well as men, young people, and not just senior clerics but laypeople in very large numbers, and would begin to connect local churches and communities in both countries. It would produce study materials and programs for Americans who knew very little about their so-called enemies, and it would give many pilgrims on visits to the churches in the USSR their first opportunity to experience something of the faith and life of the Orthodox churches.

The Nuclear Threat

During the early 1960s, representatives from both the National Council of Churches and the Russian Orthodox Church (ROC), including United Methodist bishop James K. Mathews and Protopresbyter Vitaly Borovoy, attended the Second Vatican Council in Rome as ecumenical observers, where they strengthened personal relationships. The visitations by church leaders begun by Dr. Blake's 1956 delegation continued periodically, and in 1969 an ecumenical consultation entitled "Christian Concern for the Limitation and Reduction of Arms" was convened in Saint Louis jointly by the NCC and the US Catholic Conference of Bishops.

The 1968 invasion of Czechoslovakia by the Soviet Union had triggered a number of accelerations in the nuclear arms race, including US deployment of the Sentinel ABM system, indefinite postponement of the SALT (Strategic Arms Limitation Talks) process, and the deployment by the Nixon administration of MIRVs in 1970, which unleashed a new arms race in offensive nuclear weapons. The Nixon and Ford administrations pursued détente with the Soviet Union, resulting in the 1975 Helsinki Final Act, establishing the Organization for Security and Cooperation in Europe (OSCE). At the same time, through the MIRVs, more than five thousand new nuclear weapons were added to the US arsenal. The Soviet Union did the same within the next five years, raising the specter of mutual annihilation many times over. In 1978 the Carter administration announced the planned deployment of "neutron bombs" in Europe (designed to kill without as much physical destruction), which triggered massive protests. President Carter and General Secretary Leonid Brezhnev finally signed the SALT II treaty on June 18, 1979. Seeking conservative support for SALT II, Carter approved development of the MX missile. In short, by 1979 the nuclear weapons arms race had reached levels of absurdity, with the two countries having the capacity to destroy each other and even the entire world many times over, and with no end in sight.

It was in the context of this absurdity that US and Soviet church leaders talked at a meeting of the WCC Central Committee in January 1979 in Geneva at the initiative of the Russians. They agreed to hold a formal bilateral consultation in Geneva, March 27–29, 1979, to address the nuclear arms race. Participants were acutely aware of the deadly serious nature of the policies their two countries were pursuing and knew how hard it would be to find any common ground. The conference became known by the title of its final statement, *Choose Life*.

It is hard to overstate the level of tension and consequent stiff formality in which that consultation began. It opened with addresses on the status of arms control negotiations by the US and Soviet ambassadors to the new Geneva-based permanent Committee on Disarmament of the United Nations, Adrian S. Fisher and Victor Israelyan. Israelyan remarked, "I'm also a 'Southerner' [as was President Carter]. Sometimes I face difficulties in talks with my American colleagues. Just yesterday, we had sharp divergences. But I have confidence that the American nation and the Soviet nation need peace—peace through disarmament. Slowly, step-by-step, we shall move to peace without arms and wars."[5]

The Soviet delegation was headed by Metropolitan Juvenaly of Krutitzy and Kolomna, chairman of the External Church Relations Department of the Moscow Patriarchate of the Russian Orthodox Church. The US delegation was headed by Rev. M. William Howard, president of the NCC, and Dr. Claire Randall, NCC general secretary. The Russian Orthodox participants were still clearly mourning the early death of Metropolitan Yuvenaly's predecessor at External Church Relations, Metropolitan Nikodim of Leningrad and Novgorod, who died in 1978 during a visit to Pope John Paul I at the Vatican. The attendance of the youngest member of the Soviet delegation is of note: Archbishop Kirill of Vyborg, rector of the Leningrad Theological Academy of the ROC. Kirill later became chairman of the External Church Relations Department and, in 2009, became patriarch of the Russian Orthodox Church.

Professor Bruce Rigdon set the tone of the talks as a theological exchange rather than primarily a political one through his Bible study on the "powers and principalities" in Paul's letter to the Colossians: "We have seen that the underlying problem to which the Epistle to the Colossians is addressed is the

---

5. Unpublished verbatim notes taken by Alan Geyer, technical adviser to the US delegation.

false view of reality embodied in the worldview of its citizens. This distortion of what was real and true manifested itself in idolatry and enslavement to powers, which were beyond human control. I submit that we are in fundamentally the same situation. The arms race itself is a manifestation of a distorted picture of reality and is indicative of the most bizarre and terrible form of idolatry."[6]

In his opening address, Metropolitan Yuvenaly also grounded his call for peace theologically as a mandate for the Christian church. He acknowledged the history of exchanges between church leaders of the two countries before addressing specific concerns about the arms race: "Of great imminence for the cause of peace is the circumstance that the epidemic of armament is spreading over a growing number of new regions of the world. We followed with hope the work of the Special Session of the UN General Assembly on Disarmament. At present the priority is to conclude a new Soviet-American Agreement on the basis of the SALT II and to bring it into force."[7]

A drafting committee of "the four Bs"—Arie Brouwer, general secretary of the Reformed Church in America; Alexei Buevsky, secretary of the External Church Relations Department; Alexei Bichkov, general secretary of the Union of Evangelical Baptists in the USSR; and Bruce Rigdon—plus the two technical advisers: Alan Geyer, of the Churches' Center for Theology and Public Policy, and Vladimir Kulagin, dean of the School of International Affairs in Moscow, worked into the night (as they always do) to produce a final statement. It succeeded beyond anyone's expectations in capturing the moment and giving impetus to a whole new level of relations. It began by invoking text from Deuteronomy 30:19: "I call heaven and earth to witness against you today that I have set before you life and death, blessings and curses. Choose life so that you and your descendants may live."[8]

Its opening paragraphs included the following:

We make this appeal as servants of Christ gathered from the churches of the U.S.A. and U.S.S.R. We have been drawn together across the differences of language and culture by our common Christian calling to foster life in the midst of a race towards death. . . .

Gathered in Geneva during the season of Lent, we have been especially conscious of the sufferings of our Lord, who offered Himself that we might

6. V. Bruce Rigdon, "Taming the Principalities and Powers" (unpublished manuscript), 8.

7. Metropolitan Yuvenaly, "Responsibility of Churches of the USSR and the USA for Disarmament" (unpublished manuscript), 7, 12.

8. The statement was widely distributed by the NCC in the form of a trifold brochure. All statement quotations are from that document.

have life and have it abundantly. From our faith in Christ, the All Powerful, the Conqueror of Death, we have drawn strength to choose life in spite of the spreading power of death.

The anxiety of the time is powerfully expressed in the closing plea to turn the tide of history:

Finally, our sisters and brothers, we call to your attention the authoritative predictions that nuclear war by the 1990s is an increasing probability. In that decade of high risks we will be approaching the end of our millennium. Even now, only 20 years separate us from the moment when we will be called upon to mark prayerfully the bimillenary anniversary of the coming to the world of our Lord and Saviour, Jesus Christ, the Prince of peace. How shall we meet that day!? In what state shall we present our planet to the Creator: shall it be a blooming garden or a lifeless, burnt-out, devastated land!?

The statement was endorsed by the NCC Governing Board and the Holy Synod of the ROC. It was released by the Ecumenical Press Service, the NCC Press Service, the Lutheran World Federation Press Service, and the United Methodist Press Service. The event was covered widely in leading newspapers, including several in Europe. Looking back eleven years later, US technical adviser Alan Geyer wrote, "While the statement concluded with a 'call to action' on SALT II and other disarmament issues, it was the theological and ecclesial portions that made *Choose Life* the charter of bilateral ecumenism for years to come."[9]

The next step was a second consultation with similar delegations held in Geneva, August 22–25, 1980, referred to as Choose Life II. In the interim between the two meetings, conservatives in the US Senate successfully blocked ratification of the SALT II treaty. The acute crisis of US hostages in Iran, NATO approval of Pershing II rockets and ground-launched cruise missiles in Europe, and the Soviet invasion of Afghanistan in December 1979 all took place between the two consultations, adding new levels of tension to the political context around the meeting. In spite of all this, the atmosphere within the meeting itself was somewhat more relaxed and confident of achieving useful work. This time in his opening remarks, Metropolitan Yuvenaly focused on

9. Alan Geyer, *Christianity and the Superpowers: Religion, Politics, and History in US-USSR Relations* (Nashville: Abingdon, 1990), 199.

the five years of success of the OSCE (a review conference in Madrid was pending), but did also acknowledge the new difficulties:

> Dear American sisters and brothers! There is a halt in the process of political and military détente; loss of confidence between our countries, further escalation of the nuclear threat, and therefore the strengthening of cooperation between the Christians of the Soviet Union and the United States of America acquires a special importance in the cause of preservation [of] peace on earth.
>
> It gives me pleasure to note that this cooperation has not been broken, but rather, it has gained a more positive character.[10]

The focused Bible study, "The Glory and Honor of the Nations," was given by Arie Brouwer of the Reformed Church in America, and was based on Isaiah 2:1–4 and portions of Revelation 21. A substantive paper, "Role of the Churches for the Cause of Cooperation, Disarmament and Peace," was given by Alexei Bichkov of the Union of Evangelical Baptists. This time the title of the joint communiqué, "Christ Is Our Peace," came from a study of Ephesians in a paper given by William P. Thompson, stated clerk of the United Presbyterian Church in the USA. The communiqué acknowledged the recent deterioration in the political situation and lifted up the special responsibility of the two nations for the whole of humanity. Specifically, it reached three conclusions: reaffirmation of the need to ratify SALT II; recognition of "the special regional responsibilities of Europe and North America for disarmament, economic and technological development, and human rights in the OSCE review"; and commitment to developing "continuing forums of cooperation, including educational and exchange programs."

Equally important to the communiqué itself was the memorandum of program suggestions attached to it. Three immediate steps were endorsed: distribution in the United States of films describing the life of churches in the Soviet Union, seminars for theological professors and students on Orthodox life and other topics, and exhibits in the USA of icons and other religious art and music from the USSR. The real creativity in programmatic thinking came in the list of ten program suggestions referred back to the churches for further study. These identified a variety of venues for developing exchange programs and laid the foundation for their rapid growth throughout the 1980s.

---

10. Metropolitan Yuvenaly, "Introductory Address at the Meeting of the Representatives of Churches from the USA and the USSR in Geneva" (unpublished manuscript), 5.

A Grassroots Movement

Building on the shared experience and commitments made among the US and USSR church leaders at the two Choose Life conferences, a third meeting took place in Geneva in July 1982. A joint statement resulting from that meeting noted: "The international climate at the time of our meeting was a matter of deep concern to the participants. . . . In such a time, there is much which tends to divide governments and peoples of our two countries. But we have renewed our pledge to remain together in this time when the fellowship of churches in the ecumenical movement takes on special importance."[11]

The international context the statement referenced was an escalating period of friction between the United States and the USSR that replaced the period of détente in the 1970s with what some European leaders were calling "the outbreak of Cold War II." In retrospect, Mikhail Gorbachev said, "Never, perhaps, in the postwar decades was the situation in the world as explosive and hence, more difficult and unfavorable, as in the first half of the 1980s." The NCC document stated: "Within this context of escalating tensions, church leaders at the July 1982 meeting were moved to a deeper level (of relationships) as the realities and aspirations of the life of peoples and churches were probed in formal and informal discussions. Further plans were made for our cooperative work and the broadening of our exchanges and visits to include more people from local churches and seminary students."[12]

The first of the programs that characterized the broadened exchange took place in May 1983. A group of forty American Christians, officially invited by the Russian Orthodox Church and sponsored by the NCC, visited the Soviet Union to share concerns with Christians there. Though sponsored by the NCC, the program was organized by the Presbyterian Peacemaking Program. Leadership for the program included Bruce Rigdon and John Lindner.

While preparation for the program began in 1982, by the time the group arrived in Moscow in May 1983, tensions had escalated. Two months prior to departure, President Reagan, while addressing the National Association of Evangelicals, promulgated his thesis that the Soviet Union functioned as an "evil empire," as he argued against a nuclear freeze. Reagan followed the "evil empire" speech with a proposal to create a space-based antimissile system,

11. This quote is from an NCC document titled "A Brief History of Relationships between the National Council of Churches of Christ in the USA and the Churches of the Soviet Union 1956–1988." It is undated and without authorship.

12. "A Brief History of Relationships between the National Council of Churches of Christ in the USA and the Churches of the Soviet Union 1956–1988."

the Strategic Defense Initiative (SDI). From the Soviet perspective, this would have distorted the nuclear balance to the US's advantage, and therefore the announcement was seen as further aggression.

It was in this context of rising fear of mutual destruction that the May 1983 delegation of American Christians arrived to celebrate Easter with Christians in the USSR. Members of this group arrived with a desire to witness to peace and reconciliation and to ask hard questions. As it happened, Easter occurred somewhat later than usual in 1983, and was followed on May 9 by "Victory Day," a national holiday of remembrance of Germany's surrender in 1945. The experience of huge crowds assembled to remember as well as personal conversations with Soviet people on this day left a deep impression on participants as they experienced the fear of war deeply felt by the people they met. Clearly, the emotional scars from that war lived on nearly four decades later.

The travel seminar program involved a wide range of experiences, including substantive meetings that raised hard questions, as well as times of profound worship and prayer. Perhaps nothing left a stronger impression on American participants than learning of the deep sense of loss and fear of war felt by the very people whom they themselves had grown to fear.

The May 1983 experience was a catalyst for further visits and exchanges. The 1983 group had participated in extensive study and preparation before departure and returned to their home churches and communities where they received numerous opportunities to speak and to share their experiences. Given the impact of escalating tensions, many Americans were eager to hear about the participants' experiences. A filmstrip (the visual media of that time) titled *Discovering Our Oneness* was produced and shared in congregations across the United States.

A Program of Church Relations Initiated

With extensive preparation during the summer of 1983, which included consultation among church leaders at the WCCs Sixth Assembly in Vancouver, an official NCC program of US-USSR church relations was approved and set in motion in the autumn of that year. In a memorandum of understanding (November 8, 1983), General Secretary Claire Randall wrote: "The office has been established for an experimental year, in order to begin the process of program development. It is stressed that it is precisely church relations that will be the focus of this office's work. The program will involve long-term study of implications for these relationships with corresponding resource development, as well as the implementation of four projects of exchange and visitation with the churches of the Soviet Union."[13] From the outset, this was a very ambitious project that was to include a visit to the United States by twenty Soviet church leaders in May 1984, a travel seminar to the USSR by two to three hundred American church representatives in June, an official visit of the heads of American churches to consult with their counterparts in the Soviet Union in October, and a delegation to US theological schools by Russian Orthodox seminarians in the fall. In a time prior to the common use of computers, email, and easy international communications, the logistical challenges of organizing these programs were truly enormous.

An ad hoc committee was named to administer the program and oversee the work. It was chaired by Bruce Rigdon, while John Lindner served as program coordinator, and David Weaver was an assistant. In addition, twenty-two volunteers from across the country were trained to accompany church leaders from the USSR on their visits to the United States and also to be group leaders for the June USSR travel seminar that ultimately included 266 US participants.

At the same time, several publications were produced and resources developed, including *Together on the Way: The Story of the Dialogue between the Churches of the United States and the Soviet Union*; *On the Way to Unity and Peace: A Report of the 1984 Program of US-USSR Church Relations*; and *USSR Travel Seminar Briefing Manual*.

Because of the profound sense of urgency surrounding these efforts, there was an outpouring of support for these initiatives. The two programs with the greatest public participation were the May and June events.

Communities across the United States applied for and were eager to receive Soviet religious leaders in May 1984. The nineteen religious leaders from various parts of the Soviet Union included representatives of the ROC, the Georgian Orthodox Church, the All Union Council of Evangelical Christian Baptists, the Evangelical Lutheran Church of Estonia, the Evangelical Church of Latvia, the Armenian Apostolic Church, and the Moscow Choral Synagogue. The entire delegation visited New York City, Washington, DC, and Louisville, Kentucky. In addition, divided into five small groups, they visited a total of fifteen different cities. In each community an ecumenical group arranged their visit and received them. Included were time with public officials, schools, churches, colleges, and civic groups such as Rotary Clubs, and visits

---

13. From an internal NCC "memorandum of understanding" dated November 8, 1983, from General Secretary Claire Randall to Bruce Rigdon, chair of the ad hoc US-USSR Church Relations Committee.

to private homes. Effort was made in each community to expose them to as many people as possible and to allow time for dialogue as well as informal interactions. An American volunteer host and a Russian translator traveled with each group.

Out of the visits came hundreds of stories and anecdotes, including poignant stories of personal encounters with Americans eager to meet a Soviet citizen for the first time. The Soviet visitors, for their part, reported being deeply moved by these encounters. They met with a wide range of Americans, from average working people, including a cowboy in Texas, to leading American personalities such as Coretta Scott King and Andrew Young, at that time mayor of Atlanta. Several of them reflected with appreciation on their first experience of seeing women lead in worship. While tensions between the two nations escalated almost weekly among political leaders, Soviet and American citizens in city after city were becoming friends.

Similar experiences occurred the following month in the Soviet Union, though on a much larger scale, when 266 Americans—the largest group of American Christians ever to visit the Soviet Union—arrived in Moscow. The Soviet hosts nicknamed this visit the "peace invasion."

In advance of their departure for the USSR, the Americans received a three-day briefing from leading experts from major universities, the State Department, a Soviet representative to the UN, and several human rights groups. The group had plenary sessions in both Moscow and Leningrad (now Saint Petersburg) and traveled in ten subgroups to two cities each, some to far distant areas of the USSR. Similar to the visit in the United States, they met with a wide range of Soviet officials, academics, church leaders, and ordinary citizens in both organized and informal settings. Russians too were curious about and eager to meet Americans. Substantial dialogue took place on a wide range of topics.

Among the American participants was a contingent of press, including the highly regarded AP religion writer George Cornell. Cornell arranged to crisscross the travel groups and sent back a series of syndicated articles reporting on religion in the Soviet Union and the groups' experiences. These stories appeared in many newspapers across America. Also accompanying the group was a television reporter from Michigan, Jim Reikse, who produced an hour-long documentary entitled *On the Other Side* that was broadcast by many TV stations across the United States.

Toward the end of the visit, while worshiping at a Baptist church in Moscow, the entire group witnessed a brief demonstration by dissidents unfurling a banner about religious dissenters suffering persecution in the USSR. A similar incident had taken place earlier with Billy Graham in the same Baptist church and, as happened to Graham, the US press asked members of the group about religious persecution and our visit with the churches. By the time the delegation returned home, large segments of the US press were in full attack mode condemning the visit. The *Wall Street Journal* published an editorial about the "deferential reverends."

Other media were more eager to hear about the experience of participants; for example, a select group appeared on the then-popular Phil Donahue TV show. Local newspapers typically wrote long human-interest features about the participants from their areas that were part of the visit. The visit thus attracted more attention and was of greater general interest than might otherwise have been expected. Though the office in New York received some hate mail, the overwhelming response was appreciation for the efforts to build bridges for peace. Clearly these efforts contributed substantially to a national conversation about the Cold War.

As the experimental program year concluded, the executive committee of the NCC, on the basis of careful evaluation and recommendations, adopted a four-year plan to further develop this ambitious program of encounter and dialogue. Steps were laid down to sustain these programs, and in each of the years that followed major programs of travel and exchange took place. Communities and individuals that participated in 1983 and 1984 continued their involvement through the NCC program, and many extensive local and regional programs were also created. Some organizations, such as the John Conner Center at Purdue University, initiated programs that were cosponsored with the NCC. In 1985, 1986, and 1987, for example, the Conner Center sponsored a summer school for academic credit on the subject of religion in the Soviet Union.

From 1985 through 1987, exchanges and visits continued and included two more large seminars to the USSR, which totaled 222 participants. During this period, an official visit to the United States from Soviet churches took place in April 1986, along with a visit by Russian Orthodox seminary students in November 1986 to visit six locations in which there were clusters of theological schools of various denominations.

While all these activities were taking place, many signs of change were occurring in US-Soviet relations, as well as in the Soviet Union itself. In November 1985, the first Reagan-Gorbachev summit took place in Geneva, Switzerland. As a result of the large number of exchanges and programs, many churches were eager to encourage these peace talks and to pray for their success. In a dramatic initiative, Arie Brouwer, general secretary of the NCC, invited the churches of the USSR to join American congregations in a day of prayer for the summit talks, and at the same time for leaders of churches from the United States and the USSR to meet together in a prayer vigil in Geneva.

Hundreds of congregations in both countries participated. A major ecumenical service of worship was held in Geneva in the historic Cathedral of Saint Peter. The cathedral was filled to capacity with worshipers from many countries around the world. This prayer vigil continued throughout the summit. Press people who attended a postsummit press conference with Gorbachev reported that he made a point of thanking the religious leaders for "creating a climate for change."

Other, similar witness events and activities took place over the next several years as Reagan and Gorbachev held three more summits. A major prayer vigil took place at the Washington National Cathedral at the time of the December 1987 Washington summit. Like the vigil in Geneva, parishes and congregations from across the United States and USSR held simultaneous prayers for peace in their local communities.

In 1987 and 1988, much of the focus shifted to a major effort to share in the one thousandth anniversary of the baptism of Prince Vladimir of Kiev, the event that marked the arrival of Christianity in Russian-speaking lands of the Soviet Union. The celebration of this significant event became an occasion for the publication of an ecumenical study series by Martin Bailey entitled *The People and the Churches of the USSR*, published by Friendship Press. Also, leadership training was organized for fifty-four previous seminar participants to enable them to serve as small-group leaders for travel seminar programs for the millennial celebrations of the Russian Orthodox Church. In 1988, an unprecedented number of American church leaders participated in these seminar programs. Five pilgrimages of 150 persons each took place throughout the year. Each was planned around a time of special significance in the liturgical calendar, including Easter and Pentecost.

While plans for all these events were initiated in 1984, no one could have anticipated the enormous changes that would take place in the USSR by 1988. Beginning in the early 1980s, a few closed churches were allowed to reopen, and the centuries-old Danilovsky Monastery was returned to the Russian Orthodox Church. With the coming of the Gorbachev era, restrictions on the churches were gradually eased. Both the Danilovsky and Holy Trinity Lavra (often referred to then as Zagorsk) monasteries were fully restored and renovated in advance of the thousand-year anniversary. However, the most dramatic and systemic changes began to occur in 1988; not only were more church properties returned, but in addition, the church was permitted to engage in a variety of social ministries that had previously been prohibited. These included the return of some schools and hospitals and the permission to establish a limited number of chaplaincies.

Thus the date of the millennial celebration proved to be not only a time for the churches to celebrate and reflect on a remarkable millennial heritage but also the beginning of new challenges and possibilities so radical as to suggest the opening of a new era in the history of the churches in the USSR. These changes sometimes occurred so suddenly and unexpectedly as to require major adjustments in church exchange plans that had been set in place months earlier. For example, when the delegation visiting for the Easter feast arrived in Moscow in 1988, the Holy Synod was in emergency session, having just received news of major property returns. As a result, the US delegation was taken to a local hotel to wait until the session was concluded. Emotions ran high with both hope and fear in such moments. The hope was that the changes would be real and lasting, but the fear was that, like the "Prague Spring," the new possibilities might just as quickly be crushed.

In 1989, the Coordination Committee of the Churches of the Soviet Union and the NCC was established to facilitate the possible contributions US churches might make to the enormous new tasks faced by churches in the USSR, tasks such as publishing Christian education materials, providing training for undertaking social service ministries, and rebuilding churches and church-related properties. Discussions now began to focus on ways in which American churches might offer support and assistance with such new challenges.

Efforts with the "churches of the USSR," however, would soon come to an end as the USSR itself was shortly destined to be dissolved. A new era was indeed to follow with a considerable variety of relations with churches in the nations that were reborn with the end of the USSR. This included relations between the churches in the USA and the Russian Orthodox Church.

Through all these various efforts, many Christians in the USSR and in the United States became acquainted with one another and came to perceive each other as fellow believers and not as enemies. This involved not only the over-coming of stereotypes created by national enmities but also a serious search for reconciliation among Christians who had been separated from one another by much older ecclesial divisions in the history of Christianity East and West. Many American Christians had found the encounter with Eastern Orthodox Christians to be one of the most important and life-changing aspects of their experience of dialogue and exchange.

The encounters in this final decade in particular included large numbers of clergy and laity from regional and local churches and ecumenical groups.

In this process people and communities gained new insights and understandings from one another. Most participants in the travel seminars came away describing the encounters as "life changing," often because they worshiped in traditions other than their own and encountered people that the world viewed as enemies but with whom they had become friends. These engagements created "a climate of change." Despite the conflicting government ideologies and the restrictions on the churches of the USSR, the prayers and yearning for peace by religious communities did in fact prove to be influential for many people in both nations.

What Was Achieved and What Was Learned

On February 23–24, 1989, representatives of the NCC and its member churches and of the churches in the USSR met in Moscow to evaluate the work that had been done together and to outline a very ambitious program of continuing cooperative efforts for the 1990s. In the impressive joint document that this meeting approved, the participants made a very positive evaluation of the work that had been undertaken, celebrated the particular accomplishments that years of hard work had produced, and laid out in some detail an ambitious program of thirteen proposals to be undertaken during the following five years. "The participants noted with satisfaction the traditional friendly relations which long existed between them. Almost 33 years have elapsed since the first official meeting of church delegations from the United States and the Soviet Union when conversations took place on contemporary theological issues and ethical problems, as well as on particular aspects of the churches' activities in their work for the establishment of peace in the world."[14] The joint document noted with deep appreciation the considerable progress that had been made in many areas of mutual cooperation. "We have deepened our mutual knowledge of the ways of Christian witness borne by our churches in different cultural and social contexts. We have successfully explored religious and ethical problems as well as those of mission and evangelism, Christian unity and active involvement of the churches in the cause of preserving peace." The document lifted up with gratitude the tenth anniversary of the first Choose Life conference, the gathering of church representa-

---

14. From an NCC document "For Presentation to the NCC Governing Board May 16–19, 1989" titled "Report of the NCC Delegation to the USSR: Dialogue with Soviet Churches and Visit to Armenia, February 21–27, 1989." The quotations that follow come from this document.

tives to surround each summit meeting with prayer, the programs stemming from the travel seminars, and the decennial visits dating from 1956 "which helped to reduce the alienation of the Cold War." "The Christians of our countries were actually the first people to melt the ice of mistrust between our two nations. This is our Christian contribution to the general problems with which the contemporary world is concerned and to the elimination of mistrust and alienation between our peoples." In light of a change of leadership in Washington and the impact of glasnost and perestroika in the USSR, the document pointed to a future filled with new dangers, new challenges, and new opportunities. It concluded with a very ambitious list of new programs to be undertaken by the churches and developed by a continuation committee made up of a coordinator from each nation and a minimum of two additional persons from each side. "On the basis of cooperation and as an expression of Christian unity, we see the need to continue building relationships between the churches of our two countries. We affirm our renewed commitment to building greater awareness among church people to overcome the lack of knowledge and misinformation about each other's reality, the ever-present danger of nuclear disaster, and the fragility of political relationships." The document concluded: "After a two day discussion on these opportunities, we have come to the conclusion that a new programme of our cooperation for the coming years would make us ever more united, on the one hand, and our work together more effective and fruitful, on the other. . . . We trust in God's grace which invisibly helps us, opens new opportunities for us and inspires us for tireless efforts in the name of God to choose life together."

What no one in the 1989 meeting in Moscow could have known was that the subsequent breakup of the USSR would lead to drastic changes in the churches of the former Soviet Union and in their relations with their US partners. The coordination committee held two meetings after 1989, but by 1991 found it impossible to carry out its mandate and, sadly, never met again.

After the fall of the USSR, some American churches viewed its former territories as promising new mission fields and began to send missionaries in considerable numbers. Most often this was done without consultation with the Russian Orthodox Church. Such acts led to resentment and anger on the part of the leaders of the Orthodox community. On the other hand, the churches in Russia were of necessity so preoccupied with restoring their life and work in the new situation that their priorities in relation to their US partners and the ecumenical movement as a whole underwent significant changes. Under these circumstances, it proved impossible to develop the new programs that had been outlined by the 1989 joint consultation.

The ethos that had generated so much energy and hard work around the themes related to Choose Life in the churches of both the USA and the USSR had undergone a profound change. The sense of urgency that had characterized their cooperation for several decades was no longer in evidence. Even the official decennial meetings of the leaders of the churches in the two countries was discontinued. That is all the more reason for asking what we may learn from this period of Christian witness in the years of the Cold War.

It should be said that as trust developed among the participants in this unfolding dialogue, American Christians became increasingly aware of the enormous threats and difficulties under which their brothers and sisters lived in the USSR. Where possible, Americans advocated in behalf of Christians who were in prison or for those who suffered for having taken strong stands for human rights. This often required discretion and discernment in seeking the most effective ways to be of significant help to individuals and the churches in the USSR. Suffice it to say that the NCC and its constituents also played a significant role in the wider official negotiations in Europe to achieve agreements about the status of human rights within each of the nations of Europe and internationally.

Conclusion

It is clear that for much of the American public the Soviet Union and Eastern Europe represented an evil empire that required that the United States arm itself in every way against its enemy. This dark and arbitrary view of the USSR also suggested that most Soviet citizens were not to be trusted since, for the most part, as it was often observed, people get the government they deserve. Such fears, stereotypes, and judgments made it all but impossible to see political realities very clearly or to make wise and constructive judgments and decisions. The result was that the gap between East and West grew ever more threatening, not only for Americans and Soviets but also for all of humankind.

What is most instructive and significant in this story is the fact that the National Council rejected the alternative of constructing protective walls and sought instead to build bridges. It did not begin with the assumption that Soviets were enemies, but with the conviction that all human beings are created in the image of God, that each is deeply loved by God, and that all have infinite value as a result of this extraordinary gift. With this came the conviction that the way to deal with threats and dangers to human life is not merely to protect oneself or one's nation but to talk with one's enemies, to open and sustain a dialogue, however difficult that might prove to be. What many discovered in doing this is that dialogue is a means not only to learn about others but also to come to know oneself in profoundly new ways, to see oneself in relationship to others. It may well follow that one learns most and best about oneself from those who are most different, those who are in every sense "strangers" or even enemies.

The National Council also sought to have relations with the Christian churches and communities in the USSR because they were brothers and sisters in Christ. The council sought to strengthen these connections, the more so because these were churches experiencing profound trials and suffering. To talk together, to pray together, to witness together was itself an expression of the church's mission in the world. And somehow, despite a history of tragic separations and divisions among the world's churches, the conviction continued that the church is one because that unity is God's own gift and cannot be destroyed. Indeed, it witnesses to the reality of the unity of all humankind, a unity that transcends differences of race and nation, of ideology, class, and gender. And as it reached out, the NCC created fragile but real connections and channels of communication between alienated peoples. (For example, in 1983, after the crash of Korean Airlines Flight 007, it is believed that for several days the only institutions in the United States and the USSR communicating with one another were the National Council of Churches and the Patriarchate of the Russian Orthodox Church.)

Thus it was that many American Protestants who traveled to the USSR in response to deep political concerns returned to report that one of the most unexpected results of the journey was the impact that their encounter with the life, liturgy, and people of the Russian Orthodox Church had had upon them. As a result, they saw their life as American Protestants quite differently and looked at the Christian community in the USSR through different eyes and with different hopes for the future.

Yet another lesson for many participants in the dialogue was that it would never again be possible for Americans to define Christian faithfulness in the same simple and narrow terms as before or to assume that they knew precisely what it would look like. What does it mean or require to be faithful? Life in a closed society was so full of dangers, contradictions, risks, and ambiguities that Americans had little in their own experience to help them understand it fully. Christians in the USSR sometimes had to make decisions that led to martyrdom, but they also had at times to live with compromises to protect the lives of others and to permit the church to continue to minister to a vast and needy population.

The fact that some church leaders whom Americans met in the dialogue, for example, reported regularly to the political authorities what had been said during the discussions did not necessarily mean that such people were enemies of the church. Indeed, it was often by learning to listen carefully to what such persons said that one could learn what was really happening to the churches and what as an outsider one might do to express genuine solidarity or to attempt to help. This was particularly true of the conversations among the heads of the churches from the two nations. Without romanticizing this subject, it can certainly be said that during these difficult years in the USSR some Christians quietly and powerfully exhibited in many surprising ways great loyalty to the Christian gospel. Those who were fortunate enough to visit and to talk with such Christians caught occasional glimpses of these acts and signs of genuine Christian faithfulness.

By looking more closely at our experience as Christians in the Cold War, can we learn something of value for the dialogue in which we must now engage with Islam in its many forms and contexts? And in the free market capitalist economies and societies in which we Christians now live, is there something from our recent history that can help us to provoke a serious dialogue about the urgent necessity for economic justice as an essential part of a healthy society? At a time when socialism is a dirty word in most political discourse, how do we make sure that the issues of the needy, the poor, the disabled, the sick, and the elderly challenge the intolerable assumptions about the distribution of wealth that currently prevail in most places where we live?

Ahead of us lies the challenging task of learning much more about the churches and the Cold War. We must take that task very seriously indeed. There is much yet to be discovered and understood. At the same time, let us respond to this challenge not only by looking back but also by allowing that past experience to enlighten and instruct us for the new responsibilities with which the future is already confronting us.

Niebuhrian Realism, Cold War Realities, and the Ethics of Empire

GARY DORRIEN

The Cold War traumatized US theological ethicists for over forty years. Two world wars shredded the empires that demanded world wars, yielding the possibility of a world rid of empires. But that was not to be. The United States, already a superpower, but long habituated to a benevolent self-image, emerged from World War II with a vast military empire and confronted a superpower rival armed with a Communist ideology. US theologians struggled with the novelty of this situation and the tensions built into it. Their own fear of the Soviet Union usually loomed large in the equation, as did their beliefs about the ways that the United States was, or was not, a typical empire.

One theologian towered above all others on this subject: Reinhold Niebuhr. He was the most influential US theologian of the twentieth century. On many subjects, including the Cold War, he compelled all theologians to deal with him. Every theological player in the debate over the Cold War revolved around Niebuhr and defined his or her position with reference to him. And we still do.

With Niebuhr there are always ironies; in this area, three stand out. The most influential US theologian of the twentieth century was deeply political and held little interest in formal theology. He acquired his early fame by ridiculing the Social Gospel that founded the field in which he taught and which he mostly took for granted. And this profound theologian of divine grace and transcendence became best known for his position about a very transient phenomenon, the Cold War.

Niebuhr was born in 1892, educated at Elmhurst College, and trained in a mild Social Gospel liberalism at Yale Divinity School. He took an aggressively prowar position during World War I and repented of doing so after the war, while serving as an Evangelical and Reformed Church pastor in Detroit. During the war Niebuhr anxiously enlisted German Americans in the war effort. After the war, having proved his Americanism, he vowed to preach no more sermons about saving the world for democracy or Christian civilization. In the 1920s Niebuhr wrote Social Gospel articles for the *Christian Century* magazine and rose to the presidency of the pacifist Fellowship of Reconciliation. His pacifism was always a strained affair, since Niebuhr worried that a just order could not be achieved without resorting to coercive violence. His early book *Does Civilization Need Religion?* rued that religious idealism was sentimental and very limited politically, yet he called for more of it.[1]

In 1928 he joined the faculty of Union Theological Seminary, teaching in a field—social ethics—that had no history apart from the Social Gospel. Niebuhr took for granted that Christianity has a social-ethical mission to transform the structures of society in the direction of social justice. If people suffer because of economics and politics, the church has to deal with economics and politics. He never disavowed these defining convictions of the Social Gospel, nor did he relinquish his liberal positions about theological method, authority, biblical criticism, myth, and Christology. What Niebuhr rejected, in the early 1930s, was the optimistic idealism and rationalism that permeated much of the Social Gospel movement. In 1932 he repudiated Social Gospel idealism with blistering polemical force.

Niebuhr's landmark book, *Moral Man and Immoral Society*, declared that politics is about struggling for power; it is not a vehicle for creating a good society. Human groups never willingly subordinate their interests to the interests of others. Morality belongs to the sphere of individual action. On occasion, individuals rise above self-interest, motivated by compassion or love, but groups never overcome the power of self-interest and collective egotism that sustains their existence. For this reason, Social Gospel attempts to moralize society through reason and Christian love were stupid and futile.[2]

1. Reinhold Niebuhr, "The Failure of German-Americanism," *Atlantic*, July 1916, 16–18; Niebuhr, "A Trip through the Ruhr," *Evangelical Herald*, August 9, 1923, in William D. Christal, ed., *Young Reinhold Niebuhr: His Early Writings, 1911–1931* (Saint Louis: Eden Publishing House, 1977), 124–28; Niebuhr, "Germany in Despair," *Evangelical Herald*, September 13, 1923, in Christal, *Young Reinhold Niebuhr*, 128–31; Niebuhr, "Governor Smith's Liberalism," *Christian Century* 45 (September 13, 1928): 1107–8; Niebuhr, "Protestantism and Prohibition," *New Republic*, October 24, 1928, 266–67; Niebuhr, *Does Civilization Need Religion? A Study in the Social Resources and Limitations of Religion in Modern Life* (New York: Macmillan, 1927); Richard Wightman Fox, *Reinhold Niebuhr: A Biography* (Ithaca, NY: Cornell University Press, 1996), 3–12; Charles C. Brown, *Niebuhr and His Age: Reinhold Niebuhr's Prophetic Role in the Twentieth Century* (Philadelphia: Trinity, 1992), 25.

2. Reinhold Niebuhr, *Moral Man and Immoral Society: A Study in Ethics and Politics* (New York: Scribner's Sons, 1932); Niebuhr, "Why We Need a New Economic Order," *World Tomorrow* 11 (October 1928): 397–98; Niebuhr, "Catastrophe or Social Control?," *Harper's* 165

Moral Man and Immoral Society had an air of icy omniscience, buttressed by Niebuhr's debt to Marxism, and a deep anger at the ravages of the Depression. Niebuhr predicted: "The full maturity of American capitalism will inevitably be followed by the emergence of the American Marxian proletarian." The problem with capitalism was systemic, Niebuhr argued. Mass production needed mass consumption, but capitalism was too predatory and class-stratified to sustain mass consumption. Thus it was disintegrating on the contradictions of a system that required, but could not accommodate, continually expanding markets. Liberalism and capitalism were finished. Niebuhr urged that no amount of reformist tinkering would stop the world historical drift toward fascism. The only alternative to it was radical state socialism.[3]

Liberals were soft utopians, Niebuhr said. They persisted in believing that society's problems could be solved with sufficient rationality and good will, so they refused to recognize that all social relationships and forms of political rule are permeated with violence. Marxism was wiser because it was a form of hard utopianism that spurned liberal illusions about avoiding violence. Niebuhr acknowledged that Marxist utopianism was naive in believing that Communism would bring about the end of history. In current Marxist mythology, the Soviet state was the incarnation of the absolute. This element of Marxist faith, Niebuhr said, though illusory, had a helpful role to play. Soviet utopianism was "a very valuable illusion for the moment; for justice cannot be approximated if the hope of its perfect realization does not generate a sublime madness in the soul." Communist madness, to be sure, engendered terrible fanaticism; thus it needed to be brought under the control of reason. But Niebuhr hoped "that reason will not destroy it before its work is done."[4]

Niebuhr was active in the Socialist Party and its network of New York leftist allies, which fought ferocious battles in the early 1930s over the crimes of Stalinism and the rights of American Communists. Many New York Socialists were militantly anti-Communist; Niebuhr worried that his colleague at Union Seminary, Harry Ward, lapsed into true-believing pro-Communism; and Niebuhr held a middling position between the battling factions. Until 1935 he stuck with his argument about valuable Communist illusions. Then he gave up believing that the Soviet regime would liberalize, declaring, "Here lies the

---

(June 1932): 118. This chapter contains condensed versions of arguments in Gary Dorrien, *Social Ethics in the Making: Interpreting an American Tradition* (Oxford: Wiley-Blackwell, 2011), 236–76; and Dorrien, *Economy, Difference, Empire: Social Ethics for Social Justice* (New York: Columbia University Press, 2009), 29–65.

    3. Niebuhr, *Moral Man and Immoral Society*, 144 (quote).

    4. Niebuhr, *Moral Man and Immoral Society*, 277 (quotes).

root of Marxian utopianism and all the nonsense connected with it. The state will wither away!" In the Soviet Union, Niebuhr wrote, Marxist utopianism was enforced by a repressive state: "I once thought such a faith to be a harmless illusion. But now I see that its net result is to endow a group of oligarchs with the religious sanctity which primitive priest-kings once held."[5]

Niebuhr did not lurch in the late 1930s toward militant anti-Communism, although he had numerous friends in that camp, notably Socialist Party leader Norman Thomas. For most of the 1930s Niebuhr continued to laud the Soviet Union's gains toward equality and disputed typical American condemnations of "Communist violence." To Niebuhr, Communism was dangerous because it misconstrued the social problem, not because it was extraordinarily violent. Communists wrongly dismissed political democracy as an instrument of class rule. Niebuhr acknowledged that democracy grew out of the bourgeois revolutions and that democracy in the United States and Europe was obviously overmatched by economic oligarchies. Nonetheless, he argued, democracy was not merely a ruse to control the masses, for democratic political power was an indispensable check on economic power. Whenever the rule of the capitalist class was imperiled by democratic demands, capitalists sought to abrogate democracy. Nazi Germany was the showcase example—a perverse regime of absolute cynicism toward democratic institutions.[6]

Liberal idealism was no match for the cynical evils of fascism or the ravages of capitalism. This was Niebuhr's untiring refrain in the late 1930s and early 1940s, to which he increasingly added that it was no match for the enormous savageries of Stalinism, either. Terrible things were happening in the world, yet liberals like philosopher John Dewey and Social Gospel theologian Shailer Mathews claimed that reason and good will could solve the world's problems. Niebuhr poured out a torrent of refutation, charging that liberalism was blind to human irrationality and tragedy, and the New Deal was a pathetic waste of time. Repeatedly Niebuhr blasted Dewey for purveying liberal nonsense, even though he and Dewey had nearly the same politics. Both believed that only democratic socialism could achieve social justice, which Niebuhr defined as "a tolerable equilibrium of economic power." Both used the rhetoric of progress in claiming that socialism was the next logical step for history to

5. Reinhold Niebuhr, "Religion and Marxism," *Modern Monthly* 8 (February 1935): 714; see Harry F. Ward, *The New Social Order: Principles and Programs* (New York: Macmillan, 1920); Ward, *Our Economic Morality and the Morality of Jesus* (New York: Macmillan, 1929).

6. Reinhold Niebuhr, *An Interpretation of Christian Ethics* (New York: Scribner's Sons, 1935), 117; see Niebuhr, "After Capitalism—What?," *World Tomorrow*, March 1, 1933, 204; Niebuhr, *Reflections on the End of an Era* (New York: Scribner's Sons, 1934), 17–18.

take. Both said that modern civilization had to choose between retrogression and progress.[7]

By this reckoning, fascism was not a genuine historical alternative; Niebuhr called it "a frantic effort to escape the logic of history by returning to the primitive." Fascism had no staying power, no matter how many victories it won. The real choice was between retrogression to capitalist anarchy and achieving government ownership and control of the economy. Capitalism, even as it destroyed itself, had to be destroyed before it shredded the liberal and democratic gains of the past century. Niebuhr kept saying it after capitalism did not disintegrate in the mid-1930s. He did not apply his penetrating analysis of ruling-group egotism to his own solution. Niebuhr ignored that his state-centered model of socialism would place immense power in the hands of a self-interested, technocratic planning elite and rely upon its limited capacity to get prices right. Instead he invoked a dogma about history moving forward or backward.[8]

Niebuhr's attacks on liberalism got terrible reviews from prominent liberals, who protested that Niebuhr had suddenly turned cynical, wild, mean-spirited, and not very Christian. Meanwhile, younger theological readers embraced *Moral Man and Immoral Society* for expressing their anger and disappointment. The age of religious idealism and liberal theology had passed, leaving behind the Social Gospel dream of moral community. Old-style liberals protested that Niebuhr had no alternative and his books gushed with paradoxes and exaggerations; young theologians John C. Bennett and Walter Marshall Horton countered that Niebuhr defined reality for a new generation. The liberal language of process, ideals, cooperation, and personality had lost its credibility, while Niebuhr took American theology vaguely to the left politically and vaguely to the right theologically. Then the Nazi march to war made Niebuhr's dark vision seem prophetic.[9]

Niebuhr is best known for calling the isolationist USA to war against Fascism and for subsequently championing Cold War ideology. But memory

7. Reinhold Niebuhr, "The Blindness of Liberalism," *Radical Religion* 1 (Autumn 1936): 4; Niebuhr, "The Idea of Progress and Socialism," *Radical Religion* 1 (Spring 1936): 28 ("a tolerable equilibrium"); Niebuhr, "Ten Years That Shook My World," *Christian Century* 56 (April 26, 1939): 546.

8. Niebuhr, "The Idea of Progress and Socialism," 28.

9. Norman Thomas, review of *Moral Man and Immoral Society*, by Reinhold Niebuhr, *World Tomorrow* 15 (December 14, 1932): 565, 567; John Haynes Holmes, review of *Moral Man and Immoral Society*, by Reinhold Niebuhr, *Herald Tribune Books*, January 8, 1933, 13; Theodore C. Hume, "Prophet of Disillusion," *Christian Century* 50 (January 4, 1933): 18–19; Reinhold Niebuhr, "Dr. Niebuhr's Position," *Christian Century* 50 (January 18, 1933): 91–92.

is often fitted to our stereotypes, as in these cases. Niebuhr did not spend the 1930s urging the United States to arm for a war against Fascism; in the late 1930s he hammered Franklin Roosevelt for preparing for war. Niebuhr supported League of Nations internationalism, opposed isolationism, supported passage of the Neutrality Acts of 1935 and 1937, and wanted the United States to support League of Nations sanctions against Italy in 1935. As late as March 1939, Niebuhr was passionately opposed to preparing for war. In 1937 he condemned Roosevelt's naval buildup as a "sinister" evil, declaring that it had to be "resisted at all costs." The next year he blasted Roosevelt's billion-dollar defense budget as "the worst piece of militarism in modern history." The best way to avoid war, Niebuhr insisted, was not to prepare for one; collective security was the realistic alternative to war.[10]

The fact that even Reinhold Niebuhr stridently opposed Roosevelt's preparations for war is a measure of the revulsion against war that his generation felt after World War I. *Moral Man and Immoral Society* did not lead straight to his famous call to war; Niebuhr resisted his own lesser-evil rationale for war until Hitler's determination to conquer Europe became undeniable. Then Niebuhr blasted the democracies for surrendering to the "concentrated fury" of Fascist totalitarianism and excoriated the churches for promoting antiwar cowardice.[11]

Christian Century editor Charles Clayton Morrison especially offended Niebuhr. The *Christian Century* supported Roosevelt in 1936 but opposed his reelection in 1940, charging that Roosevelt was an American-style Fascist who played to the working class and militarized a peaceable nation. Morrison held out for neutrality and called for efforts to slow down Roosevelt's march toward war. As late as December 10, 1941, in an issue that went to press just before Japan attacked Pearl Harbor, the *Christian Century* insisted: "Every national interest and every moral obligation to civilization dictates that this country shall keep out of the insanity of a war which is in no sense America's war."[12]

10. Reinhold Niebuhr, "Brief Comments," *Radical Religion* 3 (Winter 1937): 7 ("sinister"); Niebuhr, "Brief Comments," *Radical Religion* 3 (Spring 1938): 7 ("the worst piece of militarism").

11. Reinhold Niebuhr, *Christianity and Power Politics* (New York: Scribner's Sons, 1940), 71 (quote); Niebuhr, "Christian Moralism in America," *Radical Religion* 5 (1940): 16–17; Niebuhr, "An Open Letter," *Christianity and Society* 5 (Summer 1940): 30–33.

12. [Charles C. Morrison], "No Third Term!" *Christian Century* 57 (October 16, 1940): 1273; [Charles C. Morrison], "Defending Democracy," *Christian Century* 57 (June 5, 1940); [Charles C. Morrison], "Why We Differ," *Christian Century* 58 (December 10, 1941): 1534–38, 1538 (quote); see [Charles C. Morrison], "The Neutrality Act Is Discarded," *Christian Century* 58 (November 26, 1941): 1459; Morrison, *The Christian and the War* (Chicago: Willett, Clark and Co., 1942).

Morrison's pacifism was practical, not absolute, which infuriated Niebuhr all the more. Niebuhr called on America to "prevent the triumph of an intolerable tyranny." American Christianity needed to summon the moral will to fight Fascism, "lest we deliver the last ramparts of civilization into the hands of the new barbarians." No worthy peace could be brokered with a Nazi regime stoked by genocidal ambitions and a "pagan religion of tribal self-glorification." Niebuhr excoriated the appeasing moralism of America's liberal establishment: "It imagines that there is no conflict of interest which cannot be adjudicated. It does not understand what it means to meet a resolute foe who is intent upon either your annihilation or enslavement."[13]

The *Christian Century* epitomized what was wrong with American Protestantism, so Niebuhr launched an alternative to it. Liberal Protestantism needed a journal that renounced the prevailing sentiment that anything was better than war. Niebuhr already had one journal, *Christianity and Society*, published by the Fellowship of Socialist Christians, which was called *Radical Religion* until 1940. But few ministers read Socialist magazines, and very few subscribed through their churches. In February 1941, Niebuhr launched *Christianity and Crisis* as an antidote to the *Christian Century*, enlisting liberal Protestant friends who agreed that the *Century*'s isolationism had become an embarrassment. They included Sherwood Eddy, Francis McConnell, William Adams Brown, Will Scarlett, Henry Sloane Coffin, Henry Van Dusen, John R. Mott, and Niebuhr's closest colleague, Union Seminary ethicist John C. Bennett. The format of *Christianity and Crisis* was cloned after the *Christian Century*, but its editorial line spoke the Christian realist language of tragic necessities, group interests, power politics, lesser evils, and internationalism. Niebuhr and Bennett worked hard at realigning liberal Protestantism. Meanwhile, in May 1941, Niebuhr similarly gathered his left-wing political friends into a new organization, the Union for Democratic Action (UDA).

The Union Seminary liberals who founded *Christianity and Crisis*, notably Coffin, Brown, and Van Dusen, were pillars of the Protestant establishment. They supported Niebuhr but could never rub elbows with his lefty friends. Niebuhr enlisted union leaders Murray Gross and A. Phillip Randolph, intellectuals George Counts and James Isaac Loeb, and American Communist founder Lewis Corey (formerly Louis Fraina) to join him in the UDA. Essentially, the UDA consisted of New York leftists who were disgusted by the

13. Reinhold Niebuhr, "To Prevent the Triumph of an Intolerable Tyranny," *Christian Century* 57 (December 18, 1940): 1579–80 (quotes); see Niebuhr, *Christianity and Power Politics*, 44, 68; Niebuhr, "Editorial Notes," *Christianity and Society* 5 (Spring 1940): 10.

Socialist Party's isolationism. It renounced the traditional socialist denigration of religion, excluded Communists from membership, and exhorted Americans to face up to the fight against Fascism.

Niebuhr had started voting for Roosevelt in 1936, despite believing that FDR wasted his opportunity to save America. It seemed pointless to keep voting for Norman Thomas when Roosevelt carried out much of the Socialist platform. Then the Socialist Party came out against intervening in World War II, and Niebuhr canceled his membership, declaring: "Socialism must come in America through some other instrument than the Socialist Party." He had in mind a farmer-labor party, but said that would take up to eight years. In the meantime—1940—realistic radicals had to hold their noses and vote for Democrats. Niebuhr put it bluntly. FDR, though often too cunning, deserved credit for building up the military and gaining political control over the economy, and his reelection was imperative.[14]

In the spring and fall of 1939, Niebuhr delivered the Gifford Lectures at Edinburgh, which were published as *The Nature and Destiny of Man*. He worried that his abstract excursuses on theological anthropology were sadly irrelevant as Europe careened toward war, but he offered a few glosses on the crisis. Christianity, Niebuhr argued, possesses distinctive spiritual, moral, and intellectual resources to help modern people think about themselves and their world. These resources were desperately needed in a world plagued by various kinds of cynical militarism and nihilism, on the one hand, and a variety of naive idealisms on the other hand: "The fateful consequence in contemporary political life of Hobbes's cynicism and Nietzsche's nihilism are everywhere apparent."[15]

Shortly after Japan attacked Pearl Harbor in December 1941, Niebuhr lamented that the same American moralists who had resisted going to war could now be counted on to clothe America's war effort with insufferable visions of a transformed world order. He could hardly bear the idealistic calls to war that he knew were coming. Americans habitually failed to acknowledge the power of self-interest in their politics, he complained; thus they insisted on moralizing even their wars and imperial occupations. Niebuhr wanted Americans to view the world more realistically as a theater of perpetual struggles for power among competing interests. In foreign policy, realism sought a balance of power among regimes and a stable correlation of forces. Theologically,

14. Reinhold Niebuhr, "The Socialist Campaign," *Christianity and Society* 5 (Summer 1940), 4 (quote); see Niebuhr, "The London Times and the Crisis," *Radical Religion* 4 (Winter 1938–1939): 32; Niebuhr, "Willkie and Roosevelt," *Christianity and Society* 5 (Fall 1940): 5.

15. Reinhold Niebuhr, *The Nature and Destiny of Man: A Christian Interpretation*, 2 vols. (New York: Scribner's Sons, 1941, 1943), 1:25.

realism was rooted in the doctrine that the image of God in every human being is marred by selfishness and pride.[16]

In November 1943, while Roosevelt, Winston Churchill, and Joseph Stalin met in Tehran to plan the Allied invasion of Europe, Niebuhr mapped out his political philosophy. The lecture version was presented in January 1944 as the Raymond F. West Lectures at Stanford University. The book version was titled *The Children of Light and the Children of Darkness*. Niebuhr argued that Americans did a bad job of defending democracy because they rarely gave realism its due.[17]

Basically he replaced his Marxist either/or about history going forward or backward by refashioning his dialectic about soft and hard utopianism. Modern American liberals were spiritual cousins of John Locke, Adam Smith, Jean-Jacques Rousseau, Thomas Paine, G. W. F. Hegel, and all true-believing Marxists, Niebuhr said. All were "children of light" who believed that the conflict between self-interest and the general interest could be readily resolved. Locke's social contract, Smith's harmonizing invisible hand, and Rousseau's general will needed only minimal restraints on human egotism, because Locke, Smith, and Rousseau had immense confidence in reason and/or nature. Hegel believed that his philosophy synthesized the national and universal interests. Marxists even believed that no state would be necessary after the proletarian revolution occurred.

Niebuhr allowed that most children of light recognized the existence of a moral law beyond themselves, although some called it something else. But all were naive about the power of self-interest in society; thus he called them "stupid children of light." Even Marxists were guilty of "the usual stupidity" that marked modern democratic theory as a whole, he argued. Liberal naïveté yielded bad arguments for democracy, and it made the children of light inept at defending democracy against "children of darkness," who were wise and strong in their moral cynicism. The children of darkness, Niebuhr said, understood self-interest terribly well and were not constrained by a moral law beyond themselves. Hobbes and Machiavelli were children of darkness, exemplifying the toxic corruption of a realism lacking a moral dimension. The epitome of toxic darkness, Nazi barbarism, had plunged Europe into total war. The classic liberal picture of a harmless, essentially individualistic social existence was utterly refuted by the "demonic fury" and success of Fascism.[18]

16. Reinhold Niebuhr, "Editorial Notes," *Christianity and Society* 7 (Winter 1941–1942): 9.

17. Reinhold Niebuhr, *The Children of Light and the Children of Darkness* (New York: Scribner's Sons, 1944; reprint, Chicago: University of Chicago Press, 2011).

18. Niebuhr, *The Children of Light*, 32 ("stupid children of light" and "the usual stupid-

In 1944, Niebuhr had many friends who saw little difference between the barbarity of the Nazi and Soviet regimes; some had written extensively about the crimes of Stalinism. Niebuhr leaned toward their side of the argument and was repelled that Harry Ward stubbornly defended Stalin's reign of terror. In 1939 Niebuhr wrote in the *Christian Century* that he felt "genuinely sorry for my friends who seem to be under a spiritual necessity to deny obvious facts about Russian tyranny." He told Bennett and other friends that the tyrannical evil of Soviet Communism was "almost, though not quite" as bad as that of Nazi Germany. But in 1944 Niebuhr settled for a wartime evasion, mindful that American newsmagazines called Stalin "Uncle Joe." It was too soon to place Stalin unequivocally among the children of darkness, Niebuhr suggested. However, down the road, "Stalin will probably have the same relation to the early dreamers of the Marxist dreams which Napoleon has to the liberal dreamers of the eighteenth century."[19]

Modern liberals thought that democracy fulfilled an ideal that people deserved on account of their moral worth. The children of darkness, being cunning and immoral in their pursuit of power, better understood the centrality of will to power in politics and history. This dialectic yielded Niebuhr's most famous epigram: "Man's capacity for justice makes democracy possible, but man's inclination to injustice makes democracy necessary." Liberal democracy is worth defending because it is the best way to restrain human egotism and will to power, not because it fulfills a moral ideal or because modern civilized types deserve nothing less. Niebuhr espoused a realist-leaning dialectic of idealism and realism, urging that America needed to find a moral balance between cynical amorality and sentimental idealism.[20]

In 1944 Niebuhr still believed that political democracy needed to grow into economic democracy to attain social justice and protect democracy itself. But he was nearing the end of his Socialist phase, and he no longer believed that socialism was possible in his country. Niebuhr had friends in the upper reaches of the Democratic Party; he adjusted to the Cold War as soon as it came along; and he shook his head at the Henry Wallace wing of the Democratic Party that called for friendly cooperation with the Soviet Union.

---

ity"), 23 ("demonic fury"). The phrases "children of light" and "children of darkness" occur throughout the book.

19. Niebuhr, "Ten Years That Shook My World," 543 ("genuinely sorry"); Niebuhr, quoted in John C. Bennett, "Tillich and the 'Fellowship of Socialist Christians,'" *North American Paul Tillich Society Newsletter* 16 (October 1990): 3 ("almost, though not quite"); Niebuhr, *The Children of Light*, 33 ("Stalin will probably").

20. Niebuhr, *The Children of Light*, xi (quote).

Niebuhr let go of socialism and its fixation with equality, adopting the New Deal view of the federal government as an assertive countervailing power mediating between corporate capitalism and the trade unions. In 1947 he made two organizational adjustments. Niebuhr persuaded the Fellowship of Socialist Christians to change its name to Frontier Fellowship, and he folded UDA into a new organization dominated by establishment liberals, Americans for Democratic Action (ADA).

The ADA liberals stressed their anti-Communist credentials. The old leftists that came into the ADA with Niebuhr were especially valuable to it because they were veterans of the battles to expel Communists from the trade unions and Socialist Party. The best anti-Communists were Socialists or former Socialists, because they hated Communism for ruining something they prized, and they knew better than anyone how Communists subverted democratic organizations. They boasted that they were the experts on thwarting Communism. The *Christian Century* worried that Niebuhr was veering toward a middle-of-the-road conformism. He countered that the middle ground did not have to be a dead center, for everywhere the struggle for the middle ground was a fight for democracy. This fight necessarily included a long-term battle against the spread of Communism, for "we are fated as a generation to live in the insecurity which this universal evil of communism creates for our world."[21]

Fascism lacked an inspiring ideal that appealed to others; thus it could be smashed directly by armed force. But Communism had the moral power of a utopian creed that appealed to deluded leftists and to millions in the Third World. Thus it had to be fought differently. Niebuhr hung a vast ideological scaffolding on this argument, teaching that Communism was an evil religion; it was devoted to the establishment of a new universal order, not merely the supremacy of a race or nation; and thus it had to be contained through diplomatic pressure and military force.

Niebuhr charged that Communism, though tactically flexible, was inherently fanatical, because it rested on "simple distinctions between exploited and exploiter," simplistic concepts of class and exploitation, and a simplistic vision of world revolution. Old-style realists viewed Soviet Communism as merely a new form of Russian imperialism; Niebuhr countered that traditional realpolitik failed to grasp the "noxious demonry" of Communism. At the same

---

21. Reinhold Niebuhr, "Frontier Fellowship," *Christianity and Society* 13 (Autumn 1948): 4; Niebuhr and others, "Christian Action Statement of Purpose," *Christianity and Crisis* 11 (October 1, 1951): 126; Niebuhr, "Superfluous Advice," *Christianity and Society* 17 (Winter 1951–1952): 4; Niebuhr, *Christian Realism and Political Problems*, 33 ("we are fated"); see Niebuhr, "The Organization of the Liberal Movement," *Christianity and Society* 12 (Spring 1947): 8–10.

time, in the name of realism, he counseled against a crusading hot war. America's battle against Communism needed to walk a fine, patient, vigilant line between treating the Soviet state as a geopolitical Great Power rival and as an implacable Nazi-like enemy.[22]

In power politics, Niebuhr cautioned, a perverted moralism is always more dangerous than explicit evil. For this reason, Communism was capable of creating greater and longer-lasting evils in the world than fascism. Niebuhr argued that the best analogy for the Communist threat to the West was the rise of militant Islam in the high Middle Ages, not the Third Reich: "Moslem power was consolidated in the Middle Ages and threatened the whole of Christendom much as Communist power threatens Western civilization today." Just as Islam brandished a quasi-universal ideology that transcended nationalism while being rooted in the Arab world, the Communist movement wielded a pseudo-universal creed that served Russian imperial ambitions. Niebuhr believed that equating Soviet tyranny with Islam validated his conception of Soviet Communism as an evil religion. He took for granted that his audience would not object to his slur that Islam was similarly demonic, and he was not called on it. Usually he added that the Islamic concept of a holy war against infidels was "analogous to the Communist conception of the inevitable conflict between capitalism and Communism."[23]

The Niebuhr later revered by American neoconservatives was the Niebuhr of this period, the icon of Cold War liberalism. Neoconservatives claimed they became conservative Republicans only because the Democratic Party betrayed the aggressive anti-Communist liberalism of presidents Harry Truman and John F. Kennedy. Niebuhr-style liberalism was not the feminized progressivism that emerged in the 1960s and nominated George McGovern for president in 1972. It did not sentimentalize the public sphere or project moral idealism into politics. It did not shrink from fighting Communism, which Niebuhr defined in 1953 as "an organized evil which spreads terror and cruelty throughout the world and confronts us everywhere with faceless men who are immune to every form of moral and political suasion." For neoconservatives, Niebuhr epitomized the tough-minded and aggressively pro-American liberalism that disappeared in the 1960s. This rendering of Niebuhr's legacy was reinforced by Christian leftists who viewed Niebuhr chiefly as the figure who turned

22. Reinhold Niebuhr, "The Change in Russia," *New Leader* 38 (October 3, 1955): 18–19 ("simple distinctions"); Niebuhr, *Christian Realism and Political Problems*, 34 ("noxious demonry").

23. Reinhold Niebuhr, "The Peril of Complacency in Our Nation," *Christianity and Crisis* 14 (February 8, 1954): 1; Niebuhr, "The Change in Russia," 18, quotes on Islamic analogy.

American Christian ethics into a form of Cold War apologetics. Pacifist ethicist John Swomley, in a typical indictment, said that Niebuhr provided "the religious rationale for the military foreign policy that created the contemporary American empire and the policy of global intervention culminating in the war in Vietnam."[24]

These ideologically driven interpretations had a substantial basis, but they assigned a fixed position where none existed. To Niebuhr, Christian realism was not an ideology or even a method; it was a dynamic orientation, chastened by the awareness of sin and interest, that responded to social challenges of the moment. In the early 1950s, while the United States convulsed over McCarthyism and FBI agents dug for incriminating details about Niebuhr's radical past, he portrayed "Communism" as a devouring totalitarian monolith committed to world domination. Like his ADA allies, Niebuhr detested Joseph McCarthy and was determined not to allow him to monopolize the anti-Communist issue. He spurned McCarthy, demonized Communists in classic old Left fashion, and implicitly condoned parts of McCarthy's campaign to smoke Communists out of American government, education, and religion. Niebuhr strongly supported the government's execution of Julius and Ethel Rosenberg for stealing atomic secrets, and, in a 1953 article for *Look* magazine, he carelessly and mistakenly claimed that McCarthy's assistant, J. B. Matthews, accurately identified more than a dozen pro-Communist church leaders.[25]

Niebuhr later apologized for giving ballast to the smear tactics of McCarthy and Matthews. His loathing of McCarthy motivated him to burnish his own credentials as a Cold Warrior. For Niebuhr, anti-Communism was too important to be left to McCarthy reactionaries, and the McCarthy version demonized the entire political Left. Niebuhr stayed in this Cold War mode until 1954, when McCarthy self-destructed. Niebuhr's vulnerability as a former leftist was a factor, but his trump concern was to establish a progressive and realistic form of anti-Communism. Thus he opposed ideological versions

24. Reinhold Niebuhr, *Christian Realism and Political Problems* (New York, Scribner's Sons, 1953), 34 ("an organized evil"); Michael Novak, "Needing Niebuhr Again," *Commentary* 54 (September 1972): 52–61; Novak, "Reinhold Niebuhr: Model for Neoconservatives," *Christian Century* 103 (January 22, 1986): 69–71; James Nuechterlein, "The Feminization of the American Left," *Commentary* 84 (November 1987); John M. Swomley Jr., *American Empire: The Political Ethics of Twentieth Century Conquest* (London: Macmillan, 1970), 34. For a similar critique of Niebuhr's legacy, see Bill Kellermann, "Apologist of Power: The Long Shadow of Reinhold Niebuhr's Christian Realism," *Sojourners* 16 (March 1987): 15–20.

25. Reinhold Niebuhr, "Communism and the Protestant Clergy," *Look*, November 17, 1953, 37.

of anti-Communism that called America to fight wars against Communism wherever it vied for power.

National Review conservatives James Burnham and William F. Buckley Jr. implored the US government to "roll back" the Soviet conquest of Eastern Europe; they also defended McCarthy zealously. Niebuhr replied that conceiving the Cold War primarily in military terms was deeply mistaken. Niebuhr wrote in 1953 that the evil of Communism flowed "from a combination of political and 'spiritual' factors, which prove that the combination of power and pride is responsible for turning the illusory dreams of yesterday into the present nightmare, which disturbs the ease of millions of men in our generation." The following year he put it starkly: "We are embattled with a foe who embodies all the evils of a demonic religion. We will probably be at sword's point with this foe for generations to come."[26]

This view of Soviet Communism as a perverted religion shaped Niebuhr's understanding of how the Cold War should be waged. He stuck with his offensive analogy to Islam because it helped him get his bearings on what realistic anti-Communism looked like. The mistakes of the Crusaders were instructive for fighting off Communism. Precisely because Communism was a demonic religion, anti-Communist containment was not a job for ideologues or religious crusaders. Like the Islamic power during its glory years, the Communist movement was deeply entrenched, threatening, and ideologically driven. And like the Islamic power, it was more likely to disintegrate from its inner contradictions and corruptions than from external force from its enemies. Niebuhr recalled that the sultan of Turkey was unable to sustain his double role as spiritual leader of the Islamic world and head of the Turkish state. Stalin had essentially the same role "in the world of communist religion," and thus had the same problems.[27]

Niebuhr's friends included the father of containment strategy, State Department diplomat George Kennan. Like Kennan, Niebuhr believed that the Soviet regime would eventually self-destruct on the contradictions and failures of its unworkable system. The purpose of containment strategy was to keep enough diplomatic and military pressure on the Soviets to accelerate the implosion of the Soviet state. Kennan's historic "Mr. X" blueprint for containment, published in *Foreign Affairs* in 1947, argued that if the United States kept the pressure on for perhaps ten to fifteen years, and showed itself to be a more

26. Niebuhr, *Christian Realism and Political Problems*, 42 ("from a combination"); Niebuhr, "The Peril of Complacency in Our Nation," 1 ("We are embattled"); James Burnham, *The Coming Defeat of Communism* (New York: John Day, 1949); Burnham, *Containment or Liberation? An Inquiry into the Aims of United States Foreign Policy* (New York: John Day, 1952).

27. Reinhold Niebuhr, *The Irony of American History* (New York: Scribner's Sons, 1952), 110.

attractive alternative, the monolithic discipline of the governing Soviet party would be undermined: "And if disunity were ever to seize and paralyze the Party, the chaos and weakness of Russian society would be revealed in forms beyond description. Soviet Russia might be changed overnight from one of the strongest to one of the weakest and most pitiable of national societies."[28]

Niebuhr's early formulations of this belief were less eerily prophetic than Kennan's, but prescient nonetheless. He argued in 1952 that militaristic anti-Communists misunderstood the nature of the enemy: "If we fully understand the deep springs which feed the illusions of this religion, the nature of the social resentments which nourish them and the realities of life which must ultimately refute them, we might acquire the necessary patience to wait out the long run of history while we take such measures as are necessary to combat the more immediate perils." Soviet Communism was a conspiratorial religion that would eventually self-destruct if the West maintained a self-respecting and patient strategy of containment.[29]

Niebuhr reconsidered both ends of this argument after Nikita Khrushchev denounced Stalin's purges in 1956 and instituted de-Stalinizing reforms. In 1958, noting that the Soviet economy had apparently recovered and that the Soviet Union had advanced in science, technology, and military expansion, Niebuhr began to doubt that Soviet Communism was incapable of sustaining itself indefinitely. At the same time, he began to question the inevitability of the Cold War. If Communism was not certain to self-destruct, Niebuhr no longer believed that a state of warfare between the two superpowers was inevitable or sensible. In 1958, "as a kind of trial balloon to initiate discussion," Niebuhr's coeditor John Bennett proposed that the United States should give up its "perpetual official moral diatribe" against world Communism. Bennett wrote, "We should accept the fact that communism is here to stay in at least two great countries, that in them it is a massive human experiment which will have its chance." The Communist turn was irreversible, but not unchangeable.[30]

Niebuhr surprised many Niebuhrians by moving to the same view. The fate of the world, he declared, depended "upon our capacity to leaven the lump of our own orthodox conceptions of a changeable Communist orthodoxy." Niebuhr acknowledged that, officially, Soviet Communists still believed that the logic of history assured their triumph. However, "we had better, for the

28. X [George F. Kennan], "The Sources of Soviet Conduct," *Foreign Affairs* 25 (July 1947): 579–80.

29. Niebuhr, *Irony of American History*, 129.

30. John C. Bennett, "A Condition for Coexistence," *Christianity and Crisis* 18 (April 28, 1958): 53–54.

sake of the world, recognize that this belief is not tantamount to a policy of plotting for world domination by any possible means." Soviet Communism was not an immutable monolith, an overpowering enemy, a world-threatening conspiracy, or an enemy with which the USA could not learn to coexist. The following year, in *The Structure of Nations and Empires*, Niebuhr made a case for US/Soviet coexistence, urging that realism demanded "a less rigid and self-righteous attitude toward the power realities of the world and a more hopeful attitude toward the possibilities of internal development in the Russian despotism."[31]

Christian realists sharply debated these arguments. Many of Niebuhr's followers were appalled that he came out for coexistence and claimed that Communism was capable of making internal reforms. Some stuck with Cold War realism, that Soviet Communism was an evil but self-destructive religion that had to be waited out; others said that both positions were too passive, because the Soviets were racing ahead of the United States. Kennan influenced Niebuhr's turn toward coexistence, although Kennan still believed the Soviet system was inherently unstable. Kennan and Niebuhr argued that "containment" had acquired an overly militarized meaning in American policy, and that American policy makers overestimated Soviet political, economic, and military strength. Secretary of State John Foster Dulles, in particular, mythologized the Cold War into a holy war.

The Dulles problem especially troubled Niebuhr, because Dulles was dangerous and he readily quoted Niebuhr. Dulles had come into national prominence during World War II, when he chaired the Federal Council of Churches' Commission for a Just and Durable Peace. He and Niebuhr worked together (unsuccessfully) to urge the fledgling World Council of Churches to adopt a policy of forgiveness toward the defeated Axis Powers. But Dulles bristled with self-righteousness, especially about the Cold War. As secretary of state, he espoused a doctrine of massive nuclear retaliation, and he unctuously described the Cold War as a struggle between good and evil. Niebuhr recoiled at both, believing that Dulles overmoralized the Cold War and overrelied on the threat of retaliatory nuclear force. Niebuhrian realism did not indulge in nuclear brinkmanship, mythologize the Cold War, or arrogantly dismiss the power struggles in smaller nations. It did not use the nuclear threat as a

---

31. Reinhold Niebuhr, "Uneasy Peace or Catastrophe," *Christianity and Crisis* 18 (April 28, 1958): 54–55 ("upon our capacity" and "we had better"); Niebuhr, *The Structure of Nations and Empires: A Study of Recurring Patterns and Problems of the Political Order in Relation to the Unique Problems of the Nuclear Age* (New York: Scribner's Sons, 1959), 282 ("a less rigid").

substitute for aggressive and persistent diplomacy. Niebuhr told friends that Dulles and President Eisenhower were too stupid to be entrusted with America's fate, which became a favorite in-house debate topic among Niebuhrians, some of whom did not share Niebuhr's partisan dislike of Republicans. On the morning after Dwight Eisenhower was elected in 1952, an acutely distressed Niebuhr told his daughter Elisabeth, "You poor girl, you've never lived under a Republican administration, you don't know how terrible this thing is going to be." Dulles's simultaneously threatening and passive approach to foreign affairs confirmed Niebuhr's feelings about Republicans.[32]

The Eisenhower years were otherwise short on drama and divisive issues for the Niebuhrians. To them, bipartisan containment and America's foreign policy consensus were good things, including going to war in Korea. Kennan, Bennett, Arthur Schlesinger Jr., Hans Morgenthau, Kenneth W. Thompson, and Paul Ramsey were leading Niebuhrian realists in foreign policy. In 1956, the Soviet invasion of Hungary confirmed Niebuhr's belief that America had to preserve its nuclear dominance. Nuclear disarmament was impossible because the Soviets would accept only an agreement that drove America out of Europe. Very few American Christian ethicists who were not pacifists disputed this "consensus" position in the 1950s.[33]

Then came the exotic turbulence of the 1960s and the end of consensus even among Niebuhrians. President Kennedy appointed several figures from Niebuhr's inner circle to high positions, notably Schlesinger, Loeb, and Paul Nitze. McGeorge Bundy, Kennedy's national security adviser, lauded Niebuhr as the exemplary Christian realist. Niebuhr supported Kennedy while harboring misgivings about his depth and personal morality. Kennedy's disastrous attempt to overthrow the Castro government in Cuba deepened Niebuhr's misgivings. Niebuhr denounced the Bay of Pigs fiasco and Kennedy's embargo on Cuban products, protesting that his militaristic blundering inflamed anti-US sentiment throughout the hemisphere.[34]

---

32. Elisabeth Sifton, "Remembering Reinhold Niebuhr," *World Policy Journal* 10 (Spring 1993): 87.

33. Reinhold Niebuhr, "Our Moral Dilemma," *Messenger*, November 5, 1957, 5; George F. Kennan, *The Nuclear Delusion: Soviet-American Relations in the Atomic Age* (New York: Pantheon Books, 1982), ix–xxx; Walter LaFeber, *America, Russia, and the Cold War, 1945–1966* (New York: Wiley and Sons, 1967). I am grateful to John C. Bennett for his insights and recollections regarding this period of Niebuhr's career. author's interview with Bennett, January 2, 1993.

34. Reinhold Niebuhr, "Drama on the Cuban Stage," *New Leader*, March 5, 1962, 11; cited in Fox, *Reinhold Niebuhr*, 276.

The Berlin crisis convinced Niebuhr that Christian realism needed a policy overhaul. The Soviets walled off East Berlin in 1961, forcing Kennedy to decide whether to let the wall stand. American policy makers feared that destroying it would spark a Soviet nuclear or conventional-force attack. Niebuhr and Bennett agreed that if the Soviets launched a nuclear attack, America would have to reciprocate. The question was whether the United States should respond to a conventional-force attack with nuclear weapons.

In 1950 Niebuhr and Bennett had defended America's right to use nuclear weapons in a first strike to destroy invading Russian tanks. In 1961 they reconsidered. Bennett took the lead, noting that American ethicists rarely addressed the possibility that their nation might set off a nuclear holocaust. American ethicists had little to say about nuclear policy because no realistic moral choices seemed to exist. In this area, Bennett observed, the foreign policy consensus was a species of fatalism. Ever since the obliteration bombings of World War II, American ethicists had accepted that moral questions had to be subordinated to strategic questions during war. This assumption was routinely called Niebuhrian realism, but Bennett questioned the premise and its fatalistic consequences. Christian realism had to address the moral dilemmas of nuclear policy and retaliation, he urged. Even if one granted the moral legitimacy of nuclear deterrence, that did not legitimize any particular doctrine about retaliation, first use, countervalue warfare, or the use of tactical weapons. Bennett offered a proposal. Any conceivable nuclear attack on Russian cities would be an indefensible "atrocity" and should be ruled out. Moreover, "it would be almost as evil a deed to take the step that might initially involve the use of tactical nuclear weapons, knowing that it would be almost sure to result in the total conflict in which we would be both the destroyers and the destroyed."[35]

That pushed Christian realism into new territory, against tactical first use. Niebuhr took a further step, declaring, "The first use of the nuclear weapon is morally abhorrent and must be resisted." He doubted that a democratic society could survive a nuclear triumph: "Could a civilization loaded with this monstrous guilt have enough moral health to survive?" Remarkably, though typically for the time, he ignored that American democracy had already "survived" Hiroshima and Nagasaki; Niebuhr left the question hanging. The following year he declared that it might be time "to take some risks for peace

---

35. John C. Bennett and Reinhold Niebuhr, "The Nuclear Dilemma: A Discussion," *Christianity and Crisis* 21 (November 13, 1961): 200–202 (quotes); see Bennett, *Nuclear Weapons and the Conflict of Conscience* (New York: Scribner's Sons, 1962).

comparable to our ever more dangerous risks in the game of deterrence." The United States needed a more flexible position on disarmament. He proposed to begin by taking certain unilateral initiatives, such as dropping America's unrealistic insistence on foolproof inspection.[36]

The Niebuhr/Bennett shift on nuclear policy sparked a fractious debate among Niebuhrians. Paul Ramsey argued that only conventional weapons could be used in retaliation. Paul Tillich supported the Niebuhr/Bennett arguments against nuclear first use while defending the moral right to retaliate with tactical weapons against a tactical attack. Hans Morgenthau declared, "without qualification," that no resort to nuclear weapons could ever be morally justified. Norman Gottwald contended that nuclear weapons could be used morally, but only against military targets. Others were appalled that Niebuhr sanctioned this debate. Kenneth Thompson warned: "If we declare we shall not use thermonuclear weapons except in the ultimate defense, we have assisted the Soviet Union in plotting a campaign of expansion and imperialism. I would prefer the moralist to master a strategy of restraint, silence where policy dictates, and self discipline rather than merely to protest with all right-thinking men the grave hazards of the nuclear age." Carl Mayer said the danger of a nuclear war would increase if the United States came out against first use and the targeting of cities. He was astonished that some Niebuhrians no longer understood that the only way to peace was to prepare for war: "It seems that the days of what came to be known as Christian realism are about over in America. But it is somewhat ironical that the very magazine that used to be the staunchest champion of such a realism should today, in the matter of the most crucial political problem of the age, espouse views that hardly differ from those of *The Christian Century*."[37]

Niebuhr continued to support nuclear deterrence, while admitting that he had undermined his argument for it. He explained that the current balance of

---

36. Bennett and Niebuhr, "The Nuclear Dilemma," 202 ("The first use" and "Could a civilization"); Reinhold Niebuhr, "Logical Consistency and the Nuclear Dilemma," *Christianity and Crisis* 22 (April 2, 1962): 48 ("to take some risks").

37. Paul Ramsey, "Dream and Reality in Deterrence and Defense," *Christianity and Crisis* 21 (December 25, 1961): 228–32; Paul Tillich, "The Nuclear Dilemma: A Discussion," *Christianity and Crisis* 21 (November 13, 1961): 203–4; Hans J. Morgenthau, "The Nuclear Discussion: Continued," *Christianity and Crisis* 21 (December 11, 1961): 223; Norman K. Gottwald, "Moral and Strategic Reflections on the Nuclear Dilemma," *Christianity and Crisis* 21 (January 8, 1962): 239–42; Kenneth W. Thompson, "The Nuclear Dilemma: A Discussion," *Christianity and Crisis* 21 (November 13, 1961): 203; Carl Mayer, "Moral Issues in the Nuclear Dilemma," *Christianity and Crisis* 22 (March 19, 1962): 38.

terror seemed unsustainable to him, which drove him to an inconsistent position. But that was a mere prelude to the breakup of Niebuhrian realism. For more than twenty years, since the Chinese Revolution, Niebuhr had opposed US intervention in Asian civil wars. He did not think of Korea as an exception to this policy, because the Korean War was launched by a Soviet-backed invasion. But Vietnam was a tougher case, because it was both a civil war and a Soviet proxy war. In the early 1960s, Niebuhr agonized over what the USA should do about Vietnam. He accepted the domino theory that Communists would conquer Southeast Asia if the United States withdrew from Vietnam. However, the American-backed Diem regime in South Vietnam was a repressive dictatorship. The moral choices were deeply ambiguous. Niebuhr feared that his friends in the Kennedy administration often reduced Christian realism to amoral manipulation; he admonished that it also had a moral dimension. Meanwhile, he waffled on Vietnam, not anticipating that it would become the acid test of America's moral realism, and of his.

In 1964 the new president, Lyndon Johnson, awarded Niebuhr the Medal of Freedom, the nation's highest civilian honor. Later that year Niebuhr supported Johnson's election, partly because Johnson promised not to escalate in Vietnam. The following year Johnson invaded the Dominican Republic, and Niebuhr protested that force was creative only as the tool "of a legitimate authority in the community," which was lacking in this case. In Vietnam, Niebuhr looked for a third option after Johnson massively escalated in 1965. Niebuhr doubted that the United States could win a military victory in Vietnam, but losing the region to Communism seemed intolerable. Thus he urged Johnson to persuade Thailand to offer asylum to all the region's anti-Communist warriors, "and then defend this asylum with massive military power." Niebuhr implored that America needed to stand tall, reminding other nations of its superior might and will. This bizarre plan exposed his ignorance of Southeast Asian history and politics, and his enduring America-the-Great nationalism.[38]

In January 1966 Niebuhr was still exhorting Johnson to "take a stand" in Thailand, but by the end of the month he began to deal with reality. Niebuhr shook his head sadly as Vice President Hubert Humphrey, a treasured friend, gamely defended the war; Niebuhr, embarrassed for his friend, began to turn the other way. Vietnam was not really an important test of America's containment policy, he contended, contradicting Humphrey: "We are in fact dealing

---

38. Reinhold Niebuhr, "Caribbean Blunder," *Christianity and Crisis* 25 (May 31, 1965): 113–14 ("of a legitimate authority"); Niebuhr, "Consensus at the Price of Flexibility," *New Leader*, September 27, 1965, 20 ("and then defend").

with the nationalism of a small nation of Asia." Vietnam failed the tests of national security and economic interest, and it was a futile enterprise anyway. Above all, the carnage of the war was sickening to Niebuhr. On moral and political grounds he denounced America's use of chemical weapons; on strategic grounds he added that bombing North Vietnam was pointless too: "We are making South Vietnam into an American colony by transmuting a civil war into one in which Americans fight Asians. By escalating the war we are physically ruining an unhappy nation in the process of 'saving' it." The following year Niebuhr called for the United States to withdraw from Vietnam; in the *New York Times* he called for a public outcry "against these horrendous policies." Vietnam was an example of the "illusion of American omnipotence." He told friends that his lack of patriotic feeling frightened him: "For the first time I fear I am ashamed of our beloved nation."[39]

That reaction stunned and angered many Niebuhrians. Ramsey spoke for them, protesting that in the bizarre 1960s, "even Reinhold Niebuhr signs petitions and editorials as if Reinhold Niebuhr never existed." The real Niebuhr would not have supported unilateral disarmament initiatives or getting out of Vietnam, Ramsey suggested. Certainly, the real Niebuhr would not have legitimized the antiwar opposition with emotional rhetoric against his nation's policy. For Ramsey and what became the neoconservative reaction, it was all very sad.[40]

Thus did the Cold War liberals back away from the ravages of anti-Communist containment in Vietnam. A succession of Kennedy and Johnson administration officials followed Niebuhr in repenting of imperial overstretch. The catastrophe in Vietnam fueled an explosion of new social movements that challenged the dominant order. Two contrasting reactions to the exotic turbulence of the time had special pertinence for the fate of Niebuhrian theology: liberation theology and neoconservatism.

---

39. Reinhold Niebuhr, "The Peace Offensive," *Christianity and Crisis* 25 (January 24, 1966): 301 ("We are in fact" and "We are making"); Niebuhr, "Escalation Objective," *New York Times*, March 14, 1967 ("against these horrendous policies"); Niebuhr, foreword to *Martin Luther King, Jr., John C. Bennett, Henry Steele Commager, Abraham Heschel Speak on the War in Vietnam* (New York: Clergy and Laymen Concerned about Vietnam, 1967), 3; Fox, *Reinhold Niebuhr*, 285 ("For the first time").

40. Paul Ramsey, "How Shall Counter-Insurgency War Be Conducted Justly?" (paper presented at American Society of Christian Ethics Meeting, January 21–22, 1966); reprinted in Ramsey, *The Just War: Force and Political Responsibility* (1968; reprint, Lanham, MD: University Press of America, 1983), 458. For Bennett's response, see John C. Bennett, "From Supporter of War in 1941 to Critic in 1966," *Christianity and Crisis* 26 (February 21, 1966): 13–14.

Liberation theology charged that Niebuhrian realism was essentially an ideology of the dominant American order. The black social gospel of Benjamin E. Mays and Martin Luther King Jr. was a forerunner of the liberationist repudiation of Cold War dualism. In the late 1940s and early 1950s, Mays wrote weekly columns for the *Pittsburgh Courier* that refused to choose sides in the Cold War, protesting that most of the world's people were poor, nonwhite, and exploited by colonial powers. Telling black American progressives to loathe Communism contradicted their experience of finding white allies mostly among Communists. After liberation theology became a movement in the 1970s, liberationist Cornel West described Niebuhrian realism as a "form of Europeanist ideology that promoted and legitimated U.S. hegemony in the world." West explained that for Niebuhr, Western Europe and the USA comprised a superior civilization, a prejudice that underwrote Niebuhr's support of US domination of Latin America, European colonialism in Africa, and an Israeli state led by European Jews that oppressed the Palestinians. There were two streams of Niebuhrian realism, West observed. One sought to shore up a declining liberal Democratic Party establishment; West called them "desperate" defenders of a "discredited" perspective. The other group turned Niebuhr's Euro-American supremacism and Cold War militarism into an ideology of American empire.[41]

The second stream was the neoconservative movement. Many of the original neocons had backgrounds in the Socialist old Left. Others came straight from Niebuhr's circle, notably Ramsey and Ernest Lefever. Others turned to the political right after dabbling in new Left radicalism; Catholic theologian Michael Novak was a prominent example. In September 1972, one year after Niebuhr died, Novak wrote that it seemed like ten. Novak had worked recently for George McGovern's presidential campaign, but revulsion was stirring within him. He hated feminism; it appalled him that white liberals deferred to black power; the antiwar movement had become unbearable; and McGovern's idealistic whining sent him over the edge. Novak didn't know where he was

---

41. Cornel West, "Christian Realism as Religious Insights and Europeanist Ideology: Niebuhr and the Third World," in West, *Prophetic Fragments: Illuminations of the Crisis in American Religion and Culture* (Grand Rapids: Eerdmans, 1988), 148, 152 (quotes); Benjamin E. Mays, "Mays: Whether Robeson Should or Should Not Speak Is Irrelevant, U.S. Should Wake Up," *Pittsburgh Courier*, October 15, 1949; Mays, "Mays: We Must Spell Out D–E–M–O–C–R–A–C–Y at Home as Well as Abroad for Victory over Reds," *Pittsburgh Courier*, February 3, 1951, 19; Gary Dorrien, *The New Abolition: W. E. B. Du Bois and the Black Social Gospel* (New Haven: Yale University Press, 2015); Dorrien, *Daybreak of Freedom: Martin Luther King Jr. and the Black Social Gospel* (New Haven: Yale University Press, 2018).

going politically, but he realized he couldn't stand the new liberals, much less the radicals to whom they deferred. In his first phase of converting to neoconservatism, Novak accused the Democratic Party of betraying real liberalism. McGovern symbolized this betrayal, and Niebuhr symbolized what had been lost. More than ever, Novak argued, America needed Niebuhr's tough-minded, anti-Communist, antimoralistic realism: "In many ways it is as if he had lived and worked in vain."[42]

Meanwhile, numerous liberal centrist Niebuhrians retained their positions at prominent seminaries, often reminding critics that Reinhold Niebuhr spent his entire career in the liberal Left and never lost his passion for social justice. Bennett, Ronald Stone, and Charles West were prominent in this school. They urged that Niebuhrian realism at its best was an antidote to America-the-Greatest imperialism, not a species of it. The right-Niebuhrians had never taken Niebuhr seriously when he criticized America's fantasies of omnipotence and righteousness. Thus they were too surprised when he applied this critique to America's disastrous venture in Vietnam. In *The Irony of American History* (1952), Niebuhr declared: "We cannot simply have our way, not even when we believe our way to have the 'happiness of mankind' as its promise." In *The Structure of Nations and Empires* (1959), he put it ruefully: "We are tempted to the fanatic dogma that our form of community is not only more valid than any other but that it is more feasible for all communities on all continents."[43]

That grandiose self-image led to the jungles of Vietnam. King lamented in 1967 that America's "morbid fear of Communism" and injustice had perversely turned the USA into the world's leading counterrevolutionary power. Niebuhr regretted that he had endorsed the misleading idea of "containment," which acquired a simplistic military meaning that he did not support. In 1969 he explained that he had followed Kennan in shifting away from containment "to the partnership of the two superpowers for the prevention of a nuclear war." Like Kennan, he disavowed "any simple containment of Communism." Later that year, while images of America's incineration of Vietnam burned in his mind, Niebuhr confirmed that he had changed. Ten years previously, he had blasted Karl Barth's neutralism in the last exchange of a decade-long debate with Barth. Now Niebuhr took it back: "While I do not share his sneer at the

---

42. Novak, "Needing Niebuhr Again," 52 (quote); Novak, "Reinhold Niebuhr," 69–71.

43. Niebuhr, *Irony of American History*, 74; Niebuhr, *The Structure of Nations and Empires*, 295; see Ronald H. Stone, "An Interview with Reinhold Niebuhr," *Christianity and Crisis* 29 (March 17, 1969): 48–49; Reinhold Niebuhr, "Toward New Intra-Christian Endeavors," *Christian Century* 86 (December 31, 1969): 1662–63; Matthew Berke, "The Disputed Legacy of Reinhold Niebuhr," *First Things* 27 (November 1992): 39.

'fleshpots of Germany and America,' I must admit that our wealth makes our religious anti-Communism particularly odious. Perhaps there is not so much to choose between Communist and anti-Communist fanaticism, particularly when the latter, combined with our wealth, has caused us to stumble into the most pointless, costly, and bloody war in our history."[44]

The critic of group egotism recognized that his own country had become a reactionary world power through its arrogance of power.

44. Martin Luther King Jr., "A Time to Break Silence" (address at Riverside Church, New York City, April 4, 1967), in *A Testament of Hope: The Essential Writings and Speeches of Martin Luther King Jr.*, ed. James M. Washington (New York: HarperCollins, 1991), 231–44, quote on 242; Stone, "An Interview with Reinhold Niebuhr," 48–49 ("to the partnership"); Niebuhr, "Toward New Intra-Christian Endeavors," 1662–63 ("While I do not share"); see Niebuhr, "Barth's East German Letter," *Christian Century* 76 (February 11, 1959): 167–68.

"The Path Is Meant to Be Well Worn": Reflections on Full Communion in the Cold War

Frederick R. Trost

The year was 1979. The Cold War was roaring on. A delegation from the United Church of Christ in the United States (UCC) was visiting congregations and diaconal ministries in the German Democratic Republic (GDR). We met with friends we had come to know at the Deaconess Home in Dessau. Issues of disarmament were being discussed. A turning point in the conversation took place when a young woman observed that the church enters society with empty hands. "When the love of Christ is seen in our lives," she said, "the world may come to trust the message of God on our lips." She reminded us all that "full communion" between churches in East and West involves "word and deed." Not long afterward, near the site of an old monastery a few miles west of Berlin, an assistant pastor stood at the communion table as celebrant. With the communion bread in one hand and a chalice in the other, he spoke to the congregation: "We live our faith between this table where we meet Christ in bread and wine, and (pointing to a large crucifix at the far end of the nave) that cross, where we meet Christ again in the sufferings of the world. Our faith is a continuing movement; a pilgrimage between this table where we are forgiven, and the cross where we meet the risen Lord in the crucifixions of our time. The path is meant to be well worn."

In the 1970s, "full communion" between the Evangelical Church of the Union (EKU) in divided Germany and the UCC in the United States was developing momentum. Since the 1960s, many pastors and members of UCC congregations had engaged in nonviolent resistance to the wars in Vietnam and Cambodia. In both the GDR and the Federal Republic of Germany (FRG), dialogue between church and state was taking place in relation to compulsory military service, conscientious objection to war, nuclear deterrence, and disarmament.[1]

1. See, for example, the text of the Heidelberg Theses, composed in the late 1950s, which

Robert V. Moss, who was elected president of the UCC at a General Synod held in Boston in 1969, expressed the view early on that "In our kind of world, war has become dysfunctional." He urged the church "to put as much effort into defining a just peace as we have done in the past in defining a just war."[2]

This commitment was present in the UCC from its founding in 1957.[3] The EKU (in the GDR and the FRG) seemed to the UCC an almost perfect ecumenical partner abroad. The EKU in both countries felt the same way. Theology and heritage had linked them all together for generations. The EKU was a "united church" rooted in both the Lutheran and the Reformed traditions, as was much of the UCC. An abiding commitment to mission and to diaconal ministries was held in common. Numerous benevolent institutions in the UCC traced their roots and their inspiration to Germany and to the daring work of people like Philipp Jakob Spener, August Hermann Francke, Friedrich von Bodelschwingh, and others. At the time of the Cold War, German services were still being held in some of the former Evangelical and Reformed congregations in the United States, and hymnody was often inspired by some of the great German poets and musicians born in Germany. The faculties of several UCC-related seminaries included professors who received at least a portion of their academic training after World War II in places like Heidelberg, Tübingen, and Göttingen. Frederick Herzog, deeply involved in a commitment to "sound teaching" in the UCC and to North American "liberation theology," received his early theological education at the former Confessing Church seminary at Wuppertal in the Rhineland. Pastors were familiar with at least some of the writings of people like Gerhard von Rad, Claus Westermann, Günther Bornkamm, Dorothee Soelle, Jürgen Moltmann, and others. The writings of Dietrich Bonhoeffer and his resistance to idolatry were widely admired in the UCC. As early as 1936, central figures in the daring witness of the Confessing Church in Germany such as Martin Niemöller, Gerhard Jacobi, and Otto Dibelius had been awarded honorary degrees from Eden Theological Seminary. A member of the Eden faculty, Carl Schneider, was present to monitor the proceedings against Niemöller in Berlin the following year, keeping his faculty apprised. The initial publication of five thousand copies of Bonhoeffer's *Ethics*,

---

states (among other things) that "War must be abolished in a lasting and forward-moving effort" and that the church should begin to understand "the renunciation of weapons as a Christian action."

2. For the best account of the early commitment of the UCC to "just peace," see Susan A. Thistlethwaite, *A Just Peace Church* (Cleveland: United Church Press, 1986).

3. The union of the Evangelical and Reformed Church and the Congregational Christian Churches to form the United Church of Christ took place in June 1957.

edited by Eberhard Bethge, was made possible in the late 1940s by a gift from the Evangelical and Reformed Church.[4]

One could go on and on. The point is that there were many reasons the UCC and the EKU would reach out to embrace one another as the Cold War, with all its contradictions of the gospel of Christ, began to cast doubt on the future of the world. A dedication to world peace and justice is reflected in the UCC "Statement of Faith," which was affirmed by the General Synod in 1959: "God calls us into the church to accept the cost and joy of discipleship, to be servants in the service of the whole human family, to proclaim the gospel to all the world and resist the powers of evil. . . . God promises to all who trust in the gospel forgiveness of sins and fullness of grace, courage in the struggle for justice and peace, the presence of the Holy Spirit in trial and rejoicing." Significantly, at about the time this statement was affirmed, the UCC Council for Christian Social Action published its "Call to Christian Action in Society." The "call" stated in part that "God, as revealed in Jesus Christ, is the ruler of all human affairs—nations, social orders, institutions. To Him belong our souls and bodies, our possessions and cultures, our churches and communities. . . . We call upon our churches and their members to pray and work: for peace, justice, and the welfare of all nations and peoples; . . . [a] deeper awareness of the problems, legitimate interests and fears of other peoples, . . . [and] effective international control and reduction of all national armaments, including the testing of nuclear weapons."[5]

As the Cold War continued, Bishop Albrecht Schönherr and Bishop Werner Krusche, among others, were urging Christians in the GDR not to neglect the necessity of peacemaking.[6] Shortly before "full communion" between the EKU (East) and the UCC was initially voted on in 1980, they were asking the churches how Christians can "respond to the task of peace responsibly, in faithfulness to the Gospel, as a partner in the ecumenical community . . . and as a servant of the people." They called the churches to consult together on the issues, including ratification of the SALT II treaty. They requested "bilateral

---

4. This gift was mentioned by Reinhard Groscurth, retired ecumenical officer of the EKU (West), during a speech he gave in Magdeburg in 2011, as one of several impulses that helped lay the groundwork for the affirmation by the EKU of full communion with the UCC.

5. See Frederick R. Trost and Barbara Brown Zikmund, eds., *The Living Theological Heritage of the United Church of Christ*, vol. 7 (Cleveland: Pilgrim Press, 2005), 80–85.

6. Albrecht Schönherr, bishop of Berlin-Brandenburg, had been a student of Dietrich Bonhoeffer at the underground seminary of the Confessing Church at Finkenwalde. In 1980, he was serving as chairman of the Federation of Evangelical Churches in the GDR. Werner Krusche, a thoughtful and generous pastoral theologian, was then serving as bishop of the Evangelical Church Province of Sachsen.

political contacts in the spirit of détente," especially between the chairman of the Council of State in the GDR, Erich Honecker, and FRG chancellor Helmut Schmidt. "Our contribution will consist concretely of our making paths visible which the Gospel opens and which are often forgotten in political action." Their "Declaration on the Current World Political Situation," issued January 22, 1980, contained ten points and began by stating:

> The Federation of Evangelical Churches in the GDR observes the current development with great concern. The churches of the Federation are convinced that thoughtful political action on all sides must have priority in the situation which has developed. As a communion of churches which serves on the boundaries between the two great power blocs in the heart of Europe, the Federation repeats and reinforces its conviction (stated many times in recent years) that for the sake of world peace there is no reasonable alternative to the policy of détente. The Federation knows that many other churches in the ecumenical community agree with this. The security of the nations can be guaranteed only in a climate of trust and cooperation. The most recent ecumenical discussion on peace and disarmament reinforces this perception.[7]

In earlier discussions between Schönherr and Honecker, the government of the GDR acknowledged the church as a "viable force" in East German society. Chairman Honecker appeared to accept the church's commitment to peace and détente among the nations. The talks led to an easing, for the moment, of some of the tension between church and state and opened the door to in-depth discussions about the military's engagement with the security of the state, peace education in the public schools, the militarization of the country, and mutual disarmament, which included nuclear weapons. Honecker and the government were at this time very sensitive to how the GDR was being perceived abroad. The long-standing and deepening relationship with the UCC played a significant role in this.[8]

---

7. The complete text of this declaration can be found in Barbara A. Heck, "Grass Grows beyond the Wall: Witnessing for Peace in GDR Evangelical Churches" (senior honors thesis, University of Wisconsin, May 1984).

8. Among the early advocates of an "anchor in the West" during the Cold War were Bishop Hans Joachim Fränkel of the Church Province of Goerlitz and Ernst-Eugen Meckel, ecumenical officer of the EKU (East), whose commitment to deepening ecumenical relations abroad and personal friendships with UCC leadership helped prepare the way for the affirmation of full communion between the EKU and the UCC in 1980 and 1981.

The first "official" UCC delegation admitted to the GDR with the permission of the state took place in 1973. This followed the General Synod held in Grand Rapids, Michigan, in 1971, in which the delegates turned a great deal of their attention to the issue of war and peace.[9] The delegates agreed that in the next several years, the UCC should have among its priorities a commitment to the exploration of "peace and the United States power: enabling U.S. power to serve humane needs and contribute to world peace." Howard Schomer, Europe secretary of the UCC Board for World Ministries at the time, advocated a plan to deepen relationships between the UCC and the "East bloc" states. This began with a visit of East German theologians to the United States in the spring of 1972. It was followed that summer with UCC representatives visiting the GDR, Czechoslovakia, and Hungary. The initial purpose was to learn together "how to be a more creative Christian in a Marxist or a capitalist land today." Among the delegates who came to the United States from the GDR (at the invitation of the UCC and the United Presbyterian Church, USA) was the president of the Evangelical (Reformed) Church in Anhalt (GDR), Eberhard Natho. He helped set the tone in an address entitled "Reconciliation," in which he said: "Our calling remains to embrace the reconciling work of Christ in the realities of social and political life, while engaged in listening and learning in communion with one another—how we better proclaim in the broken world God's love, and bear witness to it in life . . . freed by the gospel . . . (that) more peace and more justice and more humanity become possible."[10]

This was the beginning of a journey that reflected Schomer's intention and the desire of the General Synod that "an international network of Christians working for peace" on both sides of the "dividing wall of hostility" engage one another "with open eyes, open ears and open minds, . . . while on their knees in gratitude for the gospel of peace and the ministry of reconciliation." In November 1973, President Robert Moss and a small delegation of church leaders from the UCC were welcomed by the EKU. The delegation, accompanied by Natho and Meckel, was received by the Secretary of State for Church Questions in the GDR and, in the course of ten days, visited communities of faith in all five of the EKU regional churches. Moss became the first US

9. Among the resolutions passed at Grand Rapids was an expression of profound gratitude to Philip Berrigan, then in prison for an act of civil disobedience in resistance to the Vietnam War.

10. The most complete account of this and other developments related to full communion between the UCC and the EKU and a mutual search for a way to theological understanding, genuine *koinōnia*, disarmament, and peace is contained in a remarkable book by Elga Zachau, *Gemeinsames Anliegen: Gerechtigkeit* (Neukirchen-Vluyn: Neukirchener Verlag, 2009).

theologian officially permitted to preach in the GDR. He did so at St. Nikolai Church in Greifswald on November 11, 1972, and at St. Mary's Church on Alexanderplatz in East Berlin on November 19, 1972. His theme was "What Is the Role of the Church of Jesus Christ in a Time of Great Cultural and Radical Change?" His critique of governmental policy toward the church and society in the GDR, given as part of a speech in Milwaukee in December 1973, led to complications in relations between the church and the state in the GDR, which were eventually overcome.[11] Additional delegations were sent to and from the UCC and the EKU during the 1970s, and continuing to the time of the "Velvet Revolution" in 1989.[12]

By 1975, momentum toward the establishment of full communion between the UCC and the EKU had developed significantly. The dialogue was enriched by conversations held in Toronto at the Third Ecumenical Consultation of United Churches, in which Robert Moss and Reinhard Groscurth urged deeper relations and a common witness among the churches. This picked up the Schomer initiatives. Momentum toward full communion and dialogue between the UCC and the EKU on theology and the issues of war, peace, and disarmament continued. While on sabbatical leave in Tübingen in 1975, M. Douglas Meeks, professor of Christian theology at Eden Theological Seminary, was a guest at several centers of theological education in the GDR. Conversations took place with Meckel and with the gifted Groscurth, who had served on the staff of the World Council of Churches. He had also been a theological student in Ohio. They continued preparations for an "official visit" of UCC theologians to the GDR in 1976. Meckel, Groscurth, and Schomer, with support from a "fraternal worker" in Berlin, UCC pastor Peter Meister, and the well-informed Christa Grengel, who was active in vital ways with the EKU (East) in Berlin, planned the journey, which was approved by educational officials in the government of the GDR.[13] Meeks and a professor of Christian ethics at Andover Newton Theological School, Max Stackhouse, were issued invitations. They are believed to have been the first academics from the United States allowed to lecture and engage in conversations with faculties

11. See Zachau, *Gemeinsames Anliegen Gerechtigkeit*, 55–70.

12. The first exchange delegation from the EKU to the UCC took place in October/November 1963. The first exchange delegation from the UCC to the EKU occurred in July 1964 and was led by UCC president Ben Herbster. The dedication and vision of Harold Wilkie and Ferdinand Schilingensiepen of the EKU gave birth to these exchanges, which were vital to the formation of Kirchengemeinschaft or full communion.

13. Grengel and Groscurth would later be recipients of honorary degrees from Eden Seminary.

and students in seminaries in the GDR since the building of the Berlin Wall in August 1961. Their assignment was to "assess educational institutions from congregations to universities . . . and submit a report to the Council of Bishops in Berlin" at the end of their journey. There was a further purpose: to establish "a deeper relation between the UCC and the EKU (East)." Privately, Meckel expressed his conviction to Meeks that "a deeper relationship with the UCC was the best opportunity and maybe the only one (because of historical and doctrinal reasons) for the EKU (East) to have a viable opening to the Oikoumene and, obviously, to the geopolitical situation." There was agreement that the study trip should explore the questions, How can the EKU (East) be a faithful church in a socialist country? and, How can the UCC be a faithful church in a capitalist country? As the journey commenced, Meeks and Stackhouse were quickly engaged by faculty, students, and church leaders in difficult questions about Vietnam, militarism, race, poverty, and other issues that were boiling over in the United States. Meeks has written that "these 'two-way questions' led us beyond the expected political stances to ask about the real freedom of the gospel" and thus about "the deepest theological realities" in both countries.[14] This would be among the factors that would lead to the deepening of a quest for "sound teaching" in the UCC and its relationship to public witness that took hold soon thereafter.[15]

Along the way, a seminar composed of UCC pastors and teachers began to meet in 1976, resulting in the publication of a document entitled "Towards the Task of Sound Teaching in the UCC." Its "Liberation Affirmation," significantly influenced by the Barmen Declaration of 1934, made a deep impression on many, both in the UCC and in the EKU. "Faithful teaching excludes the

14. Meeks recently wrote in a personal letter to me that "The strong experience of faith and hope and perseverance among countless people" caused him and Stackhouse to believe this was a gift they wanted "to bring back to the UCC and was one of the reasons [we] felt a more structured relationship between the two churches would be as salutary to the UCC as to the EKU. . . . I think both Stackhouse and I would say that our teaching and research were deeply changed and resourced by the trip."

15. Probst Heino Falcke of Erfurt continued the discussion related to "sound/binding teaching" by traveling to the United States in 1979 to meet with Meeks and Stackhouse, Frederick Herzog, and others. Later, in 1985, these visits were reciprocated with a "visitation" at several UCC-related seminaries by Professors Lothar Schreiner of the theological faculty at Wuppertal, Johannes Althausen of the Paulinum in East Berlin, Raimund Hoenen of Naumburg, and Traugott Staehlin of Bethel. Through the deepening friendships that emerged and the substantive dialogue that took place, a firm foundation was built for what would lead to full communion, with its commitment not only to theological substance but also to an authentic witness for peace.

unsound teaching that God is on our side, that of a rich and powerful nation. The meaning of life does not consist of a national defense of wealth, but of struggling with God for justice among all peoples. . . . Faithful teaching excludes the unsound teaching that the church can transform the nation when it allows itself to be co-opted by the powers that be. Attacked by increasing secularism in our Western nations, the church is called to be in constant conflict in various ways with principalities and powers that legitimate injustice."[16] The focus throughout the 1970s on theological substance and the public witness to peace in a world in which the idolization of the "gods of metal" was being challenged and often rebuked by the church deepened confidence in full communion. In August 1979, a statement by the Conference of Evangelical Churches in the GDR, published in *Kirche im Sozialismus*, reflected the mutual concerns of the church in East and West: "Dealing with the disarmament question for Christians and the church must be placed in the context of faith in God's creating, redeeming, and perfect action with people and humanity. At the same time there is the fundamental thought that God wants human life and not its destruction. Contrary to the opinion that the church's dealing with disarmament problems is an inappropriate question, we should recall that the Gospel's promise of peace covenants Christians and the church to commitment here and now for the necessary and possible peace. From this covenant arises a specific identity and legitimation of the church's action for disarmament."[17]

The EKU (East) Synod met at the Sprachenkonvikt (preaching seminary) in East Berlin, May 16–18, 1980. Albrecht Schönherr and Christa Grengel were present, of course, and their urging of full communion with the UCC was vital to its passing. Theological issues were a significant part of the discussion, but equally important was the eagerness of the church in the East to relate in teaching and witness to the church in the West, as Meckel had envisioned.[18] "The oneness of the Body of Christ," Bishop Schönherr said, "is a gift we must claim. Where there is a common understanding of the meaning of the gospel, the nature of the sacraments, and love of neighbor, full communion already

16. See the complete text published in Frederick Herzog, *Justice Church: The New Function of the Church in North American Christianity* (Maryknoll, NY: Orbis, 1980), 141–54. The significance of this document is reflected in the fact that shortly after it was published by the UCC Office for Church Life and Leadership, the text was translated into German and became fairly widely read, discussed, and debated among laity and clergy in the EKU.

17. "Erziehung zum Frieden," Bund der Evangelischen Kirchen in der DDR, August 24, 1979.

18. He did not live to see it, having died in retirement in 1977.

exists." The proposal related to full communion passed by the synod included four statements:

1. The Evangelical Church of the Union has on numerous occasions confirmed its intention to nurture and deepen its relationship to the united and uniting churches.
2. The Evangelical Church of the Union notes gratefully that there has been practiced and there has grown between the EKU and the United Church of Christ in twenty years of dialogue, mutual visits, and concerted theological work, full communion, as elaborated by the Ecumenical Commission.
3. The Evangelical Church of the Union sees neither theological nor legal grounds that would prevent full church communion between the EKU and the UCC. It is ready to acknowledge baptism, Holy Communion, and ministry of the United Church of Christ.
4. The Synod is hopeful and expectant that through continuing theological dialogue regarding our common understanding of the gospel, communion between the EKU and the UCC will deepen and that concrete steps on the pilgrimage to a yet stronger communion will be taken.

With the words "We are called to a common ministry of reconciliation to the world," full communion with the UCC was affirmed. Having heard the news, UCC president Avery D. Post sent a telegram to the delegates from a meeting of the UCC Ecumenical Council in New York City, in which he wrote: "We are keenly aware of the high risk of your present effort to stitch back together the fabric of the Body of Christ . . . and we admire your courage." Several weeks later, the EKU (West) passed a similar proposal following deep and probing discussions. "God's Word," it said, "clearly taught, disenthralls us from our captivity to national chauvinism or private occupations. Struggling for justice and peace in facing the world's poor, we forget ourselves and thus find ourselves as a people and as persons in new community."

The following year, at the UCC General Synod in Rochester, New York, in June 1981, a proposal titled "Toward a Covenant in Mission and Faith" was presented to more than seven hundred delegates from UCC congregations across the United States. The proposal celebrated the global partnerships of the UCC, grateful for the church's unity in Christ. It affirmed the deepening relationship with the EKU, acknowledging full communion as an opportunity to help one another "respond to the world's cry for justice and peace." The proposal urged the UCC Council for Ecumenism to develop with the UCC Office for Church and Society and with the EKU strategies for witness in common tasks of justice and peacemaking for the whole world. At this same synod, "the traditional stand of the UCC [which] has called for its members to be peacemakers and to work diligently for justice, human rights, and peace within the family of nations" resulted in a vote to become a "peace church."[19]

The commitment to full communion between the UCC and the EKU (East and West) had to do with the shadows of Auschwitz and the frightening reality of faith lived for the first time ever beneath an ominous and frightening nuclear cloud. Living in full communion in the 1980s was an act of faith and a witness to reconciliation amidst the militarization of much of the world, with vast amounts of money poured into the arms industry. It was an attempt by the UCC to make sense of events that had assaulted its soul since the union of 1957. It had to do with the secularization of society and with disillusion and the numbness of continuing violence. But it also was a summons for the UCC to lift up its heart with longing for a sane and peaceful world, to embrace a vision that, though often hanging by a thread, could not be allowed to disappear. It had to do with crucifixion and resurrection.

Following the synods of 1980 and 1981, full communion led to a series of theological colloquies in the EKU and the UCC in which representatives of both churches were engaged. The first, "Sound/Binding Teaching in the Face of Problems of Church in Society," was held at Berlin-Weissensee in June 1980. The second, "Peace as a Priority Issue/The Challenge of Peace," took place at Iserlohn, Westphalia, in June and early July 1982. The third, "Reformation Theology and Its Meaning for Today," convened at Erfurt, GDR, in June 1983. The fourth, "Consultation on Peacemaking for United Churches in Different Cultural and Social Contexts," occurred in Washington, DC, in June 1984. The fifth, "Accountable Teaching, Theological Education, Catechism, and the Life of the Church," assembled at Green Lake, Wisconsin, in October 1993. In addition, there was a series of consultations begun in January 1988 at Iserlohn and continuing in seven locations in the UCC in October 1988, and again in Erfurt in August 1989. These consultations were called a "Consultation in Process." Each was unique, but all were related to issues of justice, economics, and peace, including an attempt to understand the righteousness of God in the nuclear age.

---

19. See Thistlethwaite, *A Just Peace Church*. She notes that the "original wording of the resolution called upon the United Church of Christ to declare itself a pacifist church." "Two years later . . . the words peace church were a source of concern, and a resolution on the floor was amended to read 'peacemaking church.'"

The development of theological colloquies in the UCC was inspired in part by the work of Fritzhermann Keienburg, who directed the Evangelical Academy at Iserlohn. He was an early advocate of peacemaking during the Cold War and of ecumenical dialogue and full communion. Over a period of twenty-five years, beginning in 1977, his example at Iserlohn and, later, that of Hans Berthold, dean of the Institute for Continuing Education and Pastoral Studies at Schwerte, Westphalia, contributed to the convening of over one hundred theological convocations in the UCC, devoted to sound teaching and the witness of the church, and held in various parts of the United States.[20]

The 1982 colloquy at Iserlohn ("Peace as a Priority Issue") lasted nearly a week. It was convened at a time when more sophisticated weapons were arriving in the FRG from the United States as part of the Cold War. Attended by pastors and laity from the UCC and the EKU, it resulted in the "Iserlohn Appeal," which was addressed to the churches in East and West. Composed of seven brief sections, it stated in part:

> It is God's will that there be life on this planet. We affirm, therefore, our belief that the use of nuclear weapons and weapons of mass destruction, in military and political form, is a sin against God. . . . We urge NATO not to deploy the new Cruise and Pershing II missiles in Europe. We urge NATO and the Warsaw Pact to develop agreements on nuclear weapons and further disarmament, including the SS-20 in Europe. We urge the Congress of the United States to reverse its decision to produce chemical weapons. We urge all nations to abandon the deadly course of atomic, biological and chemical weapons. We urge the United States, the USSR and other powers to place a moratorium on the development, construction and deployment of all weapons of mass destruction as a necessary step towards the complete disarmament. We urge all governments to venture for peace and to forge new agreements in order to bring an end to the arms race and build a foundation for a lasting peace. . . . We rejoice in the gift of Kirchengemeinschaft/

20. One of these, exploring the thought of Karl Barth, took place in 1986 in the Wisconsin Conference of the UCC. Led by Professor M. Douglas Meeks and Professor Eugene Wehrli of Eden Theological Seminary, it resulted in the formation of a pastoral seminar that met monthly for the next twenty-five years. After a quarter-century, the seminar completed its study of all thirteen volumes of Barth's *Church Dogmatics*, and began again. It continues to this day and has resulted in the formation of other seminars that have focused on the thought of John Calvin, a number of feminist theologians, and Dietrich Bonhoeffer and their importance to the life and witness of the church in the twenty-first century.

Full Communion/Full Community between the United Church of Christ and the Evangelical Church of the Union, and share a common hope that the cornerstone of this ecumenical adventure shall remain the One who has broken down "the dividing wall of hostility" and called us into the service of reconciliation.[21]

A few months prior to the gathering at Iserlohn, and following the Krefeld Appeal, a petition appearing in the FRG that protested the deployment of US missiles in West Germany and was signed by more than one million people, Pastor Rainer Eppelmann, an EKU pastor in East Berlin, along with thirty-two others, issued "The Berlin Appeal" (January 25, 1982). It urged an end to the deployment of nuclear missiles in Europe (the SS-20 in the GDR and the Pershing II in the FRG). The words of the appeal expressed a breathless urgency and rang with prophetic fire:

There is only one kind of war which could take place in Europe, a nuclear war. The weapons stockpiled in East and West will not protect us but annihilate us. . . . For that reason, if we want to live—away with all weapons. First: away with nuclear weapons . . . ! A divided Germany has become the deployment area for the two nuclear superpowers. We propose an end to this life-endangering confrontation. The victors of World War II should finally negotiate peace treaties with both German states. . . . Thereafter, the former Allies should withdraw their occupation troops from Germany and agree on a policy of non-intervention in the internal affairs of the two German states. . . . Make peace without weapons. . . . The balance of terror has prevented nuclear war up to now only by postponing it until tomorrow.

Rainer Eppelmann was arrested by the state two weeks later and questioned for several days until released through the intervention of the EKU (East).

In 1985, the UCC General Synod passed a pronouncement that affirmed the United Church of Christ as a "just peace church." It placed the synod "in opposition to the institution of war." The pronouncement linked peace with justice. In its "Statement of Conviction," it described "just peace" as "the presence and interrelation of friendship, justice, and common security from violence" and as "a basic gift of God." It urged the UCC to hear "the voices of the oppressed" and stated that war "can and must be eliminated." It called

21. For the complete text of this document, see Frederick R. Trost, *We Know Only in Part: Reflections on a Journey in Faith* (Minneapolis: Kirk House Publishers, 2004), 105–10.

upon the United Nations to develop "peacekeeping forces . . . to police border disputes and the formation of peace-making teams, trained in mediation, conflict intervention, and conflict resolution," and to form "peace academies" and "international agreements to limit military establishments and the international arms trade," as well as to impose "an international ban on the development, testing, use, and possession of nuclear and biochemical weapons of mass destruction [and] an international ban on all weapons in space." It rejected "any use [of] or threat to use weapons and forces of mass destruction and any doctrine of deterrence based primarily on using such weapons," and encouraged a "mutual and verifiable freeze on the testing, production, and deployment of nuclear weapons as the most important step in breaking the escalating dynamics of the arms race."[22]

In many places in the UCC, the message was heard. During these years, the church was active on various fronts related to the issues of armament and the military. Among the resolutions, pronouncements, and proposals for action affirmed by the UCC General Synod were votes taken in relation to the following: nuclear disarmament, chemical warfare, the Middle East arms race, support for the US Catholic Bishops' "Pastoral Letter concerning Nuclear Armaments and the Arms Race," the impact of the US military policy in Central America, war tax resistance, the development of space weaponry, peace in Afghanistan, US overt and covert military intervention around the world, the elimination of nuclear forces in Europe, and US military aid to El Salvador.

In the Pennsylvania Central Conference, for example, a Peace Partner Ministry was formed. This resulted in an invitation to Uwe Dittmer, a pastor in the EKU (East), to serve as an ambassador of peace and reconciliation in congregations of the conference. The conference joined with the EKU in observing the *Friedensdekade* (Ten Days of Peace) with prayers composed for liturgies in German and in English. The *Friedensdekade* was an idea that emerged in the GDR following the synods of 1980. It resulted in services of prayer and in discussions about peace, disarmament, and reconciliation among Protestants and Catholics. This would eventually contribute to the "Velvet Revolution" of November 1989. In 1988, the Peace Academy of the conference made available a "peace candle" to all congregations to "remind us of the power of prayer in bringing God's peace to our weary and troubled world."[23] Not long after the

22. For the complete text, see Thistlethwaite, *A Just Peace Church*, 133–48.

23. It was Robert Hunsicker, a member of the UCC-EKU Working Group, along with another member of the working group, Clara Rader, and her husband, William Rader, and Erika Erskine Lauffer, a Presbyterian peace advocate, who guided the peace ministry in the

Berlin Wall collapsed in November 1989, perplexed officials of the government of the GDR are said to have exclaimed: "We forgot about the candles."

Among the emblems of the "Peace Decade" was a cloth badge that depicted a person beating a sword into a plowshare. Young people in the GDR sewed this badge into their clothing as a sign of hope, resistance, and determination in the search for peace. While initially accepted by the government, the badge soon became a source of controversy in the GDR, with the state insisting that "peace must be defended." Those wearing the badge were often harassed by the police. Teachers began requiring their students to tear the badge from their clothing. Many refused. The model was nurtured nonetheless in the regional churches of the EKU, and it also developed in several conferences of the UCC. In a dreadful time of endless warfare, of military technology never before known to humankind, of brutality beyond belief, a time of contempt for human life and the devastation of the innocent, a time when we are tempted by "cheap grace" and the sweetening of the message entrusted to us, will the church East and West, North and South, be able to regain its voice? Surely this is a legitimate and necessary question.

Are we capable of re-formation and of engaging the "powers and principalities" of our time with the gospel of peace? Have we the courage to confront the lies and arrogance that mark so much of our national dialogue? Are we willing to study our texts, to bend our knees to say our prayers, to respond to the One who continues to call us to faith, hope, and love? What shall we say? What shall we think? What shall we do? What shall we make of the wilting of the soul and the grinding assault on humane instincts in a society that so often appears indifferent to the contradictions of the gospel many of us learned when we were children? What shall we make of the descent into hell we observe taking place around us? What shall we do with the burning wish to get away from it all, to retreat to places of safety, to hide our eyes from what is now taking place in our name?

I shall always remember an encounter with a group of children that took place in the GDR years before the Velvet Revolution. Our meeting was in the village of Osterburg in the Altmark. The children came to meet me in the pastor's garden the day before I was scheduled to preach in the modest and beautiful Romanesque church that was home to the congregation of St. Nikolai, a church that dates from the thirteenth century. It was a Saturday in springtime, and the surrounding countryside was coming alive. The children carried peo-

---

conference during the 1980s and beyond. This model was nurtured in the regional churches of the EKU and in several conferences of the UCC.

nies (*Pfingstrosen* in German—"roses of Pentecost"). They offered the flowers to me as a sign of welcome. Then they lifted their voices together and sang several beautiful hymns they had carefully rehearsed and learned by heart. Outside the village, in the distance, beyond the ancient city wall, could be heard another sound: military vehicles and troops going through their weekend training exercises. I have always remembered the contrast. The children singing, waving good-bye and saying, "We'll see you in the morning." I reentered the parsonage, filled with a sense of wonder. On one of the walls in the hallway there was a small, glass picture frame that contained two simple words: *Jesus lebt!* ("Jesus lives!"). The flowers, the children's songs, and those two words captured for me the deep relevance and meaning of full communion in the face of resistance, the threat of war, the reality of struggles, and the many tears that flow from one generation to the next. It was people along the way to full communion who taught many of us in the UCC about living the faith we profess in the shadow of the cross and in the light of Easter.

Howard Thurman, Martin Luther King Jr., the Cold War, the Civil Rights Movement, and Postwar Liberal Black Protestantism

PETER EISENSTADT

The Cold War and the civil rights movement are destined to forever cohabit, somewhat uneasily, the same historical space. To give some particulars: On May 17, 1954, the US Supreme Court handed down its epochal decision in *Brown v. Board of Education*. On June 9, at the climactic moment of the Senate hearings investigating the army, Joseph V. Welch said to Senator Joseph Mc-Carthy, "At long last, sir, have you no sense of decency?"—a rebuke that finally began to break McCarthy's hold over American politics. But this hardly ended the Cold War. On June 27, left-leaning Jacobo Arbenz resigned as president of Guatemala after being toppled in a CIA-planned and -sponsored coup. And the civil rights movement continued as well. On September 1, Martin Luther King Jr. assumed the pastorate of the Dexter Avenue Baptist Church in Montgomery, Alabama.

The question of the relation of the Cold War to the civil rights movement has much exercised historians and other observers. Many have argued that the Cold War and the anti-Communism it engendered transformed the nascent civil rights movement. Some argue that it provided an impetus, the competition of American "democracy" against Soviet tyranny, but at a steep price: the destruction of the Communist and near-Communist Left and the de-emphasis of labor and industrial democracy issues, diluting the movement's militancy and putting it into the hands of ministers rather than union officials or political activists. Furthermore, the black Protestant ministers who emerged as the central figures in this fight, epitomized by Martin Luther King Jr., they argue, refashioned the cause of civil rights in a way that appealed to Cold War sensibilities.[1]

1. For accounts of the impact of the Cold War on the civil rights movement, see Gerald Horne, *Black and Red: W. E. B. Du Bois and the Afro-American Response to the Cold War, 1944–1963* (Albany: SUNY Press, 1986); Mary L. Dudziak, *Cold War Civil Rights: Race and*

The Cold War, and its domestic and international ramifications, clearly provided a background, context, and pretext for the civil rights movement. But to dismiss black liberal Protestantism in the 1940s and 1950s as simply another species of Cold War liberalism is to underestimate the complexity of its distinctive politics and to overestimate the impact of the Cold War upon it. It was non-Communist rather than anti-Communist, though any sympathy with the Soviet Union's broader social and racial goals stopped well short of fellow traveling. Its basic political stance, the belief in Gandhian nonviolence as the essential lever of social change, was a "third way," which was far more the sum of triangulated Cold War ideologies. Its adherents believed in the "American creed" as outlined by Gunnar Myrdal. But it wasn't entirely clear to them whether the United States or the Soviet Union would do a better job in realizing it.[2]

Although he was not the originator of this distinctive school of civil rights thought, Martin Luther King Jr. was certainly its best-known advocate. Many of King's biographers have argued that King moved on a trajectory from "non-ideological pragmatism" in his earlier years to a more fully expressed radicalism after 1965. Although there are elements of truth in this, it underplays King's interest in radical ideas, and Marxism, from the outset.[3]

During his 1949 Christmas vacation, home in Atlanta, back from his second year at Crozier Theological Seminary outside of Philadelphia, King spent much of his spare time reading Karl Marx's *Communist Manifesto* and *Das Kapital*.[4] (Or at least, one suspects, like so many before and since, he at least tried to read *Das Kapital*.) In some notes, written to himself, in 1951, he concluded that "capitalism has seen its best days," and that capitalism "is like a losing football team in the last quarter trying all sorts of tactics to survive."[5] His fiancée, Coretta Scott, remembers him saying around this time that while "he could never be a Communist," neither could he be a "thoroughgoing capitalist." His

---

the *Image of American Democracy* (Princeton: Princeton University Press, 2000); Thomas Borstelmann, *The Cold War and the Color Line* (Cambridge, MA: Harvard University Press, 2001); Martha Biondi, *To Stand and Fight: The Struggle for Civil Rights in Postwar New York City* (Cambridge, MA: Harvard University Press, 2003).

2. Gunnar Myrdal, *An American Dilemma: The Negro Problem and American Democracy* (New York: Harper and Brothers, 1944), 3–6.

3. See the discussion in Thomas F. Jackson, *From Civil Rights to Human Rights: Martin Luther King, Jr., and the Struggle for Social Justice* (Philadelphia: University of Pennsylvania Press, 2007), 1–5.

4. Jackson, *From Civil Rights*, 38.

5. *The Papers of Martin Luther King, Jr.* (hereafter *PMLK*), ed. Clayborne Carson (Berkeley: University of California Press, 1991–), 1:435–36.

father, Martin Luther King Sr., a thoroughgoing capitalist, remembered "sharp exchanges" and worried around this time that his son "was drifting away from the basics of capitalism and Western democracy."[6]

In the summer of 1952, after his first year at Boston University, King gave a sermon on this subject at Ebenezer Baptist Church in Atlanta, his father's pulpit, entitled "The Challenge of Communism to Christianity." The sermon states that Christianity and Communism are incompatible, but that the latter is perhaps a necessary "corrective" to a Christianity that is "passive" and a democracy that is "inert," because Communism seeks to "eliminate racial prejudice" and "transcend the superficialities of race and color."[7]

A good friend who heard King's sermon, the Reverend Melvin Watson, a Baptist minister and professor of philosophy and religion at Morehouse College (King's alma mater), liked it but pushed King to go further. He thought King had misunderstood the differences between the materialism of classical antiquity and Marxist materialism. Watson argues that Marxist materialism is less concerned with explanations of natural phenomena than with how the consciousness of individuals is determined by their relation to the means of production, an idea, Watson wrote King, that is "exceedingly difficult to deny." When King spoke of the oppression of religion in Russia, Watson claimed, he needed to recognize how tyrannical the hold of the Russian Orthodox Church had been.[8]

But Watson's major point to King was that he had underestimated the extent to which the abolition of racism had been a major policy goal of the Soviet Union. It was Stalin, Watson wrote King, who "wrote into the Soviet Constitution the proposition that makes the treatment of persons on the basis of race a *national* offense for the Soviets, and it was he who argued that the Soviet Union would make a strong appeal to the nations of the East—India, Japan, China, et al.—if she established the reputation of dealing with all races on the basis of equality. . . . I think there can be no doubt about it that the appeal of communism in the eastern nations today can be traceable to a large degree to the Soviet attitude toward race. This is a strategic policy with Russia."[9]

Watson was referring to article 123 of the Soviet Constitution, adopted in 1936, sometimes known as the Stalin constitution, which (allegedly) guaran-

---

6. *PMLK*, 2:14.

7. *PMLK*, 6:146–50. In *Stride towards Freedom: The Montgomery Story* (New York: Harper and Row, 1958), 95, King expresses himself similarly, saying that Marxism and capitalism are both "partial truths." See also Martin Luther King Jr., "How Should a Christian View Communism?," in *Strength to Love* (New York: Harper and Row, 1963), 93–100.

8. *PMLK*, 2:156–57.

9. *PMLK*, 2:156–57.

teed "equality of rights of citizens of the USSR, irrespective of their nationality or race, in all spheres of economic, state, cultural, social, and political life," and outlawed "any direct or indirect restriction of their rights" or "any advocacy of racial or national exclusiveness or hatred or contempt."[10]

This was truly a remarkable law to place in a national constitution, far in advance of anything in American law. Whether or not it was at all honored in the Soviet Union was another question entirely, but many African American Protestant liberals were, at the least, impressed by its ambition. King's response to Watson, if any, is unknown, but both men thought that Marxism and Communism had something crucial to contribute to America's racial debate, and said so at the height of the era of McCarthyism. Watson and King were hardly alone among liberal black Protestant religious thinkers in the late 1940s and early 1950s in thinking that there were admirable aspects of the Soviet Union. More precisely, when it came to the treatment of racial minorities, an area in which the United States had so abjectly and repeatedly failed, it was entirely plausible to think that the Soviet Union might be doing a better job. In the same year as King's sermon, both Morehouse president Benjamin Mays and Howard University president Mordecai Wyatt Johnson praised Stalin and the Soviet Union for their strides in overcoming racism and poverty.[11]

A key mentor and spiritual influence for both King and Watson was Howard Thurman.[12] Thurman was Watson's most important intellectual and spiritual influence and adviser. Thurman had known King from his earliest years, and by the time of King's 1952 address, King had already read and quoted (without attribution, as was King's wont) one of Thurman's books in a student paper.[13] Thurman was also the first important African American pacifist and an inspiration to several generations of civil rights activists, among them James Farmer (a founder and longtime leader of CORE [Congress of Racial Equality]), Pauli Murray, Barbara Jordan, and many others.[14]

10. For the text of the 1936 Soviet constitution, see https://constitutii.files.wordpress.com/2013/01/1936-en.pdf.

11. Jackson, *From Civil Rights*, 43.

12. For Thurman, see Quinton Dixie and Peter Eisenstadt, *Visions of a Better World: Howard Thurman's Pilgrimage to India and the Origins of African American Nonviolence* (Boston: Beacon Press, 2011), and Walter Earl Fluker, ed., *The Papers of Howard Washington Thurman* (hereafter *PHWT*) (Columbia: University of South Carolina Press, 2009–), passim. (The author of this paper was the associate editor for all the volumes of *PHWT*.)

13. Dixie and Eisenstadt, *Visions of a Better World*, 190–94. For liberal black Protestantism, see Barbara Savage, *Your Spirits Walk Beside Us: The Politics of Black Religion* (Cambridge, MA: Harvard University Press, 2008).

14. Dixie and Eisenstadt, *Visions of a Better World*, 161–64.

Howard Thurman, born in Florida in 1899, a graduate of Morehouse College and Rochester Theological Seminary, was one of the leading African American religious thinkers of his generation. He was professor and dean of chapel at Howard University, in Washington, DC, from 1932 to 1944, but left to become copastor of the Church for the Fellowship for All Peoples in San Francisco, one of the first churches in the United States organized on a consciously and deliberately interracial basis. Thurman rarely spoke about politics, not because he didn't care intensely about politics, but rather because he felt that what was more important was understanding the spiritual mechanics of devotion to a cause. (He also felt that white audiences often wanted to limit black speakers to speaking about racial politics, in a subtle form of stereotyping.)[15]

Even though he didn't always announce his politics from the pulpit, they form an essential context to his religious thinking. By the time he graduated Morehouse, he was a socialist and a pacifist; he continued to identify himself as a socialist throughout the 1930s and probably beyond. In 1935–1936 he served as chair of the Negro Delegation to British India from the American Student Movement; he and two other delegates became the first African Americans to meet with Indian independence leader Mahatma Gandhi; he wrote and spoke extensively on his return on creating an American, Christian-flavored Gandhianism.[16]

Thurman was definitely an interested observer of Communism in the 1930s. In 1935 he called a pro-Communist book by Julius Friedrich Hecker, someone who saw in the Soviet Union the realization of his former Methodist ideals, "scintillating." The book argues that Communism has made older forms of religion obsolete, and that the future Communist society will be "the most favorable environment for the development of a spiritual culture never dreamed of by prophets, sages, or poets."[17] (Unfortunately for Hecker, he was arrested by Stalin's secret police in April 1938 and murdered a few months later.)

Thurman's politics in the late 1930s were at their most radical; he said in 1937 that an individual must "put himself squarely against the possession of all personal property and . . . recognize that it is a thing making for evil in the world and . . . work in all ways for legislation and for public opinion that would

15. For Thurman, see Dixie and Eisenstadt, *Visions of a Better World*, and *PHWT*, passim.

16. For Thurman's Gandhian-inspired writings, see Dixie and Eisenstadt, *Visions of a Better World*, 117–50.

17. Julius F. Hecker, *Religion and Communism: A Study of Religion and Atheism in Soviet Russia* (London: Chapman and Hall, 1933), 273.

make private property impossible."[18] The most puzzling statement of Thurman on Communism in the decade—puzzling because there is nothing else in his work that resembles it—is an article in the *Richmond News-Leader* (a white newspaper) with the headline "Claims Communism Is Help to Church." Thurman states, if he was quoted correctly, "the present program of the Communist in America should be of great value to the organized church."[19] Whether he was being more candid than usual or was being misquoted is difficult to say.

The coming of World War II complicated Thurman's political choices, as it did for so many. As, after 1940, a national vice chairman of the Fellowship of Reconciliation, he watched with some amusement, if that is the right word, as the Communist Party moved from defenders of collective security, to a fervid and newfound opposition to militarism, to the loudest beaters of the war drums, all in the space of two years.[20] As a pacifist, he opposed America's entry into the war and the reinstitution of the draft. And yet, as an African American university minister with many souls of draft age in his care, he felt he could not simply abandon black soldiers in a Jim Crow military, and supported them unstintingly. And whatever his feeling about the war itself, he thought it crucial that black soldiers overcome widespread aspersions and demonstrate their capacity for combat and command positions.[21]

Thurman wrote in 1940 that the American government and white America tended to discover blacks only at times of national emergency. It was only during the last great war, Thurman wrote, "that the Negro became in some way aware of his citizenship." The Negro felt that he counted and that "the future of democracy was dependent on him. For one breathless, swirling moment he became conscious of being a part and parcel of the very core of the nation." But the promise of inclusion was a cruel illusion, snatched away as the war ended in an orgy of rioting against blacks and with no real change to their legal, political, or social status.[22]

World wars concentrate attention. "The simple fact is," Thurman wrote after World War II, "that during the war, we were all involved, men and women,

18. Thurman, "The Significance of Jesus III: Love," in *PHWT*, 2:65. See also Thurman's friendship with Max Yergan, the former African American official of the YMCA in South Africa who left the organization in the mid-1930s, denouncing it as complicit in imperialism and racism, *PHWT*, 2:26–27.

19. *PHWT*, 2:61.

20. *PHWT*, 2:264–65.

21. Thurman to A. J. Muste, September 20, 1940, in *PHWT*, 2:265–66; Thurman to Patricia Van Blarcom, April 17, 1942, in *PHWT*, 2:302

22. Thurman, "A 'Native Son' Speaks," in *PHWT*, 2:246–52.

old and young, rich and poor. It was total war." The country was now "state-centered," focused on victory over the Axis Powers, and almost everything that happened in the country was, in one way or another, related to the war effort.[23] Postwar planning, which began in the United States before the war started, was, for African Americans, particularly pressing. As the war ended, the portents were at best mixed. Blacks had been forced to serve in a segregated, Jim Crowed military, though opposition to this forced the Roosevelt administration to monitor discrimination in the defense industry. However, the monitoring proved rather toothless—perhaps a harbinger of stronger government interventions to come. The wartime economic boom sparked a huge migration of blacks from the South to cities such as San Francisco that often improved the lives of black workers and their families. On the other hand, conditions in northern cities for blacks, if better than the South, still left much to be desired, and their presence exacerbated racial tensions, leading to riots in Detroit, Harlem, and elsewhere. The fight against the Nazis became, for many Americans, a fight against racist ideologies. At the same time, the fight against the Japanese was often seen by Americans in explicitly racial terms, against the "yellow races" of Asia, a rhetoric that, as Thurman noted, was particularly intense in West Coast cities like San Francisco.[24]

Thurman was of two minds. Thurman worried deeply about the ugly racism the war exposed. As Thurman wrote in September 1942, "Grave indeed, is my concern as I watch with mounting concern tension all over the country. I have travelled some thirteen or fourteen thousand miles since early June, and the picture is the same everywhere—sporadic outbreaks of violence, meanness, murder, bloodshed, and a great paralysis in the presence of it all." At the same time, he hoped that the war would bring about a positive change for the status of blacks, and the realization of a more comprehensive and deeper meaning of democracy.[25]

The postwar years would indeed be a period of dramatic change in the political and legal status of black Americans. But what few anticipated in 1945 was that the heyday of the civil rights era, from 1945 to 1970, would coincide with the apogee of the Cold War. The wartime alliance with the Soviet Union would dissolve in fierce acrimony, the Communist movement in the United

---

23. Thurman, "The Quest for Stability" (1949), in *PHWT*, 3:312; "The Cultural and Spiritual Prospect for a Nation Emerging from Total War" (1945), in *PHWT*, 3:106.

24. Dixie and Eisenstadt, *Visions of a Better World*, 155–56.

25. Thurman to Kay H. Beach, September 4, 1942, in *PHWT*, 2:313–15; "The Cultural and Spiritual Prospect for a Nation Emerging from Total War."

States would wither to impotence, and the anti-Communist crusade would become a dominant current in American politics.

When the war ended, Thurman, in San Francisco, was a witness to the founding convention of the United Nations. He hoped that the new international organization would maintain the peace and the wartime alliance between the United States and the Soviet Union. He also hoped that the United States would not regress, as happened after World War I, from its all-too-vague democratic commitments at home. This greatly worried him. In 1946 Thurman published one of the most important of his rare political articles, "The Fascist Masquerade." The article was about the threat of a domestic postwar fascist resurgence. As the war came to an end, there were few higher issues on the progressive-liberal and Communist Party agenda. The *New York Times* in April 1944 published an article by Vice President Henry A. Wallace that defined an American fascist as "one whose lust for money or power is combined with such an intensity of intolerance towards those of other races, parties, classes, religions, cultures, or nations as to make him ruthless in his use of deceit or violence to obtain his ends." He asserted that there were several million American fascists, ready to agitate at war's end.[26]

Thurman agreed. In his article, Thurman quotes extensively from a remarkable army pamphlet, published in March 1945, simply called *Fascism!* (It is remarkable precisely because of its pre–Cold War tone.) It argued that "in the United States, native fascists have often been anti-Catholic, anti-Jew, anti-Negro, anti-labor, anti-foreign-born," that "fascism cannot tolerate such religious and ethical concepts as the 'brotherhood of man.' Fascists deny the need for international cooperation." Moreover, fascists employ the "indiscriminate pinning of the label 'Red' on people and proposals" they oppose. "Many fascists make the spurious claim that the world has but two choices—either fascism or communism, and they label as 'communist' everyone who refuses to support them."[27]

One of the central tenets of those worried about this phenomenon was that the American fascists would not be obvious or self-identify as fascists. Instead, manipulated by secretive and covertly operating big businesses, this fascism would be distinctively American, and these fascists would do everything they could to disguise their true colors. Hence, the title for Thurman's article, "The Fascist Masquerade." The new fascists would loudly proclaim their

---

26. Thurman, "The Fascist Masquerade" (1946), in *PHWT*, 3:145–61; Henry A. Wallace, "Wallace Defines 'American Fascism,'" *New York Times*, April 9, 1944.

27. "Fascism!," *Army Talk: Orientation Fact Sheet 64* (Washington, DC: War Department, March 24, 1945).

Americanness, advocate an intolerant fundamentalism of Christianity, and oppose both organized labor and civil rights. Thurman's article names several organizations he considered fascist. He writes of a Texas organization, the Christian American Association, supported by conservative business interests that pioneered so-called right-to-work legislation. There was the short-lived Nationalist Party, founded by a former North Carolina US senator who left the Democratic Party because, he claimed, it had been taken over by "Communists, Pinks, and Reds," a very early harbinger of the fissure of the solidly Democratic South. And finally, there was the Ku Klux Klan. What all these organizations had in common, besides racism, was conservative Christianity.[28]

Thurman argues that evangelical Christianity is one of the root causes of American racism and fascism, because "the bitter truth is that the Church has permitted the various hate-inspired groups in our common life to establish squatter's rights in the minds of believers because there has been no adequate teaching of the meaning of the faith in terms of human dignity and human worth." Part of this was inherent in Christian doctrine itself, especially the doctrine of salvation; the division between the "saved" and the "damned" was at the root, he thought, of all invidious divisions of humanity. The church must be transformed: "The Church is irrevocably committed to a revolutionary ethic but it tends to implement the ethic by means that are short of that which is revolutionary. . . . The Church must be as revolutionary in practice as it is in the genius of the ethic to which it is dedicated." In this way, Thurman thought, the church, and the inspiration of religious conviction, could fight American fascism.[29]

The concern about American fascism, by Thurman, Wallace, and others, was at once overblown and exaggerated and, at the same time, remarkably prescient. In the rooting out of subversion, the emphasis on secret conspiracies, on identifying organizations as un-American, the "Brown Scare," as it has been called, was an eerie and ironic anticipation of the Red Scare, which targeted many of those most concerned with the fascist threat. At the same time, it is not too much to say that the three groups identified by Thurman were forerunners of a postwar reaction against labor, civil rights, and the legacy of the New Deal that would provide the bulwark of opposition to racial equality and create, in the South, quasi-fascist institutions, such as the White Citizens Councils, to prevent its implementation.[30]

28. Thurman, "The Fascist Masquerade."
29. Thurman, "The Fascist Masquerade."
30. For the "Brown Scare," see Leo P. Ribuffo, *The Old Christian Right: The Protestant Far Right from the Great Depression to the Cold War* (Philadelphia: Temple University Press, 1983).

Once Thurman arrived in San Francisco in July 1944 to copastor the Fellowship Church, the question of how to deal with the Communist Party became more pressing and less abstract. The fight against rampant discrimination against black workers in the defense industry was a central cause for CIO (Congress of Industrial Organizations) unions, many of which were close to the Communist Party. The church's first assistant minister, Albert Cleage, serving in early 1944 until Thurman's arrival, was close to the Communist Party and almost caused a split in the church when he sponsored a forum on discrimination that, allegedly, led to FBI surveillance of the church.[31] A substantial minority of the church members were sympathetic to the Communist Party. Without alienating them, as he related in his autobiography, Thurman did his best to keep the church separate from any official or even unofficial affiliation with the party, and objected to efforts to connect the church to the Communist-connected California Labor School.[32] In 1948, when Henry Wallace, the former vice president, ran for president on the Progressive Party ticket, with considerable Communist support, Thurman tried to dissuade church members from bringing their political enthusiasms to church, and was mortified when an usher's "Wallace for President" button made its way into an article about the church in *Time* magazine in July 1948.[33]

However, it is likely that Thurman voted for Wallace that November. In a sermon he preached on the Sunday after the 1948 election, Thurman offered a rare discussion of Communism. "I realize that any public statement about the Communist development at once classes the individual as either a baiter of that which is Red or a believer of that which is Red, so that we find ourselves tongue tied." He was neither. Although Thurman wryly observes that Communist organizers in the South hid their atheism to attract black support, eventually it didn't matter. The basic message of Communists and other secular radicals was that "men, if they are afraid to participate in the common life, are not men." It was a religious message, one divorced from both conventional religion and conventional Communism.[34]

Other indications of Thurman's continuing interest in Communism in the late 1940s and early 1950s include references to article 123 of the Soviet Constitution, his conviction, expressed in 1949, that "the fear of Russian communism is in direct proportion to our lack of faith in democracy." He opposed loyalty

31. Alfred Fisk to Thurman, May, 6, 1944, in *PHWT*, 3:59–62.

32. "Biographical Essay," in *PHWT*, 3:xxxii, xlix–ln104.

33. "*Time*: Fellowship Church," in *PHWT*, 3:275–78.

34. Thurman, "Modern Challenges to Religion: Secular Radicalism," November 6, 1948.

oaths, renewal of the draft, and continued to support left-wing CIO unions.[35] When he left the Fellowship Church in 1953, his successor, with Thurman's enthusiastic approval, was Dryden Phelps, a former Chinese missionary who had supported the Communist revolution in China, and had been expelled from the American Baptist Foreign Mission Society for his pains.[36]

But Thurman drew a careful line. When in 1952 he was queried about the Civil Rights Congress, an organization connected to the Communist Party, he wrote that while he agreed with its goals, he did "not work through a channel merely because its goals are those towards which my own beliefs operate." He added that "the general impression is, in various parts of the country, that it is some kind of 'front' organization. What the facts are I do not know, nor have I had time to look into them. My own theory is that the channels through which I work must be channels in which I have abiding confidence. . . . If I select the channel through which to work, then I seek to satisfy the demands of my own mind about what its purposes, its methods, its supports are."[37] This did not include organizations connected to the Communist Party.

Thurman's dominant political and religious thinking, rooted in Gandhian nonviolence, had been established in the mid-1930s, and from it he did not waver. Thurman directly inspired the sit-ins and nonviolent protests characteristic of the early years of CORE, starting in 1941.[38] He outlined his views in 1943 in "The Will to Segregation," one of the most important blueprints for radical nonviolence to appear in the war years.[39] In the immediate postwar years, he called those who carried out his vision the "apostles of sensitiveness," individuals with acute and finely honed sensitiveness to oppression of all sorts. Thurman considered them apostles because they were the leaders, the avant-garde of a new movement. They were small groups of individuals who work "on behalf of tolerance . . . a spiritual interpretation of life which ascribes to each individual a basic dignity and worth as a person," creators of "social laboratories" for implementing these techniques.[40] They cannot "permit those sentiments that are genuinely democratic to become isolated. . . . They

35. Thurman, "The Protestant Dilemma concerning Race," October 1947; "The Quest for Stability" (1949), in *PHWT*, 3:312–13; "Untitled: Robert Meyners," in *PHWT*, 3:280–82; "Biographical Essay," 3:xxxii, xlix–lnn104, 105.

36. For Dryden Phelps, see Thurman, "To the Board of Trustees of Fellowship Church," May 19, 1953, in *PHWT*, vol. 4 (forthcoming).

37. Thurman to Gail Hudson, June 26, 1952, in *PHWT*, vol. 4 (forthcoming).

38. Dixie and Eisenstadt, *Visions of a Better World*, 161–64.

39. Thurman, "The Will to Segregation" (1943), in *PHWT*, 2:337–43.

40. Thurman, "Apostles of Sensitiveness" (1946), in *PHWT*, 3:170–74.

must resist every attempt to place false and misleading labels upon them, such as red, subversive, divisive. This is a very clever device inspired by fear, often bigotry, intolerance. The Apostles of Sensitiveness must stand guard first at their points of immediate and direct power."[41] This was the politics of nonviolence, a "third way" outside of the norms of either conventional American party politics or the mass politics of the radical left.

The focus of this chapter has been the early Cold War, its first decade, when, until the Twentieth Party Congress of the Communist Party of the Soviet Union in 1956, the American Communist movement, if increasingly beleaguered, was still an active political force and alternative on the American left. After 1956, civil rights leaders made fewer comparisons to Communists, foreign or domestic, because it was no longer a significant domestic presence on the left, and the Soviet Union's failure to solve the race or anti-Semitism problem was increasingly evident to all with eyes to see. But the failure of Communism was, in no way, for Thurman, King, and the others, a triumph for the "American way of life" when it came to the status of racial minorities. If Thurman and King may have on occasion used the rhetoric of the Cold War, they were in no way trapped or beholden to it.

Thurman summarized his thinking in his most influential work, *Jesus and the Disinherited*, published in 1949. In it, the Cold War and its resonances have little place or trace. Thurman argued that the religion of Jesus provided a way for small groups of individuals to overcome the crippling effects of fear, hypocrisy, and hatred to realize their vision of a better world. If Thurman's small book was centered on America's racial problems, it was by no means limited to them, and included all the injustices that "the man with his back to the wall" must confront. But Thurman, as generally was the case, was less interested in blueprints for the future than in developing the spiritual techniques that change of this sort would require. Martin Luther King Jr. was one of the first and most avid readers of *Jesus and the Disinherited*. And there are reliable accounts that King, on his many travels, often carried a copy with him. Thurman's vision of the deep spiritual resources needed to realize for all Americans, for all the citizens of the world, genuine inclusion is one he developed in the mid-1930s and remained true to for the rest of his life. It remains, in the middle of the new century's second decade, with Communism long dead and the Cold War long ago, all too relevant.[42]

41. Thurman, "Cultural and Spiritual Prospects," in *PHWT*, 3:106–7.
42. Thurman, *Jesus and the Disinherited* (New York: Abingdon-Cokesbury, 1949); Dixie and Eisenstadt, *Visions of a Better World*, 191–94.

Ecumenical Responses to Cold War Issues

James E. Will

The American churches responded to issues in the Cold War through two ecumenical ecclesial institutions: the National Council of Churches in the USA (NCC) and its relation to the World Council of Churches (WCC), with its worldwide membership of three hundred churches, and the Christian Peace Conference (CPC), with its uniquely large component of East European and Russian churches. No American church, however, was a direct member of the CPC; American churches' relation was mediated through the US Committee for the Christian Peace Conference, later renamed Christians Associated for Relationships with Eastern Europe (CAREE).

The CPC was founded by Professor Josef Hromádka, dean of the Comenius Theological Faculty in Prague, shortly after he had returned from a decade on the Princeton Theological Seminary faculty in the USA during Hitler's occupation of Czechoslovakia. Though originally joined only by Christian colleagues in Eastern Europe, it soon also had members in the West, where Hromádka also was well regarded after his decade at Princeton. When I joined the US Committee for the CPC, it was chaired by Professor Charles West, sometime dean of the Princeton Theological Seminary faculty.

Though under some suspicion because it was based in Communist-dominated Eastern Europe, the US Committee's secretariat originally was located ecumenically in the NCC. Though this suspicion was much reduced while Alexander Dubček was the Communist leader of Czechoslovakia during his attempt to create what he designated as "socialism with a human face," it came back with a vengeance after the Soviet Union invaded Czechoslovakia and deposed the Dubček government.

At that time, the US Committee for the CPC found it wise to reconstitute itself as CAREE, and its secretariat was removed from the NCC. Such was then, and sometimes still is, the difficulty in working ecumenically on issues arising out of the Cold War and its international remnants.

There were, however, several Cold War issues, though politically controversial, that the churches could address from theological perspectives. Perhaps the most prominent of them was the issue of human rights, which President Jimmy Carter made central to his foreign policy and President Ronald Reagan often used to condemn the Soviet Union's "evil empire." Because both presidents were practicing Christians, though with quite different theological perspectives, their statements on human rights often strongly affected the church's political discourse.

The churches, however, used another resource that transcended polarized discourse: the Universal Declaration of Human Rights adopted by the United Nations with its matching covenants of civil and political rights, on the one hand, and social, economic, and cultural rights, on the other. Though liberals in the West and socialists in the East continued to decry the violations of civil rights in the Soviet bloc, and of social and economic rights in Western societies, some in the churches saw the Universal Declaration with its matching covenants as providing the "possibility that humankind might become one covenantal community."

The quotation in the last sentence came from the work of the Faith and Order Commission of the NCC, published in their paper "Toward an Ecumenical Theology for Grounding Human Rights." Written by three theologians representing the Church of the Brethren, the Roman Catholic Church, and the United Methodist Church, respectively, it was based on worldwide consultative studies of the Roman Catholic Pontifical Commission on Justice and Peace, the Lutheran World Federation, and the World Alliance of Reformed Churches. All affirmed a holistic understanding of human rights comprising both UN covenants, teaching the essential dignity of every human being, and the necessity of just structures in genuine community for their flourishing.

CAREE made its own contribution to reconciling the conflict between human rights understandings in East and West by contributing to the publication of a special edition of the journal *Soundings* on "the East-West encounter over human rights." Based in large part on the work of its human rights committee chaired by a Mennonite, Paul Peachey, professor of sociology in the Catholic University in Washington, DC, it included essays by Russian, Hungarian, and Polish authors, along with American scholars, and also included the paper of the NCC.

In addition to this theological work on human rights, the NCC joined the European and the Canadian councils in creating the Churches Human Rights Commission for the Helsinki Final Act. This followed upon and was made possible by the significant steps toward resolving Cold War tensions negotiated in the Helsinki Accords, signed by President Ford of the United States and

General Secretary Brezhnev of the Soviet Union. Representatives from these church councils, chaired by a representative from the (East) German Democratic Republic, and administered by a general secretary from Switzerland, sought to examine and help resolve reported human rights abuses in both East and West.

The second Cold War issue that the churches addressed was the grave danger of nuclear war, and the stockpiling, indeed any possession at all, of nuclear arms. This issue proved to be even more controversial because it was central to the national security policies of both the Soviet Union and the United States. And those security policies had finally focused on the policy of "mutually assured destruction," that is, the necessity of their militaries having maximally destructive nuclear weapons ready to retaliate to deter the nuclear-armed enemy's use of them. The psycho-moral meaning of MAD, the acronym of this policy, seemed apt to its critics, including many in the churches, because it madly put not only the enemy but one's own nation, and indeed the entire world, at great risk of catastrophic destruction.

The ecumenical church moved strongly in the 1980s to morally condemn this policy. Indeed, many ethicists had already come to the basic conclusion that any use of nuclear weapons would violate the long-held traditional criteria of just war. Any use of them could not be limited to defense, but would violate the boundaries of just war by inevitably killing and injuring the civilian populations of the enemy nation.

It was not unexpected then that the Sixth Assembly of the WCC in 1983 called upon its three hundred member churches to advocate national security policies "based on justice and the rights of the people," and urged them to convince their governments "to begin immediately to reduce and then eliminate altogether present nuclear forces."

This ecumenical position was especially important for the churches in the Soviet bloc because it provided evidence that their critique of national policy was not that of a political opposition group, which the Communist state prohibited, but the authentic teaching of the universal church.

It was, of course, also important to American ecumenical Protestant churches, while their Roman Catholic colleagues had their own strong support. Their bishops in 1983 published a pastoral letter, "The Challenge of Peace," that condemned population-targeted warfare as "murder," declared first use of nuclear weapons "morally unjustified," and put strict moral conditions on a policy of nuclear deterrence.

Many ecumenically oriented churches at this time were also issuing statements on this issue. The Fellowship of Reconciliation published in 1983 the statements of twenty-five US denominations. My own United Methodist Church had adopted a statement opposing war as an "instrument of national policy" in 1980, which was strengthened and reaffirmed in the 1984 General Conference, and stated that "the militarization of society must be challenged and stopped, the manufacture, sale and deployment of weapons be reduced and controlled, and the production, possession or use of nuclear weapons be condemned."

The US churches faced opposition that claimed they were weakening the United States because their advocacy amounted to support of unilateral disarmament. They claimed churches in the Soviet bloc could exercise no comparable influence. Ecumenical relations in groups like the Christian Peace Conference, however, provided avenues to demonstrate that this was not true by enabling church-related authors from the West and East—the United States, the Netherlands, West Germany, East Germany, and Poland—to report the analogous efforts of their churches for peace. Supported by a grant from the Ford Foundation, the NCC published their essays in 1985 in a volume entitled *The Moral Rejection of Nuclear Deterrence.*

These large ecumenical institutional efforts, of course, were augmented by many smaller group and individual efforts across national and ideological lines with individual and group travel, and especially a series of Christian-Marxist dialogues. Influential communication also occurred through correspondence.

A major instance was the letter from CAREE to the Russian Orthodox Church on the occasion of the Soviet invasion of Afghanistan. Written by Alan Geyer, editor of the *Christian Century*, and Charles West, professor at Princeton Theological Seminary, it was adopted by the annual meeting of CAREE. The letter expressed our perception of the grave dangers to world peace when a superpower invades a small nation—dangers to the invading power, the invaded people, its region, and those caught up in the vast reach of the Cold War. The deep irony that the United States still is caught up in its fifteen-year war in Afghanistan brings home that the lessons from the Cold War are still being learned.

The development of the dialogical praxis in which I was more personally involved, seeking peace between East and West in the so-called Cold War, provides an authentic example of the ecumenical striving for authentic bridge building. Its setting in my experience was the ecumenical church, largely my United Methodist Church's place in the NCC, yet also in the less institutionally established Christian Peace Conference led by Josef Hromádka, who began the work of reconciliation between East and West in two major ways: first, by initiating a Christian-Marxist dialogue with the Marxist professor of philosophy Milan Machovec of Prague's Charles University; and second, by founding the CPC, originally only with Christian colleagues in Eastern Europe. However, because Hromádka was also well regarded in Western Europe and in the United States after his decade at Princeton, the CPC soon also had members in the West.

Despite this respected mainstream leadership and ecumenical location, the CPC was under suspicion by many American Christians because it was based in Communist-dominated Eastern Europe. It did, of course, have to accommodate to its authoritarian Communist governments, in ways certainly more severe but not entirely unlike how our US Committee for the CPC had to obey American laws and was under the surveillance of the FBI. This suspicion of the CPC was much reduced while Alexander Dubček was the Communist leader of Czechoslovakia, as he sought to create what he called "socialism with a human face"—a period during which Hromádka's and Machovec's Christian-Marxist dialogue was publicly celebrated in Prague, and Machovec served as chairman of the Prague Committee for Human Rights.

Western suspicion, however, came back with a vengeance after the Soviet Union and the Warsaw Pact invaded Czechoslovakia and deposed the Dubček government. Deeply disappointed, Hromádka resigned his presidency of the CPC, and was soon replaced by Metropolitan Nikodim, the Russian Orthodox archbishop of Leningrad (now again Saint Petersburg). At that time, the secretariat of our US CPC committee was removed from the NCC, and our American committee for the CPC found it wise to reconstitute itself as Christians Associated for Relationships with Eastern Europe (CAREE), maintaining its relation with the CPC but focusing more on ecumenical relations with churches in the Soviet Union and the rest of Eastern Europe. Such was, and often still is, the struggle when one's praxis seeks to serve ecumenical peace in a deeply divided world.

That such peace witness remained possible even under such difficult conditions, however, may be illustrated in two ways from experiences in which I was involved. One was the carefully drafted but strongly critical letter from CAREE, signed by me as its president, to colleagues in the Russian Orthodox Church shortly after the Soviet Union invaded Afghanistan. It was received by their Department of External Church Relations and undoubtedly reviewed by representatives of the Soviet government. This became evident when for the first time in my experience I had difficulty in obtaining visas for a group of students I planned to bring to the Soviet Union the next year. The visas finally were issued through the intervention of a Communist Party member for whose wife I had earlier arranged medical consultation while he was in

New York; yet when our group arrived in Moscow, the otherwise welcoming remarks of Metropolitan Yuvenaly uncharacteristically began with "although we sometimes have trouble with Prof. Will," which I understood to be a necessary nod to his government's objection to CAREE's letter.

The second experience was my attempt to share what I thought was the wisdom deriving from Americans, including American churches, courageously speaking truth to power, criticizing the burglary of the Democratic Party headquarters in the Watergate Hotel and demanding that the perpetrators, including President Nixon, be brought to justice. I was one of three invited to address the two-hundred-member Continuation Committee of the CPC, meeting in Siofók, Hungary, in September 1975. Though unsaid, it was quite apparent that the three were in part chosen as representing perspectives of the so-called First, Second, and Third Worlds, given our locations in the United States, Eastern Europe, and South America. I therefore decided to speak quite deliberately from the standpoint of an American Christian to the conference theme "The Calling of Christians to Cooperate for Peace and Justice." I described how many American citizens recently had cooperated in using our freedoms of speech, assembly, and the press to bring President Nixon's administration to justice for their criminal act.

I then took the carefully considered, but perhaps too audacious, risk of asking my colleagues in their far more difficult contexts in Eastern Europe, "Can you make your own prophetic critique of what appears to some of us to be the excessive, yes even sinful, claims to exclusive power and special privilege of some of your new ruling and bureaucratic classes?" The question was softened by citing Martin Luther King's words about all of us—East, West, and South—from his April 1967 speech against the American war in Vietnam: "Even when pressed by the demands of inner truth," King said, "men do not readily assume the task of opposing their government's policy." Nevertheless, some in the audience objected immediately; in the words of Bishop Károly Tóth of the Hungarian Reformed Church, the general secretary of the CPC, there were "consternation and indignation in the meeting." Indeed, some urged Metropolitan Nikodim, who was presiding, to exclude me from any further participation in the CPC.

It was characteristic of his wise leadership, however, that he refused any such suggestion. He was much influenced, as I had come to know, by the wisdom of the Roman Catholic pope John XXIII, on whom he had written his doctoral dissertation in a Russian Orthodox seminary. Metropolitan Nikodim's response to me, personal and off the record after the meeting, was, "You may be correct in principle, but you must not think that you as a North American know better than your brothers and sisters in the Soviet Union when the right time has come for the kind of dialogue and communication you are advocating." He, of course, was right. But a better time did surely come a decade later through the glasnost and perestroika enacted by their president Gorbachev.

These relatively small acts of personal witness are meant only to provide illustration of authentic peace praxis. No grandiose claims about their historical effect in resolving the Cold War is intended or possible. The problems at issue were too complex and the interacting factors too many to make any such claims credible.

Memoirs of a Participant in East-West Dialogues

CHARLES WEST

In East Germany (1951–1961)

Let me begin with an experience. A group came to Berlin with a special situation; they had discovered that their pastor was informing on members of the congregation to the police. That can be dangerous. There was a law against "incitement to boycott against democratic institutions." A careless critical remark, spoken in private but reported, could bring one before the court and perhaps send one to prison. But the group treated it as a pastoral problem. What made the pastor an informer? Was it fear? If so, what caused the fear? Was it concern for his family? Was it a sin (most often sexual or monetary) that he wanted to conceal from the public? The members became pastors; the pastor became the object of their care. They, of course, avoided saying anything that he would have to report, but basically they were concerned about him. They were creating a Christian community in spite of him, and around him. All week we learned about this ministry and tried to help them with it. Among such people we lived for two years. We were perhaps helpful, but we learned about the work of God the Holy Spirit from them.

There were problems of course. The principal one was fear. There was reason enough for fear. Oppression was everywhere. Soviet occupying military secured the state, and Soviet advisers controlled its policy. The goal of the state was to convert the society into something modeled after the Soviet Union, in ideology, politics, and economic structure. To this end the secret

[Editor's note: Charles West began his career as a missionary to China (1947–1950) two years before Communists took control of the country, and ended it one year later. Then he went as an ecumenical fraternal worker to Germany (1950 1953). He was on the staff of the Ecumenical Institute (Bossey) of the World Council of Churches (1956–1961). He has been chair of Christians Associated for Relationships with Eastern Europe (previously Christians for [not of] the Christian Peace Conference). These excerpts are from his memoirs.]

police (the Stasi) established a network of informers and claimed to know everything about you, even what you said and thought in private. There was, according to our tough-minded Christian friends schooled by resistance to the Nazis, about one chance in five that they did. But one never knew. There was always a chance that one could lose one's job, that one's children could be harassed or denied advancement in school, or that one could land in prison, as the theologian Johannes Hamel and his colleagues did for three months in 1953.

That was the outer fear. There was also an inner fear. Many Christians, like the majority of East Germans, profoundly resented the Communists and the Soviet occupation. There was constant temptation to live in "inner emigration" toward an idealized West, and therefore to conform to, while cutting off, the society they were in. Hamel used the image of a fist balled in one's pocket. We were often asked, "How long must we wait, until you (the Americans) come and rescue us?" All this deepened fear. It left people prisoners of their own hatreds, unable to give a free witness.

How, then, does one overcome fear? Let me add a few examples to those above. A woman student, member of the Student Christian Movement (SCM) in her university, was called in by the authorities and told that unless she joined the Free German Youth (a Communist front), she could not be admitted to final exams. For the sake of her family, which depended on her, she joined, but she continued, on the advice of her pastor, to be part of the SCM, and to pray. Finally, she could not stand the tension. She went to the authorities a few weeks before the exams and withdrew from the organization. The authorities were amazed and tried to persuade her. Finally she said to them, "Because I was afraid for myself, I came to you. Because the gospel has taken that fear away from me, I am leaving now."

Another example: Johannes Hamel [a pastor and theologian] was imprisoned in early 1953. As he described it to me later, he was not physically abused, except for the conditions of his imprisonment (solitary confinement, poor food, and a single bulb burning twenty-four hours a day in his cell), but he was psychologically manipulated almost daily by interrogators who threatened and deceived him. At one point one of them asked him sarcastically, "Where is your Jesus now?" "Why," Hamel replied, "he's here. He's been here all along. I'm surprised you haven't noticed."

A West German pastor asked an East German colleague, "How free is your congregation?" The Easterner replied, "We have as much freedom as we are willing to take." He had just held a youth rally in a local park. Christian instruction was given in his church, explicit in its repudiation of Marxist atheism. All such activities had their dangers. The three examples I have given turned out well. The student was admitted to the exams; she has exceptional character, they said. Hamel was freed and restored to his family. The pastor continued to function until the Berlin Wall fell. But it could have been otherwise. Does one live in fear, or in faith?

A second problem was lack of truthfulness. There was reason enough to say whatever was required to get along, whether it was truthful or not. The government was seeking to impose an ideology on the whole society, the ideology of Marxism in a Stalinist form of Leninist interpretation, which led to uncritical support of Soviet foreign policy. The pressure was especially hard in school. Children were not only taught ideologically; they were asked about their parents. "Dad, I lie every day in school," a boy said to his father. "If I didn't, you'd go to jail." But the pressure was on in the workplace too, and in the public sphere. Every so often a referendum was held "for peace," which denounced the Western warmongering powers, especially America, and claimed to speak on behalf of the "peace-loving" peoples of the world. Only a few resisted this hypocrisy by staying home, and they received visits that could be interpreted as persuasive or threatening depending on one's point of view. They might have consequences, or they might not. One never knew.

Christians were especially under suspicion, not only because they had a different faith, but also because the church was the only social body not under the control of the party. There, people responded to a different reality. There, a different standard of truthfulness prevailed. Martin Luther's emphasis on the Word permeated the culture, and made it difficult, despite—or perhaps because of—the Nazi experience, to prevaricate in order to get along.

This led in the churches to an intense study (continuous, for Confessing Churches, with resistance in the Nazi times) of the living word of God in Christ and the Bible. I was privileged to participate in many such studies. They took place not only among catechists who were allowed to gather children after school in church rooms for religious instruction (attendance at which was already a mark against the child and its family) but also in congregations, among members. Each time it was an encounter with the reality of God among people who were trying to understand their history, their world, and themselves in God's presence. We talked about our relations with the Communists on several levels of truthfulness. There was the level of observed fact. Just pointing out that this work crew was behaving like an army with its shovels, or that women were not necessarily liberated by being forced to work in factories, could lead to trouble. There was the moral level. When could one deceive, or hide one's convictions, in order to avoid conflict? When should one call hate or injustice by its name, in East or West, instead of excusing it by pointing to the evils of the other side? Then there was the question of faith. What is the relation of confessing Christ to Communist ideology? A few thought there was no conflict. Many regarded them as enemies. Most, however, wrestled with the problem: How can one bear witness to the truth of God's revelation in Christ in a society that dismisses religion and politically enforces its own humanist ideology?

That led to the problem of justice. It is a Hebrew-Christian, not a Marxist, concept, though Marxism arose and drew much of its strength from the injustice of early capitalist theories and practices. Marx and Lenin (and Stalin) spoke rather about the laws of history that led from a society where the vast mass of people were deprived of the fruits of their labor, and therefore of their humanity, until they rose in revolution, dispossessed their exploiters, and built together a classless society without private property leading toward Communism. The Communist Party was considered the instrument of this revolution and the planner of the future, the enlightened mind of the masses, who knew the laws of history. This determined the law and the judiciary. "There is no crime apart from some harm to the people's progress toward socialism," said one official.

What does one do when a neighbor is unjustly hauled into court for such a crime? The most general indictment was *Boycotthetze gegen demokratische Insitutionen* (incitement to boycott against democratic institutions, that is, the institutions of the German Democratic Republic). Defense in the court is already a risk. Yet many Christians, church leaders among them, using older, Christian-influenced standards of justice, did prevail in influencing judges, who were grateful for their support. One of the heroes of this legal struggle was Präses Lothar Kreyssig, a lawyer in the Provinz Sachsen (Magdeburg) church who had brought criminal suit against the Nazi government officials responsible for the killing of disabled children. The suit could not go forward, and Kreyssig landed in concentration camp, because it was disclosed that Hitler himself had given the order. Experience with the Nazis was good training for dealing with the Communists. Kreyssig, among others, used it to the full.

Then there was the area of social responsibility in which all of this played out. Five-sixths of Communist East Germany was traditionally Protestant, overwhelmingly influenced by the teachings of Martin Luther. One of these, deeply ingrained in the people, was the belief that every occupation was a vocation, a calling, from God. This had its weaknesses as well as its strengths. It led often to a failure to see one's calling as a citizen beyond one's particular vocation. The Christian Germans we knew were shocked by Germany's failure to resist Hitler on this basis. There was much discussion when we were there of the need to open the doctrine of vocation to broader responsibility in politics, economics, and culture. But people were confronted with another demand on their sense of vocation, an atheist demand to serve the collectivized system whose model was the Soviet Union. The root of the conflict was the contrast between the practice of Christian vocation based on the teaching of Martin Luther and the government-engineered plan to realize the classless society by collectivized methods.

We heard almost daily of such conflicts. What does one do when one's farm is taken over by a Communist Party–managed "cooperative" and one can no longer manage planting, cultivation, and harvesting while at the same time being required to produce certain quotas of produce on schedule? One may recognize that the old system was unjust and in need of land reform, but is this the alternative? The same is true if one owns a business, a small store or a large factory, that is collectivized, and one can no longer responsibly plan purchases, sales, or production. To be sure, in the old system profit played too large a role in these calculations, and workers were often exploited, but is total planning the answer? What does one do if it is imposed?

What is responsible Christian witness in situations such as these? Certainly to respond first of all to God's judgment and grace, to find one's hope not in tradition or ecclesiastical influence but in the victory of the risen Christ over the powers of the world. As one pastor put it, "When we talk with Westerners, they tell us of the problems confronting them, and we tell them what is happening to us." Therefore the church warned against finding salvation, or even justice, in either the solidarity of a centrally planned classless society or in the individualism of private enterprise, however attractive they may be as ideals. In other words, human problems cannot be solved either by the Communism of the East or the capitalism of the West, but by Christian hope and responsibility in both. This meant, for Easterners, accepting from God responsibility to "seek the welfare of the city" (Jer. 29:7) that had been imposed on them, to work for "an improvable socialism" (to quote one church document), and to take responsibility wherever they could, even in collective enterprises. "Send me Christians," one Communist manager cried. "They're the only ones I can depend on." All this in the context of living freely and responsibly as witnesses to the risen Christ and the kingdom of God in a society where another ideology and another power claimed to reign.

Encounter with the Russians

At the Third Assembly of the World Council of Churches in 1961, the Orthodox churches of the Soviet area became members of the World Council of Churches, after years of negotiation. Delegations from member churches was the logical next step. Thus began my encounter with Russians. In 1962, my first visit to the Soviet Union was as part of a National Council of Churches USA delegation. But there was a third party to these negotiations: the government of the Soviet Union, with which the churches had to deal. The year 1962 was the Khrushchev era. The churches—persecution having been relaxed as a result of their nationalist role in World War II—were now under new pressure. There was aggressive atheist teaching in the schools, churches were being closed, and their publications were being limited and censored. Still, the interest of the Soviet government was clear, and the church leaders used it. It was to cultivate friends among the Christians of the West and the Third World, and to use the churches of the Soviet Union, especially the Russian Orthodox Church (ROC), to do so. The government had already infiltrated the church with informers, and it demanded that the bishops and clergy of the churches report to it regularly. But the churches had another agenda: to use ecumenical contacts to increase the freedom of Soviet Christians to exercise their faith. We foreign visitors were willing servants of that agenda. The question for us was: How do we understand our Soviet Union hosts? Who was a believer, a nationalist, or a Communist, and in what mixture? We assumed that everyone we talked with would have to report our conversation to the government, but what would they say? How would they understand us, and we them?

Archbishop Nikodim, head of the Foreign Office of the Moscow Patriarchate (later metropolitan of Leningrad), was the prime puzzle. He was a clever, jolly man, and the chief negotiator with the government for ecumenical relations. As such, he joined Josef Hromádka in the Christian Peace Conference (CPC) and pushed the Soviet foreign policy there, as well as in every WCC meeting he was part of. He used to give signals in such meetings to the Russian delegation for how to vote. I remember sitting with him on two occasions negotiating as chief spokesman for the Americans. It was hard-nosed diplomacy. On the other side, he slipped favorable documentation about a dissident priest in disfavor with the government to a friend of mine who he knew would publish it. He opened doors for us and cultivated ecumenical contacts wherever he could. He respected our faith and our worship; but it was his love of the Orthodox liturgy that persuaded us that he was fundamentally a churchman. His negotiations with the government were on behalf of the church. Over time, recognizing the limits of his position, we came to trust him.

So it was with other churchmen and churchwomen we met. We participated in Orthodox and Baptist services and drank deeply of the faith of each group. The Orthodox Church was rich from the sale of candles and icons, which was the only source of income. We heard stories of candles being burned in museums where holy objects were on display. To the question of how many believers there are in Russia, the standard answer was always given: wrong question. The church embraces all the people, whether they recognize it or not. All are included in the drama of salvation that the liturgy enacts.

The next delegation I was a part of, in 1974, featured the same characters, but it was quite different. Khrushchev was gone, overthrown in 1964. With him went the intense atheist educational movement and limitation of the churches that he promoted. The Soviet invasion of Czechoslovakia to crush the "Prague Spring" had taken place in 1968 (see below), and with it came the destruction of the Marxist-Christian dialogue. The leadership of the Soviet Union, whether from policy change or weakness, was more relaxed. We were invited to visit places (e.g., Tallinn in Estonia and Riga in Latvia, where there are Lutheran churches) that had been closed to us before.

More important, substantive dialogue, based on papers from both sides, took place between the churches in the Soviet Union (dominated by the ROC) and the churches of the United States (arranged by the NCC), and occurred in open session. The theme was that of the WCC's Fourth Assembly slogan: "Jesus Christ Frees and Unites." The title of my paper was "Implications for World Peace," which was my contribution to the Moscow meeting. This paper led to a fruitful exchange, for which our friends from the churches in the Soviet Union expressed their gratitude in private conversations. I think they fed on our theological and ethical reflections, which were not available in their restricted ideological environment.

But we went a step further. We decided beforehand that we would ask for a dialogue with Marxist philosophers. The officials of the Russian Orthodox Church were taken aback. They would ask, but they weren't sure it was possible. But then Metropolitan Nikodim took over. He saw it as an opportunity. It was arranged. We put a group of learned Marxists through their paces from an angle they had never heard before, and Nikodim sat grinning the whole time. He wasn't the only one enjoying it. At the farewell dinner for our delegation, several of the philosophers turned up and sought us out to continue the conversation. One of them later sent me a book that was a critique of my book

Communism and the Theologians. I still have it, but it is in Russian, so I can't read it. Maybe I will meet Yuri Levada in heaven, where we will understand each other in God's language.

We went home, but it was not over. The church leaders in the Soviet Union wanted to continue the conversation—in the United States. Already in Moscow a group of two Americans (Bruce Rigdon and myself) and two Russians (as I remember, Rev. Vitaly Borovoy of the Russian Orthodox Church and Rev. Alexander Bichkov of the All-Union Baptists and Evangelicals) drew up a plan, including four papers and Bible study in small groups where we could talk informally. I wrote a letter to Princeton Theological Seminary president James McCord asking whether the delegation might be invited as guests of the seminary. The answer was immediate: welcome! He consulted with Claire Randall, general secretary of the NCC, who was arranging the trip, and made arrangements to accommodate some twenty Orthodox prelates, plus Baptists, Armenians, Lutherans, and others, with interpreters and American invited guests.

The meeting was held at Princeton Seminary in March 1975. It was a successful meeting in several ways. There was a reception for the seminary faculty, a public meeting for students and visitors, Bible study in small groups introduced by an American and a Russian leader, and even a protest demonstration organized by Carl McIntire. But first, in my memory, were the person and performance of the Reverend Vitaly Borovoy, protopresbyter (the highest rank available to a married priest in the Orthodox Church) in the Russian Orthodox cathedral in Moscow. He was the leading theologian, the best communicator, and the most creative thinker we met. I had met him in Moscow twice and seen him perform at the WCC Church and Society meeting in Geneva in 1966. The issue was Marxist-Christian dialogue, which at that time was at its height in Europe. The overwhelming majority from all continents were in favor of the WCC promoting it, but the Russians were against it. A heated discussion took place, and finally Father Vitaly spoke up: "I will tell you why my brethren are so opposed to dialogue," he said, and then explained tactfully that they had not been able to study Marxist-Leninist doctrine and therefore could not intelligently discuss its relation to Christian faith. We all knew the conditions in the Soviet Union. We knew what he was saying. The confrontation passed without incident. His last assignment was as representative of the ROC on the staff as of the WCC.

This spirit was reflected also in Princeton. We wanted the students to have a chance to interact with the Soviet church visitors. This was difficult because many of the visitors did not speak English (though we recruited as many interpreters as we could). But Father Vitaly had enough English by then. He spent hours talking to students in the dorms about the experience of being a pastor in a Communist country; about officials who would argue with him and then come to church, hiding behind a pillar so no one would recognize them; about weddings and baptisms that flew under the Soviet radar; about informal education of youth in a country where church education was prohibited; and about pastoral care in an atheist-dominated land. He inspired them and educated them.

The students responded, not only to Father Vitaly, but also to the whole visit. They entertained the members of the delegation in lounges after the evening sessions. And they engaged the students who came from Carl McIntire's seminary in Pennsylvania with placards to protest. They arranged with those students a discussion led by one of their faculty members and me. I was looking forward to it, but it never happened. Their seminary forbade it.

This was the first, and in some ways the most important, fruit of the visit. The second was substantive discussion of the theme: "Jesus Christ Frees and Unites." There were two papers from the Russian Orthodox side. Bruce Rigdon dealt, for the Americans, with the freedom theme. I dealt with unity. It was the only Faith and Order theme this ethicist dealt with in his life, but it was relevant to the life of faith.

I came away from this experience with a deep appreciation of the piety of the ROC. It was expressed differently in Father Vitaly Borovoy and in Metropolitan Nikodim, but it was the same piety. It was rooted in the liturgical life of the church, which was more basic than any theology or ideology or political hope. It saturated Russian culture and helped that culture survive. I could worship in that church. On the other hand, Communism required a different encounter than that of transcendence, more like that of the Lutheran/Reformed faith that I experienced in East Germany.

Since then, things have changed in both lands. In 1994 the Hungarian Reformed and Lutheran churches held an international conference entitled "Christian Faith and Human Enmity." Inspired by this, the Russian Orthodox Church invited the churches in the former Soviet Union to a similar conference in Moscow. It was the most ecumenical meeting ever held there. Will the ROC rise to the ecumenical challenge in the post-Communist era, or will it succumb to nationalism? Pray for it.

Josef Hromádka

But I next turned to a quite different theologian, one who accepted the Communist revolution and tried to find his Christian witness in it, a Protestant theologian of the Church of the Czech Brethren, Josef L. Hromádka.[1] Why Hromádka? I think for three reasons.

First, he was a leader in whom the East and the West combined. With Slavic sympathy, he experienced the drama of Russian history as his own. He probed the depths of human nature and Russian culture with Dostoevsky. He experienced the Russian Revolution as an event in the life of his world. At the same time, he was a man of Western culture, a Protestant in the tradition of the Czech Reformation, trained in Vienna, Basel, Heidelberg, and Aberdeen, steeped in the spirit of free critical inquiry, political democracy, and personal response to the word of God in the church. His mind is not a fascinating alien world to explore, as is that of Nicholas Berdyaev, for example. Nor is he part of a Western world caught behind the Iron Curtain, as are many of the articulate creative theologians of the Evangelical Church in East Germany. In Hromádka, we find a man of two worlds, united in one spirit.

Second, Hromádka's theological task is also ours: to place the history of the world in the context of the word and act of God made known in the biblical story and in the life, death, and resurrection of Jesus Christ. He was a servant of the living God, a witness to the reality of God's kingdom, in his situation, as we are called to be in ours. Our lives are in the same context of reality known by faith. It is our worlds that differ somewhat. We can learn from him, therefore, in a special way, different from the way we learn from our Western theologians, how to hear the word of God, how to live with Christ, how to be the church, and how to hope for the world.

Third, Hromádka has posed more sharply than any other theologian I know the question of the meaning of secular historical events in the context of the providence and the promise of God. We may or may not agree with his historical perceptions. I, for one, have taken sharp issue with him at times. But in all his thought and action, he was a Christian witness. Never were the judgment and grace of God absent from the events and powers of human history; never was the saving promise of God absorbed into these events. We need to learn this art from him today and practice it ourselves.

1. Excerpts from Charles West, "Josef Hromadka and the Witness of the Church in East and West," *Occasional Papers on Religion in Eastern Europe* 10, no. 2 (March 1990): 13–25. Not copyrighted.

"Looking history in the face" and being "confronted with raw history" were among Hromádka's favorite expressions. It was clear that for him the Bolshevik Revolution in Russia was the first and remained the paradigmatic expression of this history. Looking back in old age on his reaction to that revolution in 1918, he put it this way:

> Beneath all the horrors, cruelties and brutalities of the revolution and the onset of the civil war, I heard an ominous but clear cry that the division of the world into central European theocratic empires and Western liberal democracies was not the last word. There is a far deeper, an abysmal division between poor and rich, between those who have economic and financial power in their hands and those who have only empty hands or educated heads. This division pervades the whole world, characterizing both victors and vanquished. That which we call the class struggle is not just a propaganda slogan or a cheap call to action. It embraces the most serious of human problems: the fight against poverty and hunger, against the humiliation and exploitation of men and nations.[2]

There was no doubt in his mind that Soviet Communism, with its outreach in Communist parties throughout the world, was the vehicle of this struggle. "Communism is not only a doctrine, a theory or a political conviction," he wrote in 1945 to his own Czechoslovak people.[3]

Marxist-Leninist Communism was, for Hromádka, not primarily an ideology but a historical movement carried by disciplined, dedicated believers, with a systematic well-balanced philosophy guiding its policies, empowered by the will and the hope of masses of people "for a social system in which all class differences would fade away, the demonic, tyrannical power of money and private property would be crushed, and all men and women would be united on the same ground of human dignity, freedom and love."[4] This evaluation defined the context of his ministry and determined his analysis of events, in Czechoslovakia and Eastern Europe, in the East-West conflict and tension, and in the radical social and political upheavals in Africa and Asia, right up to the Soviet invasion

---

2. Josef Hromádka, *The Impact of History on Theology: Thoughts of a Czech Pastor* (Notre Dame: Fides, 1970), 28.

3. Apparently translated for Charles West by a Czech student, but he did not know the original source—[Ed.].

4. *Man's Disorder and God's Design*, The Amsterdam Series, vol. 4 (London, 1949), 129. This volume was published in the USA under the title *The Church and the International Disorder* (New York: Harper, 1949).

of Czechoslovakia on August 21, 1968. He understood the "socialism with a human face" of the Dubček government during the 1968 "Prague Spring" to be a natural development from necessary coercion and control to more participation and freedom, as the members of society became more mature.

After August 21 there was of course a change. Hromádka saw it as a tragic failure by the Soviet Union and other countries of Eastern Europe to understand and trust this natural development. "What it concerns," he wrote to the working committee of the Christian Peace Conference in October 1968, "is the question whether socialism is able to develop creatively and whether it will influence the world community, especially the young and the youngest generation by convincing ideas, moral frankness and political wisdom." As he saw it in retrospect, sterile Marxist dogmatism, administrative pressures, and pure power politics were stifling the creativity of the movement. "New socialist orders were created, the socialist house was built. However . . . we were not able to inhabit it by the socialist man." The struggle as he saw it at the end of his life would be for a democratic socialism. "For us there is no way back to bourgeois society. Our state will remain socialist in the full meaning of that word. But we desire to fill it with all the great spiritual and cultural values of freedom, equality and true humanism. This is what we are determined to do, ready for sacrifice and, if necessary, for suffering."[5]

Many critical things have been said about this judgment of historical powers and moral forces in the past seventy years. Thirty years ago[6] I wrote the following about the Hromádka–John Foster Dulles confrontation at Amsterdam:[7] "In the last analysis both men, the extremes of Christian pro- and anti-Communism, think in terms of a faith which is less than the Christian faith, a faith in culture, society and politics informed by a unifying religion which will meet Communism as friend or enemy on its own level. In both, the Christian remains bound not to Christ in the world but to the world of Communist power and pretension itself."[8]

Today I think that I was wrong about both men. Pushed by the tensions of the Cold War, each was tempted to overstate the identification of his faith with a particular set of historical powers, values, and ideas, but each finally

5. From Hromádka's letter to the Working Committee of the Christian Peace Conference, October 1968, source no longer available to the author—[Ed.].

6. That is, in 1960—[Ed.].

7. The founding First Assembly of the World Council of Churches took place in Amsterdam in 1948.

8. Charles West, *Communism and the Theologians: Study of an Encounter* (Philadelphia: Westminster, 1958).

resisted the temptation. The gospel that they both confessed bore witness to the transcending judgment and grace of God over the society in which they took responsibility as Christ's servants and witnesses.

They were both undialectical in their analysis, however, and here remains the problem. How does one throw oneself completely into the service of one's neighbor in the world, into the construction of a more just society informed with compassion and inspired by the hope of true community and freedom, and at the same time bear witness to the judgment of God on the inhumanities and idolatries of that society? How does one bear faithful witness to and within historical power?

A final question: What is out vision of community in a pluralistic world? For the past century at least, answers to this question have assumed one world. This was the message of the free-market economists. Karl Marx made it a dogma. Technocratic twentieth-century science and industry have reinforced it. In this picture, the world is basically composed of scientists and technologists, producers and consumers, managers and workers, all driven primarily by the desire to control the resources of the world for a better material life.

We are learning in the early twenty-first century that this is only part of human reality. Nations are reasserting themselves around the centers of their languages and cultures. Eastern Europe and the Soviet Union offer vivid examples. Religions, not as faiths but as communities bound together by common practices and dogmas, are both uniting and dividing various parts of the world. There is everywhere a thirst for community in a fuller and deeper sense than any ideology can provide. How does Christian faith understand human community—embodied in the church, in the town, in the culture, in the state, and in the world? We should not be complacent. We have not solved this problem in the United States of America. Perhaps we can learn from as well as contribute to the search of nations like the Soviet Union and Yugoslavia[9] for solutions to it there.

In a word, thanks in no small degree to the ministry of Josef Hromádka in his time, we are now no longer groping for mutual understanding across barriers of ideology and deeply contrasting experiences with worldly power. We are in each other's neighborhoods, just as we have always been—by faith and by God's grace in the ecumenical movement—in each other's churches. The problems of the world that we face together in faith are becoming increasingly common. In Christ we need each other more than ever to face them responsibly and with hope. This, I suggest, is our agenda in the next few years.

9. This was written prior to disintegration of these two countries—[Ed.].

Roman Catholic Approaches

Catholic Anti-Communism and the Early Cold War

Dianne Kirby

Recent scholarship has established a strong religious dimension to the conduct and nature of the Cold War that highlights the profound impact that the Cold War and American Catholicism had on each other.[1] Will Herberg notably observed in 1955 that "being a Protestant, a Catholic, or a Jew is understood as the specific way, and increasingly perhaps the only way, of being an American and locating oneself in American society."[2] The emphasis on religious affiliation and the apparently equal footing accorded the three, despite a history and some at least residual persistence of anti-Semitism and anti-Catholicism, has been attributed to the Cold War. Certainly, "Catholic anti-communism echoed American Cold War patriotism. . . . American Catholics, in expressing anti-communism, simultaneously affirmed both their Catholicism and Americanism."[3] Additionally, traditional Catholic antiradicalism was seen as facilitating convergence in the early Cold War "between the views of Catholic leaders and those of American Cold War leaders generally."[4]

On March 6, 1946, the day after Winston Churchill's famous Fulton speech, President Harry Truman declared that the survival of the civilized world required Americans to fortify their spiritual strength through a renewal of religious faith.

1. Dianne Kirby, ed., *Religion and the Cold War* (Basingstoke, UK: Palgrave Macmillan, 2003, 2013); Julius Filo, ed., *Christian World Community and the Cold War* (Bratislava, Slovakia: Evangelical Theological Faculty of Comenius University, 2012); Philip E. Muehlenbeck, ed., *Religion and the Cold War: A Global Perspective* (Nashville: Vanderbilt University Press, 2012).

2. Will Herberg, *Protestant, Catholic, Jew: An Essay in American Religious Sociology* (New York: Doubleday, 1955), 160.

3. John Haynes, *Red Scare or Red Menace? American Communism and Anti-Communism in the Cold War Era* (Chicago: Ivan R. Dee, 1996), 95.

4. D. F. Crosby, "The Politics of Religion, American Catholics and the Anti-Communist Impulse," in *The Specter: Original Essays on the Cold War and the Origins of McCarthyism*, ed. Robert Griffith and Athan Theoharis (New York: New View Points, 1974), 20.

He called upon America's key faith communities, Protestant, Catholic and Jewish, to provide the necessary impetus.[5] Initiating a process that would appropriate the rhetoric of Roman Catholic anti-Communism and the concept of a Judeo-Christian nation to buttress America's ideological struggle with the Soviet Union, Truman effected a remarkable transition that challenged not simply the nation's traditional Protestant identity but also its identity as a Christian nation.

As the United States moved to assume global leadership under the rubric of democracy, freedom, and self-determination, there was a realization that while Christianity was definitely a weapon to wield against the Soviet Union, it was also a potential hindrance. Nations in the developing world, determined to throw off the shackles of Western imperialism, linked colonialism to Christianity. Faith, however, was important in these same states, meaning Marxist atheism remained the Achilles' heel through which the appeal of Communist doctrine to the poor and dispossessed could most effectively be blunted. American laissez-faire capitalism held little appeal, being viewed outside of America as responsible for delivering slump, fascism, and war. Within America, of course, protecting its way of life, of which capitalism and Christianity were key components, was paramount in mobilizing domestic support.

Religious persecution was a staple theme of American anti-Communist propaganda, but it was largely a rhetorical device intended to strengthen the Cold War consensus by evoking strong feelings about suffering Christians behind the Iron Curtain, kept to the forefront of public consciousness, including through the popular medium of film, by American Catholics.[6] The United States had used religious liberty as an indicator for international threat since the 1930s. Catholic intelligence material prepared for American consumption naturally focused on Communist persecution of the Catholic Church. It was important for American propaganda in buttressing the proposition that Communism was ideologically driven to conquer the world and eradicate religion. Notably, however, in mid-1946, when Archbishop Stepinac, the foremost Catholic bishop in Croatia, was found guilty of collaborating with the wartime occupation Ustashe regime, America remained silent in the face of the Vatican claim that it marked "the 'first phase' in a systematic reign of terror to be meted out against the Catholic Church in Yugoslavia."[7]

5. Harry S. Truman, "Address at a Conference of the Federal Council of Churches," March 6, 1946, The American Presidency Project, http://www.presidency.ucsb.edu/ws/index.php?pid_12599.

6. T. Shaw, "'Martyrs, Miracles and Martians': Religion and Cold War Cinematic Propaganda in the 1950s," in Kirby, *Religion and the Cold War*, 211–31.

7. Charles Gallagher, "The US and the Vatican in Yugoslavia, 1945–50," in Kirby, *Religion and the Cold War*, 118–44.

The apparent unwillingness to support the papal absolution granted Stepinac reflected extant questions as to his guilt at a time when the Nuremberg trials constrained displays of American sympathy for former collaborators. Moreover, with clear-cut examples of religious persecution in Spain under a remaining Axis leader, to indict Tito and not Franco would be a gift to Soviet propaganda. Once Stalin publicly expelled Tito's Yugoslavia from the Cominform, providing an opportunity to "penetrate and disunite the Soviet bloc," the United States actively sought to minimize the Stepinac affair. On the home front, however, the National Catholic Welfare Conference waged a stirring press campaign that kept Stepinac at the forefront of Catholic anti-Communist endeavors. These included appeals from Archbishop Spellman and Monsignor Fulton Sheen and a loyalty parade of one hundred thousand Catholics sponsored by the Knights of Columbus in New York City, which in turn led to resolutions in Congress and the Senate calling on the US government for action.[8] Tito's newly acquired status as an enemy of Stalin meant, however, that the Truman administration disregarded the domestic campaigns and even a personal appeal from Pius XII and proceeded with a $25 million Export-Import Bank credit to Yugoslavia in September 1949.

Anti-Communism undoubtedly helped the acculturation of Roman Catholics into American society, but it was a process that began before the Cold War started. The cessation of immigration and the disruption to the social order caused by the Depression, the New Deal, the Second World War, and the postwar industrial revolution more than normalized the Catholic minority and removed the perception of them as immigrants and of Catholicism as an "immigrant faith."[9] Following waves of immigration, by the 1930s Catholics constituted over 20 percent of the American population. Although the defeat of Al Smith in the 1928 election reminded Catholics that they resided in an essentially Protestant nation, the power of the Catholic vote was realized with the 1932 election of Franklin Roosevelt and correspondingly warm relations between his administration and the Catholic Church.

Nonetheless, in 1933 Catholics strenuously opposed the diplomatic recognition accorded the Soviet Union. In 1934, a direction came from Rome via Father Ledochowski, the father general of the Society of Jesus, calling American Jesuits to concerted action against Communism in America. It signaled

---

8. Charles Gallagher, *Vatican Secret Diplomacy: Joseph P. Hurley and Pope Pius XII* (New Haven: Yale University Press, 2008), 189.

9. Sydney E. Ahlstrom, *A Religious History of the American People* (New Haven: Yale University Press, 1972), 1002.

the beginning of a massive, organized anti-Communist campaign, with Father Edmund Walsh of Georgetown University swiftly implementing a fourteen-point program.[10] It failed to mobilize support beyond the Catholic community.

Reinforcement for the campaign came from the Vatican in 1936, a presidential election year. Cardinal Pacelli, Vatican secretary of state and the future Pius XII, made a visit to the United States, largely organized by the archbishop of New York, Francis Spellman. The day after Roosevelt was successfully re-elected, the president and the cardinal met privately. In the absence of an official record, there was a great deal of speculation whether diplomatic relations between the Holy See and the White House, or restraining anti-Semitic radio priest Charles Coughlin, were discussed. What is known is that Pacelli made clear his conviction that the greatest threat to the future and to America was the Soviet Union, and that a time would come when all the churches would need to combine to resist and defeat atheistic Communism.[11] Roosevelt dismissed the notion of a Communist America. Nevertheless, when war came he sought to cultivate papal support, conscious of the Vatican's legitimizing, and indeed mobilizing, potential with Catholics at home and in the global arena.[12] Attempts were also made to reach and mobilize other religious leaders, but none possessed the Vatican's attributes of state status and global spiritual authority as the center of the worldwide Catholic faith.

The organized Catholic anti-Communist drive made little headway in non-Roman America, despite further reinforcement in 1937 by the papal encyclical *Divini Redemptoris*, in which Pius XI elaborated on "that infamous doctrine" and the need to combat the "fatal plague" of Communism. With the exception of the Catholic population, Roosevelt's sanguine attitude toward the Communist threat to America was shared by most of his fellow citizens in the 1930s. That the threat was very real to American Catholics can be attributed to the promotion within the American Catholic Church of a form of separatism that operated through a legion of Catholic alternatives to secular organizations and associations. It included educators; legal and medical people; a host of trades; youth, women, and union organizations; and more. There

10. Robert L. Frank, "Prelude to Cold War: American Catholics and Communism," *Journal of Church and State*, 1992, 39–56. See also Charles R. Gallagher, "Decentering American Jesuit Anti-Communism: John LaFarge's United Front Strategy, 1934–1939," *Journal of Jesuit Studies* 5, no. 1 (2018).

11. "Meeting with Protestant Clergymen," October 20, 1947, Myron C. Taylor Papers, Harry Truman Library.

12. George Q. Flynn, *Roosevelt and Romanism: Catholics and American Diplomacy, 1937–1945* (London: Greenwood Press, 1976).

were also schools and colleges and, of course, a huge variety of publications. It was an infrastructure that assured the influence of the Catholic hierarchy on their flocks and the success of an anti-Communist campaign in the Catholic community despite the lack of a credible Communist threat or support from the rest of America.

That the wider community remained largely unmoved is important because it challenges popular assumptions that 1930s American society was informed by what Michael Parenti called "the anti-Communist impulse."[13] In fact, as Robert L. Frank has pointed out, the published literature on American anti-Communism provides meager evidence of any such impulse between the post–Great War 1919–1920 Red Scare and post–Second World War McCarthyism.[14] As determined by Sydney Lens, during the 1930s, "For Americans . . . Communism became a peripheral issue, far removed from the epicenter of their deliberations."[15] For Catholics, it was a continuation of their two-centuries-old quest to be both Catholic and American.

Having survived late nineteenth-century nativist anti-Catholic movements and twentieth-century Ku Klux Klan opposition to foreigners and Catholics, the church leadership was aware of lingering suspicion that it was a Trojan horse instructed by the Vatican to create a Catholic state. Hence the motto of the first Catholic national organization, the NCWC (National Catholic War Council, subsequently National Catholic Welfare Conference), established in 1919, was For God and Country. The motto reflected the discernible preoccupation amongst the hierarchy to show that their religion was not an obstacle to Americanism.[16] In the 1930s, the fusion of ideology and religion that informed Catholic anti-Communist rhetoric seemed to Catholics an affirmation of both their faith and their patriotism as the campaign targeted the antithesis of American democracy and the foe of religion. The very different perceptions of Protestants were reflected in the pages of the liberal and nondenominational *Christian Century*, which repeatedly warned Protestants against the "Catholic Anti-Red Campaign," as the title of one article put it.[17]

---

13. Michael Parenti, *The Anti-Communist Impulse* (New York: Random House, 1969).

14. Frank, "Prelude to Cold War," 39–56.

15. Sydney Lens, *The Futile Crusade: Anti-Communism as American Credo* (Chicago: Quadrangle Books, 1964), 17.

16. Richard John Neuhaus, *The Catholic Moment* (New York: Harper and Row, 1987).

17. "The Catholic Anti-Red Campaign," *Christian Century*, September 30, 1936, 1275; "Shall Protestants Accept the Pope's Invitation?," *Christian Century*, November 25, 1936, 1550–52; "Stay Out!," *Christian Century*, December 9, 1936, 1646–48.

Additionally, Catholic attitudes toward the Spanish Civil War revealed that adhering to Vatican policy, even where a sizable number of Americans agreed with it, would inevitably prove problematic for American Catholics. Allen Guttman, documenting the impact of the Spanish Civil War on America, described the divisions it caused as a "wound in the heart." The American Catholic Church proved the vanguard for the minority that supported Franco, elsewhere regarded as a Fascist.[18] Catholics considered that in opposing a brutal Communist regime, justified by their church's domestic anti-Communist campaign and the Vatican, they were once again confirming their commitment to both their faith and their country's democratic values.

Although Catholics strenuously opposed aid to the Soviet Union following Operation Barbarossa, Pearl Harbor aligned them with every other American in supporting the Allied cause against the Axis Powers. Even more importantly, Protestant and Catholic church leaders shared a concern to be part of the new social and political order promised during the war. Christian leaders from within the ecumenical movement made clear their conviction that the church could provide the common moral code required for a just and humane world order.[19] Moreover, they "boldly asserted the right of the church as an institution to occupy itself with the problems of this world."[20] From the Catholic side, as early as 1942, a manifesto was issued by a group of European Catholics living in America that included Jacques Maritain, "the outstanding Catholic philosopher of our time." Published in *Commonweal* on August 21, 1942, the manifesto claimed that the issue at stake in the war was "the very possibility of working toward a Christian civilization."[21] The main preoccupation of the Vatican under the obsessively anti-Communist Pius XII appeared to be the exclusion of the Soviet Union.

Despite engaging meaningfully in postwar planning, church leaders were excluded from peace negotiations.[22] Yet, as American opposition to the Soviet

18. Allen Guttman, *The Wound in the Heart: American Response to and Interpretation of the Spanish Civil War* (New York: Free Press of Glencoe, 1962).

19. G. K. A. Bell, "The Christian Church and World Peace," July 22, 1957, London, Lambeth Palace Library, Bell Papers, vol. 349, pp. 44–62.

20. Darril Hudson, *The Ecumenical Movement in World Affairs* (London: Littlehapton Books, 1969), 3.

21. John Nurser, *For All Peoples and All Nations: Christian Churches and Human Rights* (Geneva: WCC Publications, 2005), 87.

22. John Foster Dulles, "Acceptance of Appointment as General Adviser to the US Delegation, San Francisco Conference," April 5, 1945, Box 292, Dulles Papers, Seeley G. Mudd Library, Princeton.

Union congealed, church advocacy of a Christian order for the postwar world was not only supported but actively promoted in America by politicians and statesmen, business and media moguls, even military men and industrialists. It was a process Jonathan Herzog aptly termed "the spiritual-industrial complex," a beneficiary of state sanction and commercial talent that "worked to foment a religious revival that was conceived in boardrooms, rather than camp meetings, steered by Madison Avenue and Hollywood suits rather than travelling preachers, and measured with statistical precision."[23]

A distinct Catholic contribution to the "spiritual-industrial complex" project derived from the Marian cults organized around apparitions, miracles, and prophecies. The cult of the Virgin of Fatima, a set of prophecies many believed foretold the apocalypse, became particularly salient. In 1942, Pius XII consecrated the whole human race to the Virgin Mary, apparently in response to warnings and prophecies made to three child shepherds at Fatima in Portugal in 1917 but not published until 1942. They included a warning to convert Russia; otherwise it would spread its errors, causing more suffering, persecution, and conflict. In the critical Cold War year of 1947, a new organization, the Blue Army of our Lady of Fatima, began attracting significant numbers of Americans. Its stated aim was to prosecute spiritual warfare against atheistic Communism and to defend against cosmic catastrophe. Its paranoid, apocalyptic style of Catholicism was well suited to the anxieties and fears generated by the McCarthy era.

In 1946, Pius XII crowned Our Lady of Fatima "Queen of the World." In 1947, Eastern and Western statues of the Virgin of Fatima began circulating the world. The arrival of the Western statue in America inspired a movement, blessed and encouraged by Pius XII, whereby the faithful were asked to pledge devotion to the Virgin of Fatima and wear a small blue ribbon as a sign of belonging to the Blue Army of Our Lady against the Red Army of atheistic Communism. Between the McCarthy hearings and the assassination of John F. Kennedy, the Blue Army attracted over five million recruits.[24]

It was, however, the adoption by the "spiritual-industrial complex" of Catholicism's theological anti-Communist doctrine as outlined in *Divini Redemptoris* that proved to be the most consequential contribution. It complemented and gave doctrinal rigor to America's most entrenched self-perceptions: "An

---

23. Jonathan P. Herzog, *The Spiritual-Industrial Complex: America's Religious Battle against Communism in the Early Cold War* (Oxford: Oxford University Press, 2011), 7.

24. Jeffrey S. Bennett, "The Blue Army and the Red Scare: Politics, Religion and Cold War Paranoia," *Politics, Religion and Ideology* 16, nos. 2–3 (2015): 263–81.

America drunk on notions of its own innocence and goodness has been able to identify the devil with its enemies, and its enemies with the devil, time and again."[25] American history is littered with political movements that adopted an evangelical fervor, exacerbated by "an ideological world view that explains everything in terms of conspiracy; that reduces complex issues to a struggle between good and evil, and that exaggerates the evil to the point of paranoia; that prompts a self-righteousness on the part of the faithful; and that ultimately rests on a blind faith."[26]

As leaders from American industries, businesses, media, churches, and government identified religious faith as "one of the most potent arrows in the quiver of domestic security,"[27] Truman reached out to the Vatican. It was the beginning of America's religious cold war, initiating a process by which Catholic theological anti-Communism came to inform American political anti-Communism, which developed discernible doctrinal characteristics specific to Catholicism. It meant that American anti-Communism served politically partisan domestic interests as well as Cold War policies. Reflecting traditional Catholic antiradicalism, it became a means by which conservative forces in America waged war against the entire Left and even moderate, reform-inclined forces that included the Democratic Party and even other Christians. Above all, however, the Catholic absolutism introduced into American anti-Communism meant a focus on "evil" that designated US-Soviet rivalry as an irreconcilable conflict that precluded the normal modes of diplomacy and led to rigid attitudes that failed to allow for change and evolution within the Soviet bloc.

Communist attitudes and practices toward organized religion varied considerably over time and according to circumstances. The Second World War revealed that, albeit for entirely pragmatic and expedient reasons, the Soviet leadership was prepared to accept and work with organized religion where it was perceived as a potential asset and not as a threat to the regime. W. A. Visser 't Hooft, the first general secretary of the World Council of Churches and a careful observer of the evolving relations between the new Communist regimes and their churches, opined that domestication, not eradication, was their objective.[28] In contrast, Catholicism, with its belief that all morality de-

25. W. Scott Poole, *Satan in America: The Devil We Know* (New York: Rowman and Littlefield, 2009), xxi.

26. Philip Brenner, "Waging Ideological War: Anti-Communism and US Foreign Policy in Central America," in *Socialist Register*, ed. Ralph Miliband, John Saville, and Marcel Liebman (London: Merlin Press, 1984), 230–60.

27. Herzog, *The Spiritual-Industrial Complex*, 6.

28. Dianne Kirby, "Harry S. Truman's International Religious Anti-Communist Front,

rives from God, emphasized the destructive drive of Communism, which, being "godless," and indeed "anti-God," lacked all moral restraint.

Pius XI composed *Divini Redemptoris* against the backdrop of the Spanish Civil War when the Catholic press was full of the atrocities perpetrated against the church. Unsurprisingly, unqualified absolutism marked the encyclical's rhetoric. Pius XI declared: "Communism strips man of his liberty, robs human personality of all its dignity. . . . No natural right is accorded to human personality, which is a mere cog-wheel in the communist system."[29] Naturally the American Catholic press presented Pius XI's claims in the context of the church being the guarantor of the key American values of freedom, democracy, and individualism.

Francois Houtart has argued that twentieth-century Roman Catholic Church documents tended "to caricature Marxist positions in order to criticize them more easily."[30] However, Communist brutality toward the Spanish Catholic Church inevitably meant that fear and misunderstanding were also factors causing Catholic anti-Communism to develop around faulty modes of representation. The same absolutism and misrepresentation subsequently became incorporated into Cold War America's brand of anti-Communism, which embraced the same distorting tendencies. Marxist atheism was used to depict Communism as godless and thus *evil*, committed to the *destruction* of Christianity as a step toward world domination. In designating the Soviet Union the "evil other," the Truman administration was, significantly, able to shift America into permanent military, political, and economic intervention on a world scale.

It is notable, therefore, that *Divini Redemptoris* failed to move majority America in the 1930s and that its themes only became influential when they were embraced by American Cold War propaganda. Notably, the claims informing Pius XI's 1937 encyclical against "Atheistic Communism," as it was entitled in the English text, not only became the core rhetorical templates for Cold War America's brand of anti-Communism, but also underwent significant adaptations. Pius XI had begun by presenting "'the all too imminent danger' of communism as attributable to the 'sad legacy of the original fall.'"[31]

---

the Archbishop of Canterbury and the 1948 Inaugural Assembly of the World Council of Churches," *Contemporary British History* 15, no. 4 (2001): 35–70.

29. *Encyclical Letter of Pope Pius XI on Atheistic Communism (Divini Redemptoris)* (Boston: St. Paul Editions, 1937), 9.

30. Francois Houtart, "Religion and Anti-Communism: The Case of the Catholic Church," in *Socialist Register* (1984), 349–63.

31. *Divini Redemptoris* 1.

The deliberate claim that the roots of Communism were moral and spiritual implied that its defeat could only be achieved by a superior moral and spiritual force, by which of course the pope meant the Catholic Church. The majority of the encyclical described Catholic doctrine and the revitalization of Catholicism as the spiritual solution to the evil of Communism.

In America's doctrine of anti-Communism, it came to mean the United States, which of course already perceived itself as a "chosen nation" with a God-given mission. In his famous anonymously written X article, George Kennan argued that it was necessary for the United States to express "a spiritual vitality capable of holding its own among the major ideological currents of the time."[32] Religious ideas were enshrined in the crucial 1950 Cold War document NSC 68, which referred to defeating the fanatic faith of Communism by mobilizing a "spiritual counter-force."[33] The Soviet Union was designated the vehicle of a godless and aggressive ideology that sought the destruction of Western civilization and Christianity, against which America was presented as a God-fearing nation, defender of the free world, and the only force able to stop Communism.[34]

Significantly, it was not until the 1930s that Catholic anti-Communism depicted Communism as seeking world domination through deceit and the dissemination of lies and propaganda. Although Communism was a negligible threat to America, Pius XI, fearing that Stalin's united front strategy could make inroads, claimed that Communism "strives to entice the multitudes by trickery of various forms, hiding its real designs behind ideas that in themselves are good and attractive."[35] He charged that ordinary Americans were susceptible to inadvertently supporting the Communist cause. These unwitting "dupes" consisted largely of liberals, teachers, writers, union activists, and others of that ilk. *Divini Redemptoris* mandated that Catholics should not work with Communists: "Communism is intrinsically wrong and no-one who would save Christian civilisation may collaborate with it in any undertaking whatsoever."[36]

32. X [George Kennan], "The Sources of Soviet Conduct," *Foreign Affairs* 25, no. 4 (July 1947): 566–82.

33. E. R. May, ed., *American Cold War Strategy: Interpreting NSC 68* (Boston: Palgrave Macmillan, 1993), 29–30.

34. Dianne Kirby, "Divinely Sanctioned: The Anglo-American Cold War Alliance and the Defence of Western Civilisation and Christianity, 1945–48," *Journal of Contemporary History* 35 (July 2000): 385–412.

35. *Divini Redemptoris* 37.

36. *Divini Redemptoris* 58.

To facilitate American aid to the Allies, including the Soviet Union, Roosevelt had looked to the pope for some modification of this particular aspect during the Second World War. With the advent of the Cold War, it was precisely the absolutism of Catholic anti-Communism that appealed to Cold Warriors, particularly illustrated by J. Edgar Hoover's penchant for the Catholic Church, relationships with its hierarchy, and preference for Catholic agents. Hoover's best-selling anti-Communist book was, significantly, entitled *Masters of Deceit: What the Communist Bosses Are Doing Now to Bring America to Its Knees.*[37] Under his direction, the FBI effectively criminalized not simply Communism but also dissent, especially dissent from the Cold War consensus. Thousands of harmless people were subjected to FBI surveillance and even persecution. Suspects included social gospel adherents, civil rights supporters, and antiwar activists, clergymen included. Herzog places Hoover at the heart of the "spiritual-industrial complex" and the managed use of societal resources to stimulate a religious revival in the late 1940s and 1950s.[38]

Herzog contends that "Fewer Americans brooded more about the dangers of domestic communism, and fewer benefitted more from the fears they helped create."[39] Hoover, a prolific writer and speaker and "America's most respected authority on Communism," was critical to the exercise of exaggerating the Communist threat. In doing so he also had the FBI emulate the dissemination tactics of the Catholic anti-Communist campaign: "The Bureau trained its field agents to cultivate a nation-wide anti-communist consensus by working with local media groups. It leaked intelligence estimates to anti-Communist allies like HUAC and established liaisons with Hollywood studios."[40]

Like Truman, Hoover established a working alliance with the Catholic Church and received information from its intelligence networks. In 1946, the same year that Truman instructed Myron C. Taylor to return to Rome, Hoover and Spellman, organizer of the 1936 US visit, coauthored a pamphlet that warned of the dangers of Communism.[41] Subsequently, Hoover addressed Congress, detailing Communism's insidious and conspiratorial nature and emphasizing its menace as a psychic and spiritual disease that

37. This was the title of the American edition (Pensacola, FL: Beka Book, 1958). The British edition was *Masters of Deceit: The Story of Communism in America* (London: J. M. Dent and Sons, 1958).

38. Herzog, *The Spiritual-Industrial Complex*, 6–7.

39. Herzog, *The Spiritual-Industrial Complex*, 84.

40. Herzog, *The Spiritual-Industrial Complex*, 84–85.

41. John Cooney, *The American Pope: The Life and Times of Francis Spellman* (New York: Times Books, 1984), 146–48.

destroyed from within.[42] In the same week in June that George Marshall proposed what became the European Recovery Program, Hoover appeared on the cover of *Newsweek*. Inside he provided an article, "How to Fight Communism," in which he linked Christianity with democracy and individualism.[43] Hoover was critical to cultivating anti-Communist sentiments in the House and the Senate, to which the FBI supplied information on Communist Party USA members and anyone suspected of sympathizing with them or the causes they promoted.[44]

Hoover, of course, also made good use of the Catholic conflation of liberalism with Communism. "Liberalism" represented to Catholics an amoral, materialistic philosophy derived from the Enlightenment. It was a perspective also adopted by anti–New Dealers, especially Republicans looking to equate Roosevelt's progressive legislation with Communism. It became a feature to which conservative Americans adhered far longer than Catholics. The 1960s brought a mandate from Vatican II that stressed that part of Catholic teaching, common in the 1930s, which posited that the Enlightenment led to laissez-faire economics and the injustices and inequalities associated with unrestrained capitalism. Catholicism in the 1930s had indicted the unrestrained competition among individuals caused by capitalism's promotion of greed and the accumulation of wealth. Ironically, by the 1960s, it was an emphasis that challenged America's anti-Communist consensus, which defended free market capitalism, to which the Catholic Church had so effectively contributed in the early Cold War.

In August 1947, Truman and Pius XII effected a letter exchange that was a spiritual corollary to the earlier efforts that same year on the political and economic planes, the Truman Doctrine (March 1947) and the Marshall Plan (June 1947). Truman was particularly anxious at this time about isolationist sentiments in Congress and public opinion. A survey conducted by the State Department had concluded that two years after American GIs embraced Red Army troops on the banks of the Elbe, 70 percent of Americans opposed a hard-line anti-Soviet policy.[45] However, "the working alliance between the world's two great anti-communist forces, the US and the Vatican, made the

42. Dianne Kirby, "J. Edgar Hoover, the FBI, and the Religious Cold War," in *The FBI and Religion: Faith and National Security before and after 9/11*, ed. Sylvester A. Johnson and Steven Weitzmann (Oakland: University of California Press, 2017), 67–84.

43. Kirby, "J. Edgar Hoover, the FBI, and the Religious Cold War."

44. Kirby, "J. Edgar Hoover, the FBI, and the Religious Cold War."

45. Martin Eve, "Anti-Communism and American Intervention in Greece," in *Socialist Register* (1984), 101–13.

spiritual children of Martin Luther uneasy,"[46] precisely as had previously happened with Roosevelt, whose example Truman followed in appointing Taylor as his personal representative to the Holy See, despite the existence of a congressional prohibition against official relations.

In both cases, Protestants were concerned about favor toward the Catholic Church and disregard for the constitutional separation of church and state. Interestingly, Roosevelt's defense was that such appointments were part of a wider effort to mobilize the moral and religious forces of the world on behalf of peace. The same defense would be proffered by Truman in the early Cold War. In both cases, there is evidence that efforts were made to reach out to such forces, but questions remain regarding substantiveness and sincerity.[47] Truman's efforts were certainly seen as suspect by Protestant leaders who feared that Catholicism sought to use American power to promote Catholic interests. Ecumenical church leaders in particular were opposed to "any kind of diplomatic relationship that seems to unite Protestantism with Catholicism in a common war against Russia."[48]

Nor were Protestant reservations eased by developments on the home front. The story of the senator from Wisconsin whose name is most associated with the early Cold War period of political repression that made Americanism synonymous with anti-Communism is well known. Looking for an issue with which to garner support for his reelection to the Senate in 1950, Joe McCarthy was receptive to the suggestion of Jesuit Father Edmund Walsh that he use Communism. McCarthy had attended the Jesuit Marquette University. Walsh, of Georgetown University, was responsible for directing the response in 1934 to the call from Rome for organized action against Communism in America. The campaign Walsh initiated was to reach its apotheosis in the McCarthy era.[49] McCarthyism, an umbrella term for the era of postwar political repression, reflected the hallmarks of Catholic anti-Communism. It was an outcome that crystallized the way in which the Christian struggle against secularization, the *bête noir* of the church in the nineteenth century, had merged in the twentieth with that against Communism.

When Pius XI promulgated *Divini Redemptoris* in 1937, declaring that Moscow's struggle "was against Christian civilization," he credited the papacy

46. R. S. Ellwood, *The Fifties Spiritual Marketplace: American Religion in a Decade of Conflict* (Brunswick, NJ: Rutgers University Press, 1997), 52.

47. Dianne Kirby, "The Religious Cold War," in *The Oxford Handbook of the Cold War*, ed. Richard H. Immerman and Petra Goedde (New York: Oxford University Press, 2013), 491–530.

48. Kirby, "Harry S. Truman's International Religious Anti-Communist Front," 35–70.

49. Frank, "Prelude to Cold War," 39–56.

with having "called public attention to the perils of Communism more frequently and more effectively than any other public authority on earth." The theology of Catholic anti-Communism partially emerged as a counter to the new ideas and thinking that were companion to modernization and progress. Many factors, including the rise of science and enlightenment thinking, caused the erosion of Christian authority in Western society, contributing to the gradual decline of church attendance and an increase in atheism.[50] The conflict between Communism and Christianity was but one component in the wider problematic confronting the church, secularization. Two years prior to Karl Marx publishing the *Communist Manifesto*, Pope Pius IX condemned "that infamous doctrine of so-called Communism which is absolutely contrary to the Natural Law" and which "would utterly destroy the rights, property and possessions of all men."[51] Within a decade, the church was preoccupied with the appeal of socialism to the lower orders as the more insidious threat.[52] Leo XIII's 1878 warning against the poisonous doctrines of socialism, Communism, and nihilism reflected papal preoccupation with the forces for change that threatened the established order and the church's place within it. To the pope, these new forces represented a "deadly plague that is creeping into the very fibers of human society and leading it on to the verge of destruction."[53]

By the twentieth century, Catholic anti-Communism had become infused with a form of anti-Semitism that went beyond the damaging charge of deicide owing to the identification of Jews with left-wing ideologies. The notion of "Judeo-Communism" combined anti-Semitism with anti-Communism, producing one of the twentieth century's most consequential myths. Representing the context in which anti-Semitic ideas evolved is a complex and perilous exercise, but certainly the negative implications about Jews in Christian teaching made them easy scapegoats for a host of ills within Christian societies well before Communism became an issue. However, and very importantly, in America the myth was challenged from the late 1930s when the anti-Fascist Left combined with Protestant neoorthodoxy to emphasize the shared heritage of Christianity and Judaism via the concept of "Judeo-Christian." Intended as a counter to anti-Semitism and Fascism, along with their Catholic supporters, the concept was part of the opposition to Catholic demagoguery as espoused

50. Adrian Hastings, *A World History of Christianity* (Grand Rapids: Eerdmans, 2000).

51. Pius IX, *Qui Pluribus*, November 9, 1846.

52. Paul Misner, "The Predecessors of 'Rerum Novarum' within Catholicism," *Review of Social Economy* 49 (1991): 454.

53. Leo XIII, *Quod Apostolici Muneris*, December 28, 1878.

by Father Coughlin's Christian Front and those seeking a Christian American identity that expressed Fascist sympathies and anti-Semitism.

Mark Silk, who charted the rise of the term "Judeo-Christian," noted how it operated as "a catchword" versus "Fascist fellow travelers and anti-Semites."[54] The concept served to highlight similarities and continuities between the two monotheistic faiths, bringing them together in opposition to totalitarianism, helping distance Jews from Communism and Christians from anti-Semitism. During the Cold War, linking Christianity with Judaism changed from being an anti-Fascist strategy to being an anti-Communist strategy, thus facilitating the Cold War transition celebrated by Herberg in 1955, whereby Catholics, Protestants, and Jews were presented as united by the shared values and ideals of Americanism. In the Vatican Secretariat, however, the anti-Judaic assumption that Jews had brought destruction upon themselves by rejecting Christ was still very much alive and included Cardinal Augustin Bea. Such assumptions persisted right up to Vatican II and *Nostra Aetate*, when the Catholic Church condemned all discrimination by race or nationality, celebrating the truth in Hinduism, Buddhism, and Islam before speaking of the Jews.[55] *Nostra Aetate* repudiated the centuries-old "deicide" charge against all Jews, emphasized the religious bond shared by Jews and Catholics, reaffirmed the eternal covenant between God and the people of Israel, and dismissed church interest in trying to baptize Jews.[56] Vatican policy, albeit belatedly, at last supported the Americanist aspirations of US Catholics.

By Vatican II, however, the Catholic Church, like its mainstream Protestant counterparts, had found that far from giving it access to the corridors of power, the advent of the Cold War in America, which initially seemed to embrace the concept of a world order informed by Christian values, in fact confronted it with a range of politico-moral dilemmas. The religious cold war had required the construction of an American anti-Communist religious identity, achieved through appropriating the spiritual and moral authority of American churches for the nation. Challenging the church's role in defining the relationship between religion and politics, it was a process of symbolic appropriation that reinterpreted religion as an increasingly abstract and moral concept, controlled and mediated by secular leaders rather than the church.

54. Mark Silk, "Notes on the Judeo-Christian Tradition in America," *American Quarterly* 36, no. 1 (Spring 1984): 65–85.

55. John Connelly, *From Enemy to Brother: The Revolution in Catholic Teaching on the Jews, 1933–1965* (Cambridge, MA: Harvard University Press, 2012), 299.

56. *Nostra Aetate*, Declaration of the Relationship of the Church to Non-Christian Religions, Second Vatican Council, October 28, 1965.

American Catholic leaders were as confounded as their mainstream Protestant counterparts when "the nation with the soul of a church" appropriated religion in general rather than Christianity per se for its Cold War agenda. In the 1950s a "Christian amendment" to the Constitution was easily defeated, reflecting congressional preference for "adhesional religious symbolism" rather than "invidious distinctions among the God-fearing."[57] The same sentiment permeated the Supreme Court, which in 1931 used the word "Christian" to describe the nation. By 1952 it was using the term "religious": "We are a religious people whose institutions presuppose a Supreme Being."[58] In addition, many mainstream church leaders, Catholic and Protestant, worried about the instrumentalization of religion and the way in which the American way of life was assigned the status of religion.[59]

The generalized religiosity and patriotic moralism that characterized America's "spiritual-industrial complex" were well captured by President Eisenhower's blunt 1954 declaration that "Our government makes no sense unless it is founded on a deeply felt religious faith—and I don't care what it is."[60] By the time Herberg celebrated the Cold War constellation of Protestant-Catholic-Jew, the Manichaean distinction drawn between the godly US and the godless Soviets affirmed the value of religion generally rather than Christianity specifically. At the same time, increases in the number and destructive capacity of nuclear weapons led to a more questioning church and demands for serious engagement with the ethical and theological issues raised by this new means of destruction. However, the logic undergirding absolutist anti-Communism, that Communism was evil and hence the *"ultimate"* threat, justified deterrence and possession of the *"ultimate"* weapon.

The proliferation of nuclear weapons and the prospect of global annihilation, the impact of the civil rights movement and the Vietnam War, meant Catholics, including those in religious orders, were, especially following Vatican II, as divided and conflicted by these challenges to the Cold War consensus as their fellow American Christians. In essence, affirmation of Catholic Americanism was a complex and messy procedure that reflected profound changes in America's politico-religious landscape and Cold War contestation of American values and patriotism.

57. Mark Silk, *Spiritual Politics: Religion and America since World War II* (New York: Simon and Schuster, 1988), 107.

58. *New York Herald Tribune*, February 21, 1955.

59. Herberg, *Protestant, Catholic, Jew*.

60. *Christian Century* 71 (1954).

American Catholicism and US Intelligence in the Early Cold War

Michael Graziano

When the Second Vatican Council convened in 1962, much of the world's attention was fixated on Rome. The ecumenical council took the Catholic world by surprise. The ceremonial nature of the proceedings was fodder for an international news media eager to document the council. Many Catholics, watching the colorful tableau of arriving bishops and church leaders, remained unsure what to make of Pope John XXIII's calls for *aggiornamento* in the church, a "bringing up to date."[1] Where some Catholics saw new and exciting developments, others saw reason for alarm. Among those unsure what to make of the council was the Central Intelligence Agency (CIA).

In May 1963, Director of Central Intelligence (DCI) John McCone sent a memo to President Kennedy in which he outlined the CIA's assessment of the council. Titled "Change in the Church," the document revealed the US intelligence community's interest in possible changes to church doctrine and practice. While many American Catholics wondered what changes might be made to the role of laypeople in the church, or to the use of vernacular languages in the Mass, the agency was concerned about the geopolitical ramifications of the council. The CIA's chief fear was that the council would usher in a new politics of permissiveness: permissiveness toward the Italian political Left, for example, or toward church intervention in international issues like nuclear nonproliferation. Some feared there might even be a new permissiveness toward Soviet Communism.[2] This chapter explores how the US intelligence community approached the Vatican and Roman Catholicism during the early Cold

1. For more on American reactions, see Colleen McDannell, *The Spirit of Vatican II: A History of Catholic Reform in America* (Philadelphia: Basic Books, 2011).
2. CIA Office of National Estimates, "Staff Memorandum No. 27–63, 'Change in the Catholic Church,'" May 13, 1963, NSF/CF/Vatican, Box 191A, John F. Kennedy Presidential Library, 2.

War, and how this relationship affected American Catholics living at a time of rapid changes for both the United States and the Roman Catholic Church.

The church's perceived softening toward Communism was the greatest concern for many in the CIA. Agency analysts surmised that Pope John XXIII's openness toward Moscow was due to two assumptions made by the pope. First, that Soviet premier Khrushchev was essentially a reformer with whom the church need not have an antagonistic relationship. Second, that warming relations toward Moscow could aid the besieged Catholic Church in Eastern Europe—locked behind the Iron Curtain—before "it is totally destroyed."[3] While the CIA made clear that they did not doubt the pope's—or his council's—good intentions, agency analysts worried that the pope was well meaning but naive. "The Vatican's grasp of broader international problems," one CIA memo noted, "may be something less than comprehensive." In light of the Second Vatican Council, they concluded that "the establishment of official relations with the USSR, Khrushchev's reception by the Pope, and even a new series of concordats with the Communist states are possibilities."[4]

The CIA's careful attention to the council, and to the activities of Pope John XXIII, may seem out of place for a national intelligence agency presumably engaged in high-stakes espionage and geopolitical intrigue. Yet the agency's interest in Catholicism was part of a larger dynamic between the American intelligence community and religious ideas, individuals, and institutions during the Cold War. The intelligence community's interest in Catholicism was linked to the church's peculiar place in American culture. American Catholic history was often turbulent, shadowed by its relationship to the Vatican. Yet during the Cold War the Vatican was a bastion of anti-Communism, making it of increasing interest to American policy makers—and thus to American intelligence officers. Catholics, as newly appreciated allies against Communism, were also necessary for internal American cohesion during the Cold War.[5] Reliably anti-Communist Catholics reinforced a popular American political narrative that prized religious belief as the ultimate bulwark against Communism. In this context, the CIA's concern about the council was simple: If the pope went soft on Khrushchev, who would be next?

The CIA was not the only institution rethinking the place of Catholics in American culture. The agency's actions were part of a larger trend in which elements of the federal government, and specifically the intelligence commu-

---

3. CIA Office of National Estimates, "Staff Memorandum No. 27–63," 3.

4. CIA Office of National Estimates, "Staff Memorandum No. 27–63," 14–15.

5. For more on this, see Kevin M. Schultz, *Tri-Faith America: How Catholics and Jews Held Postwar America to Its Protestant Promise* (New York: Oxford University Press, 2011).

nity, reworked their views of Catholicism and developed relationships with Catholic Americans. These changes were driven by concerns over foreign policy as well as the changing makeup of the US population.[6] For example, FBI director J. Edgar Hoover eagerly recruited FBI agents from Jesuit schools since he understood those institutions to produce the ideal form of "Christian manhood" demanded by the bureau.[7] By 1960, 170 of the FBI's nearly 6,000 special agents were Fordham graduates. A few years prior, Hoover provided glowing praise for the Catholic university in its alumni magazine: "I like to find men of granite, men of physical, mental, moral, and spiritual strength."[8] Hoover thought the FBI and Catholic Church shared important values, and for decades FBI agents were sent on retreats with Jesuit priests at Manresa-on-Severn.[9]

The place of the institutional Catholic Church in the United States changed tremendously during the Cold War. President Roosevelt's attempt to send an informal representative to the Vatican in 1939 elicited an uproar, while the establishment of formal diplomatic relations during President Ronald Reagan's administration was widely perceived to cap a period of intense cooperation against the "evil empire" of the Soviet Union.[10] A major contribution to this period of dramatic change was the relationship between Catholicism and the United States intelligence community.

*　　　　*　　　　*

The relationship between American Catholicism and US intelligence has roots in a genealogy of ideas about religion and American national security that predates America's founding. In the twentieth century, a central figure in this

---

6. For more on the relationship between American foreign policy and American perceptions of Catholicism, see Katherine D. Moran, "Catholicism and the Making of the U.S. Pacific," *Journal of the Gilded Age and Progressive Era* 12, no. 4 (October 2013): 434–74, doi:10.1017/S1537781413000327.

7. Quoted in Steven Rosswurm, *The FBI and the Catholic Church, 1935–1962* (Amherst: University of Massachusetts Press, 2009), 44. See also Regin Schmidt, "The FBI and the Catholic Church," in *The FBI and Religion: Faith and National Security before and after 9/11*, ed. Sylvester A. Johnson and Steven Weitzmann (Berkeley: University of California Press, 2017).

8. Rosswurm, *The FBI and the Catholic Church*, 43. This was out of 5,900 agents.

9. Rosswurm, *The FBI and the Catholic Church*, 50.

10. On the establishment of formal relations, see Gerald P. Fogarty, SJ, "The United States and the Vatican, 1939–1984," in *Papal Diplomacy in the Modern Age*, ed. Peter C. Kent and John F. Pollard (Westport, CT: Praeger, 1994); Marie Gayte, "The Vatican and the Reagan Administration: A Cold War Alliance?," *Catholic Historical Review* 97, no. 4 (2011): 713–36, doi:10.1353/cat.2011.0170; Luca Castagna, *A Bridge across the Ocean: The United States and the Holy See between the Two World Wars* (Washington, DC: Catholic University of America Press, 2014).

story was William Joseph Donovan. Donovan was a former soldier, lawyer, and statesman. In World War II, Donovan headed the newly formed intelligence agency, the Office of Strategic Services (OSS). Much about the CIA in the early Cold War—not least its leadership and staffing—is closely tied to the OSS. The agency, for its part, recognizes the OSS as its "true ancestors in spirit and deed."[11] But one adjective is notable for how infrequently it is used to describe Donovan: Catholic.

Importantly for the intelligence community's later relationship with the Catholic Church, Donovan developed working relationships with important church leaders and institutions during the war. The apostolic delegate in Washington, DC, for example, unofficially agreed to help American intelligence. In a memo to President Roosevelt, Donovan outlined the reasoning behind this unusual cooperation: "I had a long visit with the Delegate and from him obtained assurances that there would be made available for us information from all over the World that would be received from their various delegates. He recognizes that a Hitler victory might well mean a modern Avignon for the Papacy. I think that he is very anxious, unofficially, to help in every way possible."[12] American Catholics were cultivated by Donovan, too. Francis Spellman and Fulton Sheen, both pillars of postwar American Catholicism, were frequent correspondents and allies of Donovan's.

Donovan succeeded at developing unorthodox information networks, including those in and through the church. Yet the fact that a Catholic was chosen to coordinate the intelligence activities of the United States government in wartime is notable. The focal point of American anti-Catholicism had long been the Catholic's curious relationship to the American state, but American anti-Catholicism was neither uniform nor stable.[13] Debates about transubstantiation, the body of Christ, and other theological conflicts—while important in some respects—mask the way in which American anti-Catholicism drew its

11. Central Intelligence Agency, "An End and a Beginning," June 28, 2008, https://www.cia.gov/library/publications/intelligence-history/oss/art10.htm.

12. William Donovan, "Memorandum for the President No. 265," February 18, 1942, Director's Office Records, NARA Microfilm Publication M1642, Roll 22, National Archives.

13. The legacy of anti-Catholicism in US history is discussed at greater length in Susan M. Griffin, *Anti-Catholicism and Nineteenth-Century Fiction* (Cambridge: Cambridge University Press, 2004); Tracy Fessenden, *Culture and Redemption: Religion, the Secular, and American Literature* (Princeton: Princeton University Press, 2006); William R. Hutchison, *Religious Pluralism in America: The Contentious History of a Founding Ideal* (New Haven: Yale University Press, 2004); Elizabeth Fenton, *Religious Liberties: Anti-Catholicism and Liberal Democracy in Nineteenth-Century U.S. Literature and Culture* (New York: Oxford University Press, 2011); Philip Hamburger, *Separation of Church and State* (Cambridge, MA: Harvard University Press, 2004).

force from concerns about the subversive nature of Catholics in liberal democratic states. Throughout the nineteenth century, anti-Catholicism generally had more to do with (often exaggerated) fears of the Vatican as a foreign state power than it did with the place of individual Catholics in American life.[14] This distinction between pious American Catholics and a potentially dangerous Catholic foreign state never fully disappeared, even as it was reworked amid the influx of Catholic immigrants to the United States after the Civil War.

Led by the Catholic William Donovan, OSS's success working with the Catholic Church during the war helped future officers in intelligence agencies—as well as other parts of the US government—think differently about the Vatican and institutional Catholicism in the United States. This was accomplished not by dispelling notions of Vatican political power, but rather by reimagining this political power as friendly to American interests.[15] Even so, the OSS overlooked differences between the Vatican and the US government that would have consequences for the two institutions' relationship during the Cold War. The quiet alliance between the Vatican and the United States during World War II obscured many of the ways in which the two governments' interests paralleled, rather than merged. In addition, relations between the Vatican and the United States were complicated by differing assumptions about the nature of Communism, the place of US Catholics in American culture, as well as the rich history of anti-Catholicism in the United States. These assumptions exacerbated the confusion when, years later, some American officials worried that the Second Vatican Council could work against American interests.

Reading *Testem Benevolentiae* at Langley

Between World War II and Vatican II, American intelligence officers continued to shape American policy toward the Vatican at the highest levels. One

---

14. This is not to say that individual American Catholics did not face hardship or discrimination on account of their Catholic identity or practices. Rather, I suggest that American Protestants' fears of American Catholics often had as much or more to do with the "political" than the "religious." This was certainly the case in Donovan's own life. For more on this, see Douglas C. Waller, *Wild Bill Donovan: The Spymaster Who Created the OSS and Modern American Espionage* (New York: Free Press, 2012); Anthony Cave Brown, *The Last Hero: Wild Bill Donovan* (New York: Times Books, 1982).

15. This is explored at greater length in Michael Graziano, "William Donovan, the Office of Strategic Services, and Catholic Intelligence Sources during World War II," *US Catholic Historian* 33, no. 4 (2015): 79–103.

CIA report explained: "There is no reason to doubt that [Pope] John, if he felt that good would result from such a meeting [with Khrushchev] or exchange [with the Soviets], would brush aside criticism thereof (even from within the Roman Curia), just as Christ dismissed criticism of His talking with Publicans and sinners."[16] The CIA's assessment of the Vatican in the early days of the council paints a picture of an institution in the midst of great change. Young priests and laymen were excited about the liberalizing possibilities, with some even thinking that the church now endorsed a "kind of socialism." Other Vatican insiders, according to CIA sources, were "deeply disturbed" at the possible consequences.[17] In particular, the CIA worried about the papal encyclical *Pacem in Terris*, which reiterated the importance of peace, justice, and human rights in the nuclear age. A month before DCI McCone briefed Kennedy, the agency put together some "preliminary comments" on the encyclical. While the agency eventually concluded that the encyclical avoided any radical changes, they did note that the carefully chosen language of the documents left the door open to more substantial changes in the Vatican's future relationship with the Soviet Union.

This was not the first time that American intelligence officers fretted about Pope John XXIII's perceived friendliness toward Communism. Before he was Pope John XXIII, Cardinal Roncalli made a brief appearance in an OSS intelligence report during World War II. OSS informants at a Vatican social function had made note of Roncalli's overt friendliness toward the Soviet ambassador—an uncommon sight at the Vatican, even during World War II.[18] It was a brief line in a throwaway report, but it represented fears that would resurface decades later during the Cold War. A few weeks before DCI McCone sent his "change in the church" memo to Kennedy, McCone had asked the president for permission to investigate "whether there might be more than met the eye" behind the pope's recent meeting with Premier Khrushchev's son-in-law Alexei Adzhubei.[19] The president agreed, and the CIA dispatched longtime

---

16. "Preliminary Comments on the Encyclical 'Pacem in Terris,'" April 15, 1963, CIA-RDP79T00429A0013000300012–0, National Archives (CREST Database), 2.

17. CIA Office of National Estimates, "Staff Memorandum No. 27–63, 'Change in the Catholic Church.'"

18. "Special Report #80: Vatican Relations with Russia and France," March 7, 1945, RG 226, Entry 210, Box 311, Folder 2, National Archives.

19. "Memorandum of Conversation with the President with Mr. John McCone and Mr. Bundy," March 25, 1963, National Security Files, Meetings and Memoranda, Meetings with the President: General, March 1963, John F. Kennedy Presidential Library, http://www.jfklibrary.org/Asset-Viewer/Archives/JFKNSF-317-014.aspx.

diplomat Robert Murphy to the Vatican. The episode is significant not for what it uncovered, but rather because it is another reminder of Catholicism's importance in the eyes of the intelligence community.

In this way, the CIA's interest in the council was no accident. The CIA was already studying how to present American Catholicism in the most strategically beneficial light.[20] While there were plenty of unconventional topics researched by the agency in the 1950s, a lengthy report on American religious history ranks among the more unexpected. After careful study, the agency concluded that each of America's many religious groups had made a unique contribution to the history of religious freedom: Baptists provided freedom of conscience, Congregationalists modeled democratic organization, Quakers gave sanctity of conscience, and Catholics contributed respect for natural law.[21] Each American religious group had played a part in making American religion "American."

The memo demonstrated historically what the agency argued contemporaneously: that American Catholics were unabashedly "American" and felt no political allegiance toward Rome. The agency accomplished this by carefully threading the historiographical needle. The centerpiece of the agency's interpretation of American Catholic history was an analysis of the nineteenth-century papal encyclical *Testem Benevolentiae Nostrae* (1899).[22] In particular, the agency reinterpreted the so-called Americanist controversy as evidence of Catholics' undivided loyalty to the American state, since it demonstrated how American Catholics differed from their European counterparts. It was not their religion that marked American Catholics as unique—but their nationality. In this view, *Testem Benevolentiae* did not change anything about American Catholic practice because Catholic immigrants to the United States had become different solely because of "a spirit of freedom that arose from the freedom of America and had little to do with religious concepts." Thus,

20. For more information on the CIA's relationship to Catholicism, see Hugh Wilford, *The Mighty Wurlitzer: How the CIA Played America* (Cambridge, MA: Harvard University Press, 2008); Richard Gribble, "Anti-Communism, Patrick Peyton, CSC and the CIA," *Journal of Church and State* 45 (2003): 535; James T. Fisher, *Dr. America: The Lives of Thomas A. Dooley, 1927–1961* (Amherst: University of Massachusetts Press, 1997); Michael Graziano, "Religion and the Birth of the American Intelligence State" (diss., Florida State University, 2016).

21. "Christian Influences in United States Democracy," January 1959, CIA-RDP78-02771R0005000160002–5, National Archives (CREST Database).

22. Pope Leo XIII issued *Testem Benevolentiae* in 1899 in response to perceived liberal trends in the church, particularly those involving church-state separation in the United States. The encyclical was addressed to the American cardinal James Gibbons and came amidst church-state tension in Europe.

freedom for immigrants "to live their faith to the fullest" eventually resulted in a different kind of Catholicism that would later be recognized by some European Catholic leaders as threatening church unity.[23]

Yet American leaders, and their agency advisers, had no interest in American Catholics forsaking church unity so long as the Vatican stressed the importance of anti-Communism. So while the agency concluded that *Testem Benevolentiae* did not change anything about American Catholicism, it was only because "before *Testem Benevolentiae* they accepted authority in dogma and moral matters and continued to associate with non-Catholic neighbors in all things not necessarily religious—labor unions, business associations or sports. . . . This is the true badge of American Catholicism generally."[24] This historical narrative attempted to normalize Catholics in American history. American Catholics could accept the moral authority of Rome, it suggested, while remaining loyal to the political order of the United States. This "dual" identity of Catholics was complementary, not contradictory.

But the CIA was, of course, an intelligence agency enmeshed in a variety of geopolitical concerns: its work was more than simply a scholarly analysis of *Testem Benevolentiae*. The agency's goal was practical: to reassess American Catholicism in light of the pressing political demands of the Cold War. American Catholic history was an opportunity to engage with issues of religious accommodation in a religiously pluralist democracy. The CIA saw American Catholic history as an antidote for the kinds of religious bigotry that the country could not afford during the Cold War. "The problem of pluralism," the report explained, is that it "implies a plurality of incompatible religious faiths."[25]

The memo recognized Catholics' place in the complex landscape of American religious freedom.[26] "On what theory," the memo asked, "is the plurality within the community accepted in a manner not to destroy the necessary social unity? Secondly, on what theory is the consensus of the community based, in order that it does not infringe on the plurality, but permits to all the different groups the full integrity of their convictions?"[27] Tensions within American religion were all the more important in light of Cold War assumptions about the necessity of religious belief in challenging the Soviet Union.

23. "Christian Influences in United States Democracy," 17.
24. "Christian Influences in United States Democracy," 17.
25. "Christian Influences in United States Democracy," 18.
26. For more on historical approaches to understanding American religious freedom, see David Sehat, *The Myth of American Religious Freedom* (New York: Oxford University Press, 2011).
27. "Christian Influences in United States Democracy," 18.

Debates about the nature of religious freedom in a pluralist democracy—and the place of American Catholics in United States history—could have serious geopolitical consequences. In a broader sense, these efforts signaled that the value of Catholicism in American politics was being recognized anew, and that the direction of American Catholicism was being contested in ways both covert and overt. This chapter concludes by considering one such contest involving the agency and a Catholic magazine from California called *Ramparts*.

Ramparts and "Proper" Catholicism

Ramparts began publishing in 1962. The magazine described itself as a Catholic literary quarterly that would be a "forum for the mature American Catholic" focusing on "those positive principles of Hellenic-Christian tradition . . . in an age grown increasingly secular, bewildered, and afraid."[28] It lasted only seven years—going out of business in 1969—but it had a remarkable impact.[29] Radicalized in large part by the Vietnam War and the civil rights movement, the magazine negotiated its Catholic identity as its politics tilted increasingly to the left. In the interim, *Ramparts* would have the dubious journalistic distinction of being targeted by the CIA for a "run down."[30] When the magazine collapsed, *Ramparts* refugees went on to found *Rolling Stone* and *Mother Jones*. It also helped shape a generation of neoconservatives, including David Horowitz and Brit Hume, the latter a contributing editor at *Ramparts* before he went on to work for Fox News. According to Helen Keating, who cofounded the magazine with her husband Ed, *Ramparts* was designed to "present the ancient truths of the Church with intelligence and sophistication," but also to "stimulate the artists who had been stifled by the narrowmindedness of the Church in America."[31]

28. Quoted in Jeffrey M. Burns, "No Longer Emerging: 'Ramparts' Magazine and the Catholic Laity, 1962–1968," *US Catholic Historian* 9, no. 3 (1990): 323. Burns's article is a thorough, scholarly investigation of the relationship between *Ramparts* and the changing nature of American Catholicism in the 1960s.

29. The magazine would be resurrected a few years later and published until 1975 under the same name, but it was functionally a separate publication from the Catholic *Ramparts* that had come before it.

30. Quoted in Angus Mackenzie, *Secrets: The CIA's War at Home* (Berkeley: University of California Press, 1999), 17.

31. Peter Richardson, *A Bomb in Every Issue: How the Short, Unruly Life of Ramparts Magazine Changed America* (New York: New Press, 2009), 21.

Ramparts was a symbol of the changes in both the American Left and American Catholicism during the 1960s.[32] One early issue published an essay by Thomas Merton challenging white liberals on racial issues, and Merton in turn put the editors in touch with Father Daniel Berrigan and Rabbi Abraham Heschel. *Ramparts* later defended a play, *The Deputy*, that charged Pope Pius XII with ignoring the Holocaust. Editorials criticized James Cardinal McIntyre for insufficient support of the civil rights movement. The November 1964 issue excoriated Barry Goldwater, and continued criticizing Cardinal McIntyre by linking him to the GOP presidential candidate. Merton wrote the editors, cautioning them about their change in tone: "I do think that in certain areas a judicious restraint would perhaps do the magazine much more good than harm."[33] But the slide to the left continued. Editor Warren Hinckle wrote that the Catholic Left was "the best thing that has happened to the Catholic Church since probably Jesus Christ."[34]

The magazine's strident polemical tone made it unpopular with the church hierarchy, and there was a great deal of controversy over whether the magazine was actually Catholic. Finally, in 1965, the magazine announced it was now an ecumenical publication, aimed at Protestants and Jews as well as Catholics.[35] *Ramparts* had grown away from the church even as its editors felt the church had grown away from it. "The Church was a willing participant in the divorce," Hinckle later wryly observed.[36]

While *Ramparts* reimagined its relationship to Catholicism, it published a series of articles exposing the CIA on a number of fronts. *Ramparts*'s muckraking included an exposé on the CIA–Michigan State University relationship, wherein the CIA paid MSU to train South Vietnamese in "covert police training."[37] *Ramparts* dropped another bombshell when it revealed, in 1967, that the CIA was funding the National Student Association and other ostensibly independent organizations.[38]

32. Burns, "No Longer Emerging," 322. Burns argues that this is one of the most important legacies of *Ramparts*.

33. Quoted in Richardson, *A Bomb in Every Issue*, 32.

34. Quoted in Burns, "No Longer Emerging," 332.

35. Richardson, *A Bomb in Every Issue*, 19–33.

36. Quoted in Burns, "No Longer Emerging," 328.

37. Rhodri Jeffreys-Jones, *The CIA and American Democracy* (New Haven: Yale University Press, 2003), 153.

38. For an account of the *Ramparts* situation from inside the CIA, see Cord Meyer, *Facing Reality: From World Federalism to the CIA* (Lanham, MD: University Press of America, 1982), 86–89.

Particularly in regard to the Vietnam War, *Ramparts* was also highly suspicious of the church's relationship to the American state. In a 1965 article by Robert Scheer, the magazine charged the CIA with manipulating Catholic individuals and institutions.[39] Francis Cardinal Spellman, the archbishop of New York, was another of the magazine's primary targets.[40] Spellman was cast as a moral leader complicit in the immoral dealings of America's early involvement in Vietnam. In the article's infamous conclusion, Scheer asked, "If the war continues, may it not one day be called Cardinal Spellman's final solution to the Vietnam question?"[41]

In July 1965, *Ramparts* followed up with an article by Scheer and Hinckle dissecting the so-called Vietnam Lobby, an informal group of American lobbyists and decision makers supporting interventionist policy in Vietnam.[42] While the article did identify some important connections about the group—including the involvement of Cardinal Spellman—it also slipped into conspiratorial theorizing by suggesting that a nefarious network of Catholics influenced US policy in Vietnam.[43] Despite obvious factual errors, the dramatic claims helped cement the argument into popular memory.[44] As James Fisher observed, it was notable that an ostensibly Catholic publication (albeit a far-left one) relied on nativist Protestant tropes to argue its point.[45] Scheer and Hinckle's determination to demonstrate Catholic culpability for America's errors in Vietnam began, Hinckle would later explain, "in an earnest attempt to hang something on the Catholic Church. We set out looking to lay some of the blame for Vietnam

39. Robert Scheer, "Hang Down Your Head, Tom Dooley," *Ramparts*, 1965.

40. *Ramparts* viewed the war as an unjust intervention into Vietnamese attempts to free themselves of colonial oppressors. The United States, in this view, was inheriting the colonial power over Vietnam from France, which *Ramparts* saw as fundamentally un-American.

41. Scheer, "Hang Down Your Head, Tom Dooley," 28.

42. Robert Scheer and Warren Hinckle, "The Vietnam Lobby," *Ramparts*, 1965, 22.

43. It is important to note that Scheer overemphasized the role played by the CIA in the early days of American involvement. For more on this, see Peter Hansen, "Bắc Đi Cú: Catholic Refugees from the North of Vietnam, and Their Role in the Southern Republic, 1954–1959," *Journal of Vietnamese Studies* 4, no. 3 (October 2009): 173–211, doi:10.1525/vs.2009.4.3.173.

44. Scheer and Hinckle's errors, and their consequences, have been explored by a number of scholars. See James T. Fisher, "The Second Catholic President: Ngo Dinh Diem, John F. Kennedy, and the Vietnam Lobby, 1954–1963," *U.S. Catholic Historian* 15, no. 3 (1997): 119–37; James T. Fisher, "The Vietnam Lobby and the Politics of Pluralism," in *Cold War Constructions: The Political Culture of United States Imperialism, 1945–1966* (Amherst: University of Massachusetts Press, 2000); Joseph G. Morgan, *The Vietnam Lobby: The American Friends of Vietnam, 1955–1975* (Chapel Hill: University of North Carolina Press, 1997); Burns, "No Longer Emerging."

45. Fisher, "The Second Catholic President," 120.

at the silken slippers of the Pope; we succeeded only in implicating Cardinal Spellman."[46] Such voracious criticism of the Catholic hierarchy was unheard of in the Catholic press, and was one of *Ramparts*'s most important—if unorthodox—contributions to American Catholicism.[47]

The CIA devised a number of strategies to counteract *Ramparts*. DCI William Raborn ordered an investigation into the magazine, in clear violation of the agency's charter. CIA officers assembled dossiers on nearly two dozen *Ramparts* editors and writers. All the while, *Ramparts* kept publishing and the investigation widened. James Jesus Angleton, the agency's counterintelligence expert, took over the investigation on the assumption that *Ramparts* was likely a Communist plot to weaken American resolve. By 1967, Angleton had a dozen officers investigating *Ramparts*, and had pursued 127 employees and almost two hundred additional people with more tenuous connections to the magazine. In Angleton's report, he noted each time *Ramparts* described things in ways the CIA deemed dangerous, such as the US government being "sick," the Catholic Church being "reactionary," or the CIA being "evil."[48]

Meanwhile, Desmond Fitzgerald, then CIA's deputy director for plans, tasked CIA officer Edgar Applewhite with finding covert ways to damage *Ramparts*. "I had all sorts of dirty tricks to hurt their circulation and financing," Applewhite later recalled. "The people running RAMPARTS were vulnerable to blackmail. We had awful things in mind, some of which we carried off, though *Ramparts* fell of its own accord. We were not the least inhibited by the fact that the CIA had no internal security role in the United States."[49] The CIA also looked into the financial support of *Ramparts*. In a meeting between the CIA and the Internal Revenue Service (IRS), the agency made clear that it understood *Ramparts*'s promise of future exposés as a threat, and as "an attack on CIA in particular, and the administration in general." The CIA proposed that the IRS "examine" the corporate tax returns of *Ramparts* in order to find any possible financial improprieties as well as to locate information on the magazine's financiers.[50] They hoped to find evidence of Soviet funding—which would have provided a more formal entry point for the CIA's involvement—but

46. Fisher, "The Second Catholic President," 120.

47. Burns, "No Longer Emerging," 332–33.

48. Michael Howard Holzman, *James Jesus Angleton, the CIA, and the Craft of Counterintelligence* (Amherst: University of Massachusetts Press, 2008), 231–36.

49. Quoted in Evan Thomas, *The Very Best Men: Four Who Dared; The Early Years of the CIA* (New York: Touchstone, 1995), 329–30.

50. "IRS Briefing on Ramparts," February 2, 1967, CNSS Documents Collection Box 9 File C-48, National Security Archive.

they came up empty-handed.[51] In any case, for the CIA the damage was done.[52] DCI Helms later said that the *Ramparts* exposés contributed to congressional investigations of the CIA in the mid-1970s.[53]

The intelligence community was wary of changes to Catholic anti-Communism, whether it came from the lay Catholics of *Ramparts* or the church hierarchy in Rome. *Ramparts* and the liberalizing trends of the Second Vatican Council were not the kind of Catholicism the agency wanted to cultivate. It was too oppositional to US policy, too friendly to dangerous ideas like socialism and nuclear disarmament. This conflict is a reminder that changes to Catholicism were negotiated not just in Saint Peter's Basilica or in local parishes, but in US government offices.

Conclusion

The relationship between Catholicism and the intelligence community demonstrates the US government's interest in influencing religion during the Cold War. One of the defining features of the relationship between Christianity and the state during this period was the level of diffusion between the two, such as the Religious Right's involvement in US politics. Yet the relationship worked in both directions. Various government agencies took an interest in certain kinds of Christianities, convinced as they were that involvement in the spiritual life of Americans would lead to discernible geopolitical benefits.

American Catholics and American national security share overlapping histories. In much the same way that Catholics had long been threatening in the American imagination because of their perceived loyalty to a foreign state, American Catholics during the Cold War became normalized through the burgeoning national security state. The relationship between American Catholicism and the intelligence community illustrates how government attitudes toward Catholics had little to do with Catholics per se, but were instead rooted in a utilitarian appreciation of the practical benefits of using Catholicism and the institutional Vatican against the Soviet Union. Observation of international Catholic developments, as well as careful policing of varieties of Catholicism

51. "Ramparts Tax Returns," February 15, 1967, CNSS Documents Collection Box 9 File C-48, National Security Archive.

52. John Ranelagh, *The Agency: The Rise and Decline of the CIA* (New York: Simon and Schuster, 1986), 251–52.

53. Nicholas Dujmovic, ed., "Reflections of DCIs Colby and Helms on the CIA's 'Time of Troubles,'" *Studies in Intelligence* 51, no. 3 (1988): 39–56.

at home, was necessary from this point of view. The intelligence community helped reimagine the place of Catholics in American culture, and the image of the Vatican as a foreign state, by refashioning Catholic distinctiveness as an asset in America's Cold War arsenal. Specters of papal scheming and Jesuit invasions gave way to an image of an institutional Vatican friendly toward—and perhaps even in service to—American ideals.

Changing Course:
The American Catholic Bishops and the
Decline of Anti-Communism during the Cold War

Todd Scribner

In their 1980 pastoral letter on Marxist Communism, the Catholic bishops of the United States reasserted their long-standing conviction that Marxism endorsed a materialist vision of the human person and of society that is detrimental to human flourishing and at odds with a Christian one.[1] This perspective had a long pedigree in church teaching, both in the United States and at the Vatican. As early as 1846, Pope Pius IX issued a scathing condemnation of Communism and avowed that with its embrace "the complete destruction of everyone's laws, government, property, and even of human society itself would follow."[2] His successor popes—from Pope Leo XIII through Pope John Paul II—at one point or another expressed similar sentiments, although often in less catastrophic terms.[3] Some conservative bishops criticized the pastoral letter for being too philosophical and failing to take into account the real-life atrocities recently committed under the banner of Communism.[4] Most people just ignored it. Its release elicited

1. National Conference of Catholic Bishops, "Pastoral Letter of the U.S. Bishops on Marxist Communism," reprinted in *Origins* 10, no. 28 (1980).

2. Pope Pius IX, *Qui Pluribus (On Faith and Religion)*, November 9, 1846, no. 16, http://www.ewtn.com/library/encyc/p9quiplu.htm.

3. Pope Leo XIII, *Diuturnum (On the Origin of Civil Power)*, June 29, 1881, no. 23, http://www.vatican.va/holy_father/leo_xiii/encyclicals/documents/hf_l-xiii_enc_29061881_diuturnum_en.html; Patrick McNamara, *A Catholic Cold War: Edmund A. Walsh, S.J., and the Politics of American Anticommunism* (New York: Fordham University Press, 2005), 25–26; Pope Pius XI, *Divini Redemptoris (On Atheistic Communism)*, March 19, 1937, no. 14, http://w2.vatican.va/content/pius-xi/en/encyclicals/documents/hf_p-xi_enc_19370319_divini-redemptoris.html; Dianne Kirby, "The Cold War, the Hegemony of the United States, and the Golden Age of Christian Democracy," in *Christianity: World Christianities, c. 1914–2000*, ed. Hugh McLeod (Cambridge: Cambridge University Press, 2006), 293–94.

4. Bruce Buursma, "U.S. Catholic Bishops Ease Stand on Marxism," *Chicago Tribune*, November 13, 1980, 1.

little reaction from the mainstream press and went largely unnoticed even within Catholic circles.

Contrast this to the reception of their pastoral letter "Economic Justice for All" six years later, which proved contentious and elicited widespread praise and criticism from within secular and religious circles alike. "Economic Justice for All" critiqued existing economic institutions and analyzed the extent to which they promoted or undermined human dignity, assisted the poor, protected human rights, and uplifted opportunities for people to participate in the economic life of their local community. It was critical of economic injustice, including the problem of a world in which financial disparities were pronounced and economic inequality the status quo. As such, it is surprising that Communism went unmentioned, given the Catholic Church's long-held conviction that Marxism was antithetical to human flourishing and that it undermined authentic community.

The tepid response to the bishops' pastoral letter on Marxist Communism, as set against the more robust reception of their economic pastoral, points to an important change in climate within American Catholic life. Although unapologetic anti-Communists in the early years of the Cold War, by the early 1980s the US Catholic bishops had reconfigured their foreign policy priorities and, as a consequence, anti-Communism lost much of the salience that it once had in the face of other geopolitical realities. The anti-Communism that for decades had been central to the Catholic bishops' worldview became embedded in a foreign policy framework that increasingly emphasized human rights abuses, economic inequalities between countries, and problems associated with underdevelopment in the developing world. Anti-Communism as a primary motivator for the bishops' activities in public life became increasingly marginalized. The East-West divide that had defined the bishops' foreign policy during the Cold War became largely subordinate to divisions that emerged along the North-South axis.

As late as the 1960s, the anti-Communist impulse remained a defining marker of American Catholic identity, with Catholic media, the hierarchy, and the laity alike often expressing passionate hostility toward Communism.[5] And yet, despite such loud opposition coming from all quarters of American Catholic life, within little more than a decade its unapologetic and ideologi-

---

5. For example, in 1955, *America* magazine referred to Communism as essentially "brutal and inhuman," and *Commonweal* described it as an ideology with which there "can be no positive coexistence." Cited in Joseph G. Morgan, "A Change of Course: American Catholics, Anticommunism, and the Vietnam War," *U.S. Catholic Historian* 22, no. 4 (Fall 2004): 119.

cally based anti-Communism began to wane. More surprising still, for all the bluster about the dangers of the Communist threat, its diminished resonance occurred at the height of the Cold War when the Soviet Union posed its greatest peril. What accounts for this shift?

Richard Gid Powers has traced American Catholicism's move away from anti-Communism, noting that when Catholics remained outsiders in American life, their anti-Communism functioned as a marker of identity, in a way similar to the eating of fish on Fridays. As anti-Communism became freighted with the baggage associated with McCarthyism and right-wing extremism, which happened to coincide with the slow integration of the Catholic Church into American culture following World War II, a reflexive ideological anti-Communism became more problematic. Rather than demonstrating their commitment to the American experience, the identification of anti-Communism with extremism reinforced perceptions of the outsider status of the Catholic community. Paired with the Vatican's softening stance toward Communism under the leadership of Pope John XXIII, a path was provided for American Catholics to do the same.[6]

Powers's narrative has some merit. The changing social status of Catholics in American life had an important influence on how they approached questions related to foreign and domestic policy alike, as did the shift in priorities promoted by the Vatican beginning with Pope John XXIII. Nevertheless, his analysis fails to take into account changes in American Catholic thought that underlay the transition away from a reflexive anti-Communism. In an effort to at least partially rectify this oversight, this chapter will focus on the way in which the Catholic bishops of the United States used anti-Communism as a central component in their political rhetoric in the early period of the Cold War and how it diminished in importance beginning in the mid-1960s.

To do so, this essay will begin by tracing the American Catholic Church's anti-Communism from the onset of the Cold War to the early 1960s, with a particular emphasis on how the hierarchy engaged this issue. It will then focus on the transition that occurred within their political and social thought, which downplayed Communism as the central threat to international peace and emphasized issues related to human rights and economic inequality. As a way to make this study more concrete, it will close by examining the way in which the Catholic bishops of the United States engaged the political and religious upheavals occurring in Central America beginning in the late 1970s

6. Richard Gid Powers, "American Catholics and Catholic Americans: The Rise and Fall of Catholic Anticommunism," *U.S. Catholic Historian* 22, no. 4 (Fall 2004): 32–34.

and continuing into the following decade. For many, the Soviet Communist threat was central to the conflicts raging in areas including Nicaragua and El Salvador. The bishops did not share this view. As such, the focus on Central America has the added benefit of highlighting the central role that the Catholic Church played in the "war of ideas" that raged during the Reagan years on this issue.[7] Competing Catholic voices to that of the bishops' analysis will be included in this respect. Examining these differences will point to the ways in which ruptures had emerged in the Catholic Church itself, pitting competing segments of the church against one another, primarily along political and ideological lines.

American Catholicism on the Eve of the Cold War

One of the prominent figures in the Catholic Church's anti-Communist efforts to appear on the eve of the Cold War was Father John Cronin, a Baltimore-based Sulpician priest who was active in the effort to keep organized labor free from Communist influence. His work caught the attention of Catholic leadership and, at their November 1944 annual meeting, the National Catholic Welfare Conference's (NCWC) administrative board approved a proposal to finance a comprehensive study on the spread of Communism and to develop a constructive program to respond to this threat.[8] Father Cronin was chosen to lead in its development.

At nearly 150 pages, the report is expansive enough in scope so that it is impossible to adequately summarize in the space available here. In short, it found the following: that the Soviet Union was an international threat of such magnitude that it could sweep away Europe in the next two decades; that the Communist Party in the United States was a small but aggressive organization that was making inroads into organized labor and the federal government; and that popular media provided an effective platform for the spread of Soviet propaganda. An effective defense against further Communist subversion would require, first, a comprehensive education campaign that would target primary

7. Charles Strauss, "Quest for the Holy Grail: Central American War, Catholic Internationalism, and United States Public Diplomacy in Reagan's America," *U.S. Catholic Historian* 33, no. 1 (Winter 2015): 164–67.

8. The most comprehensive survey to date of the Cronin Report and its development is in chapter 4 of Steve Rosswurm, *The FBI and the Catholic Church: 1935–1962* (Amherst: University of Massachusetts Press, 2009), 133–79. The NCWC was the precursor to the United States Conference of Catholic Bishops, still in existence today.

and secondary schools and seminaries. Second, it would prove important to develop a leadership base within the church and society at large that would help to deliver a Catholic message that could counteract Communist propaganda in the public square.[9]

Once completed, the report was distributed to all the bishops of the United States, but because of its sensitivity the administrative committee of the NCWC requested that it not be distributed to any laymen, and that it be distributed only to a very selective group of clergy, depending on their professional positions.[10] Cronin's authorship of the report and subsequent appointment to the NCWC's Social Action Department in 1946, as an assistant director alongside Monsignor George Higgins, put him in a position to influence the direction of the Social Action Department over the next two decades. According to one commentator, Cronin's appointment "signaled the beginning of a reconfiguration of Catholic social action and social policy that produced an all-out war against American Communists and those who worked with them."[11]

In November 1953, the administrative board discussed and declined a proposal to develop a program to combat Communism on the parish level, but directed Cronin to continue his study of Communism. This directive resulted in the production of a second, smaller report that was presented to the bishops the following April.[12] Highlighting the continued influence of Soviet Communism around the world, he noted that the policy of containment, a central pillar in the United States' confrontation with the Soviet Union, was a failure and the threat that the Soviets posed to world peace and stability had not decreased during the previous decade.[13] Nevertheless, on the domestic front the American Communist Party had experienced "grievous losses," as public opinion had sharply turned against Communism in recent years due to ongoing investigations by both the executive and legislative branches, which had taken positive action against the party and its Communist sympathizers.[14]

In addition to its focus on the current state of international Communism, Cronin's follow-up report highlighted the way in which Cold War politics both

9. Fr. John Cronin, *The Problem of American Communism in 1945: Facts and Recommendations,* Confidential Study, Office of the General Secretary, Box 24, File 17, ACHRCUA.

10. Rosswurm, *The FBI and the Catholic Church,* 167.

11. Rosswurm, *The FBI and the Catholic Church,* 178.

12. Fr. John Cronin, *Communism Today: A Digest,* April 1954, Office of the General Secretary, Box 24, File 17, ACHRCUA.

13. Cronin, *Communism Today,* 4.

14. Cronin, *Communism Today,* 9–12.

anticipated and contributed to the reconfiguration of interdenominational relationships in post–World War II America. One initiative that he specifically pointed to was the Foundation for Religious Action, which was launched by Dr. Charles Lowry, an Episcopalian minister who had given up his pulpit to fight Communism. The foundation sought to establish a national advisory council made up of clergy and laity of all faiths and, in doing so, to demonstrate that the struggle against Communism was not merely a political problem but also a religious one. It maintained close ties to the federal government, and as such functioned in part to promote and engage religious institutions as a spiritual counterforce to atheistic Communism.[15]

Despite its efforts, the foundation's leadership struggled to achieve widespread support among liberal Protestant and Jewish circles. The Christian-oriented theological underpinnings of the foundation's rhetoric tended to alienate Jews from participation, and the deference toward Catholic influence in the group seems to have resulted in some unease among Protestants.[16] Despite these difficulties, the foundation's advisory council included prominent Protestant leaders, including Billy Graham and Norman Vincent Peale.[17] Catholic support for the foundation was forthcoming, at least among some of the powerful hierarchs in the American church, who expressed an inclination to coordinate at least some activities with non-Catholic organizations in the fight against the Soviet Union.

In his follow-up report to the administrative board, Cronin emphasized that the NCWC's participation with the foundation would *not* involve "inter-faith cooperation on religious matters," but would, in keeping with dictates of the Holy Office, provide for the "defense of religion against its enemies as an area in which cooperation is not forbidden."[18] By avoiding any explicitly religious involvement with it, the bishops were free to engage on the level of the more secular, institutional involvement in the defense of religion against an outside threat.

15. Kirby, "The Cold War," 297–98. President Eisenhower publicly endorsed the purpose of the foundation, which was to mobilize "a counter-offensive of ideas, of faith, or moral force against the powers bent on destroying religion and enslaving man through world revolution and world dictatorship." Kenneth Dole, "News of the Churches," *Washington Post*, June 12, 1954, 9.

16. K. Healan Gaston, "The Cold War Romance of Religious Authenticity: Will Herberg, William F. Buckley, and the Rise of the New Right," *Journal of American History* 99, no. 4 (March 2013): 1145–50.

17. Jonathan Herzon, "America's Spiritual-Industrial Complex and the Policy of Revival in the Early Cold War," *Journal of Policy History* 22, no. 3 (2010): 349.

18. John Cronin, *Communism Today: A Digest*, April 23, 1954, Office of the General Secretary, Box 24, File: Communism: General: April–May, 1954, 20–21, ACHRCUA.

Cronin's commentary on the foundation was accompanied by a memorandum prepared by Archbishop O'Boyle of Washington that proposed establishing a formal relationship. The administrative board authorized O'Boyle to begin negotiations, which resulted in a name change to the Foundation for Religious Action in the Social and Civil Order. While subtle, the change reinforced the notion that the church's cooperation would not involve questions that were dogmatic or otherwise religious in nature. Archbishop O'Boyle also made clear that any derogatory comments about the Catholic Church by any member of the National Advisory Council would lead to the immediate withdrawal of the church from these efforts. It was decided that two bishops would serve on the advisory committee: Bishop Michael Ready of Columbus, Ohio, and Bishop John Wright of Pittsburgh, Pennsylvania.[19]

Although the foundation had only limited success coordinating a unified front across denominational lines, an initiative of this sort would have been difficult to fathom even a decade earlier, particularly one that had Catholic bishops standing shoulder to shoulder with bishops of a Protestant variety. Throughout most of American history the relationship between Protestants and Catholics has often been strained, if not openly hostile; the literature surrounding nativist movements and their adversarial stance toward Roman Catholicism is expansive and well known. Whereas Catholics remained on the margins of American life well into the twentieth century, by the 1950s they had begun to make a place for themselves within it, even in the eyes of some of their Protestant counterparts.

By no means was this place yet secure; the anxieties that the Kennedy candidacy for president enflamed revealed that Catholics still maintained a kind of outsider status in the eyes of many Americans. Nevertheless, the hierarchy's interest in cooperating with Protestant and Jewish groups in activities aimed at defending American democracy against the Communist threat revealed that a slow thaw in interreligious relationships was under way. While not a sufficient cause unto itself, the onset of the Cold War helped to alleviate some of the tensions that existed between competing faith traditions. The emergence of an external enemy as dangerous as the Soviet Union helped to rework the relationship of the Catholic Church to the broader American community. A long-standing and ardent foe of Communism, the church could portray itself as a loyal defender of America and not a subversive threat.[20]

19. O'Boyle to Archbishop Karl Alter, August 20, 1954, Office of the General Secretary, Box 24, File: Communism: General: June–October 1954, ACHRCUA.
20. Todd Scribner, "'Not Because They Are Catholic but Because We Are Catholic': The Bishops' Engagement with the Migration Issue in Twentieth-Century America," *Catholic Historical Review* 101, no. 1 (Winter 2015): 90.

TODO

As Richard Gid Powers has pointed out, the easing of tensions between Catholics and Protestants in the decades after World War II contributed to the church's shift away from anti-Communism as a defining feature of its public identity. Nevertheless, until at least the early 1960s, the Catholic bishops of the United States—both individually and corporately—pushed an anti-Communist agenda that often coincided with foreign policies promoted by the United States government. Cardinals Richard Cushing (1944–1970) and Francis Spellman (1939–1967), to cite two prominent examples, were both unapologetic opponents of Communism who used their positions to speak forcefully against it on both the international and the domestic front. Cardinal Spellman endorsed the controversial anti-Communist senator Joseph McCarthy in April 1954, just eight months before the Senate officially censured him in December of that year; committed his support to Ngo Dinh Diem after first meeting him in the mid-1950s; and remained adamant in support of the US war in Vietnam, even as it became increasingly unpopular in American culture.[21]

For his part, Cardinal Cushing established the Missionary Society of St. James the Apostle in 1959; its primary purpose was to assist the Catholic Church in Central America by sending priests from North America to countries in the south that were in need of support. By revitalizing (it was hoped) the church in Latin America through this initiative, encroachments by both Communism and Protestantism could be halted.[22] The ongoing opposition to Communism typified "the close alliance of the national imperative and the Church's mission with regard to communism [that] was a consistent feature of Cushing's rhetoric of the time, as it was for so many others within the Catholic Church and within the broader national society."[23]

Other individual bishops could be highlighted for their anti-Communism, but just as important as what any individual bishop might have said is what the bishops stated corporately through their affiliation with the NCWC. In the immediate aftermath of World War II, and as the antagonisms between the Soviet Union and the United States increased, the bishops released a series of statements highlighting the existential threat of Communism. Some of these

21. Joshua Zeitz, *White Ethnic New York: Jews, Catholics, and the Shaping of Postwar Politics* (Chapel Hill: University of North Carolina Press, 2005), 134; Christopher Kauffman, "Politics, Programs, and Protests: Catholic Relief Services in Vietnam, 1954–1975," *Catholic Historical Review* 91, no. 2 (April 2005): 230–35.

22. James Garneau, "'Santiago Matacomunistas'? Cardinal Cushing's Crusade against Communism in Latin America and the St. James Society," *U.S. Catholic Historian* 22, no. 4 (Fall 2004): 97–115.

23. Garneau, "Santiago Matacomunistas," 103.

statements focused on the philosophical underpinnings of the Communist worldview and their antithetical character to a Christian worldview, while others highlighted specific situations of persecution, particularly as they affected bishops, clergy, and other faithful in select Communist countries. Their statement entitled "Persecution behind the Iron Curtain," for example, saluted the "Christian heroism" and love of freedom demonstrated by the bishops, clergy, and other faithful who "live and suffer in all those countries of Asia and Europe behind the Iron Curtain and under the influence of godless persecution."[24] In addition, twice in both 1952 and 1953, once in 1956, and again in 1957 the bishops issued official statements condemning the persecution perpetrated against believers behind the Iron Curtain and in other Communist-controlled areas of Eastern Europe and Asia.[25]

In one of their most pointed statements of the period, "Victory . . . Our Faith," they identified atheistic materialism as the fundamental enemy of Christian civilization, which was manifest both in Communism and, in a subtler form, in a pervasive and growing secular humanism. The only adequate response to this crisis was through a renewed and forthright Christian faith, which abandoned the "weak and vacillating Christianity" ascendant throughout much of the West. While recognizing reports that religious participation has increased in the decade after World War II, they lamented that this increase had shown few signs of moral uplift and had obscured the extent which God's law and teaching are regularly disregarded in public life.[26]

Given the measurable expansion of religious life during this period, it is surprising that the bishops expressed the degree of skepticism they did with respect to the health of religion in the United States. Between 1946 and 1949, the Southern Baptists constructed five hundred new churches. Overall, Protestant denominations invested a billion dollars in new construction. The Catholic Church built 125 hospitals, one thousand new elementary schools, and three thousand parishes in the decade following the war. The editor of *America*

---

24. NCWC Administrative Board, "Persecution behind the Iron Curtain," November 1950, reprinted in *Pastoral Letters of the United States Catholic Bishops* (Washington, DC: United States Catholic Conference, 1984), 107.

25. The following are reprinted in *Pastoral Letters of the United States Catholic Bishops*: "Persecution behind the Iron Curtain," April 22, 1952, 146–47; "Communist Persecution Particularly in China," November 27, 1952, 158–59; "Persecution in Poland," September 29, 1953, 160; "Peter's Chains," November 21, 1953, 161–63; "A Statement on Persecuted Peoples," December 20, 1956, 190; and "A Statement on Persecuted Peoples," November 17, 1957, 199.

26. The Catholic Bishops of the United States, "Victory . . . Our Faith," November 19, 1954, in *Pastoral Letters of the United States Catholic Bishops*, 172–74.

magazine, John Lafarge, declared that it was impossible "not to rejoice" at the strength of the American Catholic Church.[27] Robert Putnam has posited that in terms of church attendance and other forms of religious observance, "the 1950s was probably the most religious decade in American history."[28]

While the American people may have been religious on paper and reflected in a bricks-and-mortar reality, the bishops continued to question whether they were religious in conviction. In their 1959 "Statement on Freedom and Peace," they lamented that for too many Americans, the American way of life had become little more than the achievement of a high standard of living. Instead of remaining committed to God's law, Americans were beholden to a materialist paradigm, and that the material wealth made from industry and education had superseded their commitment to the higher values inherent to the Christian faith. In so doing, "we have tacitly accepted the materialist philosophy of Communism as our way of life. We have aimed our efforts at satisfying the body and, paradoxically, have allowed the Communists to capture the minds of men."[29]

Although the Catholic bishops continued to concentrate on Communism and the Soviet Union as the primary danger confronting the West, other emergent dangers threatened the international community. The decline of colonialism during the postwar period, a development that the bishops applauded, brought with it the rise of an excessive nationalist impulse, of which they were not so keen. Here they warned that nations that are discovering freedom for the first time must be careful to avoid building a national identity that is preoccupied with past grievances and arouses a "spirit of revenge that defrauds certain minorities of freedom and obstructs a clear vision of the constructive and peaceful paths that lead to national greatness."[30]

Complicating matters was the fact that nationalist movements and communistic propaganda often thrived in conditions created by "poverty, hunger, disease, and the bitterness engendered by social injustice."[31] Such conditions provide fertile soil for Communists and nationalists alike to appeal for support

---

27. Robert Wuthnow, *The Restructuring of American Religion: Society and Faith since World War II* (Princeton: Princeton University Press, 1988), 35–38.

28. Robert Putman, "Lecture 1: Americans Are Religious, Devout, and Divided, but Tolerant. Why?" (American Grace: The Tanner Lectures on American Values, Princeton University, October 27–28, 2010, https://tannerlectures.utah.edu/_documents/a-to-z/p/Putnam_10.pdf).

29. Catholic Bishops of the United States, "A Statement on Freedom and Peace" (Washington, DC: United States Catholic Conference, 1984), 219.

30. Catholic Bishops of the United States, "A Statement on Freedom and Peace," 216.

31. Catholic Bishops of the United States, "A Statement on Freedom and Peace," 216.

from large swathes of humanity who suffered from such indignities. While it might not resolve the problem completely, eliminating the underlying socio-economic and political realities that Communists and nationalists of various stripes often took advantage of for their own self-aggrandizement could limit the reach and influence of these extremist movements. As this conviction became ascendant over the course of the next decade, the bishops' attention to economic inequality, endemic poverty, and human rights abuses became central to their foreign policy perspective. Eliminating these abuses and inequalities would contribute to the creation of an economic and political system in which human dignity could thrive, and remove the fertile soil from which extremist political movements could grow. As socioeconomic inequalities came to the forefront in the bishops' foreign policy, their anti-Communism began to recede and became embedded in a more complex set of priorities. This shift was reinforced by a similar change occurring at the Vatican during this same period.

The Vatican, Communism, and the 1960s

Issued by Pope John XXIII on May 15, 1961, *Mater et Magistra* built on the contemporary social teaching tradition of the church that was initiated by Pope Leo XIII in his encyclical *Rerum Novarum*. Although Pope John XXIII highlighted the antithetical character of socialism as compared to the Christian worldview[32]—a central theme in *Rerum Novarum*—the altered conditions of the post–World War II world led him to emphasize aspects that were not as pressing or apparent decades earlier. Unlike *Rerum Novarum*, which focused on the changing economic and political conditions confronting Europe, Pope John XXIII's encyclical had a more international focus. It included an emphasis on the provision of foreign aid, in as disinterested a way as possible, so as to avoid new forms of colonialism (#169); the problem of concentrated wealth in the hands of a few and the need for its more equitable distribution (#168); the imperative for nations to develop a robust social insurance system (##135–136); and the importance of addressing the needs of the common good on the international level (##78–81). Critics of the encyclical, often from established conservative political and Catholic circles, criticized the pope for downplaying

32. Pope John XXIII, *Mater et Magistra*, May 15, 1961, #34–6, http://w2.vatican.va/content /john-xxiii/en/encyclicals/documents/hf_j-xxiii_enc_15051961_mater.html. Hereafter, references to this document are placed in the text.

the threat of Communism and instead attending to what they understood as less pressing issues.[33]

His following encyclical, *Pacem in Terris*, reinforced many of the themes developed in *Mater et Magistra*. One of its primary purposes was to provide a framework for how the international community might establish a lasting peace within the context of a properly constructed international community that respects the rights and duties of individual people. At one point, Pope John XXIII noted that "it is perfectly legitimate to make a clear distinction between a false philosophy of the nature, origin, and purpose of men and the world, and economic, social, cultural, and political undertakings, even when such undertakings draw their origin and inspiration from that philosophy."[34] Such a vision laid the groundwork for a dialogue to occur between Catholics and Communists, recognizing that even movements that were based on false ideas could still maintain a hint of truth and thus the foundation for further engagement.[35]

The Second Vatican Council issued commentary that further undercut the reflexive anti-Communism that had long defined the church's engagement with the world. In its *Pastoral Constitution on the Church in the Modern World*, the bishops roundly criticized the nuclear arms race, declaring that it was a "treacherous trap"; the current state of affairs that existed between the superpowers was untenable and distracted from other important problems.[36] Several bishops from the United States, including Cardinal Spellman, dissented from this position and instead argued that the possession of nuclear weapons could provide an effective form of deterrence against foreign aggression, and thus was a service to peace.[37]

The willingness to engage political movements and government entities, regardless of whether or not they would pass a kind of politically based purity test, signified a break from past practice. Whereas Pius XII resisted any substantive contact with Soviet leadership, John XXIII initiated a thaw in relations

33. John Judis, *William F. Buckley: Patron Saint of Conservatives* (New York: Simon and Schuster, 1988), 164; Niels Bjerre Poulsen, *Right Face: Organizing the American Conservative Movement, 1945–1965* (Copenhagen: Museum Tusculanum Press, 2002), 128.

34. Pope John XXIII, *Pacem in Terris*, April 11, 1963, #159, http://w2.vatican.va/content/john-xxiii/en/encyclicals/documents/hf_j-xxiii_enc_11041963_pacem.html.

35. J. Bryan Hehir, "Papal Foreign Policy," *Foreign Affairs* 78 (Spring 1990): 29–31.

36. Second Vatican Council, *Gaudium et Spes,* December 7, 1965, #81, http://www.vatican.va/archive/hist_councils/ii_vatican_council/documents/vat-ii_const_19651207_gaudium-et-spes_en.html.

37. Powers, "American Catholics and Catholic Americans," 31.

between the Vatican and Moscow. Through limited engagement with Soviet authorities, the latter promoted a strategy referred to as "Vatican *Ostpolitik*," intended to provide space for the Catholic Church in Eastern Europe. Pope John XIII's commitment to engage was demonstrated concretely through the important role he played in resolving the Cuban missile crisis in 1962.[38] His successor, Pope Paul VI, further developed on this *Ostpolitik*-oriented diplomacy and, in his encyclical *Populorum Progressio*, emphasized the importance of focusing on the developing world and responding to the unjust international structures that currently defined international relations.[39]

Populorum Progressio marked a further marginalization of Communism as the primary threat to international stability and instead highlighted the various disparities at play between the developed and developing world, and the moral obligations of the former to the latter. Appealing to Scripture, Pope Paul VI posited that one of the primary objectives of the church "involves building a human community where liberty is not an idle word, where the needy Lazarus can sit down with the rich man at the same banquet table."[40] As important as economic considerations are in his analysis, the appeal here is not aimed only at material ends. His emphasis on what has come to be known as integral human development in Catholic thought focuses on the entirety of the human person, with all its economic, political, and spiritual characteristics. Such a focus carries with it an implicit critique of Marxism, given that the latter's focus on economic forces and class conflict as the primary driver in historical development does not take into account the entirety of the human person. While implicit here, his critique of Communism was made much more explicit elsewhere.

In 1964, for example, Pope Paul VI reiterated traditional church teaching against Communism in his encyclical *Ecclesiam Suam*, where he noted that "We are driven to repudiate such ideologies as deny God and oppress the Church—We repudiate them as Our predecessors did, and as everyone must do who firmly believes in the excellence and importance of religion. These ideologies are often identified with economic, social and political regimes; atheistic communism is a glaring instance of this."[41] Communism as a po-

---

38. "Pope John XXIII and the Cuban Missile Crisis," Vatican Radio, April 23, 2015, http://en.radiovaticana.va/news/2015/04/23/pope_john_xxiii_and_the_cuban_missile_crisis_/1138957.

39. Hehir, "Papal Foreign Policy," 32–33.

40. Pope Paul VI, *Populorum Progressio*, March 26, 1967, #47, http://w2.vatican.va/content/paul-vi/en/encyclicals/documents/hf_p-vi_enc_26031967_populorum.html.

41. Pope Paul VI, *Ecclesiam Suam*, August 6, 1964, #101, http://w2.vatican.va/content/paul-vi/en/encyclicals/documents/hf_p-vi_enc_06081964_ecclesiam.html.

litical vision remains unacceptable. Nevertheless, his shift toward economic inequality as one of the central threats to international peace had become an ascendant feature of Catholic thought by the late 1960s.

A Preferential Option for the Poor and Catholic Political Thought

This change had measurable consequences for the church's public character. In particular, the influence of both popes John XXIII and Paul VI, alongside the church's opening to the world that was brought about via the Second Vatican Council, had a notable effect on the church in Central America, particularly insofar as both popes helped to lay the groundwork for the conference at Medellin and the emergence of a more socially conscious hierarchy. Allan Figuerora Deck emphasizes the seriousness with which the Latin American bishops took the writings of Pope Paul VI in particular; he used his thought as a lens to criticize the failure of Latin American countries to support effective development due to their "prevailing, oppressive, nondemocratic, and non-participatory political structures."[42]

Reflecting on some of the changes that occurred in Latin America in the fifteen years since the council ended, Archbishop James Hickey of Washington, DC, noted that the changing political posture of the church there shifted from a "socially conservative position to that of the leading voice for reform and social change, and can be traced to the experience and teaching of Vatican II" and as a consequence of the Medellin (1968) and Puebla (1979) conferences that followed.[43] Out of this matrix emerged an emphasis on the "preferential option for the poor," which focuses on the importance of maintaining solidarity with impoverished populations and engaging in efforts of social reform to improve their economic, political, and social standing. At times the commitment to this option produced tension, as revolutionaries in Nicaragua and elsewhere were seen as cooperating with Marxist rebels for political purposes.[44] Setting aside these concerns, the preferential option helped to reconfigure the way in which

42. Allan Figuerora Deck, SJ, "Commentary on *Populorum Progressio*," in *Modern Catholic Social Teaching Commentaries and Interpretation*, ed. Lisa Sowle Cahill et al. (Washington, DC: Georgetown University Press, 2005), 305.

43. Archbishop James Hickey, "The Focus of U.S. Church Concern for El Salvador," *Origins*, March 19, 1981. This was testimony given before a subcommittee of the House Foreign Affairs Committee on March 5, 1981.

44. Andrew Kirkendall, *Paulo Freire and the Cold War Politics of Literacy* (Chapel Hill: University of North Carolina Press, 2010), 141.

these conflicts were understood, with questions related to social justice coming to the forefront and the need to address the living conditions of impoverished and marginalized populations pronounced.

This reconfiguration is evident in many of the public pronouncements by the Catholic bishops of the United States, who tended to downplay the Marxist and Cold War implications of these conflicts. Instead they recognized that the political and social tensions at play in more than one Central American country, including El Salvador and Nicaragua, had been going on for decades. Long before concerns arose over outside intervention—including Communist influence from the East and American influence from the North—internal strife between various segments of society was prevalent.[45]

Communism was seen as less important as a primary factor contributing to and exacerbating the problems in the region and instead became embedded in the arena of economic disparity and widespread human rights abuses. Certainly, Communists often tried to take advantage of the socioeconomic and related political problems plaguing the region and use them to foment revolution. Nevertheless, the core problem confronting much of Latin America, alongside many other developing nations, was the disparities that laid the foundation for conflict between the United States and the Soviet Union. Examining the way in which the bishops formulated their public policy position on the conflict in Nicaragua beginning in the late seventies and continuing into the following decade will show how far removed the bishops were from emphasizing Cold War factors as primary to their foreign policy paradigm.

The US Catholic Bishops and Latin America

Formed in 1961, the Sandinista National Liberation Front (FSLN) was created with the purpose of overthrowing the authoritarian Somoza-led government in Nicaragua.[46] In less than two decades, the Sandinistas had succeeded in this objective. During the early part of the 1980s, the conflicts that continued to engage the country and the surrounding area remained a central focus for church leaders in the United States. Most important for our purposes here is the extent to which, for the US Catholic bishops at least, these conflicts were

45. Hickey, "The Focus of U.S. Church Concern for El Salvador."

46. For a more expansive analysis of the problems related to Nicaragua and the Catholic Church, see chapter 6 of Todd Scribner, *A Partisan Church: American Catholicism and the Rise of Neoconservative Catholics* (Washington, DC: Catholic University of America Press, 2015).

not so much a product of Cold War politics as of economic insecurity and human rights abuses. While foreign influences were complicating matters, they were not the source of the problem. Certainly, such entities took advantage of the underlying revolutionary impulses at play in the region, but such impulses were primarily the product of economic and social injustices already present.[47] This perspective is evident in the US bishops' 1981 statement on the crisis in Nicaragua, wherein they stated that "internal conditions of poverty and the denial of basic human rights characterize many of these societies. These conditions, if unattended, become an invitation for interventions."[48]

Given this emphasis, it is not surprising that the bishops took issue with President Reagan's dependence on a military solution to the problems there, which would likely further destabilize the region. The bishops thought the administration, instead of focusing on military options, ought to resume carefully monitored economic aid that would address the underlying problem of underdevelopment. With the resumption of economic aid, the United States should refrain from trying to unilaterally solve these difficulties and instead rely on a regional and multilateral approach to negotiations. A unilateral approach, the bishops argued, would likely fail because the United States was seen as a partisan in the debate and it would undermine their credibility.

The position of the bishops became more refined during testimony before the National Commission on US Policy in Central America. More popularly known as the Kissinger Commission, it was created to investigate the problems in Central America and report back possible solutions. Testifying on behalf of the US Conference of Catholic Bishops (USCCB), Archbishop James Hickey argued that "because the conflicts in Central America are fundamentally rooted in questions of social injustice and the persistent denial of basic human rights for large sectors of the population, the [USCCB] has always opposed interpretations of the Salvadoran and Central American conflict which place primary emphasis on the superpower or East-West rivalry." Policies that depend on a military solution to the problem will fail and could easily spin out of control, increasing the likelihood that a regional conflict would ensue. Consequently, Hickey rejected current administration policies that gave "the

---

47. See, for example, Archbishop James Hickey, Archbishop Patrick Flores, and Archbishop Peter Gerety, "Fact Finding Mission to Central America," *Origins* 12, no. 38 (March 3, 1983); Archbishop John Roach, "Toward a Diplomatic, Non-Military Solution in Central America," *Origins* 13, no. 10 (August 4, 1983); Father Bryan Hehir, "Testimony on Central America," *Origins* 13, no. 43 (April 5, 1984).

48. National Conference of Catholic Bishops, "U.S. Bishops' Statement on Central America," *Origins* 1, no. 25 (December 3, 1981): 3.

appearance of encouraging war in Nicaragua" and that "[continued] primarily in a military direction" in El Salvador. He instead called for a multilateral strategy that included other Latin American countries—rather than one that relied primarily on American power—thus undercutting any accusations related to imperialistic overreach by the United States. He also emphasized the need for a cease-fire in both Nicaragua and El Salvador, and highlighted the need for systemic reform and an emphasis on the promotion and protection of human rights.[49]

The following year Father Bryan Hehir, the director of the conference's Social Action Department, commented on the findings of the Kissinger Commission. He noted that the "report's style of stressing the complexity of the region's multiple crises—political, economic, military—rather than reducing the problem immediately to its geopolitical element, is a welcome shift of official statement. . . . [But] the inner logic of the report reaffirms and intensifies the basic direction of a policy which stands in need of fundamental redirection."[50] The central error of the report lay with its continued emphasis on a military solution rather than developing a strategy that focused on economic and diplomatic solutions.

In contrast to the position taken by the bishops, publications like *National Review*, led by the conservative Catholic William Buckley, and groups like the neoconservative Catholics, alongside their political counterparts in secular society, continued to maintain a hard-line position with respect to the Soviet Union. The Cold War remained central to these individuals' views on foreign affairs, particularly in Latin America, where it was feared the Soviet Union was making inroads through Cuba, and from there into Central America. Given the investments made by the Soviets in the region, it would be naive to assume that they were not a central player in the conflicts that were raging in the region.[51]

These same critics also accused the bishops of having capitulated to a left-wing, secular politics. In 1981, the neoconservative Catholic Michael Novak accused Thomas Quigley, a leading lay expert on Latin America at the USCCB, of holding to the position that "geopolitical considerations have nothing to do with the revolution" raging in El Salvador at the time, and of rejecting what Quigley deemed to be an outdated and "discredited 'Cold War' mentality."[52]

49. Archbishop James Hickey, "U.S. Catholic Conference Testimony on Central America," *Origins* 12, no. 41 (March 24, 1983).

50. Hehir, "Testimony on Central America," 3–4.

51. Michael Novak, "To Fight or to Appease," *National Review*, July 22, 1983, 878.

52. Michael Novak, "The Moral Minority and the Savior," *National Review*, March 6, 1981, 228.

Elsewhere, the editors of *National Review* took the Catholic bishops to task for their posturing on the situation in Nicaragua, declaring that their claim that the fundamental problems in the region are economic is akin to something Fidel Castro might utter. The National Conference of Catholic Bishops has become, the editorial concluded, "distinctive only for its predictable leftward tropism."[53]

Conclusion

By the early 1980s, anti-Communism had become an increasingly marginal category in the political rhetoric of the Catholic bishops of the United States. In its place, issues related to economic development and inequality, and concerns related to human rights, were ascendant. Less emphasis was placed on the role that the Soviet Union and other Communist states played in exacerbating these disparities. Instead, social injustices were largely a consequence of flawed institutions and political failures that were endemic to a specific country or region, and less so of the political machinations of the Soviet Union. This shift contrasted with a more conservative wing of the American Catholic Church whose thinking was still deeply enmeshed in the threat of the Soviet Union to Western ideals and values. This division signified a deep philosophical divide that existed between different segments of the church, each of which held to philosophically disparate worldviews. It is a chasm in the public life of the church that remains, and has perhaps only worsened, long after the fall of the Soviet Union and the end of the Cold War.

53. "Shepherds Astray," *National Review*, December 18, 1987, 18.

Where Should a Catholic Stand?
George Weigel and J. Bryan Hehir
Debate the Fate of Just War Theory

RAYMOND HABERSKI JR.

In April 2016, the Vatican sponsored a conference on just war theory. In reporting this event, the *National Catholic Reporter* reminded readers that "just war theory is a tradition that uses a series of criteria to evaluate whether use of violence can be considered morally justifiable."[1] While a long-held tradition, just war is also a contested one. Leaders of the event explained: "After more than 1,500 years and repeated use of the just war criteria to sanction war rather than to prevent war, the Catholic Church, like many other Christian communities, is rereading the text of Jesus' life and re-appropriating the Christian vocation of pro-active peacemaking."[2] Representatives of Pax Christi International, the organizers of the Vatican conference, have profound problems with the way just war theory has been applied. They should have held the conference in Washington, DC.

Perhaps no other country has posed a greater test for just war theory than the United States, a nation with a large, influential, and wealthy Catholic population that has been in an almost constant state of war—"cold" as well as "hot"—since 1917. In fact, as religious historian Harry Stout observes, "The norm of American national life is war. From colonial origins to the present, Americans have never seen a generation that was not preoccupied with war, threats of wars, and military interventions on foreign soils." War is among the most crucial and consistent experiences in American history, but to make sense of such experiences, Americans have called upon religion—a resource that helps them find transcendent meaning from their military history. "American wars are *sacred* wars," Stout asserts, "and American religion, with some

---

1. Joshua J. McElwee, "Vatican to Host First-Ever Conference to Reevaluate Just War Theory, Justifications for Violence," *National Catholic Reporter*, April 5, 2016, http://ncronline.org.

2. McElwee, "Vatican to Host First-Ever Conference to Reevaluate Just War Theory, Justifications for Violence."

notable exceptions, is martial at the very core of its being. The ties between war and religion are symbiotic and the two grew up intertwined."[3]

Just war theory has consistently been a way for Americans to make meaning out of war. They do so, the *National Catholic Reporter* editorialized, "in a culture awash in military images and one that spends more than most of the rest of the developed world combined on its war-making capacity."[4] And so, while the Vatican conference on just war theory is unique in the history of the church, Catholic history in the United States provides some insight into the paradox of using just war theory. In the decade following the Vietnam War, Catholic officials in the United States sparked a debate over whether just war theory was as much about defending the meaning of the United States as it was about whether it was just to kill and die for the nation.

In 1992, David Scott, the former editor of *Our Sunday Visitor*, wrote an essay for the magazine *U.S. Catholic* in which he concluded that American Catholics were hopelessly divided over the issues of war and peace. He related a somewhat sardonic story about a poll taken just a year earlier by a radio station in Erie, Pennsylvania—as he said, an all-American city. The poll pitted two threats to the United States at the height of the Persian Gulf War, Saddam Hussein and the Benedictine Sisters, who ran the Pax Christi USA (an organization based in Erie). Scott wrote: "It was a tight race, but the nuns won."[5] The point being, in mainstream America, wars fought for the nation trump a peace waged in the name of a church.

While the debate over war and peace has been more complicated than that, for the most part the Catholic Church and American Catholics have historically supported wars fought by the United States. Yet, in the wake of the historic challenges issued by Vatican II and the profound soul-searching forced over the war in Vietnam, Catholic officials in the United States began a period of deliberation and public discussion about the role religion plays in defining the moral landscape of American power. The apex of this era was the 1983 peace pastoral "The Challenge of Peace" issued by the United States Conference of Catholic Bishops (USCCB). And while much attention was paid to the way the bishops applied just war principles, their pastoral also offered a theology that spoke to the American experience of war but did so without privileging that experience. This moment demonstrated that in the United

---

3. Harry S. Stout, "Religion, War, and the Meaning of America," *Religion and American Culture: A Journal of Interpretation* 19, no. 2 (Summer 2009): 275.

4. Staff editorial, *National Catholic Reporter*, May 7, 2016, http://ncronline.org.

5. David Scott, "Fighting Words: Why Catholics Disagree about War," *U.S. Catholic*, May 1992, 6.

States, to rethink just war required rethinking nationalism and the relationship between religion and foreign policy.

Religion and US Foreign Policy

For the most part, historians have assumed that religion has always been less influential than politics in questions of war. Leo Ribuffo, an intellectual historian at George Washington University, has argued that religious groups and their institutions matter just like ethnic groups or gender or political party affiliation when it comes to considering how religion influences foreign policy.[6] In short, religion is another variable policy makers consider, but only insofar as it relates to political calculations. Continuing along similar lines, University of Notre Dame historian Wilson Miscamble cautions that we should be circumspect about measuring the influence of religion on foreign policy and, in the particular case of Catholics, limit our understanding to those historical situations that are clearly demonstrable—for example, when Catholics evidently persuaded FDR to remain neutral in the Spanish Civil War.[7] Thus Catholics neither wielded specific power over foreign policy nor influenced those who did in any appreciable way. While we might demonstrate that Catholicism offered an alternative to American foreign policy, such evidence comes from minority groups within Catholicism or from trends within the church that did not last long.

Recently, in a new history of religion and the American history of diplomacy and war, Cambridge University historian Andrew Preston has demonstrated that religion in America has contributed to the culture in which foreign policy has been crafted, understood, debated, and sold.[8] It matters that presidents, pastors, policy makers, and the people share common religious references, debate religious terms, use religion to critique and support foreign policy, and offer conflicting religious interpretations of the world. Preston's argument can only be understood through a comprehensive narrative of American history—religion in American foreign policy operates on two levels:

6. Leo Ribuffo, "Religion and the History of U.S. Foreign Policy," in *The Influence of Faith: Religious Groups and U.S. Foreign Policy*, ed. Elliott Abrams (Lanham, MD: Rowman and Littlefield, 2001), 1–32.

7. Wilson Miscamble, "Catholics and American Foreign Policy from McKinley to McCarthy: A Historiographical Survey," *Diplomatic History* 4 (Summer 1980): 223–40.

8. Andrew Preston, *Sword of the Spirit, Shield of Faith: Religion in American War and Diplomacy* (New York: Knopf, 2012).

first, as a language that allows successive generations of Americans to make common references, and second, as a tool with interpretative power calibrated to specific conditions of a historical moment. Religion provided general or national context while also being used within specific religious traditions to forward specific foreign policies.

However, measuring the influence of religion on American foreign policy usually meant considering Protestant influence, as it was the dominant source of transcendent meaning for most of American history. Protestantism underwrote the rise and dominance of the American empire. And for most of US history, Catholics supported the nation and its foreign policy in part to erode their status as outsiders.

American Catholics and War

For American Catholics, though, playing the role of outsiders had advantages. For example, traditions that exist beyond the history of any single nation, such as the United States, offer Catholics a way to be at once a part of a place while claiming to stand almost outside of any single nation's history. Moreover, because Catholic traditions have contended with the evolution of war—from medieval weaponry to nuclear arsenals—American Catholics across the ideological spectrum are nearly forced to speak to each other through a theology of war that is far bigger than themselves and their nations.

During the Cold War, such perspective seemed in desperate need. In his recent book on religion and American foreign policy, William Inboden contends that religion helped clarify what was at stake in the Cold War and how the United States should act based on those stakes. In the abstract, the use of religion and moral arguments was supposed to check as well as justify the American exercise of power. Thus, according to Inboden, God-speak provided more than merely rhetorical cover for those policies. "Differences over political structures and economic systems and even national interests, though important in their own right, paled in comparison with the prospect of a world ruled by evil, a world devoid of spiritual values, a world without God," Inboden contends. "If ever there was a cause to fight, this was it."[9]

The imperatives of the Cold War pressed religion into service of the nation. Amidst a semblance of hand-wringing, religious organizations spoke

9. William Inboden, *Religion and American Foreign Policy, 1945–1960: The Soul of Containment* (New York: Cambridge University Press, 2008), 4.

confidently about the role the United States had to play in a struggle with theological overtones. For the period following the Second World War, no other Catholic intellectual had more influence in that conversation than Jesuit priest John Courtney Murray. He and other Catholic realists argued that war was not an end in itself but a way to provide an "adequate and moral defense of America and the West." They sought first and foremost to preserve Western liberal society but, at the same time, avoided endorsing the kind of internationalism that the Holy See hoped, naively the realists argued, might prevent and perhaps even eradicate war. The issue for the realist position was not the existence of nuclear weapons and their capacity to destroy but the "moral clarity of those formulating policy" for their use.[10]

During the Cold War, the issue that galvanized debate over just war theory was the threat posed by nuclear weapons and the development of strategies bundled under the term "nuclear deterrence." Realists argued that not only was the buildup of an American nuclear arsenal morally defensible, but limited nuclear war could be waged within the boundaries of moral limits. Historian Paul Boyer points to a pamphlet produced by the Catholic Association for International Peace called *The Ethics of Atomic War* (1947) that came from a group chaired by John Courtney Murray and Bishop Fulton Sheen. The report did not denounce nuclear weapons outright, nor did it reject the targeting of civilians. "Millions might die, the report conceded, but as an unintended side-effect, not a primary objective, and thus the deaths would be 'outweighed by the good obtained, the salvation of the innocent country.'"[11]

From the beginning of the Cold War, arguments that employed religion to determine an ethical position on nuclear weapons consistently embraced an abstract defense of the United States to justify what otherwise would be unethical positions. The locus was not God, or just war principles, or even some notion of morality, but the ideal of America. In his book on Catholics and war, William A. Au explains, "Murray insisted that reappropriation of the just war tradition was essential to the development of the moral-political consensus necessary to America's ability to mount a strong and moral military deterrent."[12] At base, the realist position developed through Murray and other theologians such as William V. O'Brien, James E. Dougherty, and William V.

10. William A. Au, *The Cross, the Flag, and the Bomb: American Catholics Debate War and Peace, 1960–1983* (Westport, CT: Greenwood Press, 1985), 52.

11. Paul S. Boyer, "God, the Bomb, and the Cold War: The Religious and Ethical Debate over Nuclear Weapons, 1945–1990," in *Uncertain Empire: American History and the Ideas of the Cold War*, ed. Joel Issac and Duncan Bell (New York: Oxford University Press, 2012), 171.

12. Au, *The Cross, the Flag, and the Bomb*, 52.

Kennedy was that the Catholic position could not be sectarian or oppose the defense policies of the American government. "Their political presupposition of the priority of preserving Western liberal society," Au writes, "was easily wedded to their ecclesiological priority of preserving Catholicism as a significant part of that society."[13]

Liberal Catholics who were nuclear pacifists such as Justus George Lawler "placed such people under the judgment of Cardinal Newman, who charged that logicians are usually more interested in arguing rightly than in right conclusions." The journal *Continuum* became a serious voice for Catholic opposition to the realist position on nuclear war and deterrence. Lawler was a major force behind this journal's position on war—rethinking just war in the era of nuclear deterrence and the critique of hard-line anti-Communist, pro-American bishops. Lawler argued: "I would base my own total denial of the morality of any nuclear war not on strict logic, but on the certitude flowing from the converging probabilities created by the history of all recent major wars, by the exorbitant potential of the weapons themselves, by the consequences of the psychological strain induced by more than a decade of living on the edge of a volcano, by the fact that even in limited engagement where our vital interests are not at stake—as in Vietnam—war has been prosecuted through immoral means."[14] Lawler raised a critical issue: much of Catholic defense of just war slid toward a kind of American exceptionalism, or imagining that while both sides in the Cold War possessed dangerous weapons, only the Americans did so righteously. Without accepting a moral equivalence between the Soviets and Americans, critics such as Lawler simply pointed out that possessing weapons with the capacity to do great evil implicated those who possessed them, including the United States, in that evil. And then the experience of Vietnam badly eroded whatever moral righteousness the United States had left.

Significance of Vietnam

Because of the Vietnam War, many churches felt it imperative to stake a position publicly on the moral fate of the United States. The Catholic Church was perhaps the most surprising exemplar of that trend. Historian Mary Hanna points out that "American bishops loyally supported every war in our history. . . . World War I produced only one American Catholic conscientious

13. Au, *The Cross, the Flag, and the Bomb*, 75.
14. Justus George Lawler, quoted in Au, *The Cross, the Flag, and the Bomb*, 89, 90.

objector; World War II, about 200, nearly all of them followers of Dorothy Day's Catholic Worker movement." But by the late 1960s, "American Catholic attitudes had changed dramatically, [registering] the greatest percentage increase in conscientious objection . . . in this formerly more supportive religious group." By the 1970s, the American Catholic leadership followed, proving that the post-Vietnam church was no longer Francis Cardinal Spellman's church.[15]

This change began in earnest with the pronouncements and spirit that emanated from the ecumenical council called by Pope John XXIII known as Vatican II. The council gave all Catholics a "license to act," to involve themselves vigorously in social-justice action, to join groups promoting civil rights, antipoverty, and antiwar positions. The conscientious objector issue, though, caused problems for the Catholic hierarchy in the United States. Draft boards refused to allow Catholic men to claim such status on the grounds that the church did not have a tradition of pacifism. To respond, the National Conference of Catholic Bishops turned to the just war tradition. Renewed interest in and study of this medieval doctrine had implications for the contemporary position of the Catholic Church toward the United States. From 1968 to 1971, the American Catholic hierarchy turned away from supporting the American war effort, declaring Vietnam an unjust war and demanding its end in a resolution issued in November 1971. According to leaders of the church interviewed by Hanna in 1973, this letter was a "declaration of independence" from supporting the nation's position on war and peace. "Church leaders would now be much readier than they had been in the past to challenge political decisions they believed morally wrong." The issues that emerged most prominently included Vietnam, abortion, and the American policies on stockpiling and possible use of nuclear weapons. In fact, in the post-Vietnam period, Catholics linked war, abortion, and nuclear weapons together through the church's broad understanding of a right to life.[16]

The Challenge of Peace

In May 1983, in their pastoral letter entitled "The Challenge of Peace," the National Conference of Catholic Bishops declared their opposition to nuclear

15. Mary Hanna, "From Civil Religion to Prophetic Church: American Bishops and the Bomb," in *American Political Theology: Historical Perspective and Theoretical Analysis*, ed. Charles W. Dunn (New York: Praeger, 1984), 144, 148.
16. Hanna, "From Civil Religion to Prophetic Church," 149, 150, 153.

weapons. "In simple terms," the bishops explained, "we are saying that good ends (defending one's country, protecting freedom, etc.) cannot justify immoral means (the use of weapons which indiscriminately threaten whole societies)." Rather than trust policies of nuclear deterrence, the bishops warned, "we fear that our world and nation are headed in the wrong direction. More weapons with greater destructive potential are produced every day. More and more nations are seeking to become nuclear powers." And with a direct jab at what many people viewed as the dangerous brinkmanship of the Reagan administration, the bishops concluded, "In our quest for more and more security we fear we are actually becoming less and less secure."[17]

The pastoral letter had gone through three substantial versions before the conference officially issued it. The process that produced the final product included a good deal of debate between the more pacifist wing of the Catholic Church and those bishops who adhered to an interpretation of just war theory that, traditionally, counseled deferring to state authority in matters of war and peace. A committee of bishops and their advisers worked on the letter for over a year, during which the group held hearings, issued drafts, and invited officials from the Reagan administration to contribute testimony. In the end, though, the conference knew the letter would "prove highly controversial, not least because [it] would almost certainly voice major criticisms of U.S. defense policy in the past and probably even more of the hawkish . . . Reagan administration." In other words, the American Catholic bishops, who overwhelmingly voted in favor of the 1983 letter, wanted to strike a prophetic stand toward their nation.[18]

In this way, the letter was very much a reflection of the struggle over Catholic moral authority that emerged in the wake of Vietnam. The American Catholic Church had a pacifist faction within it, but that faction had exerted little influence over the church hierarchy. In the 1970s, though, the wars in Central America, the Supreme Court's decision in *Roe v. Wade*, and the abject and existential terror many people felt living with a nuclear standoff emboldened Catholic leaders to go beyond decrying the immorality of the Vietnam War and to influence the agenda of the nation. Father J. Bryan Hehir, the Catholic priest who served as the key architect of "The Challenge of Peace," approached the issue of nuclear weapons from within a broad understanding

17. National Conference of Catholic Bishops, "The Challenge of Peace: God's Promise and Our Response," May 3, 1983, http://www.usccb.org/upload/challenge-peace-gods-promise-our-response-1983.pdf.

18. William J. Gould, "Father J. Bryan Hehir: Priest, Policy Analyst, and Theologian of Dialogue," in *Religious Leaders and Faith-Based Politics*, ed. Jo Renee Formicola and Hubert Morken (Lanham, MD: Rowman and Littlefield, 2001), 205, 210.

of what Joseph Cardinal Bernardin had termed "the consistent ethic of life." That position embraced ending the threat of nuclear war, opposing abortion and the death penalty, and fighting against the kind of oppression and poverty that pervaded the developing world. Hehir attempted to find a point of collaboration between the pacifists, who had carried the day during the Vietnam War, and the just war advocates, who argued that nuclear deterrence was not an end in itself but a means to prevent Soviet expansion at the price of democratic freedom.

Hehir was sensitive to the criticism by conservative Catholics and observers outside the church that the letter presaged a move toward outright pacifism or the adoption of a position in direct conflict with that of the US government. This was the era during which liberation theology inspired many Catholics to imagine the church as a vanguard institution standing with the poor of Central America to resist and perhaps even topple oppressive regimes. The religious and secular Left in the United States lumped the Reagan administration in with regimes tagged as global oppressors. And so a letter that came out boldly against American defense policy might also be seen as another version of the Left's condemnation of the United States as an immoral nation.[19]

The conservative Catholic response emerged from intellectuals such as William F. Buckley Jr., America's most prominent conservative Catholic; Michael Novak (who wrote for Buckley's magazine, *National Review*); and George Weigel, attacking Hehir for what they viewed as the priest's internationalist relativism. Weigel contributed to this debate with his 1987 book *Tranquillitas Ordinis*, in which he spent over four hundred pages attempting to refute the bishops' letter and, in particular, Hehir's criticism of American foreign policy. Standing with the counterlogic of deterrence, Novak asserted in an essay entitled "Moral Clarity in the Nuclear Age" that "to abandon deterrence is to neglect the duty to defend the innocent, to preserve the Constitution and the Republic, and to keep safe the very idea of political liberty. No President by his oath of office can so act, nor can a moral people." Indeed, the sanctity of the American promise had to be protected, even at the price of endangering the material existence of the entire population.[20] Yet for Hehir, the population that concerned him extended beyond the borders of the United States.

---

19. Gould, "Father J. Bryan Hehir," 207; Au, *The Cross, the Flag, and the Bomb*, 237–39.

20. Michael Novak, "Moral Clarity in the Nuclear Age," *National Review*, April 1, 1983, 380, 383.

J. Bryan Hehir and Political Theology

Hehir arrived at a moment of great activity at the USCCB and became a significant figure, by almost all accounts, in shaping that moment.[21] Hehir performed
both intellectual and practical tasks: he researched large issues such as arms
control, often provided drafts of speeches for bishops, and at times himself
gave testimony to congressional committees on behalf of the USCCB. "He
was able to exercise so much influence because," William Gould explains, "to
a very large extent, he provided the intellectual framework within which they
came to understand and evaluate major policy questions. After extensive exposure to Hehir's policy framework, the bishops came increasingly to embrace
it as their own, which in turn frequently led them to embrace his particular
policy recommendations."[22] Gould relates that Hehir was part of, if not a key
influence in, the rift within the Catholic hierarchy over how to frame "life"
issues—the conservative bishops gave prominence to opposition to abortion
while more progressive bishops saw abortion as part of a larger agenda that
included nuclear war, poverty, and international relations under the umbrella
of a "consistent ethic of life." The peace pastoral was an expression of the new
orientation of the USCCB: Vatican II had called for "an evaluation of war in
an entirely new attitude."[23] He called on the church to undertake a version
of nuclear pacifism, to recognize its internationalism, and to emphasize the
interdependency of all nations.

Hehir offered his advice out of a particular political theology. In a series of
essays published in *Worldview*, the journal of the Carnegie Council for Ethics
and International Affairs (formally known as the Church Peace Union), Hehir
provided context for not merely a different reading of just war principles in
light of nuclear deterrence but for how those principles created a critical stance
toward the national interest of the United States.

The most significant document for Hehir's thought on the church's relationship to the nation was *Gaudium et Spes*, or the *Pastoral Constitution on the
Church in the Modern World*, which also offered the Second Vatican Council's
recognition of pacifism as a legitimate option for Catholics. Hehir explained:
"In open and optimistic language it acknowledges the problems and accomplishments of the modern world in all its technical complexity and terrifying
potential; it declares the radical solidarity of the Church with the world; and it

---

21. Gould, "Father J. Bryan Hehir," 204–5.
22. Gould, "Father J. Bryan Hehir," 207.
23. Gould, "Father J. Bryan Hehir," 209.

seeks to initiate a dialogue about the problems and possibilities both Church and world face in this post-modern period of history as they seek to serve their common constituency, the men of this age."[24]

Hehir understood Vatican II as offering something beyond an explanation or clarification for how the church thinks about natural law or religious liberty in order to establish how the church positions itself in relation to other sources of understanding and knowledge. In the essays for *Worldview*, Hehir established his own internationalist position. He built his argument in part on University of Münster theologian Johannes Metz's conception of political theology as being a response to the Enlightenment attack against religion in the public square and the consequential retreat of religion into the personal or private sphere. "His purpose in presenting a political theology," wrote Hehir, "is to prevent concern for the individual, narrowly conceived, from being the exclusive focus in which the meaning of faith is exposed to believers and unbelievers alike."[25]

In a passage that crystallized Hehir's perspective on the church's role in politics, he explained:

> To carry out its task the Church must become "an institution of social criticism" which exists neither above the world nor beside the world but *in* the world. The role of the Church as an institution of social criticism is to measure every political situation against the values of the Kingdom. To fulfill this role the Church needs a political theology. . . . Fulfilling the role of institution of social criticism has implications for the Church's posture in society and for her self-understanding as Church. In terms of her position in the political order, it requires *standing with* those who are denied a share in the values of the Kingdom by an unjust social structure; it also requires a *standing against* the forms and forces of injustice as they are incarnated in a given political context.[26]

Yet Hehir found Metz's view of political theology "too timid" because the German theologian had feared making the church just another political operator that engaged in critiquing policy development and its execution. To that, Hehir argued for a "twofold application of the teaching ministry: a prophetic

---

24. J. Bryan Hehir, "The Idea of Political Theology, I," *Worldview* 14, no. 1 (January 1, 1971): 5.

25. Hehir, "The Idea of Political Theology, I," 6.

26. Hehir, "The Idea of Political Theology, I," 6.

or negative critique and a pedagogical or positive critique." Hehir offered his idea for the church's strategic position: "conscious recognition that the Church stands in the position of a transnational actor in international affairs, and use of the concept of collegiality as an organizing principle in the international arena." For Hehir, the church was a very agile transnational actor: "universal presence, centralized decision-making process and communication system, global constituency, and a significant number of trained personnel. These features provide the raw material for a significant degree of participation in the international system." Hehir proposed using the collegiality between the papacy and national episcopal conferences in international affairs in ways similar to how these conferences carry out papal directives in national affairs. "A political theology in the international arena requires a consciously coordinated, flexible approach to unifying the approach of the universal Church and the local church. . . . If this strategy is to function effectively," Hehir concluded, "a dialectical relationship must prevail between the universal church and the local church."[27]

Thus, when Hehir and many of the bishops in the United States considered the threat nuclear weapons posed, they also addressed the universal effects of that threat (living under the constant fear of annihilation) as well as the national rationale for possessing nuclear weapons. That contrast—threat and defense—created a tension that Hehir and many of the bishops viewed as crucial to developing a new, nonnational position on war. Thus they offered an alternative, a "psychology and spirit of peace," as a way to reflect on the frustration they had with the failure to advance anything but a nation-based strategy toward dealing with nuclear weapons. Hehir related that the church hoped that its positions would "test the policies adopted by our government and others in terms of their impact on human life and dignity." And that "it is the role of the church to function in [an] ambit of public opinion, to foster a spirit and psychology of peace that will support a policy directed toward peace."[28]

27. J. Bryan Hehir, "The Idea of a Political Theology, II," *Worldview* 14, no. 2 (February 1, 1971): 5–6.

28. J. Bryan Hehir, "The Catholic Church and the Arms Race," *Worldview* 21, nos. 7–8 (July 1, 1978): 14.

George Weigel and Moral Imperatives

George Weigel turned Hehir's logic on its head, rejecting interdependency and psychology in favor of understanding world politics in binary and nationalistic terms: "Between the fire of war and the pit of totalitarianism, moral imagination in the modern world is in schism. Our choices seem reduced to either/or propositions: either resist totalitarian aggression, even by war, or run the risk of a world in Gulag; either end the threat of war, even by appeasing totalitarians, or run the risk of global holocaust."[29] Weigel built his argument around identifying and defining the context within which just war and the entire "heritage" of Catholic thought on war should be understood. He used the idea of "heritage" as a stand-in for right thinking and to call into question the context of all other uses of just war. Thus, in regard to thinkers as diverse as Gordon Zahn and Bryan Hehir, Weigel contended that many Catholics misinterpreted the church's traditional positions on war because they failed to understand the context in which just war principles might be applied to specific cases.

Weigel entered the public debate over just war theory through "The Challenge of Peace." For Weigel, the letter illustrated the general drift of Catholic leaders toward positions he argued were discordant with church traditions.

> The body of the policy iceberg, often below the surface of consciousness as well as of public debate, is, over the long haul, of even more significance than the specific choices to which it leads at one or another given moment. We may call the "body of the iceberg" the *context* out of which political judgments, which are concurrently moral judgments, are made. Context is of greater long-term importance than binary choice because context creates the possibility of coherent policy over time. Moreover, *it is at the contextual level of the argument that moral imagination and moral reasoning make their primary claims for attention.* (178–79)

While he dwelt on the issue of context, his critique of the Catholic bishops and especially of Hehir hinged on what he believed was a dramatically altered opinion of the United States. Weigel believed the bishops had "abandoned" faith or confidence in the American experiment. "For if, as Murray's project

---

29. George Weigel, *Tranquillitas Ordinis: The Present Failure and Future Promise of American Catholic Thought on War and Peace* (New York: Oxford University Press, 1987), 17. Hereafter, references from this work will be given in parentheses in the text.

suggested, the American experiment was an important prism through which to think about the peace of dynamic political community in the world, a soured view of that experiment would inevitably lead to altered understandings of both the problem of war and America's possible contribution to its resolution" (211). In a survey of elite opinion found in journals such as *Commonweal* and *America*, Weigel summed up the transition away from Murray this way: "From America as Proposition, to America as Amerika, to America as Antichrist, to America as whore: all in one generation" (214).

Of course, the catalyst for this shift was Vietnam. The war gave credence to the pacifist position and delegitimized, according to Weigel, the traditional just war idea. "American Catholics were taught that their's had been a voice of silence and accommodation," Weigel asserted. "Vatican II's call for a deepened encounter with the modern world, received in the supercharged politics of the 1960s, led rather easily to a heightened focus on prescription and a consequent diminishment of culture-formation" (243). Weigel actually incorporated his own condemnation of Vietnam into his analysis of the misapplication of just war thinking. To Weigel, Vietnam acted like a virus infecting what would otherwise be a healthy and unified body of thought. And while neither side argued that the United States was uniquely good or bad, Weigel believed that Vietnam was an anomaly of American history that could be contextualized, while the bishops saw Vietnam as an expression of a dangerous strand of American history.

Weigel acknowledged the power Vietnam had to move Catholic debate about war by creating "the cultural conditions for the possibility of the emergence of pacifism as a full partner in the American Catholic debate over war and peace, security and freedom. That partnership would be even more vigorously asserted—and this time by official leaders of the church—in the debate over nuclear weapons that erupted less than a decade after the fall of Saigon" (244). Weigel observed that in the wake of Vietnam, a vigorous discussion opened about just war theory in various communities, within the church as well as among scholars. And yet, he added, "American Catholics were regularly taught in their principal opinion journals, and by an increasing number of their bishops, that just-war theory had been developed in order to soothe the Catholic conscience during a time of Christendom, and had subsequently functioned as an ex post facto rationalization for whatever kind and degree of violence public authorities had deemed necessary for *raisons d'etat*." "Vietnam," he concluded, "was a decisive factor in this deterioration of discourse" (248–49).

The debate over just war became for Weigel an extension of a broader debate over how Catholics related to the United States. The bishops rejected just war principles, he contended, because they found the United States unworthy to defend—changing their position on just war served as a way for the bishops to pass judgment on a nation rather than on church doctrine.

Thus, when Weigel turned his attention to "The Challenge of Peace," he lumped the bishops' thought in the pastoral in with left-wing critiques of the nation that had come out of the Vietnam War. "The implicit identification of 'peace' and 'love' (in either personalist or eschatological terms) marked the key symbolic point at which 'The Challenge of Peace' definitively broke with their heritage of *tranquillitas ordinis* [or 'tranquillity of order'] which taught the possibility of a morally worth peace of political community *prior* to the world's final conversion" (284). What became apparent in Weigel's argument was the link he forged between the United States as an abstract moral entity and the just war tradition. So, whereas Weigel played the Americanist (the nationalist), Hehir assumed the role of global strategist and internationalist. Their conflict was between one who assumed the essential morality of the United States and another who assumed that the United States was no different from any other actor in history.

According to Weigel, Hehir's views or positions on a host of foreign policy questions demonstrated that "Hehir-the-strategist views the United States and the Soviet Union analytically as equally culpable and equally blundering mastodons in a world that neither of them understands very well" (317). Hehir's internationalism did not so much reject Americanism as advocate for a "transnational" role for the Catholic Church within the United States. It stood outside of all nations, including the one Weigel found as the last, best hope for a more moral politics. "There is an undercurrent in Hehir's thought," Weigel wrote with apparent consternation, "which suggests that he views himself as a mediating force in the American Catholic debate on war and peace: a figure standing between the rhetoric and analyses of post-Vietnam Catholic activists and intellectuals, and the stringencies of the Catholic social ethical tradition. Yet Father Hehir's disinclination to criticize the dominant themes in Catholic activism on the questions of nuclear weapons and Central America has been an important element in validating those themes within the Catholic debate" (323).

If in Weigel's eyes Hehir failed to bolster a role for the Catholic Church in affirming the American experiment, moral theologian David Hollenbach, SJ, criticized Weigel for going much too far the other way. In a review of Weigel's ambitious book *Tranquillitas Ordinis*, Hollenbach argued: "In Weigel's exposition, Christian faith seems to exist alongside of or above American culture, synthesized with it in concord and harmony but not challenging it in any really pointed way. Despite Murray's strong affirmation of the American proposition, he exhibited considerably more epistemological humility than does Weigel by refusing to draw an unambiguous conclusion about the full compatibility of Christian faith with the way this proposition has been lived out in history."[30]

Within the Catholic debate over just war theory, as demonstrated through the contest between Hehir and Weigel, the stakes came down to affirming the foreign policy of the United States at the risk of supporting a dangerous, potentially apocalyptic scenario, or challenging that foreign policy and implicating the United States in a struggle that assumed moral equivalency between the opposing sides. While neither Catholic officials nor Catholic intellectuals imagined that their debate would decisively influence policy makers, they did understand their ability to shape the culture in which policy was made. In this way, debates about just war theory were not only an illustration of using religion to understand the American experience with war, but were also, potentially, a method to critique that experience. After all, the historic relationship between just war theory and American wars has been characterized by alignment, not tension. In one of many essays published by the journal *Ethics* on the implications of nuclear deterrence, Colin S. Gray, a defense analyst, made an illuminating observation about the connection between moral arguments and the defense policy of the United States: "The ability of a democracy to sustain an adequate military posture year after year . . . is not unrelated to the popularly perceived compatibility of moral values with defense policy."[31] Hehir and the bishops understood how important just war theory had become to sustaining that relationship, and while they hoped to disrupt it, in the end, they failed.

30. David Hollenbach, "War and Peace in American Catholic Thought: A Heritage Abandoned?," *Theological Studies* 48 (1987): 716.

31. Colin S. Gray, quoted in Boyer, "God, the Bomb, and the Cold War," 189.

Eastern Orthodox Approaches

The Orthodox Church in America: Steering through the Cold War

Leonid Kishkovsky

On April 10, 1970, the Holy Synod of the Russian Orthodox Church granted autocephaly to the Orthodox Church in America (OCA), thus recognizing it as a self-governing church with canonical independence. The term "autocephaly" is defined as the right to elect the head or primate of a church without reference to or approval by any other church. This action was preceded by decades of separation between the Moscow Patriarchate and its North American daughter church, officially known as the Russian Orthodox Greek Catholic Church of North America, and informally known as the "Metropolia." The 1970 event occurred at the midpoint of the Cold War. The United States and the Soviet Union were engaged in a global ideological competition and military confrontation. The Russian Orthodox Church and the Orthodox Church in America were inescapably part of the Cold War tableau.

The connection between the Russian Orthodox Church and Orthodoxy in America is direct and has a long history. As the original North American missionary diocese of the Russian Orthodox Church grew to be the American Metropolia, its identity slowly changed. The historical ecclesial ties with Russia remained as a reference point. Both the missionary beginnings in Alaska in 1794 and the immigrant streams in the late nineteenth and twentieth centuries contributed to the evolving identity of the Metropolia. Gradually, the American experience grew in importance. The stages of this journey inform and illumine the Cold War period as lived by the Orthodox Church in America. It is ironic that the Russian Orthodox Church and its former American diocese achieved ecclesial reconciliation as well as mutually agreed canonical and administrative separation in the midst of the Cold War. Their previous separation from one another—a separation that can be called a schism—took place in the aftermath of the Communist revolution in Russia, long before the Cold War. In the present reflection, the little-known story of the Orthodox Church in America's original dependence on the Russian

Orthodox Church needs to be told in order to gain a full understanding of twentieth-century events.[1]

In 1794, Russian Orthodox missionaries arrived in Alaska. The missionary monks were recruited at Valaam and Konevitsa Monasteries and were sent by the church authorities to evangelize the native people of Alaska. The journey of the missionaries began on December 21, 1793, in Saint Petersburg, capital of the Russian Empire. The long pilgrimage across Siberia and the Bering Strait brought them to Kodiak. They covered 7,300 miles in 293 days. The journey from beginning to end was within the Russian Empire. Alaska was ruled by the Russian American Company. The missionaries soon discovered that their greatest challenge was the brutal behavior of the Russian colonists.

The task of evangelizing the native population was undertaken with an attitude of respect for the native cultures. For example, the burial customs of the native people were not despised or negated. Rather, these customs were given a Christian interpretation—were baptized. In their methods of evangelizing the native people, the Orthodox missionaries were unusually enlightened in comparison with other Christian missions of the eighteenth and nineteenth centuries.

Two missionaries to Alaska represent vivid examples of mission as a Christian task performed with love. The first is Saint Herman (1756–1836), who came to Alaska as a humble member of the original missionary group in 1794. Herman was not a deacon or priest, remaining a simple monk until his death in 1836. His relations with the native people were so close and loving that they began to call him "*apa*," meaning grandfather, and remembered him gratefully as grandfather long after his death. Because Herman defended his beloved native people against the abuses of the Russian American Company, relations between the holy monk and the company went from bad to worse. Finally, Herman left Kodiak to resettle on Spruce Island, where he could live and pray in peace, all the time maintaining his relations with the natives. In

---

1. As I was a participant in and witness of most of the developments during the Cold War described in this chapter, I relied on my files and recollections for the narrative. Additionally, I used the following sources: J. Martin Bailey, *One Thousand Years: Stories from the History of Christianity in the USSR, 988–1988* (New York: Friendship Press, 1987); Kent R. Hill, *The Puzzle of the Soviet Church: An Inside Look at Christianity and Glasnost* (Portland, OR: Multnomah, in cooperation with the Institute on Religion and Democracy, 1989); Robert C. Lodwick, *Remembering the Future: The Challenge of the Churches in Europe* (New York: Friendship Press, 1995); Mark Stokoe, in collaboration with Leonid Kishkovsky, *Orthodox Christians in North America: 1794–1994* (Orthodox Christian Publication Center, 1995); Constance J. Tarasar, gen. ed., *Orthodox America: 1794–1976* (Syosset, NY: Orthodox Church in America/Department of History and Archives, 1975); James E. Will, *Must Walls Divide? The Creative Witness of the Churches in Europe* (New York: Friendship Press, 1981).

August 1970, the Holy Synod of the Orthodox Church in America canonized Herman as the first Orthodox saint in America.

The second outstanding missionary personality of Russian Alaska is Saint Innocent (1797–1879). Arriving in Alaska in 1824 as the married priest John Veniaminov after graduating from the seminary in Irkutsk (Siberia), Veniaminov became a missionary of many talents and accomplishments—explorer and geographer, linguist and translator, inventor and carpenter, pastor and visionary. When Veniaminov was widowed, the Holy Synod of the Russian Orthodox Church named him bishop for Alaska and eastern Siberia, with the monastic name of Innocent. In his episcopal ministry Innocent expanded his influence as the missionary voice and conscience of the Russian Orthodox Church.

Toward the end of his long and productive life, Innocent was named metropolitan of Moscow. His appointment coincided with the 1867 sale of Alaska to the United States. In a remarkable testimony to his vision for Orthodoxy in America, he noted in a letter to the *Ober Prokurator* (lay administrator) of the Holy Synod of the Church of Russia that rumors suggesting he opposed the sale of Alaska to the United States were false, and that, to the contrary, he welcomed the sale because it would open the way for Orthodox presence and mission in the United States. Then he made specific recommendations: (1) transfer the diocesan center from Alaska to San Francisco; (2) recall the incumbent bishop to Russia from Alaska; (3) appoint a new and English-speaking bishop for the American diocese; (4) establish a school in San Francisco to train clergy, with English as the language of instruction. At the request of the Orthodox Church in America, Metropolitan Innocent was canonized by the Russian Orthodox Church in 1977.

During the following decades, the North American diocese of the Russian Orthodox Church realized much of the vision of Saint Innocent. Toward the end of the nineteenth century, immigration from eastern Europe, the Balkans, and the Middle East brought to the United States and Canada increasing numbers of Orthodox Christians representing different Orthodox cultures and speaking different languages. Among the immigrants who came from the Austro-Hungarian Empire were Slavs whose ancestors had been Orthodox but who had been received into communion with the Catholic Church while retaining their Eastern Rite. These churches and communities were known as Greek Catholics and were commonly called Uniates (referring to their unity with the pope). In the United States misunderstanding arose between the US Roman Catholics and the new arrivals who followed the Eastern Rite in communion with Rome. As a result, a movement advocating a return to Orthodoxy emerged, with considerable numbers forming new parish communities in the Russian Orthodox Diocese.

The most important personality of this period was Tikhon Bellavin (1865–1925), who served as bishop of the diocese from 1898 to 1907. As a wise and open-minded pastor, Tikhon traveled widely in the United States and Canada, gaining a sympathetic understanding of the needs of his vast diocese. He witnessed the arrival of new immigrants, the inclusion of recent converts from the Greek Catholic community, the encounter with the US and Canadian societies and their religious diversity and democratic values and habits, and the cultural and liturgical pluralism of Orthodoxy in America. He addressed challenges and solved problems energetically, always maintaining a sense of humor and a generosity of spirit. The diocesan center was transferred from San Francisco to New York, where a new cathedral dedicated to Saint Nicholas was built. A seminary was established in Minneapolis, and a monastery in South Canaan, Pennsylvania. An auxiliary bishop was appointed for Alaska, and an Arabic bishop was appointed to minister to the growing communities of immigrants from the Middle East. The active participation of clergy and laity in the decision making of the diocese was encouraged; toward this end, an assembly composed of clergy and lay delegates was convened in Mayfield, Pennsylvania, in 1907. Significantly, Bishop Tikhon encouraged translations of the liturgical texts into English, thus laying the foundation for the emergence of the Orthodox faith from ethnic confines.

Bishop Tikhon (from 1905 archbishop) described his vision of the future of Orthodoxy in America in a 1905 report to the Holy Synod in Saint Petersburg. He envisioned a church with several bishops to serve the various immigrant communities—in addition to the Arab bishop, there would be Greek and Serbian and other bishops, all united in one church, with a Russian archbishop at the head. He saw a future church with autonomy in administration, and even a possible autocephaly. After Archbishop Tikhon's departure for Russia, his successors, appointed by the Holy Synod in Saint Petersburg, continued the fruitful work of strengthening the diocese, building parishes and church organizations.

In 1914 Russia and all of Europe entered into the firestorm of World War I. At first, patriotic enthusiasm inspired the combatants. Soon the millions of dead and wounded traumatized their societies; economic and social dislocation brought bitter suffering to all—the soldiers at the fronts and the populations at home. In 1917 the storm of revolution broke out in Russia. The first stage of the revolution in February forced the abdication of Emperor Nicholas II. A provisional government proved to be confused, weak, and helpless. Since the time of Emperor Peter the Great, the office of patriarch of the Church of Russia had been abolished and the church had been ruled by a Holy Synod in which the administrative power was held by a lay *Ober Prokurator* appointed by the emperor to act as the emperor's representative. A telling detail: a throne symbolizing the emperor's presence was at the head of the room where the Holy Synod met. At the beginning of the twentieth century, debates and polemics emerged on reform in the Russian Orthodox Church. Extensive and thoughtful preparations were made for the convening of a council of the church. Emperor Nicholas II nevertheless declined to give his permission to convene a council. So long as the monarchy stood, no proposals for reform and revitalization in the church could be moved forward.

In 1917, under the provisional government, the long-awaited All-Russian Council of bishops, clergy, and lay delegates assembled in Moscow. By then, Archbishop Tikhon (Bellavin) was metropolitan of Moscow. The lively debates on reforms in church governance, parish life, liturgical life, education, and mission were under way at the time the Communist coup took place in Saint Petersburg. As fighting between the Communists and the provisional government unfolded in Moscow, the council decided to restore the office of patriarch of Moscow. After preliminary voting named three candidates for the office, the final selection was made by drawing one name from a chalice. The patriarch of Moscow was now Tikhon, the former archbishop of America.

The North American diocese was duly represented at the council. One of its delegates was Archpriest Leonid Turkevich, who many years later became the metropolitan of the Russian Orthodox Greek Catholic Church in America with the monastic name Leonty. The violent upheavals in the former Russian Empire had a profound impact on the life of the American diocese. The structures of ecclesiastical and financial support for the diocese crumbled. Communications between the American diocese and the patriarchate in Moscow became uncertain and sporadic, and often lapsed completely. Under Communist rule, there were violent persecutions of the church. The patriarch was imprisoned for a time, before dying in a hospital in 1925. Numerous bishops and many priests and lay believers were exiled, imprisoned, and murdered.

In America, this was a time for painful challenges in the midst of an agonizing struggle for the survival of the diocese. In 1924, at a council in Cleveland, a decision was made to declare the North American diocese "temporarily autonomous." Eventually three groups emerged. The largest group continued to see itself as temporarily autonomous, as the Russian Orthodox Greek Catholic Church in America, and awaited a free council of the Russian Orthodox Church to restore normal church life in Russia and in America. A smaller group aligned with the Russian Orthodox Church Outside of Russia (ROCOR), with its center first in Serbia and, after World War II, in the United States, lived in anticipation of returning to Russia after the demise of the Communist regime. A third small group of parishes maintained loyalty to the Moscow Patriarchate. These three "successor" bodies of the original Russian Orthodox diocese in North America at times came together, at other times again separated. The main body, adhering to the "temporary self-government" decision of 1924, was wary of the Soviet regime and its persecution of the church and control of church institutions. At the same time, there was continuing awareness of the need to respect the Russian Orthodox Church in her martyrdom. The parishes of the Russian Orthodox Church Outside of Russia in time adopted the conviction that the Moscow Patriarchate itself was so controlled by the Communist regime that it was no longer a legitimate church body. For the parishes remaining loyal to the Moscow Patriarchate, the highest priority was loyalty, a loyalty that trumped any other considerations.

In the wider American Orthodox context, new Orthodox dioceses emerged to serve the growing population of Greeks, Arabs, Serbs, Romanians, Bulgarians, and Albanians. The stage was set for the enduring Orthodox pattern in North America—jurisdictional pluralism in the form of "ethnic" jurisdictions. In some instances, the American Orthodox whose mother country fell under Communist domination, like the Russian Orthodox, divided into jurisdictions maintaining loyalty to the mother church, on the one hand, and on the other hand separating from it in order to protect themselves from potential dictates of Communist governments.

The main successor body of the Russian Orthodox diocese slowly grew into a Metropolia with several dioceses, church institutions such as seminaries, and regularly convened governance bodies. Indeed, the heritage received from the Russian Orthodox Church was given life in America in ways that were impossible in the Soviet Union. The All Russian Council of 1917–1918, which restored the office of patriarch, also established governance bodies— the Holy Synod; a Supreme Church Council with a mixed membership of bishops, clergy, and laity; and a regularly convened All Russian Council, also with mixed membership. The violent and genocidal persecutions in the Soviet Union for decades made it impossible for this church governance to be implemented.

The North American Metropolia, on the other hand, implemented the governance structure established by the All Russian Council. In fact, in significant ways, the approach to church governance by the beloved Patriarch Tikhon when he was bishop in America anticipated the decisions of the All

Russian Council. In the American Metropolia the church governance took the shape of Holy Synod (bishops only), Metropolitan Council (chaired by the metropolitan and mixed membership of clergy and laity), and All American Council (bishops, clergy, and lay delegates).

During the World War II alliance of the United States with the Soviet Union in the struggle against Nazi Germany, there was a mood of friendliness toward the Soviet Union in the United States. This is illustrated in the nickname "Uncle Joe" given to Joseph Stalin, turning the genocidal tyrant into a comfortable family figure. The mood of the wartime alliance also made possible an openness of the Metropolia to the Moscow Patriarchate. It was helpful that in 1943 bishops of the Russian Orthodox Church were allowed by Stalin to elect a patriarch. In the late 1940s, the Metropolia took steps toward restoring church relations with Moscow, recognizing the patriarch of Moscow as its "spiritual head." Negotiations between the Metropolia and the patriarchate, however, did not come to a satisfactory result. The Metropolia needed a fully recognized autonomy. Representatives of Moscow needed to secure for the patriarchate a real authority over the Metropolia. This involved the confirmation by the patriarchate of the election of the head of the church in America and the commitment of the church in America to refrain from criticizing the Soviet Union.

As the Cold War unfolded, the Metropolia responded to changes in society and among church members. The use of the English language in worship and in church life gradually increased. Little by little suburban parishes were created to address the shift in population patterns. Typically, the suburban parishes from their foundation were oriented toward the exclusive use of the English language. On the world scene, the Metropolia early became a member of the World Council of Churches. In the United States, the Metropolia took membership in the National Council of the Churches of Christ in the USA.

The canonical situation of the Metropolia in the US Orthodox communities became increasingly precarious. For those Orthodox who were canonically in a direct relationship with their mother churches, the status of the Metropolia was seen as "schismatic." Nevertheless, liturgical relations were maintained, and the Metropolia, as one of the larger "jurisdictions," took part in all significant Orthodox initiatives. Nevertheless, Archbishop Iakovos of the Greek Orthodox Archdiocese gave private warnings that the Ecumenical Patriarchate was moving toward severing relationships with the Metropolia. At the end of the 1960s, the Metropolia, through its primate, issued a lengthy and thoughtful letter describing the anomaly of the pluralism of jurisdictions and appealing for vigorous action by the mother churches to address the canonical problems involved. Effectively, Ecumenical Patriarch Athenagoras was petitioned to accept the Metropolia under his authority, in the hope that this would begin the process of movement toward Orthodox unity in America. The ecumenical patriarch's response was clear—to solve your problems, as Russians you must go to Moscow.

By this time, the Moscow Patriarchate had entered the World Council of Churches (1961). The delegates of the Metropolia to WCC assemblies and central committee meetings were encountering delegates of the Russian Orthodox Church. It seemed that there were new opportunities to achieve a solution for the Moscow-Metropolia issues. Informal contacts led to formal meetings. The Moscow Patriarchate reached the point of accepting the need for the full self-government of the Metropolia. The final steps were the signing of a formal agreement in Syosset, New York (then the residence of the primate of the Metropolia), on March 31, 1970, and approval and confirmation of the autocephaly of the Orthodox Church in America by the Holy Synod of the Russian Orthodox Church. The document of confirmation called the *Tomos* was signed by Patriarch Alexis I of Moscow and the members of the Holy Synod on April 10, 1970, in Moscow. Patriarch Alexis died on April 17, 1970, making his signature on the *Tomos* one of the final official acts of his life. Patriarch Alexis was the last living bishop of the Russian Orthodox Church who was consecrated to the episcopacy before the Russian Revolution. Thus the gift of autocephaly was conveyed to the Metropolia by the old Russian Orthodox Church of the Russian Empire and the renewed Moscow Patriarchate of the Soviet Union.

The autocephaly opened the way for eucharistic communion and normal ecclesial relations between the newly renamed Orthodox Church in America and the Russian Orthodox Church (Moscow Patriarchate). A beginning was made when Bishop Theodosius (Lazor) represented the Orthodox Church in America at the funeral service of Patriarch Alexis in April 1970.

A delegation of the Orthodox Church in America traveled to Moscow in May 1970 to receive the *Tomos* of autocephaly from the Russian Orthodox Church. After the death of Patriarch Alexis I, Metropolitan Pimen was the acting head of the Russian Orthodox Church as *Locum Tenens* of the patriarchal throne. At the head of the American delegation was Bishop Theodosius (Lazor), the youngest bishop, and also an American-born bishop. As bishop of Alaska, he represented the historical link between Russia and the United States, between the Russian Orthodox Church and the Orthodox Church in America. The visit included a *Panikhida*/memorial service at the grave of Patriarch Tikhon, sung by the delegation in English as a testimony to the encouragement for the use of English in the divine services given by the patriarch when he was bishop of the American diocese. A prayer service was sung at the grave of Metropolitan Innocent, the great missionary in Alaska and Siberia. To signify the American identity of the Orthodox Church in America, the delegation met with Jacob Beam, the US ambassador to the Soviet Union.

In August 1970, the first Orthodox saint in America was canonized in services and ceremonies in Kodiak, near Spruce Island, where Saint Herman had lived at the end of his life and had been buried. His remains were brought from Spruce Island to rest permanently in the Holy Resurrection Church in Kodiak. Symbolically significant at the canonization was the participation of Archbishop Paul of Finland, in whose church the New Valamo Monastery was created after the monks of Old Valaam Monastery fled from the Soviet annexation of eastern Karelia. Saint Herman of Alaska was a monk of Valaam before he came to Alaska as a missionary in 1794.

During the decades following the 1970 reconciliation between the Russian Orthodox Church and the Orthodox Church in America, there have been numerous exchanges of visits and liturgical concelebrations. Two occasions in the midst of the Cold War are worthy of notice. In May 1978 the Moscow Patriarchate celebrated the sixtieth anniversary of the restoration of the office of patriarch. Representatives of the other Orthodox churches participated in this event. The Orthodox Church in America delegation was led by Bishop Dmitri (Royster) of Hartford and New England, secretary of the Holy Synod. As a convert to the Orthodox faith, Bishop Dmitri was a living witness to the American present and future of the Orthodox Church in America. At the end of his message of greeting in Moscow, Bishop Dmitri said the following: "May the Risen Lord strengthen and support you and your Holy Church as you seek to follow Christ in communion with all the saints and martyrs who have illumined the Russian land. Christ is Risen!" The reference to the saints and martyrs, in the Soviet context, was an unmistakable tribute to the martyrs of the twentieth century. In June 1988 the Orthodox Church in America delegation to the celebration of the millennium of the baptism of Rus' was led by the primate, Metropolitan Theodosius. In his address, in the context of the canonization of several saints during the millennium celebration, Theodosius urged the Russian Orthodox Church to canonize Patriarch Tikhon: "I would like to say a few words about the memory of Patriarch Tikhon that is alive for Orthodox Christians in America. He is for us our own bishop and spiritual guide, one who led us from 1897 to 1907 with a wonderful humility and wisdom, and one who showed perceptive and clear missionary vision of the task of Orthodoxy in America. Thus, the canonization of Patriarch Tikhon by the Church of Russia would, for us, be similar to the canonization of Metropolitan Innocent (Veni-aminov). It would be the canonization of one who belongs both to America and to Russia, of one who is also a 'rule of faith and image of humility.'" At the time these words were spoken, the Communist "party line" was that Patriarch Tikhon was a counterrevolutionary who had anathematized the Communist regime for its violence against the Russian people and the Church of Russia.

After the restoration of communion between the Orthodox Church in America and the Russian Orthodox Church, the OCA's newspaper, both in its editorials and in its news stories, continued to highlight the persecution of religious communities and religious believers in the Soviet Union. Also, at the regularly convened All American Councils, resolutions were adopted on the violations of human and religious rights in the Soviet Union. To illustrate the consistency of these public appeals, the texts below begin with one from 1970 and conclude with one from 1992.

> The Council of the Orthodox Church in America deplores the current tendency, prevailing in ecumenical agencies, to identify the quest for Christian unity with political involvement. It protests, in particular, against the moral and material help given by some of these agencies to destructive revolutionary groups, while, at the same time, the suppression of Christian faith and human freedom in Communist lands is being ignored.

> All American Council, South Canaan, Pennsylvania,
> October 1970

> The All American Council expresses its profound indignation against . . . cases of religious persecution in the Soviet Union. It appeals to American public opinion for support of the persecuted Orthodox faithful. It calls all tourists visiting the USSR to inquire about the fate of the Dormition Cathedral in Vladimir and of the Monastery of Pochaev, and to express support for the persecuted Orthodox Church.

> All American Council, Cleveland, Ohio,
> November 1975

> We, the Fifth All American Council of the Orthodox Church in America, gratefully acknowledging freedom of religious belief and practice in our countries, reaffirm: a) Our support of all those who are discriminated against by reason of their belief in God, and b) Our protest against all po-

litical systems which curtail or suppress the basic human right to religious freedom. We pledge ourselves to continued effort on behalf of the human rights and religious freedom of all.

All American Council, Montreal, Quebec, Canada,
October 1977

The Orthodox Church in America, in its meeting of the Sixth All American Council in Detroit, Michigan, recommends that a Task Force on Human Rights be established under the authority of the Department of External Affairs for the purpose of monitoring the activities of all organizations concerned with religious freedom and violations thereof throughout the world.

All American Council, Detroit, Michigan,
November 1980

We, the delegates to the Seventh All American Council of the Orthodox Church in America, express our grave concern with the fate of Orthodox Christians and other believers in the Soviet Union. We are particularly concerned with the fact that leaders of the Orthodox religious revival are imprisoned. Among them are Fr. Gleb Yakunin, founder of the Christian Committee for the Defense of Believers' Rights, Alexander Ogorodnikov and Vladimir Poresh, representatives of Orthodox youth, and Zoya Krakhmalnikova, the editor of the Orthodox anthology called Nadezhda (Hope). . . . We call on the civil authorities of the Soviet Union to release these prisoners of conscience who are imprisoned for the expression of their faith.

Their imprisonment violates the Helsinki Final Act and other international covenants of which the U.S.S.R. is a signatory. . . .

We note, furthermore, that freedom is indivisible, as is shown by the fact that persons of conscience and courage such as Andrei Sakharov, while not themselves believers, have consistently spoken out in defense of the rights of believers as well as other human rights. Andrei Sakharov is in exile and subjected to intimidation and harassment and must, therefore, be considered also a prisoner of conscience. Since freedom is indivisible, we make our appeal on behalf of Andrei Sakharov, asking that his detention in exile be ended.

All American Council, Philadelphia, Pennsylvania,
August 1983

In considering how to "speak the truth to power" in today's world, the Council welcomes and affirms the principles expressed by His Beatitude Metropolitan Theodosius, in his address to the Council. "The Orthodox Church in America is committed to 'giving voice to those without voice' whether they are oppressed by the 'right' or the 'left.' . . . If our Church and other religious communities could speak with one voice in defense of those who are oppressed in south Africa and the Soviet Union, in Ethiopia and in Egypt, in Cuba and in Guatemala, in the Middle East and in Asia—in defense of all our fellow human beings in the concentration camps and gulags of the world in which we live—how much more authentic and powerful our common witness would be."

All American Council, Washington, DC,
August 1986

The collapse of communist regimes in the former USSR, central and eastern Europe, and the Balkans has brought freedom to most churches in these parts of the world. This is the case even in countries where communist structures and leaders still hold considerable power, and where renascent fascism has made its unwelcome appearance. . . . The collapse of communist ideology and state control reveals societies and peoples assaulted simultaneously by several crises, political, social, ethnic, economic and ecological. Most critically, a profound moral crisis has been produced which can only be addressed by strong, compassionate, honest, educated Christians and Christian churches. The Orthodox Churches in these regions carry tremendous responsibility for moral renewal.

All American Council, Miami, Florida,
July 1992

The inherent tensions of the Cold War period sometimes became apparent within the life of the Orthodox Church in America. For example, during the 1983 Assembly of the World Council of Churches in Vancouver, the primate of the OCA planned to welcome the Orthodox delegations at a church service in Vancouver's OCA parish church. This presupposed that Patriarch Ilya of Georgia, as the senior Orthodox figure present, would be invited to preside at the Liturgy. The delegations of churches from the Soviet bloc would all be invited, including the delegation of the Russian Orthodox Church. The parish community did not want to offer its hospitality, arguing that the delegations from Eastern Europe were not welcome. In preliminary conversations with the parish community, a representative of the administration of the OCA, at a general meeting of the parishioners, informed the troubled priest and laity of the parish that if they were unable to overcome their anxieties, the service would be held in another venue, which would be awkward for the OCA and embarrassing for the parish. In the end, the parish agreed to host the delegations.

From time to time, representatives of the Soviet government and the Moscow Patriarchate attempted to influence the policy of the Orthodox Church in America on making public statements on matters of concern within the Soviet Union. On one occasion an archbishop of the Russian Orthodox Church privately chided the American church for bringing public attention to apparent threats to close a cathedral; the response was a simple one: our criticism is directed at the Soviet authorities and not at the Russian Orthodox Church. On another occasion, the chairman of the Council on Religious Affairs, while visiting Washington, DC, requested a meeting with the primate of the OCA. During the ensuing conversation, several ideas for deepening relations between the Russian Orthodox Church and the Orthodox Church in America were put forward, among them exchanges of professors and students of theological schools and the opening of an OCA parish or "representation church" in Moscow. In addition, the point was made that the approaching millennium of the baptism of Rus' made it obvious that the Monastery (Lavra) of the Kiev Caves should be turned over to the Orthodox Church to play again its role as a place of religious pilgrimage and liturgical worship. The reply of the Soviet official was direct: so long as your churchwide newspaper prints fabricated stories about persecution of religion in the Soviet Union, your useful ideas on deepening relations between the churches are unachievable. The OCA reply: the information on repression of religious life in the Soviet Union is printed in many US publications; our parishioners have access to these publications, and if our readers see that we are silent while others speak out, our people will lose confidence in us. In the 1980s, two OCA clergymen were denied Soviet visas for several years; in one case an OCA representative was blocked from traveling to the Soviet Union as a member of a delegation of the National Council of Churches.

The Cold War context had implications for the OCA in relations with Romania and the Romanian Orthodox Patriarchate. The majority of Romanian Orthodox in the USA and Canada were separated from the Romanian Patriarchate and were determined to keep their distance from the Communist regime in their country of origin. The Romanian Episcopate joined the OCA and constituted an autonomous OCA diocese. A focused effort was made by the Romanian Patriarchate to use leverage against the OCA and its Romanian Episcopate. A high representative of the Romanian Patriarchate called on the OCA primate, Metropolitan Theodosius, offering to give full recognition to the OCA as an autocephalous church if the OCA handed its Romanian Episcopate to the patriarchate. The answer was clear and unequivocal. The Romanian Episcopate is a community of Orthodox faithful with its bishop, its parishes and priests, and its institutions. As a living community, it cannot and will not be "delivered" to the patriarchate. If this means that the patriarchate does not recognize the OCA as an autocephalous church, so be it. An effort by the Bulgarian Church to pressure the OCA to relinquish its small Bulgarian Diocese was also unsuccessful.

During the Cold War, there were two predominant and incompatible paradigms in the policies and responses of Christian churches to challenges of the time. One model was antagonism not only to the USSR but also to the churches and religious communities in the Soviet Union. Among the Orthodox churches in the United States, the Russian Orthodox Church Outside of Russia was an example of this orientation. By means of publications and statements, the ROCOR position was well known, with its condemnation of the Soviet Union and its Communist ideology, its support for the persecuted in the so-called catacomb church, and its denunciations of the official Moscow Patriarchate as a nest of KGB agents, and therefore an illegitimate church. Some other US Christians adopted a similar stance.

The second model was found in "mainline" Protestant bodies that considered the threat of nuclear war a moral priority, and assessed the burden of guilt as equally shared between the West and the East. Sometimes the guilt for the nuclear threat was even assigned especially and primarily to the United States and NATO. Those espousing such convictions were eager to have relations and dialogues with Christian churches of the Soviet Union and the Communist bloc, and were happy to join the Christian brothers and sisters in the Soviet sphere in criticizing the Western bloc for its preparations for war. There was little readiness to take note of human rights violations and persecution of religious believers. The same orientation prevailed in ecumenical organizations—specifically in the National Council of the Churches of Christ in the USA and in the World Council of Churches.

The Orthodox Church in America charted a different course, took a third path, one described and illustrated above. During the period of its break with the Russian Orthodox Church, the Metropolia blamed the Soviet Communist regime for the violence and repression characterizing its rule, but did not blame the Russian Orthodox Church for its enforced submission to the regime. By welcoming the autocephaly granted by the church of Russia and entering into eucharistic communion with the Russian Orthodox Church, the Orthodox Church in America clearly affirmed the church of Russia's ecclesial legitimacy. At the same time, the Orthodox Church in America never relinquished its moral obligation to stand with those targeted for persecution by the Communist system in the Soviet Union. This moral duty of necessity led to challenging the injustices of the Soviet system in books, editorials, and statements at All American Councils. The Orthodox Church in America saw its response to the challenges of the Cold War as a striving to take its stand in truth and as a rejection of one-sided political choices.

In the 1980s, as the Russian Orthodox Church prepared to mark the one thousandth anniversary of the baptism of Rus', there was a meaningful collaboration between the Orthodox Church in America and the National Council of Churches and its Protestant member churches. The NCC sponsored visits of US Christians to the USSR, drawing attention to the millennium of the baptism of Rus' and offering experiences and encounters with Christians of the Soviet Union, especially with Orthodox Christians. Members of the OCA, both clergy and laity, participated actively in this program of study and visits. As a result of the initiative of the NCC, many US Christians who knew little if anything about Christianity in the Soviet Union gained important insights about the witness of Christians in the officially atheist nation. At the center of this pilgrimage of discovery was the learning that the largest Christian community in the USSR was the Orthodox Church, whose twentieth-century witness in the USSR was an authentic *martyria* in the name of the gospel of Christ. For some US Christians, it was a revelatory discovery that the Orthodox were fellow Christians.

The Orthodox Church in America's forthright critique of the Soviet state and its policy of hostility to religious faith was at times seen by American Christians as ideological "anti-Sovietism," an expression of Cold War rhetoric and mentality. At times OCA leaders and representatives saw their fellow American Christians (especially the mainline Protestant churches and ecumenical organizations) as co-opted by the illusory Soviet "struggle for peace" and the illusory Soviet commitment to justice and equality.

In reality, holders of each point of view could—and did—learn from the other. There was a real threat and danger of nuclear war, and Christians bore some responsibility in helping to avert a possible nuclear holocaust. There was a real and deadly tyranny in the Communist systems of rule, and Christians bore some responsibility for standing in solidarity with the persecuted and oppressed—whether the oppression and injustice occurred in the East or the West, in the North or the South.

Sustaining the Fatherland in Exile:
Commemoration and Ritual during the Cold War

Nicholas Denysenko

This chapter examines the political theology of the Ukrainian churches in the United States during the early period of the Cold War (1947–1964). The arrival of Ukrainian immigrants in the United States after World War II resulted in an adjustment of life in the Orthodox and Greek Catholic churches. Many of the immigrants carried the bitter memories of religious persecution, the violence and death of the *Holodomor*,[1] and the failed aspirations of Ukrainian sovereignty in the wake of the Soviet retention of Ukraine and absorption of western Ukrainian territories as part of the Yalta agreement. The consolidation and stabilization of Ukrainian church life in the United States coincided with their reception of American freedom. Immigrant church leaders captured the opportunity to assess the Cold War through the lens of liberation: they articulated a political theology of martyrdom through the lens of freedom. In this chapter, two events in the Ukrainian émigré community are presented that were inspired by the Cold War and contributed to the articulation of this political theology of martyrdom: the construction of Saint Andrew Memorial Church in South Bound Brook, New Jersey, from 1955 to 1965, and the establishment of the monument to Taras Shevchenko in Washington, DC, in 1964. I will explore the following primary features of the Ukrainian émigré community's political theology: the power of commemorating contemporary martyrdom and suffering; the struggle for liberating the fatherland from Soviet tyranny; America as a symbol of freedom and a space bearing a sacred mission for seeking liberation, with Moscow as the symbol of tyranny and totalitarianism; and the tension between lament and thanksgiving within the evolution of the political theology.

---

1. *Holodomor* is the Ukrainian term for the Stalinist man-made famine of 1932 and 1933 of genocidal proportions that claimed millions of lives in Ukraine.

Background

Ukrainians have immigrated to the United States since the eighteenth century.[2] In the early twentieth century, Orthodox Ukrainians established their own churches in the United States based on ethnic identity. In the United States, Archbishop John Theodorovich presided over the Ukrainian Autocephalous Orthodox Church (UAOC) from 1924 onward.[3] This church was viewed by other members of the global Orthodox ecclesial community as illegitimate and schismatic because they consecrated their own hierarchy without the participation of bishops, thus forsaking the precious mark of churchliness universally known as apostolic succession. Despite this stigma of illegitimacy, the church provided a place for immigrants to gather, worship, and socialize in their native language while observing the traditions of the fatherland.[4]

In the meantime, the mother church in Ukraine was suffering from Stalinist persecution and liquidation. Perhaps most notable was the deliberate eradication of ecclesial intelligentsia from Ukraine, as many clergy and bishops were murdered as enemies of the people, especially during the dekulakization and collectivization campaign of 1929–1933, which devastated Ukraine with an orchestrated famine that claimed the lives of approximately four million people.[5] The famine was the climax of a series of hostile events

2. For an overview of Ukrainian immigration to the United States, see Myron Kuropas, *The Ukrainian Americans: Roots and Aspirations, 1884–1954* (Toronto: University of Toronto Press, 1991).

3. The classical study of the autocephalous church in Ukraine is by Bohdan Bociurkiw, "The Ukrainian Autocephalous Orthodox Church, 1920–1930: A Case Study in Religious Modernization," in *Religion and Modernization in the Soviet Union*, ed. Dennis J. Dunn (Boulder, CO: Westview Press, 1977), 310–47.

4. Archbishop Theodorovich's canonical status became a problem for the Ukrainian church in Western Europe and the United States. His ordination was liturgically corrected in 1949 by the exarch of the Patriarchate of Alexandria. For more discussion of Theodorovich's role in the church mergers after World War II, see Bohdan Bociurkiw, "The Ukrainian Autocephalous Orthodox Church in West Germany, 1945–50," in *The Refugee Experience: Ukrainian Displaced Persons after World War II*, ed. Wsevolod W. Isajiw, Yury Boshyk, and Roman Senkus (Edmonton: Canadian Institute of Ukrainian Studies Press, 1992), 168–69.

5. The classic study of the Soviet policy of collectivization that resulted in the *Holodomor* is by Robert Conquest, *Harvest of Sorrow: Soviet Collectivization and the Terror-Famine* (New York: Oxford University Press, 1987). Recently, Norman Naimark has argued that the Ukrainian famine was an act of genocide by Joseph Stalin. See Naimark, *Stalin's Genocides* (Princeton: Princeton University Press, 2010). For a review of scholarship, see "After the Holodomor: The Enduring Impact of the Great Famine on Ukraine," *Harvard Ukrainian Studies* 30, nos. 1–4 (2008).

orchestrated by the Soviet regime that resulted in the creation of a historical anamnesis of contemporary martyrdom and gave birth to émigré political theology.

The end of World War II and the Yalta agreement resulted in the expatriation of many Ukrainians to the West, and many of the bishops and clergy of the autocephalous church arrived in the United States from the late 1940s through the early 1950s.[6] In 1947, Bishop Mstyslav Skrypnyk was one of these immigrants who settled in Canada. He came to the United States in 1950 and established a merger of the Orthodox Ukrainians into one church led by Metropolitan John Theodorovich.[7]

Under the joint leadership of Metropolitan John Theodorovich and Archbishop Mstyslav Skrypnyk, the Ukrainian Orthodox Church of the USA (UOC) became an active and vocal critic of the Soviet Union and its religious policy, especially the Moscow Patriarchate, and advocated for religious freedom in Ukraine. Metropolitan John led the church until his death in 1971 and Archbishop Mstyslav succeeded him, guiding the small church through Gorbachev's tenure as leader of the USSR and its collapse in 1991. The new religious freedom facilitated by glasnost and perestroika permitted the rebirth of the UAOC in Ukraine, which elected and enthroned Mstyslav as its first patriarch in 1990. By the time of his death in 1993, Mstyslav was both a witness of and contributor to the legal reestablishment of the UAOC and the Ukrainian Greco-Catholic Church (UGCC) in the USSR (1989–1991) and Ukraine (1991–1993).

The UGCC had endured its own struggles in the early twentieth century. While Greek Catholics under the Austro-Hungarian Empire had flourished, the tsarist regime attempted to eradicate Greek Catholics from the Russian Empire in the nineteenth century.[8] The years between the revolution and the Yalta agreement were turbulent for Greek Catholics, who witnessed numerous changes in political borders. When western Ukraine was given to the Soviet Union in the Yalta agreement of 1945, Ukrainian Greco-Catholics became subject to the same religious persecution suffered by the Orthodox churches. In 1946, a council was held in L'viv at which the UGCC voted to liquidate itself and return to Orthodoxy under the jurisdiction of the Moscow Patriarchate,

6. See Bociurkiw, "The Ukrainian Autocephalous Orthodox Church," 167–70.

7. Bociurkiw, "The Ukrainian Autocephalous Orthodox Church," 167–69. Note the continued existence of much smaller Ukrainian Orthodox churches in the United States during this period as well.

8. For an overview, see Robert F. Taft, "The Eastern Catholic 'Uniate' Churches," *Cambridge Histories Online* (Cambridge, 2008), 413–14.

a council whose legitimacy is dismissed almost universally.[9] Greek Catholics outside of Ukraine consolidated their position under leaders such as Patriarch Josef Slipyj and Ivan Lubachivsky, and vigorously sought their legalization and restoration in Ukraine. Thus, Ukrainian Greek Catholic immigrants came to the United States bearing the dual disappointment of the coerced liquidation of the UGCC and the failure of the Ukrainian Insurgent Army to deliver sovereignty to Ukraine.

Ukrainian Catholic and Orthodox immigrants came to the United States with multiple memories and a variety of attitudes. One of the primary attitudes shared by both religious groups was a strong distrust of the Soviet regime and its capital, Moscow. In the religious literature of the émigré community, Moscow emerges as the primary antagonist, the place of the tyrant who holds Ukraine's freedom-loving people captive. In this vein, Moscow simply inherited the role of Saint Petersburg and the tsarist regime that preceded the Soviet Union. Imperial Russia's anti-Ukrainian campaigns culminated with the imprisonment of Taras Shevchenko, Ukraine's nineteenth-century poet who dreamed of his homeland's independence. In the proceedings of the 1921 council of the UAOC, which asserted its independence from Moscow, a consistent pattern of themes emerges wherein the Ukrainian Orthodox self-identify as former slaves fleeing from the shackles of their captor, the tsar and his servants. The cohort of Ukrainians who arrived in the United States after World War II retained this identity, which had evolved to include the recent memory of crimes against Ukrainians committed by the Soviets as the regime that succeeded imperial Russia and attacked notions of Ukrainian sovereignty and ecclesial independence even more viciously.

The Construction of Saint Andrew's Memorial Church

From 1947 to 1951, approximately 113,000 Ukrainians departed Austria and Germany for the United States.[10] Many of these Ukrainians joined existing

9. See the magisterial study of Bohdan Bociurkiw, *The Ukrainian Greek Catholic Church and the Soviet State, 1939–50* (Edmonton: Canadian Institute of Ukrainian Studies, 1996), and Serhii Plokhy, "In the Shadow of Yalta: International Politics and the Soviet Liquidation of the Ukrainian Greek Catholic Church," in *Religion and Nation in Modern Ukraine*, ed. Serhii Plokhy and Frank E. Sysyn (Edmonton and Toronto: Canadian Institute of Ukrainian Studies Press, 2003), 58–74.

10. Wsewolod W. Isajiw and Michael Palij, "Refugees and the Problem in Postwar Europe," in Isajiw, Boshyk, and Senkus, *The Refugee Experience*, xviii.

Orthodox or Greek Catholic parishes or formed new ones. Bishop Mstyslav Skrypnyk originally settled in Canada; he came to the United States in 1950 and presided over the unification of the two largest Orthodox Ukrainian churches. Bishop Mstyslav became the primary administrator of the newly unified Ukrainian Church and was also the central figure behind the erection of Saint Andrew's Memorial Church in South Bound Brook, New Jersey.

Saint Andrew's Memorial Church is also known as the *Tserkva-Pamyatnyk* ("Memorial Church"), an edifice designed to serve the needs of the entire Ukrainian Orthodox population in the United States. The Memorial Church was more than just an edifice providing for the liturgical needs of a suburban parish. The church constructed the edifice to honor the sacrifice of the Ukrainians who died in defense of their country; it proclaimed Ukrainian fidelity to freedom in defiance of Soviet religious persecution.

The construction of the Memorial Church was the climax of a process of establishing a global center for the UOC. The process commenced with the consecration of an administrative center in Bound Brook, New Jersey, in 1952, just two years after the unification of the churches. The consecration of the church center established the foundation for the political theology that was developed primarily with the construction of the Memorial Church. In April 1952, the UOC announced the forthcoming celebration of the consecration of the church center. The theme of the consecration was the "battle of the Christian world with the aggression of godless Muscovite communism."[11] The church leaders appealed to Orthodox Ukrainians throughout the United States to gather in New Jersey under the protection of the mother of God. The theme for this inaugural event was the mother of God's protection of Orthodox Ukrainians in the past and present, headed by the theme "Beneath your compassion, we take refuge, O virgin Birthgiver of God." The church communiqué fused the mother of God's patronage of Orthodox Ukrainians with the battle against Communism and the building of Memorial Church: "The consecration of a space beneath the structure of the Memorial Church will take place after the Divine Liturgy, which is to be a manifest sign of our respect for the memory of our relatives and all of those who gave their lives for Christian truth and the will and statehood of the Ukrainian people. The Church portion of the celebrations will conclude with a prayer to the all-holy Mother of God and the common singing of 'beneath your compassion.'"[12] The communiqué refers to the other program components, including "speeches of appointed represen-

---

11. *Ukrainian Orthodox Word* (hereafter *UOW*), April 1952, 11.
12. *UOW*, April 1952, 12.

tatives from Ukrainian and American community-political life." The speeches were devoted to the "contemporary battle of the Christian world with godless Moscow and the matter of liberating the Ukrainian people."[13] In the May 1952 issue of *UOW*, under the headline "Great Feast," the church announced the preparation of an icon of the mother of God: "The Divine Liturgy and other services will occur in the Church center itself among greens and flowers, under the protection of the mother of God, with her beautiful icon near completion. This icon will stand on the plaza the entire time, illuminated by reflectors. The clergy and faithful will present their prayers before her on the day of our feast and in the future."[14]

The celebration scheduled for June 1, 1952, was disappointing because of heavy rain, which forced the organizers to move the festivities to Washington High School nearby. The rain and venue change did not result in softened polemic, as Archbishop Mstyslav seized the opportunity to encourage the people to support the building of the Memorial Church, an edifice to honor "our ancestors and all of those brethren who died for Ukraine's freedom and the freedom of the United States of America."[15] At the conclusion of the festivities, the bishops distributed small images of the protection of the mother of God to fifty-six people who had made monetary donations for the building of the Memorial Church.[16] The consecration of the Memorial Church was designated as a sign of the triumph of the Ukrainian people. The connection with the protection of the mother of God continued with the rescheduling of the consecration of the church center, which occurred on September 21, the feast of the birth of the mother of God (according to the Julian calendar). On this day, the Liturgy was offered at an outdoor altar before the enormous image of the protection of the mother of God, bringing the inaugural events of consecrating a church center under the protection of the mother of God and in memory of those who died defending freedom and Ukrainian statehood to their conclusion.

The political theology articulated at the inaugural events fused together several staples from Orthodox devotional history, namely, the commemoration of those who defended the fatherland against a bloodthirsty foe. During the Cold War, the Orthodox Ukrainians who enjoyed the protection of the mother of God in the United States named the foe: the Bolshevik regime lo-

13. *UOW*, April 1952, 12
14. *UOW*, May 1952, 5.
15. *UOW*, June 1952, 3.
16. *UOW*, June 1952, 3. The text notes that many of these early donors were elderly and required assistance when they approached Archbishop Mstyslav to receive the image.

cated in Moscow. The commemoration refers to a local struggle. The rationale for the Ukrainian reference to the protection of the mother of God was
their continued existence outside of their native homeland. In the context of
the Cold War, the Orthodox Ukrainians in the United States drew from the
traditional repository of Orthodox political theology and its champion, the
mother of God, and fused it with American civic values: freedom and democracy. Thus, the political theology proclaimed by the small Ukrainian émigré
community had global resonances: the memory of their struggle to defeat the
Soviets, who sought their eradication, provided fuel for the global Christian
battle against the Soviet Union. The émigré battleground was the United States,
an appropriate opponent for the Soviet regime as the global symbol of liberty
and freedom.

The centerpiece of the church center was the Memorial Church itself,
and the process of building the church was elongated by difficulties in raising
the necessary funds. From 1954 to 1965, the church administration repeatedly
appealed to the people for donations. The church established 1961 as the goal
for the construction and dedication of the Memorial Church, the centennial
of Shevchenko's death. In 1954, the UOC unveiled the plan for the Memorial
Church, appointing Yurik Kodak as architect; he had designed several edifices
in Canada.[17] The UOC expressed their aspirations for the legacy of the edifice:
"As we see from the project, the Memorial Church in Bound Brook will be not
only a beautiful divine temple, before whose altar daily prayers for the souls
of our beloved relatives and martyred brothers and sisters will be offered, but
also a marvelous example of Ukrainian ecclesial architecture. . . . Besides this,
the Memorial Church in Bound Brook will surely be one of the most precious
additions to the spiritual and cultural treasury of the United States of America,
which Orthodox Ukrainians offer as expressions of thanksgiving for that will
for the liberty of soul and conscience, which they exercise in America."[18] The
initial plan included fifty-two spaces for burial crypts in the mausoleum, and
the initial estimated cost for the church was $100,000. The groundbreaking
occurred in 1955.

In 1958, the political theology of the Memorial Church gained momentum
as the Ukrainian émigré community commemorated another anniversary, the
twenty-five-year mark of the *Holodomor* in Ukraine.[19] Archbishop Mstyslav
conducted a press conference for the American press and explained that

17. *UOW*, February 1954, 11.
18. *UOW*, February 1954, 11.
19. *UOW*, March 1958.

Ukrainian Americans were building the structure in memory of their brothers and sisters who died martyrs' deaths at the hands of "red-communist Moscow."[20] The Memorial Church's political theology remained consistent with the themes established in 1952. In April 1958, the UOC stated that the new church was in memory of those who gave their lives in battle for the liberty of Ukraine and her people and her life in the fatherland. This statement again referred to the United States as a "land of freedom," a symbol of the émigré community's aspiration for Ukraine's future. By August of 1960, as construction was slowed, the polemic of the political theology thickened in the wake of the Cold War.

The UOC stated that the Memorial Church was constructed in honor of those who were sacrificed by the Muscovite Communists, and was relevant not only for the Ukrainian people but also for all humankind.[21] The essay speaks of the suffering inflicted by the Communist regime upon Ukraine, attributing the burden carried by Ukraine in the terrible battle against Communism to the will of God. The author also states that the tyranny of Communist Moscow over Ukraine remains as it was, even though Stalin had died in 1953. The article states that the tyranny of Moscow exercised on Ukraine continues the pattern of the flow of blood and the suffering of the people in Ukraine, with the exception of those who serve the Communist Party.[22] In the face of this ongoing tyranny, the Memorial Church in Bound Brook was to symbolize "all of those who perished by the will of communism." "It is to stand upon a symbolical grave for all of those who perished for the freedom of Ukraine—whether in an active battle with the raider or as evening sacrifices through their own passiveness and ignorance, they led the always active enemy to victory whereas they themselves had a martyr's death for their passiveness."[23] The author states that the Memorial Church will become a manifestation of the battle between Satan and God, and that the Memorial Church is necessary for the sake of the people of other nations who were beginning to recognize the poison produced by Communism: if the Ukrainians failed to complete construction of the Memorial Church, the idea of Communism would be victorious.[24]

In the September and October 1960 issues of *UOW*, the UOC reported that the construction of the Memorial Church had garnered the attention of the Soviet Union and that Moscow viewed its completion as a serious threat.

20. At the time, in March 1958, 25 percent of the construction was complete.

21. *UOW*, August 1960, 9. The essay is signed by "Stariy," which simply means "Old man."

22. *UOW*, August 1960, 9.

23. *UOW*, August 1960, 9–10.

24. Earlier in the article, the author states that the Ukrainians were the first people to recognize Communism as a creation of Satan, which is now manifest in Moscow.

One report states that a priest in New York attempted to steal the primary contractor away from the Ukrainians, who had not raised enough money to continue construction. By November 1960, the urgency to complete construction by 1961 reached a new height: it was necessary to coincide with the hundred-year jubilee of Shevchenko's death, a symbolic year since Shevchenko was "the greatest martyr of Ukraine's battle with Moscow."[25] The urgency of the financial appeal and the latent criticism of those who had not yet donated for the cost of construction are expressed by the report's reference to a letter written to the editor.[26]

In January 1961, a new element contributed to the political theology and the edifice itself. During the construction process, the workers added fragments from beloved shrines in Ukraine to the new edifice; they came primarily from the cathedral of Saint Sophia, the Pecherska Lavra monastery, Saint Michael's monastery, and the cathedral of Saint Nicholas (all in Kyiv). Each of these edifices has historical significance for Ukrainians, and the UOC sought the addition of the last three fragments in particular as symbols of reconstruction, since their original buildings—the Dormition Church of the Lavra, Saint Michael's church, and the cathedral of Saint Nicholas—were destroyed by the Bolsheviks.[27] The UOC now added another commemoration, the forty-year anniversary of the proclamation of ecclesial autocephaly in Kyiv by the first Ukrainian Autocephalous Orthodox Church.[28]

The UOC envisioned the Memorial Church as a shrine honoring the memory and contributions of Ukraine's ecclesial and national pioneers. The edifice's foundation was the memory of the past. However, these very pioneers were invoked to challenge the people of the UOC in the present. With the failure to raise sufficient funds lurking in the background, the UOC depicted the following scene of an encounter between the Orthodox Ukrainians of their present (in 1961) and the heroes of Ukraine's past: "The time is coming to look them all in the eyes, to look directly, not hiding from their view, and to be prepared to respond to their question: but have all of you who live and benefit from the rich mercies of God, followed the example of our life and labor even in small measure?"[29] The UOC was attempting to motivate the people to donate enough

25. *UOW*, November 1960, 13. The report refers to Shevchenko as "*Prorok Ukrainy*" and "*Velykomuchenyk(a)*," or "Prophet of Ukraine" and "Great Martyr" of the Ukrainian people.

26. *UOW*, November 1960, 13.

27. *UOW*, January 1961, 10. The author of the article states that the Memorial Church was built from the fragments of Ukrainian shrines destroyed by the Muscovite hand.

28. *UOW*, January 1961, 10.

29. *UOW*, January 1961, 10.

to complete construction by 1961, and they expressed confidence that the people would respond. The Ukrainian pioneers' hypothetical question is answered by the author of the article, who questions the moral right of Ukrainians to claim the patrimony of the people who produced "the metropolitan martyrs Vasyl and Mykolaj and the genius Taras Shevchenko."[30] The invocation of the memories of Ukraine's heroes added to the political theology of defending the fatherland and sacrificing one's life for Ukraine's liberty. The émigré community produced tangible figures from Ukraine's recent history occasioned by jubilee years; the centennial anniversary of Shevchenko's death resulted in the community's recognition of his martyrdom and prophecy, whereas the fortieth anniversary of the All-Ukrainian Council restored the memory of Ukrainian church leaders who were also patriots, Metropolitans Vasil Lypkivsky and Mykola Boretsky. Shevchenko and the two metropolitans became the unofficial saints of the new holy place, the faces of Ukrainian martyrdom in the epic battle against Moscow's Communism.

From 1961 to 1965, the political theology that began to take shape with the dedication of the church center in Bound Brook remained more or less stable, as the émigré community slowly completed the construction. America as a symbol of what Ukraine hoped to become remained vibrant with the activities of church leaders in political life. On January 23, 1961, one day before the anniversary of Ukraine declaring independence in 1918, a special prayer for Ukraine's freedom was read in both chambers of the United States Congress.[31] The UOC declared June 4, 1961, a "great feast," as the fragments from the shrines in Kyiv were installed in their designated spaces in the Memorial Church. The theology of this great feast was consistent with the foundations established since 1952; the feast commemorated the Ukrainian people's sacrifice on the altars of its battle for the justice of God in the world. The church accentuated the significance of building the Memorial Church in the free world (America), an accomplishment permitted by "divine providence."[32] The addition of the ruined fragments to the Memorial Church constituted the pilgrimage of relics from Ukraine's Jerusalem to the United States.[33] One quality of the church's description of this great feast is notable: this was not an instance of an émigré community lamenting the loss suffered as a result of their exile from their native homeland. Rather, it was an occasion for thanksgiving for the

30. *UOW*, January 1961, 11.
31. *UOW*, March 1961, 17.
32. *UOW*, March 1961, 17.
33. *UOW*, March 1961, 17.

gift of divine providence, and not an occasion for weeping while gazing upon the foreign "waters of Babylon."[34] The installation of relics from Ukraine's past shrines was designed to ignite renewed love for the fatherland in the present, an illustration of the ultimate objective of the Memorial Church: the liberation and resurrection of Ukraine, and of all people who were suffering under the tyranny of Communism.

The church was finally dedicated on October 10, 1965, which was celebrated as a day of paschal joy, a "victory of light over darkness," and an opportunity to renew the majesty of ruined Ukrainian holy places in the free world. October 10 was designated as a special feast for the Ukrainian Orthodox Church as ten thousand people attended the dedication. Metropolitan John Theodorovich's speech included a concluding exhortation that synthesized the UOC's objective for erecting the edifice:

> May our Memorial Church remain standing for the ages! May the participants of the actions of our age establish the path for remembering these experiences! May our children and their children learn about the glory and sorrow of our day and evoke love to our native land and people in us! May the shrine erected by us loudly proclaim the need for our freedom-loving American people to attentively remain on the side of freedom! . . . From all ends of the United States of America, come here, and here find the breath of everything native, find in this place peace and faith: the day is coming that our land will be free and our nation on it![35]

The Erection of the Monument to Taras Shevchenko

The 1964 erection of the monument to Taras Shevchenko in Washington, DC, established Shevchenko as a hero-martyr around whom Ukrainian immigrants gathered, and whose memory contributed to the shaping of a political theology of liberation. This was a central event in the life of the Ukrainian émigré community of the United States. President Dwight Eisenhower had signed the law authorizing the erection of the statue on September 13, 1960, and the statue was unveiled on June 27, 1964.

The celebration of the unveiling of Shevchenko's statue provided another opportunity for Ukrainians in the United States to proclaim the tenets of their

34. *UOW*, March 1961, 17.
35. *UOW*, November–December 1965, 2.

political theology. Over one hundred thousand people of Ukrainian descent attended the ceremony in stifling summer heat. While President Lyndon Johnson was not in attendance, Eisenhower was the keynote political speaker for the unveiling ceremony. The ceremony also included prayers recited by Major Archbishop Ambrose Senyshyn of the Ukrainian Catholic Church and Metropolitan John Theodorovich of the Ukrainian Orthodox Church. The themes of freedom, condemnation of Communist totalitarianism, and the notion of the United States as the primary center of contemporary liberation were expressed in the event's proceedings.

Eisenhower's remarks represent the American polemic of the Cold War, language fully supported by the Ukrainian community. Eisenhower bemoaned the prevalence of tyranny and oppression galvanized by rulers in many parts of the world.[36] He expressed hope that the establishment of the statue would mark the beginning of a "new world movement . . . dedicated to the independence and freedom of peoples of all captive nations of the entire world." Eisenhower concluded his speech by referring to the significance of erecting Shevchenko's statue in the capital city of the United States: "His statue, standing here in the heart of the nation's capital, near the embassies where representatives of nearly all the countries of the world can see it, is a shining symbol of his love of liberty."[37] Eisenhower's speech does not impart particularly original material on the polemics of the Cold War, but his participation in the honoring of an outspoken patron of freedom and national independence from a republic of the Soviet Union attests to the notion of the United States as the global patron of freedom. As an international city hosting the representatives of the global community, the erection of Shevchenko's statue in Washington projected the perception of America's commitment to emancipating the peoples enslaved by Communist regimes.

America's role as a protector country providing an international platform for the émigré community's quest for freedom and condemnation of the Soviet tyrant gained momentum with the erection of Shevchenko's statue. The leaders of the Ukrainian Catholic Church and the Ukrainian Orthodox

---

36. "We have seen the counterattacks of fascism and communism substitute for them the totalitarian state, the suppression of personal freedom, the denial of national independence and even the destruction of free inquiry and discussion. Tyranny and oppression today are not different from tyranny and oppression in the days of Taras Shevchenko. Now, as then, tyranny means the concentration of all power in an elite body, in a government bureau, in a single man." Quoted from Gen. Dwight D. Eisenhower, "Address at the Unveiling of the Monument to Taras Shevchenko in Washington," *Ukrainian Weekly* (hereafter *UW*), July 3, 1964.

37. *UW*, July 3, 1964.

Church, respectively, offered the invocation and benediction for the unveiling, and the texts of their prayers grant us insight into their comprehension and hopes for America's role in liberating Ukraine and other captive countries. Archbishop-Metropolitan Ambrose Shenyshyn invoked an elaboration of the Lord's Prayer. Portions of Archbishop Ambrose's prayer referred to immediate relief for Ukraine, including a petition for freedom of worship: "Hallowed be Thy name . . . vouchsafe, o gracious Lord, that all our brothers and sisters in Ukraine may freely glorify Thee in churches, schools and homes under the guidance of Thy clergy and hierarchy."[38] Archbishop-Metropolitan Ambrose seemed to understand the formidable challenge posed to leaders of the international community who sought peace during the Cold War, and his petitions for their wisdom and prudence evoked the fears of new outbreaks of war and nuclear Armageddon: "Thy kingdom come . . . grant Thy grace to the mighty ones of this world that they may recognize Thy eternal truth, so as to find the key to the solutions of international problems and the establishment of lasting world peace."[39] The next part of the prayer refers to the prudence needed to avoid the most catastrophic potential outcomes of the Cold War: "Enlighten, Lord, the leaders of the United States as well as the leaders of the other countries, so that, employing the attainments of the natural sciences, they would use their sources of nuclear energy, not for purposes of war and destruction of peoples, but for the welfare of future generations."[40] Ambrose's prayer represents the Ukrainian community's hope and trust in the leadership of the United States in establishing world peace with prudence, given the nuclear armaments accompanying the Cold War.

Metropolitan John's closing benediction also testified to the Ukrainian community's acknowledgment of America's role in the Cold War. It designated the unveiling of Shevchenko's monument as the inauguration of a "day of life" for the Ukrainian nation. The establishment of the monument was to awaken "national consciousness" on a "day of our national rebirth."[41] The émigré community's aspiration for national rebirth depended on America's support,

---

38. *UW*, July 3, 1964, 2. The second petition asks, "Give us this day our daily bread, give it also to our brethren in Ukraine, so that they may live and work for Thy glory and the welfare of our people."

39. Immediately after "thy kingdom come," Ambrose prayed, "Thy kingdom of Thy love and freedom and peace throughout the whole world; not the kingdom of godless rulers, a kingdom of hatred, disharmony and slavery," an implicit reference to Soviet rulers, in *UW*, July 3, 1964, 2

40. *UW*, July 3, 1964, 2.

41. *UW*, July 3, 1964, 2.

and Metropolitan John's prayer included several allusions to America's role as home and patron of the émigré community (this portion of the benediction addresses Shevchenko): "Erecting this monument to thee in this capital city of the United States of America, in the blessed land to which we came led by the will of God, we pledge not to forget thy world, we pledge to live by it." Metropolitan John's final exhortation expresses the émigré community's dual mission: ignite the spirit of national rebirth for the emancipation of Ukraine while remaining faithful citizens of the United States: "Let this monument stand firm, immovable! Let it bring out in us devotion to the destiny of our Great Country—the United States of America, and to the destiny of our native land and nation." Metropolitan John depicted Shevchenko himself as a proponent of liberty whose values are held by both Americans and Ukrainians. Shevchenko was not merely the national poet of Ukraine, but also the prophet and martyr, manifested by his courage in enduring the penalties inflicted upon him for advocating an independent Ukraine.[42]

The erection of Shevchenko's statue in Washington, DC, continued the proliferation of the political theology of Ukraine's martyrdom suffered in search of ecclesial and national independence, with America as an ally and patron of the present that provided the remnant community with the public platform to seek the emancipation of their brethren muted by Soviet tyranny. The Cold War itself contributed to the erection of the statue, as American politicians viewed Shevchenko's statue as a prophetic symbol of liberty, a glimpse of the future of all countries under Soviet tyranny. Shevchenko's statue also made a more practical contribution to the émigré community, as it provided Ukrainian Americans with a national shrine for seeking Ukraine's freedom and condemning the policies of the Soviet Union, a gathering place where they integrated the evolving polemics of the Cold War into more forceful demands for Ukrainian freedom, and a pattern of public theological demonstration that reached its pinnacle with the celebration of the millennium of the baptism of Kyivan Rus'.

Conclusion

In conclusion, I assess the Ukrainian émigré community's political theology, followed by a proposal for how the contemporary historian and theologian might receive it.

42. "Bravely he bore the penalties for his daring word which Thou, Eternal, gavest him." *UW*, July 3, 1964, 2.

1. The political theology of the Ukrainian émigré community in the United States consists of the following themes: the Ukrainian people are martyrs and confessors who have been enslaved by the godless Soviet tyrants in Moscow; the heroes of the Ukrainian martyrs are their prophet and martyr Taras Shevchenko and the bishops (Vasyl Lypkivsky and Andrei Sheptytsky in particular) who cultivated their freedom and proliferation; the mission of the émigré community is to instruct the global community on the evil deeds of the Soviet Union and inspire American political leaders to act with courage in liberating captive nations from the Communist tyrants; America has a God-given and sacred mission as the bastion of hope and freedom for captive nations. America's mission is to liberate Ukraine and all other nations suffering under Soviet tyranny.

2. America, and especially Washington, DC, becomes a sacred place and holy ground in the émigré community's mission. The political theology is expressed most fervently through events and construction, especially the Orthodox Memorial Church in Bound Brook and the Shevchenko monument in Washington. The locations become the primary stations of epic ritual events that communicate the political theology of the émigré community.

3. The purpose of the political theology is not oriented toward the past, but expects tangible deliverance in the present and future. The political theology developed by the community exhorts its faithful to take action, and the faithful consistently obey this exhortation and become quite active in the public square and in political and civic life.

4. The primary themes of the Cold War that coincide with and contribute to the émigré community's political theology are the Soviet Union's violation of human rights, especially religious freedom, and the problem of tyranny and the enslavement of people in the name of socialism. America is inscribed with Christian messianism by the émigré community in its status as the bastion of freedom for the global community.[43] Other themes of the Cold War, such as

---

43. The Ukrainian émigré community's political theology echoes earlier and contemporaneous religious aspirations for the victory of Western civilization over Eastern Communist tyranny. For examples of scholarship surveying this topic, see Dianne Kirby, "Truman's Holy Alliance: The President, the Pope and the Origins of the Cold War," *Borderlines: Studies in American Culture* 4, no. 1 (1997): 1–17; Axel Schäfer, "Religious Non-profit Organisations, the Cold War, the State and Resurgent Evangelicalism, 1945–1990," in *The US Government, Citizen Groups, and the Cold War: The State-Private Network*, ed. Helen Laville and High Wilford (London: Routledge, 2006), 175–93; and Zoe Knox, "The Watch Tower Society and the End of the Cold War: Interpretations of the End-Times, Superpower Conflict, and the Changing Geopolitical Order," *Journal of the American Academy of Religion* 79, no. 4 (2011): 1018–49.

nuclear armament, are secondary, but they do appear occasionally in émigré communications.

5. The conclusion for the historian and the theologian is twofold. First, the historian should compare the Ukrainian émigré community's political theology with other manifestations of liberation theology in émigré communities, especially Latin American, Vietnamese, and Korean. Second, the emergence of a new "cold war" in the current period suggests that the historical paths of Ukraine's ecclesial and national trajectories remain in question. The theologian is posed with a question outside the scope of this study: How does the political theology of an émigré community coincide with their pastoral mission in the United States? The ongoing reconfiguration of participation in church life in Ukraine, which has been significantly impacted by the Euromaidan, Russia's annexation of Crimea, and the war in eastern Ukraine, includes a contribution from the post-Soviet Ukrainian churches in the United States. Now that Ukraine is a sovereign state, can one anticipate an adoption of a redacted version of this political theology to address the current conflict between Ukraine and Russia? Given the continued development of theological and ecclesial narratives in Ukraine during its nascent post-Soviet period, I am convinced that the political theology developed by the Ukrainian émigré community in the United States during the Cold War will ultimately contribute to the historical path of the contemporary Ukrainian church and society.

The Russian Church Abroad, the Moscow Patriarchate, and Their Participation in Ecumenical Assemblies during the Cold War, 1948–1964

Andrei V. Psarev and Nadieszda Kizenko

The Cold War reached into unexpected spheres. Among its consequences were the attitudes of the Russian Orthodox Church Outside of Russia (ROCOR) and the Russian Orthodox Church (ROC) toward participation in such ecumenical and inter-Christian gatherings as the World Council of Churches.

This is not to say that the Cold War was the only factor in shaping the responses of both churches to ecumenical activity. Political events, personal relations among clerics, theological attitudes expressed at the assemblies—all played a part. By and large, both the ROCOR and the ROC sought to witness to "traditional" Orthodoxy. Still, the larger political struggle between Communism and its opponents created a climate that influenced the attitudes of Russian Orthodox hierarchs and clerics in both churches. Given the close relationship of the Moscow Patriarchate (MP) with the Soviet state, the ROC was often directly affected by Soviet religious policies. Despite some initial misgivings, for example, the ROC ultimately used international ecumenical assemblies as a means of advancing an agenda set in part by the Soviet state. By contrast, although the ROCOR maintained an anti-Communist stance, its attitudes to the ecumenical movement were not tied to concrete American policies. Some key moments in the relationship of both the ROCOR and the ROC with the ecumenical movement show how much they were—and were not—shaped by the Cold War context. Examining those moments provides a useful way to consider the impact of the Cold War on representatives of Russian Orthodox churches operating in Soviet and in American political structures.

ROCOR in the Interwar Period

The ROCOR's anti-Communist pedigree was clear even before the Cold War began. The Russian Church Abroad[1] was founded in November 1920 in Istanbul by bishops evacuating the Crimea with General Wrangel's White Russian Army. Opposition to Communism consistently characterized the ROCOR's political position wherever its headquarters were located, whether in Serbia from 1921 to 1944, in Munich from 1946 to 1950, or in New York from 1950 onward.[2]

The ROCOR's attitudes to inter-Christian activity were less clear-cut. In the interwar period, the ROCOR kept inter-Christian activity to a minimum.[3] Still, the ROCOR did take part in two 1937 inter-Christian conferences: one on Life and Work in Oxford, and the other on Faith and Order in Edinburgh. At both conferences, Bishop Serafim (Lade) of Potsdam represented the ROCOR Synod of Bishops.[4] His participation helped to crystallize ROCOR attitudes.[5] Should the ROCOR maintain that the Orthodox Church was the

1. Although the names the Russian Orthodox Church Outside of Russia (ROCOR) and the Russian Church Abroad (RCA) are used interchangeably, the first one is an official name.

2. For a concise English-language summary of the ROCOR, see Dimitry Pospielovsky, *The Orthodox Church in the History of Russia* (Crestwood, NY: St. Vladimir's Seminary Press, 1998), 219–27, 294–99. For the attitudes of the ROCOR to Communism, see Priest Georgii Mitrofanov, *Pravoslavnaia tserkov' v Rossii i emigratsii v 1920e gody* (Saint Petersburg: Noah, 1995), and the letters of the ROCOR's primate, Metropolitan Antonii Khrapovitskii, *Zhizneopisaniie: pis'ma k raznym litsam 1919–1939 godov* (Saint Petersburg: izd. Olega Obyshko, 2006). For the attitudes of the ROCOR to the church in Russia, see Andrei Psarev, "Looking toward Unity: How the Russian Church Abroad Viewed the Patriarchate of Moscow, 1927–2007," *Greek Orthodox Theological Review* 52, nos. 1–4 (2007): 121–43; Andrei Kostriukov, *Russkaia Zarubezhnaia Tserkov' v 1928–1938 gg. Iurisdiktsionnye konflikty i otnosheniia s moskovskoi tserkovnoi vlast'iu* (Moscow: PSTGU, 2011); and *Russkaia Zarubezhnaia Tserkov' v 1939–1964 gg. Administrativnoe ustroistvo i otnosheniia s Tserkov'iu v Otechestve* (Moscow: PSTGU, 2015).

3. By contrast, Metropolitan Evlogii represented the Russian church at the preparatory conference of the movement of Life and Work in Geneva in August 1920. In 1927, Evlogii, Father Sergei Bulgakov, and Professor Nikolai Glubokovskii participated in the conference of the movement of Faith and Order in Lausanne. For Metropolitan Evlogii's account of this, see his *Put' Moei Zhizni: vospominaniia metropolita Evlogiia (Georgievskogo)* (Moscow: Moskovskii rabochii, 1994).

4. For Oxford, see Graeme Smith, *Oxford 1937: The Universal Christian Council for Life and Work Conference* (New York: Peter Lang, 2004). For Edinburgh, see *The Edinburgh Conference on Faith and Order: Report of the Committee Appointed by the Archbishops of Canterbury and York* (London: Press and Publications Board of the Church Assembly, 1939).

5. The evolution of the views of the most noticeable representative of the "defensive" approach at the council of 1938 is worth noting. At the first Pan-Diaspora Council in Sremski

sole repository of truth, and therefore any discussions with non-Orthodox were pointless—or could inter-Christian dialogues be an opportunity for Orthodox Christian witness?

An official resolution on the attitude toward the ecumenical movement adopted by the ROCOR bishops' council of 1938 became a product of the compromise between these two visions. The first paragraph of the resolution followed the "defensive" position by stating that only the Orthodox Church was a genuine *una Sancta*.[6] The second paragraph, however, took care to distinguish between the leaders of the ecumenical movement who are "close to anti-Christian Masonic organizations and even expressed sympathy for Bolshevism,"[7] and other people in the ecumenical movement who were "full of desire, searching for the truth, loving Orthodoxy and striving toward it."[8] Therefore, witnessing to those Christians in the ecumenical movement searching for "true Orthodoxy" might be a valid reason to participate.

Before the Cold War, the more open second paragraph formed the dominant ROCOR attitude. ROCOR bishops' desire to participate reflected another concern as well. They feared that other, non-ROCOR, Orthodox representatives at the ecumenical meetings might give a distorted presentation of the Orthodox faith. Therefore, in the third paragraph of their 1938 resolution, bishops required ROCOR representatives at such meetings to "uncompromisingly [explain] the doctrine of the Orthodox church and its views on all matters arising with connection with the ecumenical movement," and "not to

---

Karlovci in 1921, the report of the Missionary Department headed by Bishop Serafim (Sobolev) of Lubny explained the mission of the Orthodox abroad: "To manifest before people of other faith in the diaspora the unfading light of Orthodoxy and the purity and magnificent beauty of her truth" (*Deiania russkago zagranichnago tserkovnago sobora sostoiavshagosia 8/21–XI–20/3 XII 1921 goda* [Sremski Karlovci, 1922], 76). At the next Pan-Diaspora Council (1938), the same hierarch, Archbishop Serafim, pointed out the example of one Catholic who had become an Orthodox, who for many years searched in his church for Saint Serafim of Sarov. This Catholic decided to join the church where Saint Serafim is found. According to Archbishop Serafim, Christian unification could only take place on the basis of pious life, and therefore the goal of the ecumenical movement was not attainable (*Deianiia Vtorogo Vsezarubezhnago Sobora RPTsZ* [Belgrade, 1939], 369).

6. For a contemporary assessment of this attitude, see the working paper of Paul Gavrilyuk, "The Future Pan-Orthodox Council on Relations with the Non-Orthodox Other: A Measured Defense of Christian Unity against Those Who Consider Ecumenism a Heresy," https://www.academia.edu/21077244/The_Future_Pan-Orthodox_Council_on_Relations_with_the_Non-Orthodox_Other_A_Measured_Defense_of_Christian_Unity_against_those_who_Consider_Ecumenism_a_Heresy_a_working_paper_.

7. The resolution of August 28, 1938. *Deianiia Vtorogo*, 373–74.

8. *Deianiia Vtorogo*, 373–74.

participate in common prayers with the participants, nor in vocal and sub-mitted resolutions restricting missionary and informational activities."[9] The ROCOR hierarchy's still-open attitude appears in a key phrase in the files of the bishops' council, which nevertheless they did not put in the printed text: "to charge Bishop Serafim [Lade] of Potsdam to participate in this [ecumen-ical] movement *for missionary purposes.*"[10] On the eve of the Second World War, then, ROCOR did admit the possibility of inter-Christian dialogue for the purposes of missionary activity.

The Cold War Begins and Ecumenical Activity Resumes:
The First Assembly of the World Council of Churches, Amsterdam 1948

Wartime years of isolation in Serbia under the Nazis, and the ROCOR bishops' position as displaced persons, largely removed the ecumenical question from the ROCOR agenda.[11] After the war, ecumenical activity tentatively resumed.

9. *Deianiia Vtorogo*, 373–74. It is important how the stance of the second Pan-Diaspora Council on ecumenism was received ten years later at the conference of the heads of the au-tocephalous Orthodox churches, held in July 1948 in Moscow. The response is found in the report by Archpriest Grigorii Razumovskii: "The Russian Orthodox Church thanks God for the understanding which He has bestowed on our Russian brothers abroad, who realized the divergence between true acts of the Church and the acts and intentions of the Oxford Confer-ence of 1937, and who restrained themselves from entering the ecumenical movement at the Karlovci [*sic*] Council of 1938" (*Major Portions of the Proceedings of the Conference of Heads and Representatives of Autocephalous Orthodox Churches in Connection with the Celebration of 500 Years of Autocephalicity of the Russian Orthodox Church: July 8–18, 1948*, trans. Mrs. O. F. Clarke, ed. Paul B. Anderson [Paris, 1952], 178). Contrarily, Grabbe gave the highest assessment to the Razumovskii report and to the general evaluation of the ecumenical movement by the 1948 conference (Grabbe to Fr. Dimitrii Dudko, 1992, Stanford University Library, Department of Special Collections, M0964, Box 2, Folder 2).

10. The State Archive of the Russian Federation (GARF), f. 6343, op. 1, d. 18.

11. Bishop Seraphim, in his report to the second Pan-Diaspora Council on the Oxford conference, mentioned that, prior to his departure to London, he was warned by "people knowl-edgeable in the spheres of the international policy and informed by the tempers of certain circles [masons] that it is doubtful that the Oxford conference will decide to make an open Anti-Bolshevik appearance" (*Deianiia Vtorogo*, 313). In 1943 Archpriest V. Zen'kovskii and L. Zander were interrogated at the *Propaganda-Abteilung* regarding the ecumenical activity (F. G. Spaskii, "Kratkaia letopis' Akademii," *Pravoslavnaia mysl': trudy Pravoslavnago Bogoslovskago Instituta v Parizhe* 5 [1947]: 149). Lodyzhenskii likely refers to Iurii Il'ich Lodyzhenskii (1888–1977), active in anti-Communist activity both in the interwar and postwar periods. His papers are in the Museum of Russian Culture in San Francisco and are microfilmed in the Hoover Institution. http://www.oac.cdlib.org/findaid/ark:/13030/kt700026jm/entire_text/.

The minutes of the synodal missionary committee record a request to ask Bishop Nafanail (L'vov) and one Dr. Lodyzhenskii to inform the committee on the work of an ecumenical conference that was to take place in Oslo in June of 1947.[12] The 1948 rescheduling in Amsterdam of the prewar planned unification of the Faith and Order and Life and Work movements into the World Council of Churches, however, revealed a new factor in the attitudes of other Christian bodies to the ROCOR. Changes in religious politics in the USSR called into question ROCOR's participation.

This quickly became clear. On September 4, 1948, the synod of bishops informed Mikhail Zyzykin that he could not be assigned to participate in Amsterdam as a representative of the ROCOR not only because "we do not participate in the ecumenical council" (which was the familiar "defensive" position) but also for the simple reason that the synod had not received an invitation from Amsterdam.[13] An anonymous article published a few months before the Amsterdam Assembly declared that representatives of the ROCOR were not invited to Amsterdam by the general secretariat of the assembly because of the fear of compromising future relations between the ecumenical movement and the "Soviet Church."[14] The assertion was not unfounded. The general secretariat of the WCC did indeed have to deal with a delicate question. Metropolitan Nikolai of Krutitsy, who *had* received an invitation from the WCC general secretariat, responded on August 1, 1948. His letter expressed both gratitude for the invitation and a refusal to participate in the ecumenical movement. For our purposes, the interesting thing is something else he wrote. As a representative of the Moscow Patriarchate, he sought to have the authority of his church accepted as the sole legitimate "Russian" church; thus he hoped that the WCC would not consider those Russians under the Ecumenical Patriarchate, the "schismatics" from the groups of Metropolitan Feofil in America,[15] and the ROCOR metropolitan Anastasii in Munich as the representatives of the Russian Orthodox Church. Indeed, he called them groups which "have nothing in common with the Russian Orthodox Church."[16]

12. Archive of the Synod of the Bishops in New York, File 80/46.

13. That is, the WCC (Archive of the Synod, File 5/48).

14. "Sredi inoslavnykh: Ekumenicheskoe dvizhenie," *Pravoslavnaia Rus'* 12 (June 11/24, 1948): 15.

15. A successor to Metropolitan Platon (Rozhdestvenskii, d. 1934), who, along with Metropolitan Evlogii, separated from the bishops in Serbia in 1926.

16. "The Moscow Patriarchate and the First Assembly of the World Council of Churches," *Ecumenical Review* 12 (Winter 1949): 188–89.

Metropolitan Nikolai's statement reflected the abrupt shift in Soviet policy with regard to the Orthodox Church. In exchange for physical survival and some room for activity at home, the ROC was expected to serve Soviet interests abroad through its international contacts. And Soviet interests after the Second World War had significantly expanded. Because of the geopolitical situation of the Cold War, the USSR could now influence, directly or indirectly, areas home to the Polish, Albanian, Czech, Romanian, Bulgarian, and Serbian Orthodox churches. It attempted to establish a unified Orthodox church in Hungary. Indeed, as Daniela Kalkandjieva has demonstrated, Stalin envisioned turning the Moscow Patriarchate into a kind of Soviet Vatican for the Orthodox.[17] But the interests of the Soviet government went beyond its newly Communist East European bloc. It also sought to foster support and sympathy in Western Europe as well as in the United States for its aims. In the pursuit of these aims, the anti-Communist stance of the Vatican was clearly an obstacle. All these represented challenges and opportunities. To implement policies directed by the Council for Religious Affairs and the Council for ROC Affairs, the ROC's Department of External Church Affairs was formed in 1949.[18]

The means that the ROCOR had at its disposal, and its aims, were more modest than they had been before the war. Its representatives had not been invited to Amsterdam. Some clerics and hierarchs continued to resist ecumenical participation in principle. After the assembly in Amsterdam, Archpriest Igor Troianov from Switzerland sent a letter[19] to Archpriest Georgii Grabbe, the secretary of the synod, expressing his hope that the ROCOR would not compromise with the Protestant tendencies of the WCC; it was important for those Protestants who were close to Orthodoxy, he thought, that the ROCOR not settle with the more liberal ones. Thus the ROCOR was driven by an urge to maintain ties to conservative Protestants disposed to Orthodoxy, not to further a Cold War agenda. This letter was heard at the meeting of the synod of bishops on April 13, 1949, in the presence of Metropolitan Anastasii, Metropolitan Serafim (Lade), Archbishop Venedikt (Bobkovskii), and Bishop Evlogii (Markovskii). That group resolved to explain to Troianov that, in ac-

---

17. See "The Growth of Moscow's Jurisdiction (1945–1946)," "The Moscow Patriarchate and the Autocephalous Churches outside the Soviet Union (1944–1947)," and "Toward an Eighth Ecumenical Council (1944–1948)," in Daniela Kalkandjieva, *The Russian Orthodox Church, 1917–1948: From Decline to Resurrection* (New York: Routledge, 2015), 207–39, 264–344.

18. Anastacia Wooden, "'The Agent of Jesus Christ': Participation of Fr. Vitali Borovoy in the Second Vatican Council as an Observer from the ROC," *Occasional Papers on Religion in Eastern Europe* 36, no. 4 (July 2016): 1–27.

19. Archive of the Synod, File 1/49.

cordance with previous resolutions of the bishops' council and the synod, the ROCOR was not participating in the ecumenical movement. The bishops' council considered it possible to be present at the various conferences only for the exposition of Orthodox teaching.[20]

The First Postwar Statement on Ecumenism

On November 29, 1950, the council of bishops in Mahopac, New York, heard Troianov's written report regarding the possibility of the ROCOR's participation in the ecumenical movement.[21] While critically mentioning the ecumenical statements of Fathers Bulgakov and Zen'kovskii, Troianov positively commented on the ecumenical participation of the representatives of Eastern Orthodoxy, who with few exceptions defended the Orthodox viewpoint. The author referred to Father Georges Florovsky, who claimed that the Orthodox must participate in the ecumenical movement in order to witness to the truth in face of the world.[22] But Troianov believed otherwise. Although the Toronto declaration of the WCC (1950) in its third section stated that "The World Council of Churches is not and must never become a Super-Church," in reality the ecumenical movement was a federated church with a Protestant worldview. All this led Troianov to suggest that the ROCOR bishops not participate in the ecumenical movement in its present form. After this report was discussed, a commission was established to compose the resolution regarding the ecumenical movement. This resolution, composed by Archbishop Ioann (Maksimovich) of Western Europe, Bishop Nafanail (L'vov), and Bishop Nikon (Rklitskii), was accepted by the council of bishops on the same day. Its text is more categorical than the resolution of the Second Pan-Diaspora Council of 1938:

1. Orthodox Christians must recognize the Holy Orthodox Church as the one and only Church of Christ;
2. Because of that, it is impossible to participate in any non-Orthodox religious movements, societies, or organizations;

20. Archive of the Synod. No reference is available.

21. Troianov was one of the ROCOR's experts on the ecumenical movement. As late as 1959, his report on the different currents within the WCC was read at a synod meeting, on November 25 of that year (Archive of the Synod. No reference is available).

22. Perhaps Florovsky was singled out also because, during the war years, he was a clergyman of the ROCOR in Serbia.

3. Cooperation with the heterodox is possible only in the spheres of social work and charity with the preservation of full independence in the efforts of faith and confession;
4. Orthodox Christians, following Christ's teaching, must show love and goodwill toward all, without differentiation of their faith and nationality, trying to help in their needs and to be thankful to those who beneficiated them.[23]

Note that, compared to the resolution of 1938, the bishops' council document does not even mention the possibility for ROCOR's representatives to participate in ecumenical discussions. Still, this appears to be a function of theology, not Cold War politics.

The Death of Stalin and Its Impact

Stalin's death in 1953 and the ascent of Nikita Khrushchev as the new chairman of the Communist Party of the Soviet Union (CPSU) brought changes both to Soviet general religious politics and to the attitude toward the Vatican. Despite a new wave of antireligious policies in the USSR, the state's expectations for the ROC to continue its international activity for the benefit of Soviet foreign interests remained unchanged.[24] Stalin's death appears to have had no effect on the now US-based ROCOR. Archpriest Georgii Grabbe submitted a memorandum containing guidelines for relations with the heterodox based on the precedents of different ROCOR dioceses to the bishops' council of 1953.[25] The authoritative status of this document as instruction for clergy was established by the council on October 26, 1953; this was confirmed by the synod on September 26, 1974. This document returned to the position of the 1938 bishops' council regarding witness for the Orthodox faith among the non-Orthodox. On the one hand, one must follow church rules, and on the other, one must be kind to benevolent non-

23. "Opredeleniia," *Tserkovnaia zhizn'* 1 (July 1951): 2. Metropolitan Anastasii expressed the same reasons for not participating in the National Council of Churches in his letter, written not long after the council, to Father Aleksei Godniaev in Wellington, New Zealand (Archive of the Synod, File 8/36).

24. Tatiana Chumachenko, "Church-State Relations between 1948 and 1957," in Chumachenko, *Church and State in Soviet Russia: Russian Orthodoxy from World War II to the Khrushchev Years*, ed. and trans. Edward E. Roslof (New York: Routledge, 2002), 87–142.

25. Archive of the Synod, File 5/48. Also found in Bishop Grigorii (Grabbe), *Tserkov' i iia uchenie v zhizni* 3 (Jordanville, 1992), 159–60.

Orthodox people. Priests and parishes were under no circumstances allowed to enter local councils of churches. Only priests having a sufficient theological background and the blessing of their bishops were allowed to participate in Protestant conferences, in order to explain dogmatic or practical questions.

The Assembly of the WCC in Evanston, Illinois, 1954

In accordance with the 1950 resolution on ecumenism, Metropolitan Anastasii refused to participate in the pre-Evanston conference of the International League of Apostolic Faith and Order, which was scheduled for July 1954 in Racine, Wisconsin. In his letter of May 27, 1954, to the Reverend Michael Bruce, organizing secretary of the conference, Anastasii wrote:

> Our Church does not participate in the Oecumenical movement, it is not a member of the Council of Churches and will not be represented at Evanston. Moreover, we are not informed sufficiently about the preparations for the Evanston conference and its points of issue. . . . But we do not think that any agreement between different Churches can be achieved in matters of Faith, and for this reason we have never applied for membership in the Oecumenical movement. Therefore I am afraid we would not be helpful in a meeting which is aimed to be preparatory to the Evanston Conference, although its members consist of most distinguished persons who, as far as I understand, are some of the nearest to our Church in regard to their Catholically minded conceptions.[26]

Nevertheless, from Archpriest Georgii Grabbe's letter to Metropolitan Anastasii of July 14, 1954, it appears that Anastasii wanted him to go to the Evanston conference in the capacity of observer. Grabbe received an invitation from Paul F. Anderson, who said that his presence as an observer would be desirable.[27] In his reply of July 20, 1954, Grabbe wrote that, although one should avoid participation in the ecumenical movement, "since we are invited as observers, I think it is possible to accept a personal invitation in accordance with our original practice."[28]

26. Archive of the Synod, File 15/51.
27. Bishop Grigorii Grabbe, *Pis'ma* (Moscow, 1998), 10–11. (Grabbe took the name Grigorii when he became a bishop.)
28. Archive of the Synod, File 15/51.

There may have been other factors in Metropolitan Anastasii's decision. The WCC had provided help to the Russian refugees in Europe and Asia.[29] Indirectly, the Cold War played a role as well. A ROCOR press release issued prior to Evanston stated: "We very much appreciate the manifestations of Christian love on the part of the World Council of Churches in regard to refugees who had to leave their countries behind the 'Iron Curtain' in order not only to save their lives but also to maintain the liberty of their conscience." The press release (August 13, 1954) of the synod of bishops contained a statement by Grabbe, who was on his way to Evanston as an observer to be informed of the activities of the WCC.[30] Stating its belief in the Orthodox Church as the only true church, the document explained why the ROCOR could not join the WCC:

> There are Orthodox Churches who find it possible to participate, with some reserve, in the World Council of Churches in order to witness the Orthodox Faith in the fold of the ecumenical movement.
>
> We however assume a different position in this respect. Since we believe the Orthodox Church to be the true Church, we consider it more consistent to withhold from being members of an organization which is founded with the aim to find what is believed as the Truth by various Christian Communities and achieve the formation of a body uniting them all. Such Truth would necessarily be found on some dogmatic minimum acceptable to all the members and such a body if ever achieved would be a new Church but not the one we believe in.[31]

In private conversation at Evanston, Grabbe was able to clarify why the ROCOR did not participate in the WCC, and his clarifications were met without any vexation. In a letter written to Anastasii from Evanston on August 21, 1954, Grabbe singled out the report of Father Georges Florovsky at the assembly as more or less satisfactory.[32] Moreover, Dr. W. F. Golterman associated Florovsky's ideas at Evanston with the position of the Second Pan-Diaspora Council:

> During a congress in Yugoslavia in 1938 of Russian Orthodox migrants, it was stated that participation in the Öecumenische movement was only tak-

29. Archive of the Synod, File 5/48.
30. Archive of the Synod, File 5/48.
31. Archive of the Synod, File 5/48.
32. Grabbe, *Pis'ma*, 12.

ing place to be able to explain the Creed of the Church and to give information. They refused to make any compromise with respect to the Creed, and will therefore not vote about points of Creed and church order. According to this principle, Mr. Florovsky said in Evanston during the discussions in Section I, that the division of the Church has to be considered as a partition of the Church. It is not for the Orthodoxy to recognize other churches as living parts of the Universal Church, because they lack completeness. Hierarchy, dogma, completeness; and to be truly church, one cannot miss one of those just mentioned. . . . The Orthodox Church is the only Church of Christ, therefore responsible to be the witness for truth in the world.[33]

In an article written not long after the assembly, Grabbe agreed with the position of the Orthodox participants regarding section 1 of Faith and Order.[34] Archbishop Michael of the Greek archdiocese clearly stated that the whole approach of the section toward the problem of reunification was completely unacceptable from the point of view of the Orthodox Church. Florovsky was also right, Grabbe notes, when he said that in ecumenical conversations and brotherly exchanges of opinion, a point had been reached beyond which it was more and more difficult to speak with a common voice, to make agreed statements or unify in common action.

Grabbe's assessment of the Evanston Assembly led to a stricter attitude of the ROCOR toward the WCC. In his letter of November 11, 1955, to the Reverend Dr. G. Merill Lennox of the Michigan Council of Churches, Metropolitan Anastasii wrote:

The Russian Orthodox Church Outside of Russia does not belong to the World Council of Churches and is not affiliated to the National Councils. We have, however, had a very fruitful and friendly period of co-operation with the World Council of Churches and with Church World Service in practical matters of welfare and resettlement for the past several years. Yet we feel that membership in the Council of Churches would involve certain implications which do not fit in with our conception of the dogma of the nature of the Church. For this reason our Church as a whole, and also our

---

33. "Eastern Orthodoxy and Oikumene" (Dutch title not available), *Gemeenschap der Kerken*, April 1955, n.p. An outline of this article is provided to Archpriest Georgii Grabbe by Jan S. F. Van Hoogstraten in his letter from June 17, 1955, written in English (Archive of the Synod, File 5/48).

34. "Evanstonskaiia konferentsiia," *Tserkov' i eia uchenie v zhizni* 2 (1970): 243–45.

local communities, have never participated in the Ecumenical movement. At Evanston, we were therefore represented only by an observer.[35]

Again, ROCOR's reluctance to actively participate in the ecumenical movement stems less from Cold War politics than from theological attitudes. Moscow's trajectory was rather different. As early as 1959, there was some discussion about ROC representatives attending Vatican II.[36] On April 27, 1961, the Synod of the Moscow Patriarchate announced that it had applied for membership in the WCC. Thus continued the integration of churches from the Soviet bloc into the WCC begun in Evanston. In November 1961, a delegation of the Moscow Patriarchate came to New Delhi for the Third Assembly of the WCC. Now, however, the ROCOR began to be more explicit about opposing Moscow's claims to Russian universality, and in equating the Moscow Patriarchate with Soviet control. Father Grabbe took the floor at an ecumenical meeting in Seneca Falls, New York, in October 1961 and stated that "the Kremlin-controlled prelates are 'not authentic representatives of the Russian Orthodox people.'"[37]

Father Lazarus (Moore), the ROCOR's clergyman in India, was assigned as the official observer at the New Delhi Assembly.[38] On March 31, 1962, Archimandrite Lazarus reported his disagreement that the WCC assembly protested against the brutality of the Portuguese in Angola but did not protest against Khrushchev's persecution in the USSR. But his overall comments were favorable: "This meeting of persons of differing persuasions helps to fix our minds on what is positive, rather than what is negative. We all have much in common in Christ, we all share a Spirit not of this world, we have and seek a supernatural grace for a supernatural life of service to God and man. . . . We need to thank God far more for the work of 'non-Orthodox Christians.' But for their zealous and devoted labors the world would be in a desperate state indeed."[39] Lazarus's irenic attitude prompted Metropolitan Anastasii to send Archpriest Georgii Romanov to New Delhi, since Father Lazarus seemed more interested in "ecumenical ideology" than in finding out more on the "malicious activity of the pro-communists." Lazarus, nevertheless, was present at the assembly in

35. Archive of the Synod, File 5/48.

36. "Non Possumus!" *Zhurnal Moskovskoi Patriarkhii* 5 (1961): 73–75; Wooden, "The Agent of Jesus Christ," 10.

37. "Moscow, Partner in Quest for Unity," *Catholic Courier Journal: Official Newspaper of the Rochester Diocese*, October 27, 1961, 5.

38. Archive of the Synod. No reference is available.

39. Archive of the Synod. No reference is available.

the capacity of official observer and was thanked for his report by the synod of bishops at their meeting on June 13, 1962.[40]

The Reception of the Moscow Patriarchate in the WCC

The December 1962 responses of Archbishop Savva of Australia and New Zealand to a questionnaire from an unnamed source provide additional insights on the relations of the ROCOR toward the WCC.[41] Regarding the question how the reception of the Moscow Patriarchate into the WCC would influence the life of the Russian church in Australia, Savva answered that if the local representatives of the WCC, because of their official relations with the Moscow Patriarchate, would decide to help them get legal status for their parishes, then the free part of the Russian church in Australia would face troubles. For Savva, it was clear that, by receiving the Moscow Patriarchate, the WCC would experience the same influence that the UN was experiencing as a result of the membership of the USSR. It might place the WCC in a difficult situation, for instance, regarding the defense of the oppressed faithful in Communist countries. Nothing good would result from Moscow's communications with the WCC; the Soviet government would not allow it. By accepting the Moscow Patriarchate, the WCC had abandoned its freedom. This is a reasonably clear example of the Cold War context in ROCOR attitudes to ecumenical participation.

Grabbe, by contrast, focused on the implications of ecumenical participation itself.[42] He criticized the Greek theologian Nikolaos Nissiotis for declaring that the term "Orthodox" was "not exclusive, but an inclusive term which goes beyond the limits of the churches which call themselves Orthodox. It includes all those churches and believers who seek to offer an honest confession and achieve a life which is untouched by heresies and schisms and to arrive at the wholeness of the divine revelation in Christ."[43] This statement contradicted all official, previously mentioned statements of the Russian Orthodox Church Outside of Russia that emphasized uniqueness of the Orthodox Church versus other Christian ecclesiastical bodies. Grabbe's negative reaction toward Nissiotis's statements was supported by theologians who did

40. Archive of the Synod, File 5/48.
41. Archive of the Synod, File 5/48.
42. "Rodos i N'iu-Deli," *Tserkov' i eia uchenie v zhizni* 2 (Montreal, 1970): 260–74.
43. "The Witness and the Service of Eastern Orthodoxy to the One Undivided Church," WCC, press release, November 24, 1961.

not otherwise have much common: Fathers Georges Florovsky and Alexander Schmemann.[44] Moreover, Grabbe explicitly engaged the words of Patriarch Aleksii of Moscow, addressed to the Third Assembly, where he stated that the Russian church never identified witness with proselytism. Such "disarming" of the Orthodox in front of the heterodox was a serious danger for the church, Grabbe argued. The ecumenical movement was a contradiction to the teaching of the Orthodox Church, since "ecumenism does not seek unity in the true faith but replaces it with the fellowship of people of different opinions (*raznomysliashchikh*)."[45]

But the picture of the Orthodox participation in the ecumenical movement had more shades than are represented in the article by Grabbe on the assembly in New Delhi. In his report to the 1962 council of bishops, Metropolitan Anastasii noted that the presence of the ROCOR's observers at the pan-Orthodox meeting at Rhodes[46] and in New Delhi did not enhance the authority of the representatives of Moscow, but helped representatives of the other churches to understand that the ROCOR had serious reasons for its stance.[47] Father Aleksander Trubnikov mentioned that at a Paris meeting, Orthodox representatives, including those of the Moscow Patriarchate, objected to what was unacceptable in the report of Pastor Vergez. The report of the missionary department was met by a similar reaction from the Orthodox representative.[48] Thus it was perfectly possible for Moscow and New York, or rather for ROC and ROCOR, to express similarly anti-ecumenical positions.

44. "Nissiotis' address expresses his private opinion only and can in no way be regarded as the common Orthodox position" (Florovsky); "I am surprised that this address was allowed to be delivered, because it must have been obvious to everyone, even the heretics, that once in print, it would cause objections" (Schmemann). "Protopresbyter George Grabbe's Correspondence with Archpriests Georges Florovsky and Alexander Schmemann," ed. Maria Psarev, trans. Anna Platt, ROCOR Studies, November 2004, http://www.rocorstudies.org /documents/2015/12/12/protopresbyter-george-grabbe-correspondence-with-archpriests -georges-florovsky-and-alexander-schmemann/.

45. "Rodos i N'iu-Deli," 274.

46. The first Pan-Orthodox Conference was convened in 1961 to set up an agenda for the future Great and Holy Council of the Orthodox Church. The ROCOR was represented there by Archpriest Georgii Romanov.

47. Archive of the Synod. No reference is available.

48. "Zasedaniia ekumenicheskago soveta v Parizhe," *Svet Khristov prosveshchaet vsekh* 8 (August 1962): 6.

Cold War Divergences, 1962–1964

The differences between the ROCOR and the ROC emerged with particular clarity soon afterward. In 1962, a ROCOR epistle of the bishops' council addressed to the Russian diaspora engaged the Soviet use of Orthodoxy in the Cold War. The first argument was theological: ecumenism was the primary threat posed by modernity. "We cannot place our Church in the same position as different factions of Protestantism, reduce her to the level of a sect. Therefore our Church cannot be a member of the WCC, which you, our spiritual children, should clearly understand."[49] But then the epistle became more political. It noted that the ROCOR and the Serbian church did not join the WCC, while the churches of the Soviet bloc entered by order of their governments. Why, the epistle asked, did the Orthodox churches of the free world join as well? The WCC had negatively influenced some Orthodox leaders, who began to repeat after the Protestants that the church was apparently divided. Such people confused the faithful and involuntarily posed a question: Is it necessary to believe in the one and holy church, as one reads in the creed? The bishops warned of many protests, particularly in Greece, against confusing statements of the leading hierarchs. They called their flock firmly to confess the dogma of the one, holy, catholic, and apostolic church, and stated that this new heresy would not be introduced into the ROCOR.

By contrast, the ROC moved decisively not only to participate in the ecumenical movement but also to establish closer relations with the Vatican. At a pan-Orthodox council in Rhodes in 1961, the Moscow Patriarchate had taken a strong antiecumenical, anti-Vatican stance, promoting a resolution for the Orthodox churches to act in ecumenical affairs only in complete consensus. But the election of Pope John XXIII, and his speeches urging a peaceful settlement of the September 1961 Berlin crisis and the October 1962 Cuban missile crisis, appealed both to Russian hierarchs and to Khrushchev.[50] As a result, even as they pursued an antireligious campaign within the USSR, Soviet diplomats and security agencies began to reach out to the Vatican, and the ROC was expected to contribute accordingly. And it did. At a pan-Orthodox

49. Archive of the Synod. No reference is available.

50. See the discussion in *Vatican II in Moscow (1959–1965)*, ed. Alberto Melloni (Leuven: Peeters, 1997); Karim Schelkens, "Vatican Diplomacy after the Cuban Missile Crisis: New Light on the Release of Josyf Slipyj," *Catholic Historical Review* 97 (October 2011): 679–712; and Vitaly Borovoi, "The Second Vatican Council and Its Significance for the Russian Orthodox Church," in *The Holy Russian Church and Western Christianity*, ed. Giuseppe Alberigo and Oscar Beozzo, Concilium 1996/6 (Maryknoll, NY: Orbis, 1996), 130–42.

conference in September–October 1963, the ROC's delegation joined Constantinople in promoting a resolution "to initiate an equitable dialogue with the Roman Catholic Church."[51] This resolution bore fruit: although *individual* Orthodox clerics and hierarchs, including Father Alexander Schmemann and the ROCOR's bishop Antonii of Geneva, attended the first session of Vatican II, for example, the ROC was the only Orthodox *church* to formally send observers.[52] ROC participation in ecumenical affairs continued through the end of the Cold War.

Conclusion

Thus the ROCOR and the ROC moved along different paths when it came to ecumenical relations during the Cold War. As a church of anti-Bolshevik refugees, the Russian Orthodox Church Outside of Russia could not tolerate the prosocialist or pro-Communist tendencies they sensed at inter-Christian meetings. They were quick to note the influence of the Soviet state on ecumenical participation by the ROC. Nevertheless, particularly in the early years of the Cold War, demand for information about traditional Orthodoxy moved the leaders of the ROCOR to come to ecumenical gatherings in order to clarify Orthodox doctrine and praxis. The aid to Russian refugees provided through the WCC and the unsatisfactory witness for the true faith by other Orthodox at ecumenical meetings also contributed to ROCOR's willingness to send observers to some WCC assemblies and to Vatican II, even as other ROCOR spokesmen like Father Georgii Grabbe used Orthodox ecclesiology and anti-Communist views for ideological purposes. But ROCOR's anti-Communist position predated the Cold War, was not directly influenced by US foreign policy, and did not affect ROCOR's participation in ecumenical meetings. By contrast, the ecumenical activity of the ROC seems more directly influenced by Soviet aims regarding foreign policy.

51. Shkarovskii, quoted in Wooden, "The Agent of Jesus Christ," 9.

52. Adriano Roccucci, "Russian Observers at Vatican II. The 'Council for Russian Orthodox Church Affairs' and the Moscow Patriarchate between Anti-religious Policy and International Strategies," in Melloni, *Vatican II in Moscow (1959–1965)*, 45–72. See also Wooden, "The Agent of Jesus Christ," 14.

Fascists, Communists, Bishops, and Spies: Romanian Orthodox Churches during the Cold War

Lucian Turcescu

Romanians have been present in North America through immigration since the middle of the nineteenth century. A large wave of Romanian Orthodox migrants, however, began arriving in 1895. Many of the initial immigrants were peasants from Transylvania, a province that was part of the Austro-Hungarian Empire until 1918, and they hoped to purchase or receive land in either Canada or the United States, to earn some money, and to return back home, while avoiding attempts at Magyarization (Hungarianization) in their home country. Efforts to organize themselves and preserve their ethnic identity led to the formation of Romanian aid societies, cultural societies, and social societies as early as 1900. By 1904, the first Romanian Orthodox parish was established in Cleveland, Ohio.[1]

In 1929, the Holy Synod of the recently recognized Patriarchate of the Romanian Orthodox Church (RomOC) established a Romanian Orthodox Episcopate to serve Romanians in North America.[2] The episcopate eventually shared the fate of the Russian Orthodox Church Outside of Russia and other Orthodox churches (Bulgarian, Serbian, Albanian, and Ukrainian) in North America that broke relations with the Soviet-backed Communist regimes in their mother countries. That led to the creation of a parallel ecclesial structure, which was no longer under Bucharest's control, and another that remained

---

1. Gabriel-Viorel Gârdan, *Episcopia Ortodoxă Română din America—Parte a Ortodoxiei Americane* (Cluj: Presa universitară clujeană, 2007), 31.

2. The Romanian Orthodox Patriarchate was recognized officially by the other Orthodox sister churches in 1925.

I want to thank the Social Sciences and Humanities Research Council of Canada for a grant that made possible the research and writing of this chapter. Special thanks are also due to Lavinia Stan, Monica Bastea, Adrian Cioflâncă, and Cristian Vasile, who helped me improve the quality of the chapter. Any remaining mistakes are my own.

faithful to the synod in Bucharest. The two ecclesial structures continue their separate lives to this day and are known as (1) the Romanian Orthodox Episcopate of America (ROEA), a diocese of the Orthodox Church in America (OCA), with headquarters in Jackson, Michigan; and (2) the Romanian Orthodox Metropolia of the Americas (ROMA), an autonomous diocese of the Romanian Orthodox Church, with headquarters in Chicago.

The schism among the Romanian Orthodox resembles the break of relations between the Russian Orthodox Church Outside of Russia (headquartered in North America) and the Moscow Patriarchate that occurred in 1924. Both events resulted from the poisoning of relations by the Communists, who saw themselves losing control over their diaspora populations (or "colonies," as the Romanian Communists referred to their diaspora). This split was followed by a long period of estrangement between the mother church and the diaspora church until they managed to reestablish relations following the dissolution of the Soviet Union in 1991.

In this chapter, I will follow the Cold War in the North American Romanian Orthodox community by looking at the actions of the leaders of the communities in North America and Romania—bishops and priests, some of them spies, as well as laypeople and politicians sent by the Romanian Communist secret police, the Securitate, to try to bring the estranged church back into the fold. The battle between the two communities was fought mainly through their priests and bishops, various messengers sent by Bucharest, exchanges of letters, court trials, diocesan and parish bulletins, and with the help of the Romanian secret police. Academic literature on the subject has appeared mostly in Romanian, with very few books published in English. Much of the existing Romanian literature does not consider documents from the Securitate archives. This chapter is the first to draw on those archival sources. It also includes details from an interview conducted with a participant in the events for a more comprehensive view of the topic.[3]

---

3. Gârdan, *Episcopia Ortodoxă Română din America—Parte a Ortodoxiei Americane*; Remus Grama, *Bishop Policarp Moruşcă—First Bishop of Romanians in America: An Exile in His Own Country* (Jackson, MI: Romanian Orthodox Episcopate of America Department of Publications, 2005). Two books by Gerald J. Bobango are as follows: *The Romanian Orthodox Episcopate of America: The First Half Century, 1929–1979* (Jackson, MI: Romanian Orthodox Episcopate of America Department of Publications, 1979) and *Religion and Politics: Bishop Valerian Trifa and His Times* (Boulder, CO: East European Monographs, 1981). Bobango did impressive archival work in the ROEA archives before becoming a lawyer, and was very knowledgeable of many details of Romanian history. He understood quite well the dirty game the RomOC played against Trifa with the help of the Securitate. Yet his interpretations of the

Fascists, Communists, Bishops, and Spies

Although the synod in Bucharest decided to establish a Romanian Orthodox episcopate in the United States in 1929, Policarp Moruşcă, its first bishop, was sent to his post only in 1935. His actual time in office was only four years.[4] Once in the United States, the new bishop found that the cathedral of the episcopate had been established in Detroit at Bucharest's request, although the oldest Romanian community and church was located in Cleveland, and hoped that the bishop's seat would be in Cleveland. Cleveland thus became the bishop's official residence and office, while his cathedral was in Detroit. Shortly thereafter, upon visiting his parishes in both the United States and Canada, Policarp attempted to regulate the priests' behavior by asking them to be more present in churches on a daily basis, not just during the weekends, and to raise the level of their theological education by taking specific tests and courses. Many priests and Romanian associations resented this order and the discipline imposed on them, and perceived his style as authoritarian.[5] Policarp himself felt somewhat demoralized by the lack of funds supposed to arrive from Romania, and by the divisiveness he encountered among Romanians, with some in western Canada embracing the old Julian calendar and listening to Russian bishops, and others embracing the new Gregorian calendar adopted by Romania in 1924. To this, one should add his difficulties in raising funds from the parishes for the episcopate's projects, including the purchase of a residence that came to be known as *Vatra Românească* (the Romanian Hearth), or simply "*Vatra*," in Jackson, Michigan, and the publication of the diocesan bulletin *Solia* (Herald).

In 1939, Policarp went to Romania to ask for more help for his American diocese, and to participate in the session of the Holy Synod of the Romanian Orthodox Church. Due to intrigues at the court of King Carol II, caused in part by denunciations by some Romanian Americans who disliked Policarp, and the outbreak of World War II, which interrupted communications between the United States and Romania, a Germany ally, he was prevented from ever returning to his post. Patriarch Nicodim Munteanu (1939–1948) did not support his return and attempted unsuccessfully to appoint someone else in his place.[6] The effective tenure of the Romanian Orthodox Episcopate's first bishop, Policarp Moruşcă, lasted only from 1935 to 1939.

---

fascist Legionary Movement and Trifa's involvement in it are very problematic, having been influenced by Trifa's attempts to distort the truth about himself in order to hide his fascist past.

4. Gârdan, *Episcopia Ortodoxă Română din America*, 244.

5. Bobango, *The Romanian Orthodox Episcopate of America*, 94–96.

6. Gârdan, *Episcopia Ortodoxă Română din America*, 278–79.

Romanian priests in the United States continued to be divided after Policarp's departure, due to personal bickering among them or differing ideological preferences about the Romanian politics happening back home or in the diaspora, with some priests advocating the return of King Carol II to the throne and others supporting the Nazi-allied Antonescu regime (1940–1944). After his forced abdication in September 1940, Carol II went into exile in Mexico during World War II. From Mexico he made generous financial "donations" to groups lobbying for his return to the throne of Romania. A group of supportive priests and laypeople in the United States requested Policarp's return to his see. Others, who disliked him and were willing to collaborate after 1945 with the newly established Communist regime in Romania, decided to take action. That action caused the "great schism" of the Romanian Orthodox diaspora in the Americas. The intrigues, political maneuvering, and egos of some of the participants in this tragedy are too complex to describe here, but they are captured excellently in other volumes.[7] No matter which way one tries to understand what happened, no party can be said to be guilt-free in having caused the schism. Everybody's head became too heated by the explosive political developments taking place in Romania during and after WWII and was unable to judge the situation rationally from a safe distance and avoid the schism. The Soviet Red Army entered Romania as soon as King Michael switched sides in the war following the arrest of Marshall Antonescu on August 23, 1944, and a Communist-controlled government was established in 1945. By 1945, the situation in Romania worsened considerably, following the country's shaky interwar liberal democracy and its Fascist alliance during the war. But nothing prepared its people for the terror that came with Soviet occupation. A full Communist government that eliminated all the other parties was put in place in 1947. The following year, the newly appointed, socialist-oriented patriarch Justinian Marina (1948–1977)[8] immediately agreed to Policarp's official removal from his position as bishop.

Meanwhile, in reaction to the political developments in Romania, the episcopate's extraordinary congress, held in Detroit, decided on March 28, 1947, to proclaim its full jurisdictional autonomy from the RomOC, while

7. Gârdan, *Episcopia Ortodoxă Română din America*, 281–364; Bobango, *The Romanian Orthodox Episcopate of America*, 125–229; Grama, *Bishop Policarp Moruşcă*, 73–144.

8. For a recent analysis of the complex figure of the former patriarch Justinian Marina and his relations with the Communist regime in Romania, see L. Turcescu and L. Stan, "Church Collaboration and Resistance under Communism Revisited: The Case of Patriarch Justinian Marina (1948–1977)," *Eurostudia* 10, no. 1 (2015): 75–103, http://www.erudit.org/revue /euro/2015/v10/n1/index.html.

continuing to maintain canonical and spiritual links with the mother church in Romania. In July 1950, the congress of the episcopate decided to continue to support Policarp's return to his see. However, unbeknownst to most priests, in May 1950 a group of priests led by Glicherie Moraru from Detroit, with the assistance of the Romanian legation in the United States, established secret contacts with the patriarchate in Bucharest and elected widowed priest Andrei Moldovan as the new bishop. Born in 1885 in Transylvania, Moldovan was sent as a missionary priest to the United States in 1922; in 1933 he was elected secretary of the episcopal council and also became a widower.

Patriarch Justinian agreed to ordain Moldovan as bishop in Romania and then to send him back to lead the episcopate overseas. Anticipating this move, Moraru registered in 1950, in the state of Michigan, the Autonomous Romanian Orthodox Episcopate of North and South America, with its see in Detroit, to provide a diocese for Bishop Moldovan. The founding document was signed by only three priests and six laymen; this meager number showed lack of support within the Romanian diaspora for the Bucharest-controlled diocese and its leader.[9] The vast majority of priests and parishes remained supportive of Father Ioan Truța, the official head of the original episcopal congress. On July 17, 1950, to his utter surprise, Father Truța received a telegram from Patriarch Justinian that confirmed Moldovan's appointment as bishop (replacing Policarp). Moldovan pretended he, too, was surprised by the news. His ordination took place in Romania in October 1950. His American parishioners were told that he went to a spa resort in Hot Springs, Arkansas, for health reasons, and they even received postcards from that resort that were signed by Moldovan but were sent by someone else on his behalf. The postcards confirmed the "ongoing improvement" in the priest's health. However, all that time Moldovan was in fact in Romania.[10] The priests around Truța, who represented the majority of the parishes, rejected Moldovan's appointment by Bucharest and the interference of the patriarchate and the Communist government in their affairs. In reaction to this and with the patriarchate's urging, Moldovan, now representing the Romanian Orthodox Missionary Episcopate of America, sued unsuccessfully the original Romanian Orthodox Episcopate to obtain its goods and property. With money from Romania, Moldovan's diocese published no fewer than five newspapers in which it made propaganda for the RomOC and the Communist regime in Romania, thus making the break inevitable.[11]

9. Gârdan, *Episcopia Ortodoxă Română din America*, 336–40.
10. Gârdan, *Episcopia Ortodoxă Română din America*, 342–44.
11. Gârdan, *Episcopia Ortodoxă Română din America*, 351–52.

In the sessions of July 1–4, 1951, the congress of the original episcopate officially broke relations with RomOC and appointed Viorel Trifa as the vicar bishop of Moruşcă, under the monastic name Valerian. A new episode thus opened for the Romanian Orthodox in America and Canada. Trifa was to become the most controversial bishop the Romanian Orthodox community in North America has had. To understand Trifa's role, background information is necessary.

Born in 1914 near Câmpeni, Alba County, in Transylvania, Viorel Trifa was the nephew of Iosif Trifa, the founder and leader of the Lord's Army, a Protestant-inspired Orthodox renewal movement for which young Viorel worked for a while. Some of the "short-term" goals of the movement were the combating of alcoholism, tobacco usage, swearing, and other sins, while in the "long term" they endeavored to contribute to "the rediscovery, maintenance and active living of the Orthodox faith . . . by energizing both clergy and lay people."[12] Initially supported by Metropolitan Nicolae Bălan of Transylvania commencing in 1921, Father Iosif Trifa was defrocked by the same hierarch over administrative and other issues in 1935 and died in 1938. Bălan was a supporter of the fascist Iron Guard (also known as the Legionary Movement) and the brother-in-law of Policarp Moruşcă. Bălan officiated at the funeral service for Ion Moţa and Vasile Marin, two prominent Legionary leaders who were killed while fighting in the Spanish Civil War on the side of Francisco Franco, upon the return of their bodies to Romania in February 1937. As a student leader, Viorel Trifa was involved at that time in the Romanian ceremonies and the transportation of the fascist leaders' bodies from Spain. In 1935 Trifa completed a bachelor's degree in theology at the Faculty of Orthodox Theology in Chişinău, Bessarabia, then part of Greater Romania.[13] Afterward, he was involved in the leadership of the Legionary Movement, also referred to simply as the Legion, a fascist interwar Romanian movement that eventually became a political party promoting ultranationalism, anti-Semitism, and a fundamentalist version of Orthodox Christianity. In 1939, Trifa and thirty other Legionary leaders (including Horia Sima) were in Germany, plotting to return to Romania to dethrone King Carol II, who proclaimed his personal dictatorship after killing the older Guard leaders (including Corneliu Zelea Codreanu). Due to territorial losses to neighboring Hungary and the Soviet Union, Carol II was forced to abdicate on September 6, 1940. The leader of

12. "Scurt istoric" (in Romanian), Oastea Domnului, accessed October 20, 2017, http://www.oasteadomnului.ro/scurt-istoric.

13. Bobango, *Religion and Politics*, 144.

the country, General (later Marshall) Ion Antonescu, under pressure from Nazi Germany, entered an alliance with the Legionary Movement to govern Romania. The new alliance, known as the National Legionary State, lasted from September 14, 1940, until January 23, 1941. During that time, young Viorel Trifa served as the president of the National Union of Romanian Christian Students, a position for which the Legionary legislation required a government nomination and confirmation by royal decree.[14] Students were viewed by the Legionaries as excellent recruits, since they were open to new ideas. The National Legionary State introduced many measures for the Romanianization of the state, including numerous anti-Semitic and anti-Roma policies that opened the gate for the Holocaust in Romania and outlasted the short-lived "marriage of convenience" between Antonescu and the Legion.[15]

On January 20, 1941, Trifa led a big demonstration in Bucharest's University Square and gave a public talk in front of a large crowd that included many students. In the talk he urged the reinstatement of the Legionary minister of the interior, General Ion Petrovicescu, who had just been sacked by Antonescu following the assassination in Bucharest on January 18 of Major Doehring, the chief of railway transport of the German army in Romania. American historian Gerald Bobango (who was very close to Trifa and had his blessing to write the book on him) alleges that the prepared speech was given to Trifa by Sima himself, without Trifa having input into it. The speech asked for the return of Petrovicescu, whom Antonescu had dismissed from office "at the behest of the British and masons," but also urged the purging of the government of "Greeks and Jews" (a Greek agent hired by British intelligence had killed Doehring) as well as a fully Legionary government. Since the Legion still controlled the Romanian national radio station, Trifa's message was replayed several times on January 21 and 22.[16] At the time of the speech, the Legion was definitely planning some action against Antonescu, since in early December 1940 the movement's head, Horia Sima, had visited Legionary commanders in many cities, and another Legionary leader, Nicolae Pătrașcu, was already making statements about an unavoidable divorce between the Legion and the general.[17] Antonescu did not wait passively for the divorce to happen, but in turn prepared to eliminate the movement from the government, having twice visited Hitler, to whom he complained about the Legionaries as murderers

14. Bobango, *Religion and Politics*, 161.
15. Elie Wiesel, Tuvia Frilling, Radu Ioanid, and Mihail E. Ionescu, eds., *International Commission on the Holocaust in Romania Final Report* (Bucharest: Polirom, 2004), 181.
16. Bobango, *Religion and Politics*, 175–76.
17. Bobango, *Religion and Politics*, 167.

and troublemakers who would endanger Hitler's war efforts directed at the Soviet Union through sabotage and disorder in Romania. In a surprise move, Antonescu began arresting some Legionaries and firing Legionary police chiefs, prefects, and other public officials on January 21, 1941.[18] In response, the Legionaries mobilized themselves by occupying buildings, police headquarters, and workplaces, to defend their comrades and to cause harm to their enemies, beginning with the Bucharest Jews in a genuine pogrom, followed by Communist activists, and ending with soldiers of the Romanian army who represented the Antonescu establishment. The rebellion lasted for three days, and with the help of the military, Antonescu defeated and removed the movement from power in order to rule the country as a dictator with a government of his own choice. He referred to himself as *Conducător* (Romanian equivalent of the German *Führer*). Some 120 Jews were killed during the Bucharest pogrom, and roughly 2,000—including children and the elderly—were tortured by young Legionary workers. Some Jews were hanged on meat hooks at a slaughterhouse in Bucharest. "At Bucharest's largest synagogues survivors found little but broken glass and ashes. A total of one thousand two hundred seventy-four buildings were attacked, among them 25 synagogues, 616 shops, and 547 homes."[19] Some nine thousand Legionaries, including leaders Sima and Trifa, were arrested by Antonescu after the rebellion. Yet Hitler negotiated the transfer of some of these leaders to special quarters of the Nazi labor camps of Rostock, Dachau, and Buchenwald in order to keep them under observation and later to use them against Romania if the country decided to change sides in the war. After King Michael arrested Antonescu and sided with the anti-Hitler allies on August 23, 1944, Hitler appointed Sima as the head of the "Romanian government in Vienna" and parachuted some Legionaries into Romania, but they were immediately captured by the advancing Soviet army.[20]

Trifa first fled to Italy after the war and then made his way to the United States on July 17, 1950, having lied to immigration authorities about his past and claimed that he was one of Hitler's prisoners of war. This "original sin" haunted him for decades, and led first to the loss of his American naturalization and citizenship, which he surrendered in 1980, and then to his deportation to Portugal in 1984, where he died in 1987. In his book *Religion*

---

18. The best documented account to date of the Legionary rebellion is that of Roland Clark, *Holy Legionary Youth: Fascist Activism in Interwar Romania* (Ithaca, NY: Cornell University Press, 2015), 229–32.

19. Clark, *Holy Legionary Youth*, 231–32. Cf. also Wiesel et al., *International Commission on the Holocaust in Romania*, 113–14.

20. Clark, *Holy Legionary Youth*, 235.

and Politics: Bishop Valerian Trifa and His Times, Gerald Bobango presented some very problematic interpretations of the Legionary Movement and its anti-Semitic, profascist policies, in order to make the case that Trifa was not a fascist and that his leadership position in the movement and his speech on the eve of the Legionary rebellion of 1941 had no major significance. Bobango claimed that the Iron Guard and its successor, the Legion of the Archangel Michael (or Legionary Movement), were not anti-Semitic or fascist organizations specifically, but only generally xenophobic;[21] that Trifa was not a card-carrying Legionary member, although he was very sympathetic to the Legion's policies; that due to his position as head of the National Union of Christian Students, "he was considered *ex officio* a 'member' or 'associate' of whatever party held power in the state at that moment"; and that his January 20, 1941, speech was prepared by Sima and had no effect on the events that followed during the rebellion.[22] As Roland Clark points out in his recent book on the Legionary Movement,

> Many of the students who had been Blood Brothers [*Frați de Cruce*] in 1940 understood the Legion primarily as a spiritual movement. . . . The way that these students described the Legion in their later writings suggests that they knew little about what happened during the interwar period and believed the romanticized hagiographies of legionaries promoted by the National Legionary State. . . . When they were arrested in the aftermath of the 1941 rebellion against Antonescu, roughly 250 Blood Brothers incarcerated at Aiud fell under the influence of Traian Trifan (1899–1990), a lawyer who had joined the Legion in 1933 and served a prefect of Brasov County under the legionary regime. Trifan emphasized prayer, introspection, and passive resistance as the most effective way of surviving prison.[23]

The Communists in Bucharest and their supporters in the Romanian Orthodox Missionary Episcopate in Detroit played a major role in trying to reveal Trifa's fascist past to prevent him from becoming a bishop. That failed, but once he became a bishop, they tried to convince him to accept the reunification of the two Romanian dioceses under RomOC. It all started with Bishop Andrei Moldovan, who began the attacks on Trifa almost as soon as the latter was elected bishop, and he requested help from Romania to provide evidence of

21. Bobango, *Religion and Politics*, 61–83.
22. Bobango, *Religion and Politics*, 32–33.
23. Clark, *Holy Legionary Youth*, 240.

Trifa's involvement with the Legionary Movement.[24] The allegations leveled over the years against Trifa can be summarized as follows: he was a former Nazi and a deserter from the Romanian army; he abandoned his wife and child in a European country; as the nephew of an excommunicated priest (Iosif Trifa) and his defender, he too placed himself outside the Orthodox Church; he embraced Catholicism; his election as a bishop by his congress in a room of the masonic temple in Chicago is proof that he was a freemason; and he incited the rebellion against Antonescu and the murder of some three thousand Jews in 1941. Efforts were made by both Moldovan and the Securitate in Romania or its agents at the Romanian legation in Washington, DC, to spread all these rumors, and to rally the Jewish community in the United States to denounce him.[25] Most of these allegations proved to be simply untrue, but one of them, his fascist past, was definitely true and came to haunt Trifa throughout his life. Charles Kramer, an American Romanian Jewish dentist whose family members died in the 1941 pogrom in Bucharest, was one of those who pursued Trifa for twenty-eight years, attempting to prove to the American authorities that he was a fascist in denial. RomOC also asked the other Orthodox patriarchates around the world neither to ordain Trifa nor to receive his diocese under their jurisdiction once he was ordained, as both actions represented interference in its internal affairs.[26]

Nevertheless, on April 27, 1952, Viorel Trifa was ordained a bishop bearing the name Valerian by three Ukrainian Orthodox bishops whose own ordinations were highly questioned by other Orthodox churches. One of them, John Theodorovich, belonged originally to a group of self-ordained bishops from Ukraine referred to as *samosveat*, or self-ordained. After he immigrated to the United States, Theodorovich's situation became canonical as two other bishops belonging to the Autonomous Polish Orthodox Church reconsecrated him, and he was no longer regarded by other churches as having received a heretical ordination without an apostolic succession.[27] In his memoirs published in 2008, metropolitan of Cluj, Bartolomeu Anania (whom we will encounter below), claims that only in 1970 did Valerian Trifa receive a valid ordination,

24. Gârdan, *Episcopia Ortodoxă Română din America*, 381–83.

25. Gârdan, *Episcopia Ortodoxă Română din America*, 384–85.

26. Gârdan, *Episcopia Ortodoxă Română din America*, 386–88.

27. Gârdan, *Episcopia Ortodoxă Română din America*, 393–95. About the validity of Theodorovich's ordination, see Ronald Roberson, *The Eastern Christian Churches—a Brief Survey*, 7th ed. (Rome: Edizioni Orientalia Christiana, 2002), and "The Ukrainian Orthodox Church of the USA and Diaspora," CNEWA, accessed October 20, 2017, http://www.cnewa.org/default.aspx?ID=42&pagetypeID=9&sitecode=HQ&pageno=1.

at the hands of the bishops of the Russian Metropolitanate in New York, a diocese that later became the Orthodox Church in America (OCA).[28] When the former titular bishop Policarp died in Romania in 1958, Trifa was promoted from vicar to titular bishop of his episcopate. He managed to put order in his diocese and introduce a number of initiatives that the faithful liked.

In 1980, following a long investigation against him ordered by the US government, numerous unsuccessful attempts to prove his innocence, and some $100,000 in legal costs, Trifa decided to surrender his American citizenship to the authorities and await deportation. In a letter to his diocese dated August 25, 1980, Trifa maintained his innocence, thanked his supporters for setting up another defense fund, and stated that he decided to give up fighting against the accusations brought against him in various tribunals.[29] In fact, he seemingly ran out of money for his defense. On November 14, 1980, Nathaniel Popp, a vicar elected by the congress, was ordained a bishop to succeed Valerian as leader of ROEA upon the latter's retirement in 1984. ROEA was an OCA diocese.

After the death of Bishop Andrei Moldovan of the ROMA on March 14, 1963, a search began for his replacement. Father Glicherie Moraru insisted that hieromonk Valeriu (or Vartolomeu) Anania, a former Legionary who spent many years in Communist prisons even though he was a protégé of Patriarch Justinian Marina, be sent to the United States to help the ROMA. Following his release from political prison in 1964, Anania, having become a reliable Communist agent of influence, was sent on October 29, 1965, to the United States to help find a replacement for Moldovan. Anania's departure was part of dictator Nicolae Ceaușescu's highly secretive Atlas Program, which allowed bishops, priests, engineers, doctors, and intellectuals to travel to the West in order to influence Western governments' policies toward Romania. According to former Securitate officer Roland Vasilievici, "This information network [of priests] was gradually educated in a nationalist, chauvinist, and xenophobic spirit. Church leaders were supervised by the intelligence and counterintelligence departments, were subjected to complex training programs, and sent abroad to serve their socialist country by collecting information, participating in nationalist-communist propaganda activities and disinformation campaigns, providing false information to emigration leaders, infiltrating Radio Free Europe, and mending the broken image of Romania and its communist leadership."[30]

28. Valeriu Anania, *Memorii* (Bucharest: Polirom, 2008), 361.
29. The letter is transcribed in Gârdan, *Episcopia Ortodoxă Română din America*, 415–16.
30. Roland Vasilievici was interviewed in Tudor Flueras, "Preoții informatori erau un

According to a 1976 Securitate overview of his activities in the United States, initially Anania was supportive of the Communist state that sent him there, but later changed his mind because he was not promoted as bishop in Romania. Because of that change in attitude, Anania was perceived by the Securitate and the patriarchate as acting against Romania's interests abroad and was recalled to Bucharest in October 1976, as the Securitate feared his defection to the United States.[31] During Anania's early years in the United States, however, Glicherie Moraru and others eyed him for bishop of the ROMA, but Anania was not interested in the job. According to a note dated November 29, 1965, an informer for the Securitate code-named "Costea" reported that Patriarch Justinian himself knew of Anania's intentions not to return to the clerical life he had before as a monk and then become bishop, but to try to become accomplished as a writer and possibly publish his literary works in English; the source added that the patriarch believed that the Romanian Communist "authorities do not really want the complete removal of V. Trifa from the religious life of the Romanians in America, since—according to the patriarch—Anania received instructions not to engage in a publishing duel with Trifa."[32] Instead, the authorities and Justinian himself favored the appointment of Victorin Ursache as bishop at ROMA. In that sense, Anania (known by his code name as agent "Apostol")[33] was to conduct work to compromise Trifa, as payback for Trifa successfully blocking the appointment of Arad bishop Teoctist Arăpaşu as bishop of the ROMA (Teoctist, another of Justinian Marina's protégés, eventually became patriarch of the

organ de sondare a opiniei publice," *Evenimentul Zilei*, June 14, 1999, quoted in Lavinia Stan and Lucian Turcescu, *Religion and Politics in Post-Communist Romania* (New York: Oxford University Press, 2007), 79.

31. The story of how the ROMA came to ask him to go to the United States and recommended him to both the patriarchate and the Department of Religious Denominations is recounted in Anania, *Memorii*, 338ff. For the Securitate overview, see ACNSAS, Fond I 1450–02, pp. 244–46.

32. ACNSAS, Fond SIE 2869–01, pp. 40–41.

33. On Anania as secret police agent "Apostol," see Mirela Corlăţan, "Mitropolitul Bartolomeu Anania: nume de cod 'Apostol,'" *Evenimentul Zilei*, February 3, 2011, http://www.evz.ro/mitropolitul-bartolomeu-anania-nume-de-cod-apostol-882223.html. Corlăţan's insight can be corroborated with information contained in ACNSAS, Fond SIE 2869–01, p. 74, where "Apostol" is mentioned as the agent of influence in the United States who is to receive instructions from the Securitate pertaining to the Romanian Orthodox communities. The Securitate files confirm what Pacepa wrote, that Anania was an agent of influence sent by the Securitate to bring the two Romanian episcopates under the control of the RomOC, and thus that the Securitate was using clergymen as agents. See Ion Mihai Pacepa, *Red Horizons: Chronicles of a Communist Spy Chief* (Washington, DC: Regnery Gateway, 1987), 284.

Romanian Orthodox Church in 1986). This is demonstrated by a "strictly confidential" document produced by the Ministry of Internal Affairs—DGI Directia "C"—on April 8, 1966, which also hints at some arrangements for his own recognition as a bishop that Trifa made with the Romanian patriarch. The document reads:

> We are in favor of postponing the congress for the election of V. Ursache as bishop until after the delegation of priests proposed by V. Trifa will be received [by the patriarch] for the following reasons:
>
> 1) We think that, regardless of the favorable [sic] result of the discussions between the Patriarchate and the above mentioned delegation, the only appropriate solution is that of the election of V. Ursache for the following reasons: a) the recognition of V. Trifa by the Patriarchate would not be recommended because up until now we undertook a series of actions to unmask V. Trifa and a recognition would point to an inconsistency on our part in evaluating this person; b) we disagree with the way in which V. Trifa will conceive of the relations with the Patriarchate after his recognition. We know about his [Trifa's] position from the discussions he conducted with Comrade D. Stancu, as well as with Metropolitan Iustin Moisescu, Nicolaescu and [theology professor] Liviu Stan; c) there is no possibility to convince V. Trifa to adopt a loyal position vis-à-vis our country and to use him in the work of rapprochement of the colony [that is, the Romanian diaspora] with the fatherland; d) Trifa's recognition would determine the alienation of the group that is loyal to our country inside the canonical Episcopate [ROMA] and, generally, of the Romanian colony.
>
> 2) The election of V. Ursache and the presence of Apostol [that is, Anania] in the USA will lead to: a) the strengthening of the canonical episcopate through the retention of the current parishes and the luring of other independent parishes and priests, retention of the vacant parishes and staffing them with priests brought from Romania, the luring of new vacant parishes that are now under V. Trifa's jurisdiction; . . . c) the annihilation of any action by V. Trifa to implicate our fatherland in the election of the bishop, as he did in the case of Teoctist Arăpaşu, since V. Ursache has already been in the USA for a long time, never visited Romania after 1946 and had no relations with the Patriarchate or Romania's representatives overseas.
>
> We are proposing that the Patriarchate convey to the canonical Episcopate the postponement of the congress for the election of Victorin Ursache, using a plausible explanation; that the Patriarchate ask V. Trifa to send his delegation of priests to Romania urgently and give them a deadline so as

not to procrastinate the election of V. Ursache. . . . In case our proposals are embraced, we deem it very useful to contact "Apostol" in order to explain to him what actions to undertake and how to proceed.[34]

In a file on Trifa, who had just been received in the OCA, the Securitate noted that in August 1970 Trifa sent a "A Personal and Unofficial Confession" to Patriarch Justinian, asking him to find a way to recognize the newly created Orthodox Church in America, but the patriarch did not respond, nor did he plan to. According to intelligence collected by the Securitate in the same file, "the US administration is dissatisfied and has ordered the CIA to take measures to prevent the unification of the Orthodox churches under the jurisdiction of the Russian church because this would constitute a basis for the spread of the Soviet influence in the United States."[35] Moreover, according to the Securitate, by accepting to join the OCA, Trifa was "in contradiction with his own propaganda which condemned the relationship between the Romanian Patriarchate and the Moscow Patriarchate" and even lost some parishes that disagreed with his move.[36]

According to Ion Mihai Pacepa's 1987 book *Red Horizons*, during one of his four visits to the United States in the 1970s, dictator Nicolae Ceaușescu (who ruled Romania from 1965 to 1989) decided to put pressure on Trifa to have him expelled from the United States. Since previous collaboration efforts by the Securitate with Trifa were unsuccessful, "at this point Ceaușescu personally stepped in and ordered Bolanu [a high-ranking Securitate official] to mount an operation aimed at getting Trifa denaturalized and deported from the United States as a Nazi war criminal."[37] Pacepa alleges that fake documents and a counterfeited photograph were produced by the Securitate and distributed through various secret agents, as well as Jewish leaders such as Romania's chief rabbi Moses Rosen, to compromise Trifa. The denaturalization lawsuit begun against Trifa in the US District Court in Detroit in 1975 was, according to Pacepa, the result of Ceaușescu's efforts. With Trifa under investigation by the US government, Ceaușescu organized a final unsuccessful attempt to recruit Trifa in 1976. An American TV series[38] claimed that Trifa gave up his citizenship for two main reasons: (1) his handwriting was certified on a num-

34. ACNSAS, Fond SIE 2869-01, pp. 73-74.
35. ACNSAS, Fond SIE 82-01, p. 22.
36. ACNSAS, Fond SIE 82-01, p. 23.
37. Pacepa, *Red Horizons*, 288.
38. *Forensic Files*, season 5, episode 13, entitled "Unholy Vows" (first aired on December 5, 2000). All the seasons and episodes in the series are available on amazon.com.

ber of postcards sent by one Viorel Trifa to friends in Romania when he was in Germany during WWII; (2) one of the postcards was certified by the FBI to contain Trifa's fingerprints. On the postcard, he boasted about his easy life in one quarter of Dachau, the infamous German concentration camp where he lived a sheltered life following his fall from grace with Romania's wartime leader Antonescu in January 1941 during the Legionary rebellion. In Dachau he was protected from the dangers of war and was treated very nicely by the Germans until the end of the war. Prior to this discovery, Trifa claimed to the American authorities that he was a prisoner of war (not a protégé of Hitler) while in Germany, and that was why he was accepted to enter the United States in 1951. Whatever the ultimate details of the Trifa case might be, on June 22, 1979, Elizabeth Holtzman, a US Democratic congresswoman, complained about the lack of serious collaboration in the Trifa case by the Romanian government and conditioned the United States's renewal of the most favored nation status for Romania on the Romanian government's collaboration to reveal Trifa's past.[39]

Other legal issues are worth mentioning here. According to Ronald Andrei Mureşan, an American lawyer (of Romanian descent) who assisted the ROEA in 1986–1993,

> Two crucial aspects stand out: (1) In September 1979, US federal District Judge Cornelia Kennedy, who had made rulings very favorable to Archbishop Valerian in the "denaturalization" court case, was "kicked upstairs," that is, appointed by the President Jimmy Carter to the 6th Circuit Court of Appeals. The judge who took over the case was much less favorable, even receptive to the government's case. (2) Then the fatal blow came in 1981 when Valerian lost his eminent and stalwart defense attorney, George E. Woods, who coincidentally was appointed by President Ronald Reagan to be a US federal court judge. It could be argued that the two judicial officers both got special presidential attention to get them off Valerian's case. Woods' loss was virtually fatal; there was no way for Woods' successor, William Swor, an honorable immigration lawyer but no George Woods, to absorb Woods' experience of the defense that had run from 1975–1981. Valerian saw his diocese bleeding hundreds of thousands of dollars on defense lawyers, only to lose Woods, then to see the Securitate brutalize his aged comrades—anyone

---

39. "Appendix A: Statement of the Honorable Elizabeth Holtzman (D.-N.Y.) before the Subcommittee on Trade, House Ways and Means Committee (June 22, 1979)," in Bobango, *Religion and Politics*, 235–38.

who gave testimony the slightest bit helpful to Valerian. . . . So, Valerian chose to give up his beloved American citizenship.[40]

Upon his deportation to Portugal, Valerian Trifa was succeeded by Nathaniel Popp as bishop of the ROEA in 1984. His Eminence Popp was still occupying the position as of 2017. Bishop Nathaniel was born William George Popp to a Romanian Greek Catholic family in Aurora, Illinois, in 1940. Having studied at the Gregorian University in Rome during the Second Vatican Council (1962–1965), young William returned to the United States in 1966, where he was ordained a Greek Catholic priest. In 1968, he converted to Orthodoxy and was received by Bishop Valerian, who encouraged him to start a monastic community at Vatra. He was also involved in the translation of various liturgical books from Romanian into English during that time. In 1975, Nathaniel was appointed a parish priest in Hermitage, Pennsylvania, and also served as priest of the nuns at the Transfiguration Monastery in Ellwood City, Pennsylvania. In 1980, he was elected vicar bishop to Valerian.[41] The pressure continued on the new bishop to come under the jurisdiction of the RomOC even after the collapse of the Communist regime in 1989. But given that he was born in the United States, Bishop Nathaniel could not be controlled or compromised by the Securitate during the Communist period.

Bishop Victorin of the ROMA was born Victor Ursache in 1912 at Mănăstioara-Siret, Rădăuți County, in northern Moldova, Romania, and died on July 16, 2001. After serving in various capacities in Romania, Jerusalem, and Jordan until 1946, he was placed by Patriarch Nicodim under the jurisdiction of the Patriarchate of Jerusalem, since the Romanian state ended the funding of his position in Jerusalem. In 1956, he arrived in the USA and began teaching at the Saint Tikhon Theological Seminary in Canaan, Pennsylvania. On August 7, 1966, he was ordained as bishop in Windsor, Ontario, Canada. In 1973 Victorin was promoted to the rank of archbishop, and in 1974 the episcopate became an archbishopric. The diocese's autonomy obtained in 1950 was recognized and renewed by the RomOC on the same occasion.[42] On February 22, 2001, the Holy Synod of the RomOC suggested that the archbishop retire due to age and administrative problems he had in his archdiocese.[43]

Although in 1966 Ursache had the approval for his appointment of both

40. Email message from Ronald Andrei Mureșan, JD, to Lucian Turcescu (April 16, 2016).

41. Gârdan, *Episcopia Ortodoxă Română din America*, 437–42.

42. Holy Synod of the Romanian Orthodox Church, "Decision No. 14079 of 12 December 1974," http://www.romarch.org/pags.php?id=23.

43. Gârdan, *Episcopia Ortodoxă Română din America*, 460–65.

the RomOC and the Romanian authorities, by 1980 the honeymoon between him, the new patriarch, and the Securitate seems to have ended. According to a Ministry of the Interior report dated December 4, 1980, Ursache, along with Father Vasile Vasilache and Father George Chişcă from Montreal, was no longer regarded as loyal to the country: the report describes "Ursache's exaggerated tendencies toward autonomy, and limiting his contacts with the Romanian Patriarchate, which in turn led to a dwindling of the number of immigrants who supported the missionary archbishopric." Along with close collaborators Vasilache and Chişcă, Ursache displayed a "hostile attitude" toward the Romanian Patriarchate when a Romanian envoy, Archmandrite Nicolae Mihăiţă, was sent on a mission to Canada to found a new parish in Ottawa without notifying Ursache. Ursache suspected that Mihăiţă was sent to replace him as a bishop.[44] An April 20, 1984, Ministry of Interior note entitled "Personnel Record regarding Victorin Ursache" expressed ongoing suspicions about the qualities of Victorin: "Currently, the Romanian Orthodox Missionary Archbishopric of the USA and Canada goes through a serious crisis due to the lack of authority and initiative of its leader, as well as the decrease of the number of faithful and clergy. Archbishop Victorin Ursache refused to allow the naming of a vicar bishop by the Romanian Patriarchate, he is opposed to the project of the founding of a Romanian Orthodox Episcopate of Canada and prevents the filling of the vacant posts in parishes with clergy sent from our country."[45] The Securitate pretended to be surprised that Ursache did not want to travel to Romania for fear of being replaced. Perhaps the Securitate officer writing the report in 1984 did not know the story of Victorin's predecessor, Policarp, or that of Anania, who in 1939 and 1976 respectively were prevented by the Romanian authorities from returning to the United States.

The collapse of the Communist regime in Romania in 1989 ushered in new hopes for the relations between the ROMA and the ROEA. Thus, in 1992 an official Dialogue Commission was set up to reestablish sacramental communion between the two dioceses and to bring about their eventual reunification. Sacramental communion was easier to establish. In May 1994, a delegation led by Bishop Nathaniel visited Romania. Bishop Nathaniel concelebrated the liturgy with Patriarch Teoctist in the patriarchal cathedral in Bucharest, and with other important officials in several Romanian cities. Mutual visits by Nathaniel to Romania and by bishops from Romania to the United States have occurred in subsequent years. In 1998, Bishop Nathaniel also was invited to participate

44. ACNSAS, Fond SIE 2869–02, pp. 2–3.
45. ACNSAS, Fond SIE 2869–02, pp. 4–5.

in the ordination as bishop of Archmandrite Iosif Pop, who became the Romanian Orthodox archbishop of western and central Europe. Most importantly, Bishop Nathaniel participated in the ordination as bishop of Nicolae Condrea, the successor to Victorin Ursache as archbishop of the ROMA, in 2002. His Eminence (later Metropolitan) Archbishop Nicolae, in turn, participated in the ordination of Irineu Duvlea as vicar bishop of the ROEA later in 2002. While the first goal of reestablishing sacramental communion was reached, the second goal, of reunification of the two dioceses, is yet to happen. Following several years of dialogue toward reunification between the ROEA and the ROMA, the former decided to unilaterally withdraw in 2006 and to reassert its belonging to the OCA, without seeking any further reunification with the ROMA and the RomOC.[46] As of 2016, the ROEA had seventy-two parishes in the United States and thirty-seven in Canada, while the ROMA has thirty parishes in the United States, twenty-six in Canada, and two in Latin America. In 2017, the Romanian Orthodox Episcopate of Canada was established under the leadership of His Holiness Ioan Casian Tunaru.[47]

Conclusion and Summary

The Romanian Orthodox Episcopate of North America (created in 1929) had a fate similar to other diaspora Orthodox churches from countries where Communist regimes took over, such as those in Russia, Ukraine, Serbia, and Albania; that is, it was split into two. The conclusion that imposes itself following the above presentation and analysis is that the Communists in the home countries contributed to the division of the churches in the diaspora in an attempt to bring the diaspora communities under their control.

The Romanian episcopate's first bishop, Policarp Moruşcă (1935–1939), was prevented from returning to his post after a visit to Romania as WWII broke out, and even more so after Communism arrived in Romania with the Soviet tanks in 1944. His place was taken by Andrei Moldovan (1950–1963), when a group of priests who decided to remain faithful to the patriarchate in Bucharest designated him as their bishop and created a parallel structure that came eventually to be known as the ROMA. In response to these developments, the initial episcopate (ROEA) congress decided to choose its own bishop in the

46. Gârdan, *Episcopia Ortodoxă Română din America*, 483–502.

47. Information obtained from the official websites of the two dioceses, www.roea.org and www.romarch.org (later https://www.mitropolia.us/index.php/en/).

person of the controversial Valerian Trifa (1950–1984), who was one of the leaders of the fascist Legionary Movement in interwar Romania, instigated the Legionary rebellion of January 1941, and profited from the Cold War to make his way to the United States as a refugee. Trifa was later succeeded by Nathaniel Popp (1984–present), and Moldovan by Victorin Ursache (1966–2001) and then by two bishops, Nicolae Condrea (2002–present) and Ioan Casian Tunaru (2017–present). At the height of the confrontation between the ROMA and the ROEA, the Communist authorities sent out controversial Archimandrite Valeriu Anania, a former Legionary Movement member who later became a Communist agent, to undermine Trifa. Trifa surrendered his American citizenship after Ceaușescu's Securitate got involved in the uncovering of Trifa's fascist past to the American authorities in the late 1970s. Post-Communist efforts at the reunification of the two dioceses have managed to reestablish sacramental communion but not reunification, with the ROMA remaining an autonomous diocese under the jurisdiction of the RomOC, while the ROEA is part of the OCA. While the ROMA's Metropolitan Nicolae Condrea and Bishop Ioan Casian Tunaru are uncompromised, educated in the West, and willing to see some form of unity between the two Romanian dioceses, the ROEA's Bishop Nathaniel bears with him the burden of the past and may not be too open to reconciliation. The split between the two ecclesiastical units is no longer justified, and hopefully the future will make it possible for them to be one.

Redressing Religious Freedom: Anti-Communism and the Rejection of Orthodox Christianity as the "Fourth Major Faith"

DELLAS OLIVER HERBEL

Beginning in the 1940s, Orthodox Christians in America went on the offensive regarding their religious freedom. Prior to this time, they had been bogged down in fights to preserve their religious rights (primarily in Alaska). In the 1940s, however, Orthodox in New York obtained recognition for "Eastern Orthodoxy" from the Selective Service. This galvanized many, especially those within the Greek Orthodox community, and led to an attempt at federal recognition of Orthodoxy as a "fourth major faith" in the 1950s. Although later successful in many state legislatures, the resolution failed to get out of committee at the federal level. As shall be shown below, one of the central reasons for this was the fear that providing such recognition to Orthodox Christians inevitably opened the door to Communist infiltration in America, a fear that some American Orthodox themselves had helped contribute to. The main antagonist to the Orthodox maneuver was Carl McIntire, a highly popular and politically active fundamentalist Presbyterian pastor. McIntire's objection built upon preexisting, widespread fear of Communism, effectively guaranteeing that the resolution died in committee.

The American Orthodox Religious Offensive for Religious Freedom

The Russian culture in Alaska had suffered a drastic decline following the American purchase of Alaska in 1867, for wide-ranging reasons, including internal dysfunctions[1] and an influx of American Protestant missionaries.[2]

---

1. A succinct summary may be found in B. D. Lain, "The Decline of Russian America's Colonial Society," *Western Historical Quarterly* 7, no. 2 (1976): 143–53.

2. For example, Sheldon Jackson, the first general agent of education for Alaska, from 1885 until 1906, had his salary paid by the Presbyterian Church. See Michael Oleksa, *Orthodox Alaska: A Theology of Mission* (Crestwood, NY: St. Vladimir's Seminary Press, 1992), 171.

Despite government support for the Protestant missionary zeal, Russian Orthodoxy expanded during this period.[3] At times, this expansion even occurred despite the local governing authorities, who simply dismissed the Orthodox.[4]

In 1897, Orthodox asked of President McKinley that the 1867 treaty, which guaranteed civil and religious rights, be enforced, and Bishop Nicholas traveled to Washington, DC, and met with President McKinley.[5] Two years later, Bishop Nicholas, as the outgoing bishop of the Russian Mission in North America, also wrote to the president, seeking religious freedoms for his flock in Alaska; this letter was published in papers across the country.[6] Bishop Nicholas's efforts fell largely on deaf or opposing ears. In the *New York Times*, an editor's parting shot in response to Bishop Nicholas's letter to McKinley read, "denunciations from some sources are strong recommendations; not conclusive to be sure, but really strong."[7]

By 1942, however, Orthodox Christianity in America had changed drastically. Immigration had flooded the lower forty-eight. Orthodox Christianity even brought in non-Orthodox Christian "converts" into its fold from a diverse range of backgrounds.[8] Despite such important changes in Orthodox demographics, Orthodox Christians registering with the Selective Service were not recognized as Orthodox Christians (for one had to declare Roman Catholic, Protestant, or Jewish faith).

In the spring of that year, John Gelsinger, of Buffalo, New York, was drafted by the Selective Service. Gelsinger intended to be ordained a priest,

---

3. For a description of the conversions of the Tlingits, see Sergei Kan, *Memory Eternal: Tlingit Culture and Russian Orthodox Christianity through Two Centuries* (Seattle: University of Washington Press, 1999), 245–77. Reasons that the Tlingits converted included worshiping in the same space (rather than in a separate "Indian church"), Orthodox tolerance for native customs that did not explicitly contradict Orthodox dogma, and a general appreciation for and tolerance of native culture. See Kan, *Memory Eternal*, 245–77.

4. Oleksa, *Orthodox Alaska*, 173. For example, Governor James Sheakley, Rev. A. E. Austin, and US Marshall W. E. Williams stole the body of a deceased Orthodox mother of two boarding students in order to prevent her from receiving an Orthodox funeral.

5. Two petitions are available in Michael J. Oleksa, ed., *Alaskan Missionary Spirituality* (Crestwood, NY: St. Vladimir's Seminary Press, 2010), 322–26. "Bishop Nicholas at the White House," *New York Times*, November 5, 1897.

6. The letter is included in Oleksa, *Alaskan Missionary Spirituality*, 327. Two examples of its publication in newspapers may be found in "Russian Grand Duke Here," *New York Times*, January 3, 1899, and "Alaska Run by Jackson," *Irish World and American Industrial Liberator*, January 7, 1899.

7. "Topics of the Times," *New York Times*, January 4, 1899.

8. For a summary of this development (as well as Orthodox convert movements of the twentieth century more generally), see my book *Turning to Tradition: Converts and the Making of an American Orthodox Church* (New York: Oxford University Press, 2014).

and so his bishop, Metropolitan Antony, ordained him and then argued that he couldn't be drafted.[9] Despite his ordination, the Selective Service's local board designated John Gelsinger as 1-A rather than 4-D (which would have exempted him as a clergyman). John Gelsinger's father, Father Michael Gelsinger, himself a convert to Orthodox Christianity and a classics professor at the University of Buffalo, maintained a friendship with a local Greek Orthodox attorney, George E. Phillies.[10] Phillies appealed to the local board and the state board in Albany but netted no change in designation. On October 9, 1942, Phillies appealed to the federal authorities, via General Lewis B. Hershey. The response from Washington, DC, was that they needed to see proof of an organized Orthodox Church in America. According to Phillies, this response galvanized the Orthodox and led to a meeting of four hierarchs: Archbishop Athenagoras of the Greek Archdiocese, Metropolitan Benjamin of the Russian Orthodox Church (Moscow Patriarchate), Bishop Dionisije of the Serbian Orthodox Church, and Metropolitan Antony of the Syrian Orthodox Church. The organizers behind this meeting were Michael Gelsinger and Boris Burden (also a convert priest but serving under the Russian Orthodox jurisdiction that was under Moscow).[11] Michael Gelsinger obtained the cooperation of Archbishop Athenagoras, the leading Greek bishop, and his own bishop, Metropolitan Antony, while Burden represented his own bishop, Met-

9. Antony to Father Michael Gelsinger, June 29, 1942, Michael Gelsinger Archives, Holy Transfiguration Monastery, Boston. George E. Phillies, "Heritages of Orthodoxy and History of the Federated Orthodox Greek Catholic Primary Jurisdictions in America," 58. Reproduced from the *Album of the Golden Jubilee of the Hellenic Community of Buffalo, New York*, George E. Phillies Papers, Publications File, 1944–64, Box 7, Truman Papers, Truman Library. See also Seraphim Surrency, *The Quest for Orthodox Church Unity in America* (New York: Boris and Gleb Press, 1973), 47.

10. For example, earlier in 1942, George Phillies had been the guest speaker at a dinner honoring Michael Gelsinger's elevation from priest to archpriest. See "Clergyman Honored at Testimonial Dinner," *Niagara Falls Gazette*, February 9, 1942. When writing the history of the Federated Orthodox Greek Catholic Primary Jurisdictions in America, Phillies specifically called himself a "family friend." See Phillies, "Heritages of Orthodoxy," 58.

11. By this time in America, there were three Russian jurisdictions. The largest of the three, which had formerly been the Russian Mission, was known as the "Metropolia" because it had organized itself under Metropolitan Platon following the chaos of the Russian Revolution. The second group was variously known as "the Synod" or the Russian Orthodox Synod Abroad, later normally called the Russian Orthodox Church Outside of Russia. The Synod was guided by a synod consisting of exiled Russian bishops in Sremski Karlovci, Serbia. The Metropolia had initially belonged to this group, but disagreements led to it declaring itself autonomous. In response to the entire situation, the official Russian Orthodox Church reconstituted its Diocese of the Aleutian Islands and North America in 1933.

ropolitan Benjamin, and successfully petitioned the Serbian bishop, Bishop Dionisije.

Burden wrote two letters to the board in defense of John Gelsinger, only to be informed by his own local Selective Service board that he needed to appear.[12] Phillies then appealed to his congressman, James W. Wadsworth, informing him that Orthodox were "lawabiding, respectors of authority, loyal Americans, and devoted patriots," and later asking Wadsworth to speak directly to the Selective Service in Washington.[13] Phillies feared that Burden's situation demonstrated his larger concern—that what had happened in Buffalo would not be an isolated case. In a letter to Metropolitan Athenagoras, his Greek bishop, Phillies expressed his true feelings on the matter: "It is more difficult than I had expected and too important to Orthodoxy. My blood is just boiling to think how the rights of the people of the Orthodox Church are ignored as if we were insignificant."[14]

On December 8, 1942, after a hearing on the matter (which included testimony from Bishop Germanos, a Greek Orthodox bishop), Major Simon P. Dunkle signed paperwork instructing the Selective Service of New York to recognize Father John Gelsinger as a priest.[15] Orthodox Christians who enlisted were to receive dog tags stamped "EO" for "Eastern Orthodox," and Orthodox priests now had the opportunity to serve as chaplains.

Americanizing the Orthodox While Defending the USSR

Although Phillies, the Gelsingers, and Burden had succeeded in obtaining recognition from the Selective Service, neither they nor the four bishops intended to stop there. Phillies began to pursue another venture: amending New York state law for religious corporations in order to incorporate the different Orthodox jurisdictions. He already had reviewed the religious incorporations of forty-eight states and found none pertaining to the Orthodox churches

12. Burden to Legal Board #225 in Brooklyn, November 8, 1942, and Burden to the director of the Selective Service, October 4, 1942, and November 2, 1942, all in Michael Gelsinger Archives.

13. Phillies to Wadsworth, October 23, 1942, and November 17, 1942, Michael Gelsinger Archives.

14. Phillies to Athenagoras, October 23, 1942, Michael Gelsinger Archives.

15. In addition to Phillies's own account, see "Church Accorded Army Recognition," *Niagara Falls Gazette*, December 14, 1942, and "1-A Classification for Clergyman," *Utica Daily Press*, December 28, 1942.

except for an 1895 provision in the New York statute, which he did not find adequate in light of other statutes pertaining to Eastern Catholic usages of the terms "Eastern," "Orthodox," "Greek," and "Catholic." Phillies obtained sponsorship for a bill from State Senator Charles O. Burney and Assemblyman Henry Reoux when it moved to the assembly.[16] On March 25, 1943, Governor Dewey signed the bill incorporating the Federated Orthodox Greek Catholic Primary Jurisdictions in America (henceforth, the Federation).[17]

The three men who acted as the driving force behind the development of the Federation believed this effort to force the American government to recognize Orthodoxy would itself lead to the "Americanization" of Orthodoxy. Burden sent a telegram to Dewey prior to the signing in which he argued that passing the legislation would "enable more speedy Americanization."[18] Gelsinger believed Americans needed to know that there was more to the Judeo-Christian tradition than Protestants, Roman Catholics, and Jews, and was particularly upset that the Orthodox were regularly left out of events, such as prayers on Armistice Day, and called for Orthodox Christians to obtain recognition from their fellow American citizens.[19] This sentiment was even expressed by the local Protestant Episcopal bishop, Cameron J. Davis: "it makes the oldest of all the branches of the Catholic Church an integral part of our social and religious structures. I hope that it may be approved."[20]

Part of this concern for "Americanization" included making an apology on behalf of the status of Orthodoxy in Russia. Burden took this need for an "apology" fairly seriously, and the *Buffalo Evening News* dedicated significant space to Burden's position. Burden, speaking on behalf of the Moscow Patriarchate in America, claimed that the Russian clergy who had been prosecuted were not prosecuted because of their faith but because they had joined "counterrevolutionary organizations." Furthermore, although the state seized

16. Phillies, "Heritages of Orthodoxy," 60. See also Surrency, *Quest for Orthodox Church Unity*, 48. Surrency mistakenly referred to it as the "McBurney" bill. No senator by that name has ever served in the New York State Senate. He clearly meant "Burney."

17. As recounted in Phillies, "Heritages of Orthodoxy," 61–62. This occurred with much fanfare. Governor Dewey had the legislature recess, and an Orthodox liturgical thanksgiving service reopened the legislative session. Metropolitan Antony led the service, assisted by Michael Gelsinger and Boris Burden. They then processed to the governor's mansion, where Governor Dewey signed the bill. Twentieth Century-Fox recorded the event, and Governor Dewey gave a radio address in which he discussed the importance of the bill.

18. Bill Jacket for Chapter 145 of the Laws of 1943. Telegram from Burden to Dewey, February 18, 1943.

19. Michael Gelsinger, "Editorial Comment," *Orthodox American*, December 1942, 1–3.

20. Davis to Phillies, March 5, 1943.

church properties, the churches were predominantly free for worship, and in the cases where their purpose had been changed, all religious valuables and sacramental items had been carefully preserved. He asserted that the Nazis persecuted the Orthodox much more directly than the Communists, and that there had been no censorship of mail being exchanged between Russia and the Moscow Patriarchate's office in New York since 1928.[21] This would not be the last time the connection between American Orthodox and Communists in Russia would collide for American Orthodox seeking recognition.

The efforts of the Federation to "Americanize" the Orthodox while simultaneously presenting Orthodox Christianity to America were soon to come to an end, however. The Federation lost steam when the Russian and Greek contingencies divided over whether George E. Phillies, who admitted to communing in both Orthodox and Protestant Episcopal parishes, should be disciplined for the canonical infraction.[22] With the Russian and Greek contingencies being the most powerful, and at odds with one another, the other Orthodox churches simply removed their involvement, though the Syrians kept the Federation alive on paper, inasmuch as it remained their articles of incorporation long after.

Anti-Communist Derailment of Recognizing the "Fourth Major Faith"

Although the Federation failed to achieve intra-Orthodox administrative unity and thus became largely defunct, it served as a launching pad for a continued Orthodox effort to gain governmental recognition of Orthodox Christianity. This movement sought to obtain officially sanctioned status as the "fourth major faith" (in addition to Judaism, Roman Catholicism, and Protestantism) and continued through the middle of the twentieth century.

This response to the Judeo-Christian construct (understood as Protestant-Catholic-Jew) began with continued frustration with the US armed forces' lack of recognition. Despite the 1942 ruling by Major Dunkle, the armed forces had not instituted a policy change. By the 1950s, the Orthodox were again asking to be recognized, this time through the introduction of Senate Bill 106 in the Eighty-Fourth Congress, claiming they were a "fourth major faith" and should

---

21. "4 Orthodox Church Hierarchs Celebrate Mass Here Sunday," *Buffalo Evening News*, August 20, 1943.

22. See Mary Nash, "Immigrant Boy Is Lay Head of 5,000,000 Christians," *Buffalo Evening News*, October 2, 1943, and Surrency, *Quest for Orthodox Church Unity*, 49–52, A133–34.

be able to have "E.O." stamped on their dog tags.[23] Initially, the Department of Defense, through the Department of the Army, refused to change its policy, but after continued lobbying, the bill was put to rest by the Department of the Army granting the change in policy.[24]

The move to have Orthodoxy recognized as a fourth major faith was guided by the Greek Orthodox archbishop, Archbishop Michael, who led the Greek Orthodox Archdiocese from 1949 until his death in 1958.[25] Archbishop Michael decided not to stop with federal military policy change but desired official governmental recognition through federal legislation. For Archbishop Michael, it was a matter of justice. In a 1956 letter to Harold Fey, editor of the *Christian Century*, a prominent Protestant-based magazine, he wrote, "when we ask for the recognition of the Eastern Orthodox Church as one of the major faiths, we, as American citizens, ask for justice and nothing else."[26] By 1961, twenty-five states would recognize Orthodox Christianity as a fourth major faith.

The federal attempt, however, failed. One of the main reasons it failed had to do with anti-Communist fears. Archbishop Michael and many Orthodox Christians expected things to go akin to how they had played out with regard to the Selective Service and recognition by the US armed forces. The attempt to obtain federal recognition in Congress was instigated through Senator Clifford P. Case of New Jersey. Senator Case even publicly agreed with the concern that there were events to which a Protestant, Catholic, and Jewish representative would be invited to the exclusion of an Orthodox representative.[27] Ultimately, Case's resolution (Senate Resolution 88) did not make it out of the Judiciary Committee, and the Senate never voted on it.[28] Unlike the efforts to gain recognition as a separate, established church, the attempt to receive "recognition" from the federal government as a faith separate from but equal to Catholicism, Protestantism, and Judaism touched a nerve.

---

23. The text of the proposed bill may be found in Record Group 46, Records of the US Senate, Committee on Armed Services, 84th Congress, Legislative Files, S. 106, Box 250.

24. See both letters of Robert T. Stevens, secretary of the army, to Honorable Richard B. Russell, chairman, Committee on Armed Services, March 7, 1955, and June 1, 1955, available in Record Group 46, Records of the US Senate, Committee on Armed Services, 84th Congress, Legislative Files, S. 106, Box 250.

25. See Archbishop Michael, letter to all Greek Orthodox Christians in America, April 1953, Archives of the Greek Orthodox Archdiocese (henceforth, AGOA).

26. Michael to Fey, March 30, 1956, AGOA.

27. "Case Plan Supports Eastern Orthodoxy," *New York Times*, February 17, 1961.

28. Legislative archives, S. Res. 88 in box 47 for SEN87A-E12 at 8E2/13/5/5.

The most vocal opponents of the American Orthodox efforts for further recognition were American Protestants who were concerned that Eastern Orthodoxy could be a vehicle for spreading global Communism.[29] By the time Harold Fey (in his role as editor) voiced his opposition to the idea of recognizing Orthodoxy as a fourth major faith in 1956, many Americans had already been eying Orthodoxy's relationship to (and internal division over) Communism, and the *Christian Century* had been fanning the flames of concern.[30] In 1947–1948, the same *Christian Century* noted the ongoing negotiations between American and Russian representatives of the Russian Orthodox faith as well as the split within the Serbian community along political lines (characterized as for or against collaboration with the Communist regime).[31] Indeed, the 1947 article accepted Bishop Dionisije's contention that the American Serb Congress was nothing more than a Communist front. In 1951, the magazine also highlighted a Supreme Court decision that ceded Saint Nicholas Cathedral in New York to the Russian Orthodox Church rather than the Russian Orthodox Greek Catholic Church of America, the ecclesiastical descendant of the prerevolution Russian diocese in North America.[32] Although the magazine noted that separation of church and state was the primary factor, it also contended that "many Americans, however, will be startled to discover from this decision the extent to which churches under foreign authority can challenge with legal impunity the convictions of the people of the United States."[33] As the New York case and Serbian split demonstrate, Protestants did not need to dig deeply to find reason for such concerns. Orthodox themselves would denounce fellow Orthodox as being too indebted to Communist regimes.

Yet it was neither internal Orthodox divisions nor even the concerns of the *Christian Century* that ultimately did in the efforts to declare Orthodox

29. In contrast, Archbishop Garbett of New York warned against declaring a "holy war" on all Communists, suggesting that it could hurt Orthodox Christians under Communist regimes. See "Deprecates 'Holy War' on Soviet," *Christian Century* 66, no. 28 (July 14, 1948): 714.

30. In addition to the articles cited here, David S. Foglesong observed that the *Christian Century* had been even more critical of the Orthodox Church in the 1930s. See Foglesong, *The American Mission and the "Evil Empire": The Crusade for a "Free Russia" since 1881* (Cambridge: Cambridge University Press, 2007), 90.

31. "Moscow Again Woos Russian Orthodox Churches," *Christian Century* 64, no. 36 (September 3, 1947): 1036–37, and "Orthodox Serbs Splitting on Political Lines," *Christian Century* 64, no. 48 (November 26, 1947): 1445.

32. "Court Decision Stresses Church Independence," *Christian Century* 59, no. 10 (December 1952): 1427–28.

33. "Court Decision Stresses Church Independence," 1428.

Christianity a fourth major faith. The loudest (and most successful) objections raised against the resolution were voiced strongly by Carl McIntire, a fundamentalist Presbyterian preacher who had founded, among other things, the Bible Presbyterian Church, a weekly newspaper known as the *Christian Beacon*, and a successful and popular radio ministry. Although McIntire is often omitted in American evangelical history (due to his caustic and dramatic reactions against his opponents), his opposition to the fourth major faith movement occurred after a decade of involving himself in American politics and at a time when anti-Communist fears were still prevalent within America.[34]

When Senator Case first introduced the bill, Communism was not a major concern. As he put it, the bill was "intended as public recognition of the fact that the American citizens of Eastern Orthodox faith constitute a substantial segment of our community, separate from the three major faiths already designated, and justly entitled to consideration in any Federal action or statement related to religious matters."[35] Although Case (and cosponsors, senators Keating of New York and Pell of Rhode Island) might not have understood the bill to be endorsing Eastern Orthodoxy, much less opening the door to Communism, that became precisely the objection to the bill.

McIntire, who had a history of involving himself in political action against "red clergy" (both Orthodox, as in the case of visiting Russian Orthodox hierarchy, and non-Orthodox, as in the case of liberal Protestants), watched congressional proceedings rather closely and responded in a month's time to Case's fourth major faith bill.[36] Although by 1961 he had suffered the setback of the congressional failure to investigate churches for such red clergy, McIntire's objection proved to be enough for Case's bill to die in committee.

34. Markku Ruotsila has recently begun correcting the overly sanitized self-history found in American evangelical scholarship. As Ruotsila noted, "In the six decades of his ministry, Carl McIntire played a key and underappreciated role in shaping fundamentalist Christian opinion on all the key public policy issues of the time." See Markku Ruotsila, "Carl McIntire and the Fundamentalist Origins of the Christian Right," *Church History* 81, no. 2 (June 2012): 379. Ruotsila's assessments of McIntire may be found in a more developed form in *Fighting Fundamentalist: Carl McIntire and the Politicization of American Fundamentalism* (New York: Oxford University Press, 2015).

35. Congressional Record, Senate, February 16, 1961, available in Legislative archives, S. Res. 88 in box 47 for SEN87A-E12 at 8E2/13/5/5.

36. For a summary of McIntire's political actions, which included attempts to block a visit by Russian Orthodox metropolitan Nikolai, see Ruotsila, *Fighting Fundamentalist*, 127-37. As Ruotsila summarized it, "Red clergy, then, were truly everywhere in the latter part of the 1950s if McIntire were to be believed" (131).

In a letter McIntire wrote to one of his political allies, Benjamin Mandel, research director of the Internal Security Sub-Committee,[37] McIntire provided two lines of argumentation. First, he claimed, "The Eastern Orthodox Church is a part of what is known as the Catholic branch." Second, the resolution would allegedly enable "Communist directed units of the Eastern Orthodox Church to have certain advantages with the United States Government." Demonstrating his usual commitment to see things through to the nth degree, McIntire asked for "at least a dozen copies" of the resolution so that it could be taken to the April convention of the American Council of Christian Churches, and to be informed of any hearing on the resolution so that he could attend and voice his objection.[38]

McIntire's letter set the tone for future considerations, and the bill died in committee. His letter was passed along to Senator Eastland, Judiciary Committee chairman, with its own memorandum, asking that it be included in the full committee file. At the same time the committee received the McIntire letter, Senator Case had written, asking that a public hearing be allowed in April, to coincide with the visit to the United States of the premier of Greece, Constantine Karamanlis, but Senator Eastland merely noted that he would discuss it with Senator Dirksen, a fellow committee member, who would get back in touch with Senator Case.[39] No such hearing was ever held.[40] Orthodox themselves feared that anti-Communism could be hindering the committee's decision, and at least two wrote directly to this point, Nicholas I. Borak of New Jersey and Rev. John A. Limberakis, head pastor of Annunciation Greek Orthodox Church in Providence, Rhode Island. Borak wrote to Senator Eastland directly, noting that "with the present intransigent behavior of the Soviet gov't in world affairs, it is hoped that the Orthodoxy bill will be completely disassociated with the government versus religion in this respect."[41] Limberakis

37. McIntire to Mandel, research director, Internal Security Sub-Committee, March 22, 1961, in Legislative archives, S. Res. 88 in box 47 for SEN87A-E12 at 8E2/13/5/5. Mandel, who had been a onetime member of the Communist Party, became a strident opponent of Communism and one of McIntire's political allies and supporters. See, for example, Ruotsila, *Fighting Fundamentalist*, 107.

38. McIntire to Mandel, March 22, 1961. The American Council of Christian Churches was established by McIntire as a reaction to the Federal Council of Churches (now National Council of Churches). Membership in the 1950s neared one million. See Ruotsila, *Fighting Fundamentalist*, 9.

39. See Legislative archives, S. Res. 88 in box 47 for SEN87A-E12 at 8E2/13/5/5.

40. In fact, a handwritten note on Senator Case's letter reads, "Nothing in the past 10 years," suggesting that someone had reviewed the status of the bill as late as 1971.

41. Borak to Eastland, March 30, 1962, available in Legislative archives, S. Res. 88 in box 47 for SEN87A-E12 at 8E2/13/5/5.

wrote his representative, Congressman John E. Fogarty, to urge that the Senate consider the bill not as something that might "cause controversy" but rather as a "moral issue."[42] Senator Eastland wrote to Senator Fogarty, noting that there were no plans to revisit the resolution. The bill would die in committee.

Conclusion

One cannot go so far as to claim that anti-Communism and Carl McIntire killed Senate Resolution 88 on their own. The State Department did point out to the Judiciary Committee that recognizing Orthodoxy might open the door to having to recognize other religious groups, and Senator Dirksen, when pressed on the resolution's status five years later (in 1966), claimed that the resolution could be interpreted as favoring a religion (in light of the recent Supreme Court decision, *Engel v. Vitale*).[43] Nonetheless, anti-Communism and Carl McIntire certainly created a mountain Judiciary refused to climb. Recommending passage of the resolution to the Senate would have meant the committee was willing to take on the anti-Communist feelings that linked Orthodoxy and Communist regimes (as both the *Christian Century* and McIntire had done). It also would have meant the committee believed in the principle of an official "fourth major faith" sincerely enough to take on McIntire and his political allies. In the end, American Orthodox Christians had gone as far to claim religious freedom as they could. From the desperation of self-preservation in Alaska, to taking on the Selective Service in New York, to official recognition as a religion by the Department of Defense in 1955, to designation as a fourth major faith by half the states in the Union, Orthodox Christianity had come a long way. Were it not for anti-Communism and the Cold War, it is conceivable that Orthodoxy, led by the efforts of Archbishop Michael and the Greek Orthodox Archdiocese, might have gone further.

42. Limberakis to Fogarty, August 25, 1961, available in Legislative archives, S. Res. 88 in box 47 for SEN87A-E12 at 8E2/13/5/5.

43. See Brooks Hays, assistant secretary of state, to Eastland, May 22, 1961, available in Legislative archives, S. Res. 88 in box 47 for SEN87A-E12 at 8E2/13/5/5, and "Orthodoxy Gains as Major Faith in United States but Recognition by Congress Unlikely Says Senator Dirksen," *Greek Star*, July 16, 1966, available in AGOA.

Evangelical Approaches

Evangelicals and Empire:
White Conservative Protestants
in US Cold War Politics and Society

Axel R. Schäfer

The rise to global power during the second half of the twentieth century posed significant challenges for a nation that had neither cultivated the imperialist outlook nor developed the permanent military and administrative capacities necessary for sustaining international dominance. America traced its origins back to a struggle against British colonial rule, yet it was now on the verge of becoming a hegemon itself. Whereas the United States had had one of the smallest armies at the beginning of the Second World War, it became the only country that owned, and had indeed used, the most powerful weapon in the world. Having in the past prided itself on avoiding "entangling alliances," the nation was now in charge of constructing an international collective security system. And a country that had a long tradition of limited government and strict civilian control of the military found that its economic fortunes were ever more tied to vast defense expenditures.

Of course, US history is blighted by many instances of colonial and imperialist exploitation and expansion—namely, the global entanglements of slavery, the colonization of the West, warfare against Native Americans, and the acquisition of imperial possessions after the Spanish-American War in 1898. This did not mean, however, that Americans accepted the ideological, institutional, and economic structures required for the exercise of global hegemony. In times of empire, nations are sacralized, power is consolidated, government expands, corporate influence grows, foreign interventions abound, and permanent military mobilization is depicted as a public good. Yet in the United States, these prerequisites of power clashed with deeply embedded traditions of anticolonialism, antistatism, antimonopolism, antimilitarism, exceptionalism, and distrust of centralized control. Indeed, popular attitudes in the immediate postwar years, rather than reflecting a "triumph of internationalism," were marked by the domestic tenacity of isolationist and noninterventionist sentiments. The postwar embrace of America's global role was thus a process marked by extensive contestation and negotiation.[1]

This chapter explores in what ways the conflicted postwar setting opened up new opportunities for conservative Protestants to assert themselves in American politics, society, and culture. For this purpose it maps resurgent evangelicalism onto the ideologies, institutions, political economy, and cultural transformations of World War II and the Cold War. It explores how evangelical interpretations and imagery permeated domestic and foreign policy. It traces the development of new partnerships between evangelical organizations and the federal government. It examines the connection between resurgent evangelicalism and the military-industrial complex. And it looks at evangelicals in relationship to the sociocultural dynamics that undermined established racial hierarchies, gender roles, and sexual norms in postwar America.

The analysis of the relationship between neoevangelicalism and American empire-building reveals how divided and contradictory postwar conservative Protestantism was. Evangelicals sanctified the global role of the "redeemer nation" but also remained ardent critics of US Cold War policy. They railed against the state but were the beneficiaries of large-scale federal spending. They wholeheartedly promoted consumer culture and liberal capitalism but simultaneously held on to the traditional moral norms that were undermined by materialism and free marketeering. They emerged as both staunch advocates of racial division and gender hierarchies at home, and supporters of antiracist and anti-imperialist causes abroad. They were nationalist, militarist, capitalist, and consumerist—but also separatist, antistatist, antiliberal, and moralistic.

Rather than being a mark of weakness, however, these tensions and conflicts constituted the strength of postwar evangelicalism because they helped the movement position itself as a crucial cultural arbiter in American society at a time when the country's postwar role was not yet ideologically, institutionally, economically, and culturally established. Evangelicalism was perfectly positioned for this task, because it was the dominant cultural tradition in the

1. On this issue, see Christopher McKnight Nichols, "The Enduring Power of Isolationism: An Historical Perspective," *Orbis* 57 (Summer 2013): 390–407; T. Jeremy Gunn, *Spiritual Weapons: The Cold War and the Forging of an American National Religion* (Westport, CT: Praeger, 2009), 23; James Sparrow, *Warfare State: World War II Americans and the Age of Big Government* (New York: Oxford University Press, 2011); Nancy Beck Young, *Why We Fight: Congress and the Politics of World War II* (Lawrence: University Press of Kansas, 2013); Michael Hunt, *Ideology and U.S. Foreign Policy* (New Haven: Yale University Press, 2009); and Walter Hixson, *The Myth of American Diplomacy: National Identity and US Foreign Policy* (New Haven: Yale University Press, 2008).

United States that had centuries of experience in negotiating the very conflict between empire-building and anticolonialist, antistatist, and antimilitarist impulses. As a result, it became an arena where conflicts over the new global role of the United States were symbolically negotiated or mediated.[2]

Constructing Empire, Generating Revival

World War II and the Cold War period witnessed a broad-based resurgence of evangelicalism in mainstream American society and simultaneous efforts by policy makers to instrumentalize religion for the domestic legitimation and global assertion of empire. On the one hand, a new generation of so-called neoevangelicals laid the foundation for the revival of white conservative Protestantism as a significant cultural and political force in American society. Seeking to show that evangelical Christianity was "an intellectually viable and vibrant faith and not a suspect cult," they sought to establish themselves as a "third force" in American Protestantism.[3] In their eyes, prewar fundamentalism had made the mistake of abandoning social engagement to secularists, while World War II had exposed the shallowness of modernist relativism and postmillennialism.

The formation of the National Association of Evangelicals (NAE) in 1942, Fuller Theological Seminary in 1947, and the magazine *Christianity Today* in 1956 gave institutional shape to this revival. Under their auspices, leading neoevangelicals, such as Carl F. H. Henry, organized lobbying efforts in Washington, set up a clearinghouse for legislative campaigns, expanded relief and missionary work, spawned the powerful National Religious Broadcasters, and fostered the training of conservative Christians for positions in government.[4]

2. See Emily Conroy-Krutz, *Christian Imperialism: Converting the World in the Early American Republic* (Ithaca, NY: Cornell University Press, 2015); Heather Curtis, *Holy Humanitarians: American Evangelicals and Global Aid* (Cambridge, MA: Harvard University Press, 2018); Emily Rosenberg, *Spreading the American Dream: American Economic and Cultural Expansion, 1890–1945* (New York: Hill and Wang, 1982); Hugh Heclo, *Christianity and American Democracy* (Cambridge, MA: Harvard University Press, 2007).

3. Carl F. H. Henry, *Confessions of a Theologian: An Autobiography* (Waco: Word, 1986), 119.

4. Carl F. H. Henry, *The Uneasy Conscience of Modern Fundamentalism* (Grand Rapids: Eerdmans, 1947), 16, 20, 29, 32, 76. On postwar neoevangelicalism, see George Marsden, *Understanding Fundamentalism and Evangelicalism* (Grand Rapids: Eerdmans, 1991), 66–70, 100–101; James Davison Hunter, *American Evangelicalism: Conservative Religion and the Quandary of Modernity* (New Brunswick, NJ: Rutgers University Press, 1983), 41–45; Nathan O. Hatch

Today evangelicalism is no longer the province of backcountry Bible-thumpers waging war on the evils of modernity. Instead, it is a technologically savvy, commercially pioneering, politically engaged, and internationally active movement that has shaped socioeconomic transformations, cultural shifts, political realignments, and state-building processes.[5]

On the other hand, the neoevangelical drive to re-Christianize America was matched by equally ardent efforts by postwar policy makers to engage in the "deliberate and managed use of societal resources to stimulate a religious revival in the late 1940s and 1950s." Eager to launch spiritual weapons against America's foes, a wide range of politicians, military leaders, captains of industry, and powerful private individuals created a "spiritual-industrial complex" in boardrooms, advertising agencies, TV studios, and government offices that harnessed the power of religion to the interests of the state.[6] Wartime and Cold War policy makers knew that religious belief in a just cause, a worldview based on a clear distinction between good and evil, and strong enemy images were effective mobilizing tools at a time when the country's postwar role was not yet ideologically and culturally established. By depicting the war and the Cold War as patriotic battles against enemies who needed to be defeated not only militarily but also spiritually and culturally, they tied national security to a renewed commitment to traditional religion. "What is our battle against communism if it is not a fight against anti-God and a belief in the Almighty?," Dwight Eisenhower asked, concluding that "when God comes in, communism has to go."[7]

and Michael S. Hamilton, "Taking the Measure of the Evangelical Resurgence, 1942–1992," in *Reckoning with the Past: Historical Essays on American Evangelicalism from the Institute for the Study of American Evangelicals*, ed. D. G. Hart (Grand Rapids: Baker, 1995), 395–412.

5. For recent books on the transformation of evangelicalism, see Darren T. Dochuk, *From Bible Belt to Sunbelt: Plain Folk Religion, Grassroots Politics, and the Rise of Evangelical Conservatism* (New York: Norton, 2011); Daniel K. Williams, *God's Own Party: The Making of the Christian Right* (New York: Oxford University Press, 2010); Steven P. Miller, *Billy Graham and the Rise of the Republican South* (Philadelphia: University of Pennsylvania Press, 2009); John G. Turner, *Bill Bright and Campus Crusade for Christ: The Renewal of Evangelicalism in Postwar America* (Chapel Hill: University of North Carolina Press, 2008); Larry Eskridge and Mark A. Noll, eds., *More Money, More Ministry: Money and Evangelicals in Recent North American History* (Grand Rapids: Eerdmans, 2000); Axel R. Schäfer, *Countercultural Conservatives: American Evangelicalism from the Postwar Revival to the New Christian Right* (Madison: University of Wisconsin Press, 2011).

6. Jonathan P. Herzog, *The Spiritual-Industrial Complex: America's Religious Battle against Communism in the Early Cold War* (New York: Oxford University Press, 2011), quote on 6.

7. Eisenhower, quoted in Richard V. Pierard and Robert D. Lindner, *Civil Religion and the Presidency* (Grand Rapids: Zondervan Academie Books, 1988), 189, 197–98. On religion and

In turn, evangelicals enjoyed unprecedented access to the corridors of power. Billy Graham's close relationship with Eisenhower symbolized the movement's newfound stature. Graham successfully urged Ike to become the first president ever to be baptized in office, and ensured that he became a member of an evangelical congregation.[8] This connection was part of a larger set of religio-political contacts in the 1950s. In February 1957, Vice President Richard Nixon enthusiastically promoted Graham's New York Crusade at the annual International Christian Leadership (ICL) meeting in Washington. ICL, led by Abraham Vereide, had long cultivated ties between political, military, business, and religious leaders through breakfast prayer meetings, conferences, and informal gatherings. Among its members were close allies of President Eisenhower, such as Kansas senator Frank Carlson and Minnesota congressman Walter H. Judd. ICL also included Chief Justice Earl Warren, Deputy Secretary of Defense Robert Anderson, and influential Missouri senator Stuart Symington.[9]

Nonetheless, the direct link between actual policies and evangelical beliefs has been difficult to prove. The Eisenhower-Graham axis did not translate into an evangelical-style Cold War policy. Nor did recurrent evangelical demands for "an aggressive spiritual-moral international policy" and strong support for John Foster Dulles's "roll back" ideology divert Ike from focusing on collective security and containment. In the words of historian William Miller, Eisenhower was "a fervent believer in a very vague religion."[10] As Ike famously remarked in 1952, "our form of government has no sense unless it

---

politics during and after World War II, see also Matthew Avery Sutton, *American Apocalypse: A History of Modern Evangelicalism* (Cambridge, MA: Harvard University Press, 2014); Kevin Kruse, *One Nation under God: How Corporate America Invented Christian America* (New York: Basic Books, 2015).

8. Richard V. Pierard, "Billy Graham and the U.S. Presidency," *Journal of Church and State* 22 (Winter 1980): 116, 118. See also *Just as I Am: The Autobiography of Billy Graham* (San Francisco: Harper, 1997), 188–206.

9. Anne C. Loveland, *American Evangelicals and the U.S. Military, 1942–1993* (Baton Rouge: Louisiana State University Press, 1996), 38; William Martin, *With God on Our Side: The Rise of the Religious Right in America* (New York: Broadway Books, 1996), 30–31.

10. William Lee Miller, *Piety along the Potomac: Notes on Politics and Morals in the Fifties* (Boston: Houghton Mifflin, 1964), 34; see also 19, 42–43; "Where Do We Go from Here?," *Christianity Today*, November 12, 1956, 17; Pierard and Linder, *Civil Religion*, 199, 184. For good discussions of Eisenhower and foreign policy, see Robert R. Bowie and Richard H. Immerman, *Waging Peace: How Eisenhower Shaped an Enduring Cold War* (New York: Oxford University Press, 1998); Campbell Craig, *Destroying the Village: Eisenhower and Thermonuclear War* (New York: Columbia University Press, 1998); and Fred J. Greenstein, *The Hidden-Hand Presidency: Eisenhower as Leader* (New York: Basic Books, 1982).

is founded in a deeply felt religious faith—and I don't care what it is."[11] Skepticism about overrating religion is also warranted by the fact that evangelicalism is a highly diverse and decentralized movement. Donald Dayton even called the term an "essentially contested concept" and suggested doing away with it completely.[12] In regard to foreign policy, a wide range of attitudes was represented in the movement. Whereas Harold John Ockenga, the first NAE president, demanded an "aggressive diplomacy . . . even if this means using atomic weapons," a 1956 *Christianity Today* poll of evangelical clergy showed significant support for "world security built on a trusting spiritual level, and less on military spending."[13]

In short, the focus on individuals and personal contacts doesn't tell the whole story of the confluence of religion and politics during the Cold War. Instead, we need to look more closely at the way in which wartime and postwar politics, institution building, economics, and culture intersected with the evangelical resurgence. In particular, four ideological, institutional, economic, and sociocultural contexts facilitated a new relationship between conservative Protestantism and governance: the crisis of liberalism, the government's need for administrative capacities for the exercise of global might, the rise of the military-industrial complex in the Sun Belt, and the mounting challenges to established race and gender hierarchies.

Evangelicals and Cold War Ideology: The Crisis of Liberalism

In many history textbooks, the triumph of Western liberalism over the totalitarian threat is depicted as the decisive legacy of World War II. What is often missed in this scenario, however, is that the war and the postwar period ushered in a time of profound questioning of modern liberalism in American

11. On this famous quote and its various uses, see Patrick Henry, "'And I Don't Care What It Is': The Tradition-History of a Civil Religion Proof Text," *Journal of the American Academy of Religion* 49 (March 1981): 35–49.

12. Donald W. Dayton, "Some Doubts about the Usefulness of the Category 'Evangelical,'" in *The Variety of Evangelicalism*, ed. Donald W. Dayton and Robert K. Johnston (Knoxville: University of Tennessee Press, 1991), 245. However, I would agree with Mark Noll that the term retains its usefulness in designating a particular strand of Protestants located somewhere between fundamentalists and mainline moderates. See Mark A. Noll, *The Old Religion in a New World: The History of North American Christianity* (Grand Rapids: Eerdmans, 2002), 155.

13. Harold John Ockenga, "The Communist Issue Today," *Christianity Today*, May 22, 1961, 12; "Where Do We Go from Here?," 17.

society, particularly its contours since the Progressive Era and the New Deal. Amidst total war, mass genocide, and the threat of global annihilation, leading secular and religious thinkers, such as Reinhold Niebuhr, Hannah Arendt, and George Kennan, criticized the liberal, pragmatist, and Enlightenment-based tendency to interpret evil as the result of the ignorance, rather than the wickedness, of man. These ideas matched to a significant extent evangelicalism's efforts to recover the concept of evil as an analytical category and its disdain for the "anthropocentric optimism" of the Enlightenment.

Seeking to counter the long-standing trend toward understanding democracy and American liberty as the result of secular values and pragmatist ethics, evangelical thinkers such as Carl Henry, Edward Carnell, and Dirk Jellema insisted that "the controlling ideas of modern philosophy . . . are not nearly as relevant to the judgement hour of western civilization as are the revelational views of man." Mingling perceptive criticism with belligerent polemics, Carl Henry maintained that, at best, liberalism's belief in humankind as inherently good and advancing was useless in understanding totalitarianism. At worst, its naturalism and assumption of man's ultimate animality made people susceptible to the totalitarian viruses of the twentieth century. Invoking in vivid language the cataclysmic doom of the period from 1914 to 1945, he concluded that only a firm belief in transcendent moral principles rooted in spiritual conversion could turn the Western concept of freedom into an intellectual potion powerful enough to ward off the threats of Fascism and Communism.[14]

Evangelicals also used the totalitarian nightmares of the twentieth century to reestablish orthodox eschatological, millennial, and prophetic themes as valid and coherent interpretive frames for life in the shadow of World War II. While most prewar Americans had found concepts such as the antichrist, Armageddon, and the apocalypse rather arcane, linking these terms to the Communist menace and the threat of impending nuclear warfare made them very real and palpable. Among the interpretations conservative Protestants advanced was the prophecy belief that identified Russia with the biblical Gog and viewed Communism as a false religion set up by Satan to both mimic and mock God. Their opposition to the United Nations was theologically informed by biblical readings that viewed "world government" as a sign of the impending advent of the antichrist. And they saw the founding of the state of Israel in

---

14. Carl F. H. Henry, *Remaking the Modern Mind* (Grand Rapids: Eerdmans, 1946), 20–22, 25–26, 267. Carl F. H. Henry, "The Fragility of Freedom in the West," *Christianity Today*, October 15, 1956, 8–9; Carl F. H. Henry, "The Christian-Pagan West," *Christianity Today*, December 24, 1956, 3–5.

1948 as a sign of the fulfillment of biblical prophecies, turning themselves from anti-Semites into some of the staunchest allies of the Jewish state.[15]

The postwar crisis of liberalism was not solely confined to the intellectual realm, however. It also manifested itself in the political arena. Indeed, the politics of the Cold War were liberal only in a very limited sense of the word. Already in the run-up to World War I, Woodrow Wilson had warned that "war is autocratic"; he feared that it promoted centralized government, big business control, intolerant patriotism, and the militarization of society. After World War II, illiberal politics found its most avid expression in the anti-Communist witch hunts of the Red Scare, starting in the early 1940s and culminating in the McCarthyist excesses of the early 1950s.

Evangelicals positioned themselves at the forefront of the anti-Communist crusade. Billy Graham declared in 1949 in Los Angeles that "Communism is not only an economic interpretation of life—Communism is a religion that is inspired, directed, and motivated by the Devil himself who has declared war against Almighty God."[16] Likewise, many Southern evangelicals "recognized in World War II the chance for southern fundamentalism, the South, and American defense to be fused in one common mission."[17] They used virulent anti-Communism to sanctify a hawkish foreign policy and to parade their patriotic credentials. Indeed, historian Dianne Kirby has suggested that, rather than becoming a bridge across the ideological divide, as Franklin D. Roosevelt had hoped, religion became one of the key means to persecute domestic opponents and to define the Cold War as a battle between good and evil.[18]

Taken together, the vilification of liberalism, the application of biblical interpretations to the world situation, and the avid pursuit of anti-Communism paved the way for a new kind of public and political engagement for conserva-

15. See Paul Boyer, *When Time Shall Be No More: Prophecy Belief in Modern American Culture* (Cambridge, MA: Harvard University Press, 1992), xii; Angela M. Lahr, *Millennial Dreams and Apocalyptic Nightmares: The Cold War Origins of Political Evangelicalism* (New York: Oxford University Press, 2007); Jason W. Stevens, *God-Fearing and Free: A Spiritual History of America's Cold War* (Cambridge, MA: Harvard University Press, 2010); Raymond Haberski Jr., *God and War: American Civil Religion since 1945* (New Brunswick, NJ: Rutgers University Press, 2012).

16. Graham, quoted in Uta Balbier, "The World Congress on Evangelism 1966 in Berlin: US Evangelicalism, Cultural Dominance, and Global Challenges," *Journal of American Studies*, 51 (November 2017): 1186–87.

17. Dochuk, *From Bible Belt to Sunbelt*, 47.

18. Dianne Kirby, "From Bridge to Divide: East-West Relations and Christianity during the Second World War and Early Cold War," *International History Review* 36 (September 2014): 721–44.

tive Protestants. In particular, it once again synchronized theological heritages and church practices with national ideologies in a manner that typifies civil religion. Evangelical teachings, while repudiating liberalism, simultaneously promoted a religious sanctification of American-style liberal capitalist democracy; biblical literalism conveyed the immediate political relevance of the Bible; and anti-Communism helped transform pietism into religious jingoism. In a sermon given in Los Angeles in 1949, Graham observed that "Western culture and its fruits had its foundation in the Bible, the word of God, and in the revivals of the Seventeenth and Eighteenth Centuries. Communism, on the other hand, has decided against God, against Christ, against the Bible, and against all religion."[19]

This blurring of the boundaries between political, spiritual, and patriotic identities was particularly apparent in the way evangelical rhetoric changed the traditional conversion narrative from a heart-wrenching spiritual transformation into a fervent sanctification of liberal capitalism and America's "providential" rise to global power. "If you would be a true patriot, then become a Christian. If you would be a loyal American, then become a loyal Christian," Graham exclaimed.[20] And Harold John Ockenga declared: "Instead of obscuring and depreciating the American dream which has built this noble society we ought to exalt the elements of it." Likewise, viewing the United States as a country blessed by God, a growing number of conservative Protestants identified the creation of world peace with Pax Americana based on American ideological, military, and economic might. "Firmness must be backed up by military strength and force," Ockenga insisted.[21]

Nonetheless, conservative Protestantism did not simply provide convenient spiritual legitimacy for the nation's Cold War policy. Indeed, "much as evangelicals loathed communism," William Inboden has noted, "they would not support what they regarded as compromising alliances with Catholic powers in the Cold War cause."[22] In fact, many evangelicals denounced American foreign policy when it supported Italian Catholics, shored up Franco's Catholic regime in Spain, or was not doing enough about attacks on Protestants in Colombia. They also retained a deeply apocalyptic, premillennialist, and anti-liberal view of world events that frequently combined paranoid invective and

19. Billy Graham, *Revival in Our Time: The Story of the Billy Graham Evangelistic Campaigns* (Wheaton, IL: Van Kampen Press, 1950), 124. See also Stephen J. Whitfield, *The Culture of the Cold War* (Baltimore: Johns Hopkins University Press, 1991), 77-91.

20. Graham, quoted in Loveland, *American Evangelicals*, 37.

21. Ockenga, "The Communist Issue Today," 12.

22. Inboden, *Religion and American Foreign Policy*, 73.

an obscure propheticism. Their foreign policy emphasis was less on collective security and more on "regime change." As the "two-star evangelical" lieutenant general William K. Harrison put it, "what Marx, Lenin, and Stalin needed was not simply an exposure to the 'Christian ethic' but to be 'born again.'"[23] In the same vein, evangelicals were for the most part conservative neoisolationists—that is, they vigorously opposed the United Nations, negotiations with the Communist world, and the admission of mainland China to the UN.[24] In the 1950s the NAE, for example, supported a neoisolationist constitutional amendment sponsored by Ohio senator John Bricker. This amendment, had it passed, would have placed severe restrictions on treaties and executive agreements entered into by the US government.

The strident religious nationalism of the Cold War period also failed to drown out evangelical voices critical of America's corruptibility and worldliness. A "vision more critical of nation and self-interest," George Marsden reminds us, "is an equally venerable part of a heritage that goes back at least to Roger Williams."[25] Throughout the 1940s, 1950s, and 1960s, significant groups within the evangelical movement expressed pacifist sentiments, retained a strong aversion to civil religion, and rejected the spiritual sanctification of US foreign policy. They called for "less emphasis on bombs and materials for war," more international disarmament negotiations, and even efforts to strengthen international relations through the UN.[26] Particularly the Southern Baptist Convention (SBC), which did not join the NAE, continued to be moderate or even liberal on international issues.[27] Even some of the neoevangelical trailblazers within the NAE, such as Carl Henry, urged evangelicals to address issues such as "aggressive warfare, racial hatred and intolerance, the liquor traffic, and the exploitation of labor or management."[28] Other conservatives, such as *Christianity Today* editor Harold Lindsell, insisted in 1967 that the

23. William K. Harrison, "Christianity and Peace in Our Day," *Christianity Today*, October 29, 1956, 16.

24. See Alfred O. Hero Jr., *American Religious Groups View Foreign Policy: Trends in Rank-and-File Opinion, 1937–1969* (Durham, NC: Duke University Press, 1973), 6–7, 13, 119–26. Evangelicalism's prewar internationalist attitude was linked to its predominance in the South, a region with a strong military tradition, a vested interest in freer trade, and a white population largely of Anglo-Saxon descent. In contrast, much of the postwar neoisolationist impetus came from Midwestern evangelicals, who spearheaded the neoevangelical revival and dominated the NAE.

25. Marsden, *Understanding Fundamentalism and Evangelicalism*, 97.

26. "Where Do We Go from Here?," 17.

27. See Hero, *American Religious Groups*, 120–25, 160–65, 172–75.

28. Carl F. H. Henry, *Uneasy Conscience*, 17.

church should avoid becoming "the voice of those who have managed to seize control of the power structures."[29]

In short, conservative Protestants in the United States failed to settle on a common foreign policy vision.[30] The concept of evil that evangelicals were so keen to reintroduce into the political debate exemplified the tensions that divided the movement. On the one hand, the obsession with defeating the Communist "other" translated into the uncritical acceptance of America's social order, since all criticism beyond a certain narrowly defined boundary was characterized as aiding the enemy. On the other hand, recognizing evil as part of the human condition stressed the need for humility, vigilance, and awareness of hubris, pride, and human limitations. It nurtured a focus on eternal values, not the national interest. Understanding the Cold War not simply as a political, military, or economic conflict, but as a spiritual struggle—as evangelicals did—thus also called for a serious confrontation with America's own unexorcised ghosts and moral pitfalls.[31] It balanced triumphalist notions of moral superiority with an awareness of the corruptions of power.

In summation, as evangelicals grafted prophetic and premillennialist imagery onto the wartime and Cold War scenario, they resurrected notions of the redeemer nation and the covenanted people, and depicted America's new global power as part of the biblical drama. Blending religious and patriotic practices, they sanctified America's social and political order, spiritualized the wartime and Cold War struggles via biblically based interpretations of US power, and redefined anti-Communism as a Christian duty. Nonetheless, many evangelicals, reading world events through a biblical lens, remained ardent critics of US Cold War policy. They were staunchly unilateralist, if not isolationist; they opposed the recognition of China and ridiculed the UN and "world government"; they attacked the alleged Cath-

---

29. Harold Lindsell, "An Evangelical Evaluation of the Relationship between Churches and the State in the United States," Consultation on the Church in a Secular World, October 11–13, 1967, 14–15, NAE Records, Wheaton College Archives and Special Collections, Buswell Memorial Library, Wheaton College, Illinois (hereafter cited as NAE Records).

30. Sarah Miller-Davenport, "Their Blood Shall Not Be Shed in Vain: Evangelical Missionaries and the Search for God and Country in Post–World War II Asia," *Journal of American History*, March 2013, 1110.

31. On critical voices within the evangelical fold, see David R. Swartz, *Moral Minority: The Evangelical Left in an Age of Conservatism* (Philadelphia: University of Pennsylvania Press, 2012); Robert Booth Fowler, *A New Engagement: Evangelical Political Thought, 1966–1976* (Grand Rapids: Eerdmans, 1987), 30–31; Augustus Cerillo Jr., "A Survey of Recent Evangelical Social Thought," *Christian Scholar's Review* 5 (1976): 277; Schäfer, *Countercultural Conservatives*, 69–105.

olic infiltration of US foreign policy; and they issued urgent calls to repent, fight materialism, and nurture one's inner spirituality. Despite their often rabid anti-Communism, unapologetic patriotism, and emphasis on a strong military, conservative Protestants often remained Christians first and Americans second. They were less interested in instilling democratic or capitalist values than in converting souls, and frequently expressed discomfort with exporting American secular culture. In short, they were both accommodationist and adversarial, custodial and marginal, attached to the "New Rome" and to the "New World Israel."

Evangelicals and the Institutions of Empire

The needs of empire were not just ideological, but also administrative. In particular, postwar planners faced the problem of the systematic underfunding of the foreign policy infrastructure during a time of expansion of international involvement. In addressing this dilemma, however, they were hampered by the growing political backlash against the Depression-era interventionist state. Although military mobilization during World War II had relied upon New Deal expertise, by 1942 a coalition of Republicans and Southern Democrats in Congress had begun to dismantle many of FDR's flagship agencies. Moreover, the unfolding Red Scare targeted many of the socially progressive advocates of 1930s-style integrative and redistributive public policies.[32]

Caught between the need for "big government" for the effective exercise of global power and the growing hostility to public control, Cold War policy makers had their work cut out for them. What they ended up constructing was quite remarkable: a vast administrative state that hid the expansion of the federal government behind a "smokescreen of anti-statism" (Michael Sherry). For this purpose they relied upon an arrangement that had historically been part of the political economy of expansion: cooperation between nongovernmental and state actors. Forsaking New Deal–style redistribution and direct public control, influential "vital center" liberals in the 1940s, such as Oscar Ewing and Leon Keyserling, designed policies that made federal funds available to private

32. On public policies and the backlash against the New Deal, see Alan Brinkley, *The End of Reform: New Deal Liberalism in Recession and War* (New York: Knopf, 1995); Richard Polenberg, *War and Society: The United States, 1941–1945* (Westport, CT: Greenwood Press, 1980); Michael S. Sherry, *In the Shadow of War: The United States since the 1930s* (New Haven: Yale University Press, 1995); and Alan Wolfe, *America's Impasse: The Rise and Fall of the Politics of Growth* (New York: Random House, 1980).

businesses and nonprofit organizations via subsidies, tax exemptions, loans, vouchers, grants-in-aid, and purchase-of-service agreements.[33]

Foreign aid in particular exemplified this quintessential Cold War arrangement by linking the expansion of government to the growth of religious agencies in the pursuit of humanitarian aid, commercial access, and containment. The main postwar church-state funding ties in foreign aid developed in the aftermath of the federal government's decision to fund ocean freight costs in 1947; to provide US surplus food distribution abroad under the Agricultural Act of 1949 and the 1954 Food for Peace legislation; and to offer international technical assistance under Truman's Point Four proposals, which later developed into the Agency for International Development (AID) program. In 1948 a subcommittee of the House Committee on Foreign Affairs acknowledged that religious voluntary agencies should be seen as "an essential counterpart of foreign assistance programs."[34] By the early 1950s, the share of revenue from federal sources was greater for religious aid agencies than for secular ones, and from 1955 to 1966, federal shares for both averaged 58 percent.[35]

One of the most striking aspects of this evolving state-nongovernmental relationship in foreign aid is that it integrated a significant part of the evangelical movement into the funding networks that underlay Cold War statebuilding. Evangelical participation in these funding arrangements, however, came about rather hesitantly. Many conservative Protestants remained outspoken critics of the foreign aid program well into the 1950s. Brandishing both separationist and anti-Catholic rhetoric, *Christianity Today* maintained in 1958

33. Sherry, *In the Shadow of War*, 75, 78. See also Brian Balough, *A Government out of Sight: The Mystery of National Authority in Nineteenth-Century America* (New York: Cambridge University Press, 2009); Peter Dobkin Hall, "The Welfare State and the Careers of Public and Private Institutions since 1945," in *Charity, Philanthropy, and Civility in American History*, ed. Lawrence J. Friedman and Mark D. McGarvie (New York: Cambridge University Press, 2003), 363–83; Donald T. Critchlow and Charles H. Parker, eds., *With Us Always: A History of Private Charity and Public Welfare* (Lanham, MD: Rowman and Littlefield, 1998); Axel Schäfer, *Piety and Public Funding: Evangelicals and the State in Modern America* (Philadelphia: University of Pennsylvania Press, 2012).

34. Fowler Hamilton to Clinton P. Anderson, November 9, 1962, NAE Records. Hamilton cites Department of State, Agency for International Development, "Involvement of Religious Affiliated Institutions in the U.S. Foreign Aid Program" (1962), NAE Records.

35. Rachel M. McCleary and Robert J. Barro, "U.S.-Based Private Voluntary Organizations: Religious and Secular PVOs Engaged in International Relief & Development, 1939–2004," NBER Working Paper No. 12238, May 2006, 3, http://www.nber.org/papers/w12238.pdf; Bruce Nichols, *The Uneasy Alliance: Religion, Refugee Work, and U.S. Foreign Policy* (New York: Oxford University Press, 1988), 208–10.

that "ecclesiastical control of foreign aid would turn this program into a power tool of the Roman hierarchy."[36] Carl Henry thundered that foreign aid led down the garden path of big government, breached the separation of church and state, constituted an undue tax burden, delegated too much control to the UN, and had been hijacked by the Catholic Church. In his view, it was driven by commercial self-interest, a desire for military strength, and "the outworn optimism of the liberal social gospel."[37]

Although the NAE was in the forefront of opposition to foreign aid, it increasingly faced a dilemma: other evangelical groups, such as the Seventh-Day Adventists and the Salvation Army, were using their overseas networks for the distribution of government surplus food. More importantly, Catholic Relief Services, which had become the largest private relief agency in the world by the 1950s, received over 50 percent of its supplies from the State Department's International Cooperation Agency in 1958, threatening the survival of Protestant aid organizations.[38] The crucial factor in the development of closer ties, however, was that conservative Protestants were increasingly aware that, despite their initial fears, government funding facilitated evangelical agency growth without interfering with spiritual witnessing. Carl Henry, for example, noted that "the Point Four program has indirectly furthered some aspects of Christian missionary effort."[39] In the same vein, World Relief Corporation (WRC) chairman Christian N. Hostetter noted in a 1963 review that in most cases "the entire operation of the relief program rests in the hands of the church agency."[40]

The result was that evangelicals had a change of heart in regard to foreign aid funding while still adhering to the traditional mantra of church-state separation. In the end, they no longer deployed separatist rhetoric to rail against government support, but used it to shore up their spiritualized foreign aid work within the framework of a growing administrative state. Republican congressman Walter H. Judd admonished *Christianity Today* readers that in the fight against Communism, the main significance of religious foreign aid was not to replace government efforts, but to "give meaning to, and put heart

36. "Pressures Rise for Federal Handouts," *Christianity Today*, May 12, 1958, 22.

37. [Carl F. H. Henry], "The Spirit of Foreign Policy," *Christianity Today*, April 29, 1957, 20–22.

38. Nichols, *Uneasy Alliance*, 92–93, 168–69, 200–206.

39. [Carl F. H. Henry], "Eisenhower, Khrushchev and History's Inevitable Course," *Christianity Today*, October 12, 1959, 26.

40. C. N. Hostetter Jr., "Government Overseas Programs and the Churches" (paper given at the NAE National Conference on Church-State Relations, March 6–8, 1963, 5, NAE Records).

and soul into the government programs," which "administer, but rarely do they minister."[41] Setting aside his previous concerns, Carl Henry called for spiritualized foreign aid regardless of the size and role of the state.[42] The long-term successes were obvious: a 1973 WRC agenda paper, for example, showed that recipients of government surplus food in Korea "were exposed to the Gospel in many different ways and their compensation and reward was WRC provided surplus food, clothing, vitamins, materials, equipment, and so forth."[43]

In turn, the number and size of evangelical aid agencies increased, and they also became more reliant upon public funds. Whereas evangelicals in 1940 had composed only 10 percent of religious aid agencies, by 2004 they constituted 48 percent. Seventh-Day Adventists, the Salvation Army, WRC (later renamed World Relief), and World Vision in particular became major players in government-funded distribution of surplus foods, hospital building, land reclamation programs, and the like. Evangelical agencies received an unprecedented average of 34 percent of their income from federal sources between 1955 and 1967. By the 1990s, only a quarter of evangelical international aid organizations received no government funds, as opposed to one-half of mainline Protestant agencies.[44]

Meanwhile, on the home front, evangelicals gained influence in the armed forces as the federal government sought to shore up the moral backbone of recruits via anti-Communist training programs, military chaplains, and church building on military sites. As historian Anne Loveland has shown, during World War II many in the upper echelons of the military establishment blamed alcohol abuse, venereal diseases, and other related ills on the "spiritual illiteracy" of young soldiers. These concerns prompted the Truman administration to implement "an unprecedented religious and moral welfare program," which included compulsory character education, increased opportunities for religious activities, and an enhanced role for chaplains in military training. In 1951, Secretary of Defense George C. Marshall made moral training a requirement

41. Walter H. Judd, "World Issues and the Christian," *Christianity Today*, June 23, 1958, 8.

42. [Carl F. H. Henry], "Spirit of Foreign Policy," 21.

43. "Agenda—Miscellaneous," Executive Committee of the World Relief Commission, November 13–14, 1973, 9, NAE Records.

44. McCleary and Barro, "U.S.-Based Private Voluntary Organizations," 11, 13–15; Stephen V. Monsma, *When Sacred and Secular Mix: Religious Nonprofit Organizations and Public Money* (Lanham, MD: Rowman and Littlefield, 2000), 10, 72–73. However, Catholics and ecumenical Protestants continued to receive the largest share of their funds from federal sources, averaging 70 and 65 percent, respectively, between the mid-1950s and the late 1980s.

for young servicemen. Many of the lectures and publications in the character guidance program promoted Bible-based morality, faith, and religious worship as a necessary part of service to the "covenant nation."[45]

Evangelicals were in the forefront of this new missionary activism among military personnel. The NAE's Commission on Chaplaincy and Service to Military Personnel, for example, led evangelization campaigns and succeeded in converting thousands of troops. This crusade received help from denominations outside of the NAE, such as the Southern Baptist Convention, and from parachurch organizations, such as the Officers' Christian Fellowship and the Navigators.[46] These collaborations also further strengthened ties between evangelicals and politics. The shared commitment to the Cold War mission was the background upon which the career of one of the most influential evangelicals in the Pentagon unfolded. John C. Broger was put in charge of implementing the Pentagon's program to fight the "spiritual illiteracy" of young soldiers and to promote their commitment to his concept of "militant liberty." As deputy director of Armed Forces Information and Education (AFIE) since 1956, and as the agency's director since 1961, Broger promoted ties to conservative and patriotic organizations, such as the American Heritage Foundation, as well as to extreme right-wing organizations, such as the John Birch Society. Broger also directed the NAE's Freedom Studies project, and his materials were widely distributed via International Christian Leadership.[47]

Finally, the growth of evangelical mission work abroad increasingly involved conservative Protestants in Cold War politics. World War II and the postwar years, as mentioned earlier, proved a particular boon for the expansion of evangelical overseas missions and aid. By the 1980s, 90 percent of American Protestant missionaries in Africa were evangelicals. From the viewpoint of policy makers, missionaries were a primary source of knowledge. In contrast to diplomatic and military personnel, missionaries established long-term and intimate ties with foreign cultures, were fluent in their languages, interacted closely with native populations, and were present in areas that were initially peripheral to US interests. In turn, as historian Philip Dow has shown, a range

45. Loveland, *American Evangelicals*, 10; see also 11–13.

46. Martin, *With God on Our Side*, 28; Taylor, "NAE Celebrates 30 Years"; Clyde W. Taylor, "NAE Celebrates 30 Years of Service," *Action*, Spring 1972, 8–12.

47. Loveland, *American Evangelicals*, 10–13, 56–64. On Broger's involvement with the NAE, see, for example, Clyde W. Taylor, "Report of the Office of Public Affairs to the Executive Committee," National Association of Evangelicals, Wheaton, Illinois, June 12, 1962, NAE Records; and Clyde W. Taylor, "Report of the Office of Public Affairs to the NAE Board of Administration," Chicago, October 7, 1963, NAE Records.

of formal and informal exchanges, including picnics, holidays, sports events, and hunting trips, linked missionaries and primary intelligence agents, who often lacked other viable intelligence sources.[48]

Africa in particular was a continent where an established evangelical missionary presence rather suddenly coalesced with Cold War government interests, and evangelical missionaries became a key link between religious and diplomatic circles. Among the most active organizations with evangelical leanings in Africa were the Billy Graham Evangelistic Association (BGEA), Moral Re-Armament (MRA), and ICL. ICL's Addis Ababa chapter provided an important contact point for Ethiopian elites, US policy makers, and evangelical missionaries. In particular, Senator Frank Carlson, Eisenhower's right-hand man, encouraged close ties between the Ethiopian ICL and Washington congressional chapters. Likewise, the influence of MRA missionaries, such as William Close (father of actress Glenn Close), combined "evangelical missionary ethos, zealous anticommunism, and connections to the international diplomatic elite."[49]

Nonetheless, the growing nexus between missionaries and policy makers did not simply turn evangelicalism into an extended arm of American hegemonic interests. Indeed, in an era of decolonization, many American Protestant missionaries, having interacted with indigenous movements, returned to America as advocates of foreign peoples and as agents of antiracist and anti-imperialist causes. These so-called "feedback effects of reverse missions" were more frequent than is often recognized. Historian David Swartz, for example, shows that leading evangelicals in the 1950s and 1960s, such as E. Stanley Jones, in part through his friendship with Mahatma Gandhi, took evangelicals to task over issues of domestic racism and international colonialism.[50]

Likewise, intermittent voices denouncing evangelical complicity in international racial oppression, such as during the 1966 World Congress on Evan-

48. Philip E. Dow, "The Influence of American Evangelicalism on US Relations with East and Central Africa during the Cold War" (PhD diss., University of Cambridge, 2012); Philip E. Dow, "Romance in a Marriage of Convenience: The Missionary Factor in Early Cold War U.S.-Ethiopian Relations, 1941–1960," *Diplomatic History* 35, no. 5 (November 2011): 859–95; Joel A. Carpenter, *Revive Us Again: The Reawakening of American Fundamentalism* (New York: Oxford University Press, 1997), 178–79.

49. Dow, "Influence of American Evangelicalism," 148–50.

50. David Swartz, "Christ of the American Road: E. Stanley Jones, India, and Civil Rights," *Journal of American Studies* 51 (November 2017): 1117–38. On "reverse missions," see also Patrick Harries and David Maxwell, eds., *The Spiritual in the Secular: Missionaries and Knowledge about Africa* (Grand Rapids: Eerdmans, 2012); "David Hollinger Explores the Returning American Missionaries," National History Center, November 10, 2010, http://nationalhistorycenter .org/david-hollinger-explores-the-returning-american-missionaries/.

gelism in Berlin, were followed in the 1970s by more insistent demands that evangelicals should focus more fully on global poverty and injustice. Political scientist Melani McAlister, for example, examines how the growing reliance on an indigenous workforce in international aid challenged American evangelicals' abject neglect of issues of racial discrimination and social exclusion.[51] In the same vein, mission work in Latin America helped evangelicals develop the social reflexivity and cultural empathy required for dismantling racist attitudes and structures. As historian Nancy Wadsworth points out, church-based relationships with illegal Hispanic immigrants changed many evangelicals' views on punitive migration policies. As one pastor noted, "watching a third grader cry because her dad is deported" opened his eyes to the injustices of the existing policy regime: "And I talk about 'family values.'"[52]

What is more, recent research on missions and foreign aid also highlights how the radical egalitarian logic of conversion theology and democratic church governance fed into indigenous self-assertion and critiques of colonialism. Particularly during the Ethiopian revolution of 1974, radicalized Christian converts who had been taught at mission schools and had been discriminated against by the Haile Selassie regime formed the leading cadres of the insurgency and helped establish democratic structures. However, the evangelical "theology of submission" also frequently reinforced deferential attitudes and ended up reasserting repression. The prime example of this is Kenya, where President Daniel arap Moi, mission-educated and zealously committed to missionary-inspired anti-Communism, effectively used Christian images to defend his authoritarian style.[53]

In summation, the confluence of postwar government efforts to mobilize the resources of religion with the newly energized and zealous evangelicalism generated a range of new partnerships between the state and conservative Protestantism. The analysis of these new ties in foreign aid, the military, and the global mission field suggests that the "antistatist" evangelicals became part of the "devolved governance" of the Cold War state and increasingly partici-

---

51. Melani McAlister, "The Global Conscience of American Evangelicalism: Internationalism and Social Concern in the 1970s and Beyond," *Journal of American Studies* 51 (November 2017): 1197–1220. See also "Minutes—Business Meeting of ESAC [Evangelical Social Action Commission] at NAE Convention," February 23, 1976, NAE Records; H. Wilbert Norton to Martin H. Schrag, June 11, 1976, NAE Records.

52. Nancy D. Wadsworth, *Ambivalent Miracles: Evangelicals and the Politics of Racial Healing* (Charlottesville: University of Virginia Press, 2014), 147, 253.

53. Dow, "Romance in a Marriage of Convenience," 859–95; Dow, "Influence of American Evangelicalism," 97, 76, 65, 166–67.

pated in the cultural practices of empire. The Cold War was thus a crucial moment in the process of integrating conservative Protestants into the framework of the national security state in ways that underwrote both the expansion of the federal government and the growth of religious agencies. At the same time, however, American evangelicalism was itself reformed by its new encounters with the world. This process has accelerated since the 1970s, when evangelicals from the global South—challenging the paternalism of the movement's American leaders—reconceived global evangelicalism as a pluralistic, participatory, multidirectional enterprise. In turn, evangelical voices critical of foreign policy and American hegemony have become ever more vocal.

Evangelicals and the Political Economy of Empire

World War II and the Cold War not only generated new visions of the "American century" and new administrative structures. They also dramatically reshaped the economic landscape in the United States. In particular, military spending, infrastructure investment, and new middle-class support programs ushered in a dramatic shift in socioeconomic power from the older commercial centers on the Atlantic coast and in the Midwest to the sprawling metropolises of the South and West—that is, regions where conservative Protestantism already had a strong institutional and cultural presence. States such as Texas, California, Florida, and Arizona experienced a major economic boost during and after the war as military expenditure, which had hovered around 15 percent of total federal spending in 1939, increased to over 50 percent by the early 1960s. In part because of 1930s New Deal spending on social welfare, public employment, and large-scale infrastructure projects, the South and the West became a magnet for defense contractors in the war and postwar years. In addition, generous postwar support programs for returning soldiers and vast federal subsidies, such as mortgage insurance for suburban tract developments, boosted consumer spending.[54]

White evangelicals were among the prime beneficiaries of the guns-and-butter spending lavished on the Sun Belt. As many studies have shown, by midcentury evangelicals in parts of the South and the West were no longer

54. By the 1980s, 46 percent of evangelicals lived in the South, 25 percent in the Midwest, 15 percent in the West, and 13 percent in the East. See George Gallup Jr. and Jim Castelli, *The People's Religion: American Faith in the 90's* (New York: Macmillan, 1989), 94. On the transfer of funds to the South and West, see Kenneth T. Jackson, *Crabgrass Frontier: The Suburbanization of the United States* (New York: Oxford University Press, 1985), 215-16.

significantly more rural, older, poorer, or less educated than the average American. Instead, they had emerged as culturally engaged and technologically initiated in an environment that combined employment in the military-industrial complex with suburban middle-class life. More money meant more ministry, too. Evangelical institutions at home and abroad continued to grow in size and widen in geographical reach. Conservative Protestantism particularly thrived in the context of postwar suburbanization, because evangelical forms of instantaneous religious community became highly attractive on the "crabgrass frontier" where people were mobile and separated from their traditional denominational contexts. Evangelical churches provided the social services that were often lacking in the Sun Belt as private developers put up suburban tract developments without including proper spaces for playgrounds, recreation facilities, community centers, and the like. Meanwhile, businessmen operating in the South, such as R. G. Le Tourneau and J. Howard Pew, welcomed federal subsidies and military expenditure while demanding local control, low taxes, open shops, and a workforce devoted to conservative economics.[55]

The term "political economy," however, encompasses the study not only of economic policies and structures but also of social attitudes and practices. Growing prosperity in the context of wartime state-building and the rise of the Sun Belt transformed evangelicals in ways that increasingly reflected the cognitive assumptions of modernity and the norms of consumer culture. Billy Graham combined the latest communications technology and up-to-date personnel mobilization with an apocalyptic and countercultural message. The popular Youth for Christ movement copied the teenage culture of the time with its fashions, celebrities, pepped-up music, fast-paced shows, and radio-style intensity. Sparkling suburban churches, such as Robert Schuller's Crystal Cathedral, emulated the car-oriented architecture of the shopping malls, while Christian supermarkets and other "born-again businesses" created a baptized counterpart to secular consumer culture.[56]

---

55. Dochuk, *From Bible Belt to Sunbelt*, 52, 56. On the postwar socioeconomic transformation of evangelicalism, see also Lisa McGirr, *Suburban Warriors: The Origins of the New American Right* (Princeton: Princeton University Press, 2001), esp. 48–51, 241–56; Bethany Moreton, *To Serve God and Wal-Mart: The Making of Christian Free Enterprise* (Cambridge, MA: Harvard University Press, 2009); Etan Diamond, *Souls of the City: Religion and the Search for Community in Postwar America* (Bloomington: University of Indiana Press, 2003); Eskridge and Noll, *More Money, More Ministry*; and James Hudnet-Beumler, *Looking for God in the Suburbs: The Religion of the American Dream and Its Critics* (New Brunswick, NJ: Rutgers University Press, 1994).

56. Robert S. Ellwood, *The Fifties Spiritual Marketplace: American Religion in a Decade*

As the idols of the age worked their way into evangelical affections, they transformed the evangelical message. The changing conversion narrative illustrates this "cognitive contamination" of evangelicalism. Evangelicals increasingly stressed the functional and therapeutic dimensions of the conversion experience, rather than self-denial, sinfulness, humility, and self-doubt. Sermons promising prosperity and well-being explored how faith empowered people and helped them become more affluent.[57] The NAE's postwar foray into the field of "industrial chaplaincy" provides a good example of the way in which religious concepts were rephrased in therapeutic terms. Seeking to build upon the growing postwar interest in personnel counseling, the chairman of the association's Industrial Chaplaincy Commission, A. Herman Armerding, explicitly touted religion as a means to a secular end—namely, to boost worker morale, efficiency, and productivity. He located the causes of industrial unrest in individual maladjustment and a "lack of experience of conversion." In response, he put forth the concepts of "theo-psychotherapy" and "pneumatology," which regarded religion as the key to employee happiness and success.[58]

In the eyes of many critics, this evangelical embrace of modern advertising techniques, state-of-the-art technology, commercialism, and consumer culture paved the way for the rise of a shallow faith. The critiques came hard and fast: Market-driven proselytizing and "cheap grace" had replaced the focus on profound inner spiritual transformation with an affirmation of established lifestyles and the status quo. Religious commitment was thus no longer a source of transcendence, but primarily an instrument of norm maintenance and social integration. The converted individual was ultimately the bourgeois individual, and conservative Protestantism a cultural expression "firmly representative of

---

of Conflict (New Brunswick, NJ: Rutgers University Press, 1997), 48; Joel A. Carpenter, "Youth for Christ and the New Evangelicals," in Hart, *Reckoning with the Past*, 357–58, 363–64; Colleen McDannell, *Material Christianity: Religion and Popular Culture in America* (New Haven: Yale University Press, 1995).

57. On this issue, see especially the essays in Hart, *Reckoning with the Past*; Marsden, *Understanding Fundamentalism*, 79–81; David Harrington Watt, *A Transforming Faith: Explorations of Twentieth-Century American Evangelicalism* (New Brunswick, NJ: Rutgers University Press, 1991); Robert Wuthnow, *After Heaven: Spirituality in America since the 1950s* (Berkeley: University of California Press, 2000); Wade Clark Roof, *Spiritual Marketplace: Baby Boomers and the Remaking of American Religion* (Princeton: Princeton University Press, 2001).

58. A. Herman Armerding, "Chaplain Counselors for Industry—a New Development in Human Relations Announced by the Industrial Chaplaincy Commission," in Minutes of the meeting of the NAE Board of Administration, National Association of Evangelicals, September 19–20, 1945, NAE Records.

the world of the American middle class."[59] Indeed, Billy Graham himself later conceded that in the 1950s he had frequently confused the kingdom of God with the American way of life.[60]

Seen from this angle, postwar evangelicalism fits into a story of cultural assimilation and secularization that is the staple narrative of much scholarship on Cold War culture and society. Historian Darren Dochuk thus comes to the conclusion that evangelicals effectively constructed cultural agencies to match the capitalist system of the Sun Belt and its military-industrial power base. They increasingly combined the affirmation of the Cold War militarized economy, social order, and national security state with an insurgent conservative message of free enterprise, entrepreneurial individualism, and moral awakening.[61] Underlying this understanding of the movement are sociological interpretations that see evangelicalism itself as a distinctly modern phenomenon. Its emphasis on the individual faith experience, for example, reflects the normative codes of modern pluralism, because it shifts the accent from an objective truth toward an existentialist focus on subjectivity. And the faith's absence of strong traditions, lack of institutional ties, and high level of organizational mobility matches the trajectories of modernity.[62]

Once again, however, the singular focus on assimilation obscures the diversity of evangelical socioeconomic attitudes during the Cold War. Indeed, as late as the 1990s, capitalism was one of the more divisive issues within American evangelicalism, as "a vociferous evangelical left . . . has become increasingly influential over the last twenty years."[63] Outside of the Left, many moderates also expressed concerns about laissez-faire economics' lack of

---

59. Hunter, *American Evangelicalism*, 47. See also Heclo, *Christianity and American Democracy*, 43, 202; Watt, *A Transforming Faith*, 24; Grant Wacker, "Uneasy in Zion: Evangelicals in Postmodern Society," in Hart, *Reckoning with the Past*, 381; Marsden, *Understanding Fundamentalism*, 79; Virginia Lieson Brereton, *From Sin to Salvation: Stories of Women's Conversions, 1800 to the Present* (Bloomington: Indiana University Press, 1991), 48.

60. Graham, quoted in Richard V. Pierard, "Billy Graham and Vietnam: From Cold Warrior to Peacemaker," *Christian Scholar's Review* 10 (Spring 1980): 38.

61. Dochuk, *From Bible Belt to Sunbelt*.

62. On evangelicalism and modernity, see James Davison Hunter, *Evangelicalism: The Coming Generation* (Chicago: University of Chicago Press, 1987), 47; Ellwood, *The Fifties Spiritual Marketplace*, 14–15; Robert Wuthnow, *The Restructuring of American Religion: Society and Faith since World War II* (Princeton: Princeton University Press, 1988), 55–57.

63. Craig Gay, *With Liberty and Justice for Whom? The Recent Evangelical Debate over Capitalism* (Grand Rapids: Eerdmans, 1991), 1–2; Robert Booth Fowler, *A New Engagement: Evangelical Political Thought, 1966–1976* (Grand Rapids: Eerdmans, 1987), 89, 185. For a recent study of the range of evangelical political orientations, see Swartz, *Moral Minority*.

moral values. Convinced that market economics was not beyond Christian criticism, Carl Henry urged the formulation of alternatives to both secular socialism and secular capitalism.[64] Likewise, by the late 1960s Billy Graham was cautiously progressive on issues such as poverty and the arms race, and urged involvement in social ministries.[65] Similarly, evangelical theologian Francis Schaeffer voiced a critique of materialism and capitalism. Reflecting a fear that evangelicalism could turn into a "culture religion," Schaeffer warned his fellow believers that "it will not do . . . to carry on Christian work with the means or techniques of the world (which so admirably sell cornflakes, cars, and strange sects), and then expect men to be convinced that God exists and that He is personal."[66]

In conclusion, a closer look at the evangelical engagement with the political economy of the Cold War once again presents no straightforward image. While espousing the old-time religion and biblical orthodoxy, the newly affluent evangelicals underwent a process of socioeconomic modernization that softened their theological attitudes and cultural practices. In its wake they became part of the corporate-controlled militarized economy, sacralized free-market capitalism, and embraced the materialist settings of the postwar era. At the same time, however, postwar evangelicalism's readiness to engage in politics also meant that conflicts raged within the movement over civil religion, militarism, capitalism, and social involvement.

Sociocultural Changes and Evangelical Identities

The changes in the American economy also had significant long-term sociocultural repercussions in the realm of race, gender, and sexual relations. World War II and the Cold War both exposed the deep racial fault lines of American society and cast the issue of gender inequality into sharp relief. In regard to race, the civil rights movement cannot be understood in isolation from a war where the United States saw itself as fighting against a brutal racist ideology while tolerating racism as a common feature of everyday life at home. This was "worth many divisions to Hitler and Hirohito," the civil rights leader A. Philip Randolph thundered in 1942. At the same time, many

64. [Carl F. H. Henry], "Future of the American Worker," *Christianity Today*, May 13, 1957, 20–22. See also Carl F. H. Henry, *Uneasy Conscience*.

65. Fowler, *A New Engagement*, 47–54.

66. Francis A. Schaeffer, "The Modern Drift: Is Nobody Home in This World?," *Christianity Today*, June 20, 1960, 6.

of the African Americans who had served in—mostly segregated—units in the armed forces returned from defending the nation with a sense of having stood up for themselves. They were skilled in the use of weapons, were often treated better in Europe than at home, and were no longer willing to accept racial segregation at home as they had in the past. Moreover, war-industry-related migration of many African Americans to the cities spurred the growth of urban black churches that in the 1950s emerged as the institutional centers of the civil rights movement.[67]

World War II also had far-reaching effects on the lives of many women, who made up almost 36 percent of the labor force. Wartime labor needs enabled women to find work in fields outside of their traditional low-paid domains. Employed in army and war plants, "Rosie the Riveter" worked as industrial lathe operator, welder, or crane driver. Once again, the rise of second-wave feminism cannot be understood outside these challenges to established gender roles.[68] The measure of liberation and emancipation afforded by wartime employment, however, was counterbalanced by a strong societal effort to enforce what historian Elaine Tyler May has called "domestic containment." Equivalent to foreign policy efforts to rein in Communist expansion, it sought to control potentially disruptive challenges to traditional gender roles and domesticity. In turn, women were accused of sexual libertinism and of abandoning the home when wartime family disruption led to the rise in juvenile delinquency and divorce rates.[69] In the same vein, Cold War policy makers conceptualized US citizens as explicitly heterosexual. As historian Rebecca Davis has shown, the "lavender scare" targeting alleged homosexuals resulted in more firings

---

67. A. Philip Randolph, "Why Should We March?" (1942), http://wps.ablongman.com /wps/media/objects/31/31959/primarysources1_27_2.html. On race and World War II, see also Daniel Kryder, *Divided Arsenal: Race and the American State during World War II* (Cambridge: Cambridge University Press, 2000); Ronald Takaki, *Double Victory: A Multicultural History of America in World War II* (New York: Chelsea House, 2000); and Aldon D. Morris, *The Origins of the Civil Rights Movement: Black Communities Organizing for Change* (New York: Free Press, 1984).

68. On gender and the war, see Susan M. Hartmann, *The Homefront and Beyond: American Women in the 1940s* (Boston: Twayne Publishers, 1982); Karen T. Anderson, *Wartime Women: Sex Roles, Family Relations, and the Status of Women during World War II* (Westport, CT: Greenwood Press, 1981); Robert B. Westbrook, *Why We Fought: Forging American Obligations in World War II* (Washington, DC: Smithsonian Books, 2004).

69. Elaine Tyler May, *Pushing the Limits: American Women, 1940–1961* (New York: Oxford University Press, 1994). On the Cold War and sexuality, see Linda Kintz, *Between Jesus and the Market: The Emotions That Matter in Right-Wing America* (Durham, NC: Duke University Press, 1997); and Moreton, *To Serve God and Wal-Mart*.

of government employees and greater surveillance of personal networks than the Red Scare.[70]

In regard to race, gender, and sexual mores, postwar evangelicals largely aligned themselves with those who sought to reassert social hierarchies and male spheres of control. Many lily-white Sun Belt conservative Protestants were in the vanguard of defending the "traditional family," battled the civil rights movement, and defended segregation. Martin Luther King's indictment, that eleven o'clock on Sunday morning was the most segregated hour in America, continued to ring true, as over 90 percent of Christians in the United States worshiped in separate racial groups. Moreover, postwar evangelicals' alignment with conservative politics, which supported the racially skewed distribution of wealth, reinforced existing inequalities. Similarly, evangelical rituals of admitting and forgiveness, as Nancy Wadsworth has noted, continued to repress "cognitive reflection, inquiry, and open conversation about power and politics."[71]

Despite their racial segregationism, antifeminism, and morality politics, white evangelicalism did not remain entirely untouched by the emancipatory dynamics unleashed by the war and postwar periods. Henry, Schaeffer, and Graham, for example, warned that liberals were stealing the thunder from evangelicals in the struggle for racial equality, even though the latter had been the ones who had spearheaded abolitionism in the nineteenth century. Graham was cautiously progressive on civil rights, led the first integrated crusade in 1953, and supported Lyndon Johnson's Civil Rights Act in 1964.[72] Many evangelicals also recognized the glaring contradiction that the same conservative theology that underlay the segregationism of the white church had nurtured the civil rights activism and social justice campaigns of the black church. Indeed, the civil rights movement could hardly have developed its moral purpose and movement infrastructure without the spiritual inspiration and organizational resources provided by black evangelicalism. Hence the faith was both deeply implicated in perpetuating racism and a key agent in efforts to overcome it. While white evangelicalism emphasized creating unchallenging spiritual environments that reassured suburban parishioners' social and

70. Rebecca L. Davis, *More Perfect Unions: The American Search for Marital Bliss* (Cambridge, MA: Harvard University Press, 2010).

71. Wadsworth, *Ambivalent Miracles*, 147.

72. Carl F. H. Henry, "Evangelicals in the Social Struggle," *Christianity Today*, October 8, 1965, 9–10; Carl F. H. Henry, *Confessions of a Theologian*, 158; Hatch and Hamilton, "Taking the Measure," 400–401; Fowler, *A New Engagement*, 46. See also Steven P. Miller, *Billy Graham and the Rise of the Republican South*.

material standing, it also emphasized the need for heart-wrenching conversion that required opening oneself up to sincere soul-searching and genuine racial reconciliation.[73]

Similarly, resurgent evangelicalism's stances on gender and moral norms are more complicated than they first appear. The prolife campaigns and visceral opposition to feminism that characterized the political resurgence of evangelicalism, historian Daniel Williams maintains, were not primarily based on age-old moral convictions. Instead, they derived from internal controversies over conservative Protestantism's experience of its own internal sexual revolution. Evangelicals in the 1960s and 1970s began celebrating marital sex, condoning masturbation as a way to prevent premarital transgression, and endorsing birth control. Indeed, well into the 1970s many rejected Roman Catholic efforts to preserve bans on abortion.[74] These liberalizing tendencies, culminating in the rise of a distinctive evangelical feminism, were advocated by religious authors such as Letha Scanzoni. While they condemned secular feminism, they promoted an egalitarian model of women's sexual desire that liberated women from traditional restrictions but simultaneously contained them within a hierarchical setting.[75] "Morality politics" was thus an effort to draw more rigid normative boundaries after evangelicals had begun to be more open about sexual relations. As Williams notes, while "evangelicals became more rhapsodic in their praise of the sexual dimension of heterosexual marriage, their opposition to perceived threats to such marriages—threats such as feminism, gay rights, and abortion—intensified and became the basis for a new series of grassroots political campaigns."[76]

To sum it up, socioculturally evangelicals were in the vanguard of containing the disruptive Cold War dynamics that undermined established racial hierarchies, gender roles, and sexual norms. From the anti-Communist crusades

---

73. Wadsworth, *Ambivalent Miracles*.

74. Daniel K. Williams, "Sex and the Evangelicals: Gender Issues, the Sexual Revolution, and Abortion in the 1960s," in *American Evangelicals and the 1960s*, ed. Axel R. Schäfer (Madison: University of Wisconsin Press, 2013), 97–118. See also Tanya Erzen, *Straight to Jesus: Sexual and Christian Conversions in the Ex-Gay Movement* (Berkeley: University of California Press, 2006); Paul L. Sadler, "The Abortion Issue within the Southern Baptist Convention, 1969–1988" (PhD diss., Baylor University, 1991), 25–26; Southern Baptist Convention, "Resolution on Abortion," June 1971, http://www.sbc.net/resolutions/amResolution.asp?ID=13.

75. Letha Scanzoni and Nancy Hardesty, *All We're Meant to Be: A Biblical Approach to Women's Liberation* (Waco: Word, 1974). See also Pamela D. H. Cochran, *Evangelical Feminism: A History* (New York: New York University Press, 2005), 12–39; Sally K. Gallagher, "The Marginalization of Evangelical Feminism," *Sociology of Religion* 65 (2004): 215–37.

76. Williams, "Sex and the Evangelicals," 111, 113.

to the antiabortion campaigns, the movement was on a collision course with the civil rights movement, second-wave feminism, and the cultural revolts of the 1960s and 1970s. Yet, even on these supposedly clear-cut issues, evangelicals underwent a kind of lifestyle liberalization. While white evangelicals were latecomers to racial reconciliation—mainly as a result of their own deep complicity in sustaining segregation—their faith also contained "tool kits" for genuine change in race relations. Similarly, instances of rigid morality politics and gender hierarchies clashed with efforts to promote alternative models of female empowerment.

Conclusion

The analysis of the relationship between evangelicalism and the ideological, institutional, socioeconomic, and sociocultural underpinnings of American empire-building after 1945 suggests that conservative Protestants were simultaneously at home in the "American century" and expressed sentiments deeply critical of American culture, society, and power. As evangelicals gained public recognition, established a media presence, lobbied in Washington, converted souls, and sent new missionaries to the farthest corners of the earth, their attitudes ran the gamut from anointing the defense-welfare state, the country's new role as "defender of the free world," and the "American way of life," to often viscerally opposing Washington bureaucrats, liberal internationalism, and cultural modernity. In short, as Joel Carpenter put it, evangelicals performed a "strange dance" driven by conflicting impulses. They positioned themselves as both effective communicators of the myth of American righteousness and die-hard supporters of conservative piety.[77]

How do we make sense of this? Were evangelicals absorbed by the secular order, instrumentalized as a cultural weapon, complicit in Cold War mobilization, co-opted as a handmaiden of the national security state, and employed as an agent of American soft power in the world? Or did they retain agency within a complex and multilayered Cold War setting that enabled their movement to constitute itself as a countervailing force? The analysis presented in this essay goes beyond either interpretation. Instead, it suggests that the evangelical conflicts and tensions were constituent components of both revivalism and American empire-building in the second half of the twentieth century. Only in the context of World War II and the Cold War did a new neoevan-

77. Carpenter, *Revive Us Again*, 242; Carpenter, "Youth for Christ," 371.

gelical faith come into its own, and only in the context of the neoevangelical revival did a conception of American empire emerge in the postwar period.

On the one hand, the war and the Cold War are the key to understanding how evangelicals were able to resurface so powerfully in American politics and culture in the second half of the twentieth century. Ironically, the very elements that had pushed the evangelical movement to the margins in American society—obscure propheticism, institutional separatism, and old-fashioned moralism—ended up enabling evangelicals to thrive under the conditions of the postwar period. World War II and the Cold War helped make arcane biblical concepts meaningful for the unconverted, bestowed national political importance on the experience of conversion, and established evangelical themes and sentiments as valid and coherent interpretive concepts for understanding the new world order. They strengthened the autonomy and salience of evangelical institutions, shored up the material basis for revivalism, and affirmed the moral codes of the old-time religion as part of the civic foundations of American society.

In the process of political reengagement, conservative Protestantism was itself transformed. Using orthodox belief as a template for understanding the postwar totalitarian threats, evangelicals connected the apolitical and individualistic born-again experience to a civil religious engagement at home and abroad. Expanded global missionary and humanitarian activism transformed the traditional church-state separatism into a new engagement with governance, global politics, and empire building. Sun Belt affluence and suburban culture ushered in a new accommodation with corporate and technological modernity. And the changing race and gender dynamics yielded new forms of evangelical feminism and racial reconciliation.

On the other hand, the religious resurgence was critical for establishing and legitimizing America's global role, which was narrated in an antiimperialist, antistatist, antimonopolist, and exceptionalist vein. The country had to construct ideologies, institutions, economic regimes, and cultural norms for the exercise of global power in the context of the salience of traditions that had historically limited the country's imperial aspirations. This was no mean task, since isolationist sentiments had to be reconciled with the exigencies of postwar global power, antistatist sentiments with the growth of the national security state, antimonopolist impulses with the rise of the corporate-controlled military-industrial complex, and established race and gender hierarchies with the dynamics of consumer capitalism.

In this setting, while the country's new hegemonic role was not yet firmly established at home and institutionalized abroad, evangelicals were able to position themselves as crucial cultural arbiters. Ideologically, neoevangelicalism's combination of pietism and custodialism outlined the "isolationist globalism" that appealed to a population trying to reconcile deeply embedded anti-imperial outlooks with the realities of global power. Institutionally, the involvement of evangelical voluntary organizations in federal funding arrangements paved the way for the "antistatist statism" that helped make the expansion of the state palatable to a public still committed to limited government. Socioeconomically, evangelicals simultaneously supported the military-industrial complex and upheld an insurgent message of free enterprise in a kind of "libertarian corporatism." This appealed to an electorate particularly in the South and the West of the country that had benefited from federal defense spending and the social service expansions but clung to the vision of self-made entrepreneurs and frontier individualism. And socioculturally, evangelicals combined morality politics and consumer capitalism into a form of "reactionary modernism." This spoke to people who were comfortable with the new technological society but felt besieged by the race and gender challenges it had generated. In summation, the resurgence of evangelicalism and America's rise to global power were not only intimately connected. They were constitutive of each other.

The Limits of Evangelical Christian Nationalism during the Cold War

Daniel G. Hummel

At the beginning of the Cold War in 1947, American evangelical pastor Harold Ockenga preached about a coming "great revival" that would sweep the globe. "What is the great revival?" Ockenga asked an audience of theologians and students at Dallas Theological Seminary. "It is the time when God's work is unusually prospered, quickened, enlarged, and vitalized."[1] Ockenga, a pivotal leader of a "new evangelicalism" movement in the 1940s, founder of the National Association of Evangelicals, and first president of Fuller Theological Seminary, insisted that the old-time practice of revival had not lost its relevance in Cold War America.[2]

Harold Ockenga also embraced a robust American exceptionalism. "Our continent was preserved to incarnate the development of the best civilization. Humanly speaking, it is almost as though God pinned His last hope on America," he preached in 1939.[3] This Christian nationalism—for evangelicals and historians alike—has become inextricably linked with calls for spiritual revival during the Cold War.[4] Indeed, most postwar evangelical leaders, from Billy Graham to Jerry Falwell, voiced similar syntheses of revival and nationalism, blending spiritual and national destinies. American evangelicals eagerly

---

1. Harold Ockenga, "The Great Revival," *Bibliotheca Sacra* 104, no. 414 (April 1947): 223.

2. On Ockenga's central role in postwar evangelicalism, see Garth M. Rosell, *The Surprising Work of God: Harold John Ockenga, Billy Graham, and the Rebirth of Evangelicalism* (Grand Rapids: Baker Academic, 2008), and George Marsden, *Reforming Fundamentalism: Fuller Seminary and the New Evangelicalism* (Grand Rapids: Eerdmans, 1987).

3. Quoted in Matthew Avery Sutton, *American Apocalypse: A History of Modern Evangelicalism* (Cambridge, MA: Belknap Press of Harvard University Press, 2014), 263.

4. On Christian nationalism in the early Cold War period, see Jonathan P. Herzog, *The Spiritual-Industrial Complex: America's Religious Battle against Communism in the Early Cold War* (New York: Oxford University Press, 2011), and Kevin M. Kruse, *One Nation under God: How Corporate America Invented Christian America* (New York: Basic Books, 2015).

called for a return to the old-time gospel, defended the economic system of capitalism, celebrated "In God We Trust" on American money and "under God" in the nation's pledge of allegiance, and supported politicians based on their religious rhetoric. After World War II, writes historian Matthew Sutton, "fundamentalists became the voices of patriotism and American exceptionalism . . . they had baptized Christian fundamentalism in the waters of patriotic Americanism."[5] They would keep this fervency throughout the Cold War and defend the notion of America as a "Christian nation."

The focus in this chapter is the relationship evangelicals constructed during the Cold War between the church and revivalism on the one hand, and the American state and nationalism on the other. The key contention is that during the Cold War, "the Church"[6] held primacy over the state in evangelical thinking. Evangelicals did not sacralize the state so much as they reimagined the church-state relationship—with its mix of separation, disestablishment, and functional support for religious organizations—as an instrument to further their principal concern: the expansion of the Church in an age of global, atheistic Communism.[7] Evangelicals constructed their nationalism with components from their inherited fundamentalist theology, which divided the world into three categories: "the Church," "Israel," and "the nations." American evangelicals saw themselves at the heart of the Church; the United States was a member of the nations.

This primacy for "the Church" over "the nations" could be found even in Ockenga's call for a great revival in 1947, in which the United States was mentioned only once. "Mass bombings, mass transferals of population, mass planned-starvation," Ockenga warned, speaking of the ravages of World War II, "are evidences of the fact that all nations including the United States have abandoned the Christian principles of civilization."[8] Moreover, Ockenga's description of the great revival was decidedly universalistic, removed from nationalistic rhetoric or overt sacralization of the American way. "The great revival marks a condition when men give primary interest and attention to the things of God above their livelihood, above their intellectual pursuits, and above their social interests. A terror of wrongdoing descends upon them. A

5. Sutton, *American Apocalypse*, 266.

6. The word "Church," when uppercased in this chapter, means the universal, invisible church.

7. Herzog, *The Spiritual-Industrial Complex*, esp. 92. On the process of the sacralization of the state and civil religion, see Raymond Haberski Jr., *God and War: American Civil Religion since 1945* (New Brunswick, NJ: Rutgers University Press, 2012), esp. 20–23.

8. Ockenga, "The Great Revival," 228.

passion for repentance seizes them. A desire for salvation characterizes them. Men go on a search for God."[9]

For Ockenga, insofar as the American nation empowered the Church, it remained the last best hope of heaven, as well as earth. But this was no unqualified patriotism. Evangelical loyalty hinged on state noninterference, on tacit public support for its priorities, and, as the Cold War progressed, on the American government's subsidizing of evangelical religious efforts to missionize and convert the world.

The limits to evangelical Christian nationalism during the Cold War were demarcated through a continuous reexamination of the success or failure of the American church (as defined by evangelicals) and the contribution or hindrance of the government to its vitality. This constant investigation depended on the categories of evangelical theology entering the Cold War—the Church, Israel, and the nations—and their synthesis with changes to fundamentalist and evangelical attitudes toward the American state as a result of World War II and the Cold War threat of atheistic Communism. For many evangelicals, these categories were assumed; for others, their differences were the subject of articles, books, and entire interpretations of the Cold War. In recognition of this diversity, this chapter draws on a wide array of evangelical voices—from movement leaders to editors of magazines such as the *King's Business* and *Moody Monthly*.

In the early Cold War period, the legacy of fundamentalism circumscribed expressions of unqualified Christian nationalism. In the later Cold War years, evangelicals fully flexed their Christian nationalism in service of the Church. By the 1970s, evangelicals saw the Church's position eroding, undermined by a more secular, pluralistic, egalitarian, and progressive set of social values that could limit the autonomy of the Church. The paradoxical "antistatist statism" of conservative evangelicals in the late Cold War—both rejecting and seeking to influence the power of the state—is a testament to the staying power of the movement's theological categories.[10]

9. Ockenga, "The Great Revival," 223.

10. Axel R. Schäfer, *Piety and Public Funding: Evangelicals and the State in Modern America* (Philadelphia: University of Pennsylvania Press, 2012), 6. This is also explored in Gary Gerstle, *Liberty and Coercion: The Paradox of American Government from the Founding to the Present* (Princeton: Princeton University Press, 2015), esp. 311–44.

The Church, Israel, and the Nations

Evangelical thinking about the Cold War was never unified or even consistent. It drew on a variety of traditions, both secular and religious. One of those religious traditions that played a prominent role in shaping evangelical Christian nationalism after World War II was the theological system of dispensationalism.[11] Beginning with John Nelson Darby, the first systematic theologian of dispensationalism in the mid-nineteenth century, dispensationalism emerged as a popular theology among conservative Protestants. Its influence has been widely studied, but some key aspects have received less attention: its taxonomic division of humanity and its conception of a divine economy of blessings. These aspects were particularly crucial for Cold War understandings of who constituted the Church and how the Church related to society.

Beginning in the late nineteenth century, American dispensationalists began to feel persecuted in their own denominations and constituted a powerful wing of the emerging fundamentalist movement.[12] Borrowing from Darby's original critique of his own Anglican Church, dispensationalists rejected the authority of the institutional church. For C. I. Scofield, the most prominent American popularizer of Darby's thinking, "the church" in the Bible referred to the "true Church . . . composed of the whole number of regenerate persons from Pentecost to the first resurrection united together and to Christ by the baptism with the Holy Spirit."[13] This "true Church" existed within the larger, "visible," institutional church. While the "true Church" was the body of true believers, the visible church "exists under many names and divisions based upon differences in doctrine or in government."[14] These "true" and "visible" bodies stand in opposition: the former, "a holy temple for the habitation of God through the Spirit"; the latter, destined to descend into apostasy.[15] Post-

---

11. For a historical explanation of dispensationalism, see Timothy P. Weber, *On the Road to Armageddon: How Evangelicals Became Israel's Best Friend* (Grand Rapids: Baker Academic, 2005), 19–44. For a theological exposition, see Darrell L. Bock and Craig A. Blaising, *Progressive Dispensationalism* (Wheaton, IL: BridgePoint Academic, 1993), 9–56.

12. See George M. Marsden, *Fundamentalism and American Culture*, 2nd ed. (New York: Oxford University Press, 2006). See also Ernest R. Sandeen, *The Roots of Fundamentalism: British and American Millenarianism, 1800–1930* (Chicago: University of Chicago Press, 1970), esp. 59–80.

13. See *The Scofield Reference Bible* (New York: Oxford University Press, 1917). Scofield's summary definition for "Church (true)" resides in his note for Heb. 12:23.

14. Scofield's summary definition for "Church (visible)" resides in his note for 1 Tim. 3:15.

15. This distinction, of course, did not originate in dispensationalism. John Calvin, citing

407

war evangelicals inherited this ecclesiology, remaining opposed to Roman Catholicism, ecumenism, and the mainline denominations in the United States.[16]

In contrast to "the Church," which could not be identified with any specific state or institution, "the nations" encompassed the rest of humanity.[17] The gentile nations resided outside the sphere of God's direct activity and were comprised of the unchosen masses of people around the globe. In the Bible, "the nations," or "the Gentiles" from Egypt, Persia, and Assyria, were mentioned only as they intersected with the story of ancient Israel.[18] Modern nations maintained a similar relationship to the Church. The United States, Europe, and emerging centers of geopolitical power were important but peripheral actors in God's plans, which always revolved around his chosen people.

The Jewish people, or "Israel," comprised the third category of humanity for dispensationalists. In the book of Acts, Scofield noted in his popular reference Bible, "The division of the race now becomes threefold—the Jew, the Gentile, and the Church of God."[19] Passages such as Genesis 12:3 ("I will bless those who bless you, and whoever curses you I will curse; and all peoples on earth will be blessed through you"), which positioned Abraham's physical descendants as the primary mediators of divine blessing, were used to make the state of Israel a major evangelical issue during the Cold War. Evangelicals increasingly regarded support for Israel, which claimed the mantle of Jewish statehood, as a necessary commitment after its establishment in 1948. Through religious organizations that supported Israel, the Church would gain blessings; through diplomatic and military support, individual nations, including the United States, would gain God's favor. By the 1950s, this tripartite taxonomy shaped virtually all evangelical and fundamentalist analysis of human activity, from ecclesiastical and geopolitical developments to missions and family life.

Underlying this taxonomy was a divine economy, or set of fixed, transactional relationships of divine blessings between Israel, the Church, and the

---

Saint Augustine, distinguished between a visible and an invisible church. Dispensationalists, however, were unique in emphasizing a near-total antipathy between these two entities.

16. For a more skeptical approach to the role of dispensationalist ecclesiology in fundamentalist thinking, see B. M. Pietsch, "Lyman Stewart and Early Fundamentalism," *Church History: Studies in Christianity and Culture* 82, no. 3 (2013): esp. 637n51.

17. Adherents pointed to Bible verses such as 1 Cor. 10:32 ("Do not cause anyone to stumble, whether Jews, Greeks or the church of God") as supporting evidence for these terms. All biblical quotations are from the New International Version (NIV).

18. See C. I. Scofield, *Rightly Dividing the Word of Truth*, edited and abridged (Danville, IL: Grace and Truth, 1996), 3.

19. *The Scofield Reference Bible*, vi.

nations.[20] Most importantly, the divine economy was based on the nations' treatment of the Church. National success or failure on this basis had biblical precedent, such as in Matthew 25 when Jesus explained to his disciples that he will divide the nations into "sheep" and "goats" based on how they treat his followers. The sheep will "receive good things from my Father," while the goats "will receive terrible things," including eternal punishment and unending fire.[21] Thus, for evangelicals entangled in this divine economy, the Cold War presented relatively straightforward choices. The United States would be judged by its treatment of Israel and the (true) Church.

The Limits of Christian Nationalism

During the same year in which John Ockenga sermonized on the coming great revival—1947—he also delivered one of his most significant speeches when he addressed the opening of Fuller Theological Seminary in Pasadena, California. Along with other postwar evangelical leaders, including Carl F. H. Henry, Charles Fuller, and Billy Graham, Ockenga sought to reverse the "decline of the West" through establishing a new seminary. He identified "immorality" as a chief symptom of decline, which was "demonstrated in Europe and America by promiscuity, divorce, and universal disregard for the seventh commandment ['You shall not commit adultery']."[22] In many ways, Ockenga issued a typical evangelical call for Americans to return to a biblical morality.

More precisely, Ockenga used his address at the founding of a seminary to argue that the decline of the West was a theological problem. After surveying the destruction of Europe, he concluded, "the basic concepts of men have changed. They have changed to such a degree that the moral effects of a Christian civilization no longer exist where the basic theories of the Christian

---

20. The metaphor of an economy is partially rooted in dispensationalist theology. See Charles C. Ryrie, *Dispensationalism Today* (Chicago: Moody Press, 1965), esp. 29–30. The formulaic, contractual, and predictable characteristics of economies were also epistemologically comforting to evangelicals. This desire for reliability stretches back to fundamentalist epistemology. See Timothy Gloege, *Guaranteed Pure: The Moody Bible Institute, Business, and the Making of Modern Evangelicalism* (Chapel Hill: University of North Carolina Press, 2015), esp. 76–84, and Branden Pietsch, *Dispensational Modernism* (New York: Oxford University Press, 2015), esp. 73–95.

21. Matt. 25:31–46.

22. Harold Ockenga, "The Challenge to the Christian Culture of the West," in *Fuller Voices: Then and Now* (Pasadena, CA: Fuller Theological Seminary, 2004), 15.

civilization are gone." The solution was theological: "to rethink and to restate the principles of Western culture. . . . This is a task for a theological institution which will specialize in apologetic literature to rebuild the foundations of society."[23] Ockenga's preference to build a seminary reveals one aspect of evangelical priorities that privileged the efforts of the Church in solving cultural and political issues. More than this, Ockenga's language utilized the categories of evangelical thinking about the world. Describing Fuller's mission, Ockenga explained, "It is our intention that we are to complete the task of the church to call out people, in Christ's name, to teach the nations all things whatsoever he hath commanded us and to occupy till he comes."[24] Thus, Western civilization hinged on transactions between the Church and the nations. Within the Christian world, threats of "Romanism, and of a possible perversion of ecumenicalism" threatened the Church. In the nations, "the menace of communism" worried Ockenga the most.

The primacy of the Church was evident even during World War II, when evangelicals radically reoriented themselves in support of the American state. "The Christian Church has a far more important duty than to bless military banners, christen battleships, sing 'praise the Lord and pass the ammunition,'" inveighed John Bradbury, editor of the *Baptist Watchman-Examiner*, at a 1943 prophecy conference.[25] William Houghton, the president of dispensationalist Moody Bible Institute, warned in the same year against presuming the unqualified righteousness of America's war effort. "It is all very, very comforting, BUT—What right has America to brazenly presume that God just must be her ally in war, when America has driven God, to a very large extent, out of her national life?"[26] Hostilities had ceased in 1945, a *King's Business* editorial explained, because God had preserved the United States in order to aid the Church: "Why the peace? There is but one answer, and that is God is giving the Church of Jesus Christ another—and last—chance."[27] Such distinctions between church and state were not new, but rooted in the legacy of dispensationalist thinking that evangelicals had inherited during the interwar period.

23. Ockenga, "Challenge to the Christian Culture," 16.

24. Ockenga, "Challenge to the Christian Culture," 17–18.

25. John Bradbury, "The Peace of the Prince of Peace," in Bradbury, *Light for the World's Darkness* (Neptune, NJ: Loizeaux Brothers, 1994), 69–70. Quoted in Paul Boyer, *When Time Shall Be No More: Prophecy Belief in Modern American Culture* (Cambridge, MA: Belknap Press of Harvard University Press, 1994), 111.

26. William Houghton, "God, Time, and Russia Are on Our Side . . . or Are They?," *Moody Monthly*, March 1943, 396.

27. Quoted in Sutton, *American Apocalypse*, 292.

These wartime distinctions indicate that for many evangelicals, patriotic and nationalistic sentiment was conditional. The decisive factor was the extent to which the goals of the Church—evangelism and expansion—coincided with the goals of the state—the defeat of Nazism during World War II and the containment of Communism in the Cold War. More generally, evangelical leaders acknowledged that the configuration of these two sets of goals was historically contingent. Church and state had aligned for much of American history—no more so than during World War II—but with the onset of the Cold War and rapid changes to postwar American society, this relationship was in jeopardy. Theologian Carl F. H. Henry, in his influential 1947 book *The Uneasy Conscience of Modern Fundamentalism*, raised this issue by criticizing the American conception of religious freedom that had developed during the twentieth century. "Democracy had meant, for early Americans, the right to worship God as patterned in the Scriptures, without the obstruction of earthly powers; between the two world wars it had narrowed down to the four freedoms, including the right to worship God any way and if one wanted to do so. That sort of brotherhood, the evangelical was aware, made brotherhood impossible, because it obscured man's relationship to God."[28]

Thus, for Henry the loss of a theistic conception of religious freedom portended a newly hostile environment for the Church in the United States. The very land that had nurtured the Church and provided a home for its followers was becoming distanced to the cause of the Church. Henry took this so far as to justify increased evangelical spending on "home-front expenditures" in the postwar period by collapsing the distinction between the United States and foreign lands. "The distinction between home and foreign missions is a generation outmoded; Christianity again faces the apostolic task of seeking to transform an environment that is quite unilaterally hostile."[29] Henry, like other evangelical leaders, was concerned for the fate of the Church in light of changing legal and cultural understandings of religious freedom.

This primacy of the Church spilled over into evangelical conceptualizations of the Cold War. For many, the term denoted a spiritual confrontation between Christianity and Communism, a face-off that required an altogether different analysis than an ideological battle between capitalism and Communism or the United States and the Soviet Union. "You see, every communist is a convert-maker," explained the popular preacher George Sweeting. "For

28. Carl F. H. Henry, *The Uneasy Conscience of Modern Fundamentalism* (Grand Rapids: Eerdmans, 1947), 20.
29. Henry, *Uneasy Conscience*, 69.

communism he gives up amusements, social life and even takes an inferior job in order to bring his message into a new place. Communism has become the greatest missionary movement of the day. The Communists have given more dedication to Karl Marx than we have to the Lord Jesus Christ. Communists have taken over the methods Christ used and meant His church to use."[30] Not only had Communism appropriated the Church's methods, but it was expanding at a rate faster than Christian missions. Sweeting hoped to provoke readers into responding to this threat by recommitting to the Church more than the nation.

Such spiritualizing of the conflict was not unique to evangelicals, but evangelicals invoked it in a unique way. Presidents, secretaries of state, and members of Congress also spoke of the spiritual dimension of the Cold War to justify American policies. What separated Sweeting and other evangelicals from this broader concern was the focus on the Church. The logical response to Communism, Sweeting continued, was to strengthen the Church and engage in spiritual rollback. This rhetoric, so similar to calls by evangelicals and others in the realm of American conduct in the Cold War, was aimed exclusively at the Church. "When the church loses compassion," Sweeting concluded, "Christianity confines itself to acts of worship; but when it is filled with love for a needy world, it grows from worship to activity. This is the hour for action. We must take the offensive. We must mobilize an all-out crusade to win the lost." Sweeting finished with a stark contrast that evinced the peculiarly evangelical bipolarity between the Church and Communism: "The hammer and the sickle demand a lot, but Christ and His cross demand all."[31] Thus, for Sweeting, the ontological distinction between the Church and other forces actually fueled his call for growing American evangelical involvement in the "needy world." Yet this involvement was framed not as an act of patriotism, or even chiefly for the sake of the nation, but in order to advance the Church's interests.

A similar distinction between Church and nation prevailed in evangelical jeremiads during the Cold War, which often focused on declining American morals and weakness in the face of Communism. Rev. Bruce W. Dunn, in the *King's Business* in 1967, wrote bitterly on "watching a nation die" through moral depravity, weak leadership, and the schemes of international Communism. Dunn called for a "blood transfusion" to save the nation. "The only people in America today that have the blood, the life to give, are the people of God."

30. George Sweeting, "Communism or Christ," *King's Business*, October 1961, 11.
31. Sweeting, "Communism or Christ."

Most strikingly, Dunn urged his readers to become like the "early Christian church . . . they were radicals, they were fanatics, they were out of step with the age." The solution in 1967 was the same used by the early church in 67 CE: "God's people giving America a blood transfusion. We watch a nation die; God help us to renew its life."[32] The striking line revealed a stark contrast between the "we" of the Church (fulfilling a sacrificial Christlike role) and the dying nation.

This framing of the Cold War as a spiritual battle between the Church and Communism could also be seen in the special role that the United States played in evangelical prophecy. Hal Lindsey, the greatest popularizer of dispensationalism during the Cold War, was typical in his ambivalence about role of the United States in God's plans. "According to the prophetic outlook," Lindsey wrote in his 1970 best seller, *The Late Great Planet Earth*, "the United States will cease being the leader of the West and will probably become in some way a part of the new European sphere of power. . . . It is certain that the leadership of the West must shift to Rome, in its revived form, and if the U.S. is still around at that time, it will not be the power it now is."[33] It is true that Lindsey, like many evangelicals during the Cold War, believed religious revival could reverse the immediate decline of American power in the 1970s. "The only chance of slowing up this decline in America," Lindsey warned, "is a widespread spiritual awakening." However, even this element of evangelical agency in the life of the nation was conceived by Lindsey in terms of the Church. Focused especially on American youth who rejected institutional churches and religion, he wrote glowingly of a growing "movement toward first century–type Christianity, with an emphasis upon people and their needs rather than buildings and unwieldy programs."[34] For Lindsey, the Church would be the engine to drive moral regeneration in the nation. National health was essentially epiphenomenal of the more essential health of the Church. Cold War evangelical concerns over the successes of ecumenism and even, in Lindsey's prophetic focus, the looming concern over a one-world church, were thus first-priority issues in light of the Church's role in safeguarding the nation.

Rounding out the divine economy during the Cold War, evangelicals also argued that America's support for the state of Israel was an existential issue for the nation. Writing in the *King's Business* in 1961, Norman Allensworth

---

32. Bruce W. Dunn, "Watching a Nation Die," *King's Business*, February 1967, 12.

33. Hal Lindsey and Carole C. Carlson, *The Late Great Planet Earth* (Grand Rapids: Zondervan, 1970), 84.

34. Lindsey and Carlson, *Late Great Planet Earth*, 172–73.

explicated the "reward for befriending the Jews." Citing Genesis 12:3, he wrote, "As a nation, the United States has been friendly to the Jews, and this country has been a refuge for them; this may account for the way God has blessed our nation so signally [*sic*]."[35] The realization by evangelicals that this aspect of the divine economy could actually decide the fate of the United States grew during the Cold War. By 1984, Jerry Falwell, the leader of the Moral Majority, could reflect, "In the past twenty years, Fundamentalists and Evangelicals, at a very rapid pace, have been 'converting' to support for Israel."[36] Falwell's own understanding mirrored the traditional evangelical conception of the divine economy. Speaking on American support for Israel, he explained: "I personally believe that God deals with all nations in relation to how these nations deal with Israel. I think history supports this."[37] More to the point, Falwell wrote elsewhere that, based on Genesis 12:3, to "stand against Israel is to stand against God."[38]

"Antistatist Statism"

The views propagated by Ockenga, Bradbury, Sweeting, Lindsey, and Falwell indicated that evangelicals during the Cold War did not merely view themselves as the moral guardians of the nation, but viewed the nation as the caretaker of the Church. Evangelical calls for cultural engagement, social commitment, and political organizing often stemmed from this basic understanding. The community's political priorities were directed by the underlying assumptions of God's divine economy.

By the 1970s, many evangelicals had embraced what Axel Schäfer has termed "antistatist statism." The 1960s upheaval both sharpened evangelical criticism of American society and reinforced the centrality of the government in deciding moral issues. As Schäfer argues about the New Christian Right, "Rather than solely reflecting a post-1960s backlash against the liberal state, it was a particular conservative way of reasserting the trajectory of Cold War state building."[39] Evangelicals during the Cold War were never antistatist or

---

35. Norman Allensworth, "The Christian's Reward for Befriending the Jews," *King's Business*, March 1961, 12.

36. Merrill Simon, *Jerry Falwell and the Jews* (Middle Village, NY: Jonathan David Publishers, 1984), 88.

37. Simon, *Jerry Falwell and the Jews*, 62.

38. Jerry Falwell, *Listen, America!* (New York: Doubleday, 1980), 215.

39. Schäfer, *Piety and Public Funding*, 175.

statist as such, but they approached the role of government through their inherited understanding of a dispensationalist divine economy. The role of the state was to safeguard, protect, and even promote the mission of the Church. Limited government and laissez-faire economics had historically been a boon to the American churches. As John F. Walvoord, president of Dallas Theological Seminary, observed in 1967: "Although the United States numbers only five per cent of the total world population, in the last century probably more than fifty percent of the missionaries and money spent has come from America. In view of the fact that it is God's major purpose in this present age to call out Jew and Gentile to faith in Christ and to have the Gospel preached in all nations, the prosperity which has been true of America has made possible this end and may have been permitted by God to accomplish His holy purposes."[40]

Hal Lindsey likewise defined America's role in terms of its protection of the Church. In his 1980 call for a renewed national commitment to the Cold War, he explained "why the U.S. has been preserved as a free country" in terms precisely dependent on the divine economy. His four reasons included the following: "that this country is made up of a large community of true believers in the Lord Jesus Christ"; that it "has supported and provided for missionaries"; that it "has stood behind Jews and the state of Israel in their times of need"; and that "God's people pray."[41]

Lindsey's thinking informed the new evangelical political activism in the 1970s and 1980s, as the specter of secular humanism—framed by leaders as an extension of atheistic Communism—threatened to diminish the position of the Church in the United States. While scholars have focused on the intense evangelical backlash in areas such as public schooling and traditional values, evangelical leaders were equally concerned about more general threats to the Church.[42] For Tim LaHaye, an evangelical activist and pastor, the threat of humanism was framed in terms of church and state. "In spite of our commitment to 'separation of church and state,'" he lamented in his 1982 book *The Battle for the Family*, "we have permitted the government to establish the state religion of humanism in our public schools and exclusively teach its religious beliefs

40. John F. Walvoord, *The Nations in Prophecy* (Grand Rapids: Zondervan, 1967), 174.
41. Hal Lindsey, *The 1980's: The Countdown to Armageddon* (Opelousas, LA: Westgate Press, 1980), 156–57.
42. See, for example, Natalia Mehlman Petrzela, *Classroom Wars: Language, Sex, and the Making of Modern Political Culture* (New York: Oxford University Press, 2015); Robert O. Self, *All in the Family: The Realignment of American Democracy since the 1960s* (New York: Macmillan, 2012); and J. Flippen, *Jimmy Carter, the Politics of Family, and the Rise of the Religious Right* (Athens: University of Georgia Press, 2011).

to our children."[43] He explained the proper relationship between church and state in dispensationalist terms. "Government must provide a peaceful environment, free of governmental interference, so that Christians living in that country can preach the Gospel, telling all men it is God's will they be saved."[44] LaHaye responded by organizing a political campaign to battle over the composition of the government, over its support or antipathy toward the Church. "The biggest army (the church and her many agencies, along with millions of other moralists and special-interest groups) is fighting with its back against the wall, as if the survival of our culture is at stake; and it is." LaHaye was indicative of the mind-set of evangelicals who made up the "foot soldiers" of the New Christian Right. Rather than seeking to maintain the autonomy of the Church by rejecting the power of the state, the New Christian Right embraced a form of statism—of promoting increased economic growth, subsidizing religious organizations, and promoting religious freedom rights abroad—in order to bolster the Church.

In the end, the implicit, often-assumed, and always present categories of Church, Israel, and the nations fundamentally shaped how evangelicals related to the Cold War and the American Cold War state. These categories did not dictate the rise of the New Christian Right, but they explain the perspective with which evangelicals came to see the Cold War. The theological categories organized evangelical energies and informed their evolving political views on American foreign and domestic policy. Moreover, they dictated the conceptualization of the Cold War that regarded the basic conflict as between the Church and the opposing "religion" of Communism. As the guardian of the most successful period of missions and church growth in modern history, the United States deserved the allegiance of Cold War evangelicals; it was a special nation among the nations. But that chosenness was not engraved in prophecy, nor was it irrevocable, unlike the biblical covenants with the Church and Israel. Evangelical allegiance to either American society or the state was contingent on their continuing deference to the Church and its mission. In the later Cold War era, this mission appeared to diverge from the nation with which it had developed a symbiotic relationship. At the end of the Cold War, the entanglement between church and state itself had indelibly marked the Church.

The evangelical Christian nationalism that took shape during the Cold War continued past its official end in 1991. For evangelical Christian nationalists, both the Cold War and post–Cold War era were bridged by the dispensa-

43. Tim LaHaye, *The Battle for the Family* (Old Tappan, NJ: Revell, 1982), 91.
44. LaHaye, *Battle for the Family*, 228.

tionalist categories of Church, Israel, and the nations. Though the ideological Cold War between capitalism and Communism appeared to be over, the spiritual Cold War between the Church and its opponents (the nations) merely entered a new phase. If the contest between the USA and the USSR was about freedom, so too was the contest between the Church and the nations. While the US government acted as the chief protagonist in the international contest to protect economic freedom, it increasingly strayed toward being an antagonistic member of the nations in the spiritual conflict to protect religious freedom at home. Progressive legislation, Supreme Court decisions, and secular humanist influence in education, cultural institutions, and government were all seen by evangelicals to forward communistic goals against the Church, only at a slower pace. Domestic incrementalism was little better than international revolution. Both posed potential existential threats to the Church. In the late twentieth and early twenty-first century, this antistatist statism became a hallmark of evangelical Christian nationalism.

Here, then, we reach the limits of an evangelical Christian nationalism indelibly shaped by its theological commitments. While systematic dispensationalist teaching has fallen out of favor even among many conservative sectors of American evangelicalism, the general categories of concern—the taxonomic distinction between Church, Israel, and the nations—still hold sway. The political implications of these terms were never fixed, but they were products of the intersection of inherited evangelical thinking and the onset of the Cold War.

The Great Undecided Group:
Billy Graham, Jerry Falwell, and the
Evangelical Debate over Nuclear Weapons

Jeremy Hatfield

"The atomic age opened with prayer," the late historian Paul Boyer wrote. As the *Enola Gay* departed Tinian Island on its fateful flight toward Hiroshima on August 6, 1945, a chaplain prayed for God's blessing upon its crew.[1] Three days later, in a radio address delivered after a second atomic bomb had fallen on Nagasaki, President Harry Truman thanked God that the atomic bomb had come first to Americans "instead of our enemies," adding, "We pray that He may guide us to use it in His ways and for His purposes"[2]

The idea that God had given the atomic bomb to Americans to be used for "His purposes" did not generate tremendous controversy in the environment of the postwar nationalist consensus. The evangelical community, represented most notably by the National Association of Evangelicals (NAE) and evangelist Billy Graham, largely supported this consensus and actively cultivated it through anti-Communist rhetoric. By the late 1970s, however, the consensus had fractured, and evangelicals could no longer be counted on to faithfully endorse the American exceptionalism of the early Cold War. The social, cultural, and political fracturing of the 1960s, coupled with the divisive war in Vietnam, divided evangelicals no less than the rest of the nation. Evangelicals, moreover, had become more concerned with global issues. As reports of a "window of vulnerability" between American and Soviet nuclear forces created renewed concerns about the possibility of nuclear war in the late 1970s, the evangelical community was drawn into debates about the morality of nuclear weapons.

1. Paul Boyer, *By the Bomb's Early Light: American Thought and Culture at the Dawn of the Atomic Age* (New York: Pantheon Books, 1985), 211. This essay is partially derived from Jeremy R. Hatfield, "For God and Country: The Religious Right, the Reagan Administration, and the Cold War" (PhD diss., Ohio University, 2013).

2. Harry S. Truman, "Radio Report to the American People on the Potsdam Conference," Harry S. Truman Presidential Library and Museum, August 9, 1945, http://www.trumanlibrary.org/publicpapers/index.php?pid=104&st=&st1.

This chapter focuses on the activities of two participants in those debates, Billy Graham and Jerry Falwell. Graham, the formerly ardent anti-Communist, embraced the new internationalism of neoevangelicals and with it concerns about global poverty and social justice. Falwell, meanwhile, sought to maintain and revive the fierce nationalist spirit of the early Cold War consensus.

As Graham and Falwell spoke out about nuclear weapons, they revealed deep fissures within the evangelical community, divisions over evangelicals' involvement in partisan politics and endorsement of American exceptionalism. These divisions underscored what historian Molly Worthen has called the "crisis of authority" in American evangelicalism.[3] When evangelicals looked to Graham and Falwell for guidance on nuclear issues, they received contradictory messages, leaving individual believers to decide which evangelist spoke for orthodox, biblical Christianity. While the colorful and bombastic Religious Right of Falwell and others drew an extraordinary amount of mainstream media attention in the late 1970s and throughout the 1980s—suggesting that the evangelical community as a whole was decidedly right-wing and hawkish on national defense issues—Billy Graham pushed back against the religious nationalism that had characterized his early ministry. Graham emerged from his antinuclear activism as a surprising symbol of a new internationalism that encouraged criticism of American foreign policy and concern for social justice on a global scale.[4]

On March 29, 1979, Billy Graham appeared on the *CBS Evening News* and declared that "the teaching of the Bible" encouraged "the total destruction of nuclear arms."[5] Graham later expounded upon his views in an interview with *Sojourners*, a periodical of the evangelical Left. "I honestly wish we had never developed nuclear weapons," Graham remarked. "We have nuclear weapons in horrifying quantities, and the question is, what are we going to do about it?" He continued, "I believe that the Christian especially has a responsibility to work for peace in our world. The issues are not simple, and we are always tempted to grasp any program which promises easy answers. Or, on the other side, we are tempted to say that the issues are too complex, and we cannot do anything of significance anyway. We must resist both temptations." Ruminating on the ongoing debate over Senate ratification of the second round of the Strategic Arms Limitation Talks (SALT II) treaty, Graham noted, "If SALT II

3. Molly Worthen, *Apostles of Reason: The Crisis of Authority in American Evangelicalism* (New York: Oxford University Press, 2014), 2.

4. David Swartz, "Embodying the Global Soul: Internationalism and the American Evangelical Left," *Religions* 3 (2012): 887–901.

5. "Billy Graham Drops the Bomb," *Christianity and Crisis*, April 30, 1979, 111.

were the final treaty we would ever negotiate for arms limitation, then relatively little has been accomplished. But these things have to be taken one step at a time. SALT II should give way to SALT III. I wish we were working on SALT 10 right now! Total destruction of nuclear arms."[6]

Graham's critique of nuclear proliferation happened at a moment of great tension over the nuclear arms race. For years, officials within the American intelligence community had disagreed over estimates of the Soviet Union's offensive weapons capabilities and the Soviets' intent in amassing those weapons. One side of the argument held that early Cold War estimates of Soviet nuclear capabilities had been wrong and the threat to American national security represented by the Soviets' nuclear weapons was overstated. On this side, many officials believed that the Soviets' nuclear weapons were primarily intended for defensive purposes and not for backing a worldwide Communist revolution. Reports commissioned from the Central Intelligence Agency's "Team B," a group of experts outside the American intelligence community, held the opposite view. Team B's reports, made public shortly after Jimmy Carter's election to the presidency in 1976, suggested not only that the Soviets held a greater offensive nuclear weapons capability than Americans had estimated previously, but also that "all the evidence" gathered by Team B's studies pointed "to an undeviating Soviet commitment to what is euphemistically called the 'worldwide triumph of socialism.'"[7] By 1979, when Graham began speaking out against nuclear proliferation, many Americans were concerned about the so-called "window of vulnerability" that existed between American and Soviet nuclear arsenals. In a November 1979 article in *U.S. News and World Report*, former secretary of state Henry Kissinger warned that unless American officials moved quickly to address this window, the 1980s could become "a period of massive crisis" for the United States.[8]

While the increasing rancor over nuclear weapons led some evangelicals like Graham to criticize nuclear proliferation as a moral blight in world affairs, it led others to double down on attempts to revive the spirit of the early Cold War nationalist consensus among evangelicals. Evangelist Jerry Falwell led this campaign. Pastor of Thomas Road Baptist Church in Lynchburg, Virginia,

---

6. "A Change of Heart: Billy Graham on the Nuclear Arms Race," *Sojourners*, August 1979, 12–14.

7. Jon Meacham, *Destiny and Power: The American Odyssey of George Herbert Walker Bush* (New York: Random House, 2015), 201–2; "New C.I.A. Estimate Finds Soviet Seeks Superiority in Arms," *New York Times*, December 26, 1976, 1.

8. Joseph Fromm, "Arms Gap: How Russia Stole a March on U.S.," *U.S. News and World Report*, November 12, 1979, 41.

Falwell had grown to prominence through his nationally syndicated radio and television program, *The Old Time Gospel Hour*, which was broadcast on 275 radio stations and 310 television stations across the country in the late 1970s, reaching an estimated eighteen million Americans each week, while his ministry's annual revenue was more than $30 million. Falwell's national visibility was such that *Esquire* magazine proclaimed him "the next Billy Graham" in an October 1978 profile.[9]

Beginning in 1975, Falwell toured the country holding "I Love America" rallies on the steps of state capitol buildings; he would be flanked by a patriotic choir from Lynchburg Baptist College (the school Falwell founded that would later be renamed Liberty University) and surrounded by American flags. Riding a wave of popularity created in part by the rise of the "electronic church" and spurred on by activists in the New Right, Falwell founded the Moral Majority in June 1979. Throughout its decade-long existence, the organization mobilized support for conservative candidates and causes. In the words of its promotional literature, the Moral Majority was "pro-life, pro-family, pro-moral, and pro-American."[10]

In August 1979, Falwell sent a "special report" on national security to followers of his ministry. Entitled "Why Every American Should Oppose SALT II," the "report" warned readers that the Soviet Union was just as bent on world domination in 1979 as it had been in the days of Lenin. Falwell argued that the SALT II treaty, which was awaiting Senate ratification at the time, would lock the United States into permanent nuclear inferiority to the Soviet Union. Accepting at face value the conclusions of the Team B studies, Falwell wrote, "The United States is becoming so weak militarily that the lives and destiny of the American people may soon rest in the hands of the Soviet Union. . . . It is time that Christians took a bold stand against the ratification of SALT II, a treaty which contains irreparable flaws and which threatens our survival as a free nation."[11] Falwell built on these arguments in his 1980 political manifesto *Listen, America!* He wrote, "The sad fact is that [in an ex-

9. Frances Fitzgerald, "A Disciplined, Charging Army," *New Yorker*, May 18, 1981, 53–141; Mary Murphy, "The Next Billy Graham," *Esquire*, October 10, 1978, 25–32; "A Tide of Born Again Politics," *Newsweek*, September 15, 1980, 28–29.

10. *Your Invitation to Join the Moral Majority*, pamphlet, Collection Mor 1-1, Folder 2, MM Brochures & Pamphlets, Liberty University Archive, Lynchburg, VA; William Martin, *With God on Our Side: The Rise of the Religious Right in America* (New York: Broadway Books, 1996), 200.

11. Jerry Falwell, "Why Every American Should Oppose SALT II," Oversize Magazines, Folder 1B, Periodical Articles, Liberty University Archive.

change of missiles] today the Soviet Union would kill 135 million to 160 million Americans, and the United States would kill only 3 to 5 percent of the Soviets because of [Soviet] antiballistic missiles and their civil defense."[12]

In the late 1970s, then, Billy Graham and Jerry Falwell, two of the most prominent leaders of the evangelical community, stood on opposite sides of one of the most pressing issues of the day. They also stood on opposite ends of the debate about the role evangelicals should play in politics. Graham remarked, in interviews, that groups like the Moral Majority were "not [his] cup of tea" and that "it would be unfortunate if people got the impression all evangelists belong to that group." Graham concluded, "I don't wish to be identified with them. . . . I'm for morality. But morality goes beyond sex to human freedom and social justice. We as clergy know so very little to speak out with such authority on the Panama Canal or superiority of armaments. . . . We have to stand in the middle in order to preach to all people, right and left." Graham defended his own decision to speak out on nuclear proliferation by noting, "I am not a pacifist—I believe we have a right to defend our country. But so many little nations are feverishly working on or have gotten an atomic bomb. When anyone has the power to destroy the whole human race in a matter of hours, it becomes a moral issue. The church must speak out."[13]

Ronald Reagan's election to the presidency in 1980 drew urgent attention to the nuclear issue. Reagan was elected on a platform that included bolstering American national defense and talking tough about Soviet Communism. Once in office, the Reagan administration initiated a buildup of nuclear weapons. The Reagan administration's defense policies encouraged the activism of the nuclear freeze movement and engendered discussion of nuclear issues in evangelical periodicals. On the left, *Sojourners* published articles encouraging evangelicals to oppose nuclear proliferation and become active in "loving the Russians."[14] On the right, Jerry Falwell's *Moral Majority Report*, which claimed a readership of 482,000 in the fall of 1980, defended the Reagan administration's policies, promoted fear of the growing Soviet nuclear threat, and encouraged evangelicals to explore the hidden motivations behind nuclear freeze activism.

12. Jerry Falwell, *Listen, America!* (New York: Doubleday, 1980), 98.

13. Garry Clifford, "Billy Graham, First of the Big-Time TV Preachers, Warns Falwell & Co. of Danger Ahead," *People*, February 16, 1981; Marguerite Michaels, "Billy Graham: America Is Not God's Only Kingdom," *Parade*, February 1, 1981, in *The New Right: Readings and Commentary*, vol. 4 (Oakland: CA: Data Center, 1981), 597–99.

14. Joseph Allegretti, "On Loving the Russians," *Sojourners* 11, no. 10 (November 1982): 22–23; Danny Collum, "Anti-Communism: Our State Religion," *Sojourners* 11, no. 10 (November 1982): 19–21; "Stacking Sandbags against a Conservative Flood," *Christianity Today*, November 2, 1979, 76.

Meanwhile, *Christianity Today*, a neoevangelical publication, took a centrist position on its editorial page, calling on evangelicals to examine nuclear issues in the light of traditional Christian doctrines of just war.[15]

While evangelicals debated nuclear issues, mainline Protestants and Roman Catholics took action. In 1982, the United Methodist Church, the Episcopal Church, the Lutheran Church in America, the American Lutheran Church, and the Southern Baptist Convention all issued statements that denounced American escalation of the nuclear arms race.[16] In November of that year, the National Conference of Catholic Bishops met in Washington, DC, to discuss nuclear weapons. Under the direction of Archbishop (later Cardinal) Joseph Bernardin of Chicago, the bishops drafted an open letter that expressed concern about the costs of nuclear proliferation, in terms of both the potential loss of life the weapons represented and the economic injustice caused by massive spending on nuclear defense.[17]

The united front presented by the mainline denominations and the Catholic bishops only underscored divisions within the evangelical community. Billy Graham's trip to Moscow in May 1982 drew further attention to evangelicals' involvement in the nuclear debate. Graham had sought an invitation to preach in Moscow for some time. When the invitation came in early 1982, it was not explicitly to preach, but rather to attend a peace conference organized by the Russian Orthodox Church. Entitled "World Conference of Religious Workers for Saving the Sacred Gift of Life from Nuclear Catastrophe," the four-day event was designed to draw attention to nuclear proliferation and in particular to highlight Moscow's efforts to rid the world of the specter of nuclear war. The announcement that Graham would attend the conference drew criticism from officials in Washington who feared, not without reason, that Graham's presence would signal an implicit endorsement of anti-American speeches delivered at the event.[18]

15. "In Matters of War and Peace . . . ," *Christianity Today*, November 21, 1980, 14–15; "SALT II: The Only Alternative to Annihilation," *Christianity Today*, March 27, 1981, 14–15.

16. Anne C. Loveland, *American Evangelicals and the U.S. Military, 1942–1993* (Baton Rouge: Louisiana State University Press, 1996), 232; "Lutherans Ask Nuclear Ban," *New York Times*, September 12, 1982, 27.

17. Loveland, *American Evangelicals*, 232; National Conference of Catholic Bishops, "The Challenge of Peace: God's Promise and Our Response," May 3, 1983, http://www.usccb.org /upload/challenge-peace-gods-promise-our-response-1983.pdf; Richard N. Ostling et al., "The Bishops and the Bomb," *Time* 20, no. 22 (November 29, 1982): 80–95.

18. "Billy Renders unto Caesar," *New York Times*, May 24, 1982, 89; "Graham Says U.S. Wavered on Moscow Trip," *Baltimore Sun*, May 17, 1982, A3; William Martin, *A Prophet with Honor: The Billy Graham Story* (New York: William Morrow, 1991), 491–513.

Graham's tour of American college campuses in the spring of 1982 compounded these concerns. In April, Graham spoke on the campuses of eight prestigious American universities, including Yale, Harvard, Northeastern, Boston College, and the Massachusetts Institute of Technology (MIT). Eschewing his traditional crusade format, the evangelist fashioned his presentation as a lecture entitled "Peace in a Nuclear Age." At Yale University, Graham remarked, "There are political and social forces moving now which seem to be pushing the world relentlessly toward the brink of chaos, because for the first time in the history of mankind, we have the technology to destroy the human race within a matter of hours." The evangelist repeated his call for "SALT 10" and reminded listeners that the assurance of God's sovereignty over world affairs was no excuse to remain passive in the face of the nuclear threat. "We have the responsibility to work for peace now," he said. "We don't know when the judgment is coming."[19]

Thus in May 1982, Graham departed for Moscow as a leading voice for nuclear disarmament. Speaking to delegates assembled at the peace conference, Graham argued that the nuclear arms race represented an economic injustice committed against the world's poor. "Every day, millions upon millions of people live on the knife-edge of survival because of starvation, poverty, and disease. At the same time, we are told the nations of the world are spending an estimated $600 billion per year on weapons," Graham noted, surmising, "If even one-tenth of that amount were diverted to long-range development programs that would help the world's poor and starving, millions of lives could be saved each year." Graham told the delegates that he "firmly believe[d] that God [would] judge" all parties involved in the arms race for their "blindness and lack of compassion" unless they recognized their "moral and spiritual responsibility concerning [the] life and death matter" of nuclear war. While renewing his call for "SALT 10," Graham charged world leaders to tone down the hostile rhetoric of the Cold War, to increase cultural exchanges between Eastern and Western nations, and to respect "the rights of believers as outlined in the United Nations Declaration of Human Rights."[20]

19. "Billy Graham at Yale," *Yale Daily News*, April 16, 1982, 4; "Graham Urges Divine Faith," *Yale Daily News*, April 20, 1982, 1, 5; "Evangelical Common Sense," *Yale Daily News*, April 21, 1982, 2; Billy Graham, "Peace in a Nuclear Age" (lecture at Yale University, April 19, 1982, Collection 26, T3921, Billy Graham Center, Wheaton, IL; Graham's Sermon: Collection 285, Records of the BGEA: Montreat Office: Billy Graham—Papers, Part I: Crusade Sermon Notebooks 1954, 1957, 1969–2005, Box 10, Folder 49, New England Universities, 1982–April 15, Peace in a Nuclear Age, Billy Graham Center, Wheaton, IL).

20. Martin, *A Prophet with Honor*, 507–8.

Unfortunately for the evangelist, a number of political gaffes committed during the trip drew attention away from his participation in the peace conference. While in Moscow, Graham preached at a Baptist church. In his sermon, the evangelist turned to Romans 13, where the apostle Paul exhorted Christians to "submit" themselves "to the governing authorities." Graham told the congregation that becoming a Christian would give one "the power to be a better worker" and a "loyal citizen." When considered in light of Marxist-Leninist political philosophy, these remarks seemed to endorse Soviet workers' oppression by the Communist state. When a reporter from Graham's hometown of Charlotte, North Carolina, asked the evangelist for a comment concerning his observations of religious freedom in the Soviet Union, Graham replied, "There are differences between religion as it's practiced here, and, let's say, in the United States, but that doesn't mean there is no religious freedom" in Moscow. Graham concluded that at least "a measure of freedom" existed for Christians to practice their faith in the Soviet Union, and "perhaps more than Americans think."[21]

Conservatives lambasted Graham in the American press. Columnist George F. Will labeled the evangelist "America's most embarrassing export." In an op-ed piece entitled "The Duping of Billy Graham," journalist and peace activist Colman McCarthy asked, "Why is there surprise that Billy Graham was snookered by the Soviets?" McCarthy labeled the evangelist "a man of weak analytic power" whose propensity for "talking too much and thinking too little" was on full display in Moscow. Graham's fellow evangelical Edmund W. Robb, chairman of the Institute on Religion and Democracy, remarked, "There is no question about [Graham's] integrity and good intentions, but he is apparently so anxious to be an apostle of peace that he's blinded to some of the realities of the world, one being Soviet oppression of the church." Finally, Jerry Falwell noted that he "sincerely hoped" that Graham "was misquoted or taken out of context because there is no religious liberty in the Soviet Union." Falwell added, "Everything the Soviets do is for propaganda purposes and for their advantage. I don't think [Graham] had any wrong intentions whatever. I think the Soviets had all the wrong intentions." Nonetheless, Falwell concluded that if Graham had not been misquoted, then he was "incredibly naïve."[22]

21. "Graham Preaches Peace, Loyalty in Moscow," *Washington Post*, May 10, 1982, A13; Edward E. Plowman, "Billy Graham: The Gospel Truth in Moscow," *Saturday Evening Post*, September 1982, 68–69, 102, 110–12; Martin, *A Prophet with Honor*, 514–18.

22. George F. Will, "Let Us Pray for a Little Skepticism," *Washington Post*, May 13, 1982, A31; "Falwell Calls Graham 'Naïve,'" *Deseret News*, May 14, 1982, A7; "Graham's Remarks on Soviet Religion Criticized," *Washington Post*, May 15, 1982, B5; Colman McCarthy, "The Duping of Billy Graham," *Washington Post*, May 23, 1982, K2.

Though Graham's political gaffes largely obscured his stirring anti-nuclear message in Moscow, the prodisarmament sentiments of America's leading evangelical did not go unnoticed in the White House, nor among the ranks of the National Association of Evangelicals (NAE). As the representative body of American evangelicals, the NAE was itself divided in the nuclear debate. At its annual convention in March 1982, the NAE adopted a resolution that expressed "deep concern about the threat of a nuclear holocaust" and called on America's "national leaders to rededicate their efforts to obtain a meaningful arms control agreement that will scale down the nuclear arms race."[23] The NAE resolution, combined with Graham's anti-nuclear rhetoric in Moscow, added to pressure that was already mounting on the Reagan administration in 1982 to curb the arms race. In June, between 500,000 and 700,000 protestors lined the streets of Manhattan, marching from the United Nations Plaza to Central Park in a rally against nuclear proliferation. In the midterm elections that November, voters in eight states passed resolutions in favor of some form of a nuclear freeze.[24] The *Moral Majority Report* advised readers that these antinuclear actions were the real threat to American security. "Although in theory, the idea of a freeze on nuclear weapons seems to diminish somewhat the possibilities of a nuclear war, in reality it will lock the Soviets into a position of ultimate superiority and lead to nuclear blackmail and surrender of the United States," an article in the August 1982 issue of the *Report* argued.[25]

Recognizing an opportunity to draw attention to evangelicals' engagement with and division over the nuclear debate, officials within the NAE invited President Reagan to address the organization's annual convention in Orlando, Florida, in March 1983. In a letter to White House Chief of Staff James Baker, the NAE's chief political liaison, Robert P. Dugan Jr., suggested that many evangelicals "were not yet firmly positionalized [*sic*] on the nuclear freeze issue," while reassuring Baker that he was working "behind the scenes" to counteract evangelicals' "drift toward the nuclear freeze position." In a separate letter to Reagan's speechwriter Tony Dolan, Dugan argued that in light of the successes of the freeze movement in 1982, the NAE speech would provide

23. "NAE's Social Awareness Grows," *Christianity Today*, April 9, 1982, 42.

24. "Throngs Fill Manhattan to Protest Nuclear Weapons," *New York Times*, June 13, 1982, 1; "Rally Speakers Decry Cost of Nuclear Arms Race," *New York Times*, June 13, 1982, 43; "Widespread Vote Urges Nuclear Freeze," *New York Times*, November 4, 1982, A22; Loveland, *American Evangelicals*, 220.

25. Deryl Edwards, "Nuclear Freeze: Blackmail of America," *Moral Majority Report*, August 1982, 6.

an ideal opportunity for the president to defend his nuclear defense policies against its critics.[26]

In his address at the NAE convention, Reagan charged evangelicals to "beware the temptation of pride" and "blithely declaring" themselves "above" debates about nuclear issues by considering both sides of the Cold War equally at fault for the continued proliferation of the arms race. The president labeled the freeze movement a "dangerous fraud" that would only create "the illusion of peace" and memorably referred to the Soviet Union as an "evil empire."[27] Exiting the stage to the melody of "Onward, Christian Soldiers," Reagan might have sensed that, in spite of a standing ovation from his audience, not all evangelicals in attendance agreed with the sentiments of his speech. NAE president Arthur Gay Jr., for instance, did not join his fellow evangelicals in standing to applaud the president's remarks.[28]

Reagan received considerable aid from Jerry Falwell and the Moral Majority in advancing the message he had delivered in Orlando. In the wake of the NAE convention, Falwell met with Reagan at the White House and persuaded the president that the case against the nuclear freeze movement needed to be simplified into a message that the average American could understand. Volunteering to take on this task on Reagan's behalf, Falwell received a briefing from National Security Council officials, who provided the televangelist with charts and graphs that could be employed in the administration's defense. In April 1983, the Moral Majority purchased a number of full-page, antinuclear freeze ads in newspapers across the United States.[29] The April 1983 issue of the *Moral Majority Report* was largely dedicated to the nuclear issue, with a front-page headline reading "Nuclear Freeze: The Big Lie."[30] Falwell appeared on the popular *Donahue* talk show to defend the Reagan administration against its antinuclear critics. In November 1983, the ABC Television Network aired

---

26. Dugan to Baker, December 3, 1982, folder 6 in Series I: Presidential Records, "National Association of Evangelicals" File, "1981–1989," Ronald Reagan Presidential Library, Simi Valley, CA; Dugan to Dolan, February 25, 1983, folder 7, Box 19 in Series I, "Speech Drafts, National Association of Evangelicals, March 8, 1983," Ronald Reagan Presidential Library, Simi Valley, CA.

27. *Public Papers of the Presidents of the United States: Ronald Reagan, 1983*, vol. 1 (Washington, DC: Government Printing Office, 1984), 359–64.

28. Beth Spring, "Reagan Courts Evangelical Clout against Nuclear Freeze," *Christianity Today*, April 8, 1983, 44–48.

29. Haynes Johnson, "A Preacher for 'Peace through Strength,' or, Maybe, the Bomb," *Washington Post*, April 2, 1983, A3; "Special Briefing Opposing an Immediate Nuclear Freeze," file 1of 4, Box 7, OA 9079, Series I: Subject File Morton Blackwell Files, Ronald Reagan Presidential Library; Loveland, *American Evangelicals*, 223–24.

30. Robert Baldwin, "Peace through Strength," *Moral Majority Report*, April 1983, 2–3.

The Day After, a film that depicted a Soviet nuclear attack against the town of Lawrence, Kansas. Falwell and the Moral Majority sought to counteract the film's implicit antinuclear message. A week before the movie aired, Falwell sent a press release to pastors, encouraging them to dissuade their congregations from watching the film. In the release, Falwell argued that *The Day After* was "a blatant attempt to undermine President Reagan's desire to achieve lasting peace and avoid nuclear war through a policy of strength leading to mutually assured survival." Falwell concluded that the film was "cheap propaganda," and that he hoped it "backfired on ABC." The December 1983 issue of the *Moral Majority Report* expressed similar sentiments under a headline reading "*Day After* TV Film Scares U.S."[31]

Falwell thus helped to turn 1983 into the year of the evangelical counteroffensive against the nuclear freeze movement. In the midst of the rancor among the evangelical community's leadership, the question remained what the great mass of American evangelicals really thought about nuclear issues. In an attempt to answer this question, the NAE commissioned in May 1983 a Gallup poll of both evangelicals and the general public concerning nuclear issues. The poll reported that 41 percent of evangelicals and 43 percent of the general public registered approval of President Reagan's nuclear weapons policies. Nonetheless, the poll also revealed that 60 percent of evangelicals and 75 percent of the general public supported "an agreement between the United States and the Soviet Union for an immediate, verifiable freeze on the testing, deployment, and production of nuclear weapons." In spite of this latter result, 76 percent of evangelical respondents and 78 percent of the general public did not believe that the Soviet Union would submit to the on-site inspections necessary to secure a workable nuclear freeze agreement.[32]

A public relations battle ensued to explain the results of this poll. The *Moral Majority Report* argued that the poll demonstrated a clear preference for the Reagan administration's nuclear policies among evangelicals. An article in the *Washington Post*, published in July 1983, emphasized evangelicals' support for a nuclear freeze agreement. That same month, in the pages of the NAE's newsletter, *NAE Insight*, Robert Dugan Jr. came to the defense of evangelicals who opposed the freeze, arguing that the *Post* had misinterpreted the results of the poll and that evangelicals were on Reagan's side when it came to matters

---

31. "Markey, Forsberg Lose Freeze Debate with Falwell, Denton," *Moral Majority Report*, June 1983, 2–3; press release to pastors (undated), Liberty University Archive; "'Day After' TV Film Scares U.S.," *Moral Majority Report*, December 1983, 1.

32. Loveland, *American Evangelicals*, 235.

of nuclear defense. *Christianity Today* offered the most accurate and dispassionate reading of the poll, however, with an article entitled "Evangelicals Are of Two Minds on Nuclear Weapons Issues." While "most evangelicals approve of President Reagan's promilitary policies on nuclear arms," the article noted, "they would support a nuclear freeze if the conditions were right." In addition, the article quoted officials from the NAE's Office of Public Affairs who noted that the results "confirm[ed] their suspicion that evangelicals" constituted "the 'great undecided group'" when it came to debates about nuclear weapons.[33]

Efforts abounded, in the wake of Reagan's speech, to unite evangelicals in substantive debate about nuclear issues. In late May 1983, a number of prominent evangelicals and evangelical organizations converged on Pasadena, California, for the "Church and Peacemaking in the Nuclear Age" conference. Sponsored in part by the NAE, the conference featured a variety of seminars and workshops on topics ranging from "The Medical Effects of Nuclear War" to "Will I Grow Up? The Psychological Impact of the Threat of Nuclear War on Children." Promotional materials touted the "balanced education approach" of the event wherein "differing responses to the nuclear arms race [would] be presented by leading evangelicals who represent conflicting political persuasions." In spite of these reassurances of a balanced approach, the conference failed to secure many commitments from evangelicals who were sympathetic to the Reagan administration's nuclear policies. The result was a conference that mainly reflected viewpoints from the left.[34]

In November 1983, Fuller Theological Seminary published a "Declaration of Conscience about the Arms Race" in *Christianity Today* and *Eternity*. The declaration primarily reflected the viewpoint expressed by Billy Graham and other proponents of disarmament. Decrying the "enormous resources" expended on the arms race and its danger to "the future of the human family on God's earth and the continuation of human civilization as we know it," Fuller's declaration asserted that "total war between the superpowers" could not "be morally justified" and called on the United States and the Soviet Union to stop the arms race, pursue bilateral disarmament, and enact "fundamen-

33. "Evangelicals Favor Peace through Strength," *Moral Majority Report*, August 1983, 8; "Poll Shows Evangelicals Support Nuclear Freeze," *Washington Post*, July 8, 1983, A5; *NAE Insight* 5, no. 7 (July 1983), File 1, box OA 9088, Morton Blackwell files, Ronald Reagan Presidential Library; "Evangelicals Are of Two Minds on Nuclear Weapons Issues," *Christianity Today*, August 5, 1983, 48–51.

34. News release, undated, file 3, box OA 9088, Morton Blackwell Files, Ronald Reagan Presidential Library; John Bernbaum, "Which Roads Lead to Peace," *Eternity*, December 1983, 20–23; Loveland, *American Evangelicals*, 236.

tal change" in the nature of their relationship. "We refuse to believe that, in a world where God is our Lord, our two nations are destined to perpetual hostility," it asserted.[35]

The most substantive effort to draw evangelicals into a debate about nuclear issues came in the NAE's Peace, Freedom, and Security Studies (PFSS) program. Conceived in 1984 partly as a result of the Pasadena conference and cosponsored by the Seattle-based World Without War Council (WWWC), the PFSS initiative was aimed at engendering debate about war and peace issues among evangelicals rather than advocating specific policy positions.[36] In October 1986, the PFSS program published a resolution entitled *Guidelines*. While *Guidelines* was ostensibly apolitical, it proffered thinly veiled criticisms of evangelicals on both the left and the right in its effort to advance a centrist approach to the issues at hand. The authors took evangelicals on the left to task for failing to recognize the perilous cost of Communist oppression in many corners of the globe. On the other hand, the authors excoriated the Religious Right for treating "enlarged American military capabilities" as the solution to "the looming horror of nuclear war." The solutions advanced in *Guidelines* reflected those offered earlier in the decade on the editorial pages of *Christianity Today*. The *Guidelines* authors advocated "an America strong enough to resist attack and to influence the course of world affairs; yet an America that is continually seeking realistic alternatives to war as a means of resolving international conflict." Reflecting concerns about the nature of just war, *Guidelines* also noted that evangelicals would have to address "the issue of whether the means" of nuclear deterrence were "appropriate to the goal" for which nuclear weapons would be deployed.[37]

The PFSS program and the resulting *Guidelines* nonetheless failed to generate a lively debate among evangelicals for two reasons. First, by the time *Guidelines* appeared in 1986, the revamped Cold War of the early Reagan years was abating. The rapprochement achieved by Reagan and Soviet leader Mikhail Gorbachev in the latter half of the 1980s quelled the urgency with which debates on nuclear issues had raged in the early part of the decade. The nuclear freeze movement, demoralized by Reagan's landslide reelection victory in 1984, vanished from the national scene. Billy Graham returned to Moscow

35. Fuller Theological Seminary, "A Declaration of Conscience about the Arms Race," September 25, 1983, appearing in *Christianity Today*, November 11, 1983, unpaginated insert; Loveland, *American Evangelicals*, 233.

36. Loveland, *American Evangelicals*, 237–46.

37. Loveland, *American Evangelicals*, 237–46; *Guidelines: Peace, Freedom, and Security Studies* (n.p.: National Association of Evangelicals, 1986).

in 1984 but did not generate the controversy that had characterized his journey there two years earlier. Jerry Falwell and the Moral Majority, meanwhile,
shifted their attention to promoting the Reagan administration's proposal for
the Strategic Defense Initiative (SDI), a space-based nuclear defense shield
derisively labeled "Star Wars" by its critics.[38]

Second, though the PFSS program was supposed to be apolitical, refrain-
ing from advocating specific policy proposals, it was never clear how the positions espoused in *Guidelines* were any less political than those promoted
by evangelicals on the left and right. As historian Anne Loveland noted, "the
motives and strategy of the PFSS program were as political as those on the
mainline and evangelical groups that the *Guidelines* criticized."[39] Not only did
Guidelines fail to unite evangelicals with its centrist suggestions, but its authors
also failed to perceive the extent to which evangelicals had fragmented into
passionate but disparate political camps by 1986. The 1983 NAE Gallup poll
had suggested not only that evangelicals were undecided on nuclear issues but
also that evangelical opinions on these matters largely reflected the opinions of
society at large. It was unclear, in other words, whether evangelicals' religious
beliefs played a significant role in defining their outlook on nuclear issues. The
struggles of the PFSS program suggest that evangelicals had become "the great
undecided group" on nuclear issues not due to lack of education, but instead
as a result of social, cultural, and political polarization.

The failures of the PFSS program should not overshadow the larger issues that the nuclear debates of the late 1970s and 1980s raised. These debates
demonstrated that evangelicals were divided not only over nuclear weapons
policies but also over whether such policies should be thought of in terms of
nationalism or internationalism. This divide would continue long after the
debates of the early 1980s had subsided, indeed, well into the early twenty-
first century. Throughout the remainder of the 1980s, Jerry Falwell and Billy
Graham continued their involvement in foreign affairs. Falwell and the Moral
Majority joined other conservative evangelicals in supporting President Reagan's proposal for a space-based nuclear missile shield.[40] Graham, meanwhile,
traveled behind the Iron Curtain on three more occasions before the 1991
collapse of the Soviet Union. Ultimately, Ronald Reagan's rhetoric toward the
Soviet Union came to resemble Billy Graham's more than Jerry Falwell's, espe-

38. J. Michael Hogan, *The Nuclear Freeze Campaign: Rhetoric and Foreign Policy in the
Teleopolitical Age* (East Lansing: Michigan State University Press, 1994), 31–32; Loveland, *American Evangelicals*, 224–25, 245–46; Martin, *A Prophet with Honor*, 520–24.

39. Loveland, *American Evangelicals*, 245.

40. Loveland, *American Evangelicals*, 224.

cially as the president sought rapprochement with new Soviet leader Mikhail Gorbachev in the latter half of the 1980s. The president and the evangelist both suggested that common human interests, especially preventing nuclear war, were key to bettering relations between the two superpowers. Graham put it succinctly in a *New York Times* interview conducted shortly after his return from Hungary and Romania in 1985. "In the atomic age," the evangelist remarked, "we have to live on the planet with these people."[41]

41. "Graham Sees Religious Urge in Eastern Bloc," *New York Times*, October 13, 1985, 52.

From Cold War to Culture Wars:
The Institute on Religion and Democracy

Steven M. Tipton

The Institute on Religion and Democracy began with a bang. It issued from a report fired across the bow of the United Methodist Church in 1980, aimed at challenging the "peace and justice" course set by leaders of the Methodist Board of Church and Society, and the Board of Global Ministries. "Most Methodist church-goers would react with disbelief, even anger," the report began, "to be told that a significant portion of their weekly offerings were being siphoned off to groups supporting the Palestine Liberation Organization, the governments of Cuba and Vietnam, and the pro-Soviet totalitarian movements of Latin America, Asia and Africa, and several violence-prone fringe groups in this country."[1]

So charged the report's author, David Jessup, a new member of the United Methodist Church in a large suburban congregation outside Washington, DC, and a longtime labor organizer then working for the AFL-CIO Committee on Political Education (COPE). Jessup concluded that funds were going to "the totalitarian left," as opposed to "the democratic left" represented by "Christian social-democratic parties, free trade unions and democratic governments" such as those of Venezuela, Costa Rica, and Colombia. Jessup also found evidence of related ideological biases in Methodist church agencies. "Judging from their financial contributions, statements, and actions,"

---

1. David Jessup, "Preliminary Inquiry regarding Financial Contributions to Outside Political Groups by Boards and Agencies of the United Methodist Church, 1977–79" (photocopied document, Washington, DC, April 7, 1980), 1; adapted as David Jessup with Cindy D. Vetters, "How United Methodist Dollars Are Given to Marxist Causes," *Good News*, September–October, 1980, 26–34.

This article is adapted from Steven M. Tipton, *Public Pulpits: Methodists and Mainline Churches in the Moral Argument of Public Life* (Chicago: University of Chicago Press, 2007), chap. 5, with the generous permission of the publisher.

he concluded, "several agencies of the Methodist church seem to be favoring the totalitarian option."[2]

Watchdog of the Left or Neocon Political Movement?

Jessup's report, entitled "Preliminary Inquiry regarding Financial Contributions to Outside Political Groups by Boards and Agencies of the United Methodist Church, 1977–1979," asked Methodists to weigh the facts and figures detailed in its twenty-six single-spaced pages and seventy-eight footnotes. It then invited them to support Jessup's petition to the 1980 Methodist General Conference for a churchwide "Committee on Accountability," in order to make sure that misguided denominational bureaucrats and leaders were not betraying the church's membership and the gospel by funding totalitarian governments, socialist movements, and left-wing political groups. After issuing his report a few weeks before the 1980 General Conference met, Jessup circulated copies to conference delegates and actively organized support for his petition. It did not pass, but the General Conference did move to make records of receipts and expenditures of boards and agencies available to annual conferences and local church administrative boards upon request.

Viewed narrowly, the Jessup Report, as it came to be called, did no more than ask United Methodist leaders to keep their long-standing promise, reaffirmed in publications such as "The Use of Money in Mission," to see that "All expenditures are open to scrutiny and are available on request to any individual or congregation."[3] But seen more broadly, in terms that link the Cold War to "culture wars," the Jessup Report triggered a chain of events that challenged the moral vision and social witness of the mainline denominations as corrupted by left-wing politicization threatening to destroy the church itself.

These broader charges stirred a controversy that brought into being the Institute on Religion and Democracy (IRD). The IRD has in turn deepened that controversy and cast its political and theological terms in new ideological light to recharge Cold War conflicts. For all its development and changes since its founding in 1981, the IRD in the eyes of its leaders and supporters has con-

2. Jessup, "Preliminary Inquiry," 1–3, 26; and David Jessup, interview, March 1992, here and below. All interviews were tape-recorded and conducted in Washington, DC, unless otherwise noted.

3. Edwin H. Maynard, "The Use of Money in Mission—an Opportunity for Understanding," by United Methodist Communications with the cooperation of the Board of Global Ministries and the Board of Church and Society, October 17, 1980, 2.

tinued to question with good reason the left-wing political bent of mainline church programs and funding, and criticize the communistic social witness of the national staff and appointed leaders of these denominations. "We are a watchdog of the religious and evangelical left," declared the IRD's president in 2015, "disputing their claims to represent millions of church members while espousing a liberal or far-left political agenda."[4]

For church leaders critical of the IRD, it embodies instead an essentially political movement rooted in the neoconservative ideology of the Reagan era and aimed at undercutting the churches' prophetic witness in public and their faithful social teaching in the pews. It misrepresents both as left-wing politics in traitorous service to a state socialism equally at odds with the gospel truth, the free market, and the American creed. For more than a generation, in this view, the IRD has persisted in declaring and waging culture wars along the polemical lines of the Cold War. It flies the benign banner of orthodox evangelical "church renewal" as a flag of convenience. Yet it actually serves the propaganda interests of a clique of neoconservative ideologues, hawkish political partisans, and right-wing foundations epitomized by Richard Mellon Scaife, the IRD's chief founding funder. The IRD and its allies "indulge in character assassination and seek to drive the church apart by the use of wedge issues, calculated to cause dissension and division."[5] They aim to discredit and muffle the social witness of the mainline churches, especially Methodism, and to gain control of their governance, as cultural-political conservatives did in the Southern Baptist Convention. So charge Methodist bishop Dale White and others who sponsored a 2003 "wake-up call" to alert church members to the great risk rising against the church's life and witness, and move them to fight back.

While attention has been paid to relations between mushrooming parachurch groups and the established denominations, relatively little notice has been given to their complex interrelations within a broader network of voluntary political associations, religious and nonreligious alike. They interact within the larger context of more polarized yet nonetheless overlapping political parties, an expanded state, and a more formally organized, densely crowded, and morally contested polity. Looking closely at the Institute on Religion and Democracy allows us to pursue such an inquiry, particularly by looking into the IRD's dynamic relations with the United Methodist Church,

4. Mark Tooley, "Letter from the President," Institute on Religion and Democracy, 2015, https://theird.org/about/letter-from-the-president/.

5. Bishop C. Dale White et al., "Preface: Wake, Awake!," in *United Methodism @ Risk: A Wake-Up Call*, by Leon Howell (Kingston, NY: Information Project for United Methodists, 2003), 4.

the Democratic Party and its neoconservative critics, the AFL-CIO and organized labor, and the political-cultural Left since the 1960s.

This inquiry allows us to see how expansion of government's moral concern and regulatory reach into a wider range of American social institutions—families, schools, and work—has in turn drawn churches and communities of faith more intricately and controversially into public life. It allows us to hear the ways religious faith in our time and society converses with other forms of cultural meaning and social arrangement, and argues with them in public. We can listen to how this conversation unfolds in contemporary American society, which is not only divided into a dozen major denominations and hundreds of smaller communities of faith but includes thousands of religious and nonreligious lobbies, moral advocacy groups, and voluntary political associations. Together they span and blur old boundary lines between church and state. They enrich and complicate the multivocal public argument that mixes politics and faith in the course of democratic self-government.

Infighting: Religion and Labor Team Up and Square Off

Between 1981 and 1982 the IRD's annual budget jumped from $200,000 to more than $350,000, with the Smith Richardson Foundation giving $81,000 and the Scaife Family Charitable Trusts donating $200,000 in 1982.[6] By early 1983, Scaife had contributed $300,000 and Smith Richardson $146,000 to the IRD. Together with $33,500 from the Olin, Earhart, Ingersoll and Cullom Davis Foundations, this totaled $479,000 of the IRD's initial revenue of $533,000. This yielded the figure of 89 percent of IRD funding coming from foundations on the political far right, which was widely reported in the mainline religious press. So was a picture of the larger pattern of funding these foundations shared: as a group they were dedicated to backing the anti-Communism and military buildup of President Reagan's foreign policy, in some cases through alleged ties to the CIA; and they were supporting Reagan's domestic policies against progressive labor, social welfare, and environmental protection. They were seeking to achieve these ends through interlocking grants to the Heritage Foundation, the American Enterprise Institute, the tax-exempt arm of the National Right

6. Steve Askin, "IRD 89% Funded by Right," *National Catholic Reporter*, February 4, 1983, 7; Paula Herbut, "Church Council Policies 'Leftist,' Institute Charges in New Booklet," *Washington Post*, March 19, 1983, B6; and Leon Howell, "Who Funds IRD?," *Christianity and Crisis*, March 21, 1983, 90–91.

to Work Committee, Ernest Lefever's Ethics and Public Policy Center, James Watt's antienvironmentalist Mountain States Legal Foundation, and the like.[7]

To the IRD's critics, following the trail of its money shed light on its contradictory identity as a group of self-described religious centrists funded by the political right wing to attack religious liberals for consorting with alleged extremists on the political left. To Penn Kemble, the anti-Communist labor activist who built the IRD's organization and funding network, such suspicions were themselves a projection of the Religious Left. "Why does the Left always assume that in this kind of relationship with someone to your right, he's manipulating you?" asked Kemble with exasperation in 1983. The IRD's funders, he affirmed, "are people who, whatever their views on domestic issues, are very seriously anti-Communist. They agree with what we're doing and what we're saying. We don't necessarily agree with what they do."[8]

Controversy over the IRD reflected the doctrinal intricacy and organizational intensity of infighting in the American labor movement since the 1960s. In late 1972 the Socialist Party split into three factions, each claiming the legacy of democratic socialism in the United States. Penn Kemble's Social Democrats, USA (SD/USA), was headed by Bayard Rustin. The Democratic Socialist Organizing Committee, led by the Catholic socialist Michael Harrington and including Congressman Ron Dellums (D-CA), later merged with the New America Movement and was renamed the Democratic Socialists of America (DSA). A relatively small and stagnant residual faction retained the Socialist Party name, while SD/USA went on to proclaim itself "the successor to the Socialist Party, USA, the party of Eugene Debs, Norman Thomas and Bayard Rustin."[9] Though numbering little more than a thousand in the

---

7. Eric Hochstein with Ronald O'Rourke, *A Report on the Institute on Religion and Democracy*, commissioned by the United Methodist General Board of Church and Society and the Board of Global Ministries, and the United Church of Christ Board for Homeland Ministries, October 1981, reprinted as "An American Dream: Neo-Conservatism and the New Religious Right in the USA," *IDOC International Bulletin*, nos. 8–9 (1982): 17–30. See Hochstein and O'Rourke, 20–21, including reported CIA ties to the Smith Richardson Foundation through its Center for Creative Leadership, which trained CIA staff personnel in a course later transferred to the CIA for in-house use. Scaife was linked to the CIA through his ownership of Forum World Features, a British-based news service closed in 1975 after it was widely identified in the press as a CIA front to counter Communist propaganda, according to Karen Rothmyer, "Citizen Scaife," *Columbia Journalism Review*, July/August 1981, 44.

8. Penn Kemble, quoted in Steve Askin, "IRD: Institute Says It Reveals Threat—Others Say It Is Threat—to U.S. Church," *National Catholic Reporter*, February 4, 1983, 1, 7, 18–19, quote on 19.

9. See, for example, the online website of the Social Democrats, USA, at www.social democrats.org.

core ranks of either, the SD/USA and the DSA waged an ideological war that continued to reverberate through the larger bodies of organized labor in the United States, with those on each side often impugning the other's motives. Jack Clark of the DSA and the Democratic Socialist Organizing Committee, who fought against Kemble in the old Socialist Party, declared in 1983 that his factional rival "came out of a Marxist tradition in which religion was actively sneered at and looked down upon. He's part of the crowd that always laughed at Norman Thomas for being a Protestant minister. I suspect this [the IRD] is just a cynical ploy on his part—he had realized that religion is just another lever to pull in his political machinations."[10] Differences between the two factions were still playing themselves out in struggles among unions within the AFL-CIO in the 1980s, observed Robert L. McClean of the United Methodist Board of Church and Society, with the Cold War hawks of the pro-Vietnam, pro-Israel SD/USA strongly aligned with the top leadership of the AFL-CIO. "Teachers, ILGWU [garment workers], and 'headquarters' persons such as Lane Kirkland, Tom Kahn and David Jessup are SD/USA leaders, while 'progressive' branches such as the Auto Workers and the Machinists leadership are primarily DSA."[11] For ideological reasons rooted in Trotskyite-Leninist debates in the labor movement of the 1920s, McClean notes ironically, the IRD was attacking the churches for marching with Communists in the Cold War of the 1980s, while church leaders, in fact, marched with David Jessup and other union members in the May Day rally for labor in Washington in 1982. They were marching in support of the rights of labor championed by the churches since their Social Creed of 1908, and nurtured by the Gospels' quest for biblical justice over millennia.

Controversy between the IRD and the churches washed back into these internal conflicts within the labor movement when mainline church leaders with ties to labor unions sought to win their repudiation of the IRD. These efforts culminated in 1984, when the executive council of the AFL-CIO's Industrial Union Department denounced the IRD for its attempts "to weaken the links between religion and labor," and its "effort to mask its neoconservative program by paying lip service to trade unionism," according to the department's vice president, Jack Sheinkman, secretary-treasurer of the Amalgamated Clothing and Textile Workers.[12] Twelve of the AFL-CIO's international

10. Jack Clark of the DSA and president, New York City Local, Democratic Socialist Organizing Committee, quoted in Askin, "IRD," 19.

11. Robert L. McClean, interview, February 1992, New York City.

12. The Executive Council of the Industrial Union Department (AFL-CIO), "Resolution on Relationships between Organized Labor and the Church," adopted June 21–22, 1984. See

affiliates likewise condemned the IRD. The international executive board of the United Auto Workers, for example, denounced "the IRD's scurrilous attacks on churches and church leaders and its shameless pandering of 'intelligence' reports on church activities to anti-union corporations." According to Philip R. Newell Jr., Presbyterian economic justice official and convener of the Religious Committee on Labor Relations to counter the IRD's labor leverage, "The committee will continue to expose the retrograde nature of the Institute." The IRD's true purpose, charged Rev. Newell, is "to silence the churches' public witness through attacks designed to put religious organizations on the defensive and undermine their credibility through half-truths and innuendo." Moreover, he added, "The Institute is a small, self-accountable body that received 89% of its seed money from a group of conservative foundations, including the Scaife, Olin and Smith Richardson Foundations."[13]

Commenting on the counterattack the mainline churches mounted against the IRD in the early 1980s, Penn Kemble recalls, "Mainline church people with union connections tried to get [AFL-CIO president Lane] Kirkland and then Sheinkman to muzzle us. It didn't work that well, because frankly the union movement doesn't really hold church people in high regard. In any strike situation, which is what it comes down to, the local clergy always wind up weaseling their way into the hands of the bosses, I don't care how left-wing they are on Vietnam or anything else," Kemble explains. "When you start going after the local powers, everyone in the labor movement is accustomed to hearing from some local clergymen's committee that the strike should be called off and the two sides should sit down together in reconciliation. When they went in and tried to see Lane Kirkland, I think he was genuinely offended. He didn't agree with them, and the idea put him off. Other people in the labor movement were kind of amused," adds Kemble, smiling, "that we had gotten these clergy politicos so hot and bothered they were trying to get us fired."[14]

Recalls David Jessup, more painfully: "People in the Methodist leadership were convinced I couldn't simply be a Methodist who cared about the church. They thought I had to be a political agent of some kind from the CIA or the Reagan administration, so they commissioned a study to expose me." Jessup was referring obliquely to charges that linked clandestine CIA funding to the

John Herling, "IUD Condemns NLRB & IRD," *John Herling's Labor Letter*, July 14, 1984, 1–2; Jean Caffey Lyles, "Liberal Church Aides Drive Wedge between Unions and Capitol Lobby," *Religious News Service*, July 10, 1984, 3; also "Labor Denounces IRD," *Christian Century*, August 15–22, 1984, 769.

13. *Christian Century*, August 15–22, 1984, 769.

14. Penn Kemble, interview, March 1992.

AFL-CIO's Committee for Political Education (COPE) through the American Institute for Free Labor Development (AIFLD) in its efforts to organize overseas labor groups and land-reform programs against Communism. "They called up my old college professor, and the minister at my church, who, I'm sorry to say, didn't have the decency to tell me what they were doing. They tried to get me fired from my job at the Committee for Political Education at the AFL-CIO," Jessup emphasizes. "They wrote letters and made calls for about a year in a campaign within the labor movement. I kept my job, but they were finally successful in getting a number of unions to issue a statement denouncing the IRD. They were playing political hardball. They went to trade-unionists who had had their help in religion-labor coalitions like the Farah boycott. They applied pressure and called in their counters."[15]

Was this political payment in kind? Replies Jessup, "We have to acknowledge, too, that on our side we weren't just questioning their teachings. When they got hit with the *Reader's Digest* and *60 Minutes* pieces, those were heavy body blows we delivered. We were operating politically, too," because the churches were politicized past the point of reform by internal theological dissent and democratic debate. What about institutional alternatives for democratic debate, resolutions, and legislated changes within the churches—for example, the United Methodist General Conferences in which Jessup took part in 1980 and 1984? "I've been to a lot of big national conventions in labor and a few in the church," he answers. "The Methodist General Conference is no different. The leadership and staff try to wire the convention as much as possible. They do a pretty good job at that. There is not much room for making change." In 1980 the Methodist General Conference passed a resolution on accountability that required all the denomination's boards and agencies to publish all their grants, Jessup acknowledged. "But the problem is that these are just resolutions at conventions. Afterwards it's up to the church bureaucrats to implement them. They didn't implement the human rights resolution we got passed in 1984. They may have paid lip service to it here and there, but they really just went about business as usual in terms of where they were spending their money and putting their energy."

Mainline church leaders insisted at the time that they were not seeking to get David Jessup fired or censored. But they were asking the AFL-CIO to repudiate his extracurricular activities and make clear that the federation did not stand behind his charges against the churches. They had no basis for this demand, because the AFL-CIO had no official relationship to the IRD,

15. David Jessup, interview, March 1992.

objected AFL-CIO organizing director Alan Kistler, cochair of the federation's Religion and Labor Conference. But members of the conference board of directors nonetheless issued a statement decrying the IRD's "pernicious attack" and protesting to the AFL-CIO Executive Board against "the active participation by certain elements and individuals within organized labor, including staff of the AFL-CIO, in this assault on labor's traditional allies in the religious community." Other union officials privately told AFL-CIO president Lane Kirkland of their support for the churches' protests against the IRD, and they reportedly intervened to block Jessup's appointment as assistant director of the AFL's Committee on Political Education in 1982.[16]

Trade unionists taking the churches' side, including Jack Sheinkman of the Clothing Workers and Machinists, and the union's president, William Winpisinger, were members of labor's more liberal wing and seen as supporters of the Democratic Socialists of America (DSA). They were aligned with church leaders in the Vietnam peace movement. They opposed the AFL-CIO's traditionally hawkish Cold War foreign policy, defended by Kirkland and anchored by the Social Democrats (SD/USA) on labor's more conservative wing. Sheinkman called the IRD "the Institute Against Religion and Democracy" for robing itself in a cloak of concern for labor while it actually "appeals to and works through members of religious organizations consistently opposed to church support of labor's efforts."[17]

Sheinkman wrote top AFL-CIO officials that IRD attacks on the churches were endangering their support of labor causes: "During labor law reform, right to work referenda, boycotts, Solidarity Day, and strikes, the labor movement asks, and in most cases, receives, the church's help. But when it comes to the church's agenda of disarmament and Third World political struggles, they are attacked by a not so covert front of the Social Democrats, U.S.A., read by the churches as AFL-CIO."[18] That was neither fair nor wise, judged Sheinkman. When his Molder's Union was striking the Magic Chef Company, and he appealed to national church leaders to write letters to the company in

16. David E. Anderson, "Labor-Church Alliance Imperiled," *Washington Post*, July 16, 1983, C10; Russ Schroeder, minutes of the Special Board Meeting, Religion and Labor Conference, June 23, 1983, United Labor Agency, Cleveland, Ohio; Steve Askin, "Church Groups Urge Union 'Distance' Itself from IRD Connection," *National Catholic Reporter*, July 29, 1983, 7; Steve Askin, "Churches Question IRD Connection," *In These Times*, August 10–23, 1983, 11; David Moberg, "Social Democrats' Christian Crusade," *In These Times*, April 7, 1982, 2.

17. IRD, "The Church Left on Workers' Rights: Activists Press Labor on Jessup Role," *Religion and Democracy*, August/September 1983; Lyles, "Liberal Church Aides," 3.

18. Sheinkman to Thomas R. Donahue, AFL-CIO secretary-treasurer, May 23, 1983.

behalf of the union, he said, "In all my years of dealing with church people on labor issues, from the farm workers and Farah right up through Hanes, this is the most anger I have encountered. For all basic purposes, I was turned down on support for the Molders by long-time allies in the United Church of Christ and the United Methodist Church."[19]

In August 1983, AFL-CIO president Lane Kirkland wrote to Claire Randall, then general secretary of the National Council of Churches, and stated that the federation would not interfere with David Jessup for criticizing the churches because he "conducts these activities entirely on his own time and at his own expense." Kirkland's spokesman charged church groups with "being pigheaded" in continuing to "make a big issue out of it."[20] What would critics of Jessup's IRD activities have the AFL-CIO do, demanded Kirkland of the NCC in his unsolicited letter, widely publicized by the IRD: "Would they have us fire or muzzle him for exercising his rights as a member of the Methodist Church? Would they have us publicly denounce the IRD—that is, to take a position on the issues now being debated within the churches? Is it seriously proposed that the AFL-CIO should review the international funding activities of the NCC and pass judgment on them—or that we should investigate the political character of the IRD, which has neither requested nor received support from the AFL-CIO?"

These issues properly belong within the church community, Kirkland contended, just as labor issues belong within the AFL-CIO's own policy-making process, in which church groups should not intervene. "While the AFL-CIO and the NCC may have some differences on foreign policy issues," Kirkland acknowledged, "the AFL-CIO does not and will not be a party to outside assaults on America's churches."[21] With backers of both sides well placed in the AFL-CIO, the dispute between the IRD and the churches remained unsettled and simmered on.

Each side saw the other breaking an earlier implicit agreement between the mainline churches and organized labor to avoid divisive issues of foreign and military policy that had been polarized between generally dovish churches and hawkish unions since the Vietnam era, when vigorous backing for the Vietnam War from national leaders of the AFL-CIO also produced bitter internal divisions with its liberal wing. By counterattacking the IRD through

19. Sheinkman to Donahue, May 23, 1983.
20. Lane Kirkland and his spokesman Murray Seeger, quoted in Robert S. Greenberger, "Divided Unions," *Wall Street Journal*, October 25, 1983, 1, 22.
21. Kirkland to Randall, August 3, 1983, 1–2.

the unions, charged Penn Kemble, church leaders were trying to "muscle into" the labor movement's internal process of setting its agenda for foreign policy. "They're saying, 'You've got to agree with our position on international issues, or we won't work with you.'"[22] Countered a UCC official, "The subterranean issue is the control of the [AFL-CIO] foreign policy apparatus by a very right-wing, cold-war, anti-Communist group."[23]

Anti-Communism in the American labor movement stretches from AFL founder Samuel Gompers through Cold Warrior George Meany, the AFL-CIO's first president. It inspired Lane Kirkland, a founding board member of the Committee on the Present Danger, a hawkish prodefense group that included Ronald Reagan until his election to the presidency. With Penn Kemble and Tom Kahn serving as two of Kirkland's top aides, the Social Democrats certainly helped stiffen the AFL-CIO's hard-line foreign policy stance, while Kirkland's more diplomatic style helped salve the wounds of Vietnam-era infighting in the AFL-CIO under the autocratic George Meany. But wider tensions on defense and foreign policy between the AFL-CIO's liberal and conservative wings surfaced early in the Reagan era.[24] Recognize "the special menace of Communist totalitarianism" and the danger of Nixon's "false and one-sided 'detente,'" the Social Democrats, USA, urged the incoming Reagan administration, in order to overcome the illusion bred by Vietnam that "American power was its own worst enemy" and to correct the growing US-USSR military imbalance.[25]

To reverse the "retreat and humiliation" of Jimmy Carter's McGovernite "New Politics liberalism" on foreign policy, resolved the SD/USA national convention in 1980, the United States must rebuild its nuclear and conventional military power. It must strengthen its political will to deter, contain, and finally unravel the Soviet empire. It must fortify NATO to reverse Europe's drift toward neutralism and overcome the Warsaw Pact's growing lead in Euro-strategic weapons. To defend the Persian Gulf, "the United States will need a permanent military presence in the region itself," established in the Sinai, if possible, after the Israeli withdrawal under the Camp David Accords. "A democratic and equitable Selective Service system should be instituted, as changing

22. Kemble, quoted in Askin, "Church Groups Urge Union," 7.
23. Kemble, quoted in Askin, "Church Groups Urge Union," 7. Also see Askin, "Churches Question IRD Connection," 6, 11.
24. Greenberger, "Divided Unions," 1, 22.
25. Social Democrats, USA, "The Global Vision of Social Democracy," resolution adopted by the national convention of SD/USA, in *New America* 18, no. 1 (January/February 1981): 1, 10–11.

circumstances require, to meet America's manpower needs." The United States must check expansion by the Soviets and their proxy forces in Afghanistan, the Middle East, and throughout the Third World, especially by backing anti-Castro freedom movements in Cuba and democratic land-reform programs in El Salvador. In the aftermath of the 1980 election, resolved the SD/USA, there is "an increasingly urgent need for an ideological realignment in American politics. The notion that 'guns and butter' cannot go together, whether adopted at the behest of the right or the left, is bound to have disastrous consequences." A labor-oriented domestic policy combined with a firm democratic foreign and defense policy is not only possible, urged the SD/USA, but is also "necessary for the creation and maintenance of a viable political majority."[26]

By contrast, some of the AFL-CIO's largest unions, such as the Auto Workers, Machinists, Food Workers, and Government Employees (AFSCME), dissented in 1982 from the AFL-CIO Executive Council's call for defense spending increases of from 5 to 7 percent beyond inflation, citing polls that showed 61 percent of union members behind them. They lobbied Congress against the MX missile, even as AFL-CIO headquarters reaffirmed its support for the MX.[27] Dissenting union groups also branded as a total failure in El Salvador the land-reform program celebrated as the cornerstone of the AFL-CIO's anti-Communist platform in the Caribbean Cold War. It was carried out by its American Institute of Free Labor Development (AIFLD) with multimillion-dollar US government funding via the US Agency for International Development (USAID), and boldly championed by the IRD in the early 1980s.[28]

Liberal labor officials tugged the federation's stance on El Salvador from unqualified support for US backing of the military government there to measured criticism of its violent excesses. They protested Kirkland's presence on President Reagan's policy commission on Central America. "It's clearly stacked in favor of Ronald Reagan," charged one, arguing that "shoring up Reagan's

26. Social Democrats, USA, "Resolutions: On the 1980 Elections," *Social Democrat*, Spring 1981, 9–10; and in the same issue, "On Foreign Policy," 10–13.
27. Greenberger, "Divided Unions," 22.
28. Kathy Sawyer, "AFL-CIO Toils in Foreign Vineyards," *Washington Post*, November 19, 1983, A2. See Douglas Fraser, Jack Sheinkman, William Winpisinger, National Labor Committee in Support of Democracy and Human Rights in El Salvador, "Labor, Terror, and Peace," July 18, 1983, in dissent from AFL-CIO headquarters in rejecting the democratic legitimacy of the El Salvador government, and indicting it for wholesale violation of human rights and trade-union freedom, including persecution of nongovernment unions by means of kidnapping, imprisonment, torture, and assassination; published as *El Salvador: Labor, Terror, and Peace* (New York: National Labor Committee, 1983).

military policy at the same time that labor is working to unseat him just doesn't make a whole lot of sense."[29] Labor conservatives such as the SD/USA argued that the AFL-CIO could resist Reagan's antilabor domestic policies yet remain staunchly anti-Communist in defending his foreign policy. Liberals in the federation dissented from its hawkish stance on foreign policy, claiming that it was wrongheaded in itself, disastrous in its impact in helping to hike defense spending and slash social welfare programs, and unwise in handcuffing AFL-CIO efforts to work against Reagan's expected bid for reelection in 1984.

Seen from either angle, the unionized drama of conflict between the churches and the IRD sheds light on its institutional backdrop. It situates the IRD within a larger alliance of cultural conservatives in the churches, with SD/USA conservatives in the labor movement, and with hawkish anti-Communist political conservatives in both the Democratic and Republican Parties during the Reagan administration. If the SD/USA hawks moved first to rally the Religious Right around Reaganite foreign policy, they did so in the midst of broader changes already under way in the de facto dynamics of church-labor relations since the 1960s, as Penn Kemble claimed in justifying the IRD as a response to New Left churches.

The postwar New Deal synthesis of strong industrial unions made up of working-class Democrats fighting for the free world, higher wages, and fuller public provision alike gave way to smaller unions and a larger middle class split by diverging fortunes in an increasingly white-collar and services economy, not only divided by Vietnam. Weakened unions in need of like-minded friends had begun forging closer ties to the peace-and-justice churches to fight plant closings, organize service workers, defend social-welfare spending, and lobby against the laissez-faire domestic policies of the Reagan White House.[30] So proclaimed the 1983 Labor Day message of John Sweeney, then-president of the Service Employees International Union, who was elected AFL-CIO president in 1995 and went on to dissolve AIFLD and its anti-Communist Caribbean campaigns:

> No more important vehicle for social change exists today than our churches and no more important alliance exists for the defense of the common people than a coalition of religion and labor. Through the six decades of the

29. Celia Weisin, president, Local 285 of the Service Employees International Union, quoted in Greenberger, "Divided Unions," 22.

30. Cf. Penn Kemble, "The New Anti-Union Crusade," *New Republic*, September 19 and 26, 1983, 18–20; and Bob Kuttner, "Can Labor Lead?," *New Republic*, March 12, 1984, 19–25.

contemporary American labor movement, working people and their organizations have had no stauncher ally than religious groups.

Just as business mounted new, sharp attacks on labor in the late seventies, so too are arch-conservative forces now training their well-financed guns on the churches. In particular, the major Protestant denominations are under scurrilous attack today, and the same money that funds right-to-work efforts is now financing smear campaigns aimed at silencing the witnesses to the laws of God.

In the past 8 months charges have appeared in *Reader's Digest, Time* magazine, and on "60 Minutes" that the major Protestant denominations are run by left-wing clerics who use Sunday collection money to buy guns for Third World revolutionaries and to produce anti-American propaganda at home.

Just as the churches have often come to the defense of working people, when they organize, so is this the time when organized labor should cry out against these assaults and denounce the attackers as the agents of reaction that they are.[31]

On the political right and left alike, significantly, these opening rounds of combat between the IRD and its foes in the mainline churches were justified by reference to many of the same exemplary cases in order to underscore the churches' important voice and influence in the larger moral argument of American public life. In 1984, business, labor, and government leaders were invited to subscribe to a new IRD newsletter monitoring the churches' economic involvements by Kerry Ptacek, then the IRD's research director, a Presbyterian layman, and a former colleague of David Jessup in Students for a Democratic Society (SDS) and Frontlash, the AFL-CIO youth organization. "Decision-makers in business, labor and government are learning that the concerns of the Christian churches can have a powerful influence on the climate of economic affairs, both in the United States and worldwide," the IRD's newsletter prospectus explained. "The significance of church-sponsored campaigns for disinvestment in South Africa, the [Nestle] infant formula boycott, and the opposition to U.S. aid programs in Central America has made that apparent to most."[32]

31. John J. Sweeney, "1983 Labor Day Address" (given at Catholic Labor Institute Breakfast, Los Angeles, 1983), 4–5; he incorporated much of the draft of the Religion and Labor Conference, "Resolution regarding Attacks on Religious Institutions," into his speech.
32. IRD, "Prospectus for a Church Economic Programs Information Service (CEPIS),"

For related reasons, explained a researcher at the progressive Institute for the Study of Labor and Economic Crisis analyzing the IRD's role in shaping "a new authoritarian populism" for the Reagan era, the neoconservatives intensified political attacks on the mainline churches in the 1980s. "One reason is that the churches have served as an effective rallying point for both social justice agitation at home and opposition to U.S.-backed repression abroad. Religiously based pacifist organizations were among the first vocal domestic opponents to the Vietnam War, and the churches have served as one of the few institutional bases for human rights demands for El Salvador, opposition to apartheid in South Africa, support for the Nestle boycott, and early support for the Nuclear Freeze initiative."[33]

Thus the IRD began by exchanging blows with mainline church leaders, with both sides moving and jabbing in ways each recognized in the other. They knew each other from long experience in a ring where religious conflict overlapped with political counterpunching and labor-movement infighting, particularly factional fighting waged with wedge issues by splinter groups. Should the churches have turned the other cheek instead? Of course, grants one of the ecclesial combatants years later, if they had it to do all over again. "They were slinging mud at us, we got mad, and we got down in the mud with them instead of rising above it all. I regret that now," acknowledges Rev. Philip Newell. "But at the time they were defaming us, and we felt we needed to defend ourselves and stick up for the truth, too."[34] Third parties to the mudslinging also expressed regrets later on. Asked in 2002 if he regretted any show in the long history of *60 Minutes*, Don Hewitt, its creator and producer, answered yes: "We once took off on the National Council of Churches as being left-wing and radical and a lot of nonsense." After receiving congratulatory calls from right-wing political sources the morning after the show, Hewitt recalls, he reflected, "We must have done something wrong last night, and I think we probably did."[35]

Whether right or wrong, inspired by faith or driven by power, this mix of moral drama and religious witness with ideologically charged political combat and propagandistic mudslinging on prime-time television is worthy

---

1984, 1; Jean Caffey Lyles, "Capital Gadfly Offers to Help Business Watch Church and Economics," *Religious News Service*, May 25, 1984, 6–7.

33. Gerda Ray, "Legitimating the Right: The Neoconservatives Build a Base," *Crime and Social Justice*, Summer 1983, 48.

34. Philip R. Newell Jr., interview, June 1992, Louisville.

35. Don Hewitt, interview by Larry King, *Larry King Live*, CNN, December 2, 2002, cited in Howell, *United Methodism @ Risk*, 41.

of note and cause for concern. It marked a striking escalation of continuing conflict and commingling, too, among denominational religious bodies and parachurch lobbies, freestanding political-action committees and decentered political parties, activist social movements and divided labor unions, big-business interests and private foundations. Did the IRD arise in an empty public square? Empty of New Deal Democrats and Taft Republicans, along with many traditionally faithful voters too doubtful or disappointed to stay involved in public life, this polity was crowded nonetheless and being transformed by the amplified voices and organizational agility of its innovative adversaries and their diverse allies.

Cold War Connections: The Vital Center of Liberal and Conservative Evangelicalism

Mark Thomas Edwards

"Today fundamentalism stands with the rest of the world in an atom-bomb environment," claimed conservative theologian Carl F. H. Henry, "and it is not quite so ready to say that the sooner the death-knell of Western culture is sounded, the better." Henry was a movement intellectual within the upstart National Association of Evangelicals (NAE), formed in 1942 to defend evangelistic enterprises against the perceived tyranny of liberal and ecumenical churches. Despite apocalyptic expectations, twentieth-century conservative Protestants had never doubted the worldly power of their pristine gospel. Institutional construction and realignment during the interwar years, bound to creative syntheses of religion and entertainment in mass cultural mediums, had set leaders' sights on a reconquering of old spiritual territory. Henry's depiction of the new evangelicalism as a "minority movement in a universally antagonistic environment" was ironic. Led by the trinity of Billy Graham's techno-corporate evangelism, *Christianity Today* (edited by Henry), and Bill Bright's Campus Crusade for Christ, new evangelicals stood poised to triumph over their religious modernist foes. They were aided by a Cold War context that made their long-standing hope of existential demise plausible. The "post-fundamentalist" desire for mainstream status effectively synced with earlier fundamentalist demands to see the world's end.[1]

---

1. Carl F. H. Henry, "The Vigor of the New Evangelicalism (pt. 1)," *Christian Life and Times*, January 1948, 31–33, 36–38, 85; Carl F. H. Henry, "The Vigor of the New Evangelicalism (pt. 3)," *Christian Life and Times*, April 1948, 32–35, 65–69. On fundamentalism, see Matthew Avery Sutton, *American Apocalypse: A History of Modern Evangelicalism* (Cambridge, MA: Harvard University Press, 2014). I follow Sutton in defining fundamentalism as a powerful interdenominational subset of conservative evangelicalism held together by shared readings of the end times. Henry's new evangelicalism, also called postfundamentalism and then simply evangelicalism, proposed to downplay the eschatological obsessions of its predecessors. However, as Sutton maintains, Cold War evangelicalism actually thrived because of its "politics

New evangelical efforts to redeem the time before Christ's return were not so different from those of their liberal and ecumenical rivals. Envisioning a progressively non–Roman Catholic "Christian century," liberal Protestant seminaries and mainline Protestant churches had joined forces around 1900 in an assortment of ecumenical organizations. The largest was the Federal Council of Churches (FCC), founded in 1908 out of earlier foreign and home missionary work. Its leaders would also help found the transnational World Council of Churches (WCC). Thereafter, the FCC merged with other groups to form the ecumenical powerhouse, the National Council of Churches (NCC), in 1950.

Before but certainly during and following the "fundamentalist-modernist controversies" of the 1920s, ecumenical and fundamentalist Christians had come to view each other as beyond the pale of true religion. The one had reconciled the revivalist tradition of immediate conversion with novel renderings of end-times prophecy. The other had eschewed revivalism out of concern to reform those socioeconomic structures that determined personality. Sensing the "death-knell" with Henry, however, liberal and ecumenical Christians began to rediscover their revivalist heritage at the same time that postfundamentalists began to talk of saving civilizations as well as souls. A public theology of "liberal evangelicalism," emanating from the FCC and Union Seminary in New York, among other places, undergirded a series of alliances between ecumenical and evangelical Christians during the early Cold War period. As the archetypical liberal evangelical of those years, Union Seminary president Henry Pitney Van

---

of apocalypse." See also Joel A. Carpenter, *Revive Us Again: The Reawakening of American Fundamentalism* (New York: Oxford University Press, 1997); Angela Lahr, *Millennial Dreams and Apocalyptic Nightmares: The Cold War Origins of Political Evangelicalism* (New York: Oxford University Press, 2007); Timothy Gloege, *Guaranteed Pure: The Moody Bible Institute, Business, and the Making of Modern Evangelicalism* (New York: Oxford University Press, 2015); and B. M. Pietsch, *Dispensational Modernism* (New York: Oxford University Press, 2015). Sutton's work joins other recent crucial studies of contemporary evangelicalism. See, in this respect, Bethany Moreton, *To Serve God and Wal-Mart: The Making of Christian Free Enterprise* (Cambridge, MA: Harvard University Press, 2009); Darren Dochuk, *From Bible Belt to Sunbelt: Plain-Folk Religion, Grassroots Politics, and the Rise of Evangelical Conservativism* (New York: Norton, 2010); Daniel K. Williams, *God's Own Party: The Making of the Christian Right* (New York: Oxford University Press, 2010); Molly Worthen, *Apostles of Reason: The Crisis of Authority in American Evangelicalism* (New York: Oxford University Press, 2014); Darren Grem, *The Blessings of Business: How Corporations Shaped Conservative Christianity* (New York: Oxford University Press, 2016); and Axel R. Schäfer, *Piety and Public Funding: Evangelicals and the State in Modern America* (Philadelphia: University of Pennsylvania Press, 2012).

Dusen, observed in 1947, "the philosophy of the world Christian mission is that of liberal evangelicalism."[2]

Henry's conservative and Van Dusen's liberal evangelicals connected during the 1950s on three issues: (1) reinventing America's Protestant Christian heritage; (2) restoring Protestant America through cultural engagement; and (3) reviving American Protestantism through promoting Billy Graham.[3] Those points of contact never canceled out the theological, liturgical, and political differences attested to by ecumenical (FCC/NCC/WCC) and evangelical (NAE) Christians. Yet those exchanges were not at all insignificant. In part, they reflected the common transatlantic evangelical heritage that American Protestants of all varieties had long shared. Those convergences also remind us of the centripetal as well as centrifugal force of geopolitical turmoil as felt within the United States. As symbolized by Arthur Schlesinger Jr.'s Cold War treatise, *The Vital Center* (1949), nothing so promised to heal American fracture as permanent revolution against a "foreign" foe. Superpower rivalry between the United States and the Soviet bloc in fact inspired new forms of cooperation across ideological lines. By the mid-1960s, the always contentious evangelical-ecumenical center would no longer hold. Still,

2. Henry Pitney Van Dusen, *World Christianity: Yesterday, Today, Tomorrow* (New York: Abingdon-Cokesbury, 1947), 202. On liberalism, see William R. Hutchison, *The Modernist Impulse in American Protestantism* (Durham, NC: Duke University Press, 1992 [1976]); Matthew S. Hedstrom, *The Rise of Liberal Religion: Book Culture and the Making of American Spirituality* (New York: Oxford University Press, 2012); and David Hollinger, *After Cloven Tongues of Fire: Protestant Liberalism in Modern American History* (Princeton: Princeton University Press, 2013). Unlike Hollinger, I distinguish the descriptors "liberal" and "ecumenical." On the ecumenical movement, see Heather A. Warren, *Theologians of a New World Order: Reinhold Niebuhr and the Christian Realists, 1920–1948* (New York: Oxford University Press, 1997); Jill K. Gill, *Embattled Ecumenism: The National Council of Churches, the Vietnam War, and the Trials of the Protestant Left* (DeKalb: Northern Illinois University Press, 2011); Andrew Preston, *Sword of the Spirit, Shield of Faith: Religion in American War and Diplomacy* (New York: Knopf, 2012); Michael Thompson, *For God and Globe: The Rise of Christian Internationalism, 1919–1945* (Ithaca, NY: Cornell University Press, 2016); and Mark Thomas Edwards, *The Right of the Protestant Left: God's Totalitarianism* (New York: Palgrave Macmillan, 2012). On "liberal evangelicalism," see Matthew Bowman, *The Urban Pulpit: New York City and the Fate of Liberal Evangelicalism* (New York: Oxford University Press, 2014). On the mainline, see Elesha Coffman, *The Christian Century and the Rise of the Protestant Mainline* (New York: Oxford University Press, 2013).

3. See Thomas C. Berg, "'Proclaiming Together'? Convergence and Divergence in Mainline and Evangelical Evangelism, 1945–1967," *Religion and American Culture* 5 (1995): 49–76, and Mark Silk, *Spiritual Politics: Religion and America since World War II* (New York: Simon and Schuster, 1988).

its very existence tells us a lot about the complexity of the world Christian community throughout the Cold War.

This Nation under God: The Bipartisan Resurgence of Christian Nationalism

Historians of American religion have documented a "second disestablishment" between 1880 and 1920. That one left the nation's Protestant heritage (the imagined as well as the actual) in question.[4] Numerous faith groups, including Catholics, Mormons, and even Jehovah's Witnesses, looked to reaffirm America as a Christian nation. Initially, fundamentalists and other conservative evangelicals seemed indifferent about their loss of spiritual and cultural capital. "There is not, and never has been, such a company of people as a Christian nation, and never will be until the Lord comes," proclaimed one prophecy pastor during World War I.[5]

However, Henry's postfundamentalists soon after the war united with Pentecostal Christians to take their country and world "back" for God. As historian Kevin Kruse has discovered, American businessmen fearful of totalitarian takeover under the guise of New Deal liberalism partnered with religious leaders to advance "Christian libertarianism." Central to the success of this new philosophy was convincing countrymen—including fundamentalists and evangelicals—that America had always been a Christian nation founded upon transcendent principles of free markets and limited government. Backed by corporate funding and mass advertising, church leaders following World War II flooded the public square with a myriad of Christian libertarian mottos such as In God We Trust and One Nation under God. New evangelicals, too, purposed to "win" America away from secularists, Catholics, and Communists (i.e., liberals). They mobilized behind Billy Graham to champion militantly anti-Communist Christian American exceptionalism.[6]

Kruse avoids descriptors like "liberal" and "conservative" to describe his insurgents, and wisely so. Ecumenical Christian agencies like the FCC-backed

---

4. Robert T. Handy, *A Christian America: Protestant Hopes and Historical Realities*, 2nd ed. (New York: Oxford University Press, 1984); Steven Green, *Inventing a Christian America: The Myth of the Religious Founding* (New York: Oxford University Press, 2015).

5. Leonard Newby, quoted in Sutton, *American Apocalypse*, 52.

6. Kevin M. Kruse, *One Nation under God: How Corporate America Invented Christian America* (New York: Basic Books, 2015); Harold John Ockenga, "Can Fundamentalism Win America?," *Christian Life and Times*, June 1947, 13–15.

National Conference on Christians and Jews (NCCJ) had embraced inter-
faith cooperation as the proper response to Fascist and Soviet dictatorship.[7]
Yet others had anticipated new evangelical efforts to manufacture Christian
America. National unity on a Protestant foundation had long been the aim
of ecumenical organizations such as the Home Missions Council (HMC), as
evident in administrator Hermann Morse's *Toward a Christian America* (1935).
The FCC joined Morse and the HMC in the late 1930s when it began sponsoring urban and university preaching missions led by celebrity evangelist
E. Stanley Jones, among others. Liberal evangelicals like Oberlin theologian
Walter Horton hoped the missions would "make the United States a Christian
nation again, as she was in the days of the Puritans."[8]

In fact, ecumenical Protestants led the Christian nationalist cause during
the early Cold War years. With the Christian libertarian banner, "This Nation
under God," literally hanging over their inaugural gathering, the NCC proudly
asserted that the "American way of life" was inseparable from Christian faith.
American and world church leaders (Toyohiko Kagawa), politicians (Dean
Acheson), and ambassadors (Francis Sayre) united in challenging their ecumenical audience of four thousand to stand aligned against "atheism," "secular
materialism," and other alien worldviews. "We dare to believe," announced
Morse, a chief NCC architect, "that a Christian and a Protestant America can
be the strongest force in the world against the new and the old paganisms that
are contending for the mastery of the world." Morse's declaration was seconded
by the NCC's first president, Henry Knox Sherrill. "Together," Sherrill concluded, "we shall move forward with renewed resolve and great hope in the
building of a Christian America in a Christian world."[9]

Sherrill's addition of "Christian world" pointed to some key differences
between ecumenical and evangelical versions of Christian nationalism. The
NCC advanced its predecessors' commitments to international governance

7. Kevin Schultz, *Tri-Faith America: How Catholics and Jews Held Postwar America to Its
Protestant Promise* (New York: Oxford University Press, 2011).

8. Walter Marshall Horton, *Can Christianity Save Civilization?* (New York: Harper and
Brothers, 1940), 214. See "Summarizing the National Preaching Mission," *Federal Council Bul-
letin* 20 (January 1937): 9–10; "The National Christian Mission: Its Purpose," *Federal Council
Bulletin* 23 (January 1940): 7–8.

9. Robbins W. Barstow, "Foreword: This Nation under God," in *Christian Faith in Action:
The Founding of the National Council of the Churches of Christ in the United States of Amer-
ica*, ed. Robbins W. Barstow (New York: NCCC, 1951); Hermann Morse, "The Church in the
Nation," in Barstow, *Christian Faith in Action*, 94–95; Henry Knox Sherrill, "The Presidential
Message," in Barstow, *Christian Faith in Action*, 143.

through the UN, to human rights, and to American aid for self-development in the global South. NCC members generally supported the Marshall Plan and NATO less from knee-jerk anti-Communism and more as stepping-stones toward global democratic collaboration. In contrast, many (but by no means all) new evangelicals doubled down on fundamentalist anti-internationalism, lest they help the antichrist effect his new world order. Cold War ecumenical groups believed that Christian America was not worthy to lead the free world until it dismantled racist structures within employment, housing, and worship. Most new evangelical leaders, reflecting their revivalist heritage, attacked racism as a matter of personal prejudice. They turned a blind eye to systemic injustices such as massive resistance and white flight, generally agreeing that the civil rights movement was rife with Communist sympathizers. Given those important divergences, though, the battle against "godless" Soviet transgressions still led both ecumenical and evangelical Christians to close ranks around their country's reimagined spiritual past. Liberal evangelicals, working through ecumenical organizations, resurrected Christian nationalism at a time when many fundamentalists were willing to let it rest in pieces.

The Uneasy Conscience of Cold War Evangelicalism: Common Patterns of Cultural Engagement

If bipartisan evangelical support for Christian America had been manufactured from outside the movement, the same could not be said of converging patterns of Protestant Christian cultural engagement. "The time has come now for Fundamentalism to speak with an ecumenical outlook and voice," Henry announced in his watershed NAE manifesto *The Uneasy Conscience of Modern Fundamentalism* (1947). He called upon postfundamentalists to "unite with non-evangelicals for social betterment." NAE leaders wanted their churches to set aside familiar squabbles and to begin recognizing what they confessed in common with all believers. "We need to rise above all organizations of men in a bigger and broader fellowship, as big and as broad as the eternal Church of God," counseled an NAE apologist. The context for this call to convergence, of course, remained fears of Soviet infiltration and world Communist coordination.[10]

10. Carl F. H. Henry, *The Uneasy Conscience of Modern Fundamentalism* (Grand Rapids: Eerdmans, 1947), 63, 80, 87; James DeForest Murch, *Cooperation without Compromise: A History of the National Association of Evangelicals* (Grand Rapids: Eerdmans, 1956), 214.

Henry anchored a group of young postfundamentalist scholars who were convinced they could and should restore Christ's reign within the West. Professors at Wheaton College, Moody Bible Institute, and elsewhere had begun demanding a "contemporary Christian literature that studies all phases of intellectual interest" during the 1930s. Their students, including Henry and Edward John Carnell, were primed for just such a challenge. "There is a parochialism in evangelicalism from which I must withdraw," Carnell confided to Henry after a taste of professional life. "I want to command the attention of Tillich and Bennett; then I shall be in a better place to be of service to the evangelicals. We need prestige desperately."[11]

Besides a desire for status, Carnell's comment also betrayed how much he and fellow new evangelicals admired and envied the work of their liberal rivals. Of course, John C. Bennett, Paul Tillich, and their associates had already established an impressive body of apologetic Christian literature by the early Cold War years, most notably Niebuhr's *Nature and Destiny of Man* (1943). Carnell's own encounter with religious liberalism had commenced at Harvard Divinity School, where he underwent "theological reeducation" while writing theses on Kierkegaard and Niebuhr. Henry similarly had entered the enemy's camps at Boston University to work with personalist Edgar Sheffield Brightman. Daniel Fuller, son of well-known fundamentalist radio evangelist Charles Fuller, led a wave of postfundamentalist youth who went to Princeton Theological Seminary to study Karl Barth and neoorthodoxy. With the elder Fuller's backing, Henry and Carnell headed the faculty of the new evangelical think tank Fuller Seminary in California (opened in 1947). Their school was to provide solutions to the "cultural crisis" of the West, according to Fuller president and NAE head Harold John Ockenga.[12]

New evangelical theologians insisted that neoorthodoxy represented the "new modernism" of chastened religious liberals. They still felt they had a lot to learn from those persons. Indeed, Henry's first apologetic work, *Remaking the Modern Mind* (1946), borrowed heavily from the writings of Niebuhr, Tillich, and Bennett. As founding editor of *Christianity Today*, Henry would court alliances with leading religious liberals, which included a friendship with Horton and dinner conversations with Barth, Brunner, and Tillich. Carnell, meanwhile, later regretted that he had not gone to Union to study with

11. Gordon H. Clark, foreword to *Remaking the Modern Mind*, by Carl F. H. Henry (Grand Rapids: Eerdmans, 1946), 13; Edward John Carnell, quoted in Carl F. H. Henry, *Confessions of a Theologian: An Autobiography* (Waco: Word, 1986), 137.

12. George Marsden, *Reforming Fundamentalism: Fuller Seminary and the New Evangelicalism* (Grand Rapids: Eerdmans, 1987).

Niebuhr. Though appalled by what he believed to be Niebuhr's antirational epistemology, Carnell found his analysis of the inevitable mixture of pride and love "profound and convincing." Billy Graham's claim that he had read all of Niebuhr's works confirmed both the new evangelicals' passion for intellectual credibility and the theologically liberal standards by which they thought they could attain it.[13]

Without knowing it, Graham's people borrowed in another way from the Cold War ecumenical playbook of cultural-intellectual engagement. The revival of interest in Christian "vocation" or whole-life ministry, which historians have traced back to the new evangelicals, in fact began among NCC and WCC members. "It is to those who, consciously or unconsciously, make their scientific and organizing activities a daily offering and prayer to God," J. H. Oldham prophesied, "that we may expect the way out of our present difficulties to be progressively revealed." Oldham had been the leader during and after his days at Oxford in resurrecting layperson vocation as a means to heal the rupture between individuals and their complex societies. The idea that one's work could become both song and service to God was an ancient Christian tradition. Van Dusen, for instance, commended the acumen of one first-century pastor—"we cultivate our fields, praising; we sail the sea, hymning"—in a paper on vocation. Van Dusen singled out Yale theologian Robert Calhoun's *God and the Common Life* (1935) as the premier twentieth-century statement on work-as-worship.[14]

The ecumenical Christian revival of vocation, as a means to re-Christianize a presumably pagan West, as well as to beat back Communism, occurred alongside and within a complementary interest in communitarianism. The "new reformation" that Horton identified while touring war-torn European countries promised to harmonize Oldham's spirit-directed professionals with participatory democratic concerns. Ecumenical Christians did not want an-

---

13. Walter Marshall Horton, *Christian Theology: An Ecumenical Approach*, rev. ed. (New York: Harper and Row, 1958), 31; Henry, *Remaking the Modern Mind*, 34, 36, 40, 47–48, 55, 58, 64, 69, 72, 163, 200, 206; Henry, *Confessions of a Theologian*, 66, 91–92, 120–22, 132–38, 179, 211–43; Edward John Carnell, *The Theology of Reinhold Niebuhr* (Grand Rapids: Eerdmans, 1950) preface; Billy Graham, *Just As I Am: The Autobiography of Billy Graham* (New York: HarperCollins, 1997), 135. On Graham's claim concerning Niebuhr, see Stephen J. Whitfield, *The Culture of the Cold War* (Baltimore: Johns Hopkins University Press, 1991), 100.

14. J. H. Oldham, *Work in Modern Society* (Geneva: World Council of Churches, 1950), 7, 38; Henry Pitney Van Dusen, "The Problem of Work and Vocation in the Modern World," paper presented before the Theological Discussion Group, March 1952, pp. 11–13, in The Theological Discussion Group Papers, Yale Divinity School Library, Box 4, Folder 42.

other "Protestant work ethic" that would reduce one's "calling" to a mask for personal or collective greed. They rather hoped that lay Protestant cell groups could offer even a small portion of the loving solidarity that the Catholic Action movement was at that time providing Rome's global flock. The WCC's Ecumenical Institute (EI) at Bossey, Switzerland, joined a host of older Protestant lay groups in 1947, among them the Sigtuna Foundation in Sweden, the Iona Community of Scotland, the eight Evangelical Academies spread around Germany, and Christian Frontier of England. These work-study centers varied from endeavors in adult education and correspondence course programs, to weeklong retreats, to seasonal monastic arrangements. Many were composed of educated, middle-class believers as well as a diverse body of displaced persons—including war resisters, veterans, and concentration camp survivors. Bennett became a staff member at EI during its first term, while Niebuhr and Horton eventually led sessions there.[15]

Ecumenical Christians asked Americans to follow up Continental developments at home. Only through time-tested spiritual disciplines practiced in "primary" communities, James Luther Adams advised, could "countermodels" be developed against "mass society." Van Dusen looked expectantly to the Laymen's Movement for a Christian World, of Greenwich, Connecticut, which had as its aim the "building of Christianity into the every-day life of the world." Evanston attendees furthermore expected to see the "cell" approach become commonplace throughout American industries and offices. "The world in which we live seems peculiarly hostile" to a new social gospel, Yale's ecumenical historian Kenneth Scott Latourette observed. "Can we not best serve the coming generations by stressing the formation and multiplication of small groups which will seek fully in their individual and collective living to realize without compromise Christian standards?"[16]

15. Walter Marshall Horton, "The New Reformation," *Current Religious Thought* 7 (January 1947): 1–6; Walter Marshall Horton, *Centers of New Life in European Christendom* (New York: World Council of Churches, ca. 1948), 4, 23; Paul A. Hutchinson, "Editorial: The Iona Idea," September 11, 1946, in *The Christian Century Reader*, ed. Harold E. Fey and Margaret Frakes (New York: Association, 1962), 43–44; Reinhold Niebuhr, "Editorial Correspondence," *Christianity and Crisis* 7 (April 28, 1947): 6.

16. Horton, "The New Reformation," 5–6; James Luther Adams, "The Place of Discipline in Christian Ethics," paper presented before the Theological Discussion Group, March 8–10, 1952, p. 9, in the Francis Pickens Miller Papers, University of Virginia, Box 17; Van Dusen, "Problem of Work," 2; "What Does All This Mean for the Church as an Organized Body?," in *Christian Hope and the Task of the Church*, ed. Van Dusen and Ehrenstrom (New York: Harper, 1954), 39–48; Kenneth Scott Latourette, *The Prospect for Christianity* (London: Religious Book Club, 1950), 30.

Francis Schaeffer, the most influential postfundamentalist next to Graham, would achieve mainstream respect by co-opting parts of the ecumenical investment in vocation and communitarianism. Sent as an emissary of Presbyterian fundamentalism to Europe after the war, Schaeffer soon found his family siding with the new evangelicals. The Schaeffers remained in Europe and established the L'Abri commune in the Swiss Alps. L'Abri became a shelter for post-Christian youth from throughout Europe and America. Before long, hundreds were dropping by the Schaeffers to work and study what went wrong with the West. During the 1960s and 1970s, Francis began receiving book deals and invitations to speak at Oxford, Cambridge, Wheaton, MIT, and Princeton. His chief legacy was his ignition of a vocational revolution in conservative Christian circles. In a series of lectures first given in 1955, Schaeffer argued that faith should make a substantial difference in society and culture. A generalist like Niebuhr and Tillich, Schaeffer lectured and wrote on modern philosophy, art, church life, Western history, "compassionate" capitalism, and eventually the proper use of nuclear weapons (the latter before Ronald Reagan's defense staff). He skyrocketed past Carnell and Henry—and John Calvin, according to a *Christianity Today* poll—as the global representative of a holistic, "worldview" approach to Christianity. If it was true that "Christ was Lord of all of life," Schaeffer urged, then Christlike faith should move believers to bring all aspects of modern secular culture under his dominion.[17]

Schaeffer's theocratic assumption approximated the liberal evangelical messiah as the "Lord of history." It developed among his legions of disciples (including Congressman Jack Kemp and President Gerald Ford) a renewed passion to take their faith into the academy, the professions, popular culture, and politics. Bennett had once proclaimed Christ "Lord of all life" as a basis for theological criticism of unchecked free enterprise. Schaeffer and his family instead inspired televangelist Jerry Falwell and other separatist fundamentalists to launch a new Christian Right.[18]

The ecumenical politics of vocation won a popular audience only when it was taken up by conservative evangelicals. The latter did not deliberately steal the ideal so much as grow it on their own. Yet there was a remarkable correspondence between their two designs. Here again, the Cold War caused

17. On Schaeffer, see Barry Hankins, *Francis Schaeffer and the Shaping of Evangelical America* (Grand Rapids: Eerdmans, 2008).

18. Roger L. Shinn, "The Christian Gospel and History," in *Christian Faith and Social Action: A Symposium*, ed. John Alexander Hutchison (New York: Scribner's Sons, 1953), 33; John Coleman Bennett, "A Theological Conception of Goals for Economic Life," in *Goals of Economic Life*, ed. A. Dudley Ward (New York: Harper and Brothers, 1953), 401.

both ecumenical and evangelical leaders to retreat into shared Christian traditions that could help them recapture everyday life. The differing outcomes of that innovative nostalgia would be more impressive, however. Conservative evangelicals made vocation the theological cornerstone of Christian libertarianism, or what Bethany Moreton has termed "Christian free enterprise."[19] As neorevivalists, they never appreciated nor even understood the ecumenical conception of democracy as "a company of human selves and their doings into which one must enter as a fellow member, able by his behavior to impoverish or to enrich the whole." The evangelical Cold War demanded a new individualism, not ecumenical forms of collectivism.[20]

United Evangelism: Billy Graham's Vital Protestant Center

Liberal and conservative evangelicals would briefly find fellowship and mainstream success in the upgrading of revivalist tradition. Youth for Christ rallies originated in major urban areas like Washington, DC, Seattle, and Chicago during the war. Their aim was to "present the gospel in as attractive a form as anything presented by the world." Organizers' union of old-timey religion and contemporary mass culture (especially popular song) culminated after the war in the nationwide evangelistic campaigns of Youth for Christ's gowned crusader, Billy Graham. Backed by large-scale production and the free publicity of the Luce publishing empire, Graham secured the popularity that new evangelicals had coveted. His mainstreaming of apocalyptic, anti-Communist, and antistatist populism would stimulate millions of religious "inquirers" to look into Christian belief and practice.[21]

Realists' reactions to Youth for Christ and Graham were mixed. Many liberal evangelicals had been raised in theologically conservative homes and had participated in revivals themselves as patrons and preachers. They had experienced "born again" conversions. Though he had been raised an Episcopalian, for instance, religion only had become vital to Van Dusen when he walked the sawdust trail as a teenager at a Billy Sunday meeting. He had even

19. See Moreton, *To Serve God and Wal-Mart*.

20. Robert L. Calhoun, *God and a Day's Work: Christian Vocation in an Unchristian World* (New York: Association, 1957), 14, 57.

21. Torrey Johnson and Robert Cook, *Reaching Youth for Christ* (Chicago: Moody Press, 1944), 22–23, 33, 38, 44–49; Billy Graham, "What Ten Years Have Taught Me," *Christian Century* 77 (February 17, 1960): 187. On Graham, see Grant Wacker, *America's Pastor: Billy Graham and the Shaping of a Nation* (Cambridge, MA: Harvard University Press, 2014).

worked as a revival preacher before entering Union for graduate study. Van Dusen and Bennett had expected any trouble from fundamentalism to come in "rural areas." They and friends were taken aback by the success of Youth for Christ's urban neorevivalism. Bennett went on to contrast the "more restrained forms of worship" and "more sophisticated presentation of the Gospel" of his ecumenical communities with the perceived ignorance and disorder of conservative churches. Religious liberals nonetheless testified enviously to the efficiency of new revivalists. One *Christian Century* reporter commented on what he believed to be Youth for Christ's crass gospel ploys. He then concluded, "they are coming soon, whether Jesus is or not. I wish them well."[22]

FCC churches had themselves been gearing up for greater effectiveness in spiritual recruitment before Graham's advent. Following the success of the preaching missions, the FCC's department of evangelism by 1946 had become its largest branch. Ecumenical churches further began to emphasize layperson-led "family visitation evangelism"—which included community-wide surveys, personal meetings at the homes of "prospects," special church services, and the securing of "decisions" for Christ and church membership. "Those who would Christianize the social order without beginning with the individual and proceeding through the regeneration of individuals," one veteran Christian sociologist warned, "have therefore made a profound psychological and sociological error."[23]

Some saw the coincidence of ecumenical and evangelical neorevivalism as an opportunity to rebuild the "center" of Protestant Christian witness to a nation and world threatened by Soviet and Maoist disorder. The WCC's "supreme call" in a "global age," Van Dusen had anticipated, was for "united evangelism." Niebuhr charged Graham with turning a blind eye to social injustice at the same time that his closest friends began inviting Graham to speak at Union and Princeton seminaries. "Many in my circles who would have rejected Graham entirely five years ago," Bennett explained, "feel that he

---

22. John Coleman Bennett, "Church Unity and Small Community," *Commonwealth Review* 22 (May 1940): 76; Elton Trueblood, "The New Comparative Religion," in *The Church and Organized Movements*, ed. Randolph Crump Miller (New York: Harper and Row, 1946), 32–33; Randolph Crump Miller, "The Discovery of Resistance and Resource," in Miller, *The Church and Organized Movements*, 13; John Ray Evers, "Youth for Christ Meets Pittsburgh," *Christian Century* 63 (October 10, 1945): 1171–72.

23. "Evangelism—the Primary Task," *Federal Council Bulletin* 29 (December 1946): 8–9; "Visitation Evangelism," *Federal Council Bulletin* 26 (February 1943): 10; "Preparing for Lay Evangelism," *Federal Council Bulletin* 28 (November 1945): 6; Charles A. Ellwood, *The World's Need of Christ* (New York: Abingdon-Cokesbury, 1940), 25–26.

has developed in a very desirable way and that he is no mere Fundamentalist evangelist." Princeton Theological Seminary president John Mackay and others asked Niebuhr to consider the positive value of Graham's prestige for their own churches and movement. They tried to arrange private meetings between the two leaders, but to no avail. Graham and associates, meanwhile, were more than pleased with the reception of their work among liberal and ecumenical guardians. The high point of the ecumenical-Graham collaborative occurred when Van Dusen and mainline church leaders supported the evangelist's New York City Crusade in 1957.[24]

The reasons for that unexpected partnership of elite and popular religionists during the 1950s are many. Though the utilitarian aspect cannot be denied—the desire for a united Protestant front against Communism, Catholicism, and secularism; the search for prestige and publicity—we should not overlook more obvious factors contributing to this unholy alliance. Both ecumenical and evangelical Christians traced their roots back to the revivalist religious culture of Moody and the early YMCA. Graham's tactics, not surprisingly, appealed to former student Christian leaders at the levels of both nostalgia and wisdom. As Van Dusen pointed out to Niebuhr, "there are many, of whom I am one, who are not ashamed to testify that they would probably never have come within the sound of Dr. Niebuhr's voice or the influence of his mind if they had not been first touched by the message of the earlier Billy." Van Dusen's implication that fundamentalist revivalism could be a gateway into cosmopolitan faith betrayed the condescension ecumenical leaders still directed toward Graham. Nonetheless, liberal and conservative evangelical "realism" culminated in a joint assumption that individuals must be persuaded, even pressured, to trust the Christian message.[25]

Realists' hope of winning Graham and new evangelicals to "highly constructive Christian purposes in the churches and in the nation" was partially

24. Mackay, quoted in Berg, "Proclaiming Together?," 54; Henry Pitney Van Dusen, "After Amsterdam," address given at Duke University, June 11, 1948, in The Henry Pitney Van Dusen Papers, The Burke Library at Union Theological Seminary in New York, Box iii; Reinhold Niebuhr, "Literalism, Individualism and Billy Graham," *Christian Century* 73 (May 23, 1956): 640–42; Mackay, quoted in Graham, *Just as I Am*, 255; Bennett to D. Robinson, June 27, 1955, in The John Coleman Bennett Papers, The Burke Library at Union Theological Seminary in New York, Box II, Folder 3; Sherwood Eddy, "Let Us Pray for Billy Graham and Norman Vincent Peale," circular letter, n.d., in The Reinhold Niebuhr Papers, Manuscript Division, Library of Congress (hereafter RNP), Box 5; Harold P. Sloan to Reinhold Niebuhr, May 28, 1956, in RNP, Box 11, Miscellaneous Folder; Mackay to Niebuhr, September 14, 1956, in RNP, Box 8, Miscellaneous Folder.

25. Henry Pitney Van Dusen, "Billy Graham," *Christianity and Crisis* 16 (April 2, 1956): 40.

fulfilled. Niebuhr, ironically, was the realist most responsible for the greatest achievement of liberal-conservative cooperation in mass evangelism. In response to pleas to moderate his criticism of Christianity's star witness, Niebuhr proposed that the Southern-born Graham use his clout to buttress the burgeoning civil rights movement—a challenge that Graham took to heart. The Niebuhr-Graham exchange occurred at a time when American claims to free-world leadership were forcing the country to confront the shame of segregation head-on. Graham and Niebuhr came together informally to aid African Americans in developing an alternative moral/political framework to the gradualist one advanced by northern liberals. Besides what he learned from his liberal evangelical professors at Boston University, Martin Luther King Jr. picked up from reading Niebuhr that collective social evils had to be actively resisted. Thereafter steeped in the prophetic tradition, King and other Southern Christian Leadership Conference (SCLC) leaders solicited advice about coordinating mass events from Graham's people. As the evangelist solidified his support for the civil rights movement by integrating his crusades, King identified himself with Graham's new evangelicalism by sharing the stage with him during one New York City rally. Niebuhr rejected King's nonviolent strategies as socially disruptive well into the 1960s. Nevertheless, the informal partnership of Niebuhr, Graham, and King suggested that the revival of personal Christianity during the 1950s could have blessed cultural consequences.[26]

Conclusions

The same anti-Communist Christian Americanism that could unite old enemies could also divide them anew. The Cold War evangelical center detailed here should not belie the fact that most religious liberals looked upon the "fundamentalist renascence" with bewilderment. Nor should we forget that new evangelicals generally followed John Flynn, William F. Buckley Jr., and others in indicting Christian liberalism as a red menace.[27] Even as Bennett

---

26. Bennett to Robinson, June 27, 1955, in JCBP, BII, F3; Graham, *Just as I Am*, 301; Reinhold Niebuhr, "Proposal to Billy Graham," *Christian Century* 73 (August 8, 1956): 921–22; John Pollock, *Billy Graham, Evangelist to the World* (San Francisco: Harper and Row, 1979), 157; Martin Luther King Jr., "Pilgrimage to Nonviolence," *Christian Century* 77 (April 13, 1960): 439–41. On the intersection of Niebuhr, Graham, and King, see David L. Chappell, *A Stone of Hope: Religion and the Death of Jim Crow* (Chapel Hill: University of North Carolina Press, 2004).

27. Arnold W. Hearn, "Fundamentalist Renascence," *Christian Century* 75 (April 30, 1958): 528–30.

and Mackay were trying to convince ecumenical Christians to support Billy Graham, religious conservatives were lambasting them for their arguments in favor of recognition of China. The NCC would join African Americans in civil rights work at the same time that more and more postfundamentalists became convinced that King was a Communist. As Jill Gill has detailed, evangelical conservatives broke finally and forever with the NCC and WCC over their contrasting attitudes toward the Vietnam War. The Cold War religious consensus fractured well before debates over racial, gender, and marriage equality.[28]

Still, we do disservice to the Christian past if we read the culture wars back into the 1940s and 1950s. In those decades, at least, superpower rivalry abroad fed great faith in liberal-conservative evangelical rapprochement at home. The new evangelicals hoped that the ecumenical churches might aid their reenchantment of the nation. Ecumenical leaders, on the other hand, believed that Graham's legions were finally ready to embrace the social gospel. Both were frustrated. The long-standing conservative evangelical belief in their ascendancy over a dying liberal Christian establishment is now giving way to recognition that classical secularization theorists might have been right about America all along. Never have Protestant Christian communities in the United States been more anachronistic. Never has it been more important for Protestant factions to learn from each other (as well as from Catholicism). Should they choose to do so, it won't be the first time.

28. Gill, *Embattled Ecumenism*. See also Andrew Hartman, *A War for the Soul of America: A History of the Culture Wars* (Chicago: University of Chicago Press, 2015).

Peace Activities

American Peace Churches and the Cold War

Walter Sawatsky

What makes a church a peace church? The following definition comes from a joint Catholic-Mennonite dialogue:

> A Peace Church is a church called to bear witness to the gospel of peace grounded in Jesus Christ.
>
> The peace church places this conviction at the center of its faith and life, its teaching, worship, ministry and practice, calling Jesus Lord and following him in his nonresistant and nonviolent way. A peace church is nothing other than the church, the body of Christ.
>
> Every church is called to be a peace church.[1]

This is a theologically ideal statement, challenging and inclusive, but it also points to the many ambiguities of a lived peace witness.

"Historic peace churches" (HPC) has been an American designation since the 1930s, applying to Mennonites, Quakers, and Brethren, who shared a commitment to conscientious objection to war and military service. In a Protestant legacy sense, "historic" referred to the "left wing of the Reformation," also called the Radical Reformation or the Anabaptist Reformation; it was charged with heresy in the Augsburg Confession for centuries, initially persecuted, and consistently marginalized. The Mennonites, Hutterians, and Amish survived to the present, transformed by many historical and cultural developments. Quakers and Baptists emerged a century later within the British Reformation, some of whom identified with the sixteenth-century Anabaptist spiritual legacy; still others emerged out of German Reformed churches during eighteenth-century

---

1. *Called Together to Be Peacemakers* (Vatican City: Pontifical Council for Promoting Christian Unity, 2003), 113. From the official final report of a five-year international dialogue between the Catholic Church and the Mennonite World Conference (1998–2003).

Pietism, in particular the Brethren, who had all immigrated to America by the late nineteenth century. There is a logic to combining three peace church traditions as pacifist, but it assumes a commonality of ecclesiology, theology, and ethics that were never uniform. Further, it has rendered the "peace churches" a benign minority ecumenical status, as "a nice icon in the ecumenical museum of interesting exotic species."[2]

A series of dialogues with Lutherans and Catholics in recent decades made clear that Mennonites were no longer regarded as heretical. A common statement from the Vatican and Mennonite World Conference contained not only an apology for persecution but also a common commitment to the "call to be peacemakers." When the Lutheran World Federation assembly met in 2009, its reconciliation liturgy became an emotionally moving time of worship and communion.[3] Indeed, other interchurch dialogues involving Reformed, Baptist, and Pentecostal communions have added to a much more inclusive sense of *koinōnia* among traditions, even though that is not yet what Jesus seemed to mean with "that they all may be one."[4] Also toward the end of the twentieth century, an important wing of the Mennonites in America began calling themselves Anabaptist as a positive claim, and fostered an Anabaptist peace theology, often associated with the late theologian John Howard Yoder. Although known and respected by the three peace church traditions, that peace theology cannot be considered normative, even for American Mennonite traditions. Indeed, the peace churches have generally maintained a theory-praxis integration that resists a systematic idiom.[5]

2. Fernando Enns, "Public Peace, Justice, and Order in Ecumenical Conversation," in *At Peace and Unafraid: Public Order, Security, and the Wisdom of the Cross*, ed. Duane K. Friesen and Gerald Schlabach (Scottdale, PA: Herald, 2005), 242.

3. Lutheran-Mennonite International Study Commission, *Healing Memories: Reconciling in Christ* (Geneva, 2010).

4. See the recent review attempt, John A. Radano, ed., *Celebrating a Century of Ecumenism: Exploring the Achievements of International Dialogue; In Commemoration of the 1910 Edinburgh World Missionary Conference* (Grand Rapids: Eerdmans, 2012). Radano's introduction includes references (as do numerous chapters) to still other international, multilateral, and bilateral dialogues.

5. In his recent instructive introduction to a composite collection of ecumenical dialogues involving Mennonites, Fernando Enns described Mennonites as "rather skeptical about written confessions"; they "interpret confessional texts within the limits of their local and temporal context." Their dialogue style involves sharing and comparing developments. Enns even declares the Mennonite self-understanding as *ecclesia semper reformanda*, and notes the appearance of the phrase "twin sister churches" during Reformed-Mennonite dialogues. Fernando Enns and Jonathan Seiling, eds., *Mennonites in Dialogue: Official Reports from International and National Ecumenical Encounters, 1975–1982* (Eugene, OR: Pickwick, 2015), 1–2, 19.

Labels from opponents, such as "Anabaptists" or "Mennists" (followers of Dutch leader Menno Simons) or "Quakers," were often in contrast to their self-designations: Brethren in Christ or Doopsgezinde or Religious Society of Friends. The self-designations refer to aspects of the relationship to Jesus Christ as Savior and Lord, that is, a commitment to discipleship. Also called free churches, denoting unwillingness to be subordinate to state rulership, they have in the course of five hundred years exploded in membership globally, and now include the bulk of the forty thousand organized Christian traditions. If there are any theoretical ties among them, it is their penchant to split into ever more denominational traditions over specifics of emphasis, whether ethical or spiritual. Central to all has been their claim to be Bible Christians, that is, to hold belief in some form of *sola Scriptura* that reduces the importance of tradition but is also heavily reliant on "experience" and some reasoned way of constructing biblical theologies.

This way of introducing what could be included under "peace churches" serves to nuance how limited is the treatment to follow. If any church is Christian, it must necessarily be a "peace church"; there cannot be "war churches" in terms of their theology and simultaneous fealty to Jesus. That should call to mind the incident in the Gospels as Jesus's triumphal march into Jerusalem began (Lukan version) where he wept and said, "Would that they knew what makes for peace." The point in what follows is to describe efforts of peacemaking, and to probe "what makes for peace"; it is also to say that cultural shaping of American churches grew ever more intense, so that the all-too-flawed human efforts at discipleship best point to intentions only partially attained, if at all. At the same time, what is striking not only in the peace church story (in the USA, Canada, or Europe) is that a discipleship-driven commitment to seek the ways of peace never quite disappeared, and reemerged at later times, since Christ's Sermon on the Mount, which is known almost as widely as the good Samaritan story, forces all to look in the mirror. By the 1980s, across the Christian spectrum East and West, that Christly challenge to love our enemies, seek their good, and so on was what made the nonviolent revolutions of 1989 and the subsequent end of the Cold War possible.

In the typological terms that ethicists and systematic theologians prefer, the contrasts have been between pacifist and just war theories, categories that have dominated the theological dialogues noted below. Yet the lived peace church theologies became rich in descriptive terms, such as the way of love, nonviolent activism, nuclear pacifism, etc., including the commonly affirmed "peace with justice" mantra in the twenty-first century. Yet, given the dominance of "redemptive violence" thinking in the USA, most Christians, peace

469

churches included, attribute the end of the Cold War to the triumph of the American military threat and Soviet capitulation. The actual story of the moral and nonviolent revolutions of 1989–1993, more broadly recognized in Europe, is unthinkable for culturally attuned Americans.

Pre-Cold War Peace Options

Standard American church histories invariably note the many peace movements formed at the end of the nineteenth century, including the Federal Council of Churches; however, most churches (and many of the free churches) became patriotic supporters of America in World War I through pulpits and church magazines. Indeed, among the "restorationist" churches common in America, at some point in their growth, the American flag trumped appeals to pure apostolic Christianity.[6] Such temptations to acclimatize to American patriotism were the setting for the closer ties developing among the historic peace churches following World War I, and for the establishment of a Continuation Committee of the Historic Peace Churches, through which in 1940 they organized the National Service Board for Religious Objectors (NSBRO) on behalf of conscientious objectors in World War II and during the conscription that continued into the 1970s. The program was controlled by the newly formed Selective Service Administration, although the peace churches managed to fund the Civilian Public Service (CPS) work camps.[7] Like so many other church groups, not only in America but across western Europe, Quakers, Mennonites, and Brethren had also formed relief and social service agencies to better channel aid to war sufferers and to foster rebuilding of structures.

After World War I, the American Friends Service Committee (AFSC, formed 1917) supported volunteers in the aftermath of the breakup of the Ottoman Empire and European reconstruction, some three hundred Mennonite and Brethren volunteers joining them.[8] The Mennonites, in response to appeals from their fellow members starving in the Russian famine (1920–1923), formed

6. See, for example, Theron F. Schlabach and Richard T. Hughes, eds., *Proclaim Peace: Christian Pacifism from Unexpected Quarters* (Urbana: University of Illinois Press, 1997).

7. Albert N. Keim, *The CPS Story: An Illustrated History of Civilian Public Service* (Intercourse, PA: Good Books, 1990), 17–38.

8. Donald F. Durnbaugh, "Reforming and Prophetic Movements in Church and Society: Significance of Historic Peace Church Witness," in *Prophetic and Renewal Movements—the Prague Consultations*, ed. Walter Sawatsky, Studies from the World Alliance of Reforming Churches, no. 47 (Geneva, 2009), 148.

a central committee in 1920 for administering relief supplies, later also development aid (1923–1928), with Mennonites in Canada, Netherlands, and Germany funneling their support through what became known as the Mennonite Central Committee (MCC).[9] The Brethren formed a Brethren Service Committee (1939) that sent volunteers to postwar Europe. Its supporting churches were by then more open to ecumenical sharing than were the Mennonites, whose ecumenical involvement got less support from the constituency, or the Quakers, who were more ready to work with anyone of good will, and distrusted institutions. For all three groups, nevertheless, the October Revolution of 1917 was a stimulus to face an already existent societal suspicion of socialism/Communism, and this American culture of anti-Communism grew. In simple terms, Brethren, Mennonites, and Quakers all developed small peacemaking initiatives toward countering the emerging East-West divide, while large sections of their membership learned to fear Communism and to trust (even if secretly and shamefacedly) American military might. Those contradictions remain to the present.

Nevertheless, to grasp the commitments of activists and their leaders in seeking ways of nonviolence, the interwar years and the post-WWII reconstruction years provided deeply personal experiences for many peace church individuals (male and female) in crossing barriers of animosity and in forming friendships and spiritual ties that bound with declared enemies (according to the American state). It turned out that although larger wings of the historic peace churches had supported alternative service for their sons during World War II than was possible in World War I, to do ministries of compassion in the occupied territories of Germany and its allies, all such agencies had to participate through a coordinating committee (Council of Relief Agencies Licensed to Operate in Germany [CRALOG])[10] that negotiated its work with the occupying armies of Britain, France, and the USA, less so with the Soviets. This structural cooperation had also been tested during the Russian famine when Mennonites and Quakers (as well as Jews) were only permitted to operate through Soviet oversight and in coordination with the semigovernmental American Relief Administration of Herbert Hoover.[11] That experience may explain why the

9. For a documentary history, see C. J. Dyck, ed., *The Mennonite Central Committee Story*, 5 vols. (Scottdale, PA: Herald, 1980).

10. Eileen Egan and Elizabeth Clark Reiss, *Transfigured Night: The CRALOG Experience* (Philadelphia: Livingston, 1994).

11. Although the negotiations among Mennonite groups for cooperating and providing details on the subsequent program were included in *The Mennonite Central Committee Story* cited above, an early popular narrative was C. N. Hiebert and Orie Miller, *Feeding the Hungry* (Scottdale, PA: Mennonite Central Committee, 1929), 465 pages. A thorough dissertation rely-

first CRALOG administrator, Eldon R. Burke, was from the Brethren,[12] and three regional directors in the occupied zones were Mennonite. We should remember that the postwar public opinion among the victorious allies against Nazi Germany was vengeful, even against the entire population. The occupying forces (British, French, American) finally agreed to permit relief services to Germans to prevent "actual starvation of masses of German civilians," following the query by General Dwight Eisenhower: "What are we going to do just to prevent on our part having a Buchenwald of our own?"[13] After three years, the CRALOG church agency support had directly aided one-third of the German population; the revived relief arm of the German Protestant church had managed to assist another third.[14] This ecumenical recovery effort changed hearts and minds; reconciliation happened silently, and through specific leadership initiatives, as the World Council of Churches (WCC) emerged in 1948. The relationships formed, and the capacity to rely on the charity of many Christians, became the framework for efforts by peace churches and others to resist the new division into a bipolar world, that is, the Cold War.

The long-delayed formation of the World Council of Churches in 1948 did not include Russian churches because of the Cold War. The remembered major speeches at its founding assembly in Amsterdam, from opposing sides, were by American John Foster Dulles (advocating containment, later becoming secretary of state) and Czech theologian Josef Hromádka (urging Christians from both sides to seek peace). A decade later, Hromádka organized the Christian Peace Conference (CPC), with national committees emerging in many countries, in-

---

ing on official Soviet documents as well as the extant secondary literature is Tatiana Nazarova, "Blagotvoritel'naia deiatel'nost' zarubezhnykh mennonitskikh orginizatsii v sovetskom gosudarstve (1920–1930gg.)" [Charitable work of foreign Mennonite organizations in the Soviet state (1920–1930)] (Volgograd State University, 2010).

12. J. Kenneth Kreider, *A Cup of Cold Water: The Story of Brethren Service* (Elgin, IL: Brethren Press, 2001), 218–26. An American Council of Voluntary Agencies for Foreign Service, formed in 1943, sent a seven-person study committee to Germany, then CRALOG was licensed in February 1946, by the president's War Relief Control Board, with eleven agencies as charter members. Those included AFSC, Brethren Service Committee, Mennonite Central Committee, and the Relief and Reconstruction committee of the FCC (Church World Service), as well as groups from Lutheran, Catholic, Unitarian, and Christian Science churches, plus three secular agencies.

13. Donald F. Durnbaugh, "The Response of American Peace Church to Relief and Rehabilitation Needs in Germany Following World War II," in Sawatsky, *Prophetic and Renewal Movements*, 211–12. Eisenhower's roots, by the way, were in the Brethren in Christ tradition.

14. Hans Thimme, "A Receiving Church Becomes a Giving Church," in *Hope in the Desert: The Churches' United Response to Human Need, 1944–1984*, ed. Kenneth Slack (Geneva: WCC Publications, 1986), 20.

cluding the USA. Mennonites in the Netherlands and Germany had joined the WCC, not so the Mennonites in the USA. The Church of the Brethren (not the other Brethren) joined the National Council of Churches of Christ (NCCC), and were active in its commissions. Mennonite and Brethren representatives from America did become active in the CPC in 1958, and were active in the post-1968 withdrawal from CPC and formation of Christians Associated for Relationships with Eastern Europe (CAREE) to seek East-West relationships nevertheless. Since a specific chapter also addresses the role of CAREE, it will get less detail below.

AFSC and Evangelical Quaker Programs during the Cold War

Whether as liberal Quakers (AFSC) or as evangelical Quakers, Friends tended to organize voluntary participatory societies (British and Foreign Bible Society, for example) through which a network of services was carried out. Early in the twentieth century, Quakers were often part of the Young Men's Christian Association (YMCA) that not only linked itself with the *Kirchentag* lay movement in West Germany after 1945, and with the Student Christian Movement (present all over Europe), but also with the YMCA in Russia. The latter involvement was more difficult following the revolution, since the YMCA had been forced out of the USSR within a decade thereof, but ties with Slavic religious and secular leaders, including Tolstoyans, persisted indirectly after 1930 when Western visits to the USSR had essentially stopped.[15]

So the Quaker role in opposing the Cold War was played out more through AFSC service programs in southeast Asia, in developing countries in Africa, and in the Caribbean. Quakers in Britain and small communities in Western Europe did develop relationships with Christians in Eastern Europe through regular visits, communicating, without publicity, with each other and with supporters. Beginning in the late 1950s, British Quakers and their counterparts in the Commonwealth or the USA were usually active in the Campaign for Nuclear Disarmament (CND). In the European continental peace movement of the 1980s, they marched alongside many other Christians in demonstrations for END (European Nuclear Disarmament). The major demonstrations in Amsterdam, Cologne, and many other cities, with up to a million demonstrators, were mostly organized by an ecumenical voluntary

---

15. For many fascinating details, see Matthew Lee Miller, *The American YMCA and Russian Culture: The Preservation and Expansion of Russian Orthodoxy, 1900–1940* (Lanham, MD: Lexington Books, 2013), based on a 2006 dissertation.

society, Action Committee Service for Peace (AGDF), a spin-off society from EIRENE: Christian Service for Peace that had been established in 1958, when West Germany introduced conscription.

Brethren Service Committee (BSC), Mennonite Central Committee (MCC), and Quaker representatives joined with German Protestant leaders to organize EIRENE, and soon obtained the right for alternative service for conscientious objectors. EIRENE also established a department of peace studies in the 1960s, which developed into a separate organization called Church and Peace, which conducted seminars and conferences where the church as peacemaker was stressed. Although Church and Peace itself only reached out to Eastern Europe after 1989, establishing new branches, nevertheless its presence within the European Protestant world, alongside Caritas and other Catholic agencies fostering service and peacemaking, contributed to the spiritual and theological transformations across Western Europe that helped account for the European peace movement and related citizen diplomacy initiatives leading up to 1989. BSC and MCC representatives from the USA were the conduits between the USA and Europe, for support and the facilitation of service exchanges (between Europe and America, and for assignments in North Africa and Central America). Since the Protestant *Kirchentag* (Church Day) met in Hannover in 1983, just when American pressure to station Pershing missiles on European soil was at its height, the planners chose to highlight the three hundredth anniversary of the first German migration to America to settle in Germantown, Pennsylvania. These were Quakers and Mennonites from Krefeld and environs, then fleeing conscription. So the peace church witness featured large at the *Kirchentag*, as did the Dutch interchurch peace movement, whose symbol was a housewife kicking the bomb out of her home.

The Quakers had established an information office in Brussels, Belgium (in addition to their offices in New York and Geneva), which tracked the issue of conscientious objection to military service. It soon was the most reliable directory of legal cases involving COs in Europe and elsewhere. Still another focus was to track human rights violations, especially after the Commission on Security Cooperation in Europe (CSCE) agreement of 1975 required the USSR and Western signatories to report on human (including religious) rights. Further, the Quaker role at the UN caused a shift over time, so that the UN included the right to conscientious objection to military service as a human right; indeed by 1990 it also affirmed the right to refuse to kill.[16]

---

16. Eileen Egan, *Peace Be with You: Justified Warfare or the Way of Nonviolence* (Maryknoll, NY: Orbis, 1999), 234–36.

Brethren Christian Service during the Cold War

By 1900 the Brethren, an essentially American peace church, had split into five denominations, reflecting varied approaches to acculturation. By 1939 the Church of the Brethren, now more culturally integrated than earlier split-off denominations like the Grace Brethren that were less actively pacifist, formed a service commission to assist sufferers from all sides in the Spanish Civil War. Brethren also sent a significant number of COs to serve in the Civilian Public Service (CPS), some of whom found more challenging roles later in war-torn Europe, including women volunteers, as did the Mennonites.

Their postwar role in European reconstruction was heavily personal. The story is told as a series of vignettes in *A Cup of Cold Water: The Story of Brethren Service* (2001),[17] through which the reciprocal impact of giving and receiving comes through. In Don Durnbaugh's more systematic and analytical reflections published a few years thereafter, the significance of American public assistance to the enemy, Nazi Germany, is central. One might say that Brethren peacemaking during the Cold War years was personal, ecumenical, and theological. There was much practical creativity, starting already with the sending of cows to Spain, then to postwar Poland; eventually the Heifer Project International became Third World driven. Other volunteers started inviting students—high school students, college students, and agricultural scientists— to visit and study in the USA; they lived with Brethren families.[18] The friendships, eventually totaling several thousand influential Polish professionals, for example, help account for sustained communication links during the worst phases of the Cold War, and help explain the perspectives of key officials in Poland and in the America-USA Institute during perestroika days, for finding the way toward arms control negotiations and the related transformations within the USSR and East European states.

The ecumenical aspect was articulated in two ways. The denomination joined the National Council of Churches and channeled much of its service and development involvement through Church World Service (itself partially initiated by the Brethren).[19] This meant that the Brethren could model a more neutral role in relationships with Eastern and Western European churches, since there was no sister church for them in Europe. Thanks to shared expe-

---

17. See n. 12 above.

18. Durnbaugh, "Reforming and Prophetic Movements," 145. See Kreider, *A Cup of Cold Water*, for chapters on each project.

19. Durnbaugh, "Reforming and Prophetic Movements," 145.

riences at relief agency meetings via the WCC, and through hosting Soviet delegations when other denominations were more cautious about the critics of Soviet churchmen, at key moments BSC leader Kurtis F. Naylor and the then-archbishop Nikodim of Leningrad, who had developed a personal friendship, were able to broker meetings to address contentious issues.[20]

Mennonite Central Committee (MCC) during the Cold War

It was the impact of World War II, its devastating aftermath, and the Cold War that followed that gave new life to MCC as an inter-Mennonite service agency. The sectarian suspicions between Mennonite denominations (at least thirteen struggled to cooperate) had been overcome sufficiently that for the sake of humanitarian relief for fellow Mennonites in Russia in the 1920s sacrificial donations had been possible. But then ties to the USSR ended, and more of those denominations reached outside themselves by starting their own overseas missions, which accounts for the rise of so many separate Mennonite denominations in the southern continents during the second half of the century.

The task of assisting with postwar relief in Germany, and soon also other West European countries, became the primary role of the MCC, through an even more varied proliferation of programs than the BSC had organized. As with the BSC history, the MCC histories appearing in anniversary years have tended to be more self-congratulatory than critical—telling the story was key to sustaining donations and volunteer involvement.[21] That reality of persons with MCC service experience, after returning to an American congregation, taking ownership of tasks, pushing the agendas they cared about, resulted in what one friendly observer called "gadfly citizenship."[22]

For several decades before the end of the Cold War, the orientation of MCC volunteers included showing the developing service agenda of MCC as a simple learning progression, but always rooted in the key lines from Matthew 25: "what you did unto the least . . ." First came relief, feeding the hungry—the Mennonites in Russia (actually many others too)—then teaching them to grow food (Western development theory for the Third World), then the discovery of justice (land for natives, advocacy for marginalized),

---

20. Kreider, *A Cup of Cold Water*, 321–36, specifically 325.

21. For example, Robert Kreider and Rachel Waltner Goosen, *Hungry, Thirsty, a Stranger: The MCC Experience* (Scottdale, PA: Herald, 1988).

22. Pamela Leach, "Gadfly Citizenship: Faithful Public Practices beyond the National Security Model," in Friesen and Schlabach, *At Peace and Unafraid*, 83–116.

and the shift in peacemaking from "nonresistance" (too passive) to nonviolent activism, to peace capacity building. One can easily describe this also as a progression from a highly biblical understanding of doing everything "in the name of Christ" (the MCC logo) to a highly instrumentalized peace teaching and skills mediation performed by professionals. It became a way to shift from being a separated people to one engaged in society (with concomitant societal approval) for "meeting human need" (the new MCC logo). Along the way, Amish and conservative Mennonite supporters could continue to contribute to relief with donations in kind, whereas other programs advocating for human rights (with the assistance of offices in Washington, Ottawa, and at the United Nations) were drawing on professionals from socially integrated denominations.

That serves as a quick overview for locating the Mennonite (largely inter-Mennonite through MCC) role during the Cold War. The Cold War (1947–1991) was actually framed by the entire story of the MCC as a bridge between the East and the West. When the largest organized body of Mennonites (120,000 across the Russian Empire) began to collapse due to famine (1920–1923), after which the churches were attacked (especially from 1929 to 1937), resulting in the total collapse of a functioning church, the Mennonite Central Committee was formed to offer relief. With the demands for relief and reconstruction services in Western Europe after 1945, MCC again sprang into the breach (again assisting many more than its fellow Mennonites). As a result, it became the primary structural entity for North American Mennonites, and, together with its modernizing denominations and related service agencies, it easily replaced the activism associated with Russian Mennonites before 1917. Concern for fellow Mennonites and other Christians in the Soviet Union was a constant theme, with even renewed initiatives after 1991, even as the shift to the Two-Thirds World as its primary agenda, starting around 1970, dominated budget and program. So the story of the Mennonite peace church role in the Cold War reflects both deep involvement and missed opportunities and challenges. In simplified terms, there was a Russian (and north European) Mennonite immigrant lobby pressing for contradictory involvement, and a Swiss/south German Americanized immigrant community resonating with stories of martyrdom for faith like those from the sixteenth-century Anabaptist martyrs, and because of their pacifism wanting to counter the climate of anti-Communism so determinative of Cold War support.

Among the major initiatives after 1945 was concern for refugees, providing them with food and shelter, then finding settlement solutions. Since a major flood of refugees came from the USSR, including ten thousand to fifteen thousand Russian Mennonites, who had no wish to return "home," relocating them in Germany, Paraguay, Brazil, and Canada became the primary story. The logistics of moving so many people—leasing ships, securing provisional identity papers, purchasing tracts of land in host countries—were long described in heroic terms. Earlier Russian Mennonite immigrants, especially from the major immigration to Canada (1923–1926), who had vivid but brief experiences of the violence of revolution, became the primary staff for ministries in and to the USSR. Storyteller Peter J. Dyck, one of the many "MCCers" overseeing this operation, traveled around the USA and Canada, including among the Amish, showing video footage of moving the refugees out of Berlin to Bremerhaven to Paraguay, and repeating "*Gott Kann*" (God can) until it became an MCC mantra. Later reflection began to include more self-criticism of the political innocence, of a willingness to overlook the Nazi leanings of a portion of the refugees, or of their profound anti-Communist attitudes, so often speaking of escaping the "Red hell." As was true of the majority of Russian German refugees, and to some extent of all Russians and Ukrainians among the refugees, some part of their family had stayed behind—already in the Gulag, in the Red Army or Workers Army (forced labor)—so reunification of families was especially urgent. The Red Cross was usually the centralized agency for tracking family members. Mennonites developed a *Suchdienst* (search service) of their own, amassing thousands of card files; as late as the 1970s, this service was still helping family members find each other.

This concern for the fate of families and their church bodies became a primary concern when contacts with the USSR gradually became possible after 1945. Contacts had never ended entirely, since family members found ways to get letters to each other, and their Aesopian descriptions of conditions for faith and life were circulated through church networks, less so through Mennonite periodicals. The family concern vacillated between fostering their out-migration and assisting their survival. The much wider-supporting American Mennonite community was interested in assisting with the spiritual rebirth of faith practice after its nearly two decades of death.

As early as 1950, when initial reconstruction pressures in Germany began to ease, MCC leaders met with West European Mennonite leaders to refocus; there was nevertheless a specific invitation to the primary MCC representatives to serve in an ambassadorial role between America and Europe, to foster inter-Mennonite relations that too long had been rather dormant.[23] By 1956 this came to include a special office for East-West concerns, at first based

---

23. This ambassadorial role was repeated at similar consultations in 1967, 1979, and 1992.

in Frankfurt. Its function was to coordinate contacts, to foster a variety of initiatives for bridging the East-West barrier. One key approach was to seek official contacts. When the Baptist-Evangelical Christian Union (formed in 1944) was permitted its first delegation to America in 1955, MCC leaders met with them for several hours in Chicago. The following year, two Mennonite leaders were able to join a Baptist World Alliance return delegation visit to Moscow. Equipped with address cards, they managed to meet with a Mennonite leader (long imprisoned) at a Moscow hotel, with whom they sought to expand their list of functioning Mennonite fellowships (not yet registered churches). They also urged the Baptist Union to offer an umbrella of support to this sister tradition (they were already known to each other since Russian Baptist and Evangelical Christian beginnings nearly a century earlier). There followed organized tours at least every other year until 1974, when two MCC representatives were invited to attend the all-Soviet congress of Evangelical Christians—Baptists, Pentecostals, and Mennonites—and managed to converse with Mennonite delegates from various hinterlands.[24]

The tour device was normally done through the Soviet travel agency Intourist, with tourist visas, which restricted visitors to open cities, usually the capital cities of the Soviet republics. However, by then the majority of Russian Mennonites were located in more distant places in Siberia, the Ural Mountains region, and central Asia, with a smaller percentage working on state farms, and more doing manual labor in urban centers. These tours usually linked with the Frankfurt office for background briefings, and upon return, key tour leaders met with denominational heads in Canada and the USA for ecclesial accounting. From this there developed strategies of ministry, which went beyond delivery of Christian literature through very controlled customs checkpoints, to planned reciprocal reporting on church life, de facto teaching moments when giving "greetings" or when local leaders gathered informally after worship. In all these cases, it was natural for the Mennonites to stress their peace church commitments, and to struggle with the critique of gullibility about official Soviet peace claims (often also articulated from that perspective by Soviet Baptist and Mennonite leaders) while seeking biblical and theological common ground on "what makes for peace" in Christian perspective.

---

24. For a recent review, stated in terms of partnership commitments, see Walter Sawatsky, "Serious Mission Partners in Eastern Europe: Reflections on 20 Years of Post-Communism," *Mission Focus: Annual Review* 20 (2012): 144–69.

The Peace Church Roles over Changing Times

Given their centuries of commitment to "nonresistance," to "love your ene-mies," the peace churches' role was characterized by their minority status. In America this meant that although they could claim full freedom of religion, including alternative service to soldiering, the cultural pressure to conform to the prevailing anti-Communism, the pressure to be seen as good Americans, steadily ate away at their earlier disciplined biblical nonresistance. Leaders and activists struggled to be creative in teaching and practicing peacemaking. It is worth attempting a bit of differentiation in such "peacemaking" during differ-ent phases of the Cold War. In what follows, one or more of the peace churches will appear, but always their efforts were informed by, and connected in some way to, the others, a kind of joint peace church witness. Further, it becomes difficult to make sense of things by sticking to American peace churches only, since the final third of the century marked much greater global cooperation within traditions and beyond them.

The primary phase of the Cold War entailed the period between So-viet (and then Maoist Chinese) production of nuclear armaments and the reaching of the status of mutually assured destruction (MAD). A second phase, as part of de-Stalinization in the USSR and the ending of the Chi-nese Cultural Revolution together with a Western posture toward détente, provided many more options for peacemaking involvement. In that phase, it must be emphasized, American peace churches rarely acted alone; there was more joint interpenetration of the East-West barrier. Then followed a heightened Cold War climate, usually associated with the presidency of Ronald Reagan and the prime ministership of Margaret Thatcher in Britain, and the "Star Wars" dimension of the armaments race. That became the time for larger people movements of "solidarity," ending with the "people's diplomacy" initiatives, until Reagan essentially reversed himself, and even Congress and the Duma conducted a dialogue via a TV bridge. Finally, then, we must identify a fourth phase of the ending of the Cold War with many new interchurch initiatives, yet also an American public and political persistence in sustaining the habits of the Cold War. Here there is space for limited critical commentary, pointing to more in-depth studies that could help us understand better.

Early Phase—Reconstruction, Reconciliation, Dialogue

During the first phase of the Cold War, the peace churches were engaged in common with West European efforts to foster postwar reconciliation; these included resumed efforts by American Mennonites to renew fellow European Mennonite commitments to peace. Anabaptist scholars among Dutch, German, and Swiss Mennonite communities emerged, keeping in regular touch with the zenith of Anabaptist studies in America (1950–1970). Numerous Mennonites, following their alternative service in Europe, stayed to complete doctorates in Basel, Zurich, and Heidelberg, others doing so in American universities.

"War is not the will of God" was the theme of the Amsterdam 1948 assembly. As a result, the peace churches submitted separate statements in 1951 on "war is contrary to the will of God," then common statements on "peace is the will of God" (1953) and "God establishes both peace and justice" (1955). At a more systematic theological level, several BSC and MCC volunteers (doctoral students) became theological spokespersons for their traditions at the Puidoux conference series, bringing together German, then other European, Protestant theologians on peace church theology—the first time since the Reformation, said Heinold Fast, that German Protestant theologians and the peace churches had a dialogue on "the theological questions raised by pacifism."[25] Such meetings were held in 1955, 1957, 1960, and 1962 on "the Lordship of Christ over church and state."[26]

That first event involved only twenty-seven persons. At the second dialogue in 1957 sixty were present, and at Puidoux III in 1960 there were eighty participants, including five from various Soviet and East European churches. The joint affirmation in 1957 that Jesus Christ "is the Lord over church and state" gained new significance with leaders from states overtly unfriendly to churches. At Puidoux IV in 1962, Jan M. Lochmann's (Czech) paper entitled "Influence of Historical Events on Ethical Decisions," followed by a response by J. H. Yoder and broad discussion, seemed to have participants returning to just-war-versus-pacifist positions, but with the difference that the new East-West dynamics, soon also Third World contexts, revealed more differences due to the situational settings than classic theological positions could sustain. Heinold Fast himself continued in smaller study commissions; by 1966 these

25. Heinold Fast, "Puidoux 1955–1969: Report about a Dialogue on the Theological Bases of the Christian Peace Witness," in *On Earth Peace: Discussions on War/Peace Issues between Friends, Mennonites, Brethren, and European Churches, 1935–75*, ed. Donald F. Durnbaugh (Elgin, IL: Brethren Press, 1978), 320–28.

26. Durnbaugh, *On Earth Peace*, contains texts with commentary.

were also linked to a Protestant study center at Heidelberg University. A newer generation of theologians was now wrestling with the church contribution to peace in the face of the nuclear threat.[27]

Détente Phase

Another way that the peace churches and International Fellowship of Reconciliation (IFOR) shifted their focus had to do with the movement toward an emphasis on church and society among WCC member churches. At the Uppsala Assembly in 1968, because of his assassination not long before, peace church participants were deeply involved in what was called the Martin Luther King Resolution; seeking to avoid getting bogged down in pacifist/nonpacifist debate, they sought "alternatives to war which were non-violent and led to social change and justice."[28] Many of the peace church representatives continued in a variety of ecumenical committee venues to pursue this peace and justice agenda; they went to the Nairobi Assembly (1975) seeking to address the armament/disarmament issue, then participated in other formations leading to the Decade to Overcome Violence. Gibble's survey ends by stressing that the peace church efforts were not "monovocal" but occurred via "a wide variety of organizational linkages"; he listed at least six major ones.[29]

Durnbaugh also observed that the role played by several Brethren leaders in WCC-related activities already before 1983 helped account for other American denominations issuing statements,[30] such as the Presbyterian Church USA statement "Peacemaking: The Believer's Calling," the United Church of Christ developing a "Just Peace" policy, and the Disciples' "Seeking God's Peace in a Nuclear Age," all of which emerged in the early 1980s when the press was full of the struggles of the National Conference of Catholic Bishops drafting its "Pastoral Letter on War and Peace" (1983).[31] For readers from the peace

27. Fast, "Puidoux 1955–1969," 322–23.

28. H. Lamar Gibble, *Ecumenical Engagement for Peace and Non-Violence* (Elgin, IL: Church of the Brethren, 2006), 41.

29. They were the American New Call to Peacemaking, the Prague Christian Peace Conference, Faith and Order consultations on "The Apostolic Character of the Church's Peace Witness," the "First and Radical Reformation" (or Prague consultations), activities in the NCCC's Peace with Justice Week, and also with the Life and Peace Institute in Uppsala, Sweden. Gibble, *Ecumenical Engagement*, 76.

30. Durnbaugh, "Reforming and Prophetic Movements," 150.

31. In the area of social ethics, the global leadership of the Roman Catholic Church

churches, those developments are evidence that being present persistently at ecumenical gatherings was fruitful, rather than harmful to dearly held "distinctives," and was helpful for the reciprocal search for options in finding the way toward peace and justice in changing contexts.

The Church and Peace organization later continued the dialogue in Western Europe at a more practical theology of service level, also bringing in a broader spectrum of keynote speakers from IFOR and other service agencies. This very abbreviated survey of theological dialogue and peace service projects, alternating between venues in Europe and America, albeit with a surprising continuity of participants from East and West Europe, and by American peace church representatives with extensive experience in Europe, seeks to convey how peace churches, dismissed in earlier centuries as irrelevant to social ethics, were now taken more seriously in light of the Cold War setting. Further, the peace churches were themselves becoming seekers, given the large social ethics issues shaping ecumenical discourse after 1968—such as racism, poverty, injustice, and widespread secularization. There was a spreading awareness that all churches in a global ecumenical sense needed clarity on what makes for peace.

Already at the assembly of the WCC in Delhi in 1961, where Orthodox and other churches of the USSR joined, and where Third World church bodies gained greater attention, their thinking influenced subsequent peace church actions. Further, since the first Christian Peace Conference (CPC) in 1958—with Mennonite, Brethren, and Quakers participants alongside European and American Protestant leaders and theologians—there was a growing personal familiarity with East European church leaders. This was the era of dialogue, not only the Christian-Marxist dialogue conducted in Prague, but the drawing in of Christians and Marxists in numerous CPC-related national settings, whether in the DDR, Yugoslavia, or Germany, Britain, and the USA. For decades sociologists met through the stimulus of a neutral research center in Vienna; Paul Peachey, as a Mennonite teaching at Catholic University of America, and an active member of the CPC in America, then of CAREE, was

---

and the Reformed churches in the 1980s shaped the thinking of many peace church leaders too. Clarifying boundaries for what governments and what churches must address (as in the *Centesimus Annus* encyclical, a century after *Rerum Novarum*; or the Reformed practice of identifying issues that deserve *status confessionis*) was particularly helpful. In 1982 the World Alliance of Reformed Churches proposed "peace" as a central confessional matter. See Rolf Wischnath, ed., *Frieden als Bekenntnisfrage* (Gütersloh: Gütersloherverlagshaus Mohn, 1984), 434–552, especially the appendix of statements from numerous church organizations responding to the 1982 statement.

a regular participant.[32] But much more was happening under the radar. The variety of service programs developed by the peace church agencies impacted other parts of the peace church constituency more than the formal dialogues did, and the East Europeans linked to such programs formed further networks.

From the Renewed Cold War Armaments Race to the End of the Cold War

If President Reagan's response to the quashing of Polish *Solidarność* by Soviet pressure that caused General Jaruzelski to declare martial law in Poland in 1981 was to introduce trade sanctions, causing the Polish economy to decline precipitously, public responses in Europe, especially Germany, were to send relief supplies and seek reconciliation between Poles and Germans. Long-established exchange ties to Poland through Brethren and Mennonite service agencies, as well as Catholic relief agency linkages, not only facilitated further relief but also resulted in steadily growing border-crossing interactions. When the WCC Vancouver Assembly in 1983 essentially declared a commitment to nuclear pacifism, this showed a global Christian resistance to the use of the nuclear threat, enabling even the representatives from the Soviet churches (Orthodox and Baptist) to fall in line, without serious consequences upon their return. In this changing context, the peace churches continued a modest peacemaking presence, adapting to new opportunities.

Early in the 1970s, for example, Eastern Mennonite Missions was already supporting an American Mennonite as a student in Zagreb; he combined his studies with assisting at a free church relief agency. Soon students had also been sent to schools in Romania, Hungary, Poland, and the GDR, mostly through MCC, which formed an East-West fraternity of such persons. Their assignment was to study and serve, to take seriously the culture and world

---

32. In his autobiography *A Usable Past: A Story of Living and Thinking Vocationally at the Margins* (Telford, PA: DreamSeeker Books, 1984), Paul Peachey provided an abbreviated history of the CPC and the American CAREE involvement. The eleventh chapter, "Cold War Bridgebuilding," is highly personal and brief, but contains at least two remarks of note. American (including Mennonite) anxiety about being manipulated by Soviet and other East European propaganda was worth the risk, he said, quoting a Viennese scholar who had refused to travel there during the Cold War, then being told by a peace activist in Moscow that the regular presence of Westerners at Soviet-sponsored peace conferences gave them hope, and did make possible short, more direct personal conversations that were not reported to authorities. The second was the recognition of how often the peace church representatives and others from the West lacked the specialist and linguistic expertise that could have made such "bridge-building" efforts more fruitful.

of ideas, engaging in dialogue with secular, Marxist, and Christian interlocutors personally. Such border-crossing initiatives were happening more broadly and included secret missionaries smuggling Bibles, etc. The Mennonite, Brethren, and Quaker exchanges of this sort normally approached the border crossing with deliberate transparency. In the MCC case, for example, the arrangements were made through universities or theological schools (in Poland and Romania) by MCC representatives, so the sponsorship was known. In Romania, an American Mennonite couple began studying at the Romanian Orthodox theological academy, while several Romanian priests were guests at the Mennonite seminary in Indiana, the Romanian students also finding opportunities to assist Romanian Orthodox parishes nearby. The Mennonite couple sang in the choir of an Orthodox parish in Bucharest, and regularly participated in Baptist worship. Another family spent three years in Leipzig, so identifying with their Lutheran hosts that they had their child baptized in solidarity, while the male student completed a doctoral dissertation on Thomas Müntzer, which he successfully defended before a committee of Reformation specialists—two Marxists and one Lutheran. Yet the later key critique of the Mennonite East-West exchanges, by a person placed in East Berlin, personally observing the Leipzig prayer marches throughout 1989, was that these profoundly experienced transformations of attitude toward persons across the bipolar global divide generated a quite limited bounce-back effect in the supporting American Mennonite constituency.[33] Regularly affirmed by the MCC executive committee, these exchanges were seen to be the right thing to do, but did not need publicity.

The Mennonites conducted their peacemaking efforts with the Soviet Union, which were of longer duration and more diverse, while constantly confronting two alternative constituent reactions. As stated by this writer in a personal reflection on his experiences, one representative group was anxious not to cause trouble for relatives still living in the USSR, warning against gullibility to Soviet peace overtures, while the other group pushed for more human and religious rights advocacy and for finding more ways to be present in Eastern Europe.[34] As it turned out, Peter Dyck, then director of the MCC Europe programs, discovered Michael Bourdeaux's Centre for the Study of Religion under Communism in 1972, which sought to research actual situations accurately and

33. Mark Jantzen, "Tenuous Bridges over the Iron Curtain: Mennonite Central Committee Work in Eastern Europe from 1966 to 1991," *Religion in Eastern Europe* 31, no. 1 (February 2011): 17–32; also appearing in *Mission Focus: Annual Review* (2011).

34. Walter Sawatsky, "On the Way to Living Globally," *Anabaptist Witness* 1 (2014): 156.

fairly. This writer was seconded to Bourdeaux's center (better known as Keston Institute before its demise) as a research scholar, an assignment retained when he moved to Germany three years later to interview Soviet emigrants, and even as a seminary professor in the USA for several decades. Three or four other scholars and writers were placed at Keston over the years and contributed to its journal and newsletter. Given constituency alignments in America for and against the underground or official Protestant churches (not just among peace churches), such background publications in the religious press did affect understanding. At the Nairobi WCC Assembly in 1975, for example, when reports on human rights violations were widely disseminated, including by three centers focused on religion (in London, Zurich, and Utrecht),[35] the Dutch Reformed leader Albert van den Heuvel called for ending the boundaries of silence tacitly observed at WCC meetings; he was helped by the distribution of documentary materials and analysis for all delegates at the beginning of a morning session. This led to a commitment for member churches to report on their situations annually, with the research institutes providing their services.

Among peace-building efforts at the specifically religious level was a joint East-West project to translate multivolume Bible commentaries (chosen by Soviet Baptists) on the New and Old Testaments, cofunded by the MCC and the Baptist World Alliance, that continued from 1977 to 1993. Clearly intended to improve quality of preaching and church life, it involved church leaders within the USSR and their counterparts in the West working openly across the East-West divide, thereby conveying over an extended time period that Christian work did measure up to high scholarly standards and was contributing to the good of society. None of this was a peace church distinctive, except perhaps in style, but given the more widespread experiential familiarization between church leaders (and their political minders/consultants) gained through WCC and CPC events, and peace conferences hosted in the USSR (such as the one in 1982 that Billy Graham attended), a gradual normalization of church-state relations in an environment of hostile tolerance of religion became evident by the late 1970s. Then, finally, by 1990 legal freedom of religion became the Soviet position, as it was also occurring across Eastern Europe. All this was adding up to broad societal attitude changes that made the end of the Cold War possible. This writer's role in writing, editing, and assisting within CAREE after 1990 when teaching in seminary in the USA was also sponsored by the MCC as part of its commitment to overcoming the walls of partition.

---

35. They were Glaube in der 2. Welt (Eugen Voss), Department of Studies of the Dutch Inter-Church Center in Utrecht (Hans Hebly), and Keston College (Michael Bourdeaux).

Assessing Peace Church Theology and Praxis

This mix of theory (ethical/theological) and praxis continued as the trajectory for the peace churches and others even as the Cold War was declared to be over. In 1994 Elisabeth Salter (British Quaker), Barbara Bazett (Canadian Quaker), and Don Miller (Brethren), all members of the WCC Central Committee, introduced a Programme to Combat Violence, along the lines of the contested Programme to Combat Racism. This got changed later to the more biblical Programme to Overcome Violence (POV), with Sara Specher (Brethren) as volunteer staff.[36] This initiative served as background when Fernando Enns, German Mennonite member of the WCC Central Committee, successfully moved (in 1998) the adoption of a Decade to Overcome Violence (DOV). The DOV ran from 2001 to 2011. By 2002, Swiss Mennonite Hansulrich Gerber (then MCC Europe director) was appointed director of the POV, which was no longer a centralized program but was a coordinating center to cause member and nonmember churches to link their peacemaking activities with others for the sake of solidarity and mutual learning.

One could say that even among the American peace churches, including their fellows in Canada to a lesser extent, much of their theological and practical peace engagement kept its distance from European developments. The Mennonite and Brethren theological literature since 1983 has been largely parochial, with minor exceptions, even as post–Cold War realignments might have stimulated deeper East-West relationships. Their focus has been on teaching peace to constituents whose convictions on the issue were in decline; therefore, the HPC New Call to Peace Making initiative was primarily internal, and gradually ended. The ethicists/theologians tended to think and write in their idiom: "What would/should you do?," using case studies to sharpen typological options. When the HPC activists looked outside American borders, it was to Central and South American countries, as well as to antiapartheid activists in South Africa, from which they chose "cases." Almost invariably, those discussions quickly shifted to what we (USA) should do, so the peace theology focused on small activities of mediation or nonviolence training, and protesting military "intervention" on behalf of human suffering.

To the degree that peace with justice became a shaping agenda for the WCC in the early twenty-first century, it was the Decade to Overcome Violence movements globally (with minimal visibility in the USA) that resulted in both the Jamaica declaration of 2011 and the current theme of pilgrimage

36. For details, see Gibble, *Ecumenical Engagement*, 68–77.

for peace and justice, usually as an expression of solidarity with the victimized. The American churches, peace churches included, may have peace theology attitudes evident at denominational leadership levels, but the education for peace of their members has drastically dwindled, given post-9/11 militarism. In the most recent, more broadly interactive Mennonite discussion on Christian involvement in public order, as published in *At Peace and Unafraid* (2005), indeed a rare Mennonite acknowledgment of social responsibility as inherent in a full-orbed peace witness, none of the essays draw on post-Communist settings, with the exception of the broad framing of Fernando Enns's chapter, "Public Peace, Justice, and Order in Ecumenical Conversation."[37] The latter, which shows the ways in which Mennonite and Brethren active engagement with the WCC at its highest levels conveys how persistent articulation of the peace church tradition in realistic and humble terms that include adopting ideas from other traditions also finding their way toward peace with justice and care for the integrity of creation, has been mutually enriching. Chapters by persons from other parts of the world—Indonesia, Paraguay, and Colombia— do indeed show how context shapes options and theology, but the primary thrust of the *At Peace and Unafraid* book speaks to Americans in their idiom.

As early as 1942, the MCC had established a "peace section" functioning parallel to program sections, the section also assigning peace representatives to cooperate with European Mennonite peace committees emerging after World War II. Focused heavily on conferences and consultations to recover a peace commitment (after its near collapse in the first half of the century), a European Mennonite peace committee was fostering alternative service advocacy and relationships internationally beyond Europe by the 1980s. By then, the MCC programs in Europe were focused on building bridges to Eastern Europe and the Soviet Union, on assisting with peace initiatives in conflict settings such as Ireland, and on engaging in interchurch relationships, all with peace and reconciliation intentions.

---

37. It is vital to point out that Duane Friesen's argument for a "realist perspective" on peacemaking (*Peacemaking and International Conflict* [Scottdale, PA: Herald, 1985]), which also reflected the praxis of the north European Mennonite tradition in many settings, proceeded by assuming that "a view of the international system as a transnational network of interconnections is both more descriptive of the world and more amenable to Christian values than the traditional balance of power view" (29). Given Friesen's key role in the *At Peace and Unafraid* book in 2003–2005, it demonstrates a shift in HPC thinking and praxis about the role of Christians in civil society and public order. My criticism seeks merely to point out how the inclusion of peace church involvements in Greater Europe (East and West) could help reduce the centrality of an Americanist perspective.

Following a gathering of American and European Mennonite peace activists in 1982 at the NATO headquarters in Brussels, a NATO Watch office and newsletter were eventually established, with shared financial support from the MCC Europe office and the European Mennonite peace committees. There was close cooperation between members of a Quaker peace office in Brussels and a Brussels Mennonite center (established by the Mennonite board of missions). Their stance was taken from Quaker Brian Stapleton's article in the first *NATO Watch* newsletter—"listen, learn, pray, be and act!" The newsletter, edited by J. Robert Charles and Jan Piet van den Berg (American and Dutch, respectively), attempted to follow the ground rules of dialogue to understand, mutual respect, and freedom to disagree. It conveyed information about what NATO (representing the United States/Canada and the European alliance over against the Warsaw Pact forces) was doing in maintaining its readiness against a Soviet incursion. That initial meeting had already caused participants to realize that the library at NATO headquarters lacked broad information on civil issues, including peacemaking initiatives, so MCC's "peace library" (about forty selected books) was presented soon after, and MCC paid for a series of subscriptions to religious journals and magazines (broadly ecumenical and related to East-West issues).[38] The newsletter grew to a thirty-two-page publication and was circulated to seven hundred subscribers at its height. Contributors included the peace church community, NATO staff members, and other specialists. It came at a time when the Cold War was in its final stages, then the Warsaw Pact was dissolved, but then NATO became more integrated with an expanded European Union from former Warsaw Pact members. NATO Watch members, both Quaker and Mennonite, conducted two seminars, in 1988 and 1990, respectively, producing documents proposing "steps to true security." A modest project, it nevertheless can be seen as a prelude to American Mennonites and Quakers engaging in consultations within the HPC on "responsibility to protect," a larger step by American Mennonites toward thinking about social order and the Christian's responsibility.

Also in the closing decade of the Cold War, Brethren, Quakers, and Mennonites became involved in another extended multilateral series of talks called the Prague consultations (1985–2003), which rarely connected with either the NATO Watch participants or peace church activists on the DOV after 2001. Participants knew each other, but the literature reflecting similar movement in thinking rarely connected. In part, this had to do with the growth in peace-

---

38. For a later review of this project, see J. Robert Charles, "Watching NATO, 1985–1991," *Mennonite Quarterly Review* 87, no. 4 (October 2014): 503–18.

building expertise applied to postcolonial conflicts in the southern world, with the eventual triumph of a nonviolent end to the apartheid regime in South Africa, which spawned a wonderful literature on forgiveness, healing of memories, and reconciliation as social/political ethics issues, but with rare intersection with similar theological and moral thought progressions in Eastern Europe and the USSR (which was easily tracked in English in the journal *Religion in Eastern Europe,* subsequently renamed *Occasional Papers on Religion in Eastern Europe*). There were exceptions, but it is striking how much the Western-oriented peace church efforts centered on the UN's expanded focus on its mandate for "responsibility to protect."[39] The contextual factor helping account for this heavier preoccupation with military force can be seen in the fact that the American "peace movement" of the 1980s, compared with anti-Vietnam War activism in the 1970s, was known as the freeze movement. That is, it was a broadly secular effort to resist the Reagan administration's efforts to renew the armaments race, specifically with what was popularly dubbed "Star Wars."[40] American peace churches were rather uninvolved in the West European peace movement, in which religious-based peace societies—and even Europeans for Nuclear Disarmament (END) was then led by Christians—focused more on civil society issues, on citizen diplomacy across the East-West border, to humanize the enemy so that alternatives for shared living space with fellow human beings could be found.[41]

Like the NATO Watch beginnings, the Prague consultations began following a tour of Czechoslovakia and East Germany, when conversations with Milan Opočenský, ethics professor at the Comenius faculty, resulted in a commitment to consult as representatives of the "First Reformation" (Hussite) and Radical Reformation, to become better acquainted, with the intent that their shared commitments to eschatology and social ethics could bring new life into

39. See the instructive reflections in Charles, "Watching NATO, 1985–1991," 514–18.

40. See David Cortwright, *Peace Works: The Citizen's Role in Ending the Cold War* (Boulder, CO: Westview Press, 1993). This still reflected the author's primary focus on armaments studies and his activism in the freeze movement. The chapter on religion opened with quick comments about the peace churches, then on the many churches morally rejecting nuclear war, but the author's real concern is how religious cultural influence in America made disarmament a public issue.

41. The MCC, as an inter-Mennonite service agency, had staff involved in both areas who reported internally, but that contrasts poorly with Roman Catholic global structures, including its official teaching, where even the American Catholic Bishops' pastoral letters "The Challenge of Peace" (1983) and "The Harvest of Justice Is Sown in Peace" (1993) reference more global perspectives. See Gerard F. Powers et al., *Peacemaking: Moral and Policy Challenges for a New World* (Washington, DC: United States Catholic Conference, 1994).

a declining ecumenical movement. This became a journey of discovery in a twofold fashion: the meeting style needed to accommodate more than academics, needed to keep the East-West alignments in mind, so the "dialogue" involved formal papers, freewheeling discussion, worship, conversations at table, and local tours. The Radical Reformation side, accustomed to its marginalized status in Western ecumenism dominated by mainline Protestant rules of discourse, now discovered the much longer marginalized role of its Waldensian and Hussite forerunners, whose representatives had persisted to seek dialogue, had even chosen to adopt sixteenth-century Reformation confessions when re-forming themselves in the nineteenth and early twentieth centuries. Then the Prague consultation expanded to include the World Alliance of Reformed Churches (in which Opočenský became its general secretary), with the Lutheran World Federation's Department of Studies (whose staff were also familiar with Eastern Europe) and the Mennonite World Conference (MWC) as sponsors. Larry Miller, already at the Prague consultations as MCC representative, had become MWC general secretary in 1990. So the final four gatherings, still bridging the East-West divide, now focused on "a more inclusive appreciation" of the sixteenth-century Reformations as a whole, but with participants also coming from those church traditions in the Two-Thirds World. Hence the justice, peace, and integrity of creation themes took on larger social problem fields, where probing them together was the assumed way. The ecumenically experienced Lukas Vischer of Switzerland, for example, caused all participants to see their own narrow perceptions about their "distinctives" by restating the theological concern behind them in twenty-first-century global terms, where all of us were rendered minority status, needing an ecclesial conversion.[42] Yet, already by the mid-1990s, shrinking budgets, retirement of experienced personnel, and the American cultural shift to wars in the Middle East accounted for the disappearance of the agenda of East-West reconciliation, well before it could provide closure for the American peace churches.

---

42. Lukas Vischer, "The Reformation Heritage and the Ecumenical Movement," in *Towards a Renewed Dialogue* (Geneva: World Alliance of Reformed Churches, 1996), 161–69. Presented at Prague IV, 1994.

"For, Not of, the CPC": Christians Associated for Relationships with Eastern Europe (CAREE) as a Study in Soft Power Peace Advocacy

Joseph Loya, OSA

The pursuit of Cold War studies calls for the employment of a hermeneutical lens that is less Hegelian dialectic and more Newtonian (third) law of motion: the opposing forces of action and reaction—Western bloc versus Eastern bloc—were commensurate to the point of effecting a frozen and tense steady state of an arm(s) wrestle between the two global counterparts, each capable of annihilating the other many times over. Competition for world supremacy was further aggrandized by the exertion of opposing forces of the type Joseph Nye described as "soft power," meaning a mode of suasion that eschews the application of direct hard-fisted power in favor of promoting the "prime currencies" of "values" and "culture" as means with which to obliquely curry favor among intended constituencies.[1] (Here the Eastern bloc's "anti-imperialism" drumbeat and the West's "rule by law" mantra come easily to mind.)

Amidst deep-seated Cold War enmity, the Prague-based Christian Peace Conference (CPC) was founded in 1958 to incarnate the Soviet effort to champion religiously sanctioned values such as peaceful coexistence and justice for the oppressed. Christians Associated for Relationships with Eastern Europe (CAREE) began as an American support group for the CPC and its values.[2]

1. Joseph S. Nye Jr., *Soft Power: The Means to Success in World Politics* (New York: Public Affairs, 2004), 31.

2. CAREE's archived materials are diligently cared for in Princeton Theological Seminary's Luce Library. The collection ranges to twenty feet of shelf space. There are of course many specific types of Library Manuscript Collection, Department of Archives and Special Collections. For this chapter, investigated types were limited to executive and general committee minutes, actions affirmed by the general meetings (and such proposals that were, even if not fulfilled, indicative of subjects of intent), published statements of self-identity and commitment, press communiqués and reports from the various specific association task forces (the term "commissions" was preferred after the 1972 reorganization of the association) as were deemed especially appropriate for carrying the soft power theme of this narrative forward.

For the sake of clarity, CAREE's previous names, Provisional US Regional Group

In the late summer of 1968, the CPC became an overtly politicized agency of a command center that countenanced the suppression of the "Prague Spring" by hard power means. In the words of CAREE veteran Walter Sawatsky, "Then a new leadership in CPC emerged where it became uncertain how to detect the authentic theological speech from the passport speeches or from political speeches that might be genuine or might not be."[3] The conference ultimately shared in the ignominious collapse of the Soviet Union. Although the work of CAREE has since slipped into abeyance, a narrative of the association's efforts to sustain a relationship "for, not of, the CPC" not only registers as a significant chapter in the Cold War story; it remains as an exemplary instruction in the effectuation of nonpoliticized fidelity to foundational Christian moral imperatives. The form of this chapter is one of expanded explications of excerpts (printed in an alternate font) selected from a concise and indispensable overview of CAREE's story entitled "Christians Associated for Relationships with Eastern Europe—Our Organization, Who We Are and Whence We Have Become," coauthored by Charles West and Paul Mojzes (hereafter, "West-Mojzes") and published in the winter 1999/2000 issue of CAREE's newsletter.[4]

> *It all started in the Cold War. It is hard to remember those days. . . . It is even harder to imagine oneself back into it. A world in which two great ideological systems, one Communist, the other pluralistic, open and less self-confident, confronted each other. . . . Believers too were divided by the Cold War. . . . Christians from that world sent confusing signals as they struggled to survive and find their witness. Many Christians in the West reached out to them in this struggle. Peace church groups were among the first with their practical, nonjudgmental serving witness. Others tried where they could. But how and to whom should one reach out? Whom could one trust? How should one understand what one hears in a society where few could speak openly? How should one*

(PUSRG), United States Committee for the Christian Peace Conference, and the Association for the Christian Peace Conference, will be provided in bold as they are treated in this chronologically ordered narrative.

3. Walter Sawatsky, "New Roles for CAREE since the Great Transformation," *Occasional Papers on Religion in Eastern Europe* 20, no. 3 (2000), article 4, http://digitalcommons.george fox.edu/ree/vol20/iss3/4.

4. Available online: the Christians Associated for Relationships with Eastern Europe (also known as the US Committee for the Christian Peace Conference) Manuscript Collection, http://manuscripts.ptsem.edu/collection/251. Footnotes referencing materials from the collection will be presented in this study in the form, "PTS Arch., Box #, folder #."

act so as to help, and not hurt, believers and the church? It was in this context that Josef Hromadka formed the Christian Peace Conference (CPC) in Prague, and invited Christians in the West and the third world to participate. The United States Committee for, not of, the Christian Peace Conference was formed in 1965 to organize and promote American participation in its work while maintaining our independence of its politics. (West-Mojzes)

Seventy or so Americans traveling in Western Europe for various personal and professional reasons attended the CPC-sponsored Second All-Christian Peace Assembly in Prague in 1964. For example, John Heidbrink, church secretary for the American chapter of the Fellowship of Reconciliation (an organization formed by European Christians amidst the maelstrom of World War I), was at the time leading a traveling seminar of churchpersons interested in European ecclesiastical matrices. One afternoon during the assembly the Americans caucused and successfully prevailed upon Heidbrink, who had previous experience with early CPC gatherings, to head an organized American churches' response to the budding phenomenon that was the CPC. Some weeks afterward, Heidbrink phoned Paul Peachey (an experienced peacebuilding worker for the Mennonite Central Committee) to inform him that he had fallen prey to serious illness and could not fulfill his mandate: Could he, Peachey, please shoulder the responsibility? Peachey at first demurred, then accepted.[5]

Peachey and eleven others gathered at Boston University in late November 1964, under the title "Meeting on Christian Peace Conference and American Church Relationships." The following items were among those that were recognized, reported, and affirmed. A committee had been appointed recently by the Methodist Division of Peace and World Order to study future relations with the CPC (thus indicating that the desire for some sort of relationship was in the air). The structure and finances of the CPC were heavily oriented to the East, and all the official church affiliations of any significance were with Eastern European and Russian church groups. There was considerable approval for the suggestion that the CPC be converted from a "pronouncement" group to a forum with many regional expressions. It was conceded that it would be difficult for Western churchpersons to accept the idea that a movement

---

5. Paul Peachey, *Building Peace and Civil Society: An Autobiographical Report from a Believer's Church*, Cultural Heritage and Contemporary Change Series I, Cultures and Values, book 34 (Washington, DC: Council for Research in Values & Cultural Heritage, 2006), 216–17.

toward West-East reconciliation could emerge from the East, given that those Easterners who came to Prague were the very ones who accepted cooperation with the Communists out of necessity. It could be that the actual working committees constituted by rank-and-file members and displaying a strong theological approach may be more significant than the CPC itself. A lack of symmetry existed in that the Westerners could be and were more critical of their governments than the Easterners ever could be. Concern was voiced about funding resources, not only for American representatives attending the CPC Working Committee and All-Christian Peace Assemblies, but also aiding representatives from Latin America and other areas. Questions were registered regarding the recent five-year crackdown on religion in Russia. (For example, were Stalinist activists attempting to demonstrate Russian Communist orthodoxy to the Chinese?) The need for initiatives for joint work with the National Council of Churches was affirmed. The Boston twelve moved and voted that they forthwith constitute a **Provisional US Regional Group** (PUSRG) to solicit the cooperation of American and church-related groups and persons, and to serve as correspondent between these and the CPC. Furthermore, this group would act in regard to all matters relating to participation in and support for the CPC. (The word "provisional" was intended to leave open possibilities for affiliation with other similar groups, and also the possible reconstitution of the group on a North American basis.) An executive committee and temporary steering committee for the group were then instituted. The search for funding would be the responsibility of the latter committee. Heidbrink or a specifically designated alternate should represent the group to the CPC. The interpretation of the CPC to the US churches was adopted as a major group task.[6]

The group's temporary steering committee met at the UN's Church Center on December 14, 1964. The steering committee specified its tasks and guiding principles, among which the latter included the following: "While at no point does the PUSRG presume to represent churches in America 'officially,' it must reflect them 'authentically.'"[7]

Early in 1965, Peachy suggested that he and Charles West (Princeton Theological Seminary) meet in the office of Carl Soule (executive secretary of the United Methodist Office for the United Nations) at the Church Center in New York to discuss how to perpetuate the momentum of these breakthrough

---

6. "Meeting on Christian Peace Conference and American Church Relationships," PTS Arch., Box 1, folder 1.

7. "Christian Peace Conference Provisional U.S. Regional Group," PTS Arch., Box 1, folder 1.

relationships. To the question, "Given the current circumstance, how were members of the world Christian Community to relate and respond to East European Christian outreaches?" West voiced his conclusion:

> There were two simple answers to this question. One was to find in the Soviet Revolution, for all its atheism, cruelty and violence, the promise of God for a society where all would share equally and the common good would replace private profit. The other was to see the atheism, and the totalitarian power of the Communists, and to image that the only true Christian is the persecuted one. CAREE embodied a third, and ecumenical, policy, which tried to undergird all the churches in Eastern Europe spiritually, aware of the piety they embodied and the fears and temptations which beset them. It was a hard way. One might misjudge an action, or a person, and we often did. But we believed it was the way of Christian responsibility toward our brothers and sisters in Christ who lived in that part of the world.[8]

The organization soon came to adopt as its official title **United States Committee for the Christian Peace Conference**, with its continuing purpose to facilitate relationships among American church groups and individuals on the one hand and the CPC on the other.

> *The participation was fruitful beyond our dreams. Thousands of personal friendships were formed, in which Christians from East and West shared each other's burdens and strengthened each other's faith. Honest dialogue took place in the Communist world about Christian faith and about freedom, justice and peace. . . . Christians met Marxists and, around the edges of CPC meetings, then independently, Marxist-Christian dialogue began. It all came to flower during the Prague Spring of 1968. (West-Mojzes)*

An early project of the committee concerned the sensed need to "initiate studies or conversations in Russian Orthodox piety in this country," and to bolster "spiritual-philosophical" probing "to prepare more fully for the Christian-Marxist encounter in Eastern Europe." The significant ferment at that time for such dialogue transpiring within the World Council of Churches in Geneva and Marxist lands alike needed to be attended.[9]

8. Charles West, "A Brief Pre-History of CAREE," *Religion in Eastern Europe* 32, no. 4 (2012): 5.
9. Peachey to Dr. Ralph Hyslop, October 4, 1966, PTS Arch., Box 7, folder 1.

Discussion at the spring 1968 meeting at the UN Church Center subjected to scrutiny Christian involvement in social change and the topic "The Disaster Decade: Is Revolution the Only Way Out? What Are the Alternatives?" The executive secretary reported that forty delegates and observers from the United States attended the Third All-Christian Peace Assembly held in Prague in 1968. The fledgling Committee, ever mindful that it was called into being by the CPC, changed its name to the **United States Association for the Christian Peace Conference** and committed to hold as priorities issues that included justice, change and order, revolution, and reconciliation. The functions of the general committee and officers, plus executive committee, were explicated and filled by election.[10]

> *Then came the Soviet invasion of Czechoslovakia. . . . The political reform was crushed. . . . Several national committees outside the Soviet bloc—the French, the German, the British and the Dutch—broke with the CPC after the 1969 Russian power-play. The Japanese Committee split. In each case the result was dissension, conflict and rival groups. The U.S. Committee pursued a different tactic. We protested vigorously. We attended only those meetings where we could make our voice heard. But we did not withdraw. (West-Mojzes)*

In the period after the Warsaw Pact invasion, association executives sought to keep the membership informed about fast-breaking CPC events transpiring in Eastern Europe, and to raise attendant questions regarding how those events impacted the association at home. The CPC meeting in Paris in October 1968 and one in Warsaw in February 1969 laid open a spectrum of interpretation of the recent Soviet power moves, the conflict between the Warsaw Pact countries and Western and Third World representatives, plus the *sub rosa* feeling of deep-seated lack of trust between the two blocs and among some of the membership. The degree of the CPC's captivity to Eastern bloc countries and the continued existence of the conference became real and pressing issues. There was a new relationship among the churches in Eastern Europe, and certainly in Western Europe, the USA, Latin America, Africa, and Asia; new ties of understanding and confidence would need to be forged as the churches sought to witness to peace. The Americans continued to receive CPC visitors, but it would be an understatement to say that the representatives

10. Minutes of the United States Association for the Christian Peace Conference, annual meeting, May 10–12, 1968, New York City, PTS Arch., Box 7, folder 1.

of CPC churches in Eastern Europe operated with a new mind-set. What was now to be the association's relationship to the Prague CPC, and what should be its relationship to the churches in this country? Could they preserve something of the freedom and character of movement in association and still support Prague while remaining responsible to the church bodies here in America? In all, this was a profound challenge to the association that transcended the matter of individuals taking sides; at issue for the members was the very nature of the most appropriate response of the body of Christ. Christians do not break fellowship because of differences in politics; indeed, they were called to come to deeper and more profound brotherhood by suffering, obedience, and love. A suggestion would be registered with the Prague CPC that a person from the United States be named a member of the International Secretariat. Fortunately, the United Methodist Church, by granting $10,000 to USA CPC, moved the matter forward in a real and practical way. Moved and passed were the composition and sending of a vote of appreciation for the work of ousted CPC general secretary Dr. Jaroslav N. Ondra.[11]

In late May 1970 those in leadership felt empowered to articulate the association's concerns to CPC president Metropolitan Nikodim of the Russian Orthodox Patriarchate. The authors presented the association as a voluntary group of churchmen concerned with the future of the CPC and also for all relationships between churches and among Christians who seek peace and justice in a divided world. Further, the association shared with the metropolitan the desire to deepen mutual understanding and fellowship with Christians in socialist countries, realize universal reconciliation in the conditions of this world through opposition to factors that lead to war, and redress injustices of imperialism, colonialism, and profiteering.[12]

In the course of the momentous November 1970 annual meeting at the Briarwood Conference Center in Monument Beach, Massachusetts, some members seriously questioned whether the entire CPC structure was so moribund and bureaucratically unresponsive as to render it useless as a vehicle for Christian encounter. The group decided to continue the US association as a means to facilitate interest in Eastern Europe even though its relationship to the CPC was becoming ever more tenuous and conditional.[13]

11. "Annual Meeting. United States Association for the Christian Peace Conference," May 9–10, 1969, New York City, PTS Arch., Box 7, folder 1.

12. Letter of May 25, 1970, to His Eminence, the Most Reverend Nikodim, signed by Charles West (chairman) and Kurtis Friend Naylor (secretary-treasurer), PTS Arch., Box 7, folder 1.

13. "Minutes: Annual Meeting at Briarwood Conference Center, Monument Beach, MA, November 6–8, 1970," PTS Arch., Box 7, folder 1.

In its November 20, 1970, letter to CPC president Nikodim and Acting General Secretary Dr. Janusz Makowski, association executives expressed assurance that the association would continue as a fellowship of churchmen concerned to "deepen mutual understanding and fellowship between us and Christians in the socialist countries [and] to seek justice for all men without which no peace is possible."[14]

At the association's general committee meeting of June 18, 1971, at the Interchurch Center, New York, attendees expressed dissatisfaction over how regional associations had been shut out of the planning process for the CPC's Fourth Assembly. The committee members voted to financially support the youth delegates already invited to the assembly, but promised only its understanding should individuals in their own name accept invitations to the assembly.[15] A report of this meeting to the membership included the following: "We also do not preclude by our decision the possibility of participating in future meetings organized by the CPC if we are invited and if the meetings be genuine exchanges and not propaganda occasions alone."[16]

On January 26, 1972, the executives clarified for the membership their position:

> We desire and intend to continue our relationship and cooperation with the CPC and to serve as the channel of communication between the CPC and our constituency in the American churches. This is not our only task, but it is an important one. In the light of our purposes, we must not only be related to the CPC, but have credibility of our witness for peace with our constituency. . . . We do intend to participate with integrity, to seek reconciliation not only between East and West but also between parts of the CPC, and to be open to negation and further clarification of what this means.[17]

In 1972 we changed the name of our group to "Christians Associated for Relationships with Eastern Europe" (CAREE). (West-Mojzes)

The convictions and proposals of the committee to consider the reorganization and future programming of the association were submitted to the

---

14. Letter to Nikodim and Makowski, November 20, 1970, PTS Arch., Box 7, folder 1.

15. "United States Association for the Christian Peace Conference, General Committee Meeting, Rooms C and D, 475 Riverside. June 18, 1971," PTS Arch., Box 7, folder 1.

16. "July 26, 1971. To Members and Friends of the United States Committee for the Christian Peace Conference," PTS Arch., Box 7, folder 1.

17. "Executive Committee Meeting, 26 January, 1972," PTS Arch., Box 7, folder 1.

membership for discussion at the annual meeting in Stony Point, New York, April 28–29, 1972. The association was affirmed to be a

> fellowship of persons concerned to promote world peace through deeper understanding and community between themselves and Christians in socialist countries, especially Eastern Europe. Their aim is to seek with brethren in those countries a form of witness and service in this divided and changing world to which all are called. The Christian Peace Conference, under the leadership of Josef Hromádka, was their occasion of the original coming together. Participants were drawn to it as a channel of understanding, community, and peacemaking out of confidence in him and in others they came to know and respect. It is now clear however that the CPC can only be one of these channels for the calling, though it is their intention to participate in its structures and to work for the reconciliation of all of its parts.[18]

Moved for further reflection, discussion, and eventual adoption was the name **Christians Associated for Relationships with Eastern Europe**.

> *For years in this way we held partisans and severe critics of the post-Hromadka CPC together in one organization with a broad agenda of which the CPC was only a part. (West-Mojzes)*

During the executive committee meeting in January of 1973, a consensus confirmed that the association should continue to be represented in the CPC's International Secretariat, but subject to periodic review by the executive committee, especially in light of the tenuous nature of the association's relationship with US churches.[19]

The newly appointed general secretary of the CPC, Bishop Károly Tóth, himself attended CAREE's annual meeting in April 1973. He spoke of the recent history of the CPC, the need for mutual trust, and the possibilities of cooperation. He called for specific contributions from CAREE in four areas: to a theology of peace from the American theological tradition; on racial discrimination and apartheid; on disarmament; and on education of public opinion

---

18. "Christians Associated for Relationships with Eastern Europe, Annual Meeting, Stony Point, N.Y. 28–30 April, 1972," PTS Arch., Box 7, folder 1.

19. "Christians Associated for Relationships with Eastern Europe Executive Committee Meeting, January 15, 1973," PTS Arch., Box 7, folder 1.

concerning the UN. Bylaws were edited to read "The name of the Organization shall be **Christians Associated for Relationships with Eastern Europe: An Ecumenical Association for International Peace and Justice and for Relationships with the Christian Peace Conference**."[20]

During the April 1974 annual meeting, the Christian Marxist Encounter Task Force recommended for the coming year a renewal of ideology with special attention to "Christian socialist ideology and its options," a motivating question being, "How active can Task Forces become without doing the necessary ideological homework?" Paul Mojzes (Rosemont College) suggested that the *Journal of Ecumenical Studies* would be interested in offering itself as a public relations resource for CAREE, along with granting favorable discount subscription rates in connection with the proposed interrelationship.[21]

In CAREE's continuing examination of self-definition, in May 1974 the executive committee published a declaration of recommitment:

> We are a diverse company of persons who profess to be Christians, who happen to be Americans, who are vocationally committed to peace, and who are particularly united in seeking fellowship with the peoples of Eastern Europe, whether Marxist or Christian. Prior to the Warsaw Pact invasion of Czechoslovakia, August 21, 1968, we greatly valued our participation in the Christian Peace Conference (Prague) as a unique opportunity for association with Christians in the socialist countries of Eastern Europe. While that participation always required a realistic acceptance of the fact that CPC's dominant orientation was toward the political interests and viewpoints of those countries, we were painfully aware of the excessive anti-communist orientation of our own country. Moreover, we found in Josef Hromadka and other CPC leaders abundant evidence of Christian integrity and personal courage within a non-liberal Marxist society.
>
> After August 21, 1968, the CPC was subjected to heavy political pressures which forced Dr. Hromadka and others from their positions of leadership, severely constricted CPC program, and led to the estrangement of many affiliated groups and persons. The subsequent death of Dr. Hromadka deepened our sorrow. For several years after 1968, we repeatedly voiced our own dismay over these events and sought to mitigate partisan political pressures within CPC. . . . [We] sought to maintain some continuing association with CPC, not only because of our concern for peace but also

20. Minutes of the CAREE annual meeting, April 27–29, 1973, PTS Arch., Box 7, folder 1.

21. Minutes of the CAREE annual meeting, Church Center for the United Nations, April 5–7, 1974, Wesley Theological Seminary, Washington, DC, PTS Arch., Box 7, folder 1.

because of the needs of our American churches for continuing fellowship with Christians and others in Eastern Europe—even and especially in the face of political tensions. . . . We now summon our friends in America to a significantly expanded program for CAREE and to a renewal of serious, if still limited, participation in CPC. Christians must not lag behind their political leaders in encouraging the processes of détente and international cooperation. The hope for peace depends upon the capacity to over-come past estrangements to accept what cannot be changed, to be responsive to the signs of redeeming change and to work for such change ourselves.

We recommit ourselves to the tasks of peacemaking which we share with our sisters and with all peoples on every continent. We seek renewal of the Christian-Marxist dialogue and ideological reconstruction in our own country. We heartily urge all who share these concerns to join us in this common witness.[22]

We participated in Christian-Marxist dialogues when they again became possible. [We became] an unofficial study and support group for the Europe Committee of the National Council of Churches. (West-Mojzes)

In fall 1974 the executive committee reported, "There is much sympathy in the NCC for the objectives and program of CAREE and a desire to unify the many initiatives concerning Eastern Europe being taken by US churches."[23] In the spring of 1975, CAREE presented itself to the NCC as a resource organization of Christians whose purpose is "the promotion of world peace deepening the understanding and community between Christians in the United States and their brothers and sisters in socialist countries, especially in East Europe." The task of the Association is "to contribute to the oneness of the Christian community throughout the world which has been broken by frequent inability to communicate and cooperate across political, ideological, socio-economic, and other barriers [based on the conviction] that it is the task of United States Christians to maintain and develop ties to Christians who live in the socialist countries, particularly of East Europe, regardless what the political relations between East and West and the Third world may be at any given time."[24]

22. "A Declaration of Recommitment," PTS Arch., Box 7, folder 1.
23. Minutes of the CAREE executive committee meeting, October 4 and 5, 1974, Princeton, NJ, PTS Arch., Box 7, folder 1.
24. "To: The National Council of Churches of Christ; From CAREE; Re: Long Range Proposal for Cooperation. May 31, 1975," PTS Arch., Box 7, folder 1.

Pertinent to and expressive of this chapter's title is the compelling matter of the compositional evolution and reaction to the content of the address by CAREE vice chairman James Will to the CPC's Committee for the Continuation of the Work in fall 1975 in Siófok, on Lake Balaton, Hungary, the content of which basically shined a light on the lack of self-criticism and respect for freedom of conscience exhibited by the micromanaging upper levels of the CPC. Will submitted his address for review to key correspondents before delivery. As to reactions to the actual address, entitled "The Calling of Christians to Cooperate for Peace and Justice," a reporter stated the following:

> Will used this opportunity to speak the truth with love, affirming that while he sympathized with socialism as an economic structure he was repelled by the portrayal of the perfection of the foreign policy of socialist nations and the total iniquity of "US imperialism." "It is characteristic," he said, "of the prophets of the Old Testament that they did not practice long range righteousness, but reserved their strongest strictures for their own society. . . . The pattern of voting in the UN by the USSR and the USA has become strangely similar. In the 29th General Assembly both countries voted for 12 and abstained on 9 disarmament resolutions." Spirited comment followed Will's address, but no earthquake rent the organization! At the end of the meeting Hungarian General Secretary Károly Tóth commented that it was good for those present to hear Will, since CPC was an ecumenical movement and elements from the West should be heard with respect, even though Eastern churchmen might not agree.[25]

Through the next few years, CAREE-CPC relations eased to the point that in 1979 the executive committee issued a clarification in response to voiced concerns from some of the membership that CAREE was in the process of becoming an official organizational extension of the CPC in the United States. Indeed, CAREE was represented by twenty members at the CPC assembly in June 1978, during which several members were elected to positions within CPC structures. While asserting that CAREE was never part of the CPC, the clarification noted that CAREE had been experiencing in recent years increasing openness on the part of CPC leaders to its initiatives in concert with

25. "Hungarian Churches Host Peace Conference" (seeming press release, no author's name attached), PTS Arch., Box 2, folder 9. Conference participant Paul Mojzes recently shared his recollection that "Will's address did cause a near pandemonium and that it was only the energetic intervention of Metropolitan Nikodim that made it possible to continue the meeting. Jim's address was both self-critical and critical." Email to this author, November 1, 2015.

CAREE's own "critical and selective" trusting and committed posture toward the CPC and its constituencies. While raising very difficult and challenging issues for the CPC leadership to deal with, CAREE was encouraging democratization and openness wherever and whenever possible. CAREE had been offering valuable insights into the special problems and possibilities of church leaders from one situation to another across Eastern Europe, for which the CPC leadership seemed appreciative. Christians who participate in the CPC were finding and developing relationships of trust and understanding that greatly increased possibilities of cooperation among the churches, East and West; many CAREE projects could not have been accomplished apart from the relationships formed in the context of the CPC. CAREE members had been seeing that their commitments to the CPC and to other agencies of a different nature were mutually viable, and sometimes even complementary. Increasing importance of the Third World participants and constituencies in the CPC contributed to broadening ideological perspectives and encouraged greater institutional openness, making Western presence in the CPC both more viable and credible. CPC leadership had extended an invitation to CAREE to nominate persons to its working committee, International Secretariat, and executive committee. Those elected were to be seen as fulfilling a liaison role between the CPC and CAREE in addition to their immediate CPC responsibilities. CAREE committed to continue its selective and critical participation in the life of the CPC and to pioneer programs and projects that would involve Christians in both East and West in a common struggle for international peace and justice.[26]

At this time publications began to emerge from CAREE such as *Christian-Marxist Encounter* (1976) and the occasionally published newsletter, *CAREE Communicator* (1978). The most significant periodical was and continues to be *Occasional Papers on Religion in Eastern Europe* (*OPREE*) (1981), which began as a publication that featured serious analyses of religious developments in all former socialist countries of Eastern Europe and the former Soviet Union. *OPREE*, with its advisory editorial board composed of sixteen internationally known scholars, was the sole publication on the subject matter in the United States, and only one of three in the world.[27] In 1980, CAREE initiated the In-

26. "Statement of Clarification concerning the Relationship of CAREE and the Christian Peace Conference," *CAREE Communicator*, no. 4 (August 15, 1979). Paul Mojzes was the editor of the periodical. This statement was drafted by Bruce Rigdon at the request of the executive committee, amended and accepted at the annual meeting, May 1–3, 1979. An official CPC organization unrelated to CAREE did attempt to establish itself in the United States in the late 1980s. Its existence was short-lived.

27. From George Fox University's Digital Commons, http://digitalcommons.georgefox

stitute for Peace and Understanding (IPU), which was dedicated to promoting serious study and discussion in serving as a "catalytic agent" in advancing Christian-Marxist dialogue while collecting pertinent scholarly information on subjects relating to the stated purposes of the organization. Included in the new organization's mission was the commitment to "conduct alone or in cooperation with other institutes and organizations specific and measurable actions, including symposia, conferences, seminars, public or private dialogues."[28]

> *Cooperation with two Vienna institutes, the Vienna University Center for Peace Research and the International Institute of Peace, resulted in about a dozen meetings of Christians and Marxists working for peace. These meetings commenced in the middle of the 1970s; three of them took place in the USA (Rosemont, PA [1978], Detroit, MI [1980], and York, PA [1990]).*
>
> *Today the whole scene has changed. Soviet power and Communist ideology are gone. So is the Christian Peace Conference. But central and Eastern Europe face challenges greater than ever before. . . . Each nation faces its own crisis of identity in relation to its neighbors. Each church, whether majority or minority, is struggling to rediscover its ministry and its mission in a world of new religious conflicts overlaid by a new form of secular power. How can Christians in America be of help? What can we learn from their experience that will help us be more faithful witnesses? These are the questions we need to explore. (West-Mojzes)*

This historical review opened with a reference to power and an introduction to Nye's notion of soft power as an authoritative impulse that privileges attraction over compulsion, pull rather than push, and "power with" rather than "power over."[29] (Alternatively but not exclusively, Saskia Sassen, cochair of the

---

.edu/ree/: "Occasional Papers on Religion in Eastern Europe (OPREE) provides articles about the religious situation in Eastern Europe and Eurasia, focusing on the communist and post-communist periods. From 2003 to 2012, the journal was titled Religion in Eastern Europe. The printed version of Religion in Eastern Europe (REE) was discontinued with the November 2012 issue (Vol. XXXII, No. 4) and Occasional Papers on Religion in Eastern Europe is now published exclusively online at http://digitalcommons.georgefox.edu/ree/. It can also be easily accessed using any search engine under the name of the publication. No subscription or fees are charged for reading and downloading any past or current articles."

28. "By-Laws of the Board of Trustees of the Institute for Peace and Understanding," PTS Arch., Box 6, folder 15.

29. Joseph S. Nye Jr., *The Future of Power* (New York: Public Affairs, 2011), see 83–90.

Committee on Global Thought at Columbia University, terms this "complex powerlessness" within which micro-actors are endowed with the human right to create a story of their own.)[30] According to commentators, we are currently moving beyond the era of public-private partnership into one in which multiple actors with particular characteristics suited for different tasks are brought into effective relationship. Soft power's role is not to enforce domination or create winners and losers; it is to inform the organizational profiles of communities, societies, marketplaces, and the world. For Moisés Naim (former director of the World Bank and editor in chief of *Foreign Policy* magazine), power is coming to be seen as softer and more relational amidst an increasingly interdependent world focused on cooperation for the common good. The world has entered a posthegemonic era of hyperconnectivity and ubiquitous communications, transformed by the phenomenon of the Internet and the explosion of mobile telephony. It is a world that serves as a matrix for the emergence of smaller, nimbler micro-actors and micro-powers. We are not witnessing the end of power as such (as current headlines from the Middle East and the Kremlin attest), but there is a discernible reactive movement against power as it has been known. The obtaining dynamic is not one of power's dissolution, but of its gradual dispersion and translation from brawn to brains, from old corporate behemoths to agile start-ups, from entrenched dictators to people in town squares and cyberspace. Erstwhile key factors—size, hierarchy, and centralized control—are becoming liabilities.[31] With its innate flexibility, soft power can be used for both zero-sum and positive-sum interactions; in a time marked by

30. See Saskia Sassen, review of *The End of Power: From Boardrooms to Battlefields and Churches to States, Why Being in Charge Isn't What It Used to Be*, by Moisés Naim, *Americas Quarterly*, Spring 2013, 105–7, http://www.americasquarterly.org/content /ithe-end-power-boardrooms-battlefields-and-churches-states-why-being-charge-isnt -what-it.

31. See reviews of Naim's *The End of Power* by Amy Zalman (*Prism* 4, no. 4 [2013]: 178–80), Nick Gillespie (*Barron's*, July 1, 2013, 42), Gordon M. Goldstein (*Washington Post*, March 10, 2013, B6; also, https://www.washingtonpost.com/opinions/the-end-of-power-from-board rooms-to-battlefields-and-churches-to-states-why-being-in-charge-isnt-what-it-used-by -moises-naim/2013/03/08/009f462c-7c56-11e2-9a75-dab0201670da_story.html), John Olinger (*National Catholic Reporter* 50, no. 21: 20), and Jeffrey Gedmin (*Journal of Democracy* 25, no. 1 [January 2014]: 166–69). Naim attributes the decay of hard power to what he calls the revolutions of "more" (of everyone and everything that overwhelm the means of control), "mobility" (which has ended captive audiences), and "mentality" (transformations in aspirations, expectations, awareness of alternatives, tailoring of incentives, specialization/niche strategizing, and universal values). Together, the "three *Ms*" have made power easier to acquire, harder to implement, and easier to lose. The three expansive revolutions intersect with and transform traditional "channels" of power. (See Naim's chapter 4, "How Power Has Lost Its Edge," 151–75.)

global information and a diffusion of power to nonstate actors, soft power will become increasingly important as a part of intelligent power strategies.

CAREE's story amply serves as a readily identifiable and substantial expression of the nature, province, utility, and dynamics of soft power in its founding *raison d'être*, in its consistent *modus operandi*, and in the essential ethos of its corporate existence. Soft power engenders environments for decisions that indirectly affect all decision making by adopting persuasion as a social construct and having as its operational principle "The best propaganda is no propaganda at all." Soft power is a dance that requires partners: the new, decentralized, so-called public diplomacy invests itself in building relationships among civil society actors in other countries and in facilitating networking among nongovernmental parties at home and abroad. In the dance, a key forward step is executed in trust that allowances for dissent and self-criticism enhance the credibility and attractiveness of the messages that are conveyed.[32] (Again, from 1970, CAREE's "dance card" was shown to be open, yet discerning: "We would talk to anyone, but we should know with whom we talk.") This trust also involves confidence that the fair-minded readily discern when hard-edged forces co-opt values talk as veneer for propaganda and proselytism, as was the case with post-1968 CPC leadership. (CAREE's 1971 assertion, "We also do not preclude by our decision the possibility of participating in future meetings organized by the CPC if we are invited and if the meetings be genuine exchanges and not propaganda occasions alone," stands as a prime case in point.) CAREE-as-applied-soft-power contributed in its own humble way to the explosion of new possibilities for various levels of interaction among West-East Christian constituencies, and to the sea change in Marxist attitudes toward religion as reconfigured in pragmatic rather than dogmatic terms. In maintaining a central and inclusive position among the conflicting ideological and political entities, CAREE was an active and stalwart steward of human rights as it gained a place on the world agenda, peace remaining a central objective but with fewer propaganda overtones than before.[33]

This author trusts that even readers who have subjected this chapter to cursory perusal would not object to giving to the estimable Charles West, to whom this effort is dedicated, the summary word about CAREE: "In short, a world is redefining itself in Eastern Europe, and we who have borne their concerns on our hearts for so long, have the wonderful privilege of modest participation in it."[34]

---

32. Nye, *The Future of Power*, 108–9.
33. Charles West, "CAREE: Our Situation and Our Calling," PTS Arch., Box 5, folder 1.
34. West, "CAREE."

An American Perspective on the Cold War's Impact on Christian-Marxist Dialogue

Paul Mojzes

Interactions between Marxists and Christians, or "Christian-Marxist dialogue," as our title puts it,[1] began long before the Cold War, during Marx's own time in the nineteenth century. Marx was neither the first nor the only socialist, and a number of Christians who witnessed the negative side effects of the development of capitalism explored and supported a number of alternative socialist ideas. Karl Marx, who considered himself the creator of a "scientific" analysis of capitalism and its alleged successor social system of socialism, leading into Communism, sharply rejected all other alternate approaches, including religious or specifically Christian socialism. He was disdainful of Christianity and the churches. The rejection tended to be mutual. Even Christian socialists rejected Marxism because of its atheism, whereas Marxism rejected religion due to its materialist philosophy. Only small numbers of Christians who were trying to organize the working class found certain aspects of Marx's analysis helpful, though they generally rejected his emphasis on the need for an increased level of violence. Marxists, however, almost never consciously adopted Christian insights and approaches. Marx was convinced that religion would wither away in the future along with many other superstructures of class society. He was not utterly negative about the role of religion, but did believe that religion was an impediment toward the kind of social change that he considered to be inevitably leading to a classless Communist society. Needless to say, Christians were generally unwilling to accept such an analysis, particularly the uncompromising materialist worldview that undergirded Marx's social and economic analysis, which in itself was of some interest to left-leaning Christians.

1. Christian-Marxist dialogue does not exist. The term "Christian-Marxist dialogue" is an abstraction, a shorthand for a dialogue between various Christians and Marxists, many of whom had rather diverse conceptions on how to be Christian or Marxist.

While some Marx-inspired socialists opted for a democratic model of governance that was not inherently inimical to Christianity, another, far more radical interpretation arose (later to be called Leninist or Bolshevik); in this view the power of the state could be obtained only by revolutions (such as the Great October Revolution of 1917 in Russia) and retained by dictatorial means. Lenin interpreted Marx in a totalitarian manner, giving this dominant socialist variant the name Marxism-Leninism, and by the late 1920s it had evolved into an even more brutal variant: Marxism-Leninism-Stalinism. In Russia this branch, despite tactical oscillations, had for its ultimate aim not merely the withering away of religion but the actual destruction of church structures and the elimination of religious sentiment. Some Christians attempted to adapt themselves to the Red Terror, such as the Renovationists among the Russian Orthodox, but it was clear that they too, sooner or later, would be slated for elimination. Dialogue would have been impossible under such conditions even if it were known at the time as a concept, which it wasn't. The goals of the two movements were radically different. Marxist-Leninist-Stalinists sought to eradicate religion; Christians sought to somehow survive what would become the single most brutal persecution in all of Christian history. Only a few former Russian Marxists exiled in the West, such as Nicholas Berdyaev, Sergei Bulgakov, and Piotr Struve, attempted to thoughtfully analyze this newly emerged phenomenon, usually called Communism or Bolshevism, helping readers in the West to see the undercurrent complexities of this system that claimed that it would inevitably come to control all humankind.

By the 1930s, Stalinism had evolved into a monstrous genocidal and politicidal apparatus that brought about the death of upward of 30 million people. These were unveiled more fully only upon the collapse of the system in the Soviet Union in 1990.

A number of Christian theologians in the twentieth century sharply criticized advanced capitalist forms of human denigration but also distanced themselves from the terror in Marxist-Leninist socialism. The most prominent such critics of the older generation were Walter Rauschenbusch, Karl Barth, Paul Tillich, Reinhold Niebuhr, Jacques Maritain, Helmut Gollwitzer, and Emmanuel Mournier. In their writings they analyzed social developments and took certain Marxian insights seriously. However, this was generally an inner dialogue within Christianity on how to come to grips with the harm created by the capitalist system, seeking to alter its harmful effects without considering the Soviet model as an alternative. The rise of Nazism and Fascism brought about a confusing and, as many quickly perceived, even greater danger that speedily led to an equally horrendous genocidal and politicidal totalitarian system. That system led to the outbreak of World War II—and tens of millions of additional deaths and incomprehensible suffering throughout the world. For Christianity and some of its churches, the impact of Nazism was worse than that of Communism because Hitler and his collaborators did not turn anti-Christian per se but succeeded in enticing numerous Christians to support Nazism as it promised to free the world of Communism. As this exceeds the scope of our topic, no further elaboration of it is appropriate here.

During World War II, alliances crystallized into the Western Allies that eventually found a common cause with the Soviet Union in fighting the Nazis and the Axis Powers. Stalin himself realized that he must ease off in his religious persecution if he was to obtain the cooperation of Russian Christians. It is also clear that many Christians welcomed the Nazi invasion, as they hoped that it would liberate them from the Bolshevik oppression. As the war progressed in numerous places, Christians worked with Communists in fighting the Nazis, often creating some form of a national liberation front (e.g., in France, Italy, Yugoslavia, Czechoslovakia, and Poland). Whether they fought as guerrillas/freedom fighters or resisted in territories not under Nazi control, practical cooperation took place between Christians and Communists, but not dialogue. The reason is simple—during a fight for your, your family's, and your country's lives, you hardly have time to conduct theoretical dialogues. In retrospect, some called this "the dialogue of life"—surviving concentration camps, fighting, working, and rebuilding next to each other and with each other, irrespective of religious and ideological differences. Eventually you come to trust each other. There was common suffering and common hope, but the question was, how long would it survive when the war ended?

European Roots of Christian-Marxist Dialogue

The Soviet Union that barely survived Nazi invasion emerged strengthened and was able to expand its influence and power into neighboring Eastern Europe. Between 1945 and 1948, Europe was divided into two irreconcilable blocs, with neither side concealing its aspiration to expand at the expense of the other. A demarcation line crystallized, which Churchill, already in March 1946, aptly named "the Iron Curtain." Bernard Baruch, Truman's adviser, about a year later, was the first to name it "the Cold War"—which often threatened to transmute itself into a regular "hot" war. By 1948, with Czechoslovakia being the last country to be pulled fully into the Soviet orbit, Europe was dramatically partitioned into Western and Eastern blocs from which, as of

1948, only Yugoslavia was able to extricate itself. There had been efforts to realign these constellations, during which Greece waged a bitter civil war, and Italy and France were on the verge of electoral victories of their respective Communist parties several times. There were, likewise, attempts by Eastern European countries to alter their own link to the USSR, such as the German Democratic Republic revolt in 1953, the Hungarian revolt in 1956, the "Prague Spring" in 1968, and toward the very end, Poland's "Solidarity" in the 1980s, each of which was initially suppressed but produced the context for the most fruitful Christian-Marxist dialogues.

Beginning right after World War II and continuing to the early 1960s, there was no possibility for the emergence of Christian-Marxist dialogue in Europe. Both the Soviet Union and Western allies were feverishly trying to rebuild after the destruction of WWII and were even more determined to solidify their gains and make sure that life in their sphere of influence would be in accordance with their respective principles of governance—Marxist "dictatorship of the proletariat" in the East and liberal democratic capitalism in the West. In the West, particularly in Italy and France, there were possibilities for positive interactions of Marxists with Christians, but the situation in the East precluded that.

In all countries of the Soviet bloc, the Stalinist policies toward organizing society and their approach toward churches and all forms of religious activity were oppressive and restrictive. Not that it was uniform: the tactics toward churches varied according to conditions in different countries. Actual religious policies varied from overt manipulation of churches, to tactical cooperation in specific cases, and to lesser or greater degrees of toleration, but the strategy was the same—the demise of religion was to be accelerated by "administrative" (i.e., coercive) means.[2] Even though the Communist governments (with the exception of Albania) proclaimed not only separation of church and state but also full constitutional protection of religious liberty and made strenuous efforts to disguise their brutal onslaught on religious communities, word of the real situation seeped out and only rare, naive Western visitors could be fooled into believing what the Communist propaganda and the intimidated Christians proclaimed. As dialogue is impossible between a captor and a captive, so dialogue was impossible between Marxists and Christians in the Soviet bloc countries. Dialogue was also impossible when Western Christians sensed

2. For a very detailed country-by-country account of policies toward religion and churches, see Paul Mojzes, *Religious Liberty in Eastern Europe and the USSR: Before and After the Great Transformation* (Boulder, CO: Eastern European Monographs, 1992), 473 pages.

or knew about the oppression. The prevalent view in the West was that Communism was the enemy not only of their system of governance but also of their coreligionists behind the "Iron Curtain" (a term which gradually ceased to apply to Yugoslavia, though Tito's government continued oppressive and restrictive policies toward religion). It was this situation that hardened into unadulterated enmity between the Marxist governing forces in the East and much of the population in the West, with the exception of the Communist parties in the West and some "fellow travelers." Conflict, yes; dialogue and cooperation, no. For many Christians in both the East and the West, this approach did not change during the entire duration of the Cold War, and they never accepted that a dialogue with Marxism was possible. Most Marxists East and West likewise did not and would not change their negative attitude toward the dialogue with Christians because, so they thought, what would be the use of engaging a reactionary, outdated mode of false consciousness that will soon sink? They thought this way, ironically, until their own boat sank.

So what happened to alter this situation?

Dialogue in Poland

Quietly and without fanfare, without the news seeping out to the West, an encounter among a small group of Polish Catholic and Marxist intellectuals began in 1956, intensified in 1962, and persisted till the end of the Cold War. The dialogue in Poland was historically the earliest, but, surprisingly, it is still not well known outside of Poland, even among scholars. Actually, many in Poland maintained that there was no dialogue but only negotiations and accommodations. However, the documentation of the dialogue is overwhelming, even though most of it was circulated only within Poland.

The context of this dialogue was unique. Polish Catholicism is so deeply ingrained in the national being and the Catholic Church had so steadfastly served its people during its many occupations, that when the Communist government that took full control in 1947–1948, they could not accuse the church of having collaborated with the Nazis. The Communist Party, on the other hand, was viewed as having been imposed by the Soviet Union due to Poland's problematic geographic position, so that the Communists knew they could not impose the same policies toward the churches as the Soviets had. Polish Catholics practiced a loyalty to their church unique in Europe, resembling what religion must have meant in the Middle Ages. Even members of the Polish United Workers' Party were not banned from church attendance—and the churches were perennially thronged and were obedient to their hierarchy. This meant that the Marxists soon learned that they needed the church to at least not actively oppose them politically. The government permitted the church to publish numerous journals and books, to keep a Catholic university in Lublin, and to have three Catholic political groups that had membership in the *Sejm* (Pax, Znak, and Christian Social Association).

Beginning with the anti-Stalinistic popular uprising in 1956, spontaneous dialogues broke out among students in the state and Catholic universities, and soon thereafter intellectuals began publishing studies and essays in which they approached topics of common interest from their respective points of view while stressing that, while differences and confrontation persist, the dialogical approach would serve the national interest best as they sought common ground. At first they focused on practical matters, as even Polish Marxists did not tend to be overtly theoretical in their approach to socialism. Topics were toleration, cooperation, peace, and détente, but soon they discussed Catholic and Marxist humanism, philosophical anthropology, the role of human freedom, and other topics that were neither purely theoretical nor purely practical. The dialogue passed through several stages but involved an ever-growing number of authors and publications.[3] It produced some of the well-known Marxist thinkers such as Adam Schaf, Leszek Kolakowski, and Adam Michnik. The latter two became dissidents later on. When Cardinal Karol Woytiła became Pope John Paul II in 1972, even Polish Marxists were enthralled by this choice and assumed that finally there would be a pope who fully understood socialism and might promote the positive results of the Polish experience in the worldwide Catholic Church. At the time there was no inkling among them that Marxist socialism might not be the wave of the future. Only gradually would it become apparent that the Polish masses had opted for something contrary to what the Communists expected. This would lead to the workers' movement "Solidarity," to the imposition of martial law by General Wojciech Jaruzelski to forestall a Soviet invasion, and ultimately to free elections and the collapse of the Communist system in Eastern Europe. Generally, neither Polish Marxists nor Catholics participated in any significant manner in the international Christian-Marxist dialogues.

---

3. For a detailed account of the dialogue in Poland, see Paul Mojzes, *Christian-Marxist Dialogue in Eastern Europe* (Minneapolis: Augsburg, 1981), 73–102.

Dialogue in Czechoslovakia

Not far behind was the emergence of the dialogue in Czechoslovakia. The conditions in Czechoslovakia could scarcely have been more different than those in Poland. In contrast to Poland, Czechoslovakia—particularly the Czech lands—is among the most secular countries of Europe, and its history between the two world wars was genuinely democratic. Although it is predominantly Catholic, there is a strong Protestant presence that goes back to the pre-Reformation Hussite period.

For two years after the end of World War II, it seemed that Czechoslovakia might return to a democratic political arrangement, but in February of 1948 its influential Communist Party carried out a *coup d'état* and it rapidly became a repressive Stalinist country in which all institutions, including the churches, were held in an iron grip. Darkness descended and widespread persecutions began. The Catholic Church, targeted by the government, took a clear anti-Communist stance. Protestants, particularly the largest among them, the Church of the Czech Brethren, took a different, more engaging stance mostly due to the influence of one of its pastors, the gifted but controversial Josef Hromádka. Hromádka had taken refuge in the United States after Czechoslovakia was occupied by the Nazis, and had taught at Princeton Theological Seminary until 1947. Just when many were escaping from Czechoslovakia, Hromádka decided to return. Having been profoundly disillusioned by liberal democracy because of its betrayal at Munich, selling out Czechoslovakia to Hitler, he believed that Western democracy was in decline, and that this would make space for a new Communist order championed by the Soviet Union. He believed that Christians should support this new world despite its atheistic orientation because he believed that Marxism was fundamentally humanistic. Christians should basically consent to these revolutionary changes so that ultimately they may be in a position to humanize the rough edges of some revolutionary excesses. By being supportive of Communism, he felt that if and when the time came, Christians might be able to deliver a resolute no should the Communist authorities make some major unjust demands. He expressed his views in books not only in the Czech language but also in English and German, and spoke out boldly both at home and abroad, especially at the First Assembly of the World Council of Churches in Amsterdam in 1948, where he engaged in a sharp debate with John Foster Dulles. This gained him credibility with the Communists and great influence among Protestants not only in his country but also in other countries in the Soviet orbit, which provided more maneuverability for those who accepted his interpretation. Many Westerners also read Hromádka attentively, but many criticized him sharply as being a tool of the Communists.[4] In the East he gained a hearing from Marxists, particularly in his country, and his views made it possible for them not to dismiss Christianity as a simply reactionary force, but one worthy of engagement.

The dialogue in Czechoslovakia was meteoric.[5] It came out of the dark of the Stalinist period. For a few years, beginning in about 1964, it lit up the sky not only at home but also abroad, and reached unrivaled brilliance in its critical involvement, with significant impact on social development, only to be suddenly extinguished by 1969–1970 after the invasion by the Warsaw Pact countries. That discussion produced a number of internationally recognized dialogue partners and had significant social consequences, some of them tragic. On the Christian side the foremost theologian was Hromádka, while on the Marxist side it was the philosopher Milan Machovec. The two formally engaged in a seminar at Charles University in Prague in 1964, which might be considered the starting date of face-to-face dialogue. The two had numerous prominent colleagues. On the Christian side were Jan Milič Lochman, Lubomír Miřejovský, Peter Haban, and Milan Opočenský, but the Marxists were more prominent, with creative thinkers such as Vitězslav Gardavský, Robert Kalivoda, Milan Průha, Erika Kadlecová, and Jaroslav Krejčí. Unlike the Polish authors, the Czechs were frequently translated into other languages and attended international dialogues, and also organized them in their own country, until the Soviet invasion in August 1968 curtailed their experiment of freedom, which was to be named "the Prague Spring."

If Hromádka was controversial among Christians, and probably not trusted by many dogmatic Marxists, his main partner in dialogue, the Prague philosopher Milan Machovec, was much more so. However, he was certainly much appreciated by Christians and deserves to be rediscovered by new generations of thoughtful Christians and atheists. He stands far above any Marxist who engaged in dialogue not only with Christians but also with other ranking intellectuals of his time. He became a Marxist during his student years under Nazism, became a professor of Marxism and philosophy, and, along with other courageous thinking persons, realized the discrepancy between Marxist theory and the Stalinist practice and rejected the vulgar Marxist attitude of religion

4. Among his most important books that impacted the dialogue were *Doom and Resurrection* (1944), *The Church and Theology in Today's Troubled Times* (1956), *Theology between Yesterday and Tomorrow* (1957), *Gospel for Atheists* (1958/1965), *Von der Reformation zum Morgen* (1959), *Das Evangelium auf dem Wege zum Menschen* (1963), and *An der Schwelle des Dialogs zwischen Christen und Marxisten* (1964).

5. Mojzes, *Christian-Marxist Dialogue*, 111–28 (section on Czechoslovakia).

as the opiate of the people. In the 1960s he started inviting noted European intellectuals to his seminars at the university, including Hromádka. Already in 1957 he had published, in Czech, the short version of his book, *The Meaning of Human Life*, which he expanded in 1965. He also added a chapter on dialogue, which he considered the highest level of human awareness. Another of his Czech publications was translated into German in 1965, *Marxismus und dialektische Theologie: Barth, Bonhoeffer, und Hromadka*, in which he paid serious and appreciative attention to modern theology and examined approaches to convergence. Before too long Machovec and a group of younger Marxist philosophers and sociologists advocated critical openness and a new form of Marxism that was dubbed "socialism with a human face." Among the many conferences organized by them, the most important was one cosponsored by the Czechoslovak Academy of the Sciences and the Paulus-Gesellschaft of West Germany and Austria at the famous Czech spa resort Mariánské Lazně in April 1967.[6] It was the only international Christian-Marxist dialogue held in a Communist country, and it had an enormous impact at home and abroad. There were 220 participants in attendance (170 from the West), many of them internationally recognized scholars.

The mid-1960s brought about relaxation of international tensions and much creative fermentation. The top Czechoslovak government leaders were the new secretary general of the Czechoslovak Communist Party, Alexander Dubček, a reformist-minded leader, and President Ludvig Svoboda, who facilitated political liberalization that affected nearly all facets of life in the country. It is impossible to count the number of spontaneous Christian-Marxist dialogues that took place during the heady days of the Prague Spring. For instance, in April of 1968 a public dialogue was organized by Machovec with an outstanding panel of Marxists and Christians, and the events were attended by between twelve hundred and three thousand listeners, who were given a chance to send questions to the panel. Hope was in the air both in the East and in the West—all roads led to Prague—and Marxian socialism showed the ability to evolve. Czechoslovakia was ready for it, and so were many humanist Marxists and most Christians. But Leonid Brezhnev and the Soviet Politburo perceived this as the unraveling of the Soviet bloc. In August 1968 the experiment of "socialism with a human face" came to an abrupt end with the Warsaw Pact troops overrunning Czechoslovakia. It also meant that the Christian-Marxist dialogue in Czechoslovakia would come to an end and that international dialogue had sustained an almost deadly blow because Marxists

6. See, below, the description of their Christian-Marxist dialogues.

no longer had permission to participate in the dialogues, and Christians did not want to out of solidarity with the Marxist partners.

The Soviets reimposed strict control and repression of Christians, but the humanist Marxists were severely punished. Machovec was removed from the university, expelled from the communist party, and given no means to sustain himself; he lived in miserable ostracism and poverty, barely surviving to the fall of Communism. His colleague Vitĕzslav Gardavský was even less fortunate. He too was relieved of his post as professor, was frequently interrogated by the police, and died in 1978, a day after he was once again taken into police custody.

While there were no longer formal Christian-Marxist dialogues, the protagonists entered a period of intense scholarly activity. Machovec wrote his remarkable masterpiece book that could not be published in Czechoslovakia but was published in German as *Jesus für Atheisten* (1972), and in English as *A Marxist Looks at Jesus* (1976), in which he doesn't merely show that he is well versed with modern biblical scholarship but provides suc h a profound portrait of Jesus and his meaning for the world that any Christian can greatly gain by studying it. In it Machovec states that he would not wish to live in a world in which there had been no Jesus.[7]

Gardavský was probably the second most open Marxist partner in the dialogue. He published *God Is Not Quite Dead* in Czech in 1967, and a year later in German, but the English translation appeared only in 1973, along with another book: *Hope out of Skepsis*. In 1969 he and another Marxist, Julius Tomin, and two Czech Christians, Lubomir Miřejovsky and Dan Drapel, traveled in the USA discussing the events in Czechoslovakia and the Christian-Marxist dialogue. Gardavský had become well known for his studies of Jacob, Jeremiah, Jesus, Augustine, Thomas Aquinas, and Pascal. Finally, the Czech theologian Jan Lochman wrote *Church in a Marxist Society* (1970) after a year of teaching at Union Theological Seminary in New York.

Among the Eastern European countries, the Christian-Marxist dialogue in Czechoslovakia made the deepest impact in the USA, by raising hope that a form of socialism may emerge that is respectful of human freedom and dignity and provides opportunities for creative interaction (during which time church life in Czechoslovakia was almost entirely unrestrained), but then came

---

7. In 1999 Machovec published another startling book, *Die Frage nach Gott als Frage nach dem Menschen*, Forum St. Stephan, vol. 11 (Innsbruck and Vienna: Tyrolia, 1999), in which he stated: "We cannot live without God as the sum of the deepest human experiences and longing. . . . We cannot live without God, who protects us from the egoistical and individualistic reduction of humanity."

the rude awakening of the temporary nature of this experiment. After the Soviet invasion, many Western Christians, and even some Marxists (e.g., the Frenchman Roger Garaudy, and a number of Italian Marxists), gave up hope that Soviet-style Marxism was capable of reforming itself. The best that could be hoped for, it seemed in 1969–1970, was to work out some accommodations that might lessen the societal repression in the Soviet bloc.

Dialogue in the West and the Paulus-Gesellschaft

More or less simultaneously with the emergence of the dialogue in Czechoslovakia (which was, unlike that in Poland, noticed in the West), a number of Western intellectuals began probing whether, in addition to occasional political cooperation between some Christians and Marxists, such as during World War II in France, and left-wing Catholic support for the Italian Communist Party, there may be a chance and even a need for dialogue on more theoretical, philosophical, and even theological issues.

One of the first proposed shiftings from conflict to dialogue came from a book by the French Marxist philosopher and politician Roger Garaudy,[8] *From Anathema to Dialogue*, which appeared first in 1965.[9] It came out in several translations, and included responses by two first-rate Catholic theologians: Karl Rahner, SJ, and Johannes Baptist Metz. The book was based on a paper that Garaudy had delivered at the Paulus-Gesellschaft meeting in Salzburg in 1965. On the Christian side, Giulio Girardi, an Italian Salesian priest, published *Marxismo e cristianesimo*,[10] the first of his several books dealing with Christian-Marxist dialogue themes. Books like these made a significant impact on intellectuals, advocating that Christians and Marxists could not only share concerns for the well-being of the world but also venture into thought categories that seemed taboo to one or the other side. The theological and political situation in the world was quite conducive to this fermentation. Pope John XXIII and the Second Vatican Council (1962–1965) had brought about the *aggiornamento* for Catholics and a vigorous boost to worldwide ecumenical activities not only among Catholics but also among Protestants and Orthodox

8. Garaudy had a very complex and controversial career that involved a number of drastic conversions. He was expelled from the Communist Party of France in 1970 for his criticism of the Soviet Union's invasion of Czechoslovakia.

9. American edition published in New York: Random House, 1968. Originally published as *De l'anathème au dialogue* (Paris: Plon, 1965).

10. (Assisi: Cittadella, 1966, 1969).

Christians and opened avenues for dialogue with Jews, Muslims, adherents of other world religions, and even atheists such as Marxists. On the other hand, Nikita Khrushchev had initiated the process of de-Stalinization, and even though he was replaced in 1964 by the much more rigid Leonid Brezhnev, there was a sense of relaxation of East-West tensions in the mid-1960s and a differentiation among Marxists inspired by the discovery of the writings of the "young Marx" who were seeking a more dynamic, humanistic interpretation of Marxism, which was opposed by the dogmatic Marxist-Leninist. Many Westerners felt that after the Cuban missile crisis there was an opening to explore less confrontational ways of encountering the Marxist world (vigorously opposed by anti-Communists, including many Christians, who thought that this was highly unrealistic and dangerous).

The Paulus-Gesellschaft saw this as a *kairos* moment and adjusted its congresses to this new opportunity. The Paulus-Gesellschaft was organized by a German Roman Catholic priest named Erich Kellner. Kellner saw that natural scientists and theologians in German-speaking regions had avoided discussing issues with each other in open for a long time. He believed that just as the apostle Paul was able to bring the Jewish ideas into a dialogue with the Hellenistic gentile world, so now Christianity needed to incorporate scientific worldviews or else it was going to become irrelevant. The meetings that took place in Germany and Austria brought together eminent scientists and theologians who produced a large array of interesting papers showing that science and religion are not enemies but are able to jointly address many social and personal problems.

The turning point in this movement took place in the spring of 1964 when Ernst Bloch, a Marxist from East Germany who had moved to West Germany, where he became an inspiration to many students eager for social change, attended a symposium in Munich entitled "Human Being: Spirit and Matter."[11] That meeting was so successful that in the fall of that year another meeting was held in nearby Salzburg, to which another Marxist was invited. This time it was the Polish philosopher and central committee member of the United Polish Workers' Party, Adam Schaff. Schaff, who was used to the much more traditional Catholicism of the Poles, was so thoroughly shocked at the diversity of theological views on the theme "Christianity and Marxism

11. The Paulus-Gesellschaft published in German the proceedings of these conferences in a limited edition. These are not easy to find. I used these books in the writing of *Christian-Marxist Dialogue in Eastern Europe*, which contains some of the information on 158–65.

Today," that he expressed his opinion that many of the theologians were no longer really Christian. Soon there would be Christians who felt that some of the Marxists who delivered papers at the subsequent meetings were no longer really Marxists—and that certainly was the view in Moscow, where the party *apparatchiks* looked upon these meetings as ideological subversion intended to weaken the unity of the socialist world.

The excitement and novelty of freely expressed creative ideas quickly led to another congress: "Christian and Marxist Future," held in Salzburg in the spring of 1965. From 250 to 300 participated, among whom were Roger Garaudy, Lucio Lombardo-Radice of Italy, and a large number from Eastern Europe, especially Yugoslavia. The Paulus-Gesellschaft meetings gained notoriety. Another followed in 1966 at Herrenchiemsee, West Germany, on the theme "Christian Humanity and Marxist Humanism." In addition to the larger number of Yugoslavs were Hungarians, of whom the Marxist Jószef Lukácz was the most prominent, and several from Czechoslovakia, the previously mentioned Hromádka, Kadlecová, and Průha.

The process of liberalization in Czechoslovakia made significant progress, while the reputation of these congresses attracted wide interest in the media and among the creative intelligentsia among Marxists and Christians. The Czechoslovak Academy of the Sciences, clearly with permission from the Communist Party leaders, agreed to cosponsor with the Paulus-Gesellschaft the next congress, which was held at Mariánské Lazně (Marienbad), April 27–30, 1967.[12] The participants were a "who's who" in the humanistic Marxist world, and a similarly weighty Christian contingent. Seminal thinkers, well known internationally among Catholic and Protestant theologians and philosophers both Marxist and Christian, still in the presence of many natural and social scientists, were reading many papers with content that clearly broke out of the strictures of their respective traditions. Hromádka and Machovec were the leading figures, and it seemed that a new day had dawned in parts of Eastern Europe, which would have the chance to reorder the East-West relationship and defuse the Cold War. Months later the Prague Spring, with its "socialism with a human face," took place. There was euphoria over the possibility that some form of democratic socialism might be able to develop that would not only remake the face of Eastern Europe but also affect Western Europeans who were sympathizers of a social democratic arrangement. This, in turn, could lead to political victories of some Euro-Communist parties

12. See reference to this congress above. For a more detailed account, see Mojzes, *Christian-Marxist Dialogue*, 120–23.

such as the Italian Communist Party. It was too good to be true—or rather, too good to last. While it is not clear how Western governments might have reacted to this opportunity, we do know that this was way too dangerous from the Kremlin's perspective. After all, Brezhnev was not Gorbachev. In August 1968, Warsaw Pact troops marched into Prague and the rest of Czechoslovakia in the name of Brezhnev's "limited sovereignty of socialist countries" and put an end to this experiment of openness. The Marxists in Czechoslovakia lost their positions, were expelled from the Communist Party, and were blatantly persecuted, while Marxists from other countries got the message that they had better retreat. Christians in Czechoslovakia and other Eastern European countries did not fare as badly, but they too had to bow in servility to the overwhelming power of repression.

The Soviets did not at once prohibit the Czechoslovakian participants from traveling, and in 1968 and 1969 both Marxists and Christians lectured widely in Western Europe and the USA as to what could have or should have happened. It was bound to fizzle out, however, as restrictions were increasing. Some decided not to return to their home countries. The Paulus-Gesellschaft held one more conference that was intended to bring together young Communists and Christians in 1968 in Bonn, Germany, but Erich Kellner felt constrained to terminate the meeting, as a group of the "new left" from the West disrupted the proceedings.

It was now obvious that Christians could not pretend that things were proceeding as usual, as their newly acquired Marxist colleagues were being persecuted. The dialogues in which Eastern Europeans had participated came to an end. Paulus-Gesellschaft remained in name only, with Kellner unable to find a new direction. Many years later, together with some Italian Communists, he organized a meeting in Florence, Italy, with the topic "Man: Guide of the Evolutionary Process," at which Italian Catholics sympathetic to the Communist Party and Italian Communists delivered eloquent (and long) impromptu speeches.[13] In 1977 a meeting in Salzburg was held with the topic "A Democratic and Social Europe of Tomorrow." Finally, in 1978, in conjunction with the World Congress of Philosophy in Düsseldorf, the Paulus-Gesellschaft cosponsored a one-day symposium with the American Philosophical Association that drew about thirty participants, most of whom were from the West. The topic was "Marxist Philosophy and Christian Values Today." These two may have been the only dialogues sponsored by the Paulus-Gesellschaft at

13. I attended the meeting. Of Eastern Europeans, only three Yugoslavs were in attendance. Practically speaking, these dialogues were with Euro-Communists.

which any Americans were present.[14] A Soviet representative, Pyotr Fedo-seev, stated that the Soviet philosophers saw much value in these dialogues, but no additional dialogues were cosponsored by the Paulus-Gesellschaft.[15] Kellner became even more of a hermit who distrusted both Moscow and the Vatican and dreamed of a democratic, social, and Christian Europe. Since no well-organized structure characterized the Paulus-Gesellschaft, its ability to organize dialogues dropped precipitously.

An assessment of these dialogues would require more space than is available here. Intellectually speaking, there was nothing to match them. The collected papers that were published only in German would be worthy of a serious analytical effort in the history of ideas created during the Cold War. The daring breakout of the normal bounds of Marxist and Christian dogma-tism and preconceived ideas, and the ability of these two great movements to encounter one another in ways other than antagonism, were nothing short of spectacular. One of the problems was that the number of participants was too large for people to personally socialize, and the time for discussion of seminal papers too short, as other papers needed to be delivered. But these were merely failures of organization that could have been remedied with better manage-ment. From the perspective of "real socialism," that is, the power structures that controlled the socialist countries, the threat was serious. A professor of Lomonosov University in Moscow asked, "Are these dialogues of ideological diversion?"[16] The reader can guess the author's affirmative answer. Ideological diversion is an act of treason—and that is what the powers that be in the East concluded about the dialogues. Eastern Europeans, with the exception of the Yugoslavs, could no longer attend.

Yugoslav Dialogues

In 1948 Yugoslavia defected from the Soviet orbit. At first that break did not influence the relationship of Yugoslav Marxists with religion: they sought to prove to themselves and the rest of the Communist world that they were as "orthodox" in their treatment of religion as the Soviets. Gradually, however, Yugoslavia's foreign policy reoriented itself to find a position between the two

14. John Sommerville and Howard Parsons were seemingly the only US participants.

15. Mojzes, *Christian-Marxist Dialogue*, 162–65.

16. Jan G. Vogeler, "Unter dem Banner des Hl. Paulus: Dialog oder ideologische Diver-sion?," *Internazionale Dialog Zeitschrift*, no. 3 (1971).

blocs during the height of the Cold War that was both advantageous and disadvantageous. Ultimately it led the country to a new anti-ideological-bloc policy, and the country even became a founder of the nonaligned group of nations, while internally, to justify its break from the Informbureau (Cominform), it looked for even more "authentic" interpretations of Marxism than Stalinism. Internally this created a conflict between the traditional "dogmatic" Marxists and those who sought to reinterpret Marx in the light of the newly discovered writings of the "young Marx" that were more humanistic in nature. By 1967 these creative intellectuals, having been given permission by Tito, created a so-called workers' management socialism, which eased the rigid control of the party and led to decentralization and relatively greater liberty. Coincidentally, the Second Vatican Council had taken place between 1962 and 1965, and among Catholic theologians a new spirit of *aggiornamento* and dialogue was in ascendance (although some remained who were dogmatic and resistant to change).

The years from 1962 to 1966 constituted a period of easing of control and gradual positive exploration, while 1967–1972 was the high-water mark of dialogue, to be restrained but not terminated by Tito due to fears of a rising spirit of nationalism that was allegedly enabled by greater liberalization in the church-state relationship. The dialogue was almost exclusively between an ethnically diverse group of Marxists (especially a group that published an avant-garde periodical, *Praxis*, which gained international notoriety) and a group of almost exclusively Roman Catholic theologians; the other Christian churches were either disinterested, fearful, or too weak to enter the conversation.[17]

It began and largely remained a dialogue of the printed word, with only a few face-to-face dialogues in public forums. A group of Marxist scholars—Branko Bošnjak, Esad Ćimić, Zdenko Roter, Srdjan Vrcan, Marko Kerševan, Andrija Krešić, and many others—began writing analyses of religion in general and Christianity in particular that ever more departed from the hackneyed assessments of dogmatists. They depended much more on empirical research and on a more levelheaded assessment of Christians' role in society. They concluded that Marx's analyses of religion being an opiate of the people could be interpreted with much greater nuance than had been done previously and that religious people, if not persecuted, might become a more active component of the population in contributing to social progress and the "building of socialism." These new studies did have a practical consequence of improving the treatment of churches and individual Christians

17. See Mojzes, *Christian-Marxist Dialogue*, 128–58.

by government officials, providing considerably more liberties than in the previous period.

A prominent group of Catholic theologians—the most important of whom were Vjekoslav Bajsić, Tomislav Šagi-Bunić, Josip Turčinović, Archbishop Frane Franić, Drago Šimundža, Jakov Jukić (alias for Željko Mardešić), Tomo Vereš, and Bishop Vjekoslav Grmič—explored new ways of responding dialogically to these overtures. The Yugoslav Marxists or Christians did not produce the kind of philosophical or theological depth of some of the Czech or Paulus-Gesellschaft dialogue participants (e.g., Hromádka, Machovec, Gardavský, Rahner, Metz, and others), but, having been afforded a longer period to engage with each other, they did produce a rather remarkable variety of approaches amid a fairly good rapport that developed among them.

Tito saw a rise of nationalism indirectly promoted by the large churches and religious communities that was leading to an increase in tension. He found various means, including administrative repression, to stem this liberal tide. Personally, he was beginning to lose clout due to illness and age. After he died in 1980, the country gradually descended into an economic and political crisis. It seemed that it might be the country that would make the easiest transition to post-Communism after the system collapsed throughout Eastern Europe, but in fact it was the opposite. The worst fears of ethno-religious conflicts were exceeded by the nightmare of the country's disintegration in the last decade of the twentieth century.[18]

Christian-Marxist dialogue in Yugoslavia deserves lengthier analysis. However, it had a negligible impact on the Cold War. The Yugoslavs deliberately stayed out of bloc politics, condemning the Cold War as potentially destroying the planet. When they did attend international dialogues, they kept a low profile and resisted getting sucked into possible manipulations by the dynamic of the East-West conflict. The larger context of East-West relationships did play an indirect role in their own interactions, but their own complex internal relationships mattered much more to them than what transpired abroad. Ultimately the dialogue was swallowed by the collapse of Marxism at home and abroad and the vicious ethno-religious hatreds that were stoked both by many former Communists now overnight turned into fiery nationalists and by some of the church leaders that likewise stoked national exclusiveness that

18. See Mojzes, *Yugoslavian Inferno: Ethnoreligious Warfare in the Balkans* (New York: Continuum, 1994), and see Mojzes, ed., *Religion and the War in Bosnia* (Atlanta: Scholars Press, 1998).

benefited their churches as the masses turned back to religion in search of their identity, which had been so rudely unsettled by the fall of both socialism and Yugoslavia.

International Peace Symposia

Just when it seemed that Christian-Marxist dialogues were dead, a new encounter began in Vienna. It was initiated in 1967 at the Catholic Theological School of the University of Vienna by two professors, of whom one, Rudolf Weiler, a social ethicist priest, became the central figure of a long series of low-key meetings focused on peace. Weiler and colleagues organized the Institut für Friedensforschung (Institute for Peace Research), which a few years later came to be supported by the University of Vienna administration. The first activity was to organize lectures by visiting Soviet scholars, followed by discussion. Another institute also operated in Vienna: the International Institute for Peace, which was a Soviet-supported institute established under the provisions of the Soviet withdrawal from the four-power Allied occupation of Austria. The director of that institute from 1971 to 1977 was Vladimir Bruskov, a World War II veteran who fully appreciated the dangers of another war in Europe. He had been a journalist and, like Weiler, inspired trust with his integrity and cooperativeness. By 1971 the two institutes formalized their contacts and organized a series of symposia in Vienna (1971), Moscow (1973), Henndorf near Salzburg (1974), and Tutsing near Munich (1975).[19] The characteristics of these symposia were carefully negotiated, and included selecting a mutually agreed-upon topic that normally included an aspiration toward peaceful coexistence viewed from a Christian and a Marxist perspective, with the majority of Marxists coming from the USSR, accompanied by a smaller number of Marxists from other Eastern European countries, and just a few Christians from the East. Western Europeans were predominantly Christian. Both sides tended to reflect the "establishment" or mainstream view and informed each other as to who the participants were going to be. The number rarely exceeded thirty. Two main papers were delivered at each symposium, one by a Marxist (almost always a Soviet scholar of high rank in academia and government) and the other by a Christian. Several response papers were invited, with enough time

19. Titles of the three symposia were as follows: "The Problem of International Peace and of Peaceful Co–Existence," "Ways and Means for the Resolution of Problems of Social Development from the Perspective of Different Worldviews," and "Worldview and Peace."

allowed for discussion and even more for free time when participants could freely interact with one another and exchange thoughts more confidentially than in the formal meetings. Generally, the Marxist papers were highly technical, dealing with the arms race. The presenters substantiated their arguments by quotes from Lenin and the secretary general of the Communist Party of the Soviet Union. Western European Catholic papers tended to represent the official stance of the Catholic Church, with plenty of papal pronouncements supporting their claims.

Up to that point no Americans had participated in these meetings. Rather accidentally, Paul Mojzes, during a visit to Vienna, met first Weiler and then Bruskov, learned about these symposia, and discovered a very strong interest, especially by the International Institute for Peace, to have such a symposium in the USA. So the next symposium was held at Rosemont College in 1977, which then led to one in Kishinyov, USSR (1978); Saltsjöbaden, Sweden (1979); Detroit (1980); Madrid (1981); Klingentahl near Strassburg, France (1987); Moscow (1988); Leusden, Netherlands (1989); and York, Pennsylvania (1990).[20] By the time of the meeting at York College, Marxism in Eastern Europe was collapsing and the symposia no longer were entitled "Christians and Marxists in Peace Dialogue" but "International Dialogue (East and West) about the Basics of Peace in a Pluralistic World." After the York symposium, only one or two additional meetings were held in Europe, but interest in the dialogue rapidly waned as Marxism imploded and as Eastern Europe entered the post-Communist period, and the nature of those meetings had changed sufficiently as to not merit attention in this chapter. This time the Christian-Marxist dialogue did die, perhaps not forever and everywhere, but the issues and players have changed so much that

20. For a more detailed description of the International Peace Symposia until 1980, see Mojzes, *Christian-Marxist Dialogue*, 102–19. Regular reports of each symposium in German are available in *Wiener Blätter zur Friedensforschung*: no. 1 (1974); no. 5 (1975); nos. 7 and 8 (1976); nos. 13 and 14 (1977); no. 18 (1978); nos. 22 and 23 (1979/1980); nos. 26 and 27 (1980/1981); nos. 34 and 35 (1983); nos. 38 and 39 (1984); nos. 42 and 43 (1985); nos. 48 and 49 (1986); and no. 53 (1988). The additional topics were the following: at Rosemont (1977), "Peaceful Co-existence and the Education of Youth"; in Kishinyov (1978), "Disarmament Problems from Different Ideological Viewpoints"; in Saltsjöbaden (1979), "Peaceful Coexistence from the Perspective of Different Worldviews"; in Detroit (1980), "The Responsibility to Safeguard Peace Regardless of Ideological Differences"; in Klingentahl (1987), "Humanism and Peace Order: The Right to Life in Peace within the Framework of Human Rights"; in Moscow (1988), "Christians and Marxists: Peace Dialogue"; in Leusden (1989), "Human Dimension of Contemporary Peace: Man, Society, State, and International Community"; and in York (1990), "Common Human Values and the Future Role of Ideologies in an Interdependent World."

it was actually difficult to find people in Eastern Europe and the West who would define themselves as Marxists.

The topics of the symposia were clearly determined by the Cold War, and the symposia aspired to make their contribution to preventing the Cold War from expanding into a hot war. An interesting pattern developed at the meetings at which American participants were present. The main Marxist paper, always presented on the first day of the symposium by a Soviet scholar, presented a sharp attack on US policies and weapons development (e.g., Pershing missiles, neutron bomb) that were presented as threatening peace, whereas the Soviet policies were claimed to promote peaceful coexistence. The Soviet participants seemed to address almost exclusively American representatives, to the point where it became embarrassing how they sidestepped the Western Europeans. American participants tended to be patriotically critical of US policies (except that the American Marxists were blatantly pro-Soviet), but under such undifferentiated broadsides we were frequently forced into defending US policies in order to correct the caricature of American Cold War positions. Then, during the back-and-forth discussions, especially when in the American group there was someone more specifically knowledgeable about weapons data, gradually a more amiable atmosphere prevailed so that toward the end of the conference a better give-and-take discussion made it easier to perceive of the usefulness of these meetings.

The American partner with the two Vienna institutes was Christians Associated for Relationships with Eastern Europe (CAREE). The International Institute for Peace, reflecting the concern from Moscow, expressed the opinion that CAREE was institutionally not on par with European institutes. To respond to those concerns, the Institute for Peace and Understanding was incorporated in the Commonwealth of Pennsylvania, which formality satisfied the Eastern European partners, as they did not realize that the word "institute" does not have the same lofty meaning in the United States as it does in Europe. American participants (i.e., North American, as a few were Canadians, and a few were Latin Americans who resided in the USA) reflected the voluntaristic character of American activism for peace. Unlike the Eastern Europeans, who were formally selected by some governmental agency of the Soviet Union and its allies, and the Western Europeans, who were more specifically invited by the Institute for Peace Research, American participants responded to a generalized announcement in CAREE newsletters and an informal network, and had to fund their own travel to the conferences. CAREE had established a task force for the Christian-Marxist dialogue, of which Paul Mojzes was the chairperson; this group had a mailing list of about three hundred potentially interested persons, to whom information about activities in Europe and the United States was mailed, and later a formal *Christian-Marxist Newsletter* was published, which was first edited by Mojzes, and later by Nicholas Piediscalzi.[21]

Most North American participants were academics or clergy who showed interest in the dialogue and, later, in Latin American liberation theology. They represented nobody but themselves. If they had any influence, it was by the power of their publications and lectures.[22] Among them were some fairly well-noted scholars, such as Charles West of Princeton Theological Seminary; James Will of Garrett-Evangelical Theological Seminary; Paul Peachey of Catholic University; Arthur McGovern, SJ, of the University of Detroit; Maurice Boutin of Montreal University; David Hunter of the Council of Religion and International Affairs; John McCombe, chaplain at Syracuse University; Alice Weimer, formerly of the National Council of Churches; Joseph Loya, OSA, and Barbara Wall, OP, both of Villanova University; Leonard Swidler, Temple University; Anne Marie Durst, SHCJ, and Paul Mojzes of Rosemont College; Marina Herrera of the Education Department of the National Catholic Conference; Gary Bittner of York College; and Nicholas Piediscalzi of Wayne State University—all Christians. On the Marxist side were relatively little-known academics such as Alan Weiss of John Abbott College, Canada; Philip Moran of State University of New York in Buffalo; and Fred Carrier of Villanova University; American Marxist contributions were nominal at best.

On the basis of the topics of the twenty or so symposia, one can see that they did focus rather consistently on various aspects of peacemaking. Due to the insistence of the Soviet organizers, it seemed imperative to present views from a Marxist or a Christian viewpoint. Clearly they feared that the kind of self-critical explorations practiced at the Paulus-Gesellschaft conferences would lead to dissent and possible social unrest. The Marxist papers and most of the Christian papers tended to reflect relatively standard ideological or ecclesiological positions. American participants seemed least beholden to some official position, as, indeed, the American participants did not represent any formal church body but represented their own convictions about threats to peace and ways of peacemaking. But because of the fairly frequent, and

21. A bound volume is in my possession.

22. The lists of the participants contain numerous inaccuracies as to who actually came to the meeting and their institutional affiliation. The lists were prepared ahead of the meeting based on insufficient information. Institutional affiliations were for identification purposes only.

exaggerated and one-sided, broadsides on alleged (and sometimes real) US government positions threatening the Soviet bloc nations, we Americans were often forced into a defensive position to try to set the record straight.

Miscellaneous Contributions to Dialogue

Apart from the above-depicted dialogues, there were individual writings and programs. One of the earliest books of a dialogical nature was Charles West's *Communism and the Theologians*, based on his doctoral dissertation, which explored the attitudes of prominent European and American theologians toward Marxism/Communism.

Based on a series of lectures sponsored by the Chicago Theological Seminary in 1968, a book, *Openings for Marxist-Christian Dialogue*, edited by Thomas Ogletree, was published in 1969. Ogletree showed considerable promise, but he almost immediately decided to pursue other topics and did not participate in any of the organized endeavors. Tom Dean published *Christian-Marxist Dialogue in Radical Perspective (Post-Theistic Thinking)*. Similar to Ogletree, Dean did not venture beyond the most fleeting interest in actual dialogues. Nicholas Piediscalzi and Robert Thobaben edited *From Hope to Liberation: Towards a New Marxist-Christian Dialogue* (1974). Roger Garaudy and the American Catholic theologian Quentin Lauer published in 1968 *A Christian-Communist Dialogue*. In 1978 Paul Mojzes edited *Variety of Christian-Marxist Dialogues*, followed in 1981 by his authored book *Christian-Marxist Dialogue in Eastern Europe*. Harvey Cox of Harvard Divinity School also participated in a number of dialogues.

Herbert Aptheker, who wrote *The Urgency of Marxist-Christian Dialogue* (1964), was a prominent Marxist thinker, a member of the upper circles of the Communist Party USA, one of the very few who transitioned from radical opposition to all religion to willingness to engage in dialogue. While he was adjunct professor at Bryn Mawr College, he accepted an invitation by Paul Mojzes to have a public dialogue at Rosemont College, which drew a fairly large audience, but Aptheker still had a tendency to drift into debate rather than practice dialogue. In 1968 Aptheker edited *Marxism and Christianity: A Symposium*.

An American Christian-Marxist dialogue was organized by Mojzes and CAREE at Rosemont College in May 1978. The most prominent Marxist speaker was Michael Harrington, a socialist member of the US Congress, while the main Christian speaker was the Protestant ethicist Max Stackhouse of Princeton Theological Seminary. Over one hundred participants attended, from a fairly wide range of institutions.

By the late 1980s, the New Era organization, funded by the Unification Church (not a Christian denomination but with semi-Christian characteristics and an ecumenical tendency to organize conferences with Christian and other religious participants), started showing interest in organizing academic conferences on East-West relations. In 1985 they organized a conference, "Are Unification and Socialism Compatible?" held in Fort-de-France, Martinique. With the financial assistance of the New Era, two very effective Christian-Marxist conferences were organized. The first one was in 1988 in Budapest with the title "Changes in the Evaluation of Religion and the Churches in the Last Decade in Hungary and the U.S.A.," with scholars exclusively from these two countries. The main Hungarian host was Tamás Földesi, a law professor who planned it together with Paul Mojzes. The significant liberalization of Hungarian Communist governing was reflected in the reception and dinners conducted by the Hungarian Academy of Sciences, the president of the State Office for Churches, and the rector of the university. J. Deotis Roberts was the sole black theologian who ever attended these dialogues and presented a paper.[23] The very next year, under the chairpersonship of Leonard Swidler, another, similarly financed conference took place in Washington, DC, entitled "Christian-Marxist Views on Human Rights: An American-Hungarian-Yugoslav Dialogue."[24] By this time the erosion of Marxism had become so evident that while a number of the Hungarians and Yugoslavs still were (reluctantly) willing to be described as Marxists, there was no doubt that they were critical thinkers assessing the quickly changing international situation in which both Marxists and Christians energetically supported human rights in its broader conceptualization. A somewhat amusing "sideshow" was that the three East German observers were greatly alarmed by the visible departure from dogmatic Marxist positions of the Hungarians and Yugoslavians; they were laughingly dismissed by these "revisionists." Marxism was clearly disintegrating in front of our eyes. Little did the Yugoslavs know that in the near future the disintegration in their own country would lead to bloody wars and genocides in which religion became a contributing factor.

23. File of the conference agenda and papers are in my possession and will be placed in CAREE archives at Princeton Theological Seminary.
24. The collected papers were edited by Leonard Swidler and published under the title *Human Rights: Christians, Marxists, and Others in Dialogue* (New York: Paragon House, 1991).

Conclusion

In an unpublished paper,[25] the American Jesuit Arthur McGovern distinguished three types of Christian-Marxist encounters in the USA. The first encompassed dialogues of worldviews that consisted mostly of the parties clarifying changing positions and points of convergence and divergence between the two. These took place under conditions of de-Stalinization in Eastern Europe and détente during the Cold War. The second was criticism of American interventionism that was the result of involvement with Latin American theologies of liberation, resulting in some Christians becoming committed to socialism. The context of the second type was the proxy Cold War fought by the superpowers in the Third World. The third type consisted of dialogues on issues of peace and justice, described above. It was only this third type that was a direct response to the threats to human survival emerging from the Cold War, and these dialogues were the only ones that were more specifically organized to involve both Marxist and Christian presentations in order to jointly promote peace and social justice.

It is clear from the above that neither American Christians nor American Marxists participated in any weighty way in the Christian-Marxist dialogue; participation was mostly by academics and intellectuals on an individual basis. The dialogue was much more a European phenomenon, just as liberation theology was a Latin American phenomenon, with Americans and Canadians observing and studying it, and joining it on the margins. Our North American contribution was small. Only in the international dialogues for peace was there a perceptible American presence, and we came into the limelight not so much because of our own efforts as because of the Soviet and Eastern European Marxist attacks on us. It is much less clear whether there would have been any Christian-Marxist dialogue in North America if there were not a Cold War. The Cold War depressed those American Christians who were interested in some sort of Christian socialism, because it became obvious that Stalinist and associated "regular" socialism greatly repressed and persecuted Christians and others.

Whether the Christian-Marxist dialogue made an impact on the course of the Cold War is debatable. Insofar as the dialogues of the Paulus-Gesellschaft had an impact on the development of "socialism with a human face" and the possibility of a better and kinder Marxism tolerant of Christianity, the an-

---

25. Arthur McGovern, "Three Worlds of Marxist-Christian Encounters" (University of Detroit, n.d.), 10–21.

swer would be affirmative. But the abrupt Soviet termination of these winds of freedom brought severe repression in which both humanist Marxists and Christians suffered persecutions.

What the Christian-Marxist dialogue did in countries like Poland, Hungary, Yugoslavia, and, for a short but bright period, Czechoslovakia was to provide a measurable softening of the hard-line Marxist attitude toward religion and a lifting of many restrictions on Christians. The reason was that the Marxists at these dialogues were impressed by the humane, social, and intellectual contribution of their Christian partners, and they, in turn, spoke up at various Communist government agencies against treating Christians as enemies of the state.

A bigger question is whether the Christian-Marxist dialogue, with its modest achievements, can provide some precedent or model for future ideological, religious, or other unanticipated conflicts. Is it better to let such conflicts fester or perhaps even get worse, in the hope that the other side will collapse the way Communist Marxism did? For those of us who have participated in various interreligious and interideological dialogues, the answer is self-evident, namely, that all efforts should be made to build bridges rather than promote war (cold or hot). Obviously the answer would depend on the nature of the opponent. As long as the opponent is not interested in even negotiating but only in destroying those who are not like-minded (e.g., certain branches of militant Islamism), then with them no dialogue will be possible. But dialogue will be possible and can be promoted and enlarged with other moderate or liberal forms of a rival (e.g., Islam) with the hope that such dialogue may even influence the radicals to abandon their extremist beliefs and practices. Abraham Lincoln is reputed to have said that he would work even with the devil for as long as the devil is right, and that seems to be a good motto for Christians—that we will dialogue with anyone for as long as the other party strives for positive accomplishments in the interest of human betterment.

Lessons Learned

American Christians and the Challenge of the Cold War

David Little

In his provocative study *Religion and American Foreign Policy, 1945–1960*, William Inboden declares, "American Protestants shared with many of their political leaders a common conviction that the Cold War was a religious conflict."[1] Thanks to the essays in this volume, we can now go further than Inboden in two respects. That common conviction was true not only of American Protestants, though it was certainly true of them. It was also true of American Catholics and American Orthodox. Moreover, the conviction lasted well beyond 1960, the end point of Inboden's study. It endured until the termination of the Cold War with the collapse of the Soviet Union in 1991.

At the same time, and in line with the findings of this volume, we must make very clear in exactly what way Inboden's claim is true. As with American Protestants, divided as they were into mainliners and evangelicals, American Catholics and Orthodox had their own internal divisions and diversity of viewpoints right on through the forty-six-year period. That meant that leaders and members of all these groups and subgroups interpreted the Cold War as religious conflict very differently.

For those at one extreme, it was a Manichaean struggle of good versus evil between the Western bloc (the United States and its allies) and the Eastern bloc (the Soviet Union and its allies), entitling the West to take exceptional measures, morally, politically, and militarily, in developing and implementing strategies and weapons necessary to defeat the forces of darkness. At the other extreme, the Cold War was a time for national spiritual self-examination and contrition, admitting flaws and shortcomings on both sides, recommending peacemaking efforts across the divide, and counseling caution and self-restraint as regards policy and weaponry, lest yielding to the passions of war

---

1. William Inboden, *Religion and American Foreign Policy, 1945–1960* (New York: Cambridge University Press, 2008), 62.

produce worldwide catastrophe. Between these extremes, there were of course many variations of opinion within and among all four American religious groups, variations often exhibited over time in the same person or group. In a word, the chapters in this volume leave no doubt about the rich complexity of theological interpretation and moral exhortation that existed among American religious groups during the Cold War. Sorting out the different and sometimes shifting lines of argument is an important part of the work of this chapter.

Something else calling for clarification, however, is the basic challenge of the Cold War to which, in their various ways, leaders and members of American religious groups responded. This consideration brings us to the behavior and perspectives of the "political leaders," also mentioned by Inboden, who directed American policy during the fifteen years after World War II and who, as a gloss on Inboden, can be said to have determined the American approach for much of the duration of the Cold War. Certainly, their interpretations and responses established decisive reference points for the reactions of the religious communities.

Crucial here is Inboden's comment that the common conviction about the Cold War as religious conflict was shared by these American political leaders as well. That is important for two reasons. It is cause for considering the role of religion to be of the greatest consequence in understanding American attitudes toward the Cold War. It is also cause for examining with care the relationship between religious people and political leaders. It can be seen that both groups are in a most significant way part of the same general conversation that occurred during the period in question. Before turning to the religious reactions, it will be useful, therefore, to sketch out some interpretations of and responses to the basic challenge of the Cold War, as identified by the actions and reflections of certain political leaders, including their religious perspectives.

Religion, American Policy, and the Cold War: Kennan versus Dulles

The basic challenge concerned the perplexities surrounding attempts to provide an accurate assessment of the interests and plans of the Soviet Union, and to work out the implications of that assessment for determining the best US response. George Kennan, then a young foreign service officer serving in the Moscow embassy, started things off in February 1946 with his "long telegram," later to appear anonymously in revised form in *Foreign Affairs* of July 1947 as "The Sources of Soviet Conduct." Partly because of his own infelicity of expression, as he later admitted, and partly because some members of his audience were disposed to read what they wanted to read, his famous communications to some extent increased, rather than reduced, the perplexities involved.[2]

He intended to say that Soviet intransigence was not the West's fault, but a product of the inner workings of the Soviet system, and, what is more, that there was very little the West could do about it for the time being.[3] Moreover, the major motivation of the Soviet leaders for describing the West as hostile was to provide an excuse "for the dictatorship without which they did not know how to rule, for cruelties they did not dare not to inflict, [and] for sacrifices they felt bound to demand," as he put it. Securing their rule was the primary objective. Therefore, despite their undoubted interest in expanding their influence, the leaders were fundamentally cautious, and were not inclined to accomplish their ends by starting wars with Western countries. What the West needed to do in response was to develop a "long-term, patient but firm and vigilant *containment* of Russian expansive tendencies." It could afford to do that because the Soviet system would eventually collapse of its own internal contradictions and defects.

But what Kennan meant exactly by a policy of containment itself became the subject of intense controversy. That was partly his fault, he acknowledged. He had argued that containing the Soviet Union would mean "the adroit and vigilant application of counterforce at a series of constantly shifting geographical and political points," without explaining what he intended by the word "counterforce" or what its limits were. A number of colleagues and observers took him to mean a policy of rather open-ended *military* deterrence that was, he said later, exactly "the sense I had not meant to give it."[4] For him, extending economic and political support as, for example, happened in the Marshall Plan for Western Europe was, he later indicated, often of greater utility than military assistance.

Also, containment for Kennan seemed to mean avoiding needless acts of isolation and ostracism against Communist regimes as illustrated, he believed, by the opposition to admitting the People's Republic of China to the UN. Such opposition would take on enormous symbolic importance, particularly for Republican anti-Communists during the Eisenhower years. They believed UN admission would legitimate the PRC, and amount to a renunciation by the

2. George F. Kennan, *Memoirs, 1925–1950* (Boston: Little, Brown, 1967), 357–67.

3. The summary of Kennan's thought here is a paraphrase combining the excellent summaries found in John Lewis Gaddis, *The Cold War: A New History* (New York: Penguin Books, 2005), chap. 1, at n. 34, and in Walter Isaacson and Evan Thomas, *The Wise Men: Six Friends and the World They Made* (New York: Simon and Schuster, 2008), 352–56.

4. Kennan, *Memoirs, 1925–1950*, 360.

West of Chinese nationalists as crucial allies against Communism. Kennan, on the other hand, believed that seating the PRC simply recognized an existing fact, a fact "created when the Communist Chinese overran the mainland of China." It was no different from having included the Soviet Union and its satellites in the UN from the beginning, and the admission should readily have been accepted.[5]

But there was further confusion about what containment meant. For one thing, Kennan specified that military support should be limited to the United States itself, the UK, the Rhine Valley and adjacent industrial areas, and Japan, but then agreed to a policy of military assistance to Greece and Turkey in 1947 in response to the threat of Communist insurgencies in those countries, and to a policy of direct US military intervention in Korea in 1950 to hold the line against a Soviet-authorized invasion of the South by the North. He made clear that his support for these policies was very limited. He did not agree with the Truman administration that aid to two countries under Communist threat implied support for all countries everywhere under such threat. Nor did he agree with the decision to take the war north in Korea. But however cautious his approach to the use of force, he was never able to articulate a clear practical principle for doing so.

For another thing, he went some way toward distinguishing his position from others as regards deploying nuclear weapons as a deterrent against the Soviet Union, but he never completely squared his recommendations with his moral abhorrence of such weapons. Because, as he said, these weapons were devastatingly indiscriminate in their effects, he rejected the view that the United States should expect to employ such weapons "deliberately, promptly, and spontaneously in any major encounter, regardless of whether [they were] first used against us."[6] Still, it is one thing to limit nuclear weapons to defense, and quite another to show on what grounds even their defensive use may be justified, or what may count as licit use in retaliation.

Finally, there was some unclarity regarding Kennan's religious assessment of containment policy. As a committed Presbyterian churchman, he left no doubt as to how as a Christian he assessed the Soviet system. It was diabolical in nature, proceeding "whole hog on the path of Godlessness," which is to "deny the Christian truth and values," "the existence of a supreme being," "all individual salvation," and "all individual moral law," and as such proves the existence of "evil as a force in this world" that requires "a spiritual

5. Kennan, *Memoirs, 1925–1950*, 490–97.
6. Kennan, *Memoirs, 1925–1950*, 472.

vitality capable of holding its own among the major ideological currents of the time."[7]

Such thinking would appear to provide plausible grounds for containing the Soviet Union, as Kennan recommended. But it also might suggest something else. If the Soviet system is so bad, why not design policies that attempt to undermine it, and support efforts that appear to be doing that? One of Kennan's answers, implicit in his long telegram, is that in the light of existing realities, such attempts are impractical and therefore bound to cause more harm than good.

But he also gives another, more puzzling answer. When it comes to diplomacy and the creation of foreign policy, the interests of the nation-state for which modern governments have responsibility—military security, political integrity, and the people's well-being—"have no moral quality," are neither good nor bad.[8] Nothing whatsoever in Christ's teachings, he says, relates to a world divided up into nation-states, "each with its own national ego, each assuming its service to be more worthy than any other with which it might come into conflict. Surely, this whole theory is an absurdity from a Christian standpoint."[9] In a world of nation-states without recognizable transnational standards, judgments against another state, like Kennan's judgments cited above against the Soviet Union, are irrelevant; they have no religious or moral weight. He even goes so far as to disdain East-West agreements concerning human rights as part of the Helsinki Accords of 1975, since human rights language is "hard to relegate to any category other than . . . high-minded but innocuous professions [of faith]."[10]

If one regards containment in the light of the first answer, then the reasons in favor are arguably moral in character. To try to roll back rather than contain the Soviet system, given the realities, would do more overall harm than good. But if one regards containment in the light of the second answer, then "harm" and "good" are beside the point, at least in the world we know. Members of various states share no common spiritual or moral perspectives; they cannot find common ground among them that is able to transcend their differing national identities. So far as international relations go, it is national ego against national ego.

A very different reading of the basic challenge of the Cold War is found in another political leader of the period, John Foster Dulles. As secretary of

---

7. Cited in Inboden, *Religion and American Foreign Policy*, 17–18.
8. Kennan, "Morality and Foreign Policy," *Foreign Affairs*, Winter 1985/1986, 206.
9. Kennan, "Foreign Policy and Christian Conscience, *Atlantic Monthly*, May 1959, 46–47.
10. Kennan, "Morality and Foreign Policy," 207.

state during most of the Eisenhower administration (1952–1959), Dulles came to oppose in the strongest terms Kennan's policy of containment of the Soviet Union, and to replace it with a more dire analysis of the Soviet threat, and, both rhetorically and to some extent in practice, a more belligerent and aggressive response to the threat.

To be sure, that had not always been Dulles's position. Through the early 1940s he had led a number of ecumenical study groups that drew much more irenic conclusions about the postwar prospects for a new world order and a compliant Soviet Union. A 1942 report of one of the committees he headed spoke of the possibility of a "world government of delegated powers" capable of imposing "new limitations on national sovereignty, and international control of all armies and navies." The report complained that "the natural wealth of the world is not evenly distributed," suggesting that wealthy nations have a moral obligation to correct the "defects of market-based economies" that produce such inequality, and contending that worldwide efforts should be undertaken to promote not only political rights but also economic rights to things like education, old-age security, health care, and opportunities for fair and safe employment.[11]

In an article for *Life* in 1946, Dulles described a Soviet Union unrecognizable compared to what he would say just a few years later. At that time, he "called upon Americans to understand that Soviet leaders, including Joseph Stalin, were rational people and that Americans should not fall into the trap of believing that a military buildup would necessarily make the United States more secure. Dulles argued that even if the buildup were designed for purely defensive purposes, Soviet leaders would be reasonable in understanding that a strong American army and navy could also be used for offensive purposes, and that creating a powerful American military would only prompt the Soviets to reciprocate with their own armed forces."[12] By being prudent and trusting in the capacity of the Soviets to behave rationally, Americans could lead the way in reducing the likelihood of military conflict.

Dulles's outlook had been radically transformed by 1952, in keeping with the growing panic over the Communist threat gripping the United States at the time, a time dominated by the unrelenting anti-Communist efforts of Senator Joseph McCarthy and Representative Patrick McCarran, leader of the House Un-American Activities Committee. In reality, the Truman administration

11. Cited in T. Jeremy Gunn, *Spiritual Weapons: The Cold War and the Forging of an American National Religion* (Westport, CT: Praeger, 2009), 92–93.
12. Gunn, *Spiritual Weapons*, 93–94.

had been anything but passive. It had instituted its own efforts to root out Communists in government, and its policies abroad succeeded in forcing the Soviets out of Iran in 1946, in preventing a Communist takeover in Greece in 1947, in resisting the Soviet challenge to West Berlin in 1948, in creating and joining the North Atlantic Treaty Organization in 1949, and in withstanding the North Korean attack on the South between 1950 and 1953.

However, for Dulles and for General Dwight Eisenhower, then campaigning for president, those achievements were not nearly enough. The foreign policy section of the 1952 Republican platform, written by Dulles, declared categorically that it was time to end "the negative, futile, and immoral policy of containment" that consigned "countless human beings to a despotism and Godless terrorism . . . and to revive the contagious, liberating influences which are inherent in freedom."[13] In another *Life* article, published in May 1952, Dulles spoke of the Democrats' "cowardly" policy of containment, and of the need to "liberate captive nations" and to eliminate Communist "stooges" around the world.[14]

The sharp antagonism between Dulles and Kennan over the idea of containment became personal when Dulles assumed leadership of the Department of State in March 1953. Dulles told Kennan there simply was no place for him in the new administration, though in ushering him out he asked his views on current thinking in the Kremlin. Kennan said later that he felt like a divorced person invited before being ejected to prepare a final breakfast for the enjoyment of the former spouse.[15] He was thereafter invited to join the CIA by brother Allen Dulles, then head of the agency, but Kennan refused, calling John Foster Dulles a "dangerous man" gripped by "emotional anticommunism."[16]

But if Dulles's policies sounded sharply at odds with Kennan's, they were not without their own unclarity and inconsistency. In January 1954, Dulles announced that the United States would henceforth rely more and more for protection on the "deterrent of massive retaliatory power," implying unmistakably expanding dependence on nuclear weapons. Not only would such a policy be much less expensive than having to depend on far-flung ground force installations around the world; this consideration was dear to the heart of President Eisenhower. It would also, Dulles thought, give the United States

13. Cited in Stephen Kinzer, *The Brothers: John Foster Dulles, Allen Dulles, and Their Secret World War* (New York: St. Martin's Griffin, 2013), 104.

14. Cited in Kinzer, *The Brothers*, 103.

15. Isaacson and Thomas, *The Wise Men*, 566.

16. Kinzer, *The Brothers*, 132.

decided advantages both in constraining Communist ambitions and eventually in rolling back Communist gains.

The problem was, the policy failed an early test. In line with his belief in reversing what he saw as a lack of American will and fortitude associated with the containment policy, Dulles had repeatedly called for the "liberation" of Eastern Europe, and his brother Allen did more, directing agents to encourage revolt throughout the area.[17] However, when Hungarian citizens, inspired by what appeared to be new opportunities for independence in the aftermath of Stalin's death in 1953, spontaneously rose up in 1956 against their Soviet-imposed government and, having been led to expect such support, appealed for assistance to the United States, they were bitterly disappointed. The United States did nothing, and the doctrine of massive retaliation was utterly ineffective in deterring a bloody Soviet military crackdown on the rebellion. In practice and contrary to its rhetoric, it looked as though the Eisenhower administration was doing little more than continuing the much-maligned policy of containment.

This experience reinforced a growing conviction on the part of Eisenhower and Dulles that new thinking was needed aimed at enabling the United States to gain the initiative against what appeared to them to be the gradual expansion of Soviet power around the world. Since massive retaliation was not working and a strategy of conventional military confrontation was very risky and costly, they settled on a policy of covert action. Such an undercover policy had the benefit of eliminating Communist "stooges," thereby reversing Communist gains, at low cost and without appearing to do so. "In the secrecy-shrouded 1950s, and for a long time afterward, the scope of this unseen war remained obscure." The Truman administration, it is true, engaged in covert operations, but drew the line at assassinating foreign leaders. "That line evaporated when [Truman] left office. Eisenhower wished to wage a new kind of war. Secretary of State John Foster Dulles plotted it. His brother, Director of Central Intelligence Allen Dulles, waged it."[18]

The policy consisted of covert efforts mounted against six leaders on the periphery of the Soviet sphere of influence taken to be Communists or potentially so, and to replace them with friends of the United States. These operations undertook to depose, eliminate, or otherwise disable Mohammad Mosaddegh in Iran in 1953, Jacobo Arbenz in Guatemala in 1954, Ho Chi Minh in Vietnam in 1954, Sukarno in Indonesia in 1958, Patrice Lumumba in Congo in

17. Kinzer, *The Brothers*, 213.
18. Kinzer, *The Brothers*, 114.

1960, and Fidel Castro in Cuba in 1960. What these operations accomplished in rolling back Communism and improving the lot of the countries affected is a subject of continuing controversy.[19]

Two other policies that reflect the same "ruthlessly confrontational view of the world"[20] were Dulles's opposition to the entry of the People's Republic of China to the UN and to the Senate ratification of the "International Bill of Rights," consisting of the Universal Declaration of Human Rights; the Covenant on Economic, Social, and Cultural Rights; and the Covenant on Civil and Political Rights. Together with the China lobby, led by figures like Representative Walter Judd, Dulles staunchly opposed China's admission to the UN because such an act would give moral support to a regime inherently opposed to freedom, and bound to collapse in the near future.

In the same way, he joined forces with those unalterably opposed to adopting the UN human rights treaties as the law of the land. The opponents were traditional isolationists set against diminishing US national sovereignty, along with many Southerners and others fearful that such treaties would introduce Communist-style socialism and overturn states' rights in favor of increased centralized government. In Judiciary Committee hearings in 1953, Dulles testified that the Eisenhower administration did not look upon the human rights treaties "as a means which we would now select as the proper and most effective way to spread throughout the world the goals of human liberty. . . . We, therefore do not intend to become party to any such covenant or present it as a treaty for consideration by the Senate."[21] As a younger man, Dulles had taken contrary positions in both cases. He had argued that admission to the UN is not a matter of moral endorsement, and that human rights constituted the "soul" of the UN charter.[22] Now, he had very different ideas.

Dulles had always believed strongly in a universal moral law very closely tied to the Western tradition and to his Calvinist religious faith acquired from a father who was a Presbyterian clergyman. His youthful confidence in international institutions like the UN and human rights treaties as the way to protect and promote the moral law gave way as the '50s approached. Assuming the position of secretary of state in the Eisenhower administration, and be-

19. Kinzer, *The Brothers*, wherein the six cases are all extensively discussed, and the consequences of the operations criticized.

20. Kinzer, *The Brothers*, 313.

21. Natalie Hevener Kaufman, *Human Rights Treaties and the Senate: A History of Opposition* (Chapel Hill: University of North Carolina Press, 1990), cited at 104.

22. John S. Nurser, *For All Peoples and All Nations: The Ecumenical Movement and Human Rights* (Washington, DC: Georgetown University Press, 2005), 1.

holding a world mortally threatened, as he thought, by Soviet Communism, he transferred his confidence to the United States, and more particularly to the Republican Party, as the best means to defend and advance the moral law. As he wrote in the 1952 party platform, "there are no Communists in the Republican Party"; "we never compromised with Communism and we have fought to expose it and eliminate it in government and American life." The Republicans recognized Communism for what it was: "a world conspiracy against freedom and religion." As they understood it, the most effective way to respond was by "spiritual faith." "Our nation will become again the dynamic, moral and spiritual force which was the despair of despots and the hope of the oppressed."[23]

American Christian Responses

Struggles of Soul

There are good reasons, from an American perspective, to think of the Cold War as a lengthy and sometimes contentious conversation between and among Christians and political leaders over the subject of religion. Our brief review of the outlooks and disagreements of George Kennan and John Foster Dulles, two very influential political figures, who in an important sense laid the foundations of American Cold War policy, demonstrates how central in their minds religion was to making that policy. Similarly, the chapters constituting this volume leave no doubt that many of the same disagreements and differences separating them also animated, and frequently consumed, the thought and action of the leaders and members of American Christian churches during the Cold War period.

What we are to make of their experience can be determined only after we have described and examined the basic themes implicit in their reactions to the complexities and perplexities of the Cold War. One key theme, and perhaps the most important of all, relates to our different characterizations of Kennan and Dulles. It concerns the deep divide in the American Christian community, apparent in the chapters, between what we may call "moderate" and "ardent" anti-Communists.

By no means were these two groups entirely different. They were both anti-Communist in some sense, and they shared a common conviction concerning the urgent relevance of the Christian gospel. At the same time, they

23. Cited in Gunn, *Spiritual Weapons*, 97.

differed over the nature of Communism and its goals and capabilities, and therefore they differed over the proper way to react. For the ardent group, Communism was unalterably alien and hostile; it was a unified, ceaselessly aggressive force, intent on world domination, which, unless checked by the most robust forms of deterrence, as well as disruptive and destabilizing counteraction, would have its way. For the moderate group, Christians and Communists shared common notions of justice and equity that were, to be sure, ignored and subverted in practice in Communist countries, but were also insufficiently honored and implemented in the West. Moreover, the ambitions and capabilities of Communism were less grand, and more dependent on conventional political and material interests than ideological devotion. It was of course an oppressive and abusive system, and must be vigilantly contained. But the means of containment—the weapons and strategies recommended—were themselves subject to abuse and potentially the cause of great harm. Therefore, they needed constantly to be reexamined and deliberated about in a spirit free of dogmatism and overconfidence.

The two descriptions are of course "ideal types," a point made very clear in the chapters. There is evidence of considerable struggle, variation, and change of mind and heart as regards most of the members of each group, such that it is sometimes hard to know when the line between the two types has been crossed. Still, the struggle, variation, and change of opinion within each group are a large part of what makes the accounts in this volume so interesting.

Moderate American Christian Anti-Communists and Their Struggles

In the light of the unmistakable excesses of the Soviet Union under Stalin, and of Stalinist governments in Eastern Europe, the moderates at one point or another all voiced rather strong anti-Communist sentiments. Charles West, a mainline Protestant voice, no doubt speaks for the group when he reports that in East Germany in the early '50s "oppression was everywhere. Soviet occupying military secured the state, and Soviet advisers controlled its policy. The goal of the state was to convert the society into something modeled after the Soviet Union, in ideology, politics, and economic structure . . . [and] to this end . . . established a network of informers [in order] to know everything about you, even what you said and thought in private."[24] In the same period, Reinhold Niebuhr, another mainline Protestant, described Communism as

---

24. See West's chapter in this book, "Memoirs of a Participant in East-West Dialogues."

"an organized evil which spreads terror and cruelty throughout the world and confronts us everywhere with faceless men who are immune to every form of moral and political suasion."[25] That strong form of anti-Communism was also unmistakable in an organization he helped found, Americans for Democratic Action, a group made up of former socialists and union supporters opposed to the Communists for subverting democratic procedures.

But both West and Niebuhr saw more dimensions to Communism than that. West, along with a number of authors, refers to what was to be learned from the Czech theologian Josef Hromádka, who returned home from the United States in 1947 and initiated a long-term dialogue with Western thinkers. If Soviet Communism was not the final answer, neither was democratic capitalism, especially of the sort practiced in the United States. The deep division between rich and poor, powerful and weak, required new institutions and new solutions, and Communism, Hromádka thought, was at least calling attention to that common reality.

As a young man, Niebuhr had showed sympathy for state socialism. Even as Stalin was beginning to show his true colors, Niebuhr thought Marxist faith, though mistaken, remained "a very valuable illusion for the moment," since justice cannot be achieved without the passion generated by "a sublime madness in the soul." He had spoken critically in the '30s and '40s of conventional Western liberalism and market capitalism, with what he saw as its complacency and persistent indifference to the severe infirmities it leaves in its wake, and while any enthusiasm he had for the Soviet Union would soon cool, he continued to cast doubt on what he thought of as the soaring self-righteousness and imprudence of US policies toward Communist nations during the '50s and '60s.

Liberal black Protestants, like Howard Thurman, manifested similar ambivalence toward Communism.[26] On the one hand, Thurman was suspicious of the purposes and methods of the American Communist Party, and by 1956 considered Soviet Communism a failure and its promises fraudulent. On the other hand, he had sincere sympathy for Marxist ideals in regard to racial and economic justice, and in the '30s took hope, like the young Niebuhr, in socialist efforts to reform radically the institutions of market capitalism and private property. He was fearful that the unrelenting anti-Communism

25. See Gary Dorrien's chapter above, "Niebuhrian Realism, Cold War Realities, and the Ethics of Empire."

26. See the chapter by Peter Eisenstadt, "Howard Thurman, Martin Luther King Jr., the Cold War, the Civil Rights Movement, and Postwar Liberal Black Protestantism."

characteristic of American rhetoric during the Cold War, especially as expressed in the idiom of evangelical Protestantism, would obscure the virulent forms of racism and fascism he found so pervasive at the time. Accordingly, Thurman is described as a moderate on the subject to the point of being a non-Communist rather than an anti-Communist. Such were the "struggles" of members of this group.

Starting in the late '40s, Niebuhr sympathized with the moderate anti-Communism of his friend George Kennan. He supported Kennan's understanding of containment as less dependent on military force than was held to be true by John Foster Dulles and the Eisenhower administration, though he modified his position in the early years of the Cold War. Kennan and Niebuhr both supported limited US military intervention in Korea, but their views on nuclear arms differed at first. From the beginning, Kennan had rejected the first use of nuclear weapons because of their devastating effects. Through the '50s, in contrast, Niebuhr and his close associate, John Bennett, justified the threat of first use against a possible Soviet land invasion of Western Europe, even though they were sharply opposed to the Eisenhower doctrine of massive nuclear retaliation. By the early '60s, however, they moved closer to Kennan. As the Cold War wore on, Niebuhr and Bennett, together with Kennan himself, began to have deeper and deeper doubts about the justifiability of even possessing nuclear weapons, let alone using them. Such questions continued to be raised and debated through the '60s, '70s, and '80s by a group of mainline Protestants in response to the policy of mutual assured destruction (MAD) initiated during the Kennedy administration. The policy involved both sides aiming nuclear weapons at each other's population centers on the assumption that the prospect of incomprehensible devastation guaranteed that the weapons would never be used.

Other mainline Protestant groups, like those represented by the National Council of Churches (NCC), founded in 1950, had a history of challenging government policy on nuclear weapons.[27] NCC president Edwin Dahlberg had called the massive retaliation doctrine of the Eisenhower administration "a feverish policy of bomb for bomb, rocket for rocket, Sputnik for Sputnik," something incompatible with the Christian gospel. Massive retaliation, he said, must be met by "massive reconciliation." By the '80s, these objections had blossomed into absolute opposition to US nuclear policy. In 1983, the World Council of Churches had called the nuclear powers to begin to adopt policies of disarmament, and the NCC followed up by publishing a volume of essays by

---

27. See above, Jill K. Gill, "The National Council of Churches and the Cold War."

church representatives from the United States, Western Europe, and Eastern Europe delivering a unified call for nuclear disarmament.

American Roman Catholics exhibited similar feelings of growing reluctance toward US nuclear policy over the years of the Cold War.[28] In the late '40s and '50s, the American Catholic Church was largely made up of ardent anti-Communists. In 1947, John Courtney Murray attempted to justify the use of nuclear weapons on just-war grounds in the name of defending liberty against Communism. He thereby took a position in effect quite close to Niebuhr's early defense of nuclear weapons, including a first use. However, Murray died in 1967, and no evidence is presented as to whether he began to experience the same changes of heart as Niebuhr.

On the other hand, there were dissenters within the church, such as Justus George Lawler, who began publishing the periodical *Continuum* in 1963, in which he persistently challenged the prevalent Catholic defense of nuclear policy. He rethought just-war thinking in the light of a position of nuclear pacifism, arguing that the weapons are so devastating in their effects as to eviscerate all possibility of making intelligible moral distinctions about their use. He also complained that defending nuclear weapons was in reality linked to a belief in American exceptionalism, implying that the United States, by dint of its special status as moral exemplar to the world, is somehow exempt from ordinary moral standards.

Lawler's opposition prepared the way for the expression of strong dissent against the nuclear weapons policy of the Reagan administration by the US Catholic Bishops in their 1983 pastoral letter "The Challenge of Peace: God's Promise and Our Response."[29] The letter condemned outright the targeting of nuclear weapons against population centers, as MAD policy dictated, and, in the spirit of Kennan's early reticence about nuclear weapons, urged the immediate adoption of a "no-first-use" strategy. In addition, it rejected the idea of limited nuclear war advanced by Henry Kissinger, secretary of state during the Nixon administration. "One of the criteria of the just-war teaching is that there must be a reasonable hope of success in bringing about justice and peace. We must ask whether such a reasonable hope can exist once nuclear weapons have been exchanged." The letter also called for verifiable agreements halting testing, production, deployment, and proliferation of nuclear weapons, as well

28. See above, Todd Scribner, "Changing Course: The American Catholic Bishops and the Decline of Anti-Communism during the Cold War."

29. The letter can be accessed at the United States Conference of Catholic Bishops website, http://www.usccb.org/upload/challenge-peace-gods-promise-our-response-1983.pdf.

as for "deep cuts in the arsenals of both superpowers," with special attention to reducing "systems that threaten the retaliatory forces of either major power." That was a reference to the Strategic Defense Initiative (SDI), a policy advocated by the Reagan administration as a way of neutralizing the effectiveness of Soviet nuclear counterstrikes.

At the same time, the letter was not entirely able to avoid the moral perplexities implicit in the arguments over nuclear weapons policy. It quotes a declaration by Pope John Paul II condoning a policy of nuclear deterrence as "morally acceptable," "not as an end in itself but as a step on the way toward progressive disarmament." However, it then makes a statement that appears to contradict the pope's claim: "No use of nuclear weapons which would violate the principles of discrimination or proportionality may be intended as a strategy of deterrence." The letter's subsequent assertion that nuclear deterrence is "justifiable" so long as it is not considered a "long-term basis for peace," but is employed "in conjunction with resolute determination to pursue arms control and disarmament," does not resolve the conflict between the two statements, since a policy of nuclear deterrence necessarily entails being perceived as willing to use the weapons under some circumstances. In a broader light, this contradiction only serves to illustrate, once again, the profound struggles of the moderate anti-Communists.

In the Catholic case, the important changes in the anti-Communist attitudes of the Vatican and the American bishops, beginning in the '60s, help explain the dramatic shift in reactions to US nuclear policy manifest in "The Challenge of Peace." To begin with, the encyclicals associated with Pope John XXIII, and the Second Vatican Council he initiated, betokened a new approach of the hierarchy to the problems of the world, including those connected to the Cold War. The burden of *Mater et Magistra* (1961) and *Pacem in Terris* (1963) was the compelling need to make peace by turning away from the war effort and finding instead constructive and broadly inclusive strategies like advancing universal human rights, strategies capable of reducing worldwide economic, political, and religious injustices at the root of violent conflict. Along those lines, the encyclicals reached out, if tentatively, to the Communist world by drawing a distinction between false doctrine—still descriptive of Communist theories, in the Catholic mind—and common practical concerns, thereby laying the groundwork for dialogue and possible cooperation.

Another related cause for change was growing Catholic sympathy for what were thought of as the victims of the wayward strategy of the Reagan administration toward several countries in Latin America. Earlier in the Cold War, American Catholics, as the result of their "reflex anti-Communism," were very suspicious of Marxist agitation in the southern part of the Western Hemisphere.[30] But in the '60s a new, Marxist-sympathetic movement called liberation theology emerged among Latin American Catholics, related, no doubt, to the powerful repercussions of Vatican II, but affected also by indigenous reform activity. A spokesperson for the US Catholic Bishops said in public testimony that the bishops strongly opposed claims that Central American conflicts were best understood as the result of "superpower or East-West rivalry." Instead, those conflicts were "fundamentally rooted in questions of social injustice and the persistent denial of basic human rights for large sectors of the population."[31] Policies centered on a military solution were unwarranted and futile, and very likely increased rather than reduced the incidence of violent conflict in the region.

Still one more reason why some American Catholic attitudes toward Communism were modified was the reaction against US policy in Indochina in the '60s and '70s, again inspired by the pronouncements of Vatican II. Those pronouncements, which gave the faithful "license to act" in opposition to poverty, racial and economic injustice, and war, encouraged new thinking about the justice of the use of force in general, and not just nuclear weapons. By 1971 American bishops had turned publicly against US military support for the non-Communist forces in Vietnam and neighboring countries, declaring the policy to be unjust, according to just war standards, and demanding an end to it. They did that in the name of what came to be called a comprehensive "ethic of life," linking efforts on behalf of peace to advocacy against abortion and the death penalty.

Mainline Protestants were similarly affected, particularly by controversies over US Indochina policy. Having stood with Kennan in supporting limited military action in Berlin and South Korea, Reinhold Niebuhr developed deep doubts about reacting in the same way in Vietnam. At first, he was inclined to sympathize with US officials about the dangers of losing Indochina. But as the policy escalated in response to a growing threat, he, like Kennan, worried that the corrupt South Vietnamese regime could not be saved and probably was not worth saving in any case. He seemed troubled by the effects of total withdrawal by the United States and offered dubious advice about taking a stand in Thailand. However, by 1968, he was unalterably opposed to US policy, even with the modifications proposed by his friend Hubert Humphrey,

---

30. See above, Dianne Kirby, "Catholic Anti-Communism and the Early Cold War."

31. National Conference of Catholic Bishops, "U.S. Bishops' Statement on Central America," *Origins* 1, no. 25 (December 3, 1981): 3.

running for president that year. Niebuhr was troubled that the US effort could not escape destroying the very ally it was supposedly defending, and turning the war into an anti-Asian conflict. Kennan had similar opinions; he found it impossible to conceive of an outcome that would be "less than disastrous," as he put it in 1967. He did think a precipitous withdrawal would genuinely hurt US prestige, but by stopping the bombing he thought "we can get out of there without great damage."

Although other mainline Protestants and groups like the NCC had been under consistent attack from the ardent anti-Communists during the early years of the Cold War, for criticizing nuclear weapons policy and favoring admission of China to the UN, they also found areas of agreement with the US government, as with the campaign for civil rights. Moreover, the spirit of ecumenism and cooperation among the mainline churches, to which the NCC was dedicated, generally held up well during those early years, and support for what was thought of as "sensible anti-Communism" tended to prevail. It was the position the NCC took on the war in Indochina that underscored the very high cost of standing up to US policies regarded by the organization as expressions of an extreme and unacceptable form of anti-Communism. As a result of embracing that position, ecumenical commitment declined, deepening tensions between laity and clergy appeared, and the very survival of the organization was threatened, such that it suffered serious loss of support and political influence in comparison with the growing power of American evangelical Protestantism.

Led by Robert Bilheimer, the NCC worked to mobilize grassroots action against the war by, for example, supporting Clergy and Laity Concerned about Vietnam (CALCAV), an organization that succeeded in consolidating antiwar efforts but also intensified friction between clergy and laity. They collaborated with Japanese and East Asian Christians, giving voice to their complaints about the excessive anti-Communism of American leaders, excesses, it was said, that blinded them to the cultural and racial biases that were part and parcel of the Indochina policy. And the NCC lobbied the US government without much success, trying by direct contact and by presenting concrete alternatives to redirect policy during the Kennedy, Johnson, and Nixon administrations.

Bilheimer argued that despite its failure to effect change, the NCC had a mission to perform, namely, witnessing to Christian principles in the face of ill-conceived and severely misguided American policies. As things worked out, the mission was delayed not only by the unproductive efforts to influence US policy makers but also by other challenges internal and external. The internal challenges came both from younger Protestant leaders, disaffected by the customs and procedures of mainline leadership, and eager to renovate existing institutions from top to bottom, and from the mainline Protestant base, which abandoned moral and financial support for the mission. The external challenges came from the powerful religious and political blowback that occurred as the result of opposition to US Indochina policy, as framed and directed by mainline organizations like the NCC. Ironically, one result of such criticism may have been the failure in 1968 to distinguish between the policy proposals of the two candidates running for president that year, Hubert Humphrey and Richard Nixon, thereby leading to the election of Nixon and the extension and intensification of the war in Indochina.

Ardent American Christian Anti-Communists and Their Struggles

As with the moderates, the group of ardent anti-Communists, made up of fundamentalist and evangelical Protestants, Catholics, and Orthodox Christians, displays considerable variation and fluctuation of viewpoint, especially among the evangelical Protestants.

One of the earliest postwar religious expressions of fervent anti-Communism appeared in 1945 with the publication of *The Rise of the Tyrants* by Carl McIntire. McIntire was a fundamentalist Presbyterian who devoted his life to exposing what he believed was pervasive Communist influence among mainline American Protestant churches and their organizations, particularly the Federal Council of Churches of Christ (FCC) (1908–1950), and then its successor, the NCC (1950–). In that book and throughout his career, he held that state socialism represented a mortal threat to biblical teaching, which provides a divine warrant for market capitalism. "The Bible teaches private enterprise and the capitalistic system, not as a by-product or as some sideline, but as the very foundation structure of society itself in which men are to live and render account of themselves to God." "Limit private enterprise and you massacre freedom."[32] The very church leaders, especially leaders of the FCC, who should be defending the freedom basic to this self-evidently Christian institution were attacking it as surrogates for Soviet Communism. In 1958, the American Council of Christian Churches, formed by McIntire to oppose the NCC, publicly denounced President Eisenhower for participating in a ceremony dedicating the new NCC building in New York.[33]

32. Cited in Gunn, *Spiritual Weapons*, 122.
33. Inboden, *Religion and American Foreign Policy*, 274.

In the late '40s, McIntire helped defeat the efforts of Orthodox Christians to become recognized as the "fourth major faith" in America because of what he believed were their close associations with Soviet Communism. They argued that the standard categorization of Americans as "Protestants, Catholics, and Jews" did not do them justice. Membership in Orthodox churches was not properly identified on Selective Service cards, nor were their officials distinctively represented in civic functions as were leaders of the Protestants, Catholics, and Jews. Although several states passed legislation in favor of so designating Orthodox Americans, proposed legislation at the federal level, initiated by Senator Clifford Case of New Jersey, was ultimately defeated by McIntire's strong opposition. He claimed that the Orthodox were really Catholics anyway, but more importantly, that identifying them as the fourth major faith in America would enable "Communist directed units of the Eastern Orthodox Church to have certain advantages with the United States Government."[34] There were several other reasons the legislation failed, but it likely would have succeeded had not McIntire campaigned against it.

Evangelical Protestant leaders like Jerry Falwell, longtime pastor of Thomas Road Baptist Church in Lynchburg, Virginia, exhibited a similarly fervent brand of anti-Communism.[35] In his sermons and writings, he defended free enterprise as a God-given economic system that must be protected at all costs against "godless Communism," and in the '70s he led several "I Love America" rallies in Washington, DC, promoting the ideal of an exceptional America, specially blessed by God, as the only true bulwark against that threat. In 1979, he founded the Moral Majority as prolife, profamily, promoral, and, above all, pro-American; he attacked the failures of American leadership; and he called "the danger of capitulation to the Soviet Union a very possible result." In the same year, Falwell opposed the second round of the Strategic Arms Limitation Talks (SALT II), warning of the growing ambition of the Soviet Union to dominate the world. The United States accepting restrictions on nuclear weapons would give the Soviets a huge advantage in a nuclear exchange, as would submitting to a freeze on the development of nuclear weapons, as proposed by the growing antinuclear movement in the early '80s. Because of these views, Falwell strongly endorsed President Reagan's campaign to increase dramatically spending on nuclear weapons and to build up the SDI program to defend against them.

34. See above, Dellas Oliver Herbel, "Redressing Religious Freedom: Anti-Communism and the Rejection of Orthodox Christianity as the 'Fourth Major Faith.'"

35. See above, Daniel G. Hummel, "The Limits of Evangelical Christian Nationalism during the Cold War."

In 1943, evangelical Protestant leaders like Harold Ockenga and Bob Jones Sr. founded the National Association of Evangelicals (NAE) in direct opposition to the political dispositions and policies of the FCC and later the NCC, particularly their emphasis on the importance of international institutions like the UN, and of the advancement of international human rights treaties. The NAE mounted a strong stand for free enterprise and American nationalism blessed by God, and against proposals, which they believed were urged by the NCC and WCC, "for world federation and world government"; they believed these organizations would lead to "disaster for our national sovereignty" and open the door to "world socialism and world dictatorship." The association added that the Universal Declaration of Human Rights should be revised to include references to God as the author of rights.[36] This particular attack reflected a deep-seated antagonism among evangelical Protestants against inhibiting US action in the world, thereby adding significant support to the successful efforts of Southern politicians and leaders of the American Bar Association to thwart Senate ratification of human rights treaties in the '50s for fear that they would modify segregation laws in the South and enhance Soviet control over America.[37]

Undoubtedly the most prominent evangelical Protestant of the Cold War period, the evangelist Billy Graham, started out in full accord with the ardent anti-Communist sentiments just portrayed. "The Cold War helped propel him into public visibility [even if] it did not keep him aloft." Still a young man in the '40s and '50s, "Graham hammered the communist threat constantly," giving more time to that subject, by his own reckoning, than to anything else besides the gospel message.[38] Anti-Communism "framed his image of the world" (232). He extolled the virtues of President Eisenhower and became something of a spiritual counselor to him, believing him to have the unique capacity to defeat Communism. Similarly, he developed close ties to Secretary of State Dulles, at a time when Dulles's relations with his former mainline Protestant friends were in decline.

In an *Hour of Decision* newsletter in 1953, Graham said: "This is no time to be lulled by the constant talk of peace. [The Communist] program of world conquest is moving ahead at a steady pace. . . . We are gradually being encircled" (232). Although Graham did not know or correspond with Senator

36. Cited in Inboden, *Religion and American Foreign Policy*, 56.
37. Gunn, *Spiritual Weapons*, 93–94.
38. Grant Wacker, *America's Pastor: Billy Graham and the Shaping of a Nation* (Cambridge, MA: Belknap Press of Harvard University Press, 2014), 231. Hereafter, page references from this work will be given in parentheses in the text.

Joseph McCarthy of Wisconsin, he fully supported his anti-Communist campaign until McCarthy lost face in 1954. He admitted that while McCarthy's investigations might have been unpopular, they served an invaluable service, namely, "exposing the pinks, the lavenders, and the reds who have sought refuge beneath the American eagle," thereby "bringing aid and help to the greatest enemy we have ever known—communism" (232–33).

Through the '60s, '70s, and '80s, part of Graham continued to represent ardent anti-Communism. He favored Nixon over Kennedy in the 1960 election partly because of his anti-Communist instincts, persuading Nixon to speak at one of his crusades, and also later at an occasion honoring Graham. He supported Johnson's Vietnam policy after Kennedy's death, and then without explicitly endorsing Nixon, clearly stood with him again in 1968 against Hubert Humphrey, expressing enormous admiration for him as a world leader. When he finally turned against Nixon in 1974, it was not so much because of the threat of the Watergate scandal to the foundations of constitutional government as because Nixon had used such bad language (212–13).

By 1969, Graham began to have private doubts about Nixon's Vietnam policy. In a memo to the president, he urged withdrawal of US forces and a shift of responsibility to the South Vietnamese, although his other recommendations were anything but dovish. He proposed training South Vietnamese special forces to use the same "brutal and cruel" methods the Communists used, and he encouraged an invasion of the North that would involve intimidating the population by bombing the dikes and ruining the economy (236), measures directly in violation of just-war standards and the Geneva Conventions. He excused the My Lai massacre of Vietnamese civilians by US forces in 1969, and he did not challenge the invasion of Cambodia in 1970, nor the Christmas bombing of Hanoi in 1972 (237).

In the late '70s and the '80s, Graham began to reveal another side of himself. He explicitly dissociated himself from Jerry Falwell and his Moral Majority. "I'm for morality," he said, "but morality goes beyond sex to human freedom and social justice," and he began alluding to problems of poverty and inequality in his sermons. Furthermore, he expressed deep uneasiness about the development and deployment of nuclear weapons, suggesting that when weapons exist that can effectively destroy the human race in a few hours, that is a serious moral matter, and "the church must speak out." Although he worked behind the scenes to defeat Jimmy Carter and elect Ronald Reagan president in 1980, and became friends with Reagan and closely shared his general worldview, he began to join forces with mainline Protestants and Catholics, sympathizing with the nuclear freeze movement that opposed Reagan's hard-line approach to nuclear weapons. In 1982, he attended a world conference in Moscow committed to ridding the world of such weapons, and the same year he toured eight New England campuses, delivering a lecture (rather than a sermon), "Peace in a Nuclear Age." Turning away from what he had said in the past, he was becoming "a leading voice for nuclear disarmament," even recommending that world leaders tone down the Cold War rhetoric.

Strikingly, the membership of the NAE in 1983 reflected Graham's changing attitudes toward the Cold War and anti-Communism. A majority of evangelical Protestants supported an agreement with the Soviet Union to an immediate, verifiable freeze on the testing, deployment, and production of nuclear weapons, even though they were doubtful about Soviet compliance. A group of evangelical academics, reflecting Graham's new position, published a "Declaration of Conscience on the Arms Race" in *Christianity Today*, the voice of evangelical Protestantism, claiming that a nuclear war could not be morally justified and calling for an end to the arms race.

Ambivalence toward the Cold War, described above, is apparently deep-seated in the collective psyche of evangelical Protestantism. It was the Cold War that created the conditions in which evangelical Protestantism rose to the political prominence it enjoys today, although members of this group were never entirely of one mind as to the proper relation between the Christian gospel and the American nation. As the United States achieved global power and influence as the result of its role in World War II, and defined itself and its mission after the war very much in response to the perceived threat of the Soviet Union, many evangelical Protestants gained favor by embracing and giving religious legitimacy to the ardent anti-Communism promoted by the rhetoric and policies of the Eisenhower administration and Secretary of State Dulles. They snatched the opportunity, as they saw it, to re-Christianize America by reinforcing the idea that the Cold War was a spiritual and not just a military or political conflict, and that Christian conversion both at home and abroad was essential to winning the competition with Communism. "If you would be a true patriot," said Billy Graham, "then become a Christian. If you would be a loyal American, then become a loyal Christian." Harold Ockenga declared that "instead of obscuring and depreciating the American dream which has built this noble society, we [Christians] ought to exalt the elements of it."[39]

---

39. Billy Graham, "Spiritual Inventory" ("Sermon of the Month," published by the Billy Graham Association, Minneapolis, 1955); Graham and Ockenga both cited in Axel R. Schäfer, *Piety and Public Funding: Evangelicals and the State in Modern America* (Philadelphia: University of Pennsylvania Press, 2012), 89.

It was this kind of thinking that led many evangelicals to find theological grounds for combining a belief in "the Cold War militarized economy, social order, and national security state with an insurgent conservative message of free enterprise, entrepreneurial individualism, and moral awakening."[40] It also led them to embrace traditional heterosexual marriage and oppose perceived threats to it such as feminism, gay rights, and abortion.

However, from the start, other evangelicals were considerably more reserved about the idea of America, along with its conventional economic and marital institutions, as a "redeemer nation." Part of the tradition had long been suspicious of worldly power and prestige, bringing with them, it was believed, the wages of sin and corruption. These other evangelicals preferred to play down the preoccupation with military buildup in favor of working for international agreements on arms control, and even cooperating with other nations through the UN. Others distanced themselves from all ideologies— free market or otherwise—and chose to concentrate on the misuse of power wherever it might be found.

For still others there was, in fact, an "antistatist" sentiment that focused not so much on US government policy as on Christian missionary work and relief activity as the best way to fight Communism. They did call for and receive substantial US government assistance for these endeavors, something that resulted in unexpected consequences. Despite the intention, evangelical goals became closely intertwined with government interests, leaving very unclear who was serving whom. On the other hand, their expanding experience in foreign countries led evangelicals to gain a new sensitivity to disease, poverty, racial and religious discrimination, and abuse of power often associated with colonialism. This reaction, in turn, worked to modify Cold War thinking in two ways: it generated conflicts with US policy abroad, as when missionaries spoke against colonialism and advocated for economic justice and indigenous control, and, in a feedback effect, it may have influenced such sympathy as has existed among evangelicals for the American civil rights movement and other progressive programs.

There is an additional perspective that further clarifies evangelical reservations about the role of America in the fight against Communism. On this view, there exists an ineradicable gap between the "nations," meaning "gentiles" or earthly political communities, and God's eternal "chosen people," and there are, as it happens, two "chosen peoples," the Christian church, made up of

40. Axel R. Schäfer, "Evangelicals and Empire: White Conservative Protestants in US Cold War Politics and Society," p. 396 above.

true believers existing within visible, institutional churches, and the nation of Israel, blessed of God from Abraham's time.[41] Gentile nations, like America, can be said to act as they should and thereby merit God's blessing only so long as they properly serve the church and Israel. Serving the church means aiding the Christian mission by protecting and promoting it, and serving Israel means assuring the defense and prosperity of the modern state of Israel. Thus, America is adjudged righteous in the battle against "godless Communism" only insofar as it performs those tasks, and unrighteous if it does not. That explains the emphasis mentioned above on mobilizing government resources for Christian missions, and it also explains what has been called "antistatist statism." The gentile state is important, but only as an instrument to a divine cause beyond itself. The danger is that a state like America will try to turn things around and subordinate the purposes of the church and Israel to its own goals and purposes, thereby provoking divine wrath. As described, this is ardent anti-Communism of an extreme form, based on highly idiosyncratic evangelical Protestant theology.

The Cold War greatly illuminates the relations of American Catholicism to the US government, as well as the changes within the church from a position of ardent anti-Communism in the early years to one of moderate anti-Communism beginning in the '60s, largely as the result of Vatican II. A strong form of Catholic anti-Communism preceded the Cold War, as expressed in Pope Pius XI's encyclical *Divini Redemptoris* of 1937, which spoke of the need to combat the "infamous doctrine" and "fatal plague" of Communism. And in 1942 a group of European Catholics living in the United States, including Jacques Maritain, declared that Communism imperiled "the very possibility of working toward a Christian civilization." However, at the time, Americans were not yet particularly troubled by Communism, and therefore regarded these warnings as parochial and possibly a ruse for advancing Catholic ambitions to take control of America. It was only as the Cold War began to dominate American thought and policy after World War II that Catholic anti-Communism came to be welcomed by Presidents Roosevelt and Truman, and especially by J. Edgar Hoover, head of the FBI, and Joseph Donovan, head of the Office of Strategic Services (OSS), forerunner of the CIA.[42] These close connections helped Catholics overcome widespread anti-Catholic prejudice

41. See above, Daniel G. Hummel, "The Limits of Evangelical Christian Nationalism during the Cold War."
42. See above, Michael Graziano, "American Catholicism and US Intelligence in the Early Cold War."

and acculturate to America. Roosevelt and Truman underscored the new affinity by appointing, despite considerable resistance, a "personal envoy" to the Vatican, and Hoover, though a Presbyterian, enthusiastically embraced Catholic anti-Communism as a model for all Americans, and proceeded to enlist a sizable number of Catholic recruits for the FBI. Donovan, for his part, cultivated close relations with Catholic leaders like Francis Cardinal Spellman and Fulton J. Sheen, themselves ardent anti-Communists.

That spirit of ardent anti-Communism, widely shared at the time by American Catholics, contributed significantly to the "spiritual-industrial complex," a combination of state and commercial initiatives conceived of in government offices and business boardrooms aimed at mobilizing a nationwide religious revival in the cause of fighting Communism. Figures like Spellman and Sheen were ready and willing to participate unquestioningly in that effort. There is even evidence that the rise of McCarthyism—the relentless efforts of Senator McCarthy, himself a Catholic inspired by a Catholic anti-Communist, to root out alleged Communists in government, the arts, the churches, and elsewhere—was influenced by Catholic anti-Communism, though evangelical Protestants like Billy Graham also played an important role, as we have seen.

The close ties between American Catholics and the US government, especially the intelligence community, began to unravel in the early '60s because of the reformist impulses of Vatican II and the new thinking they inspired toward controversies over Vietnam, nuclear strategy, poverty, racism, and other issues. Shocked by signs of defection from traditional Cold War attitudes on the part of American Catholics, the CIA undertook a sustained campaign to undermine *Ramparts*, a left-leaning Catholic periodical that challenged many US policies previously supported by the church. The magazine criticized Catholic leaders such as Cardinal Spellman for complicity as regards US Vietnam policy, but it also attacked the CIA for secretly conducting at an American university training for covert operations, and for funding supposedly independent student organizations. Though CIA efforts, thoroughly outside the agency's mandate, were unsuccessful, *Ramparts* eventually shut down anyway. Even so, the following conclusion is sobering: "In much the same way that Catholics had long been threatening in the American imagination because of their perceived loyalty to a foreign state, American Catholics during the Cold War became normalized through the burgeoning national security state. The relationship between American Catholicism and the intelligence community illustrates how government attitudes toward Catholics had little to do with Catholics per se, but were instead rooted in . . . the practical benefits of using

Catholicism . . . against the Soviet Union."[43] After the '60s, the early Cold War affinity between American Catholicism and the US government would change radically.

The thought and activity of the émigré Ukrainian Orthodox churches in America in the early Cold War years represent a final example of ardent anti-Communism. Ukrainians, having immigrated to the United States beginning in the eighteenth century, organized their own churches in 1924 as members of the Ukrainian Orthodox Church USA, with their own independent leadership.[44] The church was not recognized by the global Orthodox community, but it provided an American setting where expatriate Ukrainians could congregate and worship, safe from the severe infirmities to which Ukrainian Orthodox were subject both in tsarist Russia and in Stalin's Soviet Union.

The Ukrainian Orthodox in the United States undertook two key projects that expressed their Cold War attitudes. One was constructing Saint Andrew's Memorial Church in South Bound Brook, New Jersey, in honor of the memory of Ukrainians who died in defense of their country, and the other was erecting a statue in Washington, DC, of Taras Shevchenko, a Ukrainian poet, writer, and political figure, martyred in 1861 by tsarist agents. Both projects convey a standard Cold War picture: a Soviet Union directed by godless tyrants, guilty of enslaving Ukrainians and committing egregious and systematic human rights violations against them, and an America as the symbol of Christian messianism, mandated to liberate all peoples dominated by Communism.

The Search for Common Ground

Several chapters of this book devote attention to various efforts by American Christians to bridge the East-West divide of the Cold War by finding points of agreement and cooperation, both theologically and practically.

Not all the chapters, to be sure, tell a constructive story. The chapter by Lucian Turcescu, "Fascists, Communists, Bishops, and Spies: Romanian Orthodox Churches during the Cold War," is a record of failed efforts by the Orthodox Church in Romania and the Romanian Orthodox Churches in America to find agreement, largely because the efforts initiated from Romania, undertaken by devious means to exert control over the émigré churches, were

43. Graziano, "American Catholicism and US Intelligence," p. 257 above.
44. See above, Nicholas Denysenko, "Sustaining the Fatherland in Exile: Commemoration and Ritual during the Cold War."

consistently resisted. The chapter by Andrei V. Psarev and Nadieszda Kizenko, "The Russian Orthodox Church Abroad, the Moscow Patriarchate, and Their Participation in Ecumenical Assemblies during the Cold War, 1948–1964," describes the inability of the Russian Orthodox Church (ROC) and the Russian Orthodox Church Outside of Russia (ROCOR) to reconcile their differences. While the ROC joined the WCC in 1961, it was perceived as doing so primarily to advance the interests of the Soviet state, something ROCOR, because of its strong anti-Communism, found thoroughly objectionable. Moreover, ROCOR itself refused to join the WCC because of a belief in its unique status as the true church. A third description by Leonid Kishkovsky, in his chapter, "The Orthodox Church in America: Steering through the Cold War," presents a case in which the ROC did succeed in working out somewhat better relations with the Orthodox Church in America (OCA), called the "Metropolia" (a group gradually arising out of the ROC), by recognizing their independent legitimacy. Nevertheless, the attitude of Metropolia toward the ROC was still partially ambivalent since, because of its ardent anti-Communism, it strongly denounced the repressive practices of the Soviet state, while exempting the ROC from any direct criticism while it continued to be canonically related to the Moscow Patriarchate. Nevertheless, the Metropolia understood the limits and pressures imposed on the ROC by the intrusively antireligious one-party Soviet state. In strongly denouncing the repressive practices of the Soviet state, the OCA believed it was fulfilling its moral duty. In welcoming its canonical relationship with the Moscow Patriarchate, expressed especially in eucharistic communion, the OCA believed it was fulfilling its theological duty to witness to the Orthodox Church's unity in a divided world.

Otherwise, there are numerous positive accounts of one kind or another to find common ground. It is difficult in most cases to measure success, but some of the suggestions to that effect are arresting. In what follows, we call attention to the efforts simply by listing them and adding brief commentary.

- A US Association for the Christian Peace Conference sought to build bridges between East and West through the Christian Peace Conference (CPC), originally founded in 1958 in Prague, Czechoslovakia, by Czech theologian Josef Hromádka. It brought Christian church leaders and theologians from the East, the West, and the Third World together, fostering peacemaking and friendships, and some common understanding over matters of faith and policy, with special promise during the "Prague Spring" of 1968. However, that spirit was abruptly thwarted by the Soviet invasion of Czechoslovakia later that year. As a consequence, in 1972, the

US organization renamed itself Christians Associated for Relationships with Eastern Europe (CAREE) and expanded its activities beyond the CPC, including Christian-Marxist dialogue.[45]

- Christian-Marxist dialogues occurred in Poland, Czechoslovakia, Yugoslavia, and Western Europe.[46] At first they included only European Christian theologians and Marxist philosophers, but later Americans participated. Early on the dialogues consisted of exchanges over differences in worldview and the possibility of finding points of convergence; then they moved on to consider controversies regarding nuclear weapons and other policies; and finally they tried to find common solutions to questions of peace and justice in the face of the conflicts of the Cold War. They produced rich and important encounters, inspiring at once hope for unity and awareness of the obstacles involved.

- Peace church outreach was undertaken principally by Brethren, Mennonites, and Quakers as an extension of European relief work begun after World War I, but it expanded during World War II and the Cold War.[47] Such undertakings were aimed at developing contacts among Christians across the East-West divide by reflecting on a theology of peace, continuing relief activities and refugee assistance, and encouraging joint action for nuclear disarmament and for reducing the likelihood of military confrontation. These efforts reflect the combined objectives of the traditional peace churches to do what good they could, while at the same time standing for peace and justice no matter what.

- Contact continued throughout the Cold War between the National Council of Churches and churches in the Soviet Union, beginning in response to the call of the World Council of Churches in 1954 for greater ecumenical cooperation among the churches of the world.[48] This contact, which increased after the Russian Orthodox Church joined the WCC in 1961, involved exchanges of church people from the United States and the USSR to worship together, and to try to find common biblical and theological agreement, and to discuss subjects of common concern like the nuclear threat and the deep hostility dividing the two sides of the Cold War. As

45. See above, Joseph Loya, OSA, "'For, Not of, the CPC': Christians Associated for Relations with Eastern Europe (CAREE) as a Study in Soft Power Peace Advocacy."

46. See above, Paul Mojzes, "An American Perspective on the Cold War's Impact on Christian-Marxist Dialogue."

47. See above, Walter Sawatsky, "American Peace Churches and the Cold War."

48. See above, Bruce Rigdon, Barbara Green, and John Lindner, "US-USSR Church Relations, 1956–1991."

the result of these encounters, American Christians began to see through Cold War stereotypes. They came to see themselves and their nation in a different light, and to appreciate in a new way the meaning of Christian commitment under repressive conditions, commitment leading readily to martyrdom or painful compromise.

The Role of the American Christian Churches

As things turned out, George Kennan, in spite of some disagreements over what he meant, read the Cold War pretty accurately from the start. He perceived the depth of malevolence of the Soviet Union but at the same time understood well its essentially cautious international ambitions despite all the bluster, as well as the internal contradictions and defects that would produce its eventual demise, however mistaken his timetable. He grasped acutely the terrible perplexities associated with nuclear weapons and the strategies of force and coercive diplomacy employed to try to contain them. He was also right about the ultimately religious nature of the Cold War, underscored by his call for "a spiritual vitality capable of holding its own among the major ideological currents of the time" in response to the threat.

On the other hand, in a mystifying turn of mind, he abruptly disregarded that insight by claiming that the modern world of nation-states, each with its own "national ego" demanding total obeisance from its citizens, is "an absurdity from a Christian standpoint," and that the vital national interests of modern states— security and prosperity—"have no moral quality." In response, Reinhold Niebuhr spoke resoundingly for all the American Christians represented in this book in rejecting those claims. In *The Irony of American History*, Niebuhr conceded that making national interest the basis of foreign policy helps deflate naive idealism, and exposes the difficulties of knowing what's good for others. "Yet [Kennan's] solution is wrong. For egotism is not the proper cure for an abstract and pretentious idealism." The proper cure "is a concern for both the self and the other in which the self, whether individual or collective, preserves a 'decent respect for the opinions of mankind,'" in the words of the Declaration of Independence.[49] Interacting with others, whether individuals or nations, requires transcending self-interests in favor of common interests and common solutions, an undertaking, Niebuhr implied, that is unavoidably moral and religious in character.

49. Reinhold Niebuhr, *The Irony of American History* (New York: Scribner's Sons, 1952), 148.

That is surely the uniting premise of the wide range of American Christian opinion recorded and examined in this volume. No matter whether they were mainline or evangelical Protestants, Roman Catholic or Orthodox Christians, and no matter what their particular position in regard to Cold War policy debates, the various voices all shared the idea that the nature of the conflict between East and West, involving as it did both the threat of force and its occasional use, is of great religious and moral importance. That is not surprising. From the beginnings of Christianity, the subject of war and peace was at the heart of Christian cogitation, and the divisions of opinion evident in this volume reflect the diversity of views represented throughout its history. It is particularly not surprising in the Cold War context when, because of the prospect of nuclear war, the common fate of the world hung in the balance. If that subject had no religious or moral significance, it is hard to know what would.

Thus, the American Christian churches, in responding very vocally and very persistently to the challenge of the Cold War, took impressive advantage of the rights of free speech and the free exercise of religion guaranteed by the US Constitution. Unlike their counterparts in the Eastern bloc, American Christians, despite occasional efforts by the government to interfere, enjoyed considerable liberty to declare by word and deed, and without legal penalty, opinions in dissent or support of government policy, opinions that expressed their deepest theological and moral convictions.

In general, they made good use of that liberty. Early on, there were expressions of strong opposition to US Cold War strategy by some "moderate anti-Communists," especially members of the peace churches and mainline Protestants, and they experimented imaginatively with ways to reach across the East-West divide and find common ground with fellow Christians and Marxists. For them, the result reinforced their skepticism about policies of what they perceived as unbending belligerence, including "massive resistance," and promises to use force to "roll back" Communism around the world and to take military stands in improbable places like Vietnam. It also increased their sensitivity to the way policies of unbending belligerence obscured, as they saw it, the serious deficiencies and defects of the American system regarding racial, economic, gender, and other forms of injustice.

American Orthodox churches, perhaps understandably, given their experience, remained for the most part "ardently anti-Communist," consistently condemning the governments of the Soviet bloc for denying their citizens the very liberties the émigrés enjoyed in the United States. In the early years, evangelical Protestants and Catholics exercised their rights by expressing a similar degree of ardent anti-Communism along with general support for US policies associated with Secretary Dulles and the Eisenhower administration, believing in their respective ways that the only hope for universal peace and unity was military pressure against Communism coupled with efforts at world-wide Christian conversion. As the Cold War proceeded, both the evangelicals and the Catholics diversified their views. Billy Graham, along with some other evangelicals, changed his opinion on nuclear weapons, and became more sensitive to social and economic injustice in the United States and elsewhere. Catholics in greater numbers—prompted, thanks to Vatican II, by changes of heart at the highest levels of the church—came to speak out in bold protest against US nuclear strategy, as they had earlier against US policy in Vietnam.

At the same time, serious repercussions resulted from certain positions taken by American Christians during this period. Perhaps the most important was that mainline Protestants and their representative, the NCC—especially successful and influential in the early Cold War—began to lose prominence after the '60s and the traumas of the Vietnam War, and were gradually replaced in numbers and visibility by evangelical Protestants. Mainliners invested much of their energy and resources in opposing US policy in Vietnam and did not anticipate the political backlash that such opposition would produce, namely, a precipitous decline in financial support and membership, and deep divisions between clergy and laity throughout mainline congregations.

In keeping with their interest in bridging the East-West divide, many mainline Protestants were strongly committed in the late '40s and '50s to overcoming racial, economic, religious, gender, and international divisions, and supported national political and legal reforms and the development of international institutions like the UN, the World Bank, and the International Monetary Fund to that end. While there was a strong tendency to proclaim a theological foundation for the desired unity, they were also open to secular arrangements toward the same end. A fundamental concern was that the citizens of the United States should be treated equally according to a common constitution, just as the United States itself should be fully subject to the same common international standards, such as human rights treaties and the laws of armed combat and humanitarian law, as every other nation.

It is that approach that evangelical Protestants, who were beginning to find their voice at the time, found so offensive, and opposed so strenuously. In their view, the American nation, divinely designated as protector of the Christian message, and unique instrument for the conversion of the world, enjoyed a special place in international affairs, just as the Christian foundations of America afforded Christianity special consideration in the political life of the nation. Not all evangelicals thought that way, but many did, and as their numbers increased, so did the outlook. Such was one crucial effect of the Cold War on American Christians.

The complicated record of diverse American Christian responses to the Cold War contained in this volume is invaluable for at least two reasons. For one thing, it shows indisputably the role of the Christian churches in a critical period of American history. There can no longer be any doubt about the importance of the religious views of American leaders and citizens in understanding the Cold War. For another, there is a lesson for the churches. Laying out the record in full display provides an opportunity for present-day leaders and members to review and assess the performance of their own church and the churches of others, the better to respond to similar crises in the future.

CONTRIBUTORS

Bill Blaikie is an ordained minister in the United Church of Canada who served in the Canadian House of Commons from 1979 to 2008, during which time he held numerous positions, including Parliamentary Leader of the New Democratic Party, Deputy Speaker, Privy Councillor, and Dean of the House. He is the author of *The Blaikie Report: An Insider's Look at Faith and Politics*, and is currently an adjunct professor at the University of Winnipeg.

James Christie is Professor of Whole World Ecumenism and Dialogue Theology in the Faculty of Graduate Studies at the University of Winnipeg in Canada. He holds degrees from McGill University, the Montreal School of Theology, and the University of Toronto. An ordained minister of the United Church of Canada, he has held senior denominational positions for three decades, and is past president of the Canadian Council of Churches and chair of the Governing Council of the Peace Research Division of the CCC, Project Ploughshares. His principal engagements are in the fields of interreligious diplomacy and the creating of structures for peace.

Nicholas Denysenko is Jochum Professor and Chair at Valparaiso University. He is the author of *Liturgical Reform after Vatican II* and *Theology and Form*. He is an ordained deacon of the Orthodox Church. He has an MDiv degree from St. Vladimir's Orthodox Theological Seminary and a PhD degree from Catholic University of America.

Gary Dorrien is Reinhold Niebuhr Professor of Social Ethics at Union Theological Seminary and Professor of Religion at Columbia University. His seventeen books include *Kantian Reason and Hegelian Spirit,* which won the Association of American Publishers' PROSE Award in 2013, and most recently, *The New Abolition: W. E. B. Du Bois and the Black Social Gospel.*

Mark Thomas Edwards teaches US history and politics at Spring Arbor University in Michigan. He is the author of *The Right of the Protestant Left: God's Totalitarianism* (2012), which examines the politics of Christian realism and the world ecumenical movement. His current book project, *Writing the American Century: Public Diplomacy in a Protestant Secular Age*, is forthcoming from Lexington Books.

Peter Eisenstadt is the associate editor of *The Papers of Howard Washington Thurman* and the author of *Rochdale Village: Robert Moses, 6,000 Families, and New York City's Great Experiment in Integrated Housing* (2010). He is the coauthor (with Quinton Dixie) of *Visions of a Better World: Howard Thurman's Pilgrimage to India and the Origins of African American Nonviolence* (2011) and editor-in-chief of *The Encyclopedia of New York State* (2005). He is an independent historian who lives in Clemson, South Carolina.

Jill K. Gill is Professor of History at Boise State University and Director of the Marilyn Shuler Human Rights Initiative. She authored *Embattled Ecumenism: The National Council of Churches, the Vietnam War, and the Trials of the Protestant Left*. She received her PhD in American civilization from the University of Pennsylvania.

Michael Graziano is a scholar of American religious history at the University of Northern Iowa. His current book project is a history of the relationship between the US intelligence community and religious institutions during the Cold War. He received his PhD in religion from Florida State University.

Barbara Green is a retired Presbyterian pastor. She served as National Council of Churches representative to the Protestant churches in East Germany from 1977 to 1982. She later served many years in the Washington Office of the Presbyterian Church (USA) and as Executive Director of the Churches' Center for Theology and Public Policy.

Raymond Haberski Jr. is Professor of History and Director of American Studies at Indiana University–Purdue University Indianapolis. At the Center for the Study of Religion and American Culture he serves as Publishing Coordinator. Haberski's books include *The Miracle Case: Film Censorship and the Supreme Court* (2008), *God and War: American Civil Religion since 1945* (2012), and *Voice of Empathy: Franciscan Media in the United States* (San Diego: American

Academy of Franciscan History, 2018). He is at work on a monograph that looks at the US Catholic Bishops' pastoral letter "The Challenge of Peace."

Jeremy Hatfield is an Adjunct Instructor in History at Ohio University and its branch campuses. He is also a campus staff minister with InterVarsity Graduate and Faculty Ministries at Ohio University. He received his PhD in American history from Ohio University in 2013.

Gordon L. Heath is Professor of Christian History as well as Centenary Chair in World Christianity at McMaster Divinity College, Hamilton, Ontario. His research interests rest primarily in the area of Christians and war, or the intersection of church and state. His publications include *The British Nation Is Our Nation: The BACSANZ Baptist Press and the South African War, 1899–1902*; *A War with a Silver Lining: Canadian Protestant Churches and the South African War, 1899–1902*; and *Doing Church History: A User-Friendly Introduction to Researching the History of Christianity*. He has also edited a number of volumes, one of which is *Canadian Churches and the First World War*.

Dellas Oliver Herbel is a full-time chaplain for the Air National Guard in Fargo, North Dakota. His publications include *Turning to Tradition: Converts and the Making of an American Orthodox Church*. He received his PhD in historical theology from Saint Louis University in 2009.

Norman A. Hjelm was for many years Director and Senior Theological Editor of Fortress Press when it was located in Philadelphia. From 1986 to 1991 he was Director of Communication of the Lutheran World Federation in Geneva, Switzerland, and from 1991 to 1996 he was Director of Faith and Order for the National Council of Churches in the United States. He holds a doctorate in theology *honoris causa* from Uppsala University in Sweden.

Daniel G. Hummel is the Robert M. Kingdon Fellow at the Institute for Research in the Humanities, University of Wisconsin–Madison (2017–2018). He is currently finishing a book-length history of American evangelical support for the state of Israel to be published by the University of Pennsylvania Press. He received his PhD in history from the University of Wisconsin–Madison.

Dianne Kirby is a long-established scholar focused on the religious dimension of the Cold War, first addressing the subject in her doctoral studies in the

1980s. She also organized a pioneering London conference, "Religion and the Cold War," which was followed by an edited book of the same name in 2002. She lives in Northern Ireland.

Leonid Kishkovsky is Director of External Affairs and Interchurch Relations for the Orthodox Church in America (OCA), and has served as President of the National Council of the Churches of Christ in the USA (NCC), Moderator of Christian Churches Together in the USA (CCT), member of the Executive and Central Committees of the World Council of Churches and the Executive Committee of the NCC, Moderator of Religions for Peace, and member of the State Department's Advisory Committee on Religious Freedom Abroad. He was for many years editor of the *Orthodox Church*, the monthly publication of the OCA.

Nadieszda Kizenko is Associate Professor of History at the University at Albany (SUNY). Her first book, *A Prodigal Saint: Father John of Kronstadt and the Russian People*, won the Heldt Prize and was published in Russian by NLO as *Sviatoi nashego vremeni*. She is currently finishing *Hand in Hand: A History of Confession in Imperial Russia*.

John Lindner retired in 2013 from Yale Divinity School as Associate Dean for External Relations. He spent over a quarter century providing leadership for international, ecumenical/interfaith programs of the Presbyterian Church (USA), the National Council of Churches (NCC), and the World Council of Churches (WCC). Beyond his work for the PCUSA, he was twice seconded to the NCC, first as writer for the NCC's Middle East Policy Task Force 78–80, and again to coordinate the program of US-USSR Church Relations (1983–1985). Lindner is author/editor of several publications.

David Little is a research fellow at the Berkley Center for Religion, Peace, and International Affairs at Georgetown University. Until his retirement in 2009, he was Professor of Religion, Ethnicity and International Affairs at Harvard Divinity School, with a joint appointment in the Department of Government, and was an Associate at the Weatherhead Center for International Affairs at Harvard University. From 1999 until 2009, he was Senior Scholar in Religion, Ethics and Human Rights at the United States Institute of Peace in Washington, DC. Before that, he taught at the University of Virginia and Yale Divinity School. From 1996 to 1998, he was a member of the US State Department Committee on Religious Freedom Abroad. Little has authored numerous articles on religion and human rights, the history of rights and constitutionalism, and religion and peace. In 2015, Cambridge University Press published a book of his writings, *Essays on Religion and Human Rights: Ground to Stand On*, and a book of responses to his work by colleagues and former students: *Religion and Public Policy: Human Rights, Conflict, and Ethics*, edited by Sumner B. Twiss, Marian Gh. Simion, and Rodney L. Petersen.

Joseph Loya, OSA, is an Associate Professor in the Department of Theology and Religious Studies and the Director of the Russian Area Studies Concentration Program at Villanova University. He has served multiple terms on the executive boards of CAREE and the North American Academy of Ecumenists, and continues to serve, from 1994, as the Editor for Christian Resources for the *Journal of Ecumenical Studies*.

Paul Mojzes is Professor Emeritus of Religious Studies at Rosemont College and coeditor of the *Journal of Ecumenical Studies* and editor-in-chief of *Occasional Papers on Religion in Eastern Europe*. He is the author of seven books (including *Christian-Marxist Dialogue in Eastern Europe* and *Balkan Genocides: Holocaust and Ethnic Cleansing in the Twentieth Century*) and editor of sixteen. He is an ordained United Methodist Church minister, and he received the PhD degree from Boston University.

Andrei V. Psarev is a deacon of the Russian Church Abroad and PhD candidate in Byzantine history in Queen's University, Belfast. He teaches Russian church history, Byzantine history, and canon law in Holy Trinity Orthodox Seminary, Jordanville, New York.

Bruce Rigdon is an ordained minister of the Presbyterian Church (USA) and is the President Emeritus and Professor of Church History at Ecumenical Theological Seminary in Detroit. He was Professor of Church History at McCormick Theological Seminary in Chicago for twenty-three years and served as Senior Pastor at Grosse Pointe Memorial Church.

Walter Sawatsky is Professor Emeritus of Church History and Mission at Anabaptist Mennonite Biblical Seminary (AMBS) and was also full-time or part-time EastWest Research Scholar for Mennonite Central Committee for Europe (1973–2010) and coeditor of *Religion in Eastern Europe* (1996–2012).

Axel R. Schäfer is Professor of American Studies at Johannes Gutenberg

University, Mainz, Germany. His recent publications include *Piety and Public Funding: Evangelicals and the State in Modern America* and *Countercultural Conservatives: American Evangelicalism from the Postwar Revival to the New Christian Right.*

Todd Scribner is an independent researcher living in Washington, DC. He has published extensively on issues related to the Catholic Church in the public square. His most recent book is *A Partisan Church: American Catholicism and the Rise of Neoconservative Catholics.*

Gayle Thrift is an Assistant Professor of History at St. Mary's University in Calgary, Canada. Her research examines the response of Canadian Protestant churches to global issues that emerged during the early Cold War, including atheistic Communism, the efficacy of nuclear deterrence, and the antiwar movement. In her other research, Thrift analyzes formative events in western Canadian history through the lens of biographical narrative.

Steven M. Tipton is Charles Howard Candler Professor Emeritus at Emory University and its Candler School of Theology. A coauthor of *Habits of the Heart* and *The Good Society,* he is the author of *Public Pulpits: Methodists and Mainline Churches in the Moral Argument of Public Life* and *The Life to Come: Re-Creating Retirement.*

Frederick R. Trost is a graduate of the University of Michigan and Yale Divinity School. He served as a Vicar in the Badische Landeskirche in Germany and studied theology at Heidelberg University. He served for twenty years as Secretary of the United Church of Christ Working Group that conceived "full communion" between the Evangelical Church of the Union (Germany) and the United Church of Christ. Following twenty years in parish ministry in Chicago, he served for two decades as President of the Wisconsin Conference of the United Church of Christ. Now retired, he has devoted much of his pastoral ministry to peace building and the deepening of relationships with the church in Germany, in the United Kingdom, and in Central America.

Lucian Turcescu is Professor and Graduate Program Director, Theological Studies, at Concordia University in Montreal, Canada. He has done research, published, and taught in the areas of religion and politics in the twentieth and twenty-first centuries, as well as early Christianity. His most recent coauthored book was *Church, State, and Democracy in Expanding Europe*; his most recent edited volume is entitled *Justice, Memory, and Redress: New Insights from Romania.*

Charles West is Professor Emeritus of Social Ethics and former Academic Dean at Princeton Theological Seminary. After the end of WWII, he was a missionary in China and East Germany. He is the author of *Communism and the Theologians* and numerous other writings. He was a chairperson of Christians Associated for Relationships with Eastern Europe and participated in numerous East-West Christian meetings.

James E. Will was Professor Emeritus of Systematic Theology at Garrett-Evangelical Theological Seminary in Evanston, Illinois, and former Director of its Peace and Justice Center. He was the author of numerous scholarly works, of which the most recent is *A Contemporary Theology for Ecumenical Peace.* Professor Will died on September 10, 2016, in an automobile accident.

Lois Wilson, CC (Companion of Order of Canada, highest civilian honor in her country) is a retired minister of the United Church of Canada. She served as its first female moderator and was also President of both the Canadian and World Council of Churches. She sat as an Independent Senator in the Canadian Senate, serving as Canada's Special Envoy to the Sudan and establishing the first Standing Committee on Human Rights in the Senate. Mother of four and grandmother of twelve, she has authored eight books.

INDEX

Hoenen, Raimund, 185n15
Hollander, Paul, 31, 37, 49
Hollenbach, David, 291–92
Hollinger, David, 130
Holtzman, Elizabeth, 356
Home Missions Council (HMC), 453
Honecker, Erich, 182
Hoover, J. Edgar, 102, 558; and the
    Catholic Church, 239–40, 559; "How
    to Fight Communism," 240; *Masters
    of Deceit: What the Communist Bosses
    Are Doing Now to Bring America to Its
    Knees*, 239; recruitment of FBI agents
    from Jesuit schools, 247
Hope out of Skepsis (Gardavský), 517
*Hope to Liberation: Towards a New
    Marxist-Christian Dialogue* (ed. Pie-
    discalzi and Thobaben), 529
Hord, J. R., 28, 36–39, 43, 45, 50–51, 89;
    death of, 47; defamatory remarks of
    about the Canadian prime minister
    and his government, 44; General
    Council's censuring of for his actions,
    47, 50; influence of R. Niebuhr, Tillich,
    and Bennett/Union Theological Sem-
    inary on, 37; as prophet rather than
    politician, 51; as secretary of BESS, 29,
    36; sponsorship of a grant to support
    Canadian volunteer groups assisting
    American draft dodgers, 46
Horowitz, David, 253
Horton, Walter Marshall, 159, 453, 456,
    457
Hostetter, Christian N., 388
Houghton, William, 410
House Un-American Activities Commit-
    tee (HUAC), 103
Houtart, Francois, 237
Howard, M. William, 139
Howse, Ernest, 39, 51
"How to Fight Communism" (Hoover),
    240
Hromádka, Josef, 4, 206, 209, 210, 218,
    222–25, 472, 514–15, 520, 524, 546, 561;
    on Communism, 223–24
Human rights, 207–8; human rights
    abuses, 92
Human security, 93
Human trafficking, in the former USSR
    satraps, 86

Hume, Brit, 253
Humphrey, Hubert, 174, 550, 552
Hunsicker, Robert, 191n23
Hunter, David, 528

If You Love This Planet (film), 56
Ilya II, 22
Inboden, William, 280, 383, 535–36
Independent Commission on Disar-
    mament and Security Issues, Palme
    Report ("Common Security: A Pro-
    gramme for Disarmament"), 58
Innocent, Saint, 297
Institute for the Study of Labor and
    Economic Crisis, 447
Institute on Religion and Democracy
    (IRD), 433–48; criticisms of, 435;
    denunciation of by the labor move-
    ment, 438–39, 441–42; funding of by
    foundations on the political far right,
    436; grants to organizations on the
    political far right, 436–37; and main-
    line churches, 439–40, 446–58
Institut für Friedensforschung, 525
Inter-Church Coalition in Africa, 25
Inter-Church Committee on Human
    Rights in Latin America, 14, 24–25, 57
Inter-Church Committee on Refugees,
    25
Inter-Church Fund for International
    Development, 24
International Christian Leadership
    (ICL), 379; Addis Ababa chapter of,
    391
International Control Commission
    (ICC), 32, 34
International Fellowship of Reconcilia-
    tion (IFOR), 482
International Institute for Peace, 525
Iona Community, 457
Irony of American History, The (R.
    Niebuhr), 177, 563
Iserlohn Appeal, 189–90
Israelyan, Victor, 139

Jackson, Sheldon, 361n2
Jacobi, Gerhard, 180
Japan Christian Council for Peace in
    Vietnam, 110
Jaruzelski, Wojciech, 484, 513